EDITED BY CHRISTINA E. ERNELING
AND DAVID MARTEL JOHNSON

The Mind as a
Scientific Object

BETWEEN BRAIN
AND CULTURE

OXFORD
UNIVERSITY PRESS

2005

OXFORD

UNIVERSITY PRESS

Oxford   New York
Auckland   Bangkok   Buenos Aires   Cape Town   Chennai
Dar es Salaam   Delhi   Hong Kong   Istanbul   Karachi   Kolkata
Kuala Lumpur   Madrid   Melbourne   Mexico City   Mumbai   Nairobi
São Paulo   Shanghai   Taipei   Tokyo   Toronto

Copyright © 2005 by Oxford University Press, Inc.

Published by Oxford University Press, Inc.
198 Madison Avenue, New York, New York 10016

www.oup.com

Oxford is a registered trademark of Oxford University Press

Library of Congress Cataloging-in-Publication Data
The mind as a scientific object : between brain and culture / edited by
Christina E. Erneling and David Martel Johnson.
p.   cm.
Includes bibliographical references and index.
ISBN-13 978-0-19-513932-7; 978-0-19-513933-4 (pbk.)
ISBN 0-19-513932-1; 0-19-513933-X (pbk.)
1. Cognitive science.   2. Intellect — Social aspects.
3. Cognition — Social aspects.   I. Erneling, Christina E., 1951–
II. Johnson, David Martel, 1939–.
BF311.M552 2004
153 — dc21   2003006897

9 8 7 6 5 4

Printed in the United States of America
on acid-free paper

5278000

Preface

This book explores a special set of issues that go beyond the scope of our first companion book of collected readings, *The Future of the Cognitive Revolution* (Oxford, 1997). The issues in question are problems clustering around the question of which is more basic for providing a scientifically justified account of the human mind: physiological or cultural factors? Both the particular chapters we selected and the ways we chose to organize those chapters throw light on various aspects of that general topic.

Once again, we have designed the present book to be interesting and accessible, not just to specialists, but to a wide, interdisciplinary audience as well. With that goal in mind, we have added introductions to each of the parts that readers can use as guides for understanding the chapters contained therein and for seeing how the chapters relate to each other. We also have written the introductions to provide readers with a sense of some of the main difficulties that remain in each of the principal areas discussed. Our goal has been to try to present readers with a picture of selected, important themes in the field of cognitive science that is deeper than what is now usually available, but that still manages to be of both current and wide interest.

We gratefully acknowledge the assistance of the many people and institutions who contributed to the production of this book. In addition to all the authors themselves, we thank York University and its Departments of Philosophy, Psychology, and Biology, which helped us with the conference in 1996, "The Mind as a Scientific Object." This conference was the germ out of which this book began to grow, and where original drafts of at least some of the chapters included in the following pages were presented—namely, those of William Lycan, Ausonio Marras, Gunther Stent, David Olson, Itiel E. Dror and Robin Thomas, Timothy van Gelder, and Tadeusz Zawidzki and William Bechtel. (All the chapters in the book are original, with the exceptions of those written by Jerome Bruner and by David Bakhurst, which are revised versions of essays first published elsewhere.)

We also thank the Department of Psychology at Umeå University in Sweden and the College of Communication, Campus Helsingborg, Lund University, Sweden. Furthermore, we are indebted to several individuals at Oxford University Press, New York—in particular to former editor Philip Laughlin and, following him, to current editor Catharine Carlin. Also, comments received from several of Oxford's anonymous reviewers forced us to rethink some of our first ideas and thereby steered us in the direction of an improved final product.

Christina Erneling wishes to thank her husband, Alf, who provided some concrete good ideas as well as general encouragement. David Martel Johnson acknowledges the support and assistance of his wife, Barbara. We also want to mention Shereen Hassanein and Dan Bessey, who gave us help with the final draft.

Finally, we remember with thanks Robert Haynes, longtime member of the Department of Biology, York University, who died suddenly before having had a chance to finish his own proposed contribution to this book, tentatively titled "Is the Problem of 'Redness' Insoluble?" Bob Haynes made many helpful suggestions to us along the way. Especially, for example, we acknowledge the valuable assistance and advice he gave to David Martel Johnson at the time of the organization of the 1996 conference.

Contents

Contributors

David Bakhurst
Department of Philosophy
Queen's University
Kingston, Canada

William Bechtel
Department of Philosophy
University of California, San Diego

Jens Brockmeier
Department of Psychology
New School University
New York, New York

Jerome Bruner
Department of Psychology and
    Faculty of Law
New York University

Itiel E. Dror
School of Psychology
University of Southhampton
Southhampton, UK

Otniel E. Dror
Section for the History of Medicine
Hebrew University of Jerusalem

Christina E. Erneling
Lund University
Campus Helsingborg, Sweden

Peter Gärdenfors
Department of Philosophy
Lund University, Sweden

Vinod Goel
Department of Psychology
York University
Toronto, Canada

Rom Harré
Department of Philosophy
Linacre College, Oxford University/
    Georgetown University

Jagdish Hattiangadi
Department of Philosophy
York University
Toronto, Canada

David Henderson
Department of Philosophy
University of Memphis

Terry Horgan
Department of Philosophy
University of Arizona

Martin Ingvar
Department of Clinical Neuroscience
Karolinska Hospital/Institute
Stockholm, Sweden

I.C. Jarvie
Department of Philosophy
York University
Toronto, Canada

David Martel Johnson
Department of Philosophy
York University
Toronto, Canada

Thomas Hardy Leahey
Department of Psychology
Virginia Commonwealth University

Charles J. Lumsden
Department of Medicine and
    Institute of Medical Science
University of Toronto

William G. Lycan
Department of Philosophy
University of North Carolina, Chapel
    Hill

Ausonio Marras
Department of Philosophy
University of Western Ontario

David R. Olson
Department of Psychology
Ontario Institute for Studies in
    Education and University of
    Toronto

Don Ross
Department of Philosophy
University of Alabama at Birmingham
    and School of Economics

University of Cape Town, South
    Africa

William Seager
Department of Philosophy
University of Toronto at Scarborough

Stuart G. Shanker
Departments of Philosophy and
    Psychology
Atkinson College, York University
Toronto, Canada

Gunther S. Stent
Department of Molecular and Cell
    Biology
University of California, Berkeley

Talbot J. Taylor
Departments of English and
    Linguistics
College of William and Mary

Robin D. Thomas
Department of Psychology
Miami University, Ohio

Timothy van Gelder
Department of Philosophy
University of Melbourne

Barbara Von Eckardt
Division of Liberal Arts, Rhode Island
    School of Design
Providence, RI

Tadeusz Zawidzki
Department of Philosophy
Ohio University

The Editors

Christina E. Erneling is Associate Professor of Communication at Lund University, Campus Helsingborg in Sweden. She also has taught philosophy and psychology at Umeå University in Sweden and York University in Canada. Her book, *Understanding Language Acquisition: The Framework of Learning* (SUNY, 1993), deals with issues in cognitive science and language learning. She is co-editor, with David M. Johnson, of *The Future of the Cognitive Revolution* (Oxford, 1997).

David Martel Johnson is Professor of Philosophy at York University in Toronto. He twice has been a visiting lecturer at Umeå University, Sweden. In addition to the present volume, he also has co-edited two other books: *The Future of the Cognitive Revolution* (Oxford, 1997) with Christina Erneling; and *Aristotle and Contemporary Science, Volume 2* (Lang, 2001), with Demetra Sfendoni-Mentzou and Jagdish Hattiangadi. Open Court Press in Chicago published his authored book (based on a series of previously published articles) entitled *How History Made the Mind: The Cultural Origins of Objective Thinking* in 2003.

The Mind as a Scientific Object

Introduction: Can Cognitive Science Locate and Provide a Correct Account of the Mind's Center? Progress Toward the Literal

David Martel Johnson

People everywhere enjoy believing things that they know are not true. It spares them the ordeal of thinking for themselves and taking responsibility for what they know.

Brooks Atkinson

What holds together the various fields that—considered together—constitute the intellectual discipline called cognitive science? Practitioners of this relatively new discipline claim it is just a more or less ordinary branch of modern, empirical science (see, e.g., Chomsky, 1997). At least some of those same individuals also say that what all its subfields share is a fairly specific common focus, concern, or subject matter—which each of these fields then goes on to consider from its own viewpoint, and to which it applies its distinctive methodologies. Still more explicitly, theorists identify the common subject matter with what people nowadays refer to (in a vague, but nevertheless correct way) as "the mind."

Over the course of the century just ended, quite a few thinkers came to believe (for empirical as well as theoretical reasons) that science, understood in a general way, was more centrally concerned with ontology than with methodology. Their conclusion, in other words, was that scientists' most essential and characteristic job was to determine the identity, properties, and nature of the various objects they studied; and, as compared with that task, it was a marginal and trivial matter what methods scientists happened to use to arrive at, and justify, their ontological conclusions. Professional philosophers like me were bound to find these last ideas interesting because they seemed to hold out the promise that empirical, experimental investigations associated with cognitive science could be a source of new insights into problems associated with our ancient discipline. In particular, philosophers want to know if such investigations can provide a means of escaping the trap of "perennial philosophy"—or the situation where each generation of thinkers is condemned to "discover" virtually the same list of hypothetical questions and answers, but has no means of deciding which of the questions really are coherent, and which of the proposed answers are correct (see Bialystok, 1997; Harré, 1997; Johnson, 1997a; and Ross, 1997).

So far, however, such hope has proved forlorn, since cognitive scientists have not yet been able to agree on a single, satisfactory answer to the question of what the mind is. Instead, their statements on that subject remain manifold, unspecific, incomplete, and sometimes even contradictory.

Some commentators deny that it is a scientist's proper job to choose between ontological alternatives in the way just described, because "scientific investigation always raises more questions than it answers." This is the opinion, for example, of Ellen Bialystok (1997). A similarly skeptical position also may be implicit in certain remarks of Steven Pinker's.

> Any explanation of how the mind works that alludes hopefully to some single master force or mind-bestowing elixir like "culture," "learning," or "self-organization" begins to sound hollow, just not up to the demands of the pitiless universe we negotiate so successfully. (Pinker, 1997, p. 19)

Still more explicitly:

> All of human psychology is said to be explained by a single, omnipotent cause: a large brain, culture, language, socialization, learning, complexity, self-organization, neural-network dynamics. I want to convince you that our minds are not animated by some godly vapor or single wonder principle. The mind, like the Apollo spacecraft, is designed to solve many engineering problems, and thus is packed with high-tech systems each contrived to overcome its own obstacles. (Pinker, 1997, p. 4)

I believe, and shall argue later, that there are good reasons for rejecting this way of thinking about the mind—what one might call "the no-center theory"—as well as the general conception of science that stands behind it.

In a classic book, Howard Gardner lists six subdisciplines that almost every observer would be willing to accept as legitimate parts of cognitive science: linguistics, psychology, philosophy, artificial intelligence, neuroscience, and anthropology (1985, p. 37). Gardner evidently considers all these disciplines equally fundamental and important for the task of devising a scientifically acceptable account of mind, as shown by the fact, for example, that the diagrammatic metaphor by which he proposes to represent the whole of cognitive science is a circle around whose edge these six fields are distributed, but whose center he explicitly leaves blank and empty. But this presents the following problem. Does this proposed picture show that Gardner simply ignores what is arguably the most crucial question that any cognitive scientist needs to consider—namely, what the mind itself *is*?

As shown by the previous quotations from his book, Steven Pinker apparently believes there is an intuitively obvious, universally applicable, God- or nature-given boundary that separates everything belonging within the area, category, topic, or "container" of mind from everything that lies outside it. Yet—as far as I am aware—he never offers any justification for having made this strong assumption. Furthermore, in contrast with Pinker's view, and analogous to what the biologist Ernst Mayr often said about the term "species," see Putnam's comment about Mayr in Johnson and Erneling, 1997, p. 40), it is at least equally and perhaps even more plausible to say that the great majority of people in our society today do not think of the mind as something objectively determined by certain structures of the universe itself, but instead as a product of contingent history and (current) common sense. That is, I suspect the word "mind" as we currently understand does not refer to a theoretical concept whose proper home is in the realm of technical science, but is a word that needs to be interpreted in terms of categories of ordinary, culturally determined life.

"Cognitivism" is the theoretical conception of mind that most cognitive scientists accept today. Neither of the two accounts of mind preceded cognitivism — "structuralism" and "behaviorism"—suffered from the same ontological indecisiveness that now characterizes their successor (on this topic, see Johnson, 1997a). Both these earlier theories were not just rejections (in different ways) of the still earlier Cartesian view that depicted the mind as an inner, nonphysical source of experience and a cause of outer behavior that subjects only could know indirectly, by making inferences. In addition, these theories also included new, positive answers that were meant to replace what the proponents of the theories took to be the failed ideas of Descartes. Still more specifically, structuralists (also sometimes called "introspectionists") identified the mind with patterns of conscious experiences that subjects could know and describe in a fairly immediate manner, by means of introspective self-examination (see, e.g., Heidbreder, 1933, chapter 4). And behaviorists claimed that the mind was nothing more nor less than sets of patterns of concrete, observable behaviors and dispositions to behave.

Following Chomsky, the majority of cognitive scientists now have returned to what they think of as an improved version of the old-fashioned, Cartesian view. According to them, structuralists and behaviorists were wrong to identify mind with patterns of experiences and behavior, because recent empirical investigations have shown that the best and least misleading conception of mind is as a set of inner (but nevertheless physical)[1] structures, principles, and rules, one of whose functions is to generate experiences and behaviors. At least two other, more general points also seem to follow. First, cognitivists suppose, in the manner of Descartes, that a subject only can know his or her mind by means of indirect, inferential, reconstructive reasoning. Second (perhaps sadly, perhaps not, depending on one's viewpoint), compared with the structuralist and behaviorist investigators they claim to have refuted, present-day cognitivists are not in as good a position to propose and defend any single, precise conception of what the mind is.

For the preceding reasons, we need to examine all these matters again from the beginning. In particular, is there a plausible means of reconciling the following three seemingly contradictory points? (1) Science is a progressive means of discovering truth. (2) Cognitivists claim that their views are better, more accurate expressions of actual investigative results and methods than corresponding ideas of the structuralist and behaviorist theorists who preceded them. (3) Cognitivists' descriptions and explanations of mind are more numerous, incomplete, and tentative than the ones offered by those earlier theorists.

One possible way of reconciling these points is to say that even though recent cognitive scientists have not yet agreed on a univocal conception of the mind's basic nature, at least their researches have shown the directions in which we are entitled to look for such a thing. In other words, their investigations have narrowed the number of viable alternative forms such a view might take. For example, since structuralists' and behaviorists' accounts do not fit these alternatives as well as some of the theories cognitive scientists now offer, the latter have a better chance of being true (approaching the truth more closely) than the former. In this respect, then, cognitivists at least have taken a few steps down the path toward finding an accurate, realistic, explanatory, and authentically scientific conception of mind.

Consider a general point that stands behind some of the preceding remarks. It is tempting to picture structuralism and behaviorism as two small, visible tips projecting up from a huge, dark, mostly hidden iceberg that bears the name "romanticism." I propose to interpret this last word broadly. For instance, an artistic and cultural movement of this name began, flourished, then largely died out, first in Europe and afterwards in other parts of the world as well, in the eighteenth and nineteenth centuries. But I do not conceive of romanticism as confined just to those special times, places, and circumstances. In particular, I suggest that all humans have a tendency to think and act in unrealistic, imaginative, romantic ways under certain conditions, just by virtue of certain aspects of their genetic inheritance. In any case (no matter whether this particular physiological claim is right or wrong), we know from common experience that many enthusiastic, idealistic people find it easy to ignore the difference between what they know is (or could be) true and what, for political, religious, or other ideological reasons, they think should be the case, because of the fact that there would be benefits to themselves or society at large if those things were true.[2] Still more narrowly, like other romantics, structuralists and behaviorists fell into the mistake of illegitimately blending moral, practical, and methodological considerations, on one side, with theoretical, factual, and ontological matters, on the other.[3] However, in so far as some cognitivists have avoided doing the same thing, their accounts of mind have a claim to be better expressions of scientific progress.

As soon as one states the romantic ideal in clear, nonmetaphorical terms, it becomes obvious that it could not function as a methodological principle of genuine science, because of the "white-lie" fallacy it embodies. Two simple analogies will clarify what this means. First, in a French movie I saw long ago, one character, a radical political activist, offered the following advice to his colleagues: "Whenever in doubt, always abuse the United States; because then, even if you happen to be wrong, you also will be right!" Second—an even more elementary case— imagine that employees of the General Motors Corporation organize a series of workshops for the training of real estate salespeople titled "Success is a Cadillac!" The claim is repeatedly made in the teaching materials of the course that a key element in doing a better job of selling real estate than one's competitors is to purchase and drive a new Cadillac every year. For example, the authors say, typical consequences of taking this step are that (1) the salesperson in question will be encouraged to work longer, harder, and more scrupulously; (2) his or her mental discipline and strength of character will be improved, so as to allow him to ignore distractions; (3) the salesperson will acquire a feeling of importance, self-worth, and confidence that will impress his clients; (4) the customers themselves will gain an attitude of respectful seriousness toward the business at hand when they are transported in such a car; and so on. Furthermore, imagine that subsequent observations show that these claims are not groundless since, as compared with the average income of other salespeople at approximately the same levels of experience, those who began their careers by taking this course and then went on to buy a new Cadillac every year earn significantly more money. Would these observations have proved that the title of the course was a literally true statement?

Everyone knows the answer. On reflection, every sane and honest person would say that although buying a new Cadillac every year may be an expression of, stimulus to, or partial cause of financial success in a real-estate sales career, it is obviously wrong to claim that the one is (or could be) the very same thing as the other. Nonetheless, many imaginative and highly motivated people feel justified in setting aside boring, craven, merely commonsense remarks such as these in the interests of what they take to be their own good or the good of people generally.

I think some recent cognitive scientists are guilty of making a similar mistake. For instance, this is true of those (e.g., Gardner, Bialystok, and Pinker) who affirm a "no-center" theory of mind. Gardner, for example, apparently considers it a diplomatic, friendly, nonjudgmental, and therefore politically advantageous policy to represent his six proposed subdisciplines of cognitive science as if all of them were essentially similar and equally important. But this flies in the face of the fact that these fields are significantly different, since each works in distinctive ways. Therefore it follows that Gardner's supposition cannot be literally true. In particular, even if examination leads us to believe that some of these disciplines are relatively realistic candidates for representing the mind's basic nature, the same need not—and almost certainly will not—be true of the other fields as well.

As a means of showing this, let us now conduct a brief review of each of Gardner's six subdisciplines in turn. To begin with a case that seems especially clear, most present-day commentators would agree that the discipline of linguistics cannot belong at the center of Gardner's circle, since its theoretical focus is too narrow to allow it to underlie—and thereby unite—the other five fields. More specifically, the central concern of linguistics is with language; and while language may be a good model for understanding some, perhaps even many, other mental structures and functions, we are not justified in claiming that language somehow is crucial to everything the mind is and does.

In one of his early books (1975), Jerry Fodor apparently ignored this point. He maintained that all human mentality operated in terms of an inner "language of thought," so that every mental role, power, and function was implicitly linguistic. However, most people (even Fodor himself, see his 2000) now reject such a position. A good antidote against it is to focus on instances where there does not seem to be any means of getting the proposed assimilation started. For example, humans can recognize the faces of a great number of their fellow species-members. Some have speculated that this ability constitutes a special "mental module" that is part of the innately given intellectual resources of every normal human. Yet it would be arbitrary—an ad hoc stipulation based on programmatic, wishful thinking, rather than a reasoned conclusion from concrete observations—to say that language (or even some language-like principle) must be involved in that ability.[4]

Next, consider the case of psychology—by definition, "the study or science of the mind." In spite of its etymology, it also strikes me as an unpromising candidate for revealing the mind's basic nature, because of the fact that it is a broad, summarizing discipline. Psychology does not presuppose or employ any one special conception of mind. Instead, its practitioners consider any and all proposals on this topic that people happen to put forward at any given time. One mark of this is the fact that during its comparatively short history—no more than about 150 years—various groups and generations of psychologists have adopted and later abandoned a remarkable number and range of different intellectual programs, for example, psychophysicalism, introspectionism, behaviorism, natural selectionism, operationalism, constructivism, and cognitivism. Still another mark of this is the fact that the goal of much psychological research and experimentation is to collect "bare data," which do not depend on any particular conception of mind (see, e.g., Neisser, 1997).

What about philosophy? I think this discipline is at once too broad and too narrow to provide a key for understanding what is fundamental to mentality. The reason philosophy is too broad is that it has no subject matter of its own, but draws its concerns from problematic areas in science, art, religion, or practical life—for example, mathematics, physics, biology, psychology, art criticism, musical appreciation, law, and ethical behavior and discourse. As Kant and his successors emphasized, it is not a "substantial" discipline, but merely a "critical" or "commenting" one. On the other hand, this discipline also is too narrow to function as the foundation of cognitive science, since it is not primarily an empirical study, and most of the people who practice philosophy—myself, for instance—are neither trained nor personally suited to conduct systematic programs of observation and experiment.

Each of Gardner's three remaining disciplines has a somewhat more defensible claim to occupy the center of his circle. Consider artificial intelligence. Some reductionistically inclined theorists (e.g., Douglas Hofstadter—see his contributions to Hofstadter and Dennett, 1981—and Ned Block, 1990) have argued that this field must be crucial to all the rest of cognitive science since (1) nothing else can bind together all the ideas, problems, and topics included in this area except the abstract, informational, or logical forms that all these items share; and (2) artificial intelligence is the best and most natural means of expressing these common forms.

At present, however, the preceding ideas have fallen out of favor because they seem to entail a very implausible ontology. More specifically, people who affirm this view are obliged to provide clear, literal interpretations of their suggested metaphors; but when they try to do this, they typically say that, as contrasted with concrete objects of the ordinary, visible world, the subject matter of cognitive science is entities that are intrinsically general and abstract. But if that really were the case, then cognitive science would be concerned with something totally different than all the other sciences. In fact, this would reintroduce a Platonic, dualistic metaphysics that virtually no informed person would be prepared to accept today (on this point, see Chomsky, 1997, p. 30). In other words, such claims would force us to reject the view, repeatedly confirmed by recent science, that nature is a single, unified system and to accept the idea instead that there are two radically separate types of scientific knowledge.

If artificial intelligence cannot be the supposed center and basis of mind, that still leaves two alternatives. The first of these is neuroscience. Accordingly, many cognitivists (e.g., Chomsky, 1997) have proposed to "reaffirm internalism" by equating the mind with the brain and affirming that "the mental is the neurophysiological, considered at a higher level of abstraction." However, this neurophysiological approach suffers from the characteristic difficulty that people who accept it often assume that all the explanatory factors necessary to make sense of the mind are present in an unproblematic, illuminating, researchable way, in the brain itself. But this idea is at least doubtful, because the brain is an evolved organ whose present form has been produced by pressures in its environment—from outside rather than inside.

As a means of dealing with this difficulty, some theorists propose to look in the opposite direction. They claim that the environment itself—and, in particular, human culture—is the crucial thing that allows us to see what the mind is (see, e.g., Bruner, 1997). I consider this last approach promising and have argued in favor of one version of it myself (e.g., in Johnson, 1997b). However, this view is also not completely free of problems. For example, one of its weaknesses is that it often throws no light on the innate, precultural beginning points for knowledge, such as shared behavior, adaptations, abilities, and intelligence, as contrasted with things that humans have learned to be and to do in cultural settings.

The theme of the chapters collected in this volume is that contemporary cognitivism has developed two main, rival, hypothetical theses about the mind's basic ontology: (1) the mind is the same as the brain, and (2) the mind is a product of culture. Even though it is not yet clear which of these is correct, one of this book's main theses is that practitioners of cognitive science have made scientific progress by virtue of the following pair of points. First, many of these theorists have managed to avoid romantic fantasies about the question of the mind's ontology. Second, they have succeeded in narrowing the field of realistic possibilities to just two general items.

Other recently published collections review the first alternative—the "brain view"—in a more exhaustive way than we have been able to do here (e.g., see Squire and Kosslyn, 1998; Gazzaniga, 1996). Still others focus attention on the special problem, topic, or "confusion" of consciousness (e.g., Shear, 1997; Block, Flanagan, and Güzeldere, 1997). But, in addition to setting forth what we take to be the current situation in cognitive science, our main goal here has been to explore the second alternative—the cultural approach to mentality—in a more thorough and sensitive way than any other collection of new essays now available.

Notes

1. That is, according to these theorists, the mind only counts as something inner and hidden, relative to the skin, skull, and other bodily parts of the person who has it. The mind is not (as Descartes apparently believed) inner and hidden relative to the physical world considered generally.

2. Robert Nozick (1981, p. 613) mentions various additional "themes and emphases of the Romantic movement": "overcoming obstacles, breaking bonds, powerful irrational emotions, titanic struggle, continuous striving toward new goals, the value of change and novelty, the dynamic process of transcending limits."

3. I offer the following provisional and incomplete list of still other theories, proposed in comparatively recent times, that seem to be based on this same mistake: Berkeleyan phenomenalism, Humean empiricism, Comptean positivism, Jamesean pragmatism, Carnapian logical positivism, Bridgmanian operationalism, and—at least in some respects—Quinean radical nontranslationism.

4. Patricia Churchland (1978) made roughly this same point against Fodor's program (so interpreted). It seems to me that what she said then still is essentially correct.

References

Bialystok, E. 1997. "Anatomy of a Revolution." Pp. 109–13 in D.M. Johnson and C.E. Erneling (Eds.), *The Future of the Cognitive Revolution*. New York: Oxford University Press.

Block, N. 1990. "The Computer Model of the Mind." Pp. 247–89 in D.N. Osherson and E.E. Smith (Eds.), *An Invitation to Cognitive Science*. Vol. 3. Cambridge, MA: MIT Press.

Block, Ned, Flanagan, Owen, and Güzeldere, Güven (Eds.). 1997. *The Nature of Consciousness*. Cambridge, MA: MIT Press.

Bruner, Jerome. 1997. "Will Cognitive Revolutions Ever Stop?" Pp. 279–92 in D.M. Johnson and C.E. Erneling (Eds.), *The Future of the Cognitive Revolution*. New York: Oxford University Press.

Chomsky, Noam. 1997. "Language and Cognition." Pp.15–31 in D.M. Johnson and C.E. Erneling (Eds.), *The Future of the Cognitive Revolution*. New York: Oxford University Press.

Churchland, Patricia Smith. 1978. "Fodor on Language Learning." *Synthese*, 38 (May), pp. 149–59.

Fodor, Jerry A. 1975. *The Language of Thought*. New York: Crowell.

———. 2000. *The Mind Doesn't Work That Way: The Scope and Limits of Computational Psychology*. Cambridge, MA: MIT Press.

Gardner, Howard. 1985. *The Mind's New Science: A History of the Cognitive Revolution*. New York: Basic Books.

Gazzaniga, Michael S. (Ed.). 1996. *Conversations in the Cognitive Neurosciences*. Cambridge, MA: MIT Press.

Harré, Rom. 1997. " 'Berkeleyan' Arguments and the Ontology of Cognitive Science." Pp. 335–52 in D.M. Johnson and C.E. Erneling (Eds.), *The Future of the Cognitive Revolution*. New York: Oxford University Press.

Heidbreder, Edna. 1933. *Seven Psychologies*. New York: Appleton-Century-Crofts.

Hofstadter, Douglas, and Dennett, D.C. (Eds.). 1981. *The Mind's I: Fantasies and Reflections on Self and Soul*. New York: Basic Books.

Johnson, David Martel. 1997a. "Introduction: What Is the Purported Discipline of Cognitive Science, and Why Does It Need to Be Reassessed at the Present Moment? The Search for 'Cognitive Glue.' " Pp. 3–11 in D.M. Johnson and C.E. Erneling (Eds.), *The Future of the Cognitive Revolution*. New York: Oxford University Press.

———. 1997b. "Taking the Past Seriously: How History Shows that Eliminativists' Account of Folk Psychology is Partly Right and Partly Wrong." Pp. 366–75 in D.M. Johnson and C.E. Erneling (Eds.), *The Future of the Cognitive Revolution*. New York: Oxford University Press.

Johnson, D.M., and Erneling, C.E. (Eds.). 1997. *The Future of the Cognitive Revolution*. New York: Oxford University Press.

Neisser, Ulric. 1997. "The Future of Cognitive Science: An Ecological Analysis." Pp. 247–60 in D.M. Johnson and C.E. Erneling (Eds.), *The Future of the Cognitive Revolution*. New York: Oxford University Press.

Nozick, Robert. 1981. *Philosophical Explanations*. Cambridge, MA: Harvard University Press.

Osherson, D.N., and Smith, E.E. (Eds.). 1990. *An Invitation to Cognitive Science*. Vol. 3. Cambridge, MA: MIT Press.

Pinker, Steven. 1997. *How the Mind Works*. New York: W.W. Norton.

Ross, Don. 1997. "Is Cognitive Science a Discipline?" Pp. 102–8 in D.M. Johnson and C.E. Erneling (Eds.), *The Future of the Cognitive Revolution*. New York: Oxford University Press.

Shear, Jonathan (Ed.). 1997. *Explaining Consciousness: The Hard Problem*. Cambridge, MA: MIT Press.

Squire, Larry R., and Kosslyn, Stephen M. (Eds.). 1998. *Findings and Current Opinion in Cognitive Neuroscience*. Cambridge, MA: MIT Press.

I

Where Are We at Present, and How Did We Get There?

Introduction

Christina E. Erneling

Recently some very pessimistic voices have been raised about the future of psychology and its ability to contribute to the scientific study of the mind. Different scholars, both inside and outside of the discipline, have made such claims. For example, the neurophysiologist Michael Gazzaniga writes in his book *The Mind's Past* (1998) that psychology is dead, and its practitioners are the last to know (p. 1). Howard Gardner, the cognitive psychologist, echoes this in an interview with the popular science writer John Horgan (*The Undiscovered Mind*, 1999). Also, philosophers of mind make similarly pessimistic claims. Jerry Fodor, one of the leading figures in promoting the computational view of the mind, says in a review, "We do not know how minds work" (1995). The philosopher Colin McGinn expresses an even more negative view (1991) and does not think that we will ever solve the mysteries of the mind.

Similar views are echoed in this volume. David Martel Johnson claims that psychology has failed to provide a center for the study of the mind; and Rom Harré implies in his chapter in this part that "it is by no means sure that even after 150 years the project of a science of psychology has succeeded."

In spite of this pessimistic judgment, Harré does not want to give up the search for a scientific psychology, but he thinks that the problems psychology has encountered are the result of conceptual confusion. He claims that there are two interrelated questions that still need to be addressed and answered. One question is ontological: What demarcates the domains of psychology from other domains of inquiry? The other is methodological: What sort of inquiry should psychology as a science be modeled on? Harré thinks that answers to these two questions so far have been muddled. The objects of study in psychology typically include very diverse phenomena like animal behavior, intentional as well as unintentional behavior of humans, thought processes, and subjective experiences. Methodologically, most academic psychologists adhere to natural science as a model for their work. Yet even so-called experiments often involve the investigation not of causal connections, but of cultural conventions. This muddle or conceptual confusion needs to be cleared, he thinks, not by empirical studies, but by an examination of conceptions both of what the mind is and of how to study it—that is, a view of what science is.

Harré does not address the issue of the nature of the mind, except indirectly in his discussion of methodology. According to him, there are two opposing traditions of how to approach the mind: psychology-as-one-of-the-sciences, and psychology-as-one-of-the-humanities. Here Harré agrees with the general problem of this volume. He gives a short, but interesting characterization of psychology as one of the humanities by describing some of Wilhelm Dilthey's ideas on individuals as unique and culturally and historically situated, but does not explore this conception of the mind in detail, and how it differs from the dominating one.

What is the conception of mind that a majority of academic practitioners of psychology have accepted? All the authors mentioned earlier think of psychology as something that has developed out of the Cartesian and, to some extent, the Kantian traditions in philosophy. Psychology inherited a conception of both the mind and how best to study it from these thinkers. Such a conception is only one conception among many possible ones. Thomas Leahey's chapter presents some different conceptions of the mind, both in Western and non-Western thought. Nevertheless, as his chapter also shows, it is the Cartesian-Kantian conception that has formed and still informs the contemporary scientific conception of the mental. His chapter presents and illustrates some of the most important assumptions that Harré thinks it is crucial that we should scrutinize in order for us to move on from where we are now and create a scientific psychology. Let me briefly summarize these assumptions and the role they have played in psychology during the last 150 years.

In his quest for scientific knowledge, Descartes set out some of the assumptions that guide both modern philosophy and, through it, psychology as the science of the mind. He argued that the mind and the body were different substances that had to be studied in different ways. The mind was nonmaterial and consisted of individual private experiences. The body, as well as all material objects, fell into the domain of natural science, whereas the mind was the object of philosophical contemplation. Thus, in separating the mind from the body, in a sense he created the mind as a separate object of study (in particular as the study of inner private experience), yet also excluded it from the scientific realm. Kant, although critical of Descartes in many respects, agreed with this conclusion.

Kant focused his attention on the conditions for knowledge and argued that it was impossible to study the mind scientifically. The reason for this was that the Transcendental Ego, which organized the mind and synthesized experience, was the precondition for all empirical and scientific study and therefore could not be the object of such study. The content of the mind—the empirical self and subjective experience—also fell outside science because these items could not be studied experimentally. The content of the mind—subjective experience—could not be resolved into recombinable elements; introspection altered what was studied, and the privateness of experience ruled out intersubjectivity. Thus experience could not be approached by means of the methods of science.

In fact, all the main traditions or schools of psychology, after its inception as a separate science of the mind, for example, Wundt's structuralism, behaviorism, and, more recently, cognitive science, fall within the boundaries of this Cartesian-Kantian conception of the mind. They accept this conception of the mind, yet at the same time challenge these traditions by claiming that the mind can be studied the same way as the rest of nature and with similar methods.

For example, structuralism as developed by Wundt was an attempt to apply experimental methods to subjective experience or inner, private mental activity. He did not deny that mental life encompassed more than subjective experience and also included things like language, emotion, and different kinds of social and collective behavior, but he argued that these could not be studied by the methods of natural science. Wundt nevertheless argued that his method of systematic introspection emulated the methods of natural science and was capable of capturing something essential about the mental.

However, this first attempt to turn the internal sense or subjective experience into an objective science failed, as shown by the criticisms of it by Oswald Külpe and others. Furthermore, it also failed in the sense that it ruled out many central psychological phenomena like language and emotion, which were deemed impossible to study by conducting experiments. Nevertheless, such attempts were made by others.

In the fourth chapter in this part, Otniel Dror recounts the difficulties and failures of attempts in the early part of the twentieth century to make the study of emotion into an experimental discipline. Attempts to model the study of emotions on biology and to standardize, objectify, replicate, qualify, and control emotions failed. The limitation of the studies to the laboratory seemed to take emotions out of their natural context and thus make them into something that was artificial, rather than something that occurred naturally. Several of the researchers to whom Dror refers recognized difficulties of this kind, yet they continued to apply the experimental method to emotions.

Dror's chapter stresses researchers' preoccupation with scientific method and especially with experimental approaches (see also, for example, Danziger, 1985, 1990). Applying such methods is not only problematic in ways that are outlined in Dror's chapter and alluded to in Harré's chapter, but severely limited the phenomena studied, as Wundt recognized. Yet the application of what was taken to be scientific method was to dominate all mind studies since that time.

Perhaps the most severe limitation on the range of objects and phenomena to be studied — set by methodological concerns — was the one imposed by behaviorism when this school of thought replaced structuralism. But behaviorism, which reacted against both previously popular methods (introspection) and subject matter (subjective experience), also failed to give a satisfactory account of psychological phenomena. Although this tradition radically rejected individual private experience as the subject matter of psychology, it operated with the same fundamental ontological assumptions about mental phenomena, namely, that they are individual and inner. Because they are inner and not subject to intersubjective comparisons, they cannot be studied scientifically (and cannot even exist, some behaviorists maintained).

As with the earlier school of structuralism, behaviorism failed to account for most of the central psychological phenomena. Beginning with Chomsky's review (1959) of B.F. Skinner's book on language, *Verbal Behavior* (1957), it gave way to cognitive science.

Cognitive science not only reintroduced the mental into psychology, but also systematically developed a hypothetical-deductive conception of science to take the place of the earlier inductivist approach that once had been dominant. The mind's basic structure is not accessible directly through introspection, as the failure of structuralism clearly illustrated, but also is not directly reflected in behavior. On the other hand, the mental is accessible through a set of hypotheses about certain unobservable mental processes that can be tested by their consequences. Cognitive science promised to give an account of the hidden mental sphere and to illuminate and eventually explain all areas of psychology. Even so, the central assumptions of the Cartesian-Kantian perspective of the mental as inner individual phenomena containing representations of the world still were retained.

This approach also did not fulfill the promises it had made to give a scientific — that is, experimental and formalized — account of hidden individual mental phenomena, thereby unifying the study of all mental phenomena, nor has it been able to account for subjective experience (see, e.g., Feldman, 1997, pp. 68–74). Given this repeated failure of different psychological schools, the pessimistic judgments about the possibility of a scientific account of the mind noted earlier are perhaps not surprising. But is this venture entirely dead?

The chapters in this part show clearly that the study of the mind has been restricted by many self-imposed limitations both of an ontological and of a methodological nature. These limitations most often seem to come from outside psychology — for example, from religion or philosophy (see Leahey's and Harré's chapters) and from physics or biology (see Harré's, Hattiangadi's, and Dror's chapters). Although problems were apparent from the beginning, the shedding of these limitations seems to have been very difficult. Leahey's and Harré's chapters in this part cover quite well known ground, but they help introduce the central issues that are debated in the rest of the book. These chapters are also a useful introduction to readers who are not very familiar with the history of attempts to think about the mind in scientific terms, and with the many controversial issues that have been raised in that history. These chapters help explicate the choices that people have made in attempts to overcome the deadlock that the Cartesian-Kantian conception of the mind has produced. What is the ontology of the mind? Which scientific methods are appropriate to use in studying the mind, once one has correctly determined what its ontological nature is?

Perhaps it is true that psychology is a failure and in a sense is dead. The Cartesian-Kantian conception of what mind is and how it best should be studied has not been fruitful. But it does not follow from this point that it is impossible for the mental to be a legitimate object of scientific study. On the contrary, the question of what kind of object the mind is needs to be discussed and explored today more than ever before. Still another reconceptualization and reclassification of mental activity is needed now. One way of doing this is for one to return to the same contrariety that was a concern of Wundt (see Leahey in this part) and that Harré also explores, namely, the contrast between the mind as an object of natural science and the mind as an object of the cultural sciences. Many recent advances in neurobiology, evolutionary biology, psychology, and philosophy bear on this question. This is the particular point that most of the chapters collected in this volume explore and develop.

References

Chomsky, N. 1959. "Review of B.F. Skinner's Verbal Behavior." *Language*, Vol. 35 (Jan.–March), pp. 26–58.
Danziger, K. 1985. "The Method Language Imperative in Psychology." *Philosophy of the Social Sciences*, 15, pp. 1–13.
———. 1990. *Constructing the Subject: Historical Origins of Psychological Research.* Cambridge, UK: Cambridge University Press.
Feldman, Carol Fleisher. 1997. "Boden's Middle Way: Viable or Not?" Pp. 68–74 in D.M. Johnson and C.E. Erneling (Eds.), *The Future of the Cognitive Revolution.* New York: Oxford University Press.
Fodor, J. 1995. "West Coast Fuzzy: Why We Don't Know How Minds Work." *Times Literary Supplement* (August 25), pp. 5–6.
Gazzaniga, M. 1998. *The Mind's Past.* Berkeley: University of California Press.
Horgan, J. 1999. *The Undiscovered Mind: How the Human Brain Defies Replication, Medication, and Explanation.* New York: Free Press.
Johnson, D.M., and Erneling, C.E. (Eds.). 1997. *The Future of the Cognitive Revolution.* New York: Oxford University Press.
McGinn, C. 1991. *The Problem of Consciousness: Essays towards a Resolution.* Oxford: Blackwell.

1

The Relevance of the Philosophy of Psychology to a Science of Psychology

Rom Harré

What Is Psychology?

Taking the question "What is psychology?" very broadly, we could say that psychology is the study of people thinking, acting, seeing, hearing, touching, and feeling. So the field of study for the many versions, variations, and subdisciplines that make up psychology includes such activities as solving problems, resolving disputes, making friends, remembering one's mother's birthday, playing cards, watching baseball games, listening to music, picking out the smoothest stone, being in pain, being sad, imagining winning the lottery, and so on. This is a very diverse group of activities, states, and processes.

What demarcates the domain of psychology? If these and similar things are the topics of a possible science of psychology, what aspects of human life are outside that domain? Indigestion? Cancer? Orgasms? Bone breakages? While there seems to be nothing particularly psychic about this list of outsiders, it is apparent that each and every one has a cognitive, temperamental, and experiential dimension. All these activities, states, and feelings, central and peripheral to the domain of the psychological, are engaged in and experienced by ordinary people. They not only act in these ways and have these experiences, but critically comment upon and correct each other's performances. There is something normative about the psychological dimension. Furthermore, each of these activities involves or requires some dimension of awareness.

The Claim to Be a Natural Science

Everything in the above list was known and written about before there was any suggestion of a scientific psychology. The advent of new sciences like chemistry and metallurgy led quickly to the expansion of the domain of the known. New processes, new substances, and new phenomena were discovered. Our first test of what it would be like for psychology to become scientific in the mold of the natural sciences could be to ask what it would be like to discover a new psychological phenomenon. Would it be like a nineteenth-century chemist coming upon double decomposition and formulating the general principle that acid plus base equals salt plus water? In pressing for a close parallel between the natural and the human sciences, one might remark that all sorts of discoveries seem to have been made by psychologists. Did not Piaget (1932) discover the processes of accommodation and assimilation, important in cognitive development? (Darwin discovered natural selection, important in species development.) Did not Festinger (1957) discover cognitive dissonance, a process that drives "changes of mind"? (Fraunhofer discovered the absorption spectrum.) Did not Eysenck (1952) discover introversion and extroversion, hitherto unknown personality types? (Davy discovered sodium and calcium.) Trying to adjudicate these tentative but seemingly unproblematic parallels will prove to be much more difficult than it might seem. For example, it might be argued that Eysenck's seeming discovery was not much more than giving a fancy name to aspects of personality that we knew all along and that had been described in greater detail by novelists, poets, and dramatists for centuries. It might also be argued that the characteristics that Eysenck thought he had discovered were in part responses brought about by the kinds of questions he asked people, rather than windows into their characters and personalities. Perhaps Eysenck was really studying the range of discursive conventions for answering questions about oneself.

Lurking in the background to our studies is a fundamental question: What mode of inquiry should psychology as a discipline be modeled on? It might be modeled on one of the natural sciences such as physics, chemistry, or biology. If it is, then the just mentioned parallels should be thoroughgoing. However, there is another complication. Chemistry and physics are not themselves identical in their way of working. Chemistry postulates a substrate of unobservable substances like molecules and atoms, while physics postulates an unobservable substrate of dispositions and powers, like charges and field potentials. It would make a great difference to psychology if, to create this discipline as a science, we modeled it on one or the other of these established sciences.

However, there is another alternative. Psychology might be modeled on one of the cultural disciplines, such as history, linguistics, philosophy, or even jurisprudence. The putative parallels remarked earlier would surely fail if this route were to be taken. Again, our choice of a model discipline from among the cultural sciences would make a profound difference to the mode of inquiry we finally designed.

One of the tasks for philosophy of psychology is to look at these options in the light of our understanding of the phenomena that constitute the domain of our discipline. We will explore both sets of possible models. As philosophers, we are not bound to accept any of the claims of this or that school of psychology to have an exclusive claim to hegemony and to have just the right and the only right way of studying people.

We shall see, even as we try to design a psychology that does bear some of the marks of the mature natural sciences and, at the same time, acknowledges the irreducible role of meanings and the essential place of norms of correctness in what is constitutive of psychological phenomena, that both natural science and cultural sciences have a role in founding a comprehensive discipline. Such a discipline should be rich enough as a mode of inquiry to do justice to the diversity of the subject matter and should have the requisite explanatory power to satisfy our ambitions to have created a truly adequate science.

Some "Official" Accounts of the Nature of Psychology

What people think, what they say, what they do, what they feel, and why they think, say, act, and feel in these ways are plainly of the greatest interest to all of us. We already know a great deal about these matters. Not only must we have this knowledge, but we must be able to put it to use appropriately just to get through the day with all the different people and diverse situations we have to deal with in the daily round. Can we represent that knowledge systematically, and can we give a plausible account of the techniques and practices by which our mental and material life forms are jointly constructed?

There are various possibilities. Shall we try to emulate the methods and metaphysics of disciplines that are already going concerns? Or shall we try to found something entirely new? For the moment, two broadly opposed traditions have emerged: psychology-as-one-of-the-sciences and psychology-as-one-of-the-humanities.

The "Psychology-as-One-of-the-Sciences" Story

One might think that the best place to find out what psychology is would be textbooks of general psychology, the staple fodder of beginning psychology students. There we find various versions of the psychology-as-one-of-the-sciences project. Here is a very broad description from Gleitman (1985, p. 9):

> What is psychology? It is a field of inquiry that is sometimes defined as the science of mind, sometimes as the science of behavior. It concerns itself with how and why organisms do what they do; why wolves howl at the moon and children rebel against their parents; why birds sing and moths fly into the flame; why we remember how to ride a bicycle twenty years after the last try; why human beings speak and make love and war. All of these are behaviors, and psychology is the science that studies them. The phenomena that psychology takes as its province cover an enormous range. Some border on biology; others touch on social sciences such as anthropology and sociology. Some concern behavior in animals; many others pertain to behavior in humans. Some are about conscious experience; others focus on what people do regardless of how

they may think or feel inside. Some involve humans or animals in iso-
lation; others concern what they do when they are in groups.

Let us undertake some brief philosophical reflections on this account. One
is struck immediately by two very odd features of the language Gleitman uses to
describe the domain of psychology. The word "behavior" is used both in its
dictionary sense, for the overt activity of some organism or machine, and for
something quite different, something we ordinarily contrast with behavior, namely,
what someone does intentionally, roughly "conduct." In other texts we even find
the term extended to cover what someone thinks or feels; for instance, hearing
sounds as music has been called "listening behavior." Then there is the juxtapo-
sition of animal activities, described in notably noncognitive, nonintentional
phrases, such as "howling at the moon" and "flying into a flame," to human
activities, which are described in notably intentional, cognitive, and culturally
specific phraseology, such as "rebelling against one's parents" and "riding a bicycle." All wolves howl at the moon, since that is the way they are built. Photophilic
moths all end up in flames. However, there are plenty of places where young
people do not rebel against their parents, and even some where the bicycle is not
a common form of transport.

Here is another textbook definition:

> Psychology is the science of behavior and experience. By science we
> mean a discipline that uses systematic observation or experimentation to
> describe, explain, and predict events in the world. Behavior is any activity
> that can be observed—what we do, what we say, even how our bodies
> respond to elements in the environment. Experience is our feelings, our
> thoughts, our perceptions. (Laird and Thompson, 1992, p. 12)

One should notice how different this account is from the previous one. There is
no explicit assimilation of the lives of people and animals. Unlike the first account,
in which conscious experience slips in as almost an afterthought, it occupies half
the territory according to Laird and Thompson. However, there is one oddity.
Systematic observation or experiment could only explain events if science were to
be conceived according to the much derided positivistic principle that explanation
and prediction are logically identical, a principle that would wipe out the natural
sciences at a stroke. We should note well the implicit positivism of much that
passes as scientific in psychology.

Finally, I choose a third account, very different from either that we have seen
so far. Hilgard, Atkinson, and Atkinson (1975, p. 7) propose the following:

> We will define psychology as *the science that studies behavior and mental
> processes.* This definition reflects psychology's concern with an objective
> study of observable behavior and still recognizes the importance of un-
> derstanding mental processes that cannot be directly observed but must
> be inferred from behavioral and physiological data.

A number of points in this account are noteworthy. For example, it is assumed
that the notion of "an objective study of observable behavior" is an unproblematic

idea. "Percepts without concepts are blind" is a commonplace of the theory of knowledge that is overlooked by many psychologists; here we find it tacitly overlooked yet again. Furthermore, there is the idea that mental processes cannot be directly observed. Do they include thinking? That can certainly be directly observed in many cases by the thinker. If the cognitive process is a public discussion, everyone can observe what is going on. Or perhaps the realm of mental processes that cannot be directly observed is some neo-Cartesian machinery that generates observable behavior? The book itself does not offer us much help in trying to fathom the meaning of these cryptic and puzzling remarks. However, one philosophical point to note is the overt adherence to scientific realism in the citation of mental processes in explanation of observable behavior. This is in stark contrast to the positivism of Gleitman and Laird and Thompson.

The results of our survey are really rather discouraging. Even the very best seem to be uninformed by the developments in alternate proposals for a systematic psychology. Nor do the advances that have been made in philosophy of science in the past half century, that is, in our general understanding of the nature of the established sciences, seem to have reached most psychologists. We shall find that in its search for a place in the pantheon of the sciences, psychology has followed this or that philosophical account of the exemplary sciences, such as physics and chemistry, and has swayed back and forth as these accounts have developed, changed, or been abandoned. Most troublesome has been the persistence, both explicitly and implicitly, of a positivistic slant, the correlation of phenomena in search of reliable regularities.

The question to which we will try to find an answer is this: If psychological studies are to be a science like physics, or a cluster of sciences like biology, which exemplar of science would it be best to emulate? The answer may be hard to reach. Perhaps no one established mode of inquiry will serve as an exemplar. However, there are certain lines of development that one finds in physics that offer some hope. I will turn to a brief exposition of this possibility later in this chapter.

The "Psychology-in-the-Humanities" Story

There are various routes by which we could approach the ideal of psychology as a linked series of studies within the general framework of the humanities. One way that has a certain historical authenticity is to connect it with the intellectual history of nineteenth-century German reflections on the nature and possibilities of science in general, Wissenschaft. The famous distinction between Naturwissenschaft (natural science) and Geisteswissenschaft (perhaps best translated as "humanities," encompassing, among much else, what we could call "cultural studies" such as history and linguistics) provided a framework within which such distinctions as that between nomothetic inquiries and idiographic inquiries were to be understood.[1]

A nomothetic inquiry is a project aimed at finding a general law or principle that covers a range of similar cases, inductively extended from a sample. An idiographic enquiry is a study aimed at understanding a single case in very great detail. This basic methodological distinction is not peculiar to the human sciences. We can find it in physics and astronomy. We study the laws of motion of material things nomothetically and come up with general laws like those of Newton—for example, that every body continues in its state of rest or uniform motion unless acted on by an impressed force. We study the planets idiographically, each having its own unique characteristics and structure. As material bodies orbiting the Sun, they all obey the Newton-Kepler laws of planetary motion; but as individual material things, they each have a unique history and geology.

Suppose that the psychological diversity of the systems of meanings and the normative constraints made use of by diverse cultures, tribes, families, and individuals, when closely examined, turned out to be more important for our understanding of how things go in the human world than their commonalities. What methodological devices would be needed to look into such matters as the meanings of gender, the practices of an honor culture, the relative degree of tolerance of highly active children, the diversity of rankings of emotional displays as proper and improper, the favored schedule of development of children's cognitive competences, and so on? Let us look at some suggestions for methodologies other than those borrowed (and distorted in the process) from the natural sciences.

One of the most important authors in the era in which the question of the nature of a systematic psychology was most deeply debated was surely Wilhelm Dilthey. Indeed, his work has also served as a source of controversy in our own times. There had been nearly a century of German criticisms of naïve positivist science. I choose to focus on Dilthey's work since he was the most prominent inheritor of the antipositivistic tradition in the late nineteenth century.[2]

I will set out the relevant aspects of Dilthey's thinking in a sequence of dichotomous distinctions. Dilthey is perhaps best known for his distinction between *verstehen* (insight or sympathetic understanding) and *erklären* (explanation). This distinction between ways of knowing is realized in the difference between the natural and the human sciences, insofar as the latter are concerned with matters other than the physical being of human organisms. *Naturwissenschaft* proceeds by construction, that is, by the development of theories beyond the already given, and the testing of hypotheses by experiment. *Geisteswissenschaft* proceeds by transposition, that is, by using our "insider's" knowledge of how we live to reenact the experience of someone else.

The second distinction of importance is that between *Erlebnis* (lived experience) and *Erfahrung* (representation [of the material world]). But the latter is always part of the former. This distinction foreshadows the contemporary insight that the world that natural scientists study is an *Umwelt*, that is, the world as it is given to human beings. The lived experience in question is always someone's lived experience. This takes us to the next point.

Each individual is, according to Dilthey, a primordial unity (here we can hardly fail to note a hint of William Stern's *unitas multiplex*). A person is a "psychophysical life-unit" (Dilthey, 1989, p. 67). The account of "a person," then, requires both biological (natural science concepts) and cultural concepts. But the latter get their content from lived experience and cannot be ascribed without *verstehen*; but that is not the indeterminate process of "feeling the feelings of the other." It is grasping the *Erlebnis* of the other, which is made possible by the fact that I too am a human being.

What of the nature and status of human studies? It would be a huge mistake to set about trying to construct an *erklärende Psychologie*, since that would require the use of causal concepts as applied to fixed analytical elements in a search for laws of behavior (Dilthey, 1989, p. 88). Nor is it enough to pay attention only to intellectual movements, genres of art, or political and economic organization. Knowledge of these, of the past or the present, will not reveal the actuality of the lived experience of people. To know and understand fauvism is not yet to know, in the sense of grasp, the lived experience of Matisse, but one could not grasp the latter without some knowledge of the former. The practice of interpretative psychology leads to a grasp of a person's unique totality of purposes and the inner quality of his or her experience by description, *beschreiben*, and by analysis, *Zergliederen*. That is, psychology is not a search for laws, but an attempt to grasp the character of unique individuals in their concrete historical and linguistic contexts. This not only is a point of view that places the person at the apex of an ontological tree, but also comes close to the constructionist emphasis on the role of history and language in the formation of points of view, and thus as constituting the preexisting bridge by which human beings can understand one another. *Verstehen* is not the result of sympathy, the induction of a feeling in me that matches a feeling in you, but the intellectual apprehension of "how it is with you." This does not lack generality. "Historical research has its life in a progressively more deepened picture of the unique. Here there reigns a living relationship between the realm of the uniform and that of the individual" (Dilthey, 1989, p. 91).

The style of research exemplified by Dilthey's account of *Geisteswissenschaft*, research in a style we could call hermeneutic, the search for meanings, has also been advocated by contemporary German theoreticians of human studies, in particular Habermas (1984) in *The Theory of Communicative Action* and other works. In that book he set forth a method of inquiry that would replace the positivistic style of inquiry that he took to be the result of the application of certain scientistic conceptions of rationality to human affairs.

In the United States, where most of those who style themselves psychologists currently live and work, it seems to be taken as settled that psychology is or is to be a kind of *Naturwissenschaft*. This is very clear in the quotations from some representative psychology textbooks that I set out in the previous section. Yet on close examination, the work that people in the United States do in university psychology departments and publish in mainstream journals seems to be really *Geisteswissenschaft* dressed up in the garments of natural science so that it looks like *Naturwissenschaft*. For example, there are many studies that are called "experiments," a word from the philosophy of natural science, but that are based on getting answers to questionnaires and soliciting commentaries about vignettes. All are analyzed statistically, presumably on the bizarre assumption that questions cause answers and that vignettes cause commentaries. These studies really reveal discourse patterns for which customs, conventions, and rules should be sought. They do not display causal relations for which mechanisms should be sought. They are contributions to a cultural science of human conduct and not to some putative natural science of human behavior.

Is There a Special Place for Psychology?

If it is implausible to try to construct a natural science of thought, feeling, and action, and yet one's intuitions shrink from assimilating psychology wholly to literary or historical studies, what place in the intellectual universe might a possible psychology occupy? There are thousands of psychologists working away at *something*. Even though much of their activity can be seen to be misdirected from a dispassionate external point of view, perhaps it might be rewritten in another frame, eschewing causal interpretations in favor of some such conceptual framework as Dilthey sketched. Let us look briefly at some possibilities.

As an Alternative to What We Already Know?

In the light of the preceding discussion of alternative possibilities for forging a discipline, one might ask, "Why do we need a 'scientific psychology' when we already have novels, poems, plays, histories, biographies, ballets and operas, music, and so on?" These seem to treat of just the sorts of things we saw cataloged as the fields of "scientific" psychology in the quotes from textbooks. What would be different about courses in psychology, set up as a scientific field of study, from courses in the novel, or in jurisprudence, or in music appreciation, or in philosophy? Some people would say that there is nothing more for psychologists to classify and explain than is already dealt with by other human studies.

We have already seen that the prescriptions for a scientific psychology offered by Gleitman, though very general, do not do much more than express an old-fashioned philosophical view of science as positivism, which bears little resemblance to what physicists and chemists actually do in theorizing or in experimenting. Do we even have the possibility of creating new knowledge in psychology? To have made an authentic discovery that widens the domain of psychological knowledge, one must have done more than relabel a phenomenon or group of phenomena that are already part of the self-understanding of a culture. To call feeling "affect" does not advance our knowledge and indeed probably leads to an overall decline, since it lumps together phenomena already recognized in the culture to be of very different kinds. Nor is it a discovery to create an artifact by the adoption of some special method of inquiry, such as the IQ generated by a cluster of miniexaminations and ascribed to individuals as a measure of their relative cognitive powers.

Even more to the point, everyone needs to have at least a working set of open-ended assumptions about ways of solving problems, of resolving disputes, of reading character and predicting what people will do, of deciding what emotional displays are legitimate and what are frowned upon, and so on. Such sets of assumptions, rules of thumb, stereotypes, and so on have come to be called "folk psychologies." Two issues prompted by the recognition of the importance of common sense in the management of thought and action have recently preoccupied philosophers of psychology. Is knowledge of the folk psychology of a particular culture necessary as a foundation for any more science-oriented psychology? Do we really need psychologies modeled on the natural sciences, even when this modeling is based on an authentic, nonpositivist view of the natural sciences, when we have all we need for understanding what people do in the actual folk psychologies by which people are managing their lives anyway? Are we going to do any better in anticipating the future activities of people of a certain tribe or family than the forecasts by which people ordinarily and routinely manage their lives? I am fairly sure that in most cases, psychologists are worse at forecasting if they use their "scientific" knowledge. The usual excuse that psychology is a young science will not do, since so is organic chemistry.

As a Natural Science, in Particular, as a Branch of Biology?

In our discussion so far we have taken for granted that there is a place for a science of psychology. However, that assumption has been challenged often in the course of the history of science by various attempts at extending the natural sciences to cover all of human behavior, as well as the lives of animals and the inanimate processes of material nature. We are at present seeing a resurgence of reductionist accounts of human life, especially in psychology. Some authors have tried to build a psychological science as a branch of biology, in which the role of genetic inheritance in the genesis of patterns of action has been greatly emphasized. Thus the content of psychological generalizations has been biologized. Along with this, there has been a claim for the hegemony of the methods of the physical sciences in the study of all aspects of personal and public life (Wilson, 1998).

It is evident that this approach has led to a neglect of the symbolic aspects of human action, with a corresponding impoverishment of our view of ourselves. Not unexpectedly, there has been a strong reaction against the elimination of meaningfulness from the field of human studies, but this reaction needs to be tempered with some caution. The postmodernist response, that science is just another likely story, of no greater value to us than any other account of human life, is no less damaging than the reductionism to which it responds.

I shall sketch, albeit very briefly, a third way by which the achievements of the natural sciences in unraveling the inner workings of the human organism can be celebrated, while the essentially discursive character of human patterns of thought and action is preserved. But before I undertake that task, a further general observation is in order. The recovery of meaning as an indispensable category, for example, by making use of some such conceptual resource as Dilthey's scheme, leaves a crucial feature of human life still untouched. What people do is surrounded by a penumbra of social and personal representations of what they *should* do. How should this ubiquitous feature of real human life be incorporated in a scientific psychology? The natural science model has no place for it. Planets do what they do. Kepler and Newton were not recording prescriptions of orbital motions.

Right and Wrong Ways of Thinking, Feeling, and Acting

We touched on the problem of right and wrong ways of thinking, feeling, and acting at the beginning of this inquiry, but more needs to be said. Most people who would call themselves psychologists are in the clinical or medical professions. They are dealing with people who are thinking, feeling, and behaving in unacceptable ways. Psychopathology, the study of madness, neurosis, and so on, depends on our setting the bounds of normal behavior. Abnormal ways of thinking and acting in some particular culture at some particular moment will show up in contrast to all the normal ways of thinking and acting that are then and there recognized. Psychology is not just the neutral study of what people do. It incorporates at its very heart a distinction between what is the sane, balanced, and ordinary thing to do and what it is not proper or correct to do. There are right and wrong versions of all the human activities that have been listed as parts of the broad field of the subject matters of psychology. There are wrong ways to tackle problems, inadequate attempts to make friends, inappropriate emotions, and so on. This feature of human life, which looms so large in the field of phenomena that psychology studies, must find a place in whatever psychology turns out to be.

Natural Sciences Are Not Normative

Even at this early stage of our investigations, we are thrust hard up against a huge difference between psychology and sciences like physics and chemistry. Whatever a gas does in an ionized state, it does. Whatever an acid does in interacting with a base, it does. There is no application for the notions of correct and incorrect natural processes. Even in biology, the use of success concepts in describing organic evolution has been heavily criticized as an anthropomorphic metaphor for equilibria that have come about through the operation of processes that it makes no sense to assess as right or wrong.

> . . . [O]ne of the most crucial things about Darwinism is how it eschews teleology [that is, nature working toward goals through the medium of vital forces]. . . . Darwin . . . was adamant always that the new variations which selection acts upon . . . appeared "randomly" without respect to the needs of their possessors. (Ruse, 1989, p. 29)

If there are no goals, there can be no achieving them well or ill.

But human life is lived almost wholly within a variety of frameworks of goals both great and small, both long term and short term. I need to open the door, to do the laundry, to cook the dinner, to finish the job I am working on and by accomplishing various intermediate goals, to live a good life and achieve salvation and so on. For most of these, there are more or less tightly defined criteria for success and failure, and the means too are usually susceptible of assessment as proper or improper. To get my state chosen as the venue for the Winter Olympics, it is not proper to lavish gifts and financial incentives on the members of the Olympic Committee, nor is it proper for them to accept them and allow these considerations to influence their choice. To catch a ball, I must compute the trajectory correctly. To be understood, I must structure my utterances roughly according to the semantic and syntactical conventions of some language we share. And so on.

The Sources of Norms of Correctness and Rules of Propriety

Where do the standards that are subtly interwoven into the fabric of psychology come from? To some extent we can explain them by reference to successfully sustaining our organic life. Why is myopia a defect of the perceptual system? The answer is that it makes hunting and gathering more difficult and thus decreases the chances of survival of the near-sighted person. But to a much larger extent, standards of correctness come from culture and tradition. Some groups of people reason by attention to similarities. For example, the medieval doctrine of signatures was based on the principle that like went with like. Thus walnuts should be good for the brain because once out of their shells they showed similar convolutions to brains removed from their skulls. Other groups of people have reasoned by syllogism. For example, if one assumes some general truth about apples, say, ripe when red, then if this is an apple, it too will exhibit what is generally true of apples, namely, when it is ripe it will be red. Neither of these modes of reasoning is without defects with respect to modern ideals of correct thought. In some cases biological necessity and cultural criteria have run together to create a psychological phenomenon that is "all standards," for example, remembering. To remember something is not just to form some representation of a past event with which one was involved, but to represent it correctly.

The Framework of Physics

We already have noted the fundamental difference between the metaphysical foundations of chemistry and physics. In the former, explanations cite hidden mechanisms constituted by material substances in various degrees of decomposition. Thus reactions are explained by molecular processes, which in their turn are explained by the rearrangements of atoms, and so on. Explanations in physics go deeper, to the very boundaries of intelligibility. There we find citations of primitive and unanalyzable active beings, the sources of dynamic processes. Thus the falling of a body in the neighborhood of a large material entity such as a planet is explained by reference to a gravitational field. The behavior of a pair of bar magnets, attracting and repelling each other in various orientations, is explained by reference to magnetic poles, elementary sources of activity. The name of the game in physics is "*Cherchez la puissance.*" Charges and their associated fields are the basic explanatory items in the science of physics.

What if we were to model psychological science on what physics is really like? This would require us to develop a metaphysical foundation consisting of the elementary active beings in the domain in question. That domain is human life.

Evidently there will be more than one category of elementary active beings in that domain. Even in folk psychology, we are now accustomed to make use of references to active molecular entities in our accounts of important aspects of our lives. Why do I drink red wine? It contains antioxidants that help to diminish the destructive effect of free radicals on my body. Thus we deploy a molecular or M discourse more and more routinely. Why do I find the bodies of women more attractive than those of men? Because I am a male organism, possessed of XY chromosomes, and so subject to the exigencies of the running of certain fixed action patterns. Again, we are becoming accustomed routinely to deploy such explanatory rhetoric in an organism or O discourse. Yet I must choose the wine I drink, and I must suppress or redirect many of my "natural" impulses, shaping what I actually do within the rules, conventions, and customs of my tribe. The primitive active being in this third discursive realm is the human being as a person. Here I deploy a person or P discourse.

None of the three discourse modes is dispensable, yet none is comprehensive. There seem to be three ontological bases to human life conceived on the general model of physics as a science that grounds phenomena in the primitive powers of basic active particulars. Psychology might then be a hybrid science in which all three explanatory discourse modes are required to do justice to human life. The mistake of the bioreductionists is to try to get by without the P-discourse mode in which many of the key phenomena of real life must be described. The mistake of the postmodernists is to try to get by with the P-discourse mode alone.

How might the hybrid be rationally elaborated to build a unified psychology? Here is one suggestion. The M and O discourses can be used to describe and explain the workings of the human body, the movements of its limbs, the biochemistry of its life-sustaining internal processes, and the workings of its brain and nervous system. But to describe and explain the meanings and rules of real life, the P discourse must be used. In that mode we talk about the tasks we must perform and the right and wrong ways of carrying them out. Tasks require tools. Remembering is a P-discourse task, and the tool is mostly the brain of the one who is trying to recollect or recover a representation of some event correctly. Ten-pin bowling is a P-discourse task, and the tools are the limbs and nervous system of the player. Perhaps a unified psychology could be constructed by a comprehensive deployment of the task/tool metaphor. Though it is not "officially" recognized as yet, I think that much that goes on in neuropsychology and the intermediate studies in computer simulation of cognition makes tacit use of just this metaphor. Tasks are recognized in the P-discourse mode, and tools are analyzed in the O- and M-discourse modes.

Philosophy of Psychology

Why do we need philosophy of psychology? Simply because knowledge of any kind is created by an interaction between the concepts people have developed and the apparatus they have constructed, and the relevant aspects of the world. Psychology, though lately it has come to aspire to the style of a science, has been particularly in thrall to unexamined and highly unsatisfactory conceptual presuppositions. Ironically, this has been particularly true of those psychologists who have been most vociferous in denying any interest in philosophy and repudiating the very influence that to the outside observer is obviously paramount in the way they carry on their researches. Physicists have always been alert to their philosophical presuppositions and so have been much less likely to fall into purely conceptual confusions than psychologists. On the other hand, errors in matters of fact very soon make themselves felt and can be corrected. The claim that only human beings have the capacity to manage intentional signs was shown to be false by the Gardners' studies of the acquisition of the semantic and performative aspects of American Sign Language by their chimpanzees. Conceptual confusions are not as easy to detect, since they permeate every aspect of a discipline. It is a conceptual error to infer individual propensities from statistical distributions across a population, yet it continues to be a widespread and commonplace mistake. It is a conceptual error to adopt a discourse frame from which normative concepts are absent, if we wish accurately to describe human behavior. It is also a conceptual error to treat all cognition as if it were exclusively a function of the minds (or brains) of individual people.

The Upshot of Our Inquiries

Abstracting, analyzing, and critically examining the presuppositions of various schools of psychology will put us in a better position to answer some key questions than we were when we began. We will be able to give a reasonably good answer to the big question: What sort of enterprises are academic and clinical psychology?

With these answers to hand, we will be better able to answer the most searching question of all that the recent attempt to found a science of psychology and a clinical psychology brings up: How does academic psychology differ from physics and chemistry? Since these are indisputably paradigms of science, the claim to have inaugurated a science of psychology can best be judged by making this kind of comparison. We should note that should the difference prove to be very great, we may still want to elevate psychology to the status of a prestige discipline, but one that is more similar to some other kinds of inquiry than it is to physics. But we can go very far astray in these reflections if we are in thrall to a positivistic analysis of the natural sciences, and in particular of physics. The three discourse modes that seem to be in use in the everyday management of human life share an ontological style with physics — that is, they are grounded in presuppositions about the primitive sources of different kinds of activity. A comprehensive psychology might be created by linking all three through the task/tool metaphor. Tasks are culturally defined, while tools are, in the first instance, natural organic endowments.

How does clinical psychology differ from medicine? Since the notions of illness, cure, and the like are reasonably well defined for physical medicine, the claim to have inaugurated a genuine clinical psychology can be assessed in the light of the comparison. Even if it turns out that the differences between medicine proper and clinical psychology, psychiatry, and counseling are very great, it does not follow that the procedures of which these specialties consist may not have an important place in the amelioration of human misery, discontent, and pain. Reflection on the role of tacit conceptions of normal functioning in physical medicine may make the difference seem rather less than a crude comparison would suggest.

At first sight it might look as if the two deep questions are, in their own way, scientific questions, to be settled by collecting evidence for and against the theses implicit in answering them, one way or the other. But it is easy to see that they are not. What is at issue in each case is the cluster of implicit assumptions and presuppositions that it is the task of the philosophy of psychology to abstract from the relevant practices.

Notes

1. I am grateful to James T. Lamiell for guidance on these important distinctions and how to render them into English.

2. I am much indebted to discussions with Austin Harrington, who has helped me appreciate the power and forward-looking insights of Dilthey's philosophy of the human sciences.

References

Dilthey, W. 1989. *Introduction to the Human Sciences*. Vol. 1 of *Selected Works*. Trans. R.A. Makkreel and F. Rodi. Princeton, NJ: Princeton University Press.

Eysenck, H. 1952. *The Scientific Study of Personality*. London: Routledge and Kegan Paul.

Festinger, L. 1957. *A Theory of Cognitive Dissonance*. Evanston, IL: Row, Peterson.

Gleitman, H. 1985. *Psychology*. New York: W.W. Norton.

Habermas, J. 1984. *The Theory of Communicative Action*. Vols. I and II. Trans. T. McCarthey. Boston: Beacon Press.

Hilgard, E.R., Atkinson, R.C., and Atkinson, R.L. 1975. *Introduction to Psychology.* New York: Harcourt Brace Jovanovich.

Laird, J.D., and Thompson, N.S. 1992. *Psychology.* New York: Macmillan.

Piaget, J. 1932. *The Language and Thought of the Child.* London: Routledge and Kegan Paul.

Ruse, M. 1989. *Philosophy of Biology.* New York: Macmillan.

Wilson, E.O. 1998. *Consilience: The Unity of Knowledge.* New York: Knopf.

2

Mind as a Scientific Object: A Historical-Philosophical Exploration

Thomas Hardy Leahey

In 1953, the German philologist Bruno Snell published *The Discovery of the Mind: The Greek Origins of European Thought*. His preface exemplifies the difficulties of defining the mind as an object. Despite the bold thesis proclaimed by his title, Snell was not entirely sure that the Greeks had actually discovered something that already existed. Although he asserted that "the rise of thinking among the Greeks [after Homer] was nothing less than a revolution. . . . They discovered the human mind . . . ," he hedged his claim by writing that the Greek discovery "cannot be compared with the discovery of, let us say, a new continent" (Snell, 1953, v). Snell wrestled with possibilities that have since loomed large in psychological metatheory. He specifically rejected the possibility (now espoused by some in cognitive science, e.g., Dahlbom, 1993) that the mind might be an artifact. The mind, Snell wrote, "was not invented, as a man would invent a tool . . . to master a certain type of problem. As a rule, inventions are arbitrarily determined; they are adapted to the purpose from which they take their cue. No objectives, no aims were involved in the discovery of the intellect" (Snell, 1953, p. viii). Snell also perceived but did not fully articulate the conception of mind favored by today's constructivists. He wrote, "[I]n spite of our statement that the Greeks discovered the intellect, we also assert that the discovery was necessary for the intellect to come into existence" (p. viii), hinting that the mind was socially constructed by Greek philosophers, poets, and dramatists during the classical age.

The three alternatives raised by Snell go to the heart of the issues addressed by this book: if and how the mind can be a scientific object. If the mind was truly discovered (or awaits discovery), then psychology, ψυχή-λόγος—the study of the soul—might be a natural science in the usual sense of the term. The second possibility, that mind is a tool, an artifact, suggests that while mind exists as do hammers and modems, psychological science must be reconceived as a science of the artificial (H. Simon, 1981). Natural science concerns itself with spatiotemporal universals, objects such as electrons or quarks that are the same everywhere and always. Hammers and modems are real, but as human artifacts, they do not fall under the purview of natural science. Science explains how hammers and modems work, but hammers and modems are objects of engineering, not science (Leahey, "Psychology as Engineering," this volume).

Mind as artifact shades over into the third possibility, mind as social construction. If mind is socially constructed, then it is uncertain whether there can be any science (as science is usually understood) of mind. Perhaps the study of mind is a historical, not a scientific, undertaking. As Snell remarks, "The intellect, however, comes into the world, it is 'effected,' in the process of revealing itself, i.e. in the course of history" (1953, pp. vi–vii). Furthermore, the constructivist thesis gives rise to a darker prospect for scientific psychology. On the artifact interpretation, minds are real but lack the universality of the proper objects of science. In contrast, mind might be a social construction along the lines of the Greek gods, a profound illusion.

Psychologists tend to take for granted the Western tradition descended from the Greeks that is traced by Snell, but other cultures have different views of mind and self. For example, in *Selfless Persons*, Steven Collins (1982) discusses mind and personality as conceived by Theravada Buddhism. Collins observes with Geertz (1974) that the Western notion of mind, or person, is "a rather peculiar idea within the context of the world's cultures" (Collins, 1982, p. 2).

The Buddhist monk Nyanatiloka contrasts Buddhist with Western conceptions of mind (Collins, 1982, p. 5):

> [T]here are three teachers in the world. The first teacher teaches the existence of an eternal ego-entity outlasting death: that is the Eternalist, as for example the Christian. The second teacher teaches a temporary ego-entity which becomes annihilated at death: that is the annihilationist, or materialist. The third teacher teaches neither an eternal nor a temporary ego-entity: that is the Buddha. The Buddha teaches that what we call ego, self, soul, personality, etc., are merely conventional terms not referring to any real independent entity. And he teaches that there is only to be found this psychophysical process of existence changing from moment to moment. . . . This doctrine of egolessness of existence forms the essence of the Buddha's doctrine of emancipation. Thus with this doctrine of egolessness, or *anatta*, stands or falls the entire Buddhist structure.

Moreover, Theravada Buddhists regard the self, the mind, as a dangerous illusion from which we should free ourselves. According to the Sinhalese monk Rahula, "[T]he idea of self is an imaginary, false belief which has no corresponding reality, and it produces harmful thoughts of 'me' and 'mine,' selfish desire, craving, attachment, hatred, ill-will, conceit, pride, egotism, and other defilements, impurities and problems. . . . In short, to this false view can be traced all the evil in the world" (Collins, 1982, p. 4). For Buddhists, it appears, psychology is the study of a no-thing, a misbegotten enterprise. From the postmodern social constructivist perspective, R. Rorty (1979, 1991, 1993) heartily agrees.

A third book title, *The Discovery of the Individual, 1050–1200* (Morris, 1972), reminds us that more than the scientific character of psychology is at stake in the existence of mind, because possession of mind is strongly linked to personhood. In the West today we assign supreme importance to the individual human being, bearer of inalienable rights against the state and other humans. As Morris says, "The hard core of this individualism lies in the psychological experience . . . [of] the sense of a clear distinction between my self and other people" (1972, p. 3). Traditionally, a human being is treated as a person who transcends animal status by virtue of possessing a soul, or mind. Even in nonreligious contexts, possession of a mind is critical to one's status as a person and a citizen. A human in a persistent vegetative state may be ruled to lack a mind and therefore may be deliberately allowed to die, and the death is not regarded as murder. A human being with dementia—literally, deminded—may be stripped of civil rights and assigned a guardian or consigned to an institution. In psychology, questions of personhood manifest themselves in the study of the self, a less religious term than soul and a more personal one than mind.

Mind as a Religious Object

Western conceptions of mind began in religion before moving first to philosophy and then to science. However, for two reasons, psychologists have underestimated the influence of religious ideas of the soul—the ψυχή of our science—on conceptions of mind and self. First, psychology is an aggressively secular enterprise, and psychologists like to think that they put religion behind them when they assume their role as scientists. A more subtle reason concerns the dominance of historical scholarship by Christian belief. When we as psychologists read about past thinkers such as Plato and Descartes, not only do we look at them as protopsychologists, we see them through the eyes of historians and classicists who until recently worked within a quietly but univocally held Christian framework. That framework rarely intrudes explicitly, but it filters out the rough splinters, odd conceptions, and obscure but vital disputes concerning mind and soul held from Greek times through at least Descartes. Thus we psychologists inherit a conception of the mind subtly shaped by forces of which we know little, drain it of its specifically supernatural content (e.g., survival of bodily death), and fancy that what remains is somehow natural and therefore a proper object of science. I will try briefly to put back some of the lost splinters, conceptions, and disputes to provide a ground against which to see the figure of mind as an object of psychological science.

The Common Pattern

Although there are differences in detail, religions around the world have a remarkably concordant picture of the mind, positing the existence of two immaterial souls for two distinct reasons (Onians, 1961). The first, universal reason is to explain the difference between living and nonliving things. Objects with souls are living; those without are nonliving. The second, less universal reason is to explain human personality. Some religions propose that in addition to the breath of life, there is a soul that constitutes the essence of each person's personality, and sometimes this personal soul is believed to be able to survive the death of the material body, though this is not guaranteed. Modern Christianity, for example, teaches that each human being is composed of a material body and a nonmaterial soul. The soul is said to be the essence of the person, containing personal memories and personal identity. Moreover, while the body is mortal, the soul is immortal, leaving the body at death and traveling to an afterlife in heaven or hell.

The Greco-Roman Trek from Religion to Philosophy

Modern scientific psychology has its roots in Greek philosophy, which initiated secular inquiry into the nature of mind. Notwithstanding the Greek reputation for humanistic rationality, Greek philosophical thought was shaped by traditional Greek religious traditions (Bremmer, 1983) and by the eruptions of new religious forms during the Periclean age (Morgan, 1992).

Bronze Age Greek concepts of the soul are distinctive. In part, they participate in the common pattern just described, but possess unique features all their own (Snell, 1953; Onians, 1961; Bremmer, 1983). To begin with, the *Iliad* and *Odyssey* contain no word designating the mind or personality as a whole (but see Knox, 1993). Closest is the word ψυχή, the breath of life. To a large extent, ψυχή is the Greek version of the animating principle: its departure from a wounded warrior means his death. However, ψυχή is more than merely the breath of life, but is less than the complete individual mind or soul. During sleep or a swoon it may leave the body and travel around, and it may survive bodily death, but it is never described as being active when a person is awake, and it is never implicated in causing behavior.

Instead, behavior was attributed to several independently operating soul-like entities residing in different parts of the body. For example, there was φρήνες, located in the diaphragm, whose function was rationally planning action. Θυμός, in the heart, governed action driven by emotion. Νόος was responsible for accurate perception and clear cognition of the world. There were other, less frequently cited minisouls as well. None of these minisouls survived the death of the body, giving the afterlife of the Homeric ψυχή a rather bizarre character. Deprived of its body-souls, the ψυχή in the afterlife was a mental cripple, deprived of feeling, thought, and speech and incapable of normal movement. The appearance of the ψυχή was exactly that of the body at death, complete with wounds. Moreover, not every ψυχή went to Hades, because proper burial of the body was felt necessary to effect the transition from life to afterlife. Women, children, adolescents, and the elderly were not ritually buried, so their ψυχηαί were not believed to survive death, and warriors feared death without burial, for example, by drowning at sea.

On the other hand, buried with honor, a great warrior found an exalted place in the afterlife.

Greek religion and the concept of ψυχή underwent a profound change in the late fifth century BCE (Burkert, 1985; Morgan, 1992). Traditional Greek religious thought had insisted on a great gulf between the human and divine worlds, downplaying the idea of personal immortality. However, in the wake of the Peloponnesian War, continuity between the human and divine worlds was the theme of various new cults, often imported from the non-Greek East. In their practices these new religions induced in worshippers ecstatic states through which they might for a time join the gods, perhaps even briefly becoming the god of their veneration. The ψυχή became a personal, immortal soul, taking after death its rightful place in the divine world of the gods. Plato was influenced by these new teachings, but steered them in a less ecstatic, more philosophical and cognitive direction (Morgan, 1992). For Plato, the proper object of the soul's attention was indeed something divine, but he taught that instead of seeking salvation through ecstatic communion with the gods, the soul should seek salvation through philosophical pursuit of eternal, transcendent Truth. In Plato's hands, the mind became identified with reason, the ability to formulate and know the universal Truths underwritten by the heavenly Forms.

So far in the history of the West, the concept of mind was tied up with two concerns (R. Rorty, 1979). The first concern was for human dignity, or personhood. Having an immortal soul separated people from the material and animal worlds, making humans fundamentally divine, possessing dignity, not simply value (R. Rorty, 1979). This was the prime concern of the new ecstatic cults that Plato sought to tame. The second concern was the acquisition of knowledge. Plato said that knowledge was acquired through reason, and later philosophers followed him in this. The human soul was pure reason (Plato's spirited and animal souls are similar to the Bronze Age minisouls), separating people from the material and animal worlds and making them capable of grasping the Forms. In Plato's works there is little or no tension between the new religious conception of the personal soul and his own conception of the soul as pure, knowing reason. After Plato came his student Aristotle, who took Plato's teachings further away from religion, beginning to treat the human mind in a naturalistic, scientific fashion. In his works lie the seeds of tension and ultimate incompatibility between mind as religious object and mind as scientific object.

Aristotle continued to be influenced by the ancient tradition of soul as a life principle. For Aristotle, possession of a soul marked the difference between living and nonliving things. Thus there were plant and animal souls in addition to the human soul. More naturalistically, as a biologist, Aristotle defined the various souls functionally rather than dualistically. According to Aristotle, soul was not a thing that enters a body and gives it life, and that leaves it causing death, but the total collection of life processes that define the kind of being that a plant, animal, or human is. The soul is the formal, defining cause of a creature. Thus a cat has a cat's soul, a dog, a dog's soul, and a human, a human soul. However, the soul is not a substance separable from its material embodiment, as is the religious personal soul or Plato's rational soul. For Aristotle, the relation of soul to body is the same as the relation of the form of a statue to its matter. The form of the Venus de Milo defines it as such, but it is embodied in marble. The statue's form is not identical to the marble, because the same form may be embodied in a plaster or bronze replica, but it cannot exist without being embodied in some matter. The soul, as the formal cause of a person, thus has no existence beyond the life of the plant, animal, or person.

Aristotle's functional conception of the soul worked well for plants and animals, but difficulties arose when he and his followers (especially those working in the Muslim or Christian traditions) turned to the human soul. Following Plato, Aristotle defined the human soul—mind—as reason, the unique human ability to formulate universal truths. In part, this is consistent with his functional scheme, because mind is defined as the function of reason. However, there is a temptation to go further, saying that mind is in some sense separable from the body and perhaps divine, even immortal. First, logic—the heart of reason—exists before and after the lives of particular humans and is universal in scope, being the same in all human thinkers. Second, the universals known by mind transcend physical existence. The form of catness existed before, and will survive the demise of, all felines now living. Thus mind, reason, seems to transcend physical embodiment in particular humans because logic does, and because the objects of reason are themselves transcendent. Aristotle's treatment of mind (particularly active mind) is notoriously vague on this point, but arguments like these were adopted by Christians such as St. Augustine to establish the existence of immortal human souls (R. Rorty, 1979).

Conundrums of Medieval and Renaissance Thought

Ultimately, the religious and Aristotelian conceptions of the soul could not be reconciled, because Aristotle's *mind* was not the same as the Christian or Islamic *soul*. Religious thinkers influenced by Aristotle created two heresies about the soul that Descartes later strenuously but vainly tried to avoid (Gaukroger, 1995). Each heresy was occasioned by the fact that Aristotle's *mind* was pure reason and knowledge of universals and was therefore impersonal. Experience and personal memory—and therefore personal identity—were functions of the animal soul, which was presumably not immortal.

The first heresy was called Averroism, after Averroës, the Latinized name of the Islamic physician-philosopher ibn-Rushd (1126–1198). Averroism resulted from identifying mind with the Christian or Muslim soul. The heresy of Averroism derived from the fact that because the Aristotelian *mind* contained only general knowledge, not personal memories, it could not be the essence of one's personality capable of surviving bodily death. Mind was understood by Averroes to be a divine inner light from God that illuminates general knowledge, but that remerges with God at death. Many Christian Aristotelians, including Thomas Aquinas, tried to fend off the implications of Averroism by emphasizing the Resurrection, when the mind would be reunited with its body, reconstituting the whole Aristotelian person, form (soul) properly embodied in matter (flesh). However, by the time of the scientific revolution, the hope of imminent resurrection was fading, and Christian theology replaced it with the idea of immediate judgment of a soul that would live forever in heaven or hell.

The other heretical temptation, called Alexandrism after Alexander of Aphrodisias (fl. 200), arose from dropping Aristotle's sharp distinction of form and matter and attributing to the matter of the brain the power not only to perceive and remember, but to think and have knowledge. Alexandrism was heretical because it amounted to materialism, denying that humans are anything more than complex, mortal animals.

The Alexandrian view became increasingly popular in the Renaissance as naturalistic modes of thought began to replace supernatural ones. There is a parallel to the distinction between living and nonliving things in magnetism. Magnets seem quite mysterious, almost alive, as they attract metal and repel one another. A supernatural explanation of magnetism would locate the power of the magnet in an indwelling demon or a spell cast on the magnet by a sorcerer. Renaissance naturalists rejected such explanations, saying that magnets simply possessed their power by "a secret virtue inbred by nature, not by any conjuration," as Robert Fludd put it (Thomas, 1971, p. 266). Similarly, thinking, including the formation of universals, might be explained as an entirely natural power of the human brain. Obviously such naturalism about the soul offended theology, but it possessed a more philosophical shortcoming too, because the "secret virtue" of magnets to attract metals or brains to produce thoughts was left unexplained.

Mind as Scientific Puzzle

As we have traced its development so far, the concept of mind has been linked to the problem of personhood and human dignity and to the problem of how humans uniquely grasp universal ideas. These concerns were addressed by philosophers and by religious thinkers. The scientific revolution ushered in a new conception of mind, mind as consciousness.

The Transformation of Experience by the Scientific Revolution

The idea of consciousness as an inner mental space would have puzzled Greek or medieval philosophers (R. Rorty, 1979, 1993). The makers of the scientific revolution created the concept of consciousness as they created a radically new theory of perception that went with their new scientific epistemology. Greek and medieval philosophers believed that they knew things from the outside in; the makers of the scientific revolution believed that they knew the world from the inside out (A.M. Smith, 1990). Descartes was the last and most important artisan of this project, creating a definition of consciousness that ruled philosophical and scientific thought for centuries.

Aristotle proposed a theory of perception that was widely held by medieval philosophers (Durrant, 1993; A.M. Smith, 1990). In an act of perception the sense organ received the form but not the matter of the object perceived. For example, if I look at the Venus de Milo, my eye receives the statue's form, but does not receive the marble of which it is made. Thus I am directly acquainted with all the features that define the Venus statue, not only its size and shape but also its color and even its beauty. According to this account, there is therefore a direct, objective correlation between the formal order of the universe and my experience of it. The assertion that beauty is part of the statue's form, to be simply "picked up," as perceptual realists would say, strongly underscores how different our post-Cartesian understanding of perception is from Aristotle's. The Venus de Milo, on his account, is objectively beautiful, while we regard beauty as a culturally in-formed private judgment of the mind.[1] Because our understanding is most sure about direct experience and least sure about judgments made about that experi-ence, we know things from the outside (perception) in (to judgment).

The undoing of Aristotelian perceptual theory began with the development of rigorous logic and mathematics in the late Middle Ages and Renaissance. A conflict arose between elegant mathematical calculations applied to the universe and the messy appearances of our experience of the universe. In many respects the essence of the scientific revolution was the complete subordination of the world as we experience it to the way mathematical reason conceives it. Truth came to lie in calculation rather than perception. As Galileo wrote in his *Dialogue Concerning the Two Chief World Systems,* "There is no limit to my astonishment when I reflect that Aristarchus and Copernicus were able to make reason so con-quer sense that, in defiance of the latter, the former became mistress of their belief" (L.D. Smith, 1990, p. 738). The conquest of sense by reason created con-sciousness as an object of scientific concern, although not an object of scientific study.

In *The Assayer,* Galileo expresses the new scientific attitude to experience that regards the senses as deceptive and reason as the best guide to understanding the world. Here he distinguishes the primary and secondary properties and begins to create the modern idea of consciousness completed by Descartes:

> Whenever I conceive any material or corporeal substance I immediately
> . . . think of it as bounded, and as having this or that shape; as being
> large or small [and] as being in motion or at rest . . . From these condi-
> tions I cannot separate such a substance by any stretch of my imagina-
> tion. But that it must be white or red, bitter or sweet, noisy or silent, and
> of sweet or foul odor, my mind does not feel compelled to bring in as
> necessary accompaniments. Without the senses as our guides, reason or
> imagination unaided would probably never arrive at qualities like these.
> Hence, I think that tastes, odors, colors, and so on . . . reside only in the
> consciousness [so that] if the living creature were removed all these qual-

ities would be wiped away and annihilated.[2] (Quoted by A.M. Smith, 1990, p. 739)

The order of human experience no longer had any reliable connection to the order of the world. Instead, experience — consciousness — needs to be corrected by mathematics, which depicts in imagination the world as it really is, a perfect machine without color, taste, aesthetic value, or moral import. Burtt (1954, pp. 123–24) reminds us of how deep and profound was the gulf between the old classical and medieval understanding of mind and its place in the universe from the new scientific one:

> The scholastic scientist looked out upon the world of nature, and it appeared to him a quite sociable and human world. It was finite in extent. It was made to serve his needs. It was clearly and fully intelligible, being immediately present to the rational powers of his mind; it was composed fundamentally of, and was intelligible through, those qualities which were most vivid and intense in his own immediate experience — color, sound, beauty, joy, heat, cold, fragrance and its plasticity to purpose and ideal. Now the world is an infinite and monotonous mathematical machine. Not only is his high place in a cosmic teleology lost, but all these things which were the very substance of the physical world to the scholastic — the thing that made it alive and lovely and spiritual — are lumped together and crowded into the small fluctuating and temporary positions of extension which we call human nervous systems. It was simply an incalculable change in the viewpoint of the world held by intelligent opinion in Europe.

In Descartes's and Locke's hands, this incalculable change created the conception of mind as a scientific object upon which psychology was first erected.

The Cartesian Paradigm: The Way of Ideas

Descartes is typically presented as a philosopher who dabbled in science. In fact, he was a scientist and mathematician first, a leading participant in the scientific revolution. He was also raised as a devout Catholic and retained an earnest faith throughout his life, never letting his science become incompatible with his religion. In order to understand Descartes's legacy to psychology — a new conception of mind and its place in science — we must begin by looking at his overall understanding of the universe as a man of faith and of science.

Descartes was closely connected with a circle of reforming Catholics led by the scientist and theologian Marin Mersenne (1588–1648) who were worried about the scientifically appealing but religiously dangerous ideas of Renaissance naturalism. Renaissance naturalism was scientific in that it explained the world without reference to supernatural powers, but it was suspect religiously because it seemed to grant supernatural powers to matter itself. Naturalism was especially dangerous to religious orthodoxy when applied to living things, particularly people. If all mental functions were functions of the body, then the existence of the Christian soul was placed in doubt. To counter Renaissance nature philosophy, Mersenne and his followers, including Descartes, believed and taught that matter was completely inert, possessing no active powers of any kind—including magnetism and gravity. Active power to initiate motion was reserved to God alone. Matter moved or changed only when physically pushed by another piece of matter. Theirs was truly a clockwork view of the universe.

Descartes's conception of mind and body was very carefully worked out within this religious-scientific framework, and it decisively shaped the scientific psychology that was yet to come. Descartes was committed to viewing animals as complex automata, machines whose operations could be fully explained as physical processes without resort to vital forces of any kind. Thus Descartes rejected the idea that the heart was a spontaneously working pump circulating blood through the body because its action seemed self-caused by an internal power, little different from attributing attractive power to magnets. However, the "mental" powers of the beast-machine were considerable, including everything Aristotle had attributed to the sensitive soul, and to the extent that people were animals, their mental powers had to have a purely mechanical explanation. The place of the immortal human soul in a mechanical world and a mechanical body had become a serious problem.

Although Descartes began his scientific investigations in physics, he expanded them to include physiology, especially the operations of the brain and nervous system. In a letter to Mersenne of December 1629, Descartes described watching butchers slaughter cattle and taking parts back to his lodgings for his own dissections. Three years later, he wrote to Mersenne that he would now "speak more about man than I had intended to before, because I shall try to explain all of his principal functions. I have already written about those that pertain to life such as . . . the five senses. Now I am dissecting the heads of different animals in order to explain what imagination, memory etc. consist of" (quoted by Gaukroger, 1995, p. 228).

In order to understand the fundamentally new conception of mind and body that emerged from Descartes's science and philosophy—and therefore the new conception of mind as scientific object that gave rise to scientific psychology—it is important to understand the goal Descartes set for himself. From the time of Aristotle right through the Middle Ages, physicians, philosophers, and theologians had attributed most psychological functions to the animal soul, and therefore to the animal—including the human—body. Islamic physician-philosophers had proposed specific locations in the brain in which the Aristotelian mental faculties were located. Within Descartes's renovated Christian framework, however, these older treatments of the faculties were unacceptable precisely because they endowed matter with soul-like powers the way Renaissance naturalism endowed matter with magical powers such as magnetic attraction. Saying that a given piece of brain tissue has the power of memory is not a scientific explanation at all because it does not specify any mechanism by which memories are created and retrieved.

Moreover, by endowing matter with active powers, Renaissance naturalism was inconsistent with the mechanico-religious worldview being developed by Mersenne and his followers. Therefore, "Descartes' aim was to show that a number of psychophysiological functions *that had always been recognized as being corporeal* [by Aristotelians] could be accounted for in a way which did not render matter sentient" (Gaukroger, 1995, p. 278; emphasis in original).

In his work on physics, *Le Monde*, Descartes described a mechanistic universe that behaved exactly like ours, inviting us to believe that it *is* ours. In his work on physiological psychology, *L'Homme* (never completed and posthumously published), Descartes asked his readers to imagine "statues or earthen machines"—indeed, a "man-machine"—whose inner operations he described in detail, inviting us to believe that these machine *are* us, except that they lack souls. His optimism that the behavior of animals (and much of that of humans) could be explained mechanistically was fed by the high artisanship of contemporary craftsmen, who built mechanical animals and people that behaved in lifelike ways. Seeing mechanical statues move and respond to stimuli helped Descartes think that animals too were sophisticated machines.

Struggling to oust magical, occult powers from matter, Descartes set in motion the reduction of mental functions to mechanical processes—and perhaps the extirpation of mind as a scientific object—that has tempted some psychologists and repelled others. Although the details of Descartes's physiological psychology are not important here (see Gaukroger, 1995), the conceptual difficulties his approach created for his treatment of the human mind are. The problems for Descartes's psychology, and therefore for all later psychologists, begin when we turn to the human soul, which Descartes as a Christian had to exempt from mechanistic explanation. Descartes's account is usually presented as clean and simple, but it is in fact slippery and elusive, a tortured attempt to preserve a fragmentary Christian soul in a mechanistic universe.

In *L'Homme*, the human soul is distinguished from the functions of the animal body it inhabits by the power to think, which had three important facets for Descartes. Defining the soul by the power of thought, or reason, is consistent with the ancient Greek view described earlier. What is new is Descartes's account of how thinking separates humans from animals in experience, in behavior, and in the possession of language.

Thought makes human experience different from that of animals. Descartes never denied that animals have experiences, that is, that they are aware of their surroundings. What they lack is reflective, thoughtful awareness of their own awareness. Descartes wrote (quoted by Gaukroger, pp. 282 and 325):

> [A]nimals do not see as we do when we are aware that we see, but only as we do when our mind is elsewhere. In such a case the images of external objects are depicted on our retinas, and perhaps the impressions that they make in the optic nerves cause our limbs to make various movements, although we are quite unaware of them. In such a case we too move just like automata.

As did William James centuries later, Descartes here drew a sharp dividing line between simple awareness and self-awareness. James pointed out that much of our behavior occurs by virtue of ingrained habits and without being accompanied by thought, as when a driver responds to a traffic light turning red while at the same time carrying on a conversation with a friend. The impression of the light on the retina causes the driver's foot to carry out the movement of hitting the car's brakes. The driver experiences the light becoming red, but does not think about it, because his or her mind "is elsewhere," in conversation.

Thought makes human behavior more flexible than animal behavior. Animals, Descartes wrote, require some preset "disposition for every particular action" (quoted by Gaukroger, 1995, p. 276). Hitting the brakes when the light turns red is a preset habit that is automatically and thoughtlessly activated by the stimulus of the red light. Descartes viewed animals as machines that always responded in such reflexive ways. We, on the other hand, can respond to entirely novel situations by thinking about them. If you come to an intersection where all the lights are out, you will drop your conversation and think carefully about what to do. An animal, lacking any stimulus to control its behavior, would be frozen into inaction or spurred by some other stimulus into inappropriate action. Behavioral flexibility became the hallmark of mind for James.

The third outcome of human thinking was language. In *L'Homme*, language played a crucial role in Descartes's understanding of the human mind, being critical to human self-awareness. While engaged in conversation, you reflexively applied the brakes upon seeing a red traffic light. Seeing-eye dogs are trained to stop themselves and their master when they see a red light. At this level of reflexive response there is no difference between you and the dog. However, according to Descartes's analysis, only you, as a human being, can think about traffic lights and think the thought that the red light means stop. The trained dog stops as you do, but it cannot formulate the proposition "Red means stop." Being able to think about red lights in this way gives humans the ability to think about experience reflectively, rather than simply having it.

Animals, said Descartes, do not think as we do (if they think at all) because they cannot think with linguistically stated propositions. For Descartes, the ability of the human soul to formulate propositions did not, however, depend upon acquiring any particular human language. He proposed that there is an innate human language of the mind of which actual human languages are outward translations (cf. Jerry Fodor's [1975] *mentalese*). Thus while you say, "Red means stop," and a German says, "Rot bedeutet halten," at a deeper level you think the same thought linking the concepts of "redness of traffic light" to "need to stop one's motor vehicle."

Observe here that Descartes has retained but importantly altered the traditional conception of reason as the power to formulate universals. For Plato and Aristotle, universals retained a perceptual character. Plato's Forms were things that existed in the empyrean and could be experienced by the disembodied soul in heaven. In this life, too, Plato intimated, the Forms could be seen by a good soul rightly taught by a good philosopher. In the Ladder of Love in the *Symposium*, the Form of Beauty clearly retains sensuous and lovable character. One starts by loving a beautiful body, then the beautiful soul inside, then the Form of Beauty itself, which one may ultimately see in a sort of rapturous vision. Aristotle's philosophy is less ecstatic, but he also treats universals as perceptual entities. Mind observes similarities and differences among things belonging to a common class, such as *cat*, stripping away the accidental features and leaving the universal ones that define the form of the class, an ideal, universal cat of no particular color, size, or fur length. Descartes reformulated knowledge as abstract propositions that can be stated in language. This move reinforces the subordination of experience to rational calculation begun by Galileo.

Descartes never completed the part of *L'Homme* in which he planned to give a scientific treatment of the human soul. In November 1633, on the eve of the publication of *Le Monde*, Descartes learned of the condemnation by the Roman Inquisition of Galileo's advocacy of the Copernican hypothesis. To Mersenne, Descartes wrote that he was so surprised by Galileo's fate of house arrest for life that "I nearly decided to burn all my papers," because his own system of the world depended so much upon Galileo's. Nevertheless, "I wouldn't want to publish a discourse which had a single word that the Church disapproved of; so I prefer to suppress it rather than publish it in mutilated form" (quoted by Gaukroger, 1995, pp. 290–91).

Because Descartes's physics proved to be so erroneous and his philosophy so influential, it is rarely appreciated that he developed his foundational philosophy to save his science from Galileo's fate. Thus began the second, primarily philosophical phase in Descartes's career. He decided that in order for his scientific views to win the acceptance that Galileo's had not, they needed careful and convincing philosophical justification. For the development of psychology, Descartes's new direction was fateful. In his philosophical treatment of the mind, Descartes created the idea that mind was consciousness and only consciousness. Psychology thus would be born by definition as the science that studies consciousness. In the end, Descartes's legacy to psychology was a set of deep, perhaps intractable problems with which psychology has struggled to the present day (Searle, 1994; Dennett, 1991).

Descartes had fitfully worked on philosophical topics from the beginning of his career. Most important was his project of discovering or creating methodological rules by which the mind might reliably know the truth in science and philosophy. As Aristotle's physics crumbled before the research of the scientific revolution, it became widely believed that Aristotle had erred because he had relied on poor methods for theorizing about and investigating nature. Descartes wanted the new science to be guided by a better methodology, and for some years he worked on writing *Rules for the Direction of the Mind*, but eventually abandoned it, although it was published posthumously in 1684. In 1635 he returned to giving science its epistemological foundation in *Discourse on the Method of Rightly Conducting One's Reason and Seeking Truth in the Sciences*, published in 1637.

He describes the famous moment that inspired his philosophy. Returning home after military service from the coronation of Holy Roman Emperor Ferdinand II, he spent one day, possibly November 10, 1619, in a stove-heated room meditating on his own thoughts and formulating the basic principles of his philosophy. Writing in 1635, Descartes wanted to offer a firm philosophical foundation for the apparently dangerous science he was developing, and he returned to the method of radical doubt he had adopted in 1619. Then he had resolved to systematically doubt every belief he had—even those no sane person would doubt—until he found something so self-evidently true that it could not be doubted. His aim was not to actually cast doubt upon commonsense truths, but to force himself to find sound reasons for believing them.

Descartes found that he could doubt the existence of God, the validity of his sensations, and the existence of his body. He continued in this way until he found one thing he could not doubt, his own existence as a self-conscious, thinking being. One cannot doubt that one doubts, for in doing so, one makes real the very action supposedly in doubt. Doubting is an act of thinking, and Descartes expressed his first indubitable truth as the famous "Cogito, ergo sum": I think, therefore I am. I am a thing that thinks, and that is all. The soul, the thinking thing, was a spiritual substance wholly without matter, not occupying space (unextended), and completely separate from the body. Descartes proposed a radical new dualism in which soul and body are utterly unalike, sharing neither matter nor form in common. Nor is the soul conceived as the form of the body. Instead, the soul dwells within the mechanical body as a sort of ghost (as Ryle [1949] called it later), receiving sensations from it and commanding it by acts of will.

Descartes's dualism of soul and body was a way of explaining the dualism of secondary and primary sense properties. According to Descartes, the material world was made of corpuscles, or atoms, which possess only the properties of extension in space and physical location. In addition to that material world, including the body, there is a subjective world of consciousness and mind. Perhaps this second world is spiritual as well, for God and the soul are not material. In any case, as far as human knowledge is concerned, Descartes concluded that there are two worlds, an objective, scientifically knowable, mechanical-material world (the world as it really is) and a subjective world of human consciousness known through introspection (the world of a person as a thinking being).

Descartes was not the first to prove his own existence from mental activity. St. Augustine had said, "If I am deceived, I exist," and Parmenides had said, "For it is the same thing to think and to be." What was new and of profound implications was Descartes's radical reflexivity (Taylor, 1989), his focus on the self and his invention of consciousness as a thing that could be studied. Augustine had turned inward and found God. Descartes turned inward and found only himself. It was a momentous point in the history of psychology and philosophy, and we need to examine it and its implications carefully.

Descartes's argument of the *cogito* created consciousness as an object of scrutiny by radically dividing the self from conscious experience. Prior to the scientific revolution, people had assumed that the world was as it seemed to be and had simply lived in and through experience. However, the division of the primary and secondary sense properties destroyed the traditional naive belief in the validity of experience. Descartes built on this distinction by claiming that we can step back from our experience and examine it as a collection of objects—sensations—that are not part of the self.

Imagine looking at a green leaf. Now I ask you to look at the green more closely. In the older Aristotelian view, you would simply take yourself to be carefully attending to one of the leaf's special sensibles, the green that the leaf really is. Descartes, however, asks you to do something different, to think about your sensation of green, how greenness appears in consciousness. Looking in this way, you are no longer inspecting the leaf, but are introspecting a bit of consciousness, the sensation of green.

Dennett (1991) usefully calls Descartes's model of mind the Cartesian Theater. A viewer, your inner self, the existence of which Descartes has (apparently) proved by the *cogito*, looks at a screen upon which the visual stimuli from the retina are projected. Naïvely, when we see the image of a leaf, we believe that we are seeing an actual leaf outside us. If, however, the Cartesian Theater is true, what the self actually sees is not a leaf but the projected *image* of a leaf. Introspection then consists of thinking of the image as an image and of then inspecting the image without reference to the object outside.

With the Cartesian Theater the psychology of consciousness was born, although it was not yet a science. After Descartes it was generally taken for granted that consciousness is a collection of sensations projected to the mind that the self can then reflectively examine. Natural science continued to examine the world naïvely as a collection of objects to be carefully observed and about which theories might be propounded and tested. Mind was a special inner place, an object needing special methods to be studied scientifically. Psychological science became defined as the reflective, introspective study of a special inner world made up of sensations qua sensations. By submitting experience to experimental control, sensations could be carefully observed, and theories about them might be propounded and tested. Thinking of experience as an object, consciousness, apart from the things causing it gave rise in the mid-nineteenth century to both scientific psychology and modern art. Modern art began when painters rebelled against the idea of art as representation and asked viewers to look at the surface of the canvas. Traditional art, like traditional theories of perception, focused on the thing represented. The goal of a landscape, for example, was to show how a mountain or lake really was. Modern artists, however, wanted viewers to look at the canvas, seeing not what the artist saw, but the subjective impression created in the artist by the mountain or lake.

By splitting off experience from the self and making it a thing, consciousness, that might become a scientific object, Descartes made psychology possible, and he made it philosophically important, too. As a philosopher and scientist, Descartes wanted to know how the world really is. For traditional philosophies this was not a problem, because experience was thought to reveal the world directly to us. However, in Descartes's scheme the thinking self is trapped in the Cartesian Theater, seeing only a projection of the world, not the world itself. Consciousness was indelibly subjective, a presentation of how the world is for us; for it to be the basis of science and of knowledge more generally, it had to be purged of its subjectivity. As Galileo observed, experience was full of subjective traps and needed to be subordinated to the disciplines of reason. Galileo and Descartes made it imperative to study us—to practice psychology—so that the subjective contributions to experience might be subtracted, leaving only objective truth (Gaukroger, 1995).

It is generally recognized today that Descartes's philosophy failed to negotiate its way between the heresies he wished to avoid. Specifically, by denying personal memory to the soul he fell into Averroism, and his works were in fact placed on the Catholic Church's Index of prohibited books in 1663. Nevertheless, his new conception of mind triumphed and was spread by others. For the Anglo-American tradition, the most important Cartesian was John Locke. Traditionally, in the history of psychology Locke is usually paired off against Descartes as the empiricist to Descartes's rationalist. In fact, however, the differences between Locke and Descartes were not deep, because they shared the key idea of the Cartesian Theater, which became known to British philosophers as the Way of Ideas (Leahey, 2004).

Locke (1690/1975) wrote, "Since the Mind, in all its thoughts and Reasonings, hath no other immediate Object but its own Ideas . . . it is evident, that our Knowledge is only conversant about them." This is the Cartesian Theater summarized in a nutshell. Like Descartes, Locke held that ideas are mental representations of objects. The mind does not know Forms or forms, or even objects themselves, but its own ideas only. Where do our ideas come from? "To this I answer, in one word, From Experience: In that, all our knowledge is founded and derived. Our Observation employed either about external, sensible objects; or about the internal Operations of our Minds . . . is that which supplies our Understandings with all the materials of thinking. These two are the Fountains of Knowledge, from whence all the Ideas we have, or can naturally have, do spring." (pp. 104–5). The first fountain of knowledge, or kind of experience, was sensation, resulting in ideas about the objects that cause the sensations, including pleasures and pains. The second fountain of experience was reflection, observation of our own mental processes. When Kant later denied that the self can know its own operations, the stage was set for important debates about the possibility of introspection and the status of mind as an object of science.

Consequences of the Cartesian Paradigm: Mind as Scientific Object

The Cartesian-Lockean Way of Ideas created a set of questions and issues that drove philosophical and psychological theory and research for more than three hundred years. In this section, I briefly tour the psychologically most important of these questions and issues as they developed through the rise of cognitive science.[3] As R. Rorty (1979) and Searle (1994) have noted, the Cartesian view of mind as consciousness created a new challenge to philosophers, the challenge from which scientific psychology sprang. It was the challenge of subjectivity and had many facets. The old Aristotelian, Scholastic theory of perception said that humans are in direct contact with the formal features of every object we perceive. There was no subjective realm of consciousness filled with ideas having nonobjective, purely subjective sensory features. Once the realm of consciousness was defined, however, it begged for an explanation. At its inception, scientific psychology aimed to explain consciousness, the world of "immediate experience," as it was called, leaving natural science to tackle its mathematicized world-machine of "mediate experience."

Where Do Secondary Qualities Come From?

The simplest question about the subjective realm of consciousness appeared to be finding out where the secondary qualities come from. If objects themselves lack color or taste or beauty, why do our ideas of them have these qualities? A great deal of psychological research was devoted to this question as psychologists studied topics such as color and tone perception. Some secondary properties could be linked to objective "powers" (as Locke called them) possessed by objects themselves. For example, while objects are not colored, our perception of color is caused by the ability of the cones in the retina to respond differently to different wavelengths of light reflected by objects.

More problematical—and of greater moment for the history of Western culture—were properties such as beauty that had once been thought objective but that could not be directly linked to physical "powers"—causal properties—at all. Clearly in some sense the beauty of a painting depends upon (supervenes on, we now say) physical features of paint-on-canvas, because if they were to change, the beauty of the painting would change, too. However, judgments of beauty depend on factors lying beyond physical causation or even individual conscious perception. Many nineteenth-century academic paintings once praised for their beauty are now regarded as unpleasant kitsch; many people, including some critics, liked the Sistine Chapel better before it was restored to the glory that impressed the Renaissance (Zalewski, 1998). Judgments of beauty are clearly bound to historical time and place. So controversial, because it is subjective, is the concept of beauty, in fact, that it is rarely used in contemporary art criticism. It is also interesting to observe that the psychology of aesthetics has had its ups and downs throughout the history of psychology. Gustav Theodor Fechner studied aesthetic judgment with psychophysical techniques (Fechner, 1876) and when the American Psychological Association was reorganized in 1945, there was a division of aesthetic psychology. It died, though today a few psychologists hope to resurrect, if not a division, at least a group interested in the psychology of beauty. Similarly, notwithstanding Kant's and Lawrence Kohlberg's attempts to ground ethics in pure reason, moral judgments once thought to be objectively grounded in external reality are now seen as subjective emotional responses, and "judgmental" is a term of abuse.

How Are Mind and Body Connected?

Historically, the first problem created by the new Cartesian conception of mind as consciousness was the problem of mind-body interaction. Descartes thought that mind and body interact and even provided the location of interaction, the pineal gland. Sensory processes threw images onto the surface of the pineal gland for inspection by the soul, and the soul could move the pineal gland to affect the movements of the body.

However, the implausibility of Descartes's position was quickly spotted by one of Descartes's many correspondents, Princess Elisabeth of Bohemia (1615–80). In June 1643, Elisabeth wrote that she could not comprehend "how the soul (non-extended and immaterial) can move the body"; how can "body be pushed by something immaterial . . . which cannot have any communication with it? And I admit it would be easier for me to concede matter and extension to the soul, than the capacity of moving a body and of being moved, to an immaterial being" (Blom, 1978, pp. 111–12). Descartes replied with a vague argument about the "unity" of mind and body, but the princess remained perplexed, writing in July, "I too find that the senses show me that the soul moves the body; but they fail to teach me (any more than the understanding and the imagination) the manner in which she does it." Perhaps "there are unknown properties in the soul" that make interaction possible, but the matter remains mysterious; "I will despair of finding certitude in any matter unless you provide me with it" (Blom, 1978, p. 117). In his next letter, Descartes became concerned about the princess's health, and the correspondence left mind-body interaction unresolved.

Princess Elisabeth's puzzle over understanding how mind and body connect became the "world-knot" of philosophers and bane of psychologists. After Descartes came occasionalism, which held that mind and body are separate, but that God coordinates events in consciousness with events in the body. Then came Leibniz's psychophysical parallelism, which is the same theory with God left out. Parallelism was widely adopted by early psychologists, despite its implication that consciousness does not do anything. In his behaviorist manifesto, Watson (1913) denounced the mind-body problem (and parallelism in particular) as an issue that psychologists could and should avoid by adopting behaviorism.

It should be noted that the troubling question of mind-body interaction (or lack of it) was occasioned as much by Descartes's conception of matter as by his conception of mind (Gaukroger, 1995). Aristotle thought of living matter in a quasi-vitalistic way, as fundamentally different from nonliving matter, specially capable of being informed by soul (Burnyeat, 1992), and his conception was retained by the Scholastics. For Aristotle, the soul was the collection of life functions of a living body; when those processes ceased, the soul's existence ended. Soul and living flesh formed a natural unity that could not be formed by soul and inanimate matter, and since the soul simply was the functions of the body, the problem of mind-body interaction did not arise. Renaissance naturalism continued this line of thinking, albeit in a different way, seeing mental processes as the outcome of special, but natural, powers possessed by the brain. Since mind was produced naturally by the brain, again the problem of mind-body action did not arise. But Descartes deliberately and forcefully erased the difference between living organisms and clockwork machines and explained everything save consciousness and thinking as mechanical functions of the body. The soul was set radically off as a nonmaterial, unextended substance utterly distinct from the clockwork human body in which it somehow dwelled. Soul and body did not form a natural unity (as they could not if souls were to dwell bodiless in heaven), nor was thinking a brain process, as the naturalists held. Thus the mystery of soul-body interaction was created.

Do Mental Processes Exist?

For Aristotle and the Scholastics, soul was a set of processes.[4] Each of Aristotle's three souls was defined by its characteristic functions. The nutritive soul of plants had the functions of nutrition, growth, and reproduction. The sensitive soul of animals included these and added sensation, common sense (sensory integration), imagination, and memory. Sensation gave rise to motivation and behavior as good things were approached and bad ones avoided; Aristotle called this sensitive appetite. The human soul added the function of acquiring universal knowledge that Aristotle called *mind*. He divided mind into passive mind, which stored universals, and active mind, which produced them. It was active mind in particular that Aristotelians were sometimes tempted to make immortal. Possession of universals created a uniquely human motive, rational appetite, pursuing good for its own sake.

Descartes radically changed the West's conception of mind by equating it with consciousness and assigning it but one function, thinking. Functions previously thought to belong to the soul were assigned to the body, reconceived as a clockwork reflex machine. The consequences of so redefining mind and body were considerable.

Descartes's severing of soul and body provoked a new form of materialism, more radical than Aristotelian (or Renaissance) naturalism because it accepted Descartes's mechanical conception of matter. In one sense, Aristotle was a materialist, because soul could not exist without material embodiment. However, because he did not think of the body as a machine, but as a special form of matter capable of being informed by soul, his materialism did not threaten to extinguish the soul. The new materialism did. In *L'Homme*, Descartes had argued that human beings were machines wherein dwelled a soul. In *L'Homme machine* (1748), physician J.-O. La Mettrie argued that human beings were solely machines, consciousness and thought being functions of the body. The guiding belief of materialism after Descartes has been that mind (or soul or consciousness) does not exist as a separate substance apart from matter.

As it subsequently developed throughout the history of psychology, materialism adopted a variety of forms that defy easy characterization. Usually, materialism is presented as involving the relation of mind to brain, but I am going to propose an alternative way of thinking about materialism more useful to discussing mind as a scientific object. In this scheme, the main division among materialists is between those who believe that mind is an illusion that should be explained away by science, and those who believe that minds are in some sense real (though not Cartesian substances) and should be explained by science. Using conventional terms in an unconventional way, I will call the first group eliminativists and the second group reductionists. These categories are not meant to be mutually exclusive, because some theorists' treatments of mind vacillate between them.

Reductionism is a roomy mansion, embracing a wide variety of opinions and perspectives, each having different implications for treating mind as a scientific object. The general idea is that mentalistic theories are appropriate for their level of analysis, but that more detailed, less mentalistic theories undergird and explain mentalistic theories, as in other historical cases of reduction. For example, the classical gas laws developed by early physicists relating pressure, volume, and temperature of gases were later reduced to the kinetic theory of gases associated with atomic theory. The gas laws remain valid for the molar behavior of gases, but the kinetic theory explains how gases work at a molecular level. Similarly, Mendel's concept of the gene remains valid in population genetics despite having been reduced to coding sequences of DNA in molecular genetics, which explains in detail how genes construct body and behavior.

Reductionism is what I have called elsewhere (Leahey, 1997) the path through physiology to scientific psychology, and in a broad way it has been advocated by multifarious psychologists, many of whom would not regard themselves as reductionists because of psychologists' tendency to equate reductionism with eliminativism. Reductionism thus includes the early Wundt of Heidelberg, the early Freud of the "Project for a Scientific Psychology," the James of *The Principles of Psychology*, and Titchener before the posthumously published *Systematic Psychology* (Leahey, 1997). Gestalt psychology was sometimes phenomenological and sometimes reductionist (Koffka, 1935/1963; see Leahey, forthcoming). Today, reductionism is a common theme in cognitive neuroscience. Pinker (1997, p. 24), in his widely read *How the Mind Works*, writes, "The mind is not the brain but what the brain does" (see also Kosslyn and Koenig's *Wet Mind*, 1992).

It is of some significance to note that at some point in their careers, Wundt, Freud, James, and Titchener all stepped off the reductive path through physiology. Freud's reasons for doing so remain shrouded in obscurity and protected by a bodyguard of lies (Esterson, 1993; Sulloway, 1979; Webster, 1995), but in the other cases the motive seems to have been at least in part a desire to protect mind from explanation or elimination by natural science. After moving to Leipzig, Wundt implicitly adopted the distinction between *Naturwissenschaft* and *Geisteswissenschaft* (discussed later in this chapter), holding that the higher mental functions such as thought and language could be studied only by history, not laboratory science, a view echoed by Snell, as we have seen. James's deep involvement with spiritualism (L. Simon, 1998) suggests that the cerebralism of the *Principles* was a hypothesis pragmatically adopted to advance the cause of scientific psychology (James, 1892) rather than his own personal belief. James's later radical empiricism was a form of idealism, and of course idealists reject the existence of matter altogether. In *Systematic Psychology: Prolegomena*, Titchener (1929/1972) abandoned the idea of explaining consciousness for its close description. This lumps him with the phenomenologists, for whom consciousness is the primary given reality (Grossman, 1995).

Broadly speaking, eliminativists adopt the constructivist thesis that the concept of mind is a social construction on a par with the Greek gods: "mind" is a mythological object fated to be replaced by science. Eliminativism itself comes in two quite different forms, sharing the idea that mind is a myth, but differing on how to get rid of it. The first is neurophysiological eliminativism, which looks to replace mind talk with brain talk. It was probably La Mettrie's own view, was part of Comtean positivism, was advanced in the 1920s by Karl Lashley (1923) and a few others, was flirted with by Clark L. Hull (see Leahey, 2004), and is advocated today in philosophy by the Churchlands (P.M. Churchland, 1985, 1988, 1995; P.S. Churchland, 1986) and R. Rorty (1979, 1991, 1993). The second form of eliminativism is Skinnerian radical behaviorism (e.g., Skinner, 1953, 1971, 1985), which looks to replace mind talk with behavior talk.

Although it appears that eliminativism (especially in its neurophysiological form) is simply reductionism *à outrance*, it is in fact sui generis. R. Rorty (1991), for example, calls it "nonreductive physicalism," and its claims are more radical than reductionism's. Eliminativists regard mentalists the way the first atomic chemists regarded alchemists, as hopelessly wrong and out of date (P.M. Churchland, 1989). As modern chemistry developed in the seventeenth and eighteenth centuries, alchemical concepts such as phlogiston were not reduced to chemical ones; they were extirpated root and branch, replaced by a completely different understanding of matter. Similarly, say neurophysiological eliminativists, mentalistic concepts such as "feeling pain" will someday be replaced (or at least ought to be replaced) root and branch by terms such as "C-fibers firing" (R. Rorty, 1991) or "engaging in pain behavior" (Rachlin, 1985), and our understanding of ourselves will be revolutionized. Mind will cease to be an object of science because we will learn that it is not an object at all. Eliminativists tend to regard reductionists as cowards who see the truth of materialism but who cannot bring themselves to give up faith in "mind" (P.M. Churchland, 1988).

Some theoretical positions on the nature of mind hover uncertainly between eliminativism and reductionism. The old Australian central-state identity thesis said that the mind *is* the brain rather than what the brain does: Mental events are identical to brain events the way lightning is identical to atmospheric discharges of electricity. Central-state materialism sometimes seemed to be a reductive explanation of mind as brain activity and behavior (e.g., Armstrong, 1968) and sometimes an effort to eliminate the vocabulary of the mental (Place, 1956/1992).[5]

Ryle's influential book *The Concept of Mind* (1949) clearly attempted to dismantle and destroy Descartes's myth of "the ghost in the machine" and redefine mental terms as behavioral descriptions, but Ryle denied being a behaviorist. Dennett owes much to his old Oxford teacher Ryle, and his *Consciousness Explained* (1991) reveals a philosopher torn between reductionism and eliminativism. The title promises a reductive explanation of consciousness, but Dennett writes that consciousness is "just about the last surviving mystery" (p. 21) to "fall to science," (p. 24) suggesting that he has come to eliminate consciousness, not explain it. Dennett's strategy of heterophenomenology gives the believer in consciousness what she or he wants—to be taken seriously—but then takes it away by treating talk of consciousness as on a par with primitive tribes' talk about their gods (Leahey, 1994b). Finally, a related view well known in philosophy but virtually ignored in psychology is Davidson's anomalous monism (Davidson, 1980). Davidson holds that any psychology deploying intentional concepts, such as folk psychology, cannot be reduced to—that is, explained by—neurophysiology, because folk psychological discourse relies on concepts such as intentionality and logical coherence that have no corresponding concepts in biology. However, Davidson's arguments imply that psychology cannot be a science precisely because it cannot be woven into the greater fabric of the other natural sciences (Rosenberg, 1994). Mind—or, more precisely, mentalistic explanation—is real but an unnatural anomaly in the scientific scheme of things.[6]

Is Mind a Scientific Object?

Gaukroger (1995) reminds us that a primary goal of Descartes's tortured analysis of mind was to rescue the Christian concept of the soul from the threat of reduction to the brain by Renaissance naturalism. The soul for Descartes fell within the realm of religion, not science, but his new definition of mind and consciousness nonetheless invited later materialists to capture it for science or to eliminate it altogether in a victory for scientism. In the coming centuries, religiously minded philosophers and psychologists fought against naturalistic destruction of the immortal soul or its assimilation by natural science. In America, for example, the Old (Scottish commonsense) Psychology that had dominated college curricula resisted the intrusion of the New (scientific and value-free) Psychology of the German laboratory. For the former, the soul was "an emanation of the Divine" (Dunton, 1895), not an object to be weighed and measured. Although he was a president of the American Psychological Association, G.T. Ladd (1892) was also a minister and sharply criticized James's treatment of psychology as a natural science.

At the end of the eighteenth century, Kant provided quite different reasons for thinking that mind was real but transcended science. Kant famously rejected the British empiricist version of the Way of Ideas, including Descartes's identification of mind with consciousness. For Kant, consciousness was the relatively trivial Empirical Ego, which could be inventoried by introspection. Such an inventory, however, would be no more than mental butterfly collecting, falling short of the mathematical rigor of genuine Newtonian science. Deeper and more important than the Empirical Ego was the Transcendental Ego, whose Categories of Apperception created the phenomenal world of the Empirical Ego. Because the Transcendental Ego created the phenomenal world, it was not a part of it and thus could not be observed even by introspection. Therefore the Transcendental Ego—the soul of the mind, as it were—could not be an object of science.

In Germany, Kantian arguments came together with the historicist theses of Counter-Enlightenment figures such as Giambattista Vico and Johann Gottfried von Herder, who, like religious thinkers, resented making the soul an object of scientific scrutiny. Various philosophers and humanists, most notably historian Wilhelm Dilthey, rejected the positivist notion of unity of science and sharply demarcated the study of the human realm, *Geisteswissenschaft*, from the study of the natural world-machine, *Naturwissenschaft*. The method of *Naturwissenschaft* was observation and experiment, and its goal was describing the laws of nature, knowledge of which allowed us humans to predict and control the workings of the world-machine; the model natural science was physics. The method and goal of *Geisteswissenschaft* was *verstehen*, understanding, and its model discipline was history. The historian immerses him- or herself so deeply in past times and past lives that he or she comes to see and think as past people did.

Empiricism and positivism run so deep in British, American, and French philosophy and psychology that the Vico-Herder-Dilthey thesis has exerted little influence in these countries. In Germany there was a methodological struggle between a positivist faction in social science (led in psychology by Hermann Ebbinghaus) and Dilthey's historicists, and this war was essentially won by the positivists. Nevertheless, historicism has sometimes influenced psychologists; pockets of resistance hold out, occasionally sending little invasions to the New World (e.g., Gergen, 1973, 1982). Wundt's Leipzig program, as I noted earlier, divided psychology into a physiological-experimental branch and a social-historical branch. The human brain and body belong to *Naturwissenschaft*, while the human higher mental processes (the soul) belong to *Geisteswissenschaft*. As always since Descartes, consciousness and its study were perched awkwardly between them. Unfortunately, perhaps, Wundt's *Völkerpsychologie*, his version of psychology as *Geisteswissenschaft*, went unread anywhere (Jahoda, 1997).

The later philosophy of Wittgenstein staked out a position on mind as a scientific object that resembles historicism's, although it is unclear if they are connected by anything more than similarity. Wittgenstein, like Ryle and Dennett (who counts himself a follower of Wittgenstein), sought to disabuse his readers of Descartes's notion of an inner theater of ideas and an inner, thinking substance, the soul. Like the historicists, Wittgenstein gave mind an ineluctable social dimension (Leahey, 1997). Mental talk—folk psychology—is a socially defined and historically developing language game, and intentional explanations of behavior are moves in that game (R. Rorty, 1979, 1993). It is possible that other cultures with other histories might never develop the folk psychology language game, and we might find such people utterly strange and inexplicable.[7]

There is a final way of setting mind outside science, with which American psychologists are familiar because it has dominated American psychology since the first decade of the twentieth century: methodological behaviorism. The radical behaviorists attempted to expunge mind altogether, from everyday life as well as from science (Lashley, 1923; Skinner, 1971). Methodological behaviorists in their own quite different way agree with the historicists and Wittgenstein (by whom they were not influenced) that mind exists, but that it is not an object for scientific study. Methodological behaviorism stems directly from logical positivism and operationism, which demand that all scientific terminology be reducible to directly observable facts.[8]

From the 1920s on, mainstream psychologists adopted methodological behaviorism. They followed Descartes in identifying mind with consciousness. Because consciousness is private, not public, it cannot be studied by the scientific method, which demands publicly accessible subject matter. Consciousness belongs to the arts, not science. Although cognitive scientists do not think of themselves as methodological behaviorists, they are (Leahey, 1992, 2004), because they continue to exclude consciousness from psychology. Dennett (1991) calls them "zombists" (p. 256) for seeing people as zombies, that is, as behaving human bodies sans consciousness. The only new development with cognitive science is that it has broken away from the Cartesian equation of mind with consciousness, being willing to call cognitive processes "mental." However, E.C. Tolman's and Clark L. Hull's theories posited internal processes, too, only they did not usually think of them as mental (Lealey, 2004). "Mental" terms were typically thought of either as fictitious constructs useful if operationally defined or as placeholders for neurophysiological concepts yet to be developed.[9] The difference between the great golden age theorists and contemporary cognitive scientists is that the former did not have the computer model of the mind, which has made feasible detailed and sophisticated theories of mental processes. Methodological behaviorists and cognitive science's zombists share the same attitude toward consciousness—it is not our job to explain it.

What Is the Self?

Unlike earlier philosophers of an introspective bent such as Augustine, Descartes looked inward and found only himself, not God. In doing so, Descartes altered Western understanding of the self. In their conception of mind as consciousness, Descartes and Locke created the modern "pointlike" self (Taylor, 1989).[10] According to Descartes, the soul was a mathematical point, located in, but not actually occupying any, space and doing but one thing, thinking. Thinking of the soul as a point was radically new. For Aristotelians, a person had been taken to be the embodied soul, including the faculties of the animal soul that were directly connected to the world outside. According to the argument of the *cogito*, on the other hand, our essence is a small, self-aware point of pure thought, dwelling in the Cartesian Theater, detached from the body and even from experience, which it receives at second hand via projection on the screen of the Cartesian Theater.

Such a small self became easy to erase and, ironically, to inflate. David Hume (1740/1984), committed to the empiricist maxim that one should regard as illusory (or at least dubious) anything one cannot sense, set out to find himself in conscious experience. He failed to do so, finding nothing in consciousness that was not a specific sensation of world or body. His failure to locate an inner self created the problem of personal identity with which philosophers still wrestle today. Hume treated self or personal identity as he did causation, as a secondary result of simpler psychological processes rather than as a primary, directly perceived reality. In Germany, post-Kantian idealism inflated the self into a sort of black hole that swallowed — or became — the world (Solomon, 1988). Like Hume, Kant did not find the self — the Transcendental Ego — given in sensory intuition. Unlike Hume, Kant did not decide that the self was an illusion. He deduced its existence as a transcendental necessity, the a priori condition of all cognition. Later German idealists dispensed with Kant's things in themselves and said that the self posited the outside world in an act of will. As Johann Fichte wrote, according to idealism, "the independence of the thing [in itself] should be sacrificed to that of the self" (Scruton, 1994, p. 196).

As I observed earlier idealism affected early German psychology. Wundt often cited Fichte, and in his Leipzig system of psychology placed the higher mental processes of the self outside experimental study. Although Freud was a materialist, I think that the Freudian unconscious is a remnant of idealism. The unconscious is a spacious realm unknown to introspection, with its own distinct principles of operation (the pleasure principle and the primary process), and it yearns autistically to impose its own fantasized order on recalcitrant external reality. The famous imageless-thought controversy (Leahey, 2004) was in part a battle between Lockean empiricism and post-Kantian idealism. Wundt's erstwhile pupil Oswald Külpe, like many of the second generation of German psychologists, was much influenced by positivism (Danziger, 1979). Apparently believing in the Lockean power of reflection, Külpe proposed to investigate the higher mental processes by observing them introspectively. Külpe's friend Titchener undertook the same quest, but (in an echo of Hume vis-à-vis Kant) where Külpe found imageless thought, Titchener found only bodily sensations (Leahey, 2004). Wundt, who in his early Heidelberg years had shared Külpe's ambition (van Hoorn and Verhave, 1980), now rejected it (Wundt, 1907–8) as inconsistent with the Kantian view that the Transcendental Ego was beyond observation. To many American psychologists, at least, the imageless-thought episode demonstrated that the mind was too slippery an object for science to grasp, providing an important motive for the adoption of behaviorism (Leahey, 1992, 2004).

In the Anglo-American tradition of psychology, the self has always been about as elusive as it was for Hume. James (1890, 1892) wrestled mightily with the problems of self and personal identity. He realized that the existence or nonexistence of the soul was a profound question, and he possessed a clear sense of himself as a thinking, willing, striving creature. However, working within the Humean tradition, James went far to dissolve the self into a collection of disparate things and processes. The Me (the Empirical Ego of Kant) "is an empirical aggregate of things objectively known" (James, 1892b/1992, p. 208), including the body and the social selves, of whom there are as many as there are individuals one knows. James recognized that "the I, or 'pure ego' is a very much more difficult subject of inquiry than the Me" (James, 1892b/1992, p. 191). He considered its existence at length, finally concluding that psychology could and should do without it, leaving its puzzles to theology and metaphysics. Later psychologists went further in dissolving the self into, finally, nothing. John Dewey saw the self as a social construction and regarded belief in the self as a vestige of aristocratic ideology (Leahey, 2004). Watson dissolved the self into private vocalization. The end point of the process was perhaps Skinner's statement at the end of his autobiography that he had written the life of a nonperson (Skinner, 1983 p. 412). Today, the psychology of the self is experiencing a modest resurgence, though to what end it is too early to tell.

Am I Free?

The existence of free will is intimately tied up with the existence of the self, because there must be some self or I to exert free will and bear burdens of personal responsibility. As James tried to keep some notion of self for psychology while ironically pointing the way to its dissolution, so did James try to retain will as a psychological concept, only to set the stage for its destruction at the hands of his successors. James refuted the reigning theory of will, which rested upon the mythical existence of so-called feelings of enervation in the motor nerves, whose reinstatement by will caused bodily actions to occur. James proposed instead an "ideo-motor" theory of will, by which consciousness attentively focuses on the thought of an action that the body automatically executes (Leahey, 1995). Moreover, he suggested that will is primarily the active inhibition of behaviors provoked by external stimuli. As with the existence of the pure ego, or soul, James happily turned the problem of free will over to metaphysics and theology. As in the case of the self, later psychologists built upon James, but ultimately discarded his ideas. In his American Psychological Association Presidential Address, Thorndike (1913) devastated James's theory of ideo-motor action, saying that it was equivalent to believing in magic. As determinism overtook psychology—after all, we cannot have a science of behavior if there are no determining causal laws of behavior—will became a taboo concept. As with the self, will may be making a comeback, though in disguised form, as "self-efficacy."

Does Consciousness Do Anything?

The appearance of evolutionary theory in the nineteenth century added a new puzzle to the list bequeathed by Descartes and Locke. Accepting that consciousness exists in the Cartesian sense, is it adaptive? What, if anything, does consciousness do to aid the struggle for existence?[11] Psychophysical parallelism had already disconnected consciousness from behavior, but the growing acceptance of the path through physiology raised the specter of impotent consciousness in a new form. Is consciousness perhaps an accidental, epiphenomenal feature of the brain with no more survival value than male nipples? Herbert Spencer first treated psychology from an evolutionary point of view, but added nothing original to the Cartesian paradigm, simply saying that consciousness was adaptive because it provided internal representations of the world (Leahey, 2004). Darwin said little about consciousness, but his bulldog T.H. Huxley articulated what James called the automaton theory of consciousness, that consciousness is secreted by the brain, but is not causally connected to behavior.

The problem is very simple, flows directly from the Cartesian conception of soul (consciousness) and body, and was magnified by advances in neurophysiology in the nineteenth century. The emerging reflex theory of the brain seemed to vindicate Descartes's idea of the body as a clockwork machine. Thus it seemed that it must be possible in principle if not in contemporary practice to trace a complete neural reflex circuit from instigating stimulus to resulting behavior. Such a tracing would provide a mechanical, material, causal account of the behavior in question, and nowhere in this account would consciousness have to be mentioned. To use Gould and Lewontin's (1979) later term, for Huxley and other followers of the automaton theory, consciousness was a spandrel, not an adaptation. The automaton theory provided another argument that mind, identified as it was then with consciousness, was not a proper object of science.

Characteristically, James (1890) heroically resisted the automaton theory, calling it an "impertinence." James argued that consciousness "loaded the dice" of the cerebral machine, transforming survival from a mere hypothesis into an imperative decree. Consciousness was a "fighter for ends," giving its bearer interests and motives and the ability to choose more adaptive over less adaptive courses of action. For James, consciousness arose precisely when mechanical, reflex behavior was inadequate to cope with changed conditions.

Also characteristically, James's arguments carried the seeds of their own deconstruction. A key example of this occurs in James's treatment of emotion. Emotions provide our motives, guiding adaptive behavior. In the traditional view, fear motivates escape from and avoidance of danger; sexual desire motivates reproduction. Yet as is well known, the James-Lange theory of emotion reverses the traditional causal sequence of emotion, saying that we are afraid because we run rather than the other way around. Running is a reflexive or learned habit that occurs automatically when triggered by an appropriate stimulus, and the emotion follows upon the occurrence of the behavior. However, if the emotion is a consequence of behavior, it did not cause the behavior. James's line of thought was later developed into the more general motor theory of consciousness by Hugo Münsterberg, John Dewey, and others (Leahey, 1994a). The motor theory of consciousness accepts the idea that, as Münsterberg wrote, "For the preservation of the individual, it is obviously irrelevant whether or not a purposeful motion is accompanied by contents of consciousness or not" (quoted by Hale, 1980, p. 41). The causes of behavior lie in the environment (as Skinner later asserted many times). Consciousness simply reflects the environment it sees and the behavior its body is up to, but it is the brain, not the mind, that connects the two.

The motor theory of consciousness was worked out well before the advent of behaviorism, but provided a reason for psychologists to accept methodological behaviorism. The motor theory of consciousness accepts that consciousness exists, but says that it does nothing. For American psychologists eager to build a useful psychology, the study of consciousness was just intellectual navel gazing. Usefulness was to be found in studying how behavior is caused and shaped by the environment (Leahey, 1994a). E.C. Tolman, who wrote eloquent arguments for methodological behaviorism (Tolman, 1935, 1936), first studied psychology under Münsterberg at Harvard, where he found that although Münsterberg insisted that "*the* method in psychology was *introspection*," actual laboratory work was "primarily objective in nature" (Tolman, 1952, p. 326). Encountering Watson's behaviorism in Yerkes' comparative psychology class came as a relief to Tolman, because it showed that the real method of psychology was behavior study.

Are There Other Minds?

From the standpoint of considering the status of mind as an object of science, the problem of other minds is perhaps the most fundamental one. Historically, debates about the problem of other minds have led to proposals that mind is an object that science, and perhaps society at large, should do without. The problem of other minds did not arise before Descartes. For Aristotelians, soul was the sum total of a creature's life processes, so that any living being, even a plant, had a soul. All behaviors—broadly defined as self-initiated change of any type from growth through movement—indicated life and, therefore, presence of soul. Certain problems did arise with regard to the distinct human mind, but as we have seen, they involved immortality and personal individuation, not whether other human beings than ourselves have minds. Platonic and Christian concerns about soul and mind similarly centered on immortality, human dignity, and individuation.

The modern problem of other minds was created by Cartesian dualism, the doctrine Ryle called the ghost in the machine. I know that I have such a ghost, because it is my immediate self-awareness. However, because I am cut off from any consciousness but my own, it is logically possible that mine is the only mind in the universe. Indeed, if I follow Descartes, I know that there are many behaving but mindless creatures—animals—whose "mental" powers such as perception and memory are but functions of their nervous systems. In contrast to Aristotle, for Descartes the mindless, mechanical processes of body cause most behaviors. Thus is created the new problem of figuring out what behavior or behaviors mark the presence of consciousness indwelling in other humans. It is important to bear in mind that the problem of other minds has two facets. The more obvious one is establishing what behavior univocally indicates the presence of consciousness. The less obvious one is the new Cartesian notion that detecting mind in other creatures is a matter of inference rather than observation. For Aristotle, soul was for all intents and purposes directly visible in the life of plants and animals; its presence was observed rather than inferred. For Descartes, consciousness was an inner secret known only to its possessor, manifested through symptoms that had to be detected and correctly interpreted by others. As Cartesian dualism became the reigning way of thinking about mind, the second issue faded into the background, leaving the first highlighted.

Interestingly, Descartes himself never directly addressed the problem of other minds (Mathews, 1986). In *L'Homme*, as we have seen, Descartes described the difference between minded humans and mindless animals at some length, but he was not there concerned to find grounds for thinking that other people have minds. Nevertheless, we can draw on *L'Homme* and other works to construct a plausible picture of how Descartes would have treated the problem of other minds. Descartes ruled out the possibility of mind in animals because they were machines without consciousness. At the same time, animals provided a useful compass in the search for mind-indicating behaviors: Whatever behavior was the mark of the mental, no animal had it, and it is clear from *L'Homme* that Descartes regarded language as the decisive external behavior produced by thinking consciousness rather than mechanical brain processes.

The problem of other minds has a complex and tangled history. Here I will focus on the problem as it arose historically in debates over animal mind, over computer mind, and in the neorealist movement in American philosophy.

Animal Mind

La Mettrie was the first to propose that animals might have minds. In fact, he suggested the project of teaching apes language that came to fruition only in the 1970s. La Mettrie thought that if such a project should succeed, animals would be little gentlemen, a statement that attacks Descartes while conceding his criterion of the mental. The existence of linguistic apes would threaten human uniqueness (and perhaps human dignity), but at the same time La Mettrie accepted Descartes's argument that language was the mark of the mental. Like Dennett (1991) 150 years later, La Mettrie said that mind is installed by the acquisition of language.

In any event, the problem of animal mind lay dormant until it was powerfully revived after 1859 by the acceptance of evolution. Evolutionary continuity between humans and animals undermined Descartes's treatment of mind in two ways. First, Descartes treated consciousness as an all-or-none possession. Either one has self-awareness and thus a mind, or one does not. However, if this were true, it would mean that protohumans evolved without consciousness for thousands of years, suddenly crossing a mental Rubicon in a moment. The Cartesian perspective suggests that hominid animals went to sleep one night and woke up the next morning as self-aware men and women, or that hominid animals suddenly started having human infants, or that the scenario depicted in the movie *2001* actually took place, that hominid animals encountered an alien artifact that made them human. It seems more plausible—though not necessary—that the evolution of mind was gradual, that consciousness was possessed in increasing degrees by successive forms of hominids.

Such speculative questions about the evolution of the human mind were not taken up in the nineteenth century, though answers abound today in the burgeoning literature on the nature of consciousness. A more concrete and seemingly empirical question was first addressed: Do animals have minds of any sort? Descartes drew an absolute line between humans, on the one hand, and animals, on the other. Darwin erased that line, creating two new mutually exclusive alternative possibilities: Either animals had minds (albeit simpler than humans'), or no one, animal or human, had a mind, or at least a mind worth considering.

The first animal psychologists took the former possibility for granted and attempted to investigate the mental capacities and conscious experiences of animals. They recognized that their search for evidence of animal mentality was intimately connected with the problem of other minds in humans and saw that if making inferences from behavior to mind were to be forbidden in animal psychology, it would soon be forbidden in human psychology, too. Romanes (1883, pp. 5–6) wrote, "Skepticism of this kind [about the feasibility of inferring animal mind from animal behavior] is logically bound to deny evidence of mind, not only in the case of lower animals, but also in that of the higher, and even in that of men other than the skeptic himself. For all objections which could apply to the use of [inference] . . . would apply with equal force to the evidence of any mind other than that of the individual objector."

The legitimacy of inferring mind from behavior was soon thrown into greater doubt as psychology expanded its scope and methods. Because animals could not introspect, their behavior had to speak indirectly for their minds. In addition to animals, psychologists began to study subjects such as children and the insane, whose introspective abilities were nil or minimal, adding to the roster of the introspectively silent. The new method of mental testing dispensed with introspection in the case of normal adult humans, substituting objective for subjective data (Cattell, 1896). The status of introspection as *the* method in psychology, and therefore the status of mind as a scientific object, became suspect. The trouble with animal psychology, said E.C. Sanford in his 1902 American Psychological Association Presidential Address, is that it "tempts us beyond the bounds of introspection," as did studies of children, the retarded, and the abnormal. But, Sanford asked, should we be "content with a purely objective science of animal or child or idiot behavior?" Sanford thought not, recognizing with Romanes the necessary end point of an objective psychology:

> I doubt if anyone has ever seriously contemplated [a purely objective psychology] in the case of the higher animals, or could carry it to fruitful results if he should undertake it. Nor would anyone seriously propose to treat the behavior of his fellow men in the same way, i.e., to refuse to credit them with conscious experience in the main like his own, though this would seem to be required logically. (Sanford, 1903, p. 105)

In these passages, the ground is being laid for the behaviorism that was only a decade away. Romanes and Sanford defended inference to mind and introspection as essential to psychological science, but clearly there were psychologists unnamed by Romanes or Sanford who wished to change psychology fundamentally.[12] Romanes's and Sanford's defense of mentalistic psychology depended upon what they took to be an obvious and unassailable assumption: All human beings have minds, animals may have minds, and the job of the psychologist is to use behavior to construct pictures of human and animal mind. But the manifest difficulties of doing so soon became apparent. Comparative psychologists searched for a more plausible criterion of the mental than language, but the search proved frustrating (Leahey, 2004). Watson (1909) thought the search futile. Watson and his allies took up Sanford's implied challenge, treating their fellow men as if they were animals and denying that psychology needs to study the mind (the argument of methodological behaviorism) or that mind exists at all (the argument of eliminativism).

Neorealism: Challenging the Cartesian Theater

Psychologists were not the only ones wrestling with the nature of mind and consciousness around the turn of the twentieth century. American philosophy of mind was turned upside down when in 1905 James—who had defined psychology as the science of mental life in his *Principles of Psychology*—published a provocative article titled "Does Consciousness Exist?" James was moving toward his mature metaphysical system, radical empiricism, and in this article he questioned the distinction between experience, on the one hand, and conscious*ness*, on the other. Descartes said that the soul is a thinking thing (*res*) that has experience, and the post-Kantian idealists' Transcendental Ego (already rejected by James in the *Principles*) was similarly a thing that has experience. The—*ness* ending that turns conscious (experience) into a noun suggested to James a lingering but no longer tenable faith that there is a soul or Transcendental Ego standing behind and possessing experience. James wanted to strip consciousness of its nounness, asserting that pure flowing experience was the primary reality, given in itself, not *to* a soul or Transcendental Ego.

James's article set off a searching rethinking of mind by American philosophers. Most important for psychology was the revival of eighteenth-century Scottish commonsense realism by American neorealists, led by James's biographer, Ralph Barton Perry. Following Aristotle (but without adopting his metaphysics), the Scottish realists asserted that perception of objects is direct, unmediated by the Cartesian veil of ideas. Although Scottish commonsense psychology exerted great influence in American higher education, in philosophy the impact of its perceptual realism was not great. More important for psychology, the consequences of adopting realism in psychology were not apparent in the eighteenth century. However, when realism was revived by the American neorealists around 1910, the realist challenge to psychology quickly became apparent (Leahey, 2004). Quite simply, if one accepts realism, consciousness vanishes, taking with it the psychology of consciousness and its method, introspection (Dunlap, 1912; Perry, 1904; Singer, 1911). Traditional psychology's subject matter was the private inner world comprising the ideas projected onto the screen of the Cartesian Theater, and psychology used a special method, introspection, to get at its subject matter. However, if there is no veil of ideas, no Cartesian Theater, then psychology's subject matter dissolves. Introspection on the realist account is not looking inward into a mental realm, but simply observing sensory features of the world (including private bodily states) with an artificially heightened degree of attention. If one follows realism, then psychology, had to become the study of the relationship between the world and the behaving organism, and this was the definition of psychology offered by the early Tolman and is the basis of Skinner's radical behaviorism (L.D. Smith, 1986).

James (1905) had suggested that consciousness was a fallacious reification of experience based on psychologists' implicit unwillingness to give up on some remnant of a substantial soul. James rejected such reification and moved toward idealism, making pure experience the primary reality. The philosopher E.A. Singer (1911, 1912b) similarly regarded consciousness, along with mind and soul, as a reification, but moved toward a reductive or even eliminative materialism. Although Singer was not officially one of the neorealists, his ideas had much in common with theirs. Singer essentially went back to the original postulation of mind or soul by the Greeks. What, exactly, is mind supposed to explain? The ancient answer was life: when a body is ensouled, it lives; when the soul leaves, it dies. Singer argued that this answer was out-of-date and drew a parallel with thermodynamics to support his claim. The medieval and early scientific theory of heat said that a fluid, caloric, caused heat. When caloric flowed into an object from a fire, it became hot. Moved away from the fire, the object shed caloric and cooled. A hot object such as a heated piece of iron was thus composed of two substances, iron plus caloric. However, the fluid theory of heat was replaced by the kinetic theory of heat, which said that an object's temperature was its state of atomic excitation. At absolute zero there is no atomic movement and hence no heat; as energy enters a system, its state of excitation rises, and we sense it as some degree of heat. Heat is not a fluid, but a bodily state. The parallel to the soul is clear. In dualistic systems, a living being is matter plus soul. But as with heat, we may discard the soul substance, recognizing that life is a complex state of biological functioning, not a thing apart from that functioning. Descartes had gone a long way in this direction, explaining everything but thought and self-awareness as material and mechanical, operations of the nervous system. With James, Singer believed that consciousness was just the last echo of the soul in the scientific age. Against James, Singer wished it to be replaced by materialism rather than idealism. The first physiological eliminativist, Singer said that mind as an object of science was as doomed as caloric.

Singer (1912a) also addressed a thought experiment proposed by James in *Pragmatism* (1907/1955). James proposed this thought experiment[13] to show that the problem of other minds was a vital and important one, not a silly, pointless academic exercise along the lines of asking how many angels can dance on the head of a pin. James's automatic sweetheart has since become a staple of science fiction.[14] Suppose you are in love with someone and believe that s/he is in love with you. You know that you are in love from your own private thoughts and feelings. Inferring mind from behavior, you take your lover's every sigh and caress to be signs that s/he has similar thoughts and feelings, loving you as you do him/her. Suppose, however, that one day you discover that your lover is a machine constructed to behave in affectionate ways. Would you—could you—continue to love it? James thought not, and concluded that however the problem of other minds might be resolved, it mattered to human life. James intimated in this argument that believing in other minds should continue, that mind is an important object. Singer agreed that one would fall out of love with an automatic sweetheart, but not because it did not have soul or mind or consciousness, but because we would no longer trust it. We understand and predict other people's behavior by putting ourselves in their places and anticipating how we would act, expecting others to act as we would. Discovering that another person was in fact a machine would render it psychologically opaque, and we would lose faith in our ability to predict its actions. Love depends on trust, and trust would be gone.[15]

Computer Mind

Automatic sweethearts bring us to computer mind, the leading way of thinking about mind as a scientific object in the second half of the twentieth century. While we do not (yet?) have automatic sweethearts, we do have automatic chess masters, personal secretaries (PDAs and their ilk), and industrial workers (robots). Do they have minds? Could they have minds? In his presentation of the automatic sweetheart, James (1907/1955) implicitly assumed that the answer was no. However, following the development of computers during World War II, the answer became less clear, lending poignancy to later fictional treatment of androids and robots. The possibility of machine mind was first raised by A.M. Turing (1950), ushering in the era of artificial intelligence (AI). Suddenly, it seemed that science was not limited to studying existing minds; it might design new ones, too (Haugeland, 1981; Dennett, 1998). Space limitations preclude any general survey of (AI) and the changes it has wrought to philosophy of mind and cognitive psychology. I want briefly to connect AI to the historical currents I have tried to map in the preceding discussion.

　　Out of AI came a new answer to the mind-body problem called functionalism. While functionalism comes in various flavors, it is the now familiar idea that mind : body :: program : computer. The goal of functionalism was to make mind respectable as a scientific object. One could talk about the mind as a set of computations without fear of falling into religious dualism or the apparent "junk-shop" theory of folk psychology (Leahey, 2004). A prestigious Research Briefing Panel on Cognitive Science and Artificial Intelligence convened by the National Academy of Sciences advised the government whose money it was spending that "the [functionalist] hypothesis anchors the study of all the higher processes of mind to the same scientific world of mechanism as all the other natural sciences" (Estes and Simon, 1980/1983).

Superficially, functionalism appears to break with i ' rtesian tradition because it does not identify mind with consciousness. In :   , it has been claimed that Aristotle was a functionalist because he defined soul ::: terms of life processes and rejected substantial dualism, yet nevertheless saw soul and body as in some sense separable.[16] One can also make comparisons with the methodological behaviorists such as Tolman and Hull, whose models of the mind bear some resemblance to functionalism's (Leahey, 1997). Nevertheless, in important ways functionalism continues the Cartesian tradition. First, as the Research Briefing Panel makes clear, functionalism espouses the mechanistic view of the universe begun by Descartes. Second, functionalism may fairly be construed as in some regards dualistic (Searle, 1997), because one's mind might be copied as a program to be downloaded into a computer (Dennett, 1980). Third, consciousness is left a mystery (Leahey, 1994b; Searle, 1997). Most functionalist treatments of mind leave consciousness out of their theories altogether, as did the methodological behaviorists (Leahey, 1992, 2004). Others hope that consciousness will "fall to science" (Dennett, 1991). So hard is fitting conscious experience into the functionalist perspective that some thinkers are trying to revive old-fashioned dualism (e.g., Chalmers, 1996).

It is too soon to tell how successful functionalism has been in legitimating mind as an object of science. The connectionist challenge seems to have been weathered, as almost everyone in cognitive science now thinks that the conscious mind is a serial-processing virtual machine running on the massively parallel machine that is the brain (e.g., Dennett, 1991). On the other hand, it may yet turn out that functionalism may not be able to handle conscious experience (Searle, 1997) or some of the more social dimensions of mind (Leahey, 1994b). One straw in the wind indicating the possible demise of functionalism is Dennett's recent statement that Good Old Fashioned Artificial Intelligence (GOFAI) is "dead."[17] In the same place, Dennett endorses cognitive neuroscience as the best way to carry on the project of strong AI.

Where Are We?

There now are, as I see it, the following options for regarding mind as an object of science. Not all are mutually exclusive.

- The category "mind" is a natural kind. That is, minds naturally exist and are instances of a spatiotemporal universal analogous to electrons.
- The category "mind" is a social construction that refers to nothing, such as "God." Therefore, individual minds do not exist any more than Zeus exists or existed.
- Minds exist in nature, but "mind" is not a natural kind. That is, minds exist in nature, but are spatiotemporally local constructions—natural artifacts—such as leopards or Mount Everest.

• Minds are social constructions—human-made artifacts—(Searle, 1995) with genuine causal power, such as money.

A critical feature of the categories I propose is distinguishing between "mind" as a conceptual category and minds as individual things that may or may not exist. An important commitment of science is to carve nature at the joints, getting our conceptual categories to map as neatly as possible onto the lineaments of nature. A category that maps onto a spatiotemporally universal feature of nature, such as "electron" onto electrons, is a natural kind. Many objects in the physical world for which we have names are not natural kinds. "Furniture" is not a natural kind, because tables, chairs, and the like, while physically real, are constructed by human beings and are not instances of spatiotemporal universals. Mount Everest exists as a naturally made object, but "Mount Everest" and "mountain" are human concepts that map only vaguely onto nature. "Mount Everest" is a name for a single, local, geographical feature of planet Earth; it is not a universal, nor are its boundaries fixed by nature. When my family and I drive west out of Richmond, the ground gets hillier and hillier, but deciding when we are "really" in the Appalachian Mountains is pretty much a matter of taste. Similarly, mountains are real, but "mountain" is a human construct that only arbitrarily maps onto nature. We, not nature, decide the boundary between "hill" and "mountain." Drawing on the historical portion of my exploration of mind as a scientific object, I will ask a series of philosophical-scientific questions.

Is "Mind" a Natural Kind?

I closed the historical section of this chapter with a reference to cognitive neuroscience. While the most obvious construal of cognitive neuroscience is to see it as part of the projects of reductionism or eliminativism, its results can be taken to point in a very different direction—namely, support for an artifactual view of "mind" and minds. Quite instructive in this regard is the following passage written by a working neuroscientist, David Gaffan (1997). He is reviewing a tome of reductive/eliminative import compiled by Llinás and P.S. Churchland (1996).

> The idea that mental activity is brain activity has retarded research in neuroscience. We have gone into the brain expecting to find such things as memories and percepts waiting there to be discovered, and systems for attention, action, and so on—all corresponding to traditional mental events or faculties. The better we understand any of the brain processes we study, however, the clearer it becomes that they do not correspond in any sense to mental activities in folk psychology.... [F]or example, the concept of "attention" for a neuroscientist is, at best, an intuitive label for a set of questions whose answers in the end are given by reference to a general account of cortical competition, an account that goes far beyond the topic of attention. The search for an attention system or

an attentional mechanism in the brain has hindered, not helped the finding of these answers. Similarly, the search for memory systems in the brain, and the idea that cortical plasticity will instantiate the association-ism of folk psychology, have hindered progress. This hardly seems surprising if one considers that the claim to remember an event is not a description of one's brain, but rather a move in a rule-governed social game carrying, for example, the implied promise that one can supply further details about the event if requested. So I am sceptical about the idea, presented in [P.S.] Churchland's chapter, that neuroscience is simply an improved version of folk psychology and that folk psychology is nothing more than neuroscience-in-waiting. Rather, the two are parallel activities with different aims, a situation that one could tendentiously describe as: "the posit of a radical discontinuity between the mental and the neural" but more properly is described as common sense. (Gaffan, 1997, p. 194)

Accepting that Gaffan is right, we may draw several important conclusions from his argument. First, we can rule out reductionism. "Attention" will not map onto cortical competition or "association" onto neural plasticity the way "gene" maps onto coding sequences of DNA. Second, therefore, "mind" is not a natural kind. Third, our usual way of explaining behavior — folk psychology — is ineluctably social in nature, a game constituted by social rules the way a set of rules constitutes football or baseball (Leahey, "Psychology as Engineering," this volume).

Do Minds Exist?

It is important to observe that from the fact that folk psychology is a social construction — a sort of game — it does not follow that particular minds do not exist. "Furniture" and "mountain" are social constructions, but settees and mountains are quite real. It could turn out that individual minds have no more reality than the Greek gods had, though I think it unlikely.

Does Mind Exist?

If "mind" is not a natural kind, then minds are artifacts, natural or social constructions.

Mind as Natural Construction

Snell (1953) wrote that mind "was not invented, as a man would invent a tool ... to master a certain type of problem. As a rule, inventions are arbitrarily determined; they are adapted to the purpose from which they take their cue."

However, he missed or passed over the possibility that mind was "invented" by nature as an adaptation to the Darwinian purpose of surviving the struggle for existence. Although psychologists since the mid-nineteenth century have asked what the mind is good for, it has only been in the last twenty years or so that genuine Darwinian analysis has been applied to the evolution and functioning of animal and human minds. In an evolutionary view, minds are spatiotemporally local adaptations to prevailing selection pressures. That is, like opposable thumbs or binocular vision, minds are solutions to problems of survival and reproduction prevailing at particular times in a particular ecosystem. Minds are therefore natural constructions and real, but they are not natural kinds. The study of minds is therefore more similar to engineering, the discipline devoted to solving particular problems, than it is to science, the discipline of finding the laws that govern nature in all times and all places. I explore the evolutionary-engineering perspective on mind in my chapter "Psychology as Engineering" in this volume.

Mind as Social Construction

The idea that mind is a social construction seems at first glance to rule out the possibility that mind is a legitimate object of science. Eliminativists argue that mind is a socially constructed myth on a par with Zeus or caloric and, like them, is doomed to be discarded from science and ultimately from the discourse of educated people. Social constructionists and hermeneuticists argue that because mind is a social construction, its study belongs with the humanities (or the *Geisteswissenschaften*), not with science. However, being a social construction does not entail that something cannot be an object of science (Searle, 1995).

A good example of a social construction around which a science has been organized is money. Money is spatiotemporally local. The first coins were issued in the Near East around 700 BCE, and coins did not come into widespread circulation in the West until the Hellenistic period. For centuries, the value of money was tied to the medium of coinage. The value of a coin depended less on its face value than on the weight of the metal of which it was made. Inflation occurred when monarchs debased the coinage by mixing base with noble metals, or when ordinary people clipped bits of the edges off coins and passed them off as whole. Isaac Newton's first job as master of the British mint was stamping new coins with milled edges so that clipping would be immediately apparent (White, 1997). Paper money for a long time derived its value from governments' promise that it could be redeemed on demand for gold or silver, though this is no longer the case. More important, the money supply of a country is not limited to the total face value of the bills and coins in circulation at a given moment. Banks create money through lending. They take in, say, $10,000 in deposit and then loan it out. The depositor may write checks on her/his $10,000 at the same time the borrower spends her/his $10,000, and thus $20,000 are now in existence where only $10,000 existed before, even though no coins have been minted nor bills printed. Money is an intentional object (Searle, 1995). It exists because — and as long as — people believe that it exists, together with its intentional derivatives such as interest rates and bond yields. Yet no one, to the best of my knowledge, has challenged economics' right to be a (dismal) science on the grounds that its object is a social construction, not a natural kind.

Money need not be embodied in order to exist or in order to have real causal effects on human behavior. Surely, mind is the premier intentional object (Searle, 1997) and may have real causal effects on human behavior even if it cannot be reduced to or even tied to some physical reality. Mind, like money, can be a real object of a real science.[18]

Notes

1. Technically, we "pick up" directly only what Aristotle called the "primary sensibles," the particular sensory features an object possesses. Because we perceive the primary sensibles directly, our knowledge of them is infallible. Judgment, and therefore the possibility of epistemological error, arises at the level of the "common sensibles," our apprehension of the object comprised by the primary sensibles. For example, I might see an intact statue of the Venus of Milo at a distance and think that I was seeing a real woman. Because they share the same (or very similar) perceptual features (the primary sensibles), such as shape and beauty, I make an error in judgment as to what object I am seeing (two different common sensibles). However, this distinction does not alter the point that for Aristotle, perception involves the infallible apprehension of all the perceptible features of an object. Error results from mistaken judgment rather than from the subjective character of sensory processes.

2. Here is an early formulation of Nagel's view from nowhere discussed in Leahey ("Psychology as Engineering," this volume).

3. R. Rorty (1979) focuses on the philosophically important issues, primarily how epistemology became the central concern of philosophy after Descartes.

4. Islamic and Christian physician-philosophers elaborated on the number of mental faculties and added the idea of localization of function in the brain, but they did not change Aristotle's basic functional orientation. See Harvey, 1975; Leahey, 2004; and Kemp, forthcoming.

5. O'Connor (1969) provides a useful collection of articles on this movement, plus some very early papers on functionalism.

6. I discuss Davidson's ideas more fully in "Psychology as Engineering" elsewhere in the present volume. I also take up there related arguments that psychology cannot be a science because mental talk is necessarily moral talk.

7. R. Rorty (1979) presents an extended science-fiction thought experiment to illustrate the Wittgensteinian view. He imagines the discovery of an alien, but human, race with no mental language at all. Instead, they explain themselves and others by deploying neuroscientific language.

8. It is interesting to observe that while positivism is often associated with tough-minded materialism, it began as a form of tough-minded idealism along Berkeleyan lines. For the positivists, the ultimate ground of fact was sensation. Ernst Mach strongly opposed the introduction of theoretical terms such as *atom* into physics, and the later logical positivists admitted them only grudgingly. The whole idea of opera-

tional definition was to ensure that theoretical terms refer not to something materially real, but to a set of directly observable events such as measurement operations. Because the mental is private, it eludes such operations, while behavior, being public, does not. Thus sensationistic idealism as much as transcendental idealism puts the mind outside science.

9. This is particularly true of Hull, who thought of them as mechanical or physiological; Tolman vacillated between various treatments of his theoretical constructs. See L.D. Smith, 1986; Leahey, 2004.

10. Taylor (1989, p. 159) actually uses the term "punctual," but I believe that this has unfortunate connotations.

11. This question is obviously related to the question of free will, but is not the same. One might reject the idea of free will, but accept consciousness as playing a causal, but determined, role in producing behavior. The question I take up here is whether consciousness is an epiphenomenon of bodily processes, having no more bearing on human behavior than the color of a car has on its operation.

12. Ogden (1911), in a discussion of the imageless-thought controversy, mentions two psychologists ready to jettison introspective method from psychology. One wishes to know their names.

13. In a footnote.

14. My favorites are the movie *Blade Runner* and an episode from *Star Trek: The Next Generation* called "Data's Day."

15. In "Data's Day," a young woman in a brief relationship with the android Data falls out of love when he answers her question "What were you thinking when you kissed me just now?" Data replies that he was calculating how much force he could apply to the back of her head without crushing it. Data has too much introspective access to his mental processes to count as human.

16. See Nussbaum and Rorty, 1992. My own view is that while there is some similarity between functionalism and Aristotle's theory of soul, this should not be pushed too far. To begin with, there is no historical connection between them. More important, as Burnyeat (1992) points out, Aristotle's conception of living matter is radically different from our own. While Aristotle did separate form and matter, he would never have thought that a machine could be ensouled, a key notion of AI and functionalism.

17. In his reply to Searle's review of *Consciousness Explained*, reprinted in Searle, 1997, p. 119.

18. Psychologists should also bear in mind the instrumentalist alternative. Many philosophers believe that a theory need only acceptably describe and predict the phenomena in its scope. Whether or not the entities postulated by a theory actually exist (realism) is, on this view, a burden that no theory can bear. Therefore, a respectable scientific psychology might be constructed on the notion of mind whether or not "mind" or minds exist, as long as it is capable of adequately dealing with human behavior.

References

Armstrong, D.M. 1968. *A Materialist Theory of the Mind*. London: Routledge and Kegan Paul.

Beakely, B., and Ludlow, P. (Eds.). 1992. *The Philosophy of Mind*. Cambridge, MA: MIT Press.

Blom, J.J. 1978. *Descartes: His Moral Philosophy and Psychology*. New York: New York University Press.

Boring, E.G., Langfeld, H.S., Werner, H., and Yerkes, R.M. (Eds.). 1952. A *History of Psychology in Autobiography*. Vol. 4. Worcester, MA: Clark University Press.

Bremmer, J.N. 1983. *The Early Greek Concept of the Soul*. Princeton, NJ: Princeton University Press.

Bringmann, W., Lück, H., Miller, R., and Early, C. (Eds.). 1997. A *Pictorial History of Psychology*. Chicago: Quintessence.

Bringmann, W., and Tweney, R.D. (Eds.). 1980. *Wundt Studies*. Toronto: Hogrefe.

Burkert, W. 1985. *Greek Religion*. Cambridge, MA: Harvard University Press.

Burnyeat, M. 1992. "Is an Aristotelian Theory of Mind still Credible?" in M. Nussbaum and A.-O. Rorty (Eds.), *Essays on Aristotle's* De Anima. Oxford: Clarendon Press.

Burtt, E.A. (1954). *The Metaphysical Foundations of Modern Science*. Garden City, NY: Doubleday.

Cattell, J.M. 1896. "Address of the President." *Psychological Review*, 3, pp. 134–48.

Chalmers, D. 1996. *The Conscious Mind: In Search of a Fundamental Theory*. Oxford: Oxford University Press.

Churchland, P.M. 1985. *Matter and Consciousness*. Cambridge, MA: MIT Press.

———. 1988. "The Ontological Status of Intentional States: Nailing Folk Psychology to Its Perch." *Behavioral and Brain Sciences*, 11, pp. 507–8.

———. 1989. A *Neurocomputational Perspective: Toward a Unified Science of the Mind-Brain*. Cambridge, MA: MIT Press.

———. 1995. *The Engine of Reason, the Seat of the Soul: A Philosophical Journey into the Brain*. Cambridge, MA: MIT Press.

Churchland, P.S. 1986. *Neurophilosophy*. Cambridge, MA: MIT Press.

Collins, S. 1982. *Selfless Persons: Imagery and Thought in Theravada Buddhism*. Cambridge: Cambridge University Press.

Dahlbom, B. 1993. "Mind Is Artificial." Pp. 161–83 in B. Dahlbom (Ed.), *Dennett and His Critics*. Oxford: Blackwell.

Danziger, K. 1979. "The Positivist Repudiation of Wundt." *Journal of the History of the Behavioral Sciences*, 15, pp. 205–30.

Davidson, D. 1980. *Essays on Actions and Events*. Oxford: Clarendon Press.

Dennett, D.C. 1980. "Where Am I?" in D.C. Dennett (Ed.), *Brainstorms*. Cambridge, MA: MIT Press.

———. 1991. *Consciousness Explained*. Boston: Little, Brown.

———. 1998. *Brainchildren: Essays on Designing Minds*. Cambridge, MA: MIT Press.

Dunlap, K. 1912. "Discussion: The Case against Introspection." *Psychological Review*, 19, pp. 404–12.

Dunton, L. 1895. "The Old Psychology and the New," in L. Dunton, H. Münsterberg, W.T. Harris, and G.S. Hall (Eds.), *The Old Psychology and the New: Addresses before the Massachusetts Schoolmaster's Club, April 27, 1895*. Boston: New England Publishing Co.

Durrant, M. (Ed.). 1993. *Aristotle's* De Anima *in Focus*. London: Routledge and Kegan Paul.

Esterson, A. 1993. *Seductive Mirage: An Exploration of the Work of Sigmund Freud*. Chicago: Open Court.

Estes, W.K. and Simon, H. 1980/1983. "Report of the Research Briefing Panel on

Cognitive Science and Artificial Intelligence," in *Research Briefings 1983*. Washington, DC: National Academy Press.

Fechner, G.T. (1876). *Vorschule der Aesthetik*. Leipzig: Breitkopf and Hartel.

Fodor, J. (1975). *The Language of Thought*. Cambridge, MA: MIT Press.

Gaffan, D. 1997. "Review of *The Mind-Brain Continuum*." *Trends in Cognitive Sciences*, 1, p. 194.

Galileo. 1960. "The Assayer," in *The Controversy on the Comets of 1618*. Trans. S. Drake and C.D. O'Malley. Philadelphia: University of Pennsylvania Press.

Gaukroger, S. 1995. *Descartes: An Intellectual Biography*. Oxford: Clarendon Press.

Geertz, C. 1974. " 'From the Native's Point of View': On the Nature of Anthropological Understanding." *Bulletin of the American Academy of Arts and Sciences*, 27 (1).

Gergen, K. 1973. "Social Psychology as History." *Journal of Personality and Social Psychology*, 26, pp. 309–20.

———. 1982. *Toward Transformation in Social Knowledge*. New York: Springer-Verlag.

Gould, S.J., and Lewontin, R. 1979. "The Spandrels of San Marco and the Panglossian Paradigm: A Critique of the Adaptationist Paradigm." *Proceedings of the Royal Society*, B205, pp. 581–98.

Grossman, R. 1995. "Phenomenology," in T. Honderich (Ed.), *The Oxford Companion to Philosophy*. Oxford: Oxford University Press.

Hale, M. (1980). *Human Science and Social Order: Hugo Münsterberg and the Origins of Applied Psychology*. Philadelphia: Temple University Press.

Harvey, E.R. 1975. *The Inward Wits: Psychological Theory in the Middle Ages and the Renaissance*. London: Warburg Institute.

Haugeland, J. (Ed.). 1981. *Mind Design*. Cambridge, MA: MIT Press.

Hume, D. 1740/1984. *A Treatise of Human Nature*. London: Penguin.

Jahoda, G. 1997. "Wilhelm Wundt's *Völkerpsychologie*." Pp. 148–52 in W. Bringmann, H. Lück, R. Miller, and C. Early (Eds.), *A Fictional History of Psychology*. Chicago: Quintessence.

James, W. 1890. *The Principles of Psychology*. 2 Vols. New York: Henry Holt.

———. 1892a. "A Plea for Psychology as a Natural Science." *Philosophical Review*, 1, pp. 146–53.

———. 1892b/1992. *Psychology: Briefer Course*. G. Myers (Ed.). New York: Library of America.

———. 1905. "Does Consciousness Exist?" *Journal of Philosophy*, 1, pp. 477–91.

———. 1907/1955. *Pragmatism*. New York: Meridian.

Kemp, S. 2000. "Medieval Psychology." *Encyclopedia of Psychology*. Washington, DC: APA; New York: Oxford University Press, pp. 383–85.

Kenny, A. (Ed.). 1994. *The Oxford History of Western Philosophy*. Oxford: Oxford University Press.

Knox, B. 1993. *The Oldest Dead White European Males and Other Reflections on the Classics*. New York: Norton.

Koffka, K. 1935/1963. *Principles of Gestalt Psychology*. San Diego, CA: Harcourt Brace and World.

Kosslyn, S.M., and Koenig, O. 1992. *Wet Mind: The New Cognitive Neuroscience*. New York: Macmillan/Free Press.

Kraut, R. (Ed.). 1992. *The Cambridge Companion to Plato*. Cambridge: Cambridge University Press.

Ladd, G.T. 1892. "Psychology as a So-Called Natural Science." *Philosophical Review,* 1, pp. 24–53.

Lashley, K.S. 1923. "The Behavioristic Interpretation of Consciousness." *Psychological Review,* 30, pp. 237–72, 329–53.

Leahey, T.H. 1992. "The Mythical Revolutions of American Psychology." *American Psychologist,* 47, pp. 308–18.

———. 1994a. *A History of Modern Psychology.* 2nd ed. Englewood Cliffs, NJ: Prentice Hall.

———. 1994b. "Is This a Dagger I See before Me? Four Theorists in Search of Consciousness: Essay review of D.C. Dennett, *Consciousness Explained,* O. Flanagan, *Consciousness Considered,* N. Humphrey, *A History of the Mind,* and J. Searle, *The Rediscovery of the Mind." Contemporary Psychology,* 39, pp. 575–82.

———. 1995. "Ideo-motor Action." P. 30 in R. Audi (Ed.), *The Cambridge Dictionary of Philosophy.* Cambridge: Cambridge University Press.

———. 2004. *A History of Psychology: Main Currents in Psychological Thought.* 6th ed. Upper Saddle River, NJ: Prentice Hall.

———. Forthcoming. "Gestalt Psychology and Phenomenology," in *Cambridge History of Modern Philosophy, 1870–1940.* Cambridge: Cambridge University Press.

Llinás, R., and Churchland, P.S. (Eds.). 1996. *The Mind-Brain Continuum.* Cambridge, MA: MIT Press.

Locke, J. 1690/1975. *An Essay Concerning Human Understanding.* Variorum ed. P. Nidditch (Ed.). Oxford: Clarendon Press.

Mathews, G. 1986. "Descartes and the Problem of Other Minds." Pp. 141–51 in A.-O. Rorty (Ed.), *Essays on Descartes' Meditations.* Berkeley: University of California Press.

Morgan, M.L. 1992. "Plato and Greek Religion." Pp. 227–47 in R. Kraut (Ed.), *The Cambridge Companion to Plato.* Cambridge: Cambridge University Press.

Morris, C. 1972. *The Discovery of the Individual, 1050–1200.* New York: Harper Torchbooks.

Nussbaum, M., and Rorty, A.-O. (Eds.). 1992. *Essays on Aristotle's* De Anima. Oxford: Clarendon Press.

O'Connor, J. (Ed.). 1969. *Modern Materialism: Readings on Mind-Body Identity.* New York: Harcourt, Brace and World.

Ogden, R.M. 1911. "Imageless Thought." *Psychological Bulletin,* 8, pp. 183–197.

Onians, R.B. 1951. *The Origins of European Thought: About the Body, the Mind, the Soul, the World, Time, and Fate.* Cambridge: Cambridge University Press.

Perry, R.B. 1904. "Conceptions and Misconceptions of Consciousness." *Psychological Review,* 11, pp. 282–96.

Pinker, S. 1997. *How the Mind Works.* New York: Norton.

Place, U.T. 1956/1992. "Is Consciousness a Brain Process?" *British Journal of Philosophy.* Reprinted in B. Beakely and P. Ludlow (Eds.), *The Philosophy of Mind.* Cambridge, MA: Harvard University Press.

Rachlin, H. 1985. "Pain and Behavior." *Behavioral and Brain Sciences,* 8, pp. 43–83.

Romanes, G.J. 1883. *Animal Intelligence.* New York: Appleton.

Rorty, A.-O. (Ed.). 1986. *Essays on Descartes' Meditations.* Berkeley: University of California Press.

Rorty, R. 1979. *Philosophy and the Mirror of Nature.* Princeton, NJ: Princeton University Press.

———. 1991. "Nonreductive Physicalism," in *Objectivity, Relativism, and Truth*. Vol. 1 of *Philosophical Papers*. Cambridge: Cambridge University Press.

———. 1993. "Holism, Intrinsicality, and the Ambition of Transcendence." Pp. 184–203 in B. Dahlbom (Ed.), *Dennett and His Critics*. Oxford: Blackwell.

Rosenberg, A. 1994. *Instrumental Biology; or, The Disunity of Science*. Chicago: University of Chicago Press.

Ryle, G. 1949. *The Concept of Mind*. New York: Barnes and Noble.

Sanford, E.C. 1903. "Psychology and Physics." *Psychological Review*, 10, pp. 105–19.

Scruton, R. 1994. "Continental Philosophy: Fichte to Sartre." Pp. 193–238 in A. Kenny (Ed.), *The Oxford History of Western Philosophy*. Oxford: Oxford University Press.

Searle, J.R. 1994. *The Rediscovery of the Mind*. Los Angeles: University of California Press.

———. 1995. *The Construction of Social Reality*. New York: Free Press.

———. 1997. *The Mystery of Consciousness*. New York: New York Times Books.

Simon, H. 1981. *The Sciences of the Artificial*. 2nd ed. Cambridge, MA: MIT Press.

Simon, L. 1998. *Genuine Reality: A Life of William James*. New York: Harcourt Brace.

Singer, E.A. 1911. "Mind as Observable Object." *Journal of Philosophy*, 8, pp. 180–86.

———. 1912a. "Consciousness and Behavior." *Journal of Philosophy*, 9, pp. 15–19.

———. 1912b. "On Mind as Observable Object." *Journal of Philosophy*, 9, pp. 206–14.

Skinner, B.F. 1953. *Science and Human Behavior*. New York: Macmillan.

———. 1971. *Beyond Freedom and Dignity*. New York: Knopf.

———. 1983. *A Matter of Consequences: Volume 3 of an Autobiography*. New York: Knopf.

———. 1985. "Cognitive Science and Behaviorism." *British Journal of Psychology*, 76, pp. 291–301.

Smith, A.M. 1990. "Knowing Things Inside Out: The Scientific Revolution from a Medieval Perspective." *American Historical Review*, 95, pp. 726–44.

Smith, L.D. 1986. *Behaviorism and Logical Positivism: A Reassessment of the Alliance*. Stanford, CA: Stanford University Press.

Snell, B. 1953. *The Discovery of the Mind: The Greek Origins of European Thought*. Reprint edition, New York: Harper, 1953; *The Discovery of the Mind in Greek Philosophy and Literature*. New York: Dover Books, 1982.

Solomon, R.C. 1988. *Continental Philosophy since 1750: The Rise and Fall of the Self*. Oxford: Oxford University Press.

Sulloway, F.J. 1979. *Freud: Biologist of the Mind*. New York: Basic Books.

Taylor, C. 1989. *Sources of the Self: The Making of the Modern Identity*. Cambridge, MA: Harvard University Press.

Thomas, K. 1971. *Religion and the Decline of Magic*. Harmondsworth: Penguin.

Thorndike, E.L. 1913. "Ideo-motor Action." *Psychological Review*, 20, pp. 91–106.

Titchener, E.B. 1929/1972. *Systematic Psychology: Prolegomena*. Ithaca, NY: Cornell University Press.

Tolman, E.C. 1935. "Psychology vs. Immediate Experience." Pp. 94–114 in E.C. Tolman, *Behavior and Psychological Man*. Berkeley: University of California Press, 1951/1966.

———. 1936. "Operational Behaviorism and Current Trends in Psychology." Pp. 115–

129 in E.C. Tolman, *Behavior and Psychological Man*. Berkeley: University of California Press, 1951/1966.

———. 1951/1966. *Behavior and Psychological Man*. Berkeley: University of California Press.

———. 1952. "Edward Chace Tolman." Pp. 323–39 in E.G. Boring, H.S. Langfeld, H. Werner, and R.M. Yerkes (Eds.), *A History of Psychology in Autobiography*. Vol. 4. Worcester, MA: Clark University Press.

Turing, A.M. 1950. "Computing Machinery and Intelligence." *Mind*, 59, pp. 433–60.

van Hoorn, W, and Verhave, T. 1980. "Wundt's Changing Conception of a General and Theoretical Psychology." Pp. 71–113 in W. Bringmann and R.D. Tweney (Eds.), *Wundt Studies*. Toronto: Hogrefe.

Watson, J.B. 1909. "A Point of View in Comparative Psychology." *Psychological Bulletin*, 6, pp. 57–58.

———. 1913. "Psychology as the Behaviorist Views It." *Psychological Review*, 20, pp. 158–77.

Webster, R. 1995. *Why Freud Was Wrong*. New York: Basic Books.

White, M. 1997. *Isaac Newton: The Last Sorcerer*. Reading, MA: Addison-Wesley.

Wundt, W.W. 1907–8. "Über Ausfragenexperimenten und über die Methoden zur Psychologie des Denkens." *Psychologische Studien*, 3, pp. 301–60.

Zalewski, D. 1998. "Restoration Drama: The Art Historian Who Loves Dirty Pictures." *Lingua Franca*, April, pp. 42–51.

3

The Emergence of Minds in
Space and Time

Jagdish Hattiangadi

Is it incoherent to claim that minds emerged as irreducible causal agents in the physical universe as we know it? Jaegwon Kim, in a very careful, general, and thorough analysis of the concept of supervenience, has suggested that it is (Kim, 1993). After remarking upon the intuitive attraction of doctrines of emergence, he issues a challenge to produce a coherent account of emergence that can allow for the realization of the causal powers of emergent entities like minds while allowing, in some sense of that word, for "physicalism." It is perhaps the most thorough analysis of the concept of supervenience in the literature, is therefore deserving of careful study, and requires a response. In this chapter, I will show that Kim's analysis is quite cogent if we assume a certain deterministic conception of physics that was prevalent in the later eighteenth and early nineteenth centuries, known as Newtonian or classical physics. It seems, however, that a contemporary and indeterministic account of the physical world, a part of what is often called the orthodox interpretation of quantum phenomena, would suggest that emergence is not only quite coherent with it, but the best account available to us. Although Kim does not raise the question of determinism, and it is not customary to discuss determinism or indeterminism in this context, it will be shown to be relevant, and even crucial, to the development of an adequate theory of minds as they emerge in space and in time.

Kim has thoroughly reviewed the literature on, and analyzed the doctrine of, what he calls "nonreductive physicalism" (Kim, 1993). He concludes that it is untenable. Consequently, he rejects the doctrine of emergence, which, he says, is a particular expression of the general form of what he calls "nonreductive physicalism."[1] His characterization of the doctrine of emergence, as exemplified in the layered model of nonreductive physicalism, is very sympathetically stated.

> The ontological picture that has dominated contemporary thinking on the mind-body problem is strikingly different from the Cartesian picture.

The Cartesian picture of a *bifurcated* world has been replaced by that of a *layered* world, a stratified structure of "levels" or "orders" of entities and their characteristic properties. It is generally thought that there is a bottom level, one consisting of whatever micro-physical entities that are going to tell us the most basic physical particles out of which all matter is composed (electrons, neutrons, quarks, or whatever). And these objects, whatever they are, are characterized by certain fundamental physical properties and relations (mass, spin, charm, or whatever). As we ascend to higher levels, we find structures made up of entities belonging to the lower levels, and, moreover, entities at any level are thought to be characterized by properties distinctive to that level. Thus, at a certain level, we find accumulations of H_2O molecules, with such properties as transparency, the power to dissolve sugar and salt, their characteristic density and viscosity, and so on. At still higher levels we will find cells and organisms with their "vital properties," and farther up we will find organisms with consciousness and intentionality. Beyond them are social groups of organisms and perhaps groups consisting of such groups" (Kim, 1993, p. 337)

But his conclusion, upon analyzing this account, is far from optimistic about the prospects for the doctrine of emergence, or nonreductive physicalism: "Nonreductive physicalism, like Cartesianism, founders on the rocks of mental causation" (Kim, 1993, p. 339). The analysis that he proposes concludes in the form of a challenge, which will be taken up in this chapter.

He first describes the layered or stratified conception as endorsing the view that "all concrete existents are physical—there are no nonphysical particulars, no souls, no Cartesian mental substances, and no 'vital principles' or 'entelechies.' " (Kim, 1993, p. 340). He is, of course, quite right. But what exactly is entailed by the word "physical" here? Plausibly, Kim suggests the following: "Minimally, perhaps, a physical entity must have a determinate location in space and time.[2] But that may not be enough. Perhaps an entity is physical just in case it has some physical property or other. But what makes a property a physical property? Perhaps, the best answer we could muster is . . . : explain 'physical' with reference to current theoretical physics. *Nothing in the discussion to follow will depend on precise general definitions of 'physical' and 'mental'*" (Kim, 1993, p. 340; emphasis added). In a curious way, the last sentence neglects a detail that undermines, as I will argue, an otherwise very thorough and cogent argument. The issue depends very much on what we understand by "physical" and "current physical theory."

Kim's argument begins by characterizing the doctrine of emergence as an endorsement of four principles:

1. [Physical monism] All concrete particulars are physical.
2. [Antireductionism] Mental properties are not reducible to physical properties.
3. [The physical realization thesis] All mental properties are physically realized.[3]

4. [Mental realism] Mental properties are real properties of objects and events; they are not merely useful aids in making predictions or fictitious manners of speech. (Kim, 1993, p. 344)

Again quite plausibly, Kim takes "mental realism" in principle 4 to imply "that mental properties bring with them *new causal powers, powers that no underlying physical-biological properties can deliver*" (Kim, 1993, p. 350). This, too, seems precisely what the theory of emergence requires. He argues cogently that this implies "downward causation" or causal effects of mental properties and events on physical-biological properties. I will not repeat his argument here. Having developed his sympathetic description so far, however, Kim suggests that downward causation has severe difficulties, because the nonreductive physicalist wants "downward causation" (as implied by principle 4, mental realism) combined with "upward determination" (as implied, he thinks, in principle 3, physical realization). This is, he claims, incoherent. As these are described, he is quite right.[4]

To demonstrate this incoherence in the doctrine of emergence, he proposes that in accepting principle 3, the nonreductive physicalist must accept the causal inheritance principle:

If M is instantiated on a given occasion by being realized by P, then the causal powers of this instance of M are identical with (perhaps a subset of) the causal powers of P. This, of course, has the consequence that there is no causal power that M possesses that is not reducible to P, and so in fact it denies the anti-reductive thesis. (Kim, 1993, p. 355)

This principle, if adopted, reduces the theory of emergence to incoherence. It constitutes an assurance to us that nothing can emerge, on the ground that "physicalism" must enjoin us to accept the principle.

Kim recognizes that every theory of emergence need not incorporate a principle that is the equivalent of the causal inheritance principle. "And I would challenge those non-reductivists who would reject this principle to state an alternative principle on just how the causal powers of a realized property are connected with its realization base" (Kim, 1993, p. 355). This is the challenge that is met in this chapter.

The obviousness of the incoherence of nonreductive physicalism to Kim in any account of how a physical state is realized is quite understandable, I suggest, if we assume a deterministic form of the Newtonian conception of the physical world, but not if we substitute for it the nonclassical picture that emerges with quantum mechanics. This will be argued later. If we investigate the exact way in which a concept is said to be "physical," then, given the rest of Kim's analysis, we may come around to doubt the obviousness of the claim that if we accept the principle of causal realization, then we accept the causal inheritance principle, too.

As a preliminary to further developing Kim's careful study, we should review the two conditions that are necessary for a reduction of one class of entities downward to a lower level of entities. This may be the same as the "determination upwards," as Kim refers to it, of a mental property above by the physical properties below, though he tries valiantly to find some account of a difference. First, the properties of the higher level must be definable in terms of properties at the lower level. By "definable" we mean that we can give a case-by-case correlation. We do not demand a "meaning" reduction, such that the terminology of one level actually means what is correlated at the lower level. Second, on the basis of such correlational definitions, the laws governing the entities of the higher level must be deducible from the laws governing the entities of the lower level.[5] If both conditions are satisfied, then we would agree that a reduction has been successful. An example of a successful reduction may be the reduction of color to the wave theory of light, in which different wavelengths are correlated with different colors, case by case, and all the phenomena of colors in light are shown to be deducible from the new wave theory of light. Another famous example of reduction is the definition of temperature and heat in terms of energetic properties of aggregates of particles in motion, and the derivation of the laws of heat from those of statistical (Newtonian) mechanics governing those particles. Note that one does not need to make it a requirement that the reducing theory be true. We may not accept the wave theory of light, except as an approximation, but still accept that the reduction of color to wavelength is a successful reductive exercise.

Classical or deterministic Newtonian physics is a very abstract subject. The laws of motion that are used to describe the world are invariant with respect to place and to direction. Invariance is very important in physical theory. The laws are claimed to be true everywhere, because it does not matter where a motion originates and where it ends. This level of generality is achievable in physics only because it does not describe any actual arrangements of things in the universe. It is not a description of things, in that sense. The equations of classical physics are conditional laws about such possible arrangements. For certain classes of initial conditions of things at a time, the future conditions will be calculable. This form of the laws of motion is very characteristic of the way physics describes the entire universe, seemingly, by abstracting from a few experiments that have been conducted nearby.

Laplace is famous for suggesting that if only we knew the position and momentum of every particle in the universe, we could, on the basis of the laws of physics, predict the position and momentum of any particle in the world at a future time. In order to have such a determination of a future state of all particles, we need not only the bare laws of motion, but also the laws governing the forces, the distribution of all forces, and the assurance that these, indeed, are all the forces in nature. It is important to note that the state of a system, so understood, is not determined exclusively by the laws, or the abstract equations of physics. It is only when we are also given the state of a system antecedently that we can predict a future state on the basis of the laws and the given state. Prediction is of course an epistemological feature, but its use is to mimic a metaphysical issue. The state of the universe at a given time may be thought to determine all future states under the laws of physics, or we may imagine that its effect on other states is merely statistical. This is a difference of some importance to us.

Laplace's optimism that the laws of physics are complete in deriving any future states, once we are given a system's state at a time, is also known as the doctrine of physical determinism. If we assume determinism, then it seems that Kim's analysis of the determination of higher-level properties by lower-level properties is unassailable. We could argue as follows: If a new property M were to emerge, its existence would follow inexorably from an antecedently given state with properties P, together with the laws of mechanics and of the forces in play. But whatever causal effect the property M produces can be shown to be produced in turn by whatever one invokes in the determination of the property M, based on the laws, and the antecedently given state.[6]

If we abandon the principle of determinism in mechanics, however, we have a very different situation. Laws are still general in an indeterministic universe and exhibit many fascinating forms of invariance and symmetry. Each determination of a future state of a system, however, relies upon a previous state that must be newly specified each time. Suppose, for instance, that we can only specify statistical consequences for the future state of the system. This could happen for one of two very different reasons: because the laws of mechanics are inherently statistical in character, or because, though the universe is supposed to be deterministic in principle, all that we can know about the state of a complex system is of a statistical nature. The description of an ideal gas by statistical mechanics is a celebrated classical theory, or a Newtonian result, of this latter kind. In both models for statistical laws, predictions about the future state of a system will depend crucially on the prior state that has been described. The latest state that can be described as an antecedent state will always give the most detailed descriptions about the state or states to follow. But if each time a calculation has to be made, we must specify the initial conditions, then the actual arrangement of initial conditions, from time to time, can leave room for apparently emerging entities. If the system is truly indeterminate, then these entities will be real and emergent. Otherwise, they will have only the appearance of emergence, being in themselves "upwardly determined" by the prior conditions. In any system in which the arrangement of physical conditions in the state of the system is not fully determined by the laws, together with the previous states of the system, emergence is possible.

Suppose that we imagine a situation in which the likelihood of a certain configuration of atoms is highly unlikely, given any state of the system that we come across until time t. This particular configuration of atoms, once it comes together at t, however, happens to possess the peculiar property that it is stable after t. Stable structures of atoms are those that do not easily (i.e., are less likely to) break up. A structure may also be metastable, in a certain sense, in that it increases the likelihood dramatically of more atoms in the neighborhood forming similar stable structures under certain conditions that otherwise may be themselves antecedently not very likely. Such a stable entity in an indeterministic universe will possess emergent properties.

We note that the property of stability that is possessed by the complex of atoms we have been imagining is not fully describable in terms of properties of the most basic antecedent entities, be they atoms or be they even lower-level, subatomic entities. We cannot describe the properties that follow from the stability of these structures without making reference to these higher-level structures as they are formed. Every underlying structure may be comparatively unstable even while the overlying whole that is composed is more stable. Indeed, that is exactly what happens when stable things emerge. Moreover, we note that the very existence of the stable structure forms the basis for changing our predictions about the future state of the system in respect of the underlying elements. We can now predict that there is a high likelihood that the elements of the stable structure will be observed characteristically together, even though it was antecedently perhaps highly unlikely that they should have been found together. The emergent stable structure, therefore, possesses genuine causal powers that change the statistical property of the arrangement of subsequent substrate atoms. Moreover, these causal powers, or properties, are quite irreducible to the statistical properties of the atoms themselves without reference to the distributional initial conditions.

The model of how atoms can get together to form larger structures here is a schematic picture of how crystals are understood in solid-state physics, given the statistical laws of thermodynamics. The molecules in a solution in which crystals are formed are not quite as predictable as the behavior of the components of the crystals formed within the fluid solution. A fluid is more thermodynamically energetic than a crystal formed within. Any theory of emergence will need to invoke a chance event or events that lead to the formation of a particular configuration of lower-level things. This configuration has a stability that is very different from the usual expectations of the lower-level things. Any stable structure will now have properties that the substrate fails to exhibit. A crystal, for instance, has a characteristic geometric shape. It may also have the effect in the solution of facilitating the creation of more crystals like itself. Neither of these is determined by the previous properties of the substrate, though they are quite compatible with them.

Let us express this in terms used in Kim's third thesis. The physical realization of the property of stability in a higher-level entity L is in terms of properties of the entities of the lower-level C. But this is possible only because the laws governing C cannot be fully expressed without making reference to the possible higher-level entities. Suppose, for instance, that we were to imagine a different kind of stability than the ones we are accustomed to, so that from the C or chemicals on Earth, no life or L properties (of the form we encounter) appeared, but other kinds of stable structures did. Since in an indeterministic world there are many possible stable structures, of which L is just one, this is entirely possible. The future states of the system after the appearance of the L' (stable structures other than L) will not be the same as those of L. The future states of the world after the point at which L or L' or other L-type entities might emerge are underdetermined by antecedent conditions. The future determination of the world will depend crucially upon which of the possible L-type stable structures are accidentally present (L being but one of many possible stable structures).

Let us look at a typical primitive living cell. It may have molecules of nucleic acid in it, configured in a certain way; some very specific proteins; and a skin that is semi-impervious. There will also be special proteins and structures in the cell that assist in the production of proteins, in the reproduction of RNA and DNA and of the skin, and, of course, in the absorption of energy from the ambient waters in order to power these activities. The cell we examine could be the most primitive of all recognizable living cells, but it would still have these various parts in it.

Consider now in this earliest of cells that there is a particular protein that aids in the production of other proteins by utilizing information coded in RNA. This kind of protein is one of the so-called aminoacyl synthetase molecules. Its chemical composition, like that of all organic chemicals, is that of a complicated hydrocarbon. Its peculiarity and usefulness to the cell are simply these: At one end it fits a particular nucleotide sequence in the nucleic acid very precisely, and no other sequence, and at the other it attaches to one particular amino acid quite exactly. A series of such molecules is thus needed in order to transcribe the information in some coded nucleotide sequence into a series of amino acids that link serially together, in that very order, to form that particular protein. This is how proteins are synthesized, and it is a celebrated account of how the whole machinery of life works. Three and a half billion years ago, one particular aminoacyl synthetase molecule may have been the very first molecule of its kind in the universe (i.e., in linking one particular codon to one particular amino acid). Its protein product (a string of amino acids) may have been the first synthesis of that particular organic chemical ever. Its production was in a cell, and its stable continued existence since then is in some living cell or other (for which, if it is still around, it must have provided some survival benefit.) It may very well be true and (I have no wish to challenge the physical realization thesis) that the aminoacyl synthetase molecule itself is just a hydrocarbon, so far as its chemical composition is concerned. It is only a protein and nothing more, but this is not to deny that its natural occurrence is in a living cell. It may well be the case that it is only in some living cell or other that the particular molecule will ever be created, in which it will be a part of the life cycle of the cell. We cannot understand the existence of this molecule in its host cell without noting how chemicals interact with living cells, even though we accept the fact that living cells are made up only of chemicals. This is the kind of interaction between wholes and the types of things that are its constituents that needs to be studied more carefully.

We may ask: If synthetase molecules are needed to synthesize protein, and proteins are needed to duplicate nucleic acids, and nucleic acids are needed to program how synthetases and other proteins are produced, how did it all begin? How was the first synthetase synthesized? Perhaps it is best to begin by allowing that we do not know. Nor do we need to pursue this fascinating issue. We need only note that every emergent entity is in this sense a stable whole whose origin needs a special explanation. Once it has arisen, its stable existence can be understood as self-perpetuating. Those who accept a deterministic point of view may not want to distinguish between an evolutionary account of origins and a just-so story. But for any indeterminist, nature must have a narrative structure.[7] Since every emergent entity has an origin in time, and since its accidental emergence changes the interactions that take place in a certain part of the universe, there cannot be an acceptable account given of things that does not allow for historical development, or a narrative structure to nature.

The cell is a higher-level entity that has the property L of producing that particular aminoacyl synthetase molecule. The lower level entities are the chemical elements, of which it is a property C that they could form the aminoacyl synthetase molecule. (Nothing in their structure prohibits this.) But it may be that the only way in which the property L is ever realized is when a living cell evolves in a certain way, out of the myriad ways in which it might well have evolved. Thus the property L is chemically realized as a hydrocarbon, and merely as a hydrocarbon, but we cannot understand how it comes to exist and continues to be produced for three and a half billion years without making some reference to the way in which it is a stable part of the organization of a particular type of living cell, which is itself a stable structure emerging out of a less stable world of chemicals. If fully understanding the laws of the chemicals themselves is to include the understanding of the realization of the emergent property as a property of the substrate, then no full description of the substrate can be given without making reference to properties of the entities of the higher level. Or else we must agree that the properties of the entities at a higher level cannot be understood in terms of the properties of the entities of the next lower level. There is no other possibility to consider. This is how reduction fails, even though the emergent L is chemically realized by C.

We must examine the case of quantum mechanics, too. The wave equations for motions that govern the subatomic wave particles are of an unusual kind. There is one law in which the wave train being described evolves predictably in time, but another that describes how the same wave suddenly changes through a process called the reduction of the wave packet, which is unpredictable on the basis of the previous equation. In physical terms, the smooth wave begins to behave like a discrete and somewhat unpredictable particle whenever it bounces off, or interacts with, or radiates out of a classical atom in certain ways. But classical atoms are composed of subatomic particles or waves, and of nothing else. Stable atoms, entirely composed of subatomic particles or waves, must be understood to interact with these very entities of the micro level. If, therefore, we ask for a description of the entities of the micro level on their own, then they are incomplete. The description of the subatomic phenomena cannot be complete when the laws of interactions with classical wholes (atoms) are omitted. If our descriptions were to include interactions of quantum-level stuff with entities at the macro level, then they must allow for the reality of the entities at the higher level. Emergence is the only way to describe the stability of atoms arising out of the subatomic entities, with which these atoms then interact. Reduction cannot succeed if Niels Bohr has provided us with the true description of the ultimate affairs.

Quantum mechanics is not being invoked because it is authoritative. This is not an argument from Bohr's authority. It is relevant to our study because it lies at the lowest level that physics itself addresses.[8] The main reason for citing it is that reductivists always allude to reduction to the lowest level, and as it is supposedly established in "the latest theories of physics." Usually, this is included in the very definition of physicalism. Physicalism is the doctrine that all the expressions needed for understanding human beings can be defined in the language of physics. Even when they are defined explicitly in terms of a list of expressions, it is tacitly understood that this list must be satisfactory to pursue any legitimate project in physics, at the very least. So it is important to note that it is in microphysics, at the level below the atomic, that the doubt about reductionism is clearest. The analysis carries this antireductive feature all the way up to the highest of levels whenever entities are emergent and irreducibly so. What this analysis shows is that though a whole is always composed of its parts, sometimes the types of things that constitute the parts cannot be fully described in all causally relevant respects without describing how they interact with the types of things that are wholes *as wholes* that are composed out of them.

There is another reason the ultimate or most basic physical level is important. Much depends on our account of the ultimate things of microphysics, whatever they are. If the ultimate particles behave deterministically, as Laplace had hoped, then (even if we do not know it) there must be an account that can be given (even if we cannot give it) of how the properties of the whole, or the macrostates, are fully determined by the properties of parts, or the microstates. In that case the apparent reality of mental properties would be just that—merely apparent. In the converse case, in which no account of the properties of the microstates by themselves is in principle complete without reference to their interaction with macroentities, we must allow for the concept of emergence to apply. A list of properties is never enough to distinguish any one particle from any other. The determination of the identity of an atom is ultimately made by its numbers (x, y, z, t) in space-time. The key question here is whether any ultimate particle or entity has a unique trajectory that would ensure its being a different entity from any other, no matter how similar it is in any other respect. Should trajectories themselves turn out to be emergent phenomena, then we cannot accept a deterministic account of the ultimate parts of reality. With it goes the dream, or the nightmare, of the ultimate reduction of all of reality to the physical.

It is worth noting why the quantum theory is antireductivist on the orthodox interpretation of it, particularly because there have been many ingenious claims in the last seventy years about how the quantum level is directly relevant to the study of mind. None of these quantum hypothetical effects, even if they are real, are being invoked here to account for the mind. In fact, an account of mind as an emergent entity places minds in certain very local developments, not at the fundamental level of the laws of quantum physics, as some have sought to show.

The new quantum mechanics, from 1927, is worth exploring a bit further for our purposes. It has its roots in the failed theory of Niels Bohr, Hendrik Kramers, and John Slater in 1925. Bohr, Kramers, and Slater proposed a very reasonable account of the laws of conservation of energy and momentum in situations in which "quantum jumps" take place. Consider a model of a particle moving in a straight line. If we examine this model line very minutely, we find that there are gaps in the motion at regular very-low-energy-level intervals in accordance with the quantum principle. Similarly, we find gaps between the orbital states of electrons around atoms, as set out in the 1912 Bohr model of the atom. These gaps are to be found because the kinetic energy of the particle itself has a minimum value (based upon the quantum of action), and so its motion must be a little jerky when the particle is slow enough, when examined in our model. But if so, we are faced with the following peculiar situation: The energy and the momentum of the particle will be conserved over the whole line segment representing a smooth-looking motion, in accordance with classical conservation laws, but they will not be conserved in the smallest parts that compose it, because there the conservation laws will break down at each quantum jump. Here we see the beginning of the eventual breakdown of microreductive theory. But this was not the most surprising part of the story.

Bohr, Kramers, and Slater suggested, in a paper in 1924 (Bohr, 1972), that the conservation laws only hold on average, or, in our model, over the entire line segment that represents the motion of the particle, but not in the smallest parts. This seems to be an excellent description of the experimental facts and what we have noted in our model. But their wave equation for motion yielded statistical averaging consequences for all sorts of phenomena in which quanta are involved, such as for collisions between subatomic particles. Some of its factual averaging consequences were shown to be erroneous in an experiment conducted by Hans Geiger and Walther Bothe, and independently by Arthur Holly Compton. It seems, on the basis of these experiment, that even energy and momentum are conserved quite as thoroughly in each action as in the aggregate, as exactly as in the collisions between classical particles. But this is impossible in our model of a smooth-looking line segment that has minute gaps embedded in it. If all the classical conservation laws continue to hold, then it would have to be smooth all the way through. What happened to the quantum principle? This seemed to have spawned a contradiction in our most basic assumptions, between the quantum principle and the conservation of energy. The only possibility for resolving this contradiction is that we are unknowingly assuming something in this account that is false. Perhaps, thought the physicists of the time, this false assumption gives rise to the apparent difficulty.

The new quantum mechanics, formulated in 1925 and 1926, addressed this extraordinary difficulty by proposing an equally extraordinary theory, giving up an unexpected assumption, namely, that everything happens in our familiar space-time. Werner Heisenberg and Erwin Schrödinger independently came up with different but new formulations of the fundamental laws of motion, but their equations turned out to have the same experimental consequences. This became the new quantum theory. The new quantum theory was immensely successful in reconciling a very large number of very puzzling phenomena concerning light interpreted sometimes as waves and at other times as particles. To achieve this, the laws of conservation of energy and momentum are situated, not in Newtonian space, our familiar three-dimensional space with Cartesian coordinates, but in an infinite-dimensional vector space in which the defining operations govern complex numbers (called a Hilbert space after its inventor, David Hilbert). In this new kind of mechanics, energy and momentum are fully conserved in this space (Hilbert space) that is mostly hidden from us. What appears to us as the motion of the particle that we were studying is that part of the total motion that is manifest in Cartesian space as the jerky motion we observe. But the wave itself, if it proceeds on its own, without interacting with classical particles, is highly predictable in Hilbert space. But since we are trapped in our own space, we can observe the effects of the wave only when it interacts with the classical particles.

There was one additional complicating factor. It turns out that the interaction of the waves, defined in the other space, with our classical particles, defined in our space, introduces an irreducible element of chance. (Imagine that our space is smaller, like a bubble imbedded in the larger space.) Even though the wave equation describes the wave as proceeding quite smoothly when it evolves on its own, its manifestation to us, when we interact with it in our bubble, will always be unpredictable. The way in which this happens is also of interest.

The wave itself is described in terms of complex numbers. Complex numbers have two components, a real number and an imaginary number, and are expressed as $a + ib$, where a and b are real numbers (numbers representing lengths on a line), but i is equal to the imaginary number the square root of -1. Whenever we multiply any real number n by itself, whether n itself is positive or negative, it yields a square, which is positive, because two negative real numbers multiplied give a positive real number. We cannot for that reason find a real number, on a line, corresponding to the square root of a negative number i, or to the square root of a multiple of it. So these imaginary numbers do not represent lengths on any straight line in our space. They are not part of the three-dimensional space in which we exist. They are not in our bubble, so to speak. Their existence is only manifest to us as measurable lengths in terms of real numbers. When certain quantities associated with waves do not "appear" to us, but are nevertheless real, according to the calculation of conservation laws, this is because certain solutions to the complex equations will have purely real-number solutions, involving no imaginary component. Thus a number of the form $a + ib$ multiplied by the number $a - ib$ will yield $a^2 + b^2$. This can be represented on a line (in our bubble, so to speak), and so it is a physically measurable quantity. It can be said to appear to us, or be a product of measurement. This appearance is sometimes interpreted as if it had to do with our mental or perceptual capacities, but this interpretation is not warranted. The reason they do not appear to us at all at other times is that they are not represented in our space at all. To appear in this sense has nothing to do with its appearance to our senses, but with its manifestation in classical three-dimensional Cartesian space.

Those quantities given in purely real numbers are called observables by physicists, but this does not require them to be actually observed in order to have classical space-time numbers associated with them.[9] Various people have tried to account for mind by studying how it enters into quantum measurement, but that is not the reason for reporting on quantum mechanics here. It is rather—the point is worth repeating—that quantum mechanics describes the most basic level in physics. If the laws governing this level are incomplete, without including their interaction with the next higher level (of classical matter, or of "our bubble"), and if these laws therefore do not allow for the microreduction of the next higher level to it, then the consequences of this indeterminism will be felt all the way up to the highest macro levels, because if determinism were true, then it would have been fully determined by the microstates, and so, if it is false, then there is no reason to suppose that determinism is true at any higher level.

Bohr concluded, therefore, that we must interpret quantum mechanics to say that the laws of energy and momentum are conserved outside of our classical space. But he suggested, all the same, that our measuring instruments, which record various results, are in our space, that is, in classical, Cartesian, three-dimensional space. So he suggested that both the ordinary world of particles and the rarified subatomic world of wave-particles (for it is hard to distinguish these entities as clearly waves or as clearly particles) are real and complementary.

Most physicists found this approach satisfactory, but this was not true of a minority of very distinguished physicists, including Albert Einstein, Erwin Schrö-dinger, Louis-Yiator de Broglie, and David Bohm, and most philosophers who took an interest in the matter. Some have followed Einstein in supposing that the real world of three dimensions (including all its resident particles within it) is all there is. On this view, all the results of quantum mechanics eventually will have to be explained as statistical results based on real classical particles in an extended form of three-dimensional space (perhaps a multidimensional real space like the one used in Newtonian statistical mechanics). Another approach is to suppose that wave/particles in the infinite-dimensional vector space described by complex numbers (or Hilbert space) are all the entities there are in the universe. All things, we ourselves included, exist in it. Classical particles are merely how things appear to us. This describes a tree of possibilities, except that all the possibilities are realized, of which our experienced universe is just one. All the possibilities are real, but only one seems real to us. Our own apparent three-dimensional space itself is like a prison, and its apparent bars are just an illusion provided by our location on the tree of possibilities in that other space.

Experiments, so far as they have been able to discriminate between these three rival interpretations of the equations of quantum mechanics, have uniformly favored Niels Bohr's interpretation, but the issue is far from decided, since there are many variant interpretations that still remain beyond the reach of an experimental test. It is worth noting, though, that many physicists and philosophers hold very commonly that from a philosophical point of view the assumption of a unified field theory is to be preferred. This doctrine of preference for unified theories is an error. It would seem that we should not prefer unified theories if we want our philosophical problems to be solved. If determinism turns out to be true, we must, of course, accept it, but we have no philosophical reason for preferring it and every philosophical reason for not preferring it. Indeed, all the arguments for those who believe in some form of dualism are fundamentally their reason for dissatisfaction with the deterministic/reductionist account of the universe. These are all philosophical reasons for preferring the new, emergentist account provided or inspired by Niels Bohr. Although Bohr did not express himself in a manner that was suitable for all scientifically minded philosophers to appreciate his point and sometimes invoked philosophical theses that he would have done well to avoid, his main thesis concerning physics and mechanics is a breath of fresh air for modern philosophy.[10] His message is that we do not need to accept the doctrine of reduction. The reason is that even physics is not reducible to mechanics. The most basic laws of the world cannot be understood without studying their interaction with the next higher level of entities. There is no reason why we should expect life or mind to reduce to mechanics, or even to an intermediate level.

Bohr suggested a conception of levels of reality, according to which the next more complex level of reality would be a stable formation that would be governed by its own laws. These would be irreducible to the lower level (not definable in that level, nor deducible from its laws). This is the hallmark of an antireductive account (Broad, 1925). Consider, for instance, the emergence of life itself. Because there is an element of chance in all interactive physical processes, some chance arrangement of physical things makes life possible, but once life is present, living organisms will be governed by its own laws (e.g., of genetics and of evolution by natural selection) as they are determined by chance circumstances at the time of its origin and stable existence. In logical terms we could say the following three things about this: (1) The laws of physics are not complete; (2) the laws of life do not follow logically from the laws of physics; and (3) the laws of life are compatible, all the same, with the laws of physics.

On the experimental evidence available today, the antimechanistic interpretation of quantum theory is probably the best, but there has been a minority of very distinguished physicists who disagree, as we have noted. It cannot be ruled out of the realm of possibility that a unified field theory will be proposed one day that fits the experiments best. Were this to happen, it would make the antireductivism of the recent orthodox interpretation of quantum mechanics factually mistaken. Let us first of all grant that. Even so, no philosopher can claim now, or in the future, on purely conceptual or a priori grounds that have nothing to do with experimental fact, that antireductionism is incoherent. If we are to embrace what Kim calls reductive physicalism, or the variant known as eliminativism, or even if we fall back on the idea that there are two noninteracting worlds, an internal world of reason and an external physicalist, reductive, causal world, we cannot do so on a priori grounds, or on analytic grounds, which is the same thing, but must do so only after a careful review of the physical experiments pertaining to the microstructural laws of the universe.

The causal efficacy of the emergent whole upon the entities at the level that constitute its parts (downward causation) is a feature that can be illustrated at every level of emergence. I have so far given biochemical and physical examples, but an example from our social lives may also be illuminating in this regard, to illustrate the scope of the claim. It is a well-known fact about people that they can be unpredictable in the acquisition and disposal of property. When people own stocks and shares in a company, to take one such case, we cannot predict how they will react to news—whether individuals will buy, hold, or sell. There are many reasons for this. One is that some people may buy or sell on a whim, while others may sell on principle, only when they anticipate others to be selling, and still others may sell when they anticipate others to be buying the stock rather than selling it. Still others will hold stocks, come what may. Nevertheless, if there are enough people who are willing to buy, hold, and sell a type of property, for all their varying and unfathomable reasons, something called a market for it develops. If the laws governing market transactions are reasonable, generally followed, and also diligently enforced, and if there are enough buyers and sellers of the stock, then a price is quoted in the market that tends to be relatively stable from day to day. Markets and stable prices are properties of a whole social structure, rather than of the individuals who comprise it. Although the individual buyers and sellers of the stock may behave quite unpredictably, the stock itself will often behave with a higher degree of predictability. This is the basis of the idea of a stable price and of an orderly market. Moreover, in a typical stock exchange, stocks with large numbers of daily transactions usually have specialists assigned to them who buy and sell those types of stocks (in a particular enterprise) just in order to make the price changes even smoother, and therefore more stable, than they already are. We note, however, that if the stocks were as unpredictable as the decisions of individuals, no specialist would be able to survive for long as a specialist.

A stock market consists only of people, there being no social entities in addition to people and what they do or produce. Yet the properties we have noted about the price, the relative stability of the price of some stocks, and the opportunity for some individuals to make a living, and sometimes quite a good living, by becoming a specialist in a stock are all properties of groups of people. These properties are irreducible to the antecedent properties of individual humans. They can be described as properties of individuals only as they form a part of certain groups. We see, moreover, that the individual who is a specialist has a role in society that cannot be understood without making reference to the stock market, even though we would all agree that the individual, as a category or level, is antecedent to and a substrate of the social category or level known as a market.

If we pay close attention to these cases, we can see precisely why, in a system that is not deterministic, the properties of a whole may sometimes be irreducible to those of entities of the substrate level that antecedently compose it. If we define or correlate the properties of the whole with particular properties of the entities of the substrate composing it, we find in the interesting cases that while the whole, and the laws of the whole, can be shown to arise in certain situations in the substrate, we cannot predict their occurrence on the basis of what we know antecedently, or derive the macrolaws from the laws governing entities solely at the substrate level. At the very least we have to state how these lower-level entities will behave when the unlikely structure is realized. This is the reason the reduction fails. This very failure defines the general form in which all emergence is found — by invoking accidental concatenations of events that lead to the formation of the whole. The failure of reduction shows, first, that the properties of the whole are consistent with the laws of the substrate.[11] Recognizing the strength of the critiques offered by Kuhn (1962) and Feyerabend (1963) of any ahistorical conception of the language of physics, I wonder if any form of the doctrine of physicalism remains defensible. This is, of course, a debatable issue, since Paul Churchland argues in defense of physicalism from the very fact of the changing language of physics, as follows (Churchland, 1979): He suggests that the language of folk psychology is perhaps ultimately eliminated, not subsumed under the final account, since the subsumption seems impossible (for the reasons given in note 3). My difficulty with Churchland's argument is just this: If the future language of physics is always uncertain, and therefore we can find that we have eliminated folk psychology, we can with equal credibility suppose that it will not be folk psychology but vulgar materialism that is eventually eliminated. Then again, perhaps that elimination of vulgar materialism is not so far into the future. Next, failure of reduction shows how these wholes can become stable in the substrate (a statistical description of consequences of the formation of a whole). Last, it can show the effect of the stable structure on the distribution of entities and properties in the substrate (downward causation). In general terms, on this account, what we call "real" is merely what is relatively stable in a world of flux.[12]

Since the systematic anthropological study of stable societies began early in the twentieth century, the relation between stability and function has become quite well known. So has their relation, in turn, to emergence. Looking at a new entity as emergent is to focus on its novelty against the background history of the substrate that precedes it. Looking at the same entity as a stable structure among the lower-level entities and interacting with them, we recognize that very entity as a functioning whole. The role, as we see it, of certain internal arrangements, or of formations of certain parts within it, is to keep the whole stable. These substructures exhibit functional features of these wholes. For instance, in a cell, the function of metabolism is to procure energy in order to keep the stable cell from losing its dynamic stability. Functionalism is therefore closely allied to the doctrine of emergence. The emergent entity, as an entity, is on a par with the other entities of the universe that precede it, even though it is composed of the antecedently existing entities.

It is worth noting why scientists are quite justified in being reductive in their approach to their own specialism, even if the reductive assumption is erroneous on the whole. Aiming for a reductive account of everything in terms of one's own level of entities in one's chosen field of study is usually a very good scientific practice. This follows from the fact that emergence is a rare phenomenon. Even when emergence occurs, the laws governing the emergent entity remain consistent with the laws of the next lower level. Except in the extremely rare instance when accidental arrangements of initial conditions give rise to a stable higher-level structure, reduction is the most accurate description of how any level of entities is organized. No scientist can ever go far wrong in the pursuit of explanation in his or her own professional field by assuming a thoroughgoing reductive approach that attempts to reduce every phenomenon whatsoever to the entities allowed as real in his field. Emergent entities are so rare at the level of the entities thus studied that as a matter of policy, one can almost always ignore their effects. It is, of course, essential to any science that its own entities, if emergent, are not reduced to a lower level. For instance, sociologists will not want to assume that social structures are reduced to biology, biologists that living cells are merely chemical in nature, nor chemists that chemicals are reduced to physics. But once the entities proper to one's own study are admitted, the claims of reductive analysis of other levels to its own level always seem quite strong, since the cases of emergence that are exceptions in any level of entities are rare enough not to be a factor in conducting routine science.

It is therefore not surprising that chemists studying biochemistry can operate very well under the assumption that life is nothing but chemistry, and even assuming that one day the reduction will be successful. There is nothing in such an assumption that will interfere with the practice of good chemistry in supporting this attitude. On this analysis of emergence, therefore, it is not surprising that reductive accounts seem to be successful, going by the attitudes of successful scientists working in their own respective fields. It is only when we try to make sense of the different sciences together that the reductive account that seems so successful in each science shows itself, nevertheless, to be clearly mistaken as a whole.

Antireduction, however, seems to reductivists to be not just false, but impossible. This needs to be understood. Reductionism presupposes the view that the properties of an underlying physical system are closed under certain algebraic operations, and that for the derivation of these properties so defined within the closed system (so-called physical properties), the laws of the system are complete. One way of defining completeness is this: An axiomatic system is complete if and only if any well-formed statement is either derivable from the laws (or axioms) of the system or is inconsistent with them. When a system is complete, there is no third possibility. I suspect that when Kim suggests that antireduction and physicalism are incompatible, he has in mind a conception of physics as a complete system of laws that determine all the properties that are closed under the operations applicable to the system (what he calls "physical properties"). If we grant him that assumption, moreover, his argument is valid. Evidence for the fact that he does make this assumption is to be found in his remark that he assumes, as a physicalist, "the causal closure of the physical domain."[13] But that assumption, I suggest, is mistaken. More to the point, it is a factual assumption. This shows, at least, that emergence is a coherent doctrine, even if it were — unknown to us — factually mistaken. But it is not at all surprising that if we assume that physics is complete, then the belief in any emergent property will seem to us to be incoherent, since this is precisely what the presumed completeness of the laws of physics implies.

Among analytic philosophers who are not particularly concerned with the study of the physical sciences, there is a widespread tendency to assume that the state of modern science is much like the state of science in the days of Hume and Kant, with more details thrown in.[14] The hypothesis that metaphysics is meaningless has led to the factual assumptions of the physicalist being left to comparative neglect. Analytic philosophy is supposed to be conducted without regard to the facts of a science, whatever they are. The proper response to Kim's clear and troublesome writing on a metaphysical dilemma by a thoroughgoing analytic philosopher is to say, "I do not understand the claims being made here by Kim." This is, of course, a more polite version of the expression "this is meaningless" or "Kim is entertaining nonsense as if they were statements." One must allow that it takes a person of exceptional analytic ability to say, sincerely, "But, honestly, I just do not understand it," when Kim has provided such a clear and compelling account of the metaphysical difficulty in understanding the mind with his close analysis of the concept of supervenience. In fact, the concept of mind has changed in some rather fundamental ways since then. Concepts like that of the mind that once were thought to be problematic (e.g., concepts of forms or species, of functions or purposes, or of life itself) have now been integrated into an account of the natural sciences. The task of making the (apparently) impossible antireductive account work is accomplished with the use of accidental events and temporal sequence and by appealing to evolution by natural selection. Darwin's theory was the first great breakthrough, but there have been others.

The latest story along these lines that has unfolded is the story of life itself, as based on DNA. Schrödinger, in his book *What Is Life?* (1944), was inspired by the account of the properties of crystals given in quantum mechanics, assuming a basic statistical conception of the world. He went on to suggest, following an idea of Max Delbrück, that there must be an "aperiodic crystal" at the basis of life, and that it would be stable at room temperature, though less stable, even at room temperature, under radiation pressure. This book, written as it was by the author of a basic equation of quantum mechanics (the wave equation that goes by his name), inspired a whole army of young physical scientists to study the relation of thermodynamics and crystals to the carrier of heritable information in living systems. Among these were James Watson and Francis Crick, who went on to discover the structure of DNA. This led to the later discovery of the genetic code by Crick, which he describes as "a frozen accident of history." The extraordinary success of the biophysics and biochemistry of heredity in the last fifty years is partly the result of the liberation of these subjects from their earlier reductive presuppositions.

Kim's pessimism about a doctrine of emergence is, however, shared by many philosophers. The pessimism is a legacy from Kant, who suggested that reconciling the understanding of the "starry heavens above" and the "moral law within" is impossible. We must live dual lives, incomprehensibly divided between an internal moral world, a world of reason and value, and an external scientific world, a world that is governed by the deterministic law of physical causation.

David Chalmers, also struck by the apparent impossibility of reduction, has described the problems of mind and matter as two: an easy problem that concerns the actual and ascertainable mechanisms that underlie mental activity, and a hard problem, namely, how there could be such a thing as a mind at all, given the physical universe in which we live:

> The easy problems of consciousness are those that seem directly susceptible to the standard methods of cognitive science, whereby a phenomenon is explained in terms of computational or neural mechanisms. The

hard problems are those that seem to resist those methods. . . . The really
hard problem of consciousness is the problem of experience. When we
think and perceive, there is a whir of information-processing, but there
is also a subjective aspect. As Nagel (1974) has put it, there is something
it is like to be a conscious organism. This subjective aspect is experience.
When we see, for example, we experience visual sensations: the felt quality of redness, the experience of dark and light, the quality of depth in a
visual field. Other experiences go along with perception in different modalities: the sound of a clarinet, the smell of mothballs. Then there are
bodily sensations, from pains to orgasms; mental images that are conjured
up internally; the felt quality of emotion, and the experience of a stream
of conscious thought. What unites all of these states is that there is something it is like to be in them. All of them are states of experience. (Chalmers, 1995)

This division of the problem into an easy and a hard problem is itself a
manifestation of the reductive point of view about the realm of matter, even if it
does not ask for the reduction of experience to matter. It supposes that the easy
problem can tell us nothing to help solve the hard problem. I would suggest that
this is a mistake. Whether mind is an emergent property or one that is reducible
or irreducible to its "physical" substrate level (be that what it may) is an issue that
will depend not on fine conceptual distinctions, but on how the world is. We will
have to decide this by experiment. If the doctrine of emergence is to be developed,
in this manner, as a factual account of the mind, we must allow for the following
theoretical possibility. There must be a series of emergent entities, at sequential
levels, each of which can be explained on the basis of an accidental birth, followed
by a stable history, leading up to the emergence of animals of which we can ask,
as Thomas Nagel does, what it is like to be one of them.[15] This may be part of
the easy question. But this is also what we must address and investigate in order
to answer the hard question. So, notwithstanding the heroic realism of Kant, which
has been adopted in a different way by Thomas Nagel and since then by David
Chalmers, and notwithstanding Jaegwon Kim's pessimism about the coherence of
the doctrine of emergence, we must address the central questions themselves in
all seriousness. How did the complex structure called conscious experience develop and in what stages or levels? Why was it stable and successful as a product
of evolution? These questions will be addressed in a chapter also included in this
volume, titled "The Mind as an Object of Scientific Study."[16]

Notes

1. I employ scare quotes in this context because the word "physicalism" describes
the doctrine that all meaningful expressions can be reduced to the language of physics. But Kim sometimes uses the expression more generously, as synonymous with the

much older idea of materialism; and this is how I have used the term in this instance, rather than in O. Neurath's original sense, which is closer to the sense given in note 14.

2. Of course, subatomic entities do not meet even this minimal condition, but one always can imagine extending the system of space and time to a more accommodating spatiotemporal system.

3. The concept of physical realization traces farther back than the literature on theories of computation, as Kim suggests in his note 8 to chapter 17. There was an exchange on this topic between Karl Popper and Wilfrid Sellars in 1953–55. The main theses of this chapter first suggested themselves to me in an attempt to defend Sellars's idea that whatever there is must have arisen out of the physical world (Sellars, 1955, p. 23) to answer Popper's apparently insuperable objection to it (Popper, 1953) when he claimed the following: "Our thesis is that a causal realization of the name-relation cannot exist" (Popper, 1989, p. 297). Popper's objection supposes that the name-relation is the simplest semantic relation, and therefore it needs to be taken very seriously. However, he refers this idea even farther back to Karl Bühler's *Sprachtheorie*, 1934, pp. 25–28. Note that Popper, too, is an indeterminist, but he does not therefore conclude that he can circumvent the need to adopt a form of dualism. To show that Popper is in error here was at one time the main point of this chapter, though, of course, I concur with Popper in rejecting a two-language account of the mind-body problem.

4. The general theory of emergence has not been carefully stated in recent times, but among its defenders is Karl Popper, in his later writings (Popper and Eccles, 1977). This may seem surprising in view of note 3, but we recall that this was only his first publication concerning it. Popper also discusses the relevance of the doctrine of indeterminism to the problem of body and mind in his later writings, but on the whole he seems to propose a form of dualism, or at least leaves himself open to that charge. I believe that he may be understood more sympathetically to be developing an indeterministic account of emergence and of interaction between emergent and sub-strate entities, similar to what I have proposed in this chapter.

5. This is an old and well-known account of reduction, as provided, for example, in E. Nagel's *The Structure of Science*. (1961).

6. Kim's remarks on excluding one of two sufficient causes for the same event (Kim, 1993, chapter 18, "Postscript on Mental Causation") seem to be essentially an anticipation of just this point, though explored and argued much more thoroughly there, with a view to responding to the apparent exceptions to it that are suggested in the literature.

7. The expression, but perhaps not the view, is van Fraassen's (van Fraassen, 2000).

8. Paul Humphreys has also proposed an interesting counterexample to Kim's thesis on the basis of quantum mechanics (Humphreys, 1997). He suggests that emergent properties are a "fusion" of substrate properties to find a way around Kim's challenge. But if P and Q are fused into property R, then it is true that either $\{P, Q\}$ logically implies R or it does not. If it does, then the so-called emergent property R is fully reducible to $\{P, Q\}$. If, however, it does not, then the intuition that R is fused out of P and Q is irrelevant, and we must treat P, Q, and R all as basic properties of the system, on a par with one another. Therefore none of them is emergent. Humphreys has quantum entanglement in mind as his key example of a fused property. He interprets

entangled states as fused classical states. My remarks suggest an alternative but more complicated relationship of classical to entangled states than this. Classical objects must be regarded as emerging from quantum states, rather than vice versa; and entangled states are the result of the causal interaction of (emergent) classical atoms and (substrate) subatomic objects.

9. This is a somewhat controversial point of view, and many distinguished physicists have thought otherwise. An argument for my view can be found in Hattiangadi, 1998.

10. Some philosophers have taken Bohr's main thesis to be entirely different—namely, to deny realism. For an interesting alternative and relativistic account, following Feyerabend's lead (Feyerabend, 1975), see Gonzalo Munévar, "Bohr and Evolutionary Relativism" (Munévar, 1998, chapter 3).

11. This may be thought to be a weak form of the doctrine of physicalism that is actually defensible, if only there were such a thing as an eternal language of physics.

12. My preferred metaphysical stance is that there is no such thing as a "substance" (Hattiangadi, 2000). Individuals are not ultimate, as Aristotle suggested, nor are forms, as Plato said. The modern doctrine that matter, in space and time, is all there is has now been experimentally overthrown. The assumption that there is some one kind of thing that is primary as a being is dubious because its "being" seems much too closely bound up with "becoming" to be a basis for any future metaphysics. On the whole, it seems that the idea of a substance from classical metaphysics is best discarded. Beings are merely stable things, and since things can be stable at different levels of organization and still interact with other levels, all of them are equally real, and none is primary in a metaphysical or atemporal sense.

13. Kim (1993, p. 356) invokes the principle of "causal closure." He suggests that to give up this principle is to "acknowledge that there can be no complete physical theory of physical phenomena, that theoretical physics, insofar as it aspires to be a complete theory, must cease to be a pure physics and invoke irreducibly nonphysical causal powers—vital principles, entelechies, psychic energies, élan vital and whatnot." In this statement I believe that Kim has made a very rare mistake of analysis. To believe in a complete physical realm and then also to believe, defiantly, in higher-level entities is to invoke all those other extraordinary things. The person who believes in an indeterministic universe, however (or in the essential incompleteness of physical theory), is in a position to explain all the higher-level entities, including their emergence and stable functions, in terms of the organization of entities previously defined at the lower level, starting with the lowest level and proceeding up, all without recourse to ghosts or hobgoblins.

14. Kim does not define the word "physicalism." It is worth noting that as originally defined by Neurath, it is merely the thesis that everything factual can be expressed in "the language of physics." This doctrine is both about metaphysics and about language at once. It is misdirected for the very reason Popper states—that the name-relation cannot be causally realized in physics and hence cannot be part of physics proper (see note 3). But it has been seen as a metaphysical issue, which I think is a mistake. The reason this analytic issue is so hard to unravel is that in speaking of "the language of physics," we have usually understood it to mean the language presupposing eighteenth century physics, even while calling it "the latest physical theory," or meaning roughly what Kant and Hume (and Euler and Laplace) understood it to mean. Consequently, the linguistic turn of phrase makes false factual presuppositions about physical reality,

insofar as physics has made any basic advances. These false presuppositions have the danger of becoming almost like Kantian synthetic a priori truths (were they but true) within the analytic tradition in philosophy. As a consequence of this relegation of the assumption to the background, which then tends not to be discussed, metaphysical problems seem intractable to avowed "physicalists."

15. If we compare one level of entities with another level above them, after skipping a layer in between, the very existence of the higher level seems to be well-nigh miraculous. This tempts one to propose heroic solutions, like those of Kant. On the other hand, when I postulate intermediate levels, where I do not know the evolutionary story or even a plausible story of emergence, I can be accused of being gullible. I therefore have dubbed my own point of view, from time to time, "gullible realism" or "gullible emergent realism."

16. My thanks are due to Joseph Agassi, Jeanette Bicknell, Christina Erneling, Ian Jarvie, David Johnson, Anandi Hattiangadi, and Slobodan Perovic for their comments and suggestions on, and contributions to, the emerging chapter.

References

Bohr, Niels. 1972. *Collected Works*. L. Rosenfeld (Ed.). Vol. 6, *Foundations of Quantum Physics* I, J. Kalckar (Ed.). Amsterdam: North-Holland.

Broad, Charles D. 1925. *The Mind and Its Place in Nature*. London: Routledge and Kegan Paul.

Chalmers, David. 1995. "Facing the Problem of Consciousness." *Journal of Consciousness Studies*; also at http://www.u.arizona.edu/~chalmers/papers/facing.html.

Churchland, Paul. 1979. *Scientific Realism and the Plasticity of Mind*. Cambridge, UK: Cambridge University Press.

Feyerabend, Paul. 1963. "Explanation, Reduction, Empiricism," in *Minnesota Studies in the Philosophy of Science, Vol. 3*. Minneapolis: University of Minnesota Press.

———. 1975. *Against Method*. London: NLB.

Hattiangadi, Jagdish N. 1998. "On Interacting Systems of Space: Or Coefficient Fields," in G. Hunter, S. Jeffers, and J.-P. Vigier (Eds.), *Causality and Locality in Modern Physics*. Dordrecht: Kluwer.

———. 2000. "Meditations on Substance in Aristotle, Descartes and Bohr," in Demetra Sfendoni-Mentzou (Ed.), *Aristotle and Contemporary Science*. Vol. 1. New York: Peter Lang.

Humphreys, Paul. 1997. "How Properties Emerge," *Philosophy of Science*, March.

Hunter, G., Jeffers, S., and Vigier, J.-P. (Eds.). 1998. *Causality and Locality in Modern Physics*. Dordrecht: Kluwer.

Kim, Jaegwon. 1993. *Supervenience and Mind*. New York: Cambridge University Press.

Kuhn, Thomas S. 1962. *The Structure of Scientific Revolutions*. Chicago: University of Chicago Press.

Munévar, Gonzalo. 1998. *Evolution and the Naked Truth*. Aldershot: Ashgate Publishing.

Nagel, Ernest. 1961. *The Structure of Science: Problems in the Logic of Scientific Explanation*. New York: Harcourt, Brace and World.

Nagel, Thomas. 1974. "What Is It Like to Be a Bat?" *Philosophical Review*, Vol. 83, pp. 435–50.

Popper, Karl R. 1953. "Language and the Body-Mind Problem," in *Proceedings of the 11th International Congress of Philosophy*. Reprinted in Popper, *Conjectures and Refutations*, 5th edition, and all previous editions. London: Routledge, 1989.

Popper, Karl R., and Eccles, John C. 1977. *The Self and Its Brain*. New York: Springer International.

Schrödinger, Erwin. 1944. *What Is Life?* Cambridge, UK: Cambridge University Press.

Sellars, Wilfrid. 1955. "A Note on Popper's Argument for Dualism." *Analysis, 15*, pp. 23–24.

Sfendoni-Mentzou, Demetra (Ed.). 2000. *Aristotle and Contemporary Science*. Vol. I. New York: Peter Lang.

van Fraassen, Bas. 2000. "Does Nature Have Narrative Structure?" in Demetra Sfendoni-Mentzou (Ed.), *Aristotle and Contemporary Science*. Vol. I. New York: Peter Lang.

4

Is the Mind a Scientific Object of Study?
Lessons from History

Otniel E. Dror

During the late nineteenth and early twentieth centuries physiologists, psychologists, and clinicians transformed emotions into objects of scientific knowledge. They manipulated, isolated, replicated, standardized, quantified, and recorded emotions; invented new technologies for visualizing and representing emotions in curves and numeric tables; and propagated their practices and instruments beyond the narrow confines of the laboratory and clinic. Their travails redefined emotions in laboratory terms and repositioned issues of pragmatic implementation at the center of scientific efforts to study emotions and the mind. The successful realization of this new laboratory approach became the sine qua non for the scientific study of the mind and its operations.

In this chapter I examine the question of whether the mind is a scientific object of study by exploring the early attempts to develop a pragmatic and experimental approach to emotions. The question of whether the mind is a scientific object of study thus becomes the following: Can the mind yield universal, quantitative, standardized, replicable, and objective knowledge?

My aim is to explore the failures and partial successes of this late-nineteenth- and early-twentieth-century scientific cohort as it attempted to transform this elusive element of the mind—emotion—into an object of scientific knowledge. As I will argue, the mind had to be constructed in particular ways in order to become an object of scientific knowledge. The significance of this active construction of the mind as an object will be analyzed in the discussion.

The Laboratory: Problems and Stipulations

Before we begin our study, a small digression is necessary in order to explain the basic model that was most commonly employed in studying emotions. Basically, an experiment in emotion consisted of a subject (human or animal) in which the

TABLE 4.1. Major Problems of Experimenters

Stipulations	Problems of Experiments
1. The ability to create and abolish emotions on demand.	1. No reliable technique for producing or eliminating emotions on demand.
2. Control over quality and type of emotion produced (e.g., fear, anger, joy, etc.)	2. Failure to devise dependable stimuli which generate the quality and type of emotion desired.
3. Procedures for purifying emotions (i.e., procuring a pure form of each emotion—working with each emotion on its own).	3. Many emotions, especially subtle ones, came in mixed forms; great difficulty in ensuring that the subject did not generate, unintentionally, other emotions during the protocol.
4. Procedures for isolating emotions (i.e., the need to eliminate all other factors from the mind, except the emotion).	4. Can the mind ever be isolated and investigated as a clean slate with only one stimulus acting at any time?
5. Quantification	5. What is the meaning of quantification in emotion studies? And what did they really quantify?
6. Instruments for recording physiological changes during emotions.	6. Lack of direct access to the mind required the design of peripheral markers: problem of referent.
7. Replication	7. Problematic both conceptually and pragmatically: can one ever really replicate an emotion? Can one replicate the same emotion across space (in different laboratories), minds (in different subjects) and time (in the same subject over time)?
8. Standardization	8. Problematic both conceptually and pragmatically: what does it mean to standardize an emotion? The relationships between cause and effect (stimulus and emotional reaction) were very complex, unpredictable, and depended on the individual mind under investigation.
9. The need to investigate various types of emotions.	9. Can one invent techniques for evoking every possible emotion under laboratory conditions, or is one limited to only a limited number of readily induced emotions?
10. Animal models	10. Emotions were species specific; many emotions were unique to humans.
11. Emotions produced in the laboratory must have a definite and clear relationship to natural emotions occurring outside of the laboratory.	11. Many laboratory techniques are artificial and do not generate natural emotions.

experimenters attempted to produce an emotion (isolated, standardized, and replicated) and of a series of measurements, recordings, and observations of various physiological processes.

In implementing this model, experimenters followed two paths. In the majority of cases, they began each experiment by producing a nonemotional state or, as one experimenter put it, by taking a preliminary reading "without emotional influence."[1] Then they generated an emotion in the subject. The physiological differences between these two emotional states and their development over time were studied as the emotion.

Alternatively, experimenters produced a particular emotion in one group of subjects (animals) and compared these subjects to a second group that had been maintained in a neutral emotional state. The differences between the two groups were studied as the emotion. Significant results were obtained only when the laboratory succeeded in operationalizing one of these two schemes.

In spite of the conceptual simplicity of this basic approach, and despite its wide and common implementation in physiology as a whole, its realization in emotion research failed, and as a consequence, jeopardized the modern project of studying the emotions. In order to examine these failures, I have listed some of the major problems that plagued experimenters as they attempted to integrate emotions into the contemporary paradigm of the biological sciences.

Zero Emotion

The first step in every experiment on emotion was the production of a zero or neutral emotional state. This preliminary condition of the mind served two basic purposes: It functioned as a baseline—shared, standardized, and replicated across subjects—that ensured that each and every mind would begin the protocol from the same mind state; and it represented the ideal starting point of any physiological investigation—a zero state from which all background noise had been eliminated.[2]

The production of this prestimulus state was achieved by several techniques. Human subjects were usually instructed to bring themselves to this zero state through self-manipulation. They were "asked to relax," required to "compose" themselves, or told to remain as "quiet as possible" in order to eliminate emotional excitement from their minds. Alternatively, subjects were told to "read a newspaper or a textbook" or talk with companions about "indifferent topics" in order to produce the basal, de-emotional state.[3]

In animals, the creation of a zero state was achieved by new laboratory manipulations that were developed specifically in the context of the research on emotions. Animals were petted on the back, stroked on their bellies, or held gently on the keeper's lap in order to eliminate emotional excitement.[4] In rare cases, anesthetics were used on animals, as well as on humans, in order to purge emotions from the mind.[5]

The concept of zero emotion, however appealing, was reputed by many investigators to be nonexistent in the awake mind. Minds, they argued, could not attain a level of complete emotional absence. It was "not possible to induce a psychologic vacuum," one experimenter explained.[6] As another stated, " 'We always have weather, but occasionally we have a storm.' And, in a manner of speaking, it is the 'storms' to which we refer when we speak of emotions."[7]

In addition, each individual mind had a different basal state, a different level of background emotional noise that one could not eliminate. The starting point of each experiment differed from one subject to the other. To complicate matters further, each individual mind followed an idiosyncratic rhythmic oscillation of its emotional level throughout the day.[8]

In spite of the pragmatic difficulties involved in establishing a basal state, most experimenters did not go to great lengths in order to resolve this fundamental obstacle.[9] They simply carried out their experiments as if the basal state had been attained in its ideal or near-ideal standard.

A minority of investigators did emphasize these difficulties. They rejected wholesale the notion of an absolute measurement of emotion. Instead, they focused on the added effect of various emotional states, over and above an unavoidable baseline of emotional noise.[10]

The demand for a zero state introduced additional complications. Experimenters who studied humans relied on the active cooperation of their subjects and, more important, on an attribute that, for lack of a better term, was referred to as the subject's "will." The exercise of this second faculty of the mind produced the desired zero emotional state.

Different subjects differed in their ability to exercise the will, and experimenters began to select "good" subjects, that is, subjects who attained a low level of emotional noise, for their experiments on emotions.[11] Labels such as "apprehensive," "irritable," "cold," or "phlegmatic" identified in a nonformalized language the different types of available subjects and eliminated various subgroups.[12]

A similar process of preferential selection also took place in laboratories that studied animals. In these laboratories, experimenters introduced a new qualitative terminology that distinguished between the different "temperaments" of individual animals.[13] This language of temperaments explained why the experimenter discarded certain minds and chose a subset of all the available minds for his experiment. These preferred minds could be operationalized as objects of knowledge in the context of the stipulations and constraints of the new science.

The attention to and selection of individual minds in the midst of an endeavor that strove to produce objective and universal knowledge was one of the major characteristics and paradoxes of this new science. The selection process established the new science of the mind on a particular set of selected minds—and explicitly so. These minds were characterized by a particular type of plasticity that was deemed necessary for the implementation of the experimental model and hence for the production of scientific knowledge.

Creating an Emotion

The second stage of every experiment—the generation of an emotion—immediately followed the production of a zero state. The laboratory of emotions demanded a constant supply of standardized, replicated, purified, and isolated emotions.

There were numerous techniques for generating and for engineering emotions to suit the particular specifications of experimental settings. These practices, together with an assemblage of new emotion-gauging technologies, constituted the core foundations of the new science of the mind. Their development and elaboration extended over a period of years. Each had its own drawbacks and major failings (see table 4.1).

The first general observation we can make concerning the production of emotions in laboratory settings was the complete lack of a standard stimulus across laboratories, or even across subjects. A list of only a fraction of these stimuli will give an idea of their variety and nature: memories, hypnosis, spoken words, reading passages from books on the Bible, threats of physical attack or pain, music (classical/technical), honk of klaxon horn, pictures, movies, morphine, conversation, nonsense syllables, and more.[14]

The variety of laboratory stimuli and, more important, the absence of a fixed and shared set of stimuli across laboratories stemmed from the intractable difficulties that emerged as experimenters attempted to conceive and to produce standardized emotions. Some investigators searched for a set of standard stimuli that would evoke a standard emotional response in all subjects. These standard stimuli (e.g., a "sure-fire joke," or pornographic pictures) would serve as the basis for the new science of emotions.

A minority reported that they had indeed discovered a number of universal stimuli that evoked a specific and standardized reaction from subjects. These types of stimuli usually involved an acute provocation that succeeded in generating only a very limited set of very basic emotional reactions, for example, the induction of acute fear by a sudden and abrupt loss of balance.[15]

Other investigators abandoned the search for ideal stimuli.[16] They said that it was inconceivable that such a series of universal stimuli existed, because of the special nature of emotions (and of the human mind). Subjects, they explained, had particular histories, singular constitutions, and unique idiosyncrasies and would react in very different ways to the same stimulus and in a similar manner to very different stimuli. Thus no two minds would produce even roughly similar results under the same physical conditions. As William Marston explained, "We may make all our subjects see blue, or taste sweet, or feel skin pressures. But these identical sensation responses are not followed by identical emotional responses."[17] This was one of the major problems of the new science: The relationships between stimulus and emotion depended on the individual mind and on the intensity of the subjective experience of the outer world, irrespective of the objective accuracy or the actual external conditions to which the subject was exposed. Each mind required an individual stimulus and an individual interpretation.

Similar issues were raised in animal studies. As numerous physiologists observed, it was indeed feasible to devise a small number of stimuli that would evoke a standard emotional response qualitatively, but it was quite impossible to standardize these stimuli or the emotional response, quantitatively. For example, the most frequent and studied routine for producing a standard response was to bring about a confrontation between a cat and a barking dog. Yet even during this relatively simple setup, experimenters could not standardize the bark of one dog in one laboratory with the bark of another dog in another laboratory.[18] Moreover, there were always too many idiosyncratic minds that did not react as predicted. Finally, in those rare cases where experimenters attempted to go beyond fear or anger and strove to evoke a richer variety of emotions (e.g., anxiety), they faced the same problems as experimenters who worked with humans.[19]

One method for overcoming the problem of individual minds was for the experimenter to spend a preliminary period of time with the subject. During this learning period, which lasted from a couple of hours to years, the experimenter studied the specific mind of the subject and constructed appropriate stimuli in order to produce the desired emotional reactions.[20] This approach was practiced by some psychologists who worked with human subjects and by a number of physiologists working with animals. Both of these groups knew their subjects' minds and either chose the appropriate stimulus for each individual or the appropriate individual for the desired emotional reaction from their pool of available minds.[21]

A second method for generating specific emotional states depended on the same principle that guided experimenters in the production of the zero baseline. It relied on the subject's ability to elicit specific emotions by conjuring up various memories. Experimenters told subjects what emotion to produce, and the subject generated the appropriate emotion.[22] In these experiments, as in many other instances, the referent was the subject's introspective report. Alternatively, the experimenters told the subject what s/he was to think about. This was an intermediate type of stimulus, in which the experimenters decided on the content of the ideational stimulus and the subjects had to produce it in their minds.[23]

Isolating an Emotion

Generating the required emotion was only a first step. Experimenters had to isolate it from other mind processes and to eliminate any concomitant emotions. One of the major difficulties was that subjects (human and animal minds) could not produce emotions directly, merely by exercising some innate mechanism. The generation of an emotion was achieved indirectly, for example, by conjuring up specific memories or by being exposed to specific external stimuli. This indirect methodology always introduced additional factors, be they "memories" or other stimuli, into the protocols. These interfering processes had to be eliminated or controlled, leaving only emotion as a factor in the activation of the mind.[24]

In addition, any accidental external or internal stimulus could immediately activate physiological mechanisms other than those responsible for the emotion. For example, the ambient temperature, pain, various stimuli falling on the sense organs, or other concurrent mental processes all activated the mind. They, too, had to be eliminated.[25]

Compounding these difficulties was the stipulation that one had to study one emotion at a time and to eliminate all other emotions from the subject's mind. This particular constraint placed a heavy, if not impossible, burden on the experimenter, because any factor could become a stimulus and evoke an emotion in the subject's mind: for example, the experimenter (his demeanor, tone of voice, aesthetic appearance, familiarity with the subject, and so on), the instruments, the manipulations, or other animals/subjects in the laboratory.[26]

The hypersusceptibility of the mind was, in fact, responsible for the discrepancies observed between experimenters and the persistence of local, as opposed to universal, knowledge of the mind. Local circumstances produced local, uncontrollable, and irreproducible emotions during the protocol. As some experimenters argued, it was practically impossible to universalize emotion-dependent knowledge because of this local element.[27]

Eliminating emotional artifacts from protocols was thus a major concern for these experimenters and was perceived by some as either insurmountable or, at least, requiring extreme measures and new methodologies. The preoccupation with the elimination of emotional artifacts from the mind was visible in the elaboration of new rules and practices for emotion-proofing the experimental protocols and ensuring that the subject would be exposed to one pure emotion at a time.[28]

Quantifying an Emotion

Experimenters participating in the new science of the mind presented their results in quantitative terms—as numeric tables or graphical representations. This quantitative imperative was a crucial element in the objectification of the mind and was integral to the new science from its earliest beginnings.[29]

Experimenters quantified a number of different parameters during an emotion. The oldest, though minor, experimental form of quantification entailed measurements of blood flow to the brain. This was achieved by directly observing changes in the caliber of cranial blood vessels through "windows" in the skull during an emotion.[30] This method was used quite extensively before the twentieth century and was replaced during the twentieth century by alternative technologies for recording blood flow to the brain or by other brain-focused technologies, such as the electroencephalograph (EEG) or direct electrophysiological recordings from cerebral neurons.[31]

The primary method for quantifying emotions during the late nineteenth and early twentieth centuries was to identify a peripheral physiological referent of the emotion and to measure this referent as an indicator of the emotion. These peripheral concomitants of the emotion—"habitually taken as outward expression of an inward feeling"—were the major experimentally available physiological parameters that provided quantitative and objective information regarding the emotion.[32] Heart rate, blood pressure, psychogalvanic reflex, and other physiological parameters provided information regarding the duration, pattern of appearance, pattern of dissipation, intensity, "incubation period," and even quality of the emotion.[33]

These quantitative measurements were important not only for objectifying emotions, but also for understanding the mechanism of emotion, communicating between experimenters, comparing emotions, and classifying subjects according to new quantitative criteria. By representing emotions in numeric terms, experimenters could compare emotions evoked by very different means, under different circumstances, at different times, and by different individuals. These representations collapsed the fear of one individual with that of another and even that of the animal with that of the human—all produced spatiotemporal tracings (or numbers).[34]

Artificial versus Wild-Type Emotions

One of the fundamental and recurring concerns of many of the pioneers of the new science was the nature of the relationship between laboratory-generated emotions and natural kinds: Did laboratory-generated emotions have the same quality, intensity, duration, and other characteristics as wild-type emotions?[35] The limitations of the laboratory were often discussed, even by its most ardent supporters. The laboratory setting—necessary for the scientific study of emotions—imposed substantial constraints on the investigation of the mind, for example:

1. The techniques for generating emotions, such as hypnosis and morphine, evoked emotions by artificial means. Did they produce the same emotions as real-life situations?
2. The laboratory focused on a very small number of emotions and evoked them at unnatural levels and intensities. What were the relationships between these emotions and the normal emotions of everyday life?
3. Emotions produced in the laboratory lasted from a few seconds to a couple of hours, at most. How could one investigate such emotional phenomena as moods, which required long exposures and constant surveillance over extended periods of time?

One problem in particular occupied numerous experimenters. The laboratory, they argued, had successfully produced a discrete number of emotions, mostly in animals (e.g., fear and rage). Yet it had failed dramatically to induce real emotions in human subjects under experimental conditions. As one experimenter put it in articulating the wider consensus, "The production of genuine emotional states under laboratory conditions has proved much more difficult when dealing with humans than when dealing with animals."[36]

The induction of emotions demanded situations that the laboratory could not supply. How could one produce real joy, real embarrassment, or real shame in the setting of the laboratory? Even fear, the most investigated of emotions (together with anger), was often uninducible in the laboratory setting.[37] Real pleasant emotions were even more difficult to generate in the laboratory, except in children.[38] Moreover, many "subtle" emotions either could not be evoked at all or, if they were generated, could not be standardized because their method of production entailed complex experimenter-subject interactions (e.g., a "heart-to-heart talk").[39] Reports from observations outside the laboratory only reinforced these tensions by demonstrating that emotions in natural settings were much more intense than emotions produced in the laboratory.[40]

Some suggested that experimenters leave the laboratory and sample/explore the phenomenon of emotion in the social sphere (e.g., football games, theater productions, condemned criminals before execution, and the front).[41] In fact, many investigators, at one time or another, ventured outside their laboratories and studied subjects in their natural habitats. In these natural settings, experimenters forsook the laboratory and its myriad advantages, but gained access to a rich variety of authentic emotions.

Other investigators deliberately blurred the boundaries between laboratory and real life in the hope of eliciting authentic emotional reactions inside the laboratory. They asked their subjects to read their unopened real mail in the laboratory, or they created situations in the laboratory, such as fabricating a fire in the building, that their subjects would take for real. Still others took advantage of opportune moments, such as measuring the subject during a real air-raid alarm in the midst of World War I.[42] The underlying tension that permeated these attempts to transgress the laboratory was that the necessary stipulations for a scientific study of the mind (control, replication, standardization, quantification, and so on), found ideally in the laboratory setting, were detrimental for the production of the phenomenon itself—or so many experimenters argued.

Animal Models

The final impediment for launching the new science was the difficulty of finding suitable animal models for human emotions. The absence of many human emotions in animals or, at least, the assumption that animals shared only a very small and "primitive" set of emotions with humans precluded the investigation of many emotions in animals.[43] One contemporary and common example of this was the failure to produce peptic ulcers in dogs. Though the investigation of peptic ulcers was part of a different research agenda, it became relevant because peptic ulcer was believed to result from specific kinds of emotions. The absence of peptic ulcers in dogs and the failure of concerted attempts to induce peptic ulcers in dogs under laboratory conditions signified that animals simply did not have the emotions that were assumed to cause peptic ulcers.[44] The conclusion of many experimenters was that animals could only be used for a defined and limited set of emotions.

Some investigators classified animals according to an emotional repertoire, in

which specific species were endowed with particular emotions.[45] These classifications suggested either that specific emotions demanded particular species as
models, or that no model existed at all.[46] In practice, only a very limited number
of emotions were investigated in animals. Research involving animals and emotions during this early period focused almost exclusively on anger and fear, with
some experimenters including anxiety, joy, and jealousy.[47] In human subjects, by
comparison, the number of emotions that experimenters at least strove to investigate was much more expansive and included such emotions as joy, sadness, fear,
disgust, anger, shame, embarrassment, and frustration. The animal model was thus
of limited value in the study of human emotions.[48]

Discussion

When late-nineteenth-century experimenters attempted to transform emotions into
objects of modern scientific knowledge, they faced intractable practical and conceptual difficulties. Though these challenges surfaced in the particular context of
research on emotions, they illuminate the kinds of impediments that arise in trying
to transform various aspects of the mind (or the mind altogether) into scientific
objects. They also suggest two different approaches to the larger question of
whether the mind is, or can be, a scientific object of study.

In the first approach, methodologies for standardizing, objectifying, replicating, quantifying, and the like must be developed in spite of the special difficulties
posed by the mind. In the second approach, the mind, as a unique object, will
demand a unique science of the mind. This unique science will have its own
standards and stipulations, which might overlap only in some domains with other
biological endeavors. Let us examine briefly each of these possibilities.

If the mind is to become a scientific object of study, then a number of
fundamental problems must be resolved. The first is the central role that subjectivity played in the new science of the mind. As I have demonstrated earlier,
laboratory procedures relied ultimately on the subjectivity of the investigators, or,
in other words, on nonobjectifiable knowledge. This subjective aspect of experimentation expressed itself in the following ways:

1. As we have seen, at the beginning of each protocol, experimenters manipulated the mind in order to bring subjects to their zero emotional state. In humans,
this basal state depended on particular individuals and their aptitude for self-
manipulation. In animals, various uncodified practices—petting, stroking, caress-
ing, and so on—achieved the same goal. The creation of the basal emotional state
depended ultimately on the individual, personalized, and special (local) relationships between experimenters, animal keepers, and their organisms or subjects.
These special relationships introduced an important subjective and local element
into the crucial phase of creating a zero emotional state.

2. I also have discussed the infusion of subjective and impressionistic terms
into laboratory protocols as a way of describing and identifying different kinds of
minds according to a qualitative emotional typology. The frequent invocation of

these new categories (e.g., "nervous" or "cold") extended the subjective strand into the heart of the selection process and defined in noncommunicable terms the class of appropriate minds for the study of emotions.

3. Last, subjective evaluations were crucial during the actual protocol itself. During each and every protocol, the experimenters had to ensure that no second emotion intruded on the observations. Investigators constantly reviewed their subjects and evaluated their emotional status during the experiment.[49] This crucial control over the experiment depended on the subjective judgment of observers and not on any definable set of practices or instruments.

I also suggested that the operationalization of the mind entailed a series of constructions that transformed the mind into an appropriate object of scientific knowledge. The normal mind on the street corner was incapable of functioning as a true object of science. This process of engineering appropriate minds carried certain implications. For example, it entailed the neglect of most human emotions; the collapsing together of various different forms of other emotions (e.g., there was supposed to be only one form of fear, independent of the context of its production); the assumption of a single, universal, and essentialistic notion of emotion; the elimination of most minds as unsuitable for experimentation; the generation of emotions by "artificial" means, for example, morphine; and the active training of animal and human minds in order to transform them into objects of knowledge. These practices had the effect of constructing a mind for science, as contrasted with simply constructing a science of the mind.

I also argued that the notion of a standard and replicated emotion did not have an acceptable referent, a concrete meaning, or a proper methodology. Emotion itself was embroiled in similar confusion: Was it the subject's introspection, the experimental situation, or discrete physiological patterns that defined the emotion? Many experimenters working with humans or animals were well aware of these problems.

It is necessary for a science of the mind to overcome many problems. For example, it must objectify its practices, resolve the problems posed by the idiosyncratic nature of individual minds, define in precise terms the relationships between laboratory-engineered minds and their extralaboratory counterparts and face the practical and conceptual issues that emerge whenever laboratory workers attempt to standardize and replicate difficult theoretical concepts, such as emotions.

The second approach that this historical analysis suggests is quite different. Many of the difficulties and failures of the new science stemmed from an unreflective attempt to incorporate the study of mind into existing scientific templates, and more specifically, those of the biological sciences. I have argued that the drive for quantification, for instance, was an important aspect of the new study of the mind. Experimenters invented quantifiable variables, such as levels of "excitement," in their attempts to integrate the mind into the biological sciences. Yet this transformative practice, when applied to the mind, collapsed potentially different kinds of emotions into just one, unidimensional category.[50]

The fundamental question of whether the mind was in fact a quantifiable object, or whether, on the other hand, it was inherently qualitative, was not addressed in any meaningful way by these investigators. Failures to quantify were perceived as problems in implementation, rather than as invitations for a fundamental reappraisal of the essence of mind.

Other aspects of the new science suggest that existing models of biological inquiry may be unsuitable to apply to the study of mind. We noted that, for example, unlike most other forms of experimentation in biology, the study of emotions required whole organisms. Furthermore, the absence of isolated brain preparations (organ cultures of the brain) also differentiated the study of mind from many other physiological research programs.

In addition, our historical study suggested that the study of the mind requires a second human mind. This second mind—that of the experimenter—must be present in order to make subjective judgment calls, for example, concerning the affect of the subject/organism. These subjective evaluations were necessary in order to produce universal, replicable, and standardized knowledge.[51] The study of the mind finally may depend on such interactive evaluations by experimenters, with the ultimate aim of producing universal, standardized, and replicable knowledge.

In conclusion, the study of the mind must not proceed by adopting wholesale the methodologies and stipulations found in contemporary biology. Although the mind is a biological system, it demands a mind-specific science, a mind-specific set of practices, and, more important, a unique formulation of such basic terms as standardization and replication.

Notes

1. Erich Wittkower, "Studies on the Influence of Emotions on the Functions of the Organs," *Journal of Mental Science*, 81 (1935): pp. 533–682 (especially p. 568).

2. It is important to emphasize at this early point that there were numerous and different reasons for producing emotions inside laboratories and clinics: as tests or as diagnostic procedures; in clinical investigations that focused on the effects of emotions on health and disease; as part of the collective effort to standardize routine physiological measurements; and in the context of numerous theoretical debates and laboratory investigations that focused specifically on the nature of emotions. In this chapter I will focus mostly on the latter group, but will also mention some of the techniques that were employed by other groups.

3. W.E. Blatz, "The Cardiac, Respiratory, and Electrical Phenomena Involved in the Emotion of Fear," *Journal of Experimental Psychology*, 8 (April 1925): pp. 109–32 (especially p. 127); W.E. Blatz, "A Physiological Study of the Emotion of Fear," Ph.D. diss. (University of Chicago, 1924); "Measuring the Emotions," *Literary Digest*, 68 (February 12, 1921): p. 23; T. Izod Bennett and J.F. Venables, "The Effects of the Emotions on Gastric Secretion and Motility in the Human Being," *British Medical Journal*, 2 (October 30, 1920): pp. 662–63 (especially p. 662).

4. W.B. Cannon, H.F. Newton, E.M. Bright, V. Menkin, and R.M. Moore, "Some Aspects of the Physiology of Animals Surviving Complete Exclusion of Sympathetic Nerve Impulses," *American Journal of Physiology*, 89 (1929): pp. 84–107 (especially p. 92); H.F. Newton, R.L. Zwemer, and W.B. Cannon, "Studies on the Conditions of

Activity in Endocrine Organs: XXV. The Mystery of Emotional Acceleration of the Denervated Heart after Exclusion of Known Humoral Accelerators," *American Journal of Physiology*, 96 (1931): pp. 377–91 (especially p. 379).

5. In these new laboratories anesthetics were tools for eliminating emotions, not analgesics. The use of anesthetics was very problematic for a variety of reasons and was therefore limited. On anesthetics and emotions, see H.I. Schou, "Some Investigations into the Physiology of Emotions," *Acta Psychiatrica et Neurologica*, and Suppl. 14 (1937): pp. 3–111 (especially p. 82); and Frederick Hillis Lumley and L.B. Nice, "Blood Sugar of Adrenalectomized Rats," *American Journal of Physiology*, 93 (May 1930): pp. 152–55.

6. J.C. Whitehorn, M.R. Kaufman, and J.M. Thomas, "Heart Rate in Relation to Emotional Disturbances," *Archives of Neurology and Psychiatry*, 33 (1935): pp. 712–31 (especially p. 723).

7. Frederick H. Lund, *Emotions: Their Psychological, Physiological, and Educative Implications* (New York: Ronald Press, 1939), p. 200.

8. A.D. Waller, "Galvanometric Observations of the Emotivity of a Normal Subject (English)," *Lancet*, 1 (June 29, 1918): p. 916.

9. But see Walter B. Cannon, *Bodily Changes in Pain, Hunger, Fear and Rage: An Account of Recent Researches into the Function of Emotional Excitement* (New York: Appleton, 1929, 2nd edition), p. 172; Madeleine E. Field, "The Effect of Emotion on the Blood-Platelet Count," *American Journal of Physiology*, 93 (1930): pp. 245–48 (especially p. 246); and A.D. Waller, "The Measurement of Human Emotion and of Its Voluntary Control," *Proceedings of the Royal Society of Medicine*, 13 (1920): pp. 41–56 (especially p. 46).

10. "Measuring the Emotions."

11. Wittkower, "Studies on the Influence," p. 635; Ernest Lyman Scott, "The Content of Sugar in the Blood under Common Laboratory Conditions," *American Journal of Physiology*, 34 (1914): pp. 271–311; and Walter B. Cannon, *The Mechanical Factors of Digestion* (New York: Longmans, Green and Co., 1911), p. 217.

12. For "apprehension," see A.D. Waller, "The Emotive Response to Ordinary Stimulation, Real and Imaginary," *Lancet*, 1 (March 9, 1918): pp. 380–81 (especially p. 381). For "irritable," see A. Binet and J. Courtier, "Influence de la vie émotionnelle sur le coeur, la respiration, et la circulation capillaire," *L'Année Psychologique*, 3 (1896): pp. 65–126 (especially p. 70). For "cold," see G. Marañon, "Les Variations de la glycémie chez les aviateurs," *Comptes Rendus Hebdomadaires des Séances et Mémoires de la Société de Biologie*, 82 (1919): pp. 631–33 (especially p. 31). For "phlegmatic," see Ferrari, mentioned in Cannon, *Bodily Changes*, p. 178.

13. Cannon et al., "Some Aspects," p. 103; Joseph Barcroft, "Some Effects of Emotion on the Volume of the Spleen," *Journal of Physiology*, 67 (1930): pp. 375–82 (especially p. 375). See also J. Barcroft and R.H.E. Elliott, "Some Observations on the Denervated Spleen," *Journal of Physiology*, 87 (1936): pp. 189–97 (especially pp. 192–93); and Estes H. Hargis and Frank C. Mann, "A Plethysmographic Study of the Changes in the Volume of the Spleen in the Intact Animal," *American Journal of Physiology*, 75 (1925): pp. 180–200 (especially p. 198).

14. See, e.g., Otniel E. Dror, "Techniques of the Brain and the Paradox of Emotions, 1880–1930," *Science in Context 14* (Winter 2001): pp. 643–660; Wittkower, "Studies on the Influence"; E.T. Elliot, "The Control of the Suprarenal Glands by the Splanchnic Nerves," *Journal of Physiology*, 44 (July 15, 1912): pp. 374–409; W. Whately Smith, *The Measurement of Emotion* (New York: Harcourt, Brace, 1922);

Carney Landis, "Studies of Emotional Reactions: II. Ge   Behavior and Facial Expression," *Journal of Comparative Psychology*, 4 (1924):   447–509; William Moulton Marston, "Bodily Symptoms of Elementary Emotions," *Psyche*, 10 (October 1929): pp. 70–86; and David Brunswick, "The Effect of Emotional Stimuli on the Gastrointestinal Tone: I. Methods and Technique," *Journal of Comparative Psychology*, 4 (February 1924): pp. 19–79.

15. See, e.g., Blatz, "Cardiac, Respiratory, and Electrical Phenomena." In addition, it was conceptually, though not empirically, impossible to predict the quantitative dimension of emotional stimuli (the relationships between the type of stimulus and the magnitude of the emotion produced). For example, it was discovered that often the anticipation of a harmful stimulus produced a larger emotional response than the actual stimulus itself. See, e.g., A. Binet and, J. Courtier, "Circulation capillaire de la main dans ses rapports avec la respiration et les actes psychiques," *L'Année Psychologique*, 2 (1895): pp. 87–167 (especially p. 141).

16. See, e.g., William M. Marston, "Primary Emotions," *Psychological Review*, 34 (September 1927): pp. 336–63. See also Wittkower, "Studies on the Influence," p. 572: "The ideal of uniform stimuli — qualitatively and quantitatively equal emotions — can, for obvious reasons, never be attained." Many experimenters did not argue for either position, but attempted to create standard stimuli while including various nonstandardized and accidental events in their protocol. This practice was so common that W.E. Blatz included "accidents" in his survey of methods for generating emotions. See Blatz, "Physiological Study," p. 36.

17. Marston, "Bodily Symptoms," p. 73.

18. See, e.g., Newton, Zwemer, and Cannon, "Studies," p. 379: "It is impossible to regulate the struggles so that they are uniform"; and p. 380: "Obviously no quantitative statement can be made regarding this phenomenon because the struggles themselves are not of uniform intensity." See also W.B. Cannon and S.W. Britton, "Studies on the Conditions of Activity in Endocrine Glands: XV. Pseudaffective Medulliadrenal Secretion," *American Journal of Physiology*, 72 (April 1925): pp. 283–294 (especially p. 283). Some did not try to produce a standard emotion and asked a series of questions in which standardization was irrelevant. Their only interest was in producing emotions in the laboratory and measuring various physiological phenomena that occurred during the emotion.

19. Barcroft, "Some Effects of Emotion," p. 375. See also Barcroft and Elliott, "Some Observations," pp. 192–93.

20. Marston, "Primary Emotions"; and Bennett and Venables, "Effects."

21. Angelo Mosso, *Fear*, trans. E. Lough and F. Kiesow, 5th ed. (London and New York: Longmans, Green and Co., 1896), p. 13; and S.W. Britton, A. Hinson, and W. H. Hall, "Neural and Hormonal Influences on Bodily Activity: Differential Factors Controlling the Heart Rate during Emotional Excitement," *American Journal of Physiology*, 93 (1930): pp. 473–479 (especially p. 474).

22. "Measuring the Emotions," p. 23.

23. The suggestion was made in an individualized manner. The experimenters chose specific biographical details from the subject's history.

24. Cannon, *Bodily Changes*, pp. 180–81; Binet and Courtier, "Influence de la vie," p. 100; and Wittkower, "Studies on the Influence," pp. 568–69.

25. Christian A. Ruckmick, "Emotions in Terms of the Galvanometric Technique," *British Journal of Psychology*, 21 (1930): pp. 149–59 (see especially p. 150).

26. See, e.g., Landis, "Studies of Emotional Reactions," p. 454. The epistemologist

of the life sciences Georges Canguilhem has argued that an earlier version of Werner Heisenberg's indeterminacy principle was discovered in physiology long before its "rediscovery" by physicists of the twentieth century. See Georges Canguilhem, *The Normal and the Pathological*, trans. Carolyn R. Fawcett (New York: Zone Books, 1991 [1966]), pp. 146–47.

27. The problem was, in fact, much more complicated: human subjects came into the laboratory already loaded with various emotional burdens from their extralaboratory life. These moods, upsets, excitements, and other emotions persisted in the laboratory. See Otniel E. Dror, "Creating the Emotional Body: Confusion, Possibilities, and Knowledge," in Peter N. Stearns and Jan Lewis (Eds.), *An Emotional History of the United States* (New York: New York University Press, 1998), pp. 173–94.

28. These various practices require a separate discussion and are examined in detail in Otniel E. Dror, "The Affect of Experiment: The Turn to Emotions in Anglo-American Physiology, 1900–1940," *Isis*, 90 (June 1999): pp. 205–37. The use of trained animals or subjects served this purpose as well.

29. See, e.g., Claude Bernard, "Sur la physiologie du coeur et ses rapports avec le cerveau," in Claude Bernard, *Leçons sur les propriétés des tissus vivants*, coll., ed., and arranged M. Émile Alglave (Paris: Germer Bailliere, 1866), pp. 421–71; Otniel E. Dror, "Counting the Affects: Discoursing in Numbers," *Social Research* 68 (Summer 2001): pp. 357–78.

30. On windows and their history, see Mosso, *Fear*; and James Rowland Angell and Helen Bradford Thompson, "A Study of the Relations between Certain Organic Processes and Consciousness," *Psychological Review*, 6 (1899): pp. 32–69.

31. These latter techniques take us beyond the time period covered by this chapter.

32. For the quotation, see Charles S. Sherrington, *The Integrative Action of the Nervous System* (New Haven, CT: Yale University Press, 1906), pp. 251–52.

33. Some experimenters argued that specific peripheral physiological patterns indicated the type of emotion produced, but this was contested. There was a substantial literature on peripheral signifiers of emotions. See, e.g., Hugo Münsterberg, *On the Witness Stand: Essays on Psychology and Crime* (New York: McClure, 1908); Marston, "Systolic Blood Pressure;" and Frederick Peterson, "The Galvanometer as a Measurer of Emotions," *British Medical Journal*, 2 (1907): pp. 804–6 (see especially p. 805). For "incubation period," see Henry S. Upson, "Emotions as Symptoms," *American Medicine*, 6 (August 1903): pp. 228–29 (especially p. 228). On the specificity of emotional states and physiological patterns, see Fernand Papillon, "Physiology of the Passions," *Popular Science Monthly* (March 1874): pp. 552–64; William James, "What Is an Emotion?" *Mind* 9 (1884): 188–205; and William James, "The Emotions," *The Principles of Psychology*, chapter 25 (New York: Henry Holt, 1890). Both are in Carl Georg Lange and William James, *The Emotions* (Baltimore: Williams and Wilkins, 1922).

34. Mary D. Waller, "The Emotive Response of a Class of 73 Students of Medicine," *Lancet*, 1 (April 6, 1918): pp. 510–11, 511; W.H. Adolph, T.Y. Wang, and P.C. Wang, "Emotional Glycosuria in Chinese Students," *Chinese Journal of Physiology*, 5 (March 15, 1933): pp. 1–4; and Marston, "Systolic Blood Pressure," pp. 5–6. These quantitative measurements and determinations were also extended to include a second parameter. This second numeric variable typified different minds according to a new emotional quotient (EQ). As some experimenters explained, the EQ characterized whole minds according to their emotional reactivity. See Harry G. Armstrong, "The Blood Pressure and Pulse Rate as an Index of Emotional Stability," *American Journal of the Medical Sciences*, 195 (February 1938): pp. 211–20; and A.D. Waller, "The

Emotive Response to Ordinary Stimulation, Real and Imaginary," *Lancet*, 1 (March 1918): pp. 380–81. On the difficulties of this endeavor, see David Wechsler, *Conference on Experimental Study of Human Emotions*, October 15, 1926, p. 22, NAS-NRC Archives Div A&P Rec Grp: DNRC: A&P: "Com on Experimental Study of Human Emotions: Conf on Experimental study of Human Emotions: Third," October 1926, Washington, D.C. See Otniel E. Dror, "The Scientific Image of Emotion: Experience and Technologies of Inscription," *Configurations*, 7 (September 1999): pp. 355–401.

35. Lund, *Emotions*, p. 97.

36. Lund, *Emotions*, p. 97. On these difficulties, see also Ruckmick, "Emotions," p. 151.

37. Whitehorn, Kaufman, and Thomas, "Heart Rate," p. 716. The focus on anger and fear followed not only from on their relative ease of production under laboratory conditions, but also from the assumption that they had a biological, rather than a social, basis.

38. Binet and Courtier, "Influence de la vie," pp. 67, 87.

39. Whitehorn, Kaufman, and Thomas, "Heart Rate," p. 717.

40. See, e.g., Don P. Morris, "The Effects of Emotional Excitement on Pulse, Blood Pressure, and Blood Sugar of Normal Human Beings," *Yale Journal of Biology and Medicine*, 7 (May 1935): pp. 401–20 (especially p. 415); and Frank Bolles Wakeman, "Some Biochemical Aspects of Emotional States," Ph.D. diss. (Catholic University of America, 1935).

41. Wendell S. Dysinger and Christian Ruckmick, *The Emotional Responses of Children to the Motion Picture Situation* (New York: Macmillan, 1933); and *New York Times*, December 29, 1922, p. 3.

42. Otniel E. Dror, "Dangerous Liaisons: Science, Amusement, and the Civilizing Process," forthcoming in Penelope Gouk, Helen Mills (eds.), *Representing Emotions: New Connections in the Histories of Art, Music and Medicine* (Ashgate, 2004). A. D. Waller, "Galvanometric Records of the Emotive Response to Air Raids," Correspondence, *Lancet*, 1 (February 23, 1918), p. 311.

43. Even Darwin, who attributed to animals many human emotions and characteristics, argued that animals were incapable of shame. See Charles Darwin, *The Expression of the Emotions in Man and Animals* (New York: D. Appleton, 1872), chapter 13; and Janet Brown, "Darwin and the Expression of the Emotions," in David Kohn (Ed.), *The Darwinian Heritage* (Princeton, NJ: Princeton University Press, 1985), pp. 307–26.

44. See, e.g., Samuel C. Robinson, "On the Etiology of Peptic Ulcer," *American Journal of Digestive Diseases and Nutrition*, 2 (August 1935): pp. 333–43.

45. George W. Crile, *The Origin and Nature of the Emotions: Miscellaneous Papers*, ed. Amy F. Rowland (Philadelphia: W.B. Saunders, 1915), p. 52: "The skunk, the porcupine, the turtle, have little or no fear."

46. Ernest L. Scott and Thomas H. Ford, "The Concentration of Sugar in the Blood of the Rabbit during Inanition and after the Ingestion of Glucose," *American Journal of Physiology*, 63 (1923): pp. 520–34 (see especially p. 522): "The most common emotion in the cat is anger, rather than fear as in the rabbit."

47. J. Barcroft and J.G. Stephens, "Observations upon the Size of the Spleen," *Journal of Physiology*, 64 (1927–28): pp. 1–22; Barcroft, "Some Effects of Emotion," p. 375; and Barcroft and Elliott, "Some Observations." In this chapter I have focused on attempts to produce normal emotional reactions. In parallel with the experimental production of normal emotions in laboratories, there were laboratories that focused on the

production of emotional pathologies. These included the work of, e.g., Horsley Gantt, Howard Liddell, and Jules Masserman and focused on animals.

48. However, some argued that the animal mind was preferable for research on emotions. As Julian Huxley explained, "In birds the advance on the intellectual side has been less, on the emotional side greater: so that we can study in them a part of the single stream of life where emotion, untrammeled by much reason, has the upper hand." See Julian Huxley, "Emotions in Feathers," *Living Age*, *317* (May 19, 1923): pp. 418–25 (especially p. 425). Moreover, animals were extremely important in the anatomical localization of brain functions and pathways, including those of emotions. See John R. Durant, "The Science of Sentiment: The Problem of the Cerebral Localization of Emotion," in P.P.G. Bateson and Peter H. Klopfer (Eds.), *Perspectives in Ethology* 6 (New York: Plenum Press, 1985).

49. See, e.g., the laboratory notebooks of Ernest Lyman Scott, Ernest Lyman Scott Papers, MS. C, p. 165, National Library of Medicine, Bethesda, MD.

50. For a similar argument concerning Gustav Fechner's revolutionary work in psychophysics, see Jonathan Crary, *Techniques of the Observer: on Vision and Modernity in the Nineteenth Century* (Cambridge, MA: MIT Press, 1990), p. 147.

51. Objectivity would thus be defined as intersubjectivity. See Theodore M. Porter, "The Death of the Object: *Fin de siècle* Philosophy of Physics," in Dorothy Ross (Ed.), *Modernist Impulses in the Human Sciences, 1870–1930* (Baltimore: Johns Hopkins University Press, 1994), pp. 128–51.

II

Is the Study of Mind Continuous with the Rest of Science?

Introduction

David Martel Johnson

Let us tentatively assume that the human mind both can be and is a legitimate object of scientific investigation. Even when that point is granted, one still is not entitled to suppose that the mind is such an object, in exactly the same way and sense that applies to other, more standard cases—entities like neutrons, electromagnetic fields, viruses, species of African antelopes, volcanoes, periods of geological history, galaxies, and so forth. Accordingly, everyone who thinks of him- or herself as a cognitive scientist needs to consider the following questions: (1) What constitutes the (scientific) distinctiveness of the human mind? (2) For example, is its distinctiveness just a matter of degree, or of kind? (3) Still more narrowly, what types of scientific research are capable of throwing light on mind's nature and properties? (4) What makes these particular disciplines, methods, and conceptions both suited and able to perform that role? The authors represented in this second part of the book propose answers to these and related problems from the perspective of the knowledge, experience, values, and priorities that each of them brings to the task.

To begin, Thomas Leahey ("Psychology as Engineering") follows the lead of people like Daniel Dennett and Steven Pinker in suggesting that the best way to think about cognitive science—the "science of mind"—is as a practical or helping discipline as opposed to a theoretical, descriptive one. More particularly, Leahey argues that setting aside the currently popular idea of psychology as just another, more or less ordinary natural science[1] would have the good effect of showing how its practitioners can respond to important criticisms made by so-called social constructivists without thereby having to sacrifice psychology's rigor and empirical force. Still more concretely, Leahey claims there is a strong connection between psychology, correctly conceived, on one hand, and (post-Darwinian) biology, on the other, by virtue of the fact that—similar to the case of biology—psychology's main goal is to piece together an account of how humans and other animals "work" by means of reverse engineering. Thus Leahey's position apparently implies that the mind does not really count as a part of the objectively describable world at all, or, at least, that would-be natural scientists who tried to describe and explain mind in that particular way would be wasting time pursuing a misleading and hopeless task. Rather, thinking of psychology as one of the healing arts (and therefore as a discipline not well suited to reveal the nature of "things in themselves") leaves one free to conclude that the principal raison d'être of this field is simply to help make the world a better (more satisfactory and effective) place for human habitation.

Gunther Stent ("Epistemic Dualism") rejects the currently popular dogma that the position of dualism is completely discredited. He maintains that the general approach represented by dualism can provide the basis for an insightful, explanatory, and scientifically defensible theory of mind if one interprets it in epistemological rather than ontological terms. He then proposes to revive a view first adumbrated by Kant and later reworked and given a more concrete and empirical form by the biologist Konrad Lorenz. According to this theory, the basic reason the mind has all the characteristics it now possesses is simply that it is an ordinary biological entity (or set of functions) that has been shaped by forces of natural selection. However, Stent admits that this view contains one central, glaring problem (even though it shares this difficulty with virtually all other recent accounts of mind as well): what humans like ourselves are and do, insofar as we are physical objects, is not the same as what we are and do when we are considered as active, intelligent, intentional, moral agents. Furthermore, while it presumably is true that these two aspects of human beings are intimately (ontologically) related, it is hard for us to understand or express how this can be the case since, as far as we can tell, these two dimensions of "humanness" seem to have little to do with one another. At this point (similar to what Hattiangadi maintained in his contribution to the previous part), Stent appeals to Niels Bohr's notion of complementarity, a familiar idea adopted from the area of quantum microphysics, as the key to a solution of the puzzle. For instance, he points out that the characteristic answer of twentieth- and twenty-first-century physicists to the question "Does light energy take the form of particles or of waves?" is "Both." Or, to state the same point more positively and less paradoxically, physicists have come to see that in some circumstances, light behaves like particles (i.e., its implicit, particle-like features then assume more prominence), and in other conditions, it behaves more like a wave phenomenon. Stent claims that this is not just a suggestive parallel or metaphor for helping us think more clearly about the "twoness" naturally associated with human beings. Instead, it is a clue that guides us in the direction of literally understanding what it means to say that every human is "one entity compounded of two dissimilar parts."

David Olson ("Mind, Brain, and Culture") claims that Stent's remarks about natural selection (Olson has almost nothing to say about Stent's views on quantum mechanics) are too general and indeterminate to be a genuinely informative, legitimately scientific theory of mind. Why does he take this attitude? The reason is that although it is obvious that the human mind is special and distinctive in the realm of nature, simply pointing out that it is a product of evolution by natural selection does nothing to account for what is special about it. Thus—and here I am elaborating somewhat on Olson's statements—it is a primary goal of cognitive science to discover what distinguishes humans, on one side, from the rest of the living world, on the other. But appealing to the principle of natural selection cannot explain this difference, since all other creatures—and their "minds," if any—were produced by the very same type of selective pressures that also led to humans. Still more narrowly, Olson says that Stent's general strategy cannot be adequate because it fails to take account of at least two important matters. The first is the clear fact that culture (interpreted broadly as one's relations to other people) exerts a profound influence on any human mind. The second omitted point is that Stent pays no attention to the temporal stages through which all humans pass in order to become full members of a particular cultural group.

Don Ross argues in his chapter "Chalmers's Naturalistic Dualism: The Irrelevance of the Mind-Body Problem to the Scientific Study of Consciousness" that there is no room in cognitive science for a priori speculations about the mind's relation to the body, or the metaphysical status of consciousness. Ross claims—in roughly the same way as Pinker, Leahey, and Dennett—that we should think of this field as organized around practical and pragmatic principles, rather than theoretic ones. Moreover, one of the most important of these practical principles is a commitment to safeguard the scientific rigor and objectivity of the conclusions of cognitive science by assessing each of them in terms of a type of empirical verificationism. This last point implies that no theorist has a right to dictate the future course of the mind sciences by laying down conceptual limits within which their practitioners must proceed. For example, David Chalmers has argued that cognitive scientists should recognize a realm of conscious experience, separate from and irreducible to matter, simply because they can conceive (introspectively) of another world like our own in every respect except that it contains no such experiences. However, Ross rejects this idea on the grounds (following Dennett) that the "philosophical zombies" Chalmers claims he can picture in his mind's eye—that is, individuals who look and act exactly like us, but lack inner experiences—are not really conceivable. (To express this same point another way, zombies of that sort are not, and cannot be, legitimate objects of scientific investigation.) That is, Ross and Dennett believe that part of what it means to be a scientist is to form one's idea of what is and is not conceivable exclusively by induction from scientific practice and past scientific history, and not on the basis of what certain people, at certain times, claim that they are able to conceive.

The approach of William Seager ("Emergence and Efficacy") is very different from that of Ross. Seager imagines a future time when scientists have arrived at the final physical micropicture of the world—one that provides them with the means, at least in principle, of reducing all material objects to their ultimate, subatomic constituents. He then asks whether such a development would allow for the complete explanation of all aspects of the mind. We noted before that Ross, following Dennett, answers yes to a question of this sort on the basis of a certain type of verificationist reductionism. But Seager agrees instead with Chalmers that the right answer is no, since, according to him, scientists in that ultimate situation still would have no means of accounting for the existence and properties of consciousness. In this chapter, Seager does not give an exhaustive account of his reasons for choosing this alternative and rejecting the other. Instead, he invites readers who want to explore the matter further to consult his book.

But let us engage in a bit of speculation. Saul Kripke (1972) and Thomas Nagel (1974) once argued that consciousness must be irreducible to matter, because reduction centrally involves a movement from subjective to objective thought and knowledge, and since conscious experience is essentially subjective, it is impossible to know it objectively. One sign that Seager might be taking a similar approach is that he is happy to accept the title "mysterianism" for his view—a word Owen Flanagan (1992), following McGinn (1991), used as an abusive designation for the general type of theory about consciousness just mentioned. Of course, however, Seager proposes to interpret this term in a complimentary or at least neutral sense, not (as originally intended) in a negative, dismissive, and scornful way.

Finally, I want to mention that we originally intended to include a chapter by biologist Robert Haynes titled "Is the Problem of 'Redness' Insoluble?" at the end of part II. We were not able to do this because even though Haynes read one tentative version of his projected chapter at the 1996 conference, he never had time to complete the chapter in a way that satisfied him because of a sudden onset of sickness that finally ended in his death. The outline of the chapter, which we included in the literature for the conference, runs as follows:

> Science is "the art of the soluble" (P.B. Medawar). Scientists who grapple with insoluble problems, *as scientists,* are deemed by their colleagues to be artless, unwise, or foolish. On the other hand, there are many *presently unsolved* problems in science—for example, the basic problems of aging in organisms. (I deliberately exclude here the *social* problems of aging in humans.) Yet biologists expect that these problems will be largely solved, in the not-too-distant future, as a result of ongoing research programs in the physiology, genetics, and cellular and molecular biology of aging. Thus, for scientists, unsolved problems are not necessarily *insoluble* problems. History shows that the unsolved problems of the day often have been solved later by more hard work and hard thinking, or by new discoveries and/or the development of new technologies. Thus it is important for scientists to distinguish between unsolved and insoluble problems. Unfortunately, to make such distinctions unequivocally in all cases might itself be an insoluble problem, for no one can predict with assurance the discoveries of tomorrow.
>
> In this paper I will review the ideas that have been put forward on the nature and origin of *qualia*—that is, the *subjective qualities* of mental experiences such as the "redness" of red. I will then argue that "the problem of qualia" might be an insoluble problem in science, although it is usefully discussed and analyzed by philosophers. If it can be shown that the problem of "redness" is insoluble, then the problem of qualia is

not a scientific problem. Since qualia are part of the problem of consciousness, then mind cannot be *wholly* an object of science.

All of this is obviously relevant to the dispute described earlier, between Ross and Seager. Haynes asked the methodological metaquestion of whether there are two separate questions that theorists interested in describing and accounting for the nature of mind traditionally have considered—one of which it is possible to answer, the other not. The answer he proposed was yes (at least, from the viewpoint of practicing scientists like Haynes himself). Thus according to him, to consider just one typical example, appealing to the techniques of modern empirical science does *not* provide a suitable means of solving problems about the character and function of the conscious experience of "redness."

If Haynes' suggestion here is correct, it follows that traditional concerns about the nature of mind can be no more than partly, and not wholly, scientific in character. Thus his position seems to be at least roughly similar to Chalmers's theory, but with one crucial difference. While Chalmers argued for his view by employing the tools of metaphysical analysis and introspection, Haynes chose to support his by invoking considerations drawn from hardheaded, practical experience. I am sure that all the readers of this book would like to know more about this. And therefore it is very unfortunate that Robert Haynes died before having had a chance to explain his ideas more fully, in a completed chapter.

Note

1. Recall the following statement made by Harré in chapter 1: "In the United States, where most of those who style themselves psychologists currently live and work, it seems to be taken as settled that psychology is or is to be a kind of *Naturwissenschaft.*"

References

Flanagan, Owen. 1991. *Consciousness Reconsidered.* Cambridge, MA: MIT Press.
Kripke, Saul A. 1972. "Naming and Necessity." Pp. 253–355 in G. Harman and D. Davidson (Eds.), *Semantics of Natural Language.* Dordrecht: Reidel.
McGinn, C. 1991. *The Problem of Consciousness.* Oxford: Blackwell.
Nagel, Thomas. 1974. "What Is It Like to Be a Bat?" *The Philosophical Review,* October, 1974, pp. 435–450.

5

Psychology as Engineering

Thomas Hardy Leahey

In treating the history of mind as a scientific object in chapter 2, I mentioned various objections to the idea that psychology can and/or should aspire to be a science. In this chapter, I consider some of the objections more fully as philosophical arguments and find them persuasive, if not decisive.[1] I then discuss an alternative conception of psychology as a form of engineering, a view recently advanced by Daniel Dennett (1995) and Steven Pinker (1997) and put into practice by the new field of evolutionary psychology (e.g., Barkow, Cosmides, and Tooby, 1992). I try to correct misunderstandings about engineering and try to show that thinking of psychology as engineering allows us to retain the rigor and empirical quality of science while forcefully and sympathetically addressing the concerns of critics who claim that psychology cannot be a science.

Science as the View from Nowhere

Numerous philosophers have variously explicated the nature of science. For the purposes of this chapter I will not review or evaluate their proposals. Instead, I will work within the conception of natural science proposed by Thomas Nagel in *The View from Nowhere* (1986). Nagel embraces a robustly realistic conception of science, but recognizes and articulates the difficulties it faces in attempting to explain human life, including consciousness. Accepting Nagel's conception of science as a framework, I will review various objections to psychology as a natural science, discuss the character of engineering, and consider the virtues of seeing psychology as a form of engineering.

According to Nagel, natural science searches for purely objective knowledge, that is, for a description of the world in which people's thoughts or needs play no part at all: knowledge that has no point of view. He characterizes this viewpoint-that-is-not-a-viewpoint of natural science—the physical conception of objectivity—as follows (Nagel, 1986, pp. 14–15):

> The development [of the view from nowhere] goes in stages, each of which gives us a more objective picture than the one before. The first step is to see that our perceptions are caused by the actions of things on us, through their effects on our bodies, which are themselves part of the physical world. The next step is to realize that since the same physical properties that cause perceptions in us through our bodies also produce different effects on other physical things and can exist without causing any perceptions at all, their true nature must be detachable from their physical appearance and need not resemble it. The third step is to try to form a conception of that true nature independent of its appearance either to us or to other types of perceivers. This means not only not thinking of the physical world from our own particular point of view, but not thinking of it from a more general human perceptual point of view either: not thinking of how it looks, feels, smells, tastes, or sounds. These secondary qualities then drop out of our picture of the external world, and the underlying primary qualities such as size, shape, weight, and motion are thought of structurally.
>
> This has turned out to be an extremely fruitful strategy [that makes science possible]. . . . Our senses provide the evidence from which we start, but the detached character of this understanding is such that we could possess it even if we had none of our present senses, so long as we were rational and could understand the mathematical and formal properties of the objective conception of the physical world. We might even in a sense share an understanding of physics with other creatures to whom things appeared quite different, perceptually—so long as they too were rational and numerate.
>
> The world described by this objective conception is not just centerless; it is also in a sense featureless. While the things in it have properties, none of these properties are perceptual aspects. All of those have been relegated to the mind. . . . The physical world as it is supposed to be in itself contains no points of view and nothing that can appear only to a particular point of view.

In my earlier chapter, I discussed the most important historical source of science's view from nowhere, the scientific revolution's rethinking of the nature of the human mind, most completely worked out by Descartes and Locke. In common with other early scientists, they drew a radical division between con-sciousness (which Descartes identified with the soul) and the material world. Consciousness is subjective; it is the perspective from which each of us observes the world; it is how the world appears to me, to each of us in his or her private, subjective Theater of Consciousness. Science, on the other hand, describes a world from which consciousness and subjectivity have been subtracted. Science views the universe without any personal perspective: It is the view from nowhere.

Many of the often-noted characteristics of science that make it unique among human undertakings flow from adopting the view from nowhere. Quantified measurement eliminates any one observer's or theoretician's point of view; careful checking of papers by peers purges the originating scientist's point of view; replicating experiments guarantees that what is true for one scientist is true for all; proposing universal laws holding throughout the universe purges even the generic human point of view, because the same knowledge could be found by other species. Adopting the view from nowhere has been critical to the success of natural science.

Using Nagel's characterization of science, I now will consider some important objections to psychology's aspiration to be a science. Arguments against psychology's claim to scientific status fall into two classes that I will call arguments from imperfection and arguments from impossibility. The former hold that although the ideal of scientific psychology is a worthy one, psychology will never achieve the perfection of physics or chemistry. The latter hold that by its very nature psychology cannot be a natural science; therefore either the definition of science must be altered to include psychology, or psychology must define itself in a different way. I wish to stress that in what follows I touch on issues over which there is deep and angry controversy. I will not attempt to recount the arguments, but simply to pose important questions that motivate redefining psychology as something other than natural science.

Arguments from Imperfection

John Stuart Mill (1872/1987) was one of the most important and influential advocates of creating a psychology that was a natural science. Nevertheless, he carefully considered the possibility that psychology might never achieve the degree of sophistication and precision possessed by physics.

One can somewhat anachronistically state the gist of Mill's concerns as follows: The subject matter of psychology is vastly—perhaps infinitely—more complex than the subject matter of physics. The number of forces that affect matter are at most four (gravity, electromagnetism, and strong and weak nuclear forces), while the number of human motives is large and unknown. The basic particles composing all physical objects number somewhat more than a dozen and have the same character throughout the universe, while no two humans are alike, and we are affected by historical and cultural contexts that have no parallel in nature. Physical things do not know that we are studying them and are indifferent to our theories about them. People participating in experiments or filling out tests know that they are being studied, and that awareness may alter their behavior from what it would be elsewhere. Moreover, the very existence of a discipline of psychology may alter human behavior. As we learn the causes and mechanisms of human action, we can reflect on them, perhaps weakening the hold they have on us.

Electrons and sofas cannot read physics texts and decide whether or not to co-operate with the laws of nature.

Such considerations suggest at least that psychology is a much more complex science than physics, perhaps so complex that no amount of research, statistics, or sophisticated theorizing can take it to the same stage of scientific perfection as physics. Mill recognized this, but still believed that having an imperfect scientific psychology was better than having none at all. Mill drew a parallel between psychology and sciences such as meteorology (his example was a hypothetical "tidology"). Although it is a physical system, the earth's weather is so complex that it defies adequate description or prediction, much less control. Even today, with satellites and supercomputers, predicting local weather conditions past twenty-four hours is uncertain, and long-term forecasts are virtually worthless. It may be that predicting the weather will never be like predicting eclipses. Nevertheless, weather predictions are useful, and incremental progress has been made. For example, meteorologists save lives by effectively predicting many hours in advance where hurricanes will come ashore so that people can be evacuated.

The study of the weather may never be as good a science as physics, but the scientific study of the weather has paid off. Similarly, Mill (1872/1987, pp. 33–34) thought that while psychology might forever remain an imperfect science, people could be studied scientifically, and such study might bear useful fruit:

> The phenomena with which this science is conversant being the thoughts, feelings, and actions of human beings, it would have attained the ideal perfection of a science if it enabled us to foretell how an individual would think, feel, or act throughout life, with the same certainty with which astronomy enables us to predict the places and the occultations of the heavenly bodies. It needs scarcely be stated that nothing approaching to this can be done. The actions of individuals could not be predicted with scientific accuracy, were it only because we cannot foresee the whole of the circumstances in which those individuals will be placed. . . .
>
> It is evidently possible, with regard to all such effects, to make predictions, which will *almost* always be verified, and general propositions, which are almost always true. And whenever it is sufficient to know how the great majority of the human race, or of some nation or class of persons, will think, feel, and act, these propositions are equivalent to universal ones. For the purposes of political and social science this is sufficient. . . . [A]n approximate generalization is, in social inquiries, for most practical purposes equivalent to an exact one; that which is only probable when asserted of individual human beings indiscriminately selected, being certain when affirmed of the character and collective conduct of masses.
>
> It is no disparagement, therefore, to the science of Human Nature that those of its general propositions which descend sufficiently into de-

tail to serve as a foundation for predicting phenomena in the concrete are for the most part only approximately true.

Mill saw psychology (and the other social sciences) as a genuine science fated always to be less perfect than physics. I now turn to arguments that human beings are so radically different from physical objects that psychology cannot be a science at all.

Arguments from Impossibility

You Cannot Eliminate the Mind: Intentionality and the Failure of Behaviorism

In hopes of making psychology a science like any other, behaviorists abandoned the study of private consciousness for the study of publicly observable behavior. Because it was private, consciousness seemed to elude scientific investigation, but behavior appeared to be amenable to scientific inquiry because it was public in the same way as the movements of the stars and planets. Behaviorists hoped in this way to avoid the apparent difficulties of studying the mind.

Behaviorists inherited the founders of psychology's Cartesian identification of mind with consciousness (Leahey, chapter 2 in this volume) and thought that by avoiding consciousness, they could avoid mind altogether. However, they failed to realize the intimate connection between behavior and the psychological aspects of mind. For the definition of any behavior, and thus its explanation, depend on mental states to which it is connected.

Not every movement a person makes counts as behavior.[2] Coughing and breathing are behaviors in one sense—they are things human bodies do—but in another they are not. Coughing and breathing are mindless reflexes carried out by our nervous systems, and they do not require psychological explanation any more than does the rising of the sun. Observe that coughing or even breathing might sometimes have a psychological cause and then count as behaviors. If we are being ignored at the checkout counter of a store, we often "cough" to get a clerk's attention; in the movie The Andromeda Strain, a scientist breathes fast in order to throw his blood into oxidosis and thereby kill the alien virus with which he has been infected. In these cases, what are ordinarily mere physical movements become behaviors because they are done voluntarily; they are intended. In general, a bodily movement counts as a behavior only when it falls under an intentional description (Davidson, 1980) connecting it to the psychological beliefs and desires that caused it. Because psychological states define what behavior a set of movements constitutes, psychologists cannot limit themselves to studying only publicly observable movements, as the behaviorists hoped, but must probe the mind as well.

Let us look at an example of why intentional descriptions cannot be omitted from attempts to understand behavior. In an episode from the old television series

Perry Mason, Perry visits the home of a man thought to be connected with a long-unsolved bank robbery. While the man is out of the room making coffee, Perry discovers a $100 bill that probably came from the robbery and decides to hide it by rolling it up in a window blind. He pulls the blind down, inserts the bill near the top of the roller, and raises the blind. He then leaves the man's house. Unknown to Perry, the police have staked out the house. The detectives see Perry enter the house and a little later see his shadowy figure raise and lower the blind. Soon after he leaves, they become suspicious, enter the house, and find the body of the man whom Perry had come to see. Later in court, one detective testifies that he saw Perry signal to his client—whom they think guilty of the murder—to escape before the police could arrest her. Perry denies that he ever signaled his client, outraging the district attorney, who screams, "But you can't deny it—*the police saw you do it!*" Perry then takes the witness stand, saying that yes, he did raise and lower the blind, but he was not warning his client that the police were about, he was hiding the $100 bill.

We have here a single set of bodily movements—raising and lowering the blind—that has two quite different intentional descriptions, as a signal for an accomplice to flee or as the hiding of paper money. The point seems obvious, even trivial, but it has serious consequences for behaviorism, because it means that the psychological concept of mind cannot be avoided by defining psychology as the science of behavior. What a behavior is depends on the motives and beliefs of the actor. Perry might in fact have been signaling his client, as the police thought. In order to determine what needs to be explained—Why did Perry hide the bill? versus Why did Perry signal his client?—we need to look beyond his movements into his mind, into what he intended by the act. Perry's movements by themselves do not reveal their motivation and cannot be satisfactorily explained without knowing the intentional description under which they actually fall.

The fact that we cannot even define what a behavior is, and thus cannot explain it, until we know the motives and beliefs behind it means that psychology cannot simply do away with mind altogether, as behaviorists hoped. Instead, psychology must study mind and behavior together as closely and inextricably intertwined.

You Cannot Eliminate Points of View: The Failure of the View from Nowhere

There is a second aspect of intentional descriptions that poses an additional problem for scientific psychology. Science is about causes: What causes seismic events to occur and comets to return? We can answer these questions within the view from nowhere. There would be seismic events and comets even if there were no people; the universe is indifferent to human interests. Perry's actions with the window blinds had causes in psychological motives and beliefs and in physiological processes of his nervous system and musculature. Unlike the movements of comets or the Sun, Earth, and Moon, however, what Perry did had meaning. To the police his actions meant, "Run away, client, the police are near," while to him they meant, "Here's a safe place to hide what might be valuable evidence." Meanings cannot be encompassed within natural science's view from nowhere because they depend crucially upon being linked to a point of view. From Perry's point of view he was hiding a $100 bill; from the police's, he was warning his client.

John Shotter, a long-standing critic of psychology's pretensions to be a science, has discussed this problem in the context of attribution theory. Attribution theory is supposed to be about "man the intuitive scientist," seeing folk psychology as a sciencelike search for the causes of behavior. However, Shotter points out that in everyday life, much of the time "one is puzzled not by one's ignorance of what led up to a person's action, but by what their action actually is, by what it is that the person is actually trying to do in performing it" (Shotter, 1981, p. 166). That is, we usually find ourselves deciphering the meaning of a behavior the way a literary critic deciphers the meaning of a text, rather than trying to discover the causes of behavior the way a physicist tries to discover the cause of an event. In the Perry Mason incident, the police incorrectly deciphered the meaning of his actions.

A further difficulty raised by intentionality for the scientific conception of psychology is that interpreting the meaning of an action depends upon background assumptions that vary from culture to culture and across time in single cultures. This means that even if we discover rules governing intentions, actions, and interpretation of actions, they will probably hold true only for specific places and times, lacking the universality of the laws of natural science. Regardless of whose point of view one takes, Perry's actions can only be understood in a culture that possesses money, attorneys, law, police, and rules of evidence.

Even within a single culture, historical changes can alter the meaning of a behavior, even if the actor's intentional description of the action stays the same. Consider, for example, the plight of a male business executive with regard to his female personal secretary. Near Christmas, her boss gives her an expensive perfume that she knows is advertised in a sexually suggestive way. What is the meaning of her boss's action? Did he dash through the nearest department store's cosmetics section, buying for every female on his shopping list the perfume most heavily advertised during the pro football playoffs? Is he making up for yelling at her last week? Is he giving everyone an expensive gift because the company did well this year? Did he just rush out at the last minute and buy a gift, not knowing that it had a sexual connotation? Has he become fond of her and is suggesting so by the gift? Is it an attempt at seduction? Is it sexual harassment? In short, is it a nuance-free or nuance-laden gift?

The answer depends partly upon his intention, but also partly on the historical-cultural context in which the behavior is performed. Some of the secretary's reasoning about her boss's present does involve causal attribution of intention (or the lack of it) to her boss and inferences (or lack of inferences) from them to his dispositions, but much of her quandary concerns the act itself, as Shotter suggests. Consider, for example, deciding if the gift constitutes sexual harassment. If he did give it to every woman on his list, mother and mother-in-law included, the gift of perfume is probably not a case of sexual harassment. Besides, the gift may be well meant, even if it does indicate romantic fondness. Had the same man met her at church or at the gym and become fond of her, the gift at Christmas might be a way of shyly indicating his fondness without words. At work, however, the same shy gesture — caused by the same internal dispositions — becomes threatening.

According to the *Wall Street Journal* (April 23, 1996), Secretaries' Day is becoming a social minefield for bosses anxious to avoid offending women in "politically correct times." Although fancy lunches and flowers remain the most frequent way bosses honor secretaries, they are giving way to more earnest and less sexually-laden gifts such as computer classes.

Imagine an aging boss who has for decades given his secretaries flowers or perfumes for Christmas or Secretaries' Day simply out of Christmas spirit and as a small way of recognizing their work. The reasons for his behavior remained unchanged from 1959 to 1999, but the meaning of his action has shifted because the social context in which he operates has changed. Natural science searches for the universal and ahistorical causes of what happens in the world and has no place for shifting mores and altered cultural standards. The view from nowhere cannot explain how and why the meaning of the boss's gifts is not as unchanging as their causes because it must ignore the boss's point of view, the secretaries' points of view, and the wider culture's point of view, and without these, the gifts cannot be comprehended, much less explained.

The Construction of Social Reality

These considerations converge to suggest that the rules that govern human behavior are different from those that govern nature.[3] As Vico and Herder said, we live in a world we ourselves create, and natural science has no way of coping with this evolving creative process (Berlin, 1976). Moreover, social-cultural rules do not simply regulate how we do behave; they regulate how we ought to behave.

Constitutive Rules: Cultures as Games

Philosophers distinguish between regulative and constitutive rules. The law of gravity is an example of a regulative rule: Gravity inexorably controls the behavior of all physical objects in the universe. The rules of games are constitutive rules: They constrain the behavior of the players, but, more important, they define, or constitute, the game itself. The game of baseball is constituted by the set of rules of baseball that regulate the behavior of baseball players; the game of football by the set of rules that regulate the behavior of football players. Constitutive rules are importantly unlike scientific laws. Scientific laws apply to all things equally everywhere, but constitutive rules apply to particular places and times. You cannot be offside in baseball or steal second base in football. Constitutive rules change with time and may differ with place. In American League baseball, the pitcher does not bat but is replaced with a designated hitter; National League baseball follows the older rule in which the pitcher takes turns batting like his fellow players.

This analysis suggests an important way of looking at human life that sets it apart from the world of natural science. We can think of cultures as being like games defined by sets of constitutive rules, of which we are typically unaware. For example, North and South Americans differ in the distance at which they feel comfortable having a conversation: North Americans prefer greater distance than South Americans. Thus at a mixed cocktail party there occurs an odd dance in which a South American keeps closing in on a North American who keeps retreating as each tries to maintain what they intuitively feel is the right conversational distance. No doubt the South American comes to feel that the North American is emotionally cold and "remote," while the North American feels that the South American is emotionally hot and "rude."

The important point is that we cannot hope to understand and explain human behavior without referring to constitutive, cultural rules. If I explain to a foreign friend why a football referee blew his whistle and threw a yellow flag on the ground, I will have to explain that football rules decree that all the players from each team must stay on their side of the ball until it is snapped, that throwing the flag meant that a rule had been violated, and that blowing the whistle temporarily stopped the game, so that until the whistle was blown again, players could wander wherever they wanted on either side of the ball. Without knowledge of the rules, the whole scene is quite bizarre, and there is no natural science explanation of why for some minutes you have to be on only one side of the ball while during other minutes you may stand where you please.[4]

Constitutive rules differ from natural laws in another respect: They generally must be enforced. Natural laws cannot be disobeyed. The universe does not need a team of cosmic referees to keep the planets in line or to keep electrons from masquerading as protons. Constitutive rules, being human conventions, can be disobeyed and must be enforced by informal sanctions and by more formal institutions such as referees, police, and courts of law. Constitutive rules are thus moral rules. Like scientific laws, we invoke them to explain why people behave as they do, but unlike scientific laws, they prescribe what we ought to do.

The Moral Dimension of Psychology

Within its view from nowhere, natural science is above all concerned with what is, not what ought to be. Sciences seek to give an accurate and precise description of nature, free of human wishes and hopes. In nature there is no right or wrong, there are no moral values. Tornadoes do not seek out mobile-home parks to ravage; they are neither gleeful nor repentant killers but facts of nature that we find frightening. The human immunodeficiency retrovirus is scarcely living and is itself not evil; its clever means of reproduction causes a human scourge to which it is utterly indifferent. Tornadoes and viruses are evils only from the human point of view.

However, the explanation of human behavior—psychology—cannot be easily stripped of moral concerns. We have learned that mind cannot be separated from the definition or explanation of behavior and must therefore be included within any workable psychology. But the definition of mind is itself laden with moral and social values. One of *The Oxford English Dictionary*'s definitions of *mind* shows this quite clearly:

> "The healthy or normal condition of the mental faculties, the loss or impairment of which constitutes insanity."

"Having a mind" is not a neutral fact about a person on a par with "having brown hair." "Healthy" and "normal" are value-laden terms: Being healthy is good, being sick is bad; being normal is good, being abnormal is bad. Human beings whose minds are seriously defective are treated as less than real persons. A person judged insane is set legally apart from other people. A criminal judged insane is held to have no moral responsibility for his or her acts and is sent to a mental institution rather than a prison; ordinary people judged insane may have caretakers appointed to mind their affairs and may, in extreme cases, be confined against their will in mental hospitals.

We can use another shortcoming of attribution theory to illustrate the difficulty of explaining human behavior from the value-free natural science view from nowhere. Attribution theory is not about behavior itself, but about how people naively explain behavior; and attribution theories are therefore intended to be explications of folk psychology. The scientific status of attribution theory is put in doubt by the observation that folk psychology is constitutive and normative as well as explanatory. Folk psychology not only attempts the scientific job of explaining behavior, but the moral job of laying down rules about how we ought to evaluate behavior and link it to personal responsibility.

Thus when an attribution theory fails to predict people's behavior, psychologists are put in a quandary. For example, ample research has demonstrated that contrary to all attribution theories, people often commit the fundamental error of attribution, the powerful tendency to explain behavior as the result of personality factors while neglecting situational causes. What to make of the fact, however, is unclear. It might be the case that all existing attribution theories are incorrect explications of folk psychology. If this is true, then phenomena such as the fundamental error of attribution reflect failures of theoretical psychologists to correctly characterize folk psychology, and we need a better attribution theory.

On the other hand, if attribution theorists have correctly characterized folk psychology, then phenomena such as the fundamental error of attribution reflect failures of folk psychology itself, and we might conclude that folk psychology is not an adequate scientific theory of behavior. Is folk psychology, then, wrong? Normative, constitutive rules of behavior are not discarded simply because people do not always act in accord with them. We do not repeal laws against murder because some people commit murder; the National Football League does not rescind the offside rule because every Sunday afternoon some players are offside. Similarly, should we discard what appears to be a rational rule of the attribution process—compelled behaviors tell us little about a person's character—simply because sometimes observers of behavior do not follow it? These considerations suggest that any sound attribution theory, that is, one that correctly explicates folk psychology, will, like folk psychology itself, not be merely a scientific theory. The very fact that social psychologists talk about the fundamental *error* of attribution betrays a difference between psychology and physics. "Error" is a moral term. Physicists do not criticize electrons for making "errors," because electrons must follow the regulative laws of nature that physics hopes to discover.

There are, then, serious reasons for doubting that psychology can be a science, or at least one on the same plane of development as physics. In evaluating these arguments, one should remember psychology's great diversity. Some aspects of psychology have more realistic aspirations to science than others do. Physiological psychology concerns the operations of the brain and nervous system and so need grapple little with problems of intentional description or right and wrong. A physiological psychologist wants to understand how Perry Mason's body worked as he raised and lowered the window shade and need not worry about why Perry did it or whether his conduct was ethical. Similar considerations apply to the study of sensation, perception, memory, and the simpler cognitive processes. However, once psychologists address the distinctive human aspects of behavior, beginning with thinking and including language, social behavior, personality, and psychopathology and its treatment, psychology begins to look less and less like a natural science. In my earlier chapter I looked at the old alternative definition of (much of) psychology as among the humanities, or *Geisteswissenschaften*. I will now take up the recent proposal that (much of) psychology be viewed as akin to engineering.

The Nature of Engineering

We tend to think of engineering as "merely" applied science. Creative scientists discover how nature works, while engineers merely translate science into useful products.

However, the history of engineering is older than the history of science, and until the nineteenth century, the two were largely independent. The ancient Romans and Egyptians, along with non-Western cultures such as the Inca, the Chinese, or the Indian, built large and magnificent structures long before there was any serious science of physics. Medieval artillery engineers had a poor understanding of how their missiles flew through the sky, but their gunfire was accurate and effective. Engineers artfully design objects that have functions; that is, engineering is about building things that perform useful services for human beings. Engineering, while resembling science in being rigorous, mathematical, and based upon research, is nevertheless different from science in important ways.

Engineering Does Not Adopt the View from Nowhere

Engineers create things that are useful from the human point of view, typically things that are useful in particular times and places, not everywhere in the universe. For example, in the eighteenth century, artisans (who may be regarded as small-scale engineers) built pipe holders. In British pubs and American taverns, men would smoke long clay pipes. At the end of the day, the tavern owner gathered up the pipes, placed them in a sort of metal rack—a pipe holder—and placed it in the tavern's fireplace, where the heat cleansed the pipes for use the next day. Before tobacco was raised, cured, cut, and placed into clay pipes, pipe holders were not needed and did not exist. Only when two historically local events came together—smoking and public taverns—did the need to clean clay pipes arise, and some engineer or artisan designed the pipe holder to fulfill this new function. Now that smoking is in decline—especially clay-pipe smoking—pipe holders are no longer needed and have become valuable antiques. Indeed, so remote is the function of clay-pipe cleaning from modern life that only antique collectors and dealers know a pipe cleaner when they see one.

Engineering Does Not Seek Universal Laws

Because engineers focus on building things that fulfill particular functions, they do not need, or seek, universal laws of nature. Consider the mousetrap. A mousetrap is defined by its function, what it does, namely, catching mice. However, there are many ways to catch mice. There is the traditional snapping mousetrap. There are mousetraps consisting of squares of adhesive-covered material that hold a mouse's foot when it steps on it. Many people now find both kinds of traps inhumane and set box traps that catch mice alive for relocation. There is a new mousetrap consisting of a Y-shaped plastic tube mounted on a pivot; the mouse enters one branch of the Y and moves further toward the bait at the base of the Y, causing the tube to tilt, which releases a small ball from the other branch of the Y, trapping the mouse in the tube. Of course, there is the very traditional cat, which—although not designed by engineers—was designed by evolution to be a predator and therefore can be used by humans as a mousetrap. Unlike electrons, protons, quarks, or the atomic elements they form, there is no single, universal, physical form of the mousetrap. Mousetraps are defined by what they do, not by what they are.

In Engineering, Facts Are Not the Ultimate Arbiter of What to Believe

Science describes nature as it is; engineers change nature. It is a fact that humans cannot fly; we have invented airplanes. It is a fact that humans cannot see as well as eagles; we have invented telescopes and microscopes. It is a fact that humans cannot breathe under water; we have invented scuba gear. Unlike science, engineering, because it is not a view from nowhere, embodies human hopes and values. We hope to fly to the stars, so we invent spacecraft; we value life, so we invent medicine. Although engineers cannot violate the laws of nature, they can exploit them and work around them; it is the engineer, not the scientist, who makes it so.

Engineering, then, offers a model for psychology that in many respects is more congenial to psychology than is natural science. Engineering possesses science's virtues—it is rigorous, precise, and empirical—without embodying the unhuman view from nowhere. What might an engineering-oriented psychology look like?

Scientific Psychology as Engineering: Mind as Evolved Functions

Although Descartes excluded mind from science, he approached the mind from the universal perspective of science, asking what sort of thing a mind was and concluding that it was a thing, a soul, that thinks. He then thought of the soul in traditional religious terms as a nonmaterial substance that is the same in all people. Even though this definition of the soul was consonant with religion, it was also consonant with the universal nature of the objects of science, being the same sort of thing in all people at all times. Kantian idealism continued Descartes's tradition. The Transcendental Ego is the same in all human beings, indeed, in all minded creatures. The post-Kantian idealists pushed the idea further. For them, there was really just one universal Mind, not many human minds (Solomon, 1988).

A mousetrap is a thing that catches mice the way the soul is a thing that thinks. But as we have seen, from the engineering perspective, what defines a mousetrap is what it does, not what sort of thing it is. A mousetrap can be a piece of wood fitted with metal springs and catches, a square of sticky paper, a box with a trap door, a pivoting plastic tube, or a cat. There is no universal physical substance common to all mousetraps.

Similarly, we may apply the engineering perspective to Descartes's definition of mind, "mind is a thing that thinks," defining mind in terms of what it does—thinking—rather than in terms of what it is. Just as a mousetrap, being defined by its function, need have no particular physical form, a mind, defined by the function of thinking, need have no particular physical (or nonphysical) form. Employing the engineering point of view, we might rewrite Descartes this way, "Mind is the functions of thinking and feeling." Or, as Pinker (1997, p. 21) writes, "The mind is what the brain does."

Cognitive "science" is based on the analogy between people and computers, and this analogy is rooted in a functional, engineering perspective on psychology. A computer is a physical device whose conduct is controlled by the program that is running on it. A program is not a physical (or nonphysical) thing separate from the computer; it is a set of instructions—logical and mathematical functions—that tell the hardware of the computer what to do. A computer is a product of engineering, defined by what it does, not by what it is. The same computer program—word processor, spreadsheet, or game—may be implemented in physically different computers, IBM PCs and their clones using Intel processors, IBM PC clones using physically different but functionally identical non-Intel microprocessors, Apple Macintoshes, and even big mainframes. A computer's "mind" is in its software—its functions—not in its hardware.

Similarly, we may think of the mind as a set of functions—thinking and feeling—that are implemented in a human nervous system. From this standpoint, a human (or animal) body is a physical device whose conduct is controlled by the mind that is running on it. A mind is not a physical (or nonphysical) thing separate from the body; it is a set of cognitive and emotional functions that tell the hardware of the body what to do. From the scientific point of view—the view from nowhere—mind is an anomaly: It is neither a physical thing nor a physical force. From the engineering point of view, a mind is a set of functions that might be implemented in various physical means, such as a living body or a computer.

Cognitive "science" has two interrelated aspects, artificial intelligence and cognitive psychology. In the field of artificial intelligence, computer engineers perform practical mind design, trying to build computer programs capable of doing the same things that human beings do. In the field of cognitive psychology, psychologists act like engineers trying to reverse-engineer the human mind. In reverse engineering, engineers take an already working device and try to implement the same functions by different physical or computational means. For example, engineers working for Intel's rivals take an Intel microprocessor and carefully study its input-output functions until they can duplicate them with their own microprocessor, having never opened up the Intel chip or looked at its design specifications, which would violate copyright and patent laws. Like different mousetraps, the two chips are physically different but functionally identical.

Cognitive psychologists use experiments to examine the input-output functions of the human mind and theorize about the internal mental functions that connect stimulus and response. The engineers of artificial intelligence try to duplicate the same functions in physically different but functionally identical machines, computers rather than living bodies.

In addition to making the mind less mysterious and freeing psychology from the impossible ideal of finding universal laws, the engineering perspective on psychology is better able to accommodate the normative aspect of psychology than is natural science. Because it is concerned with function—with designing things that work—engineering, unlike science, can ask if things are good or bad. It makes no sense in science to ask, "Is this the best gravity we can get?" or say, "Today's batch of electrons is much better than those defective ones we got yesterday." It does make sense to ask, "Is this the best airplane we can get?" and say, "Today's batch of memory chips is much better than those defective ones we got yesterday." Functions define norms, because a given function can be performed well or badly. Computer programs, like minds, can be defective—have bugs—and can be improved or repaired.

Similar considerations apply to natural functions as well as to engineer-created functions carried out by artifacts. A heart is a device whose function is to pump blood, and a heart that does it badly is defective, that is, diseased. Similarly, the engineering perspective on the mind accommodates the idea of mental health. One of the functions of the mind is to think rationally, which constitutes sanity. If a mind fails to fulfill this function, it is defective — diseased — and needs to be treated, or, if untreatable and dangerous, isolated from others.

As I said earlier, function and design are closely linked concepts, because engineers design artifacts to carry out specific functions. In the case of artifacts, the connection is obvious, because human engineers consciously design them to meet human needs — to fulfill useful functions. Who is the designer of devices that fill natural functions, such as the heart and the mind? The answer is evolution. Engineering results from human beings solving the problems of living. Evolution results from living beings solving the problems of living, the most important of which are survival and reproduction. Before it could draw on science, much of engineering was a trial-and-error process of finding out what works, and to some degree it still is. Evolution is a trial-and-error process by which living beings, plants and animals, try out different ways of surviving and reproducing. As in engineering, successful ways are kept and unsuccessful ones discarded. In engineering, teaching transmits the good ideas and omits mention of the failures. In evolution, successful means of survival and reproduction are transmitted by the flourishing of the genes that caused them, and failures are omitted because the genes that caused them do not reproduce. Cats — the natural mousetrap — were designed by evolution and survive because they work well. Evolution and engineering are the same: the continuing search for designs that do things better and better.

Instead of defining the research and theorizing side of psychology as a science, we can define it as a form of reverse engineering. Human beings have been designed by evolution to have minds — sets of functions — that guide behavior, and to live in cultures, which do much of the programming of the rules constituting the human mind. The job of the psychologist is to study behavior, striving to infer the mental functions that define and cause it. Because many of our mental functions are constitutive and installed by our culture, theories in much of psychology will lack the universality of science's view from nowhere. Moreover, like engineers, psychologists work to help people function better.

Applied Psychology as Engineering: Expertise as Knowing What Works

The engineering perspective also provides a different way of defining the expertise of the applied psychologist. While today's engineers are, of course, well trained in science, much of what they do is based on simpler, more directly practical knowledge. For example, in building bridges and buildings, it is important to know how different materials respond to different kinds of stresses. Whether a given material responds to stress by stretching or breaking is determined by the nature of the atomic bonds holding its molecules together, but engineers do not need to know such details in order to do their work. Engineers built bridges and buildings long before quantum theory was developed. They simply experiment with materials themselves, subjecting them to stresses and strains and observing how each material responds. It is disciplined, rigorous research, but it produces practical principles rather than universal laws of nature.

Applied psychology rests upon similar practices. For example, often little guided by general psychological theories, clinical psychologists devise microtheories about different disorders that they treat. They then conduct experiments in order to see how people with different personalities or mental disorders respond to different treatments, and they constantly tinker with treatments to improve them. Similarly, since the time of Alfred Binet, mental tests have been developed in an engineering spirit. Tests are designed to fulfill a specific function, such as predicting school performance, and are developed by disciplined trial and error. Items that predict well are kept; those that do not are discarded, and the process of refining tests continues. Like the engineer, the mental test developer wants to design something that works, the test of adequacy being success, not universal truth.

One incident from the history of applied psychology demonstrates that the drive for universal truth can be positively dangerous in psychology. Freud wanted psychoanalysis to be a science, not merely a workable technique for helping troubled people (Leahey, 2004). To take one glaring example, Freud could have concluded from his self-analysis and clinical research that some people in some cultures sometimes form Oedipal attachments to their parents and that these attachments may sometimes cause trouble for them as adults, and that psychotherapy might help them deal with their feelings. Instead, driven by his "consuming passion" that psychology be a science, Freud concluded from his own (reconstructed) childhood memories that Oedipal feelings were "a universal event in early childhood" (letter from Freud to Wilhelm Fliess, October, 15, 1887; Masson, 1985, p. 272). Upon this thin reed Freud then built a pseudoscientific theory of human development. Had he stuck to particular cases, he might have been a more effective healer.

Applied psychologists need not claim to be scientists in order to be experts deserving of authority. Like physicians—the applied engineers of biology—they know more about what works than laypeople and therefore possess authority. Clients should trust applied psychologists not because they are scientists, as the Boulder model says, but because they possess the same kind of practical expertise—informed by science—that is possessed by engineers and physicians.[5]

Conclusion

I find the idea of practicing psychology as a form of engineering attractive. It recognizes the important criticisms of natural science psychology made by social constructionists, but deals with them in a way that preserves psychology's rigor and experimental character. While it gives up on the notion of psychology as a natural science, it still connects psychology strongly to biology. It provides a rigorous model—reverse engineering—by which to pursue research and theorizing about both mind and behavior. In short, it gives us a way of approaching mind and behavior that recognizes that human beings are natural and social animals, recognizes the role of meaning and culture in shaping human thought and action, but preserves the best features of natural science, objectivity and rigor.

Notes

1. I will not take up idealist objections that depend upon the concept of the Transcendental Ego, because I believe they are now merely of historical interest.

2. In what follows, I use "behavior" to mean what philosophers traditionally call "action"—intended movements.

3. I take the title of this section from Searle (1995).

4. As an exercise in the importance of constitutive rules for explaining human behavior, I recommend watching an unfamiliar sport being played, such as Australian-rules football, cricket, or team handball. You see behavior—people running around—but absent knowledge of the rules of the game, their movements make no sense, and you cannot explain what is going on to yourself, much less to another person.

5. According to the Boulder, or scientist-practitioner, model, clinical psychologists are to be trained as scientists first—learning the same research skills as scientific psychologists—and as therapists second. Graduates of Boulder programs receive the scholarly Ph.D. The alternative Vail model trains clinicians primarily as healers who receive a Psy.D, a degree parallel to the M.D.

References

Antaki, C. (Ed.). 1981. *The Psychology of Ordinary Explanations of Social Behaviour.* London: Academic Press.

Barkow, J.H., Cosmides, L., and Tooby, J. (Eds.). 1992. *The Adapted Mind: Evolutionary Psychology and the Generation of Culture.* New York: Oxford University Press.

Berlin, I. (1976). *Vico and Herder.* London: Hogarth.

Davidson, D. 1980. *Essays on Actions and Events.* Oxford: Clarendon Press.

Dennett, D.C. 1994. "Cognitive Science as Reverse Engineering: Several Meanings of 'Top-down' and 'Bottom-Up.'" Pp. 679–89 in D. Praywitz, B. Skyrms, and D. Westerstahl (Eds.), *Logic, Methodology, and Philosophy of Science.* Vol. 9. Amsterdam: Elsevier. Reprinted in D. Dennett, *Brainchildren,* Cambridge, MA: MIT Press, 1998, pp. 249–59.

———. 1995. *Darwin's Dangerous Idea: Evolution and the Meanings of Life.* New York: Simon and Schuster.

Leahey, T.H. 1997. *A History of Psychology.* 4th ed. Upper Saddle River, NJ: Prentice Hall.

Masson, J.M. (Ed. and trans.). 1985. *The Complete Letters of Sigmund Freud to Wilhelm Fliess, 1887–1904.* Cambridge, MA: Belknap Press of Harvard University Press.

Mill, J.S. 1872/1987. *The Logic of the Moral Sciences*. La Salle, IL: Open Court. Originally published as *Book VI: On the Logic of the Moral Sciences*, in Mill's *A System of Logic*. 8th ed. London: Longmans, Green, Reader, and Dyer.

Nagel, T. 1986. *The View from Nowhere*. New York: Oxford University Press.

Ogden, R.M. 1911. "Imageless Thought." *Psychological Bulletin*, 8, 185–97.

Pinker, S. 1997. *How the Mind Works*. New York: Norton.

Praywitz, D., Skyrms, B., and Westerstahl, D. (Eds.). 1994. *Logic, Methodology, and Philosophy of Science*. Vol. 9. Amsterdam: Elsevier.

Searle, J.R. 1995. *The Construction of Social Reality*. New York: Free Press.

Shotter, J. 1981. "Telling and Reporting: Prospective and Retrospective Uses of Self-Ascription." Pp. 157–81 in C. Antaki (Ed.), *The Psychology of Ordinary Explanations of Social Behaviour*. London: Academic Press.

Solomon, R.C. 1988. *Continental Philosophy since 1750*. Oxford: Oxford University Press.

6

Epistemic Dualism

Gunther S. Stent

Two things fill the mind with ever-increasing wonder and awe, the
more often and more intensely the mind of thought is drawn to
them: the starry heavens above me and the moral law within me.
                    Immanuel Kant, *Critique of Practical Reason* (1788)

Kant's epigram epitomizes the thesis that to be human means to live in two metaphysically distinct domains of the world. One of them is the natural domain of
things that are governed by physical laws. That natural domain includes not only
the starry heavens above Kant but also the species of animals of which he happened to be a member. The other is the supernaturalistic domain of persons who,
like Kant, are governed by the moral law within them. It is in this sense of mankind
coexisting in natural and supernaturalistic domains of the world that the dualism
of mind and body, which most contemporary biologists and philosophers regard
as a long-defunct doctrine, is not dead at all. On the contrary, dualism is likely to
persist for as long as there are people who live as social beings.

The Mind-Body Problem

The earliest philosophers of sixth-century BCE Greece distinguished between *substances* and *attributes*. According to them, a substance is something—such as a
stone—that can exist in the world on its own, independently of anything else. An
attribute, by contrast, is something—such as weight—that cannot exist on its own
and must ultimately refer to something that is a substance. The Greek philosophers
formulated what came to be known as the mind-body problem by asking whether
mind is a substance or an attribute of the body (figure 6.1).

Supporters of the view that mind is a substance, who included Plato, came
to be called "dualists." They were led to favor *dualism* because the (physicalist)
statements we make about peoples' bodies are obviously different in kind from the
(mentalist) statements we make about their thoughts and feelings. This difference
between physicalist and mentalist statements is especially acute in the context of
ethics, where peoples' mental volitions loom large in judgments of moral responsibility for their deeds.

144

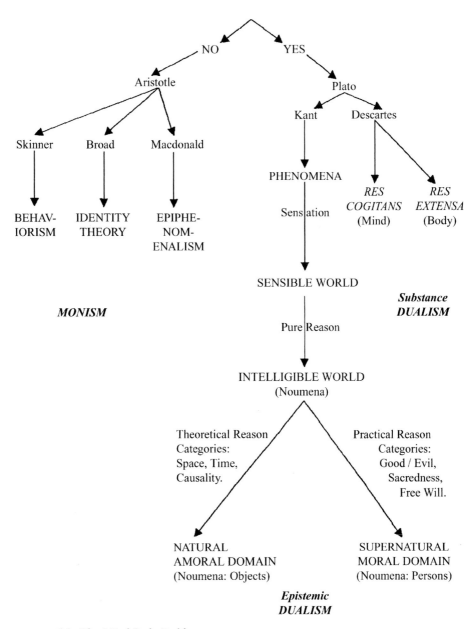

NO
YES

Aristotle
Plato

Skinner
Broad
Macdonald

Kant
Descartes

BEHAV-
IORISM
IDENTITY
THEORY
EPIPHE-
NOM-
ENALISM

PHENOMENA

Sensation

RES
COGITANS
(Mind)

RES
EXTENSA
(Body)

MONISM

SENSIBLE WORLD

Substance
DUALISM

Pure Reason

INTELLIGIBLE WORLD
(Noumena)

Theoretical Reason
Categories:
Space, Time,
Causality.

Practical Reason
Categories:
Good / Evil,
Sacredness,
Free Will.

NATURAL
AMORAL DOMAIN
(Noumena: Objects)

SUPERNATURAL
MORAL DOMAIN
(Noumena: Persons)

Epistemic
DUALISM

FIGURE 6.1. The Mind-Body Problem

Supporters of the alternative view, namely that mind is *not* a substance but merely an attribute of the human body, who included Plato's student Aristotle, came to be called "monists." They favored *monism* because they were beholden to the *materialist* doctrine about the nature of the world. According to materialism, physical matter is the world's only essential reality, with all being and all phenomena being accountable as manifestations or attributes of matter. Hence materialism holds that, as far as our presence in the natural the world is concerned, there is obviously nothing but the body.

Aristotle attributed mind to the heart, an ancient Egyptian attribution that still survives in modern language and ritual (for instance, in referring to the heart as the organ of love or in placing one's right hand over the heart while reciting the pledge of allegiance to the flag). Aristotelian monism received a strong boost in the second century CE when the Hellenist physician Galen demonstrated that the brain (rather than the heart) is the seat of consciousness and sensation. Galen's experiment, which involved vivisection of condemned Alexandrian prisoners, made it plausible that mentalist statements do in fact refer to brain states.

In the context of modern brain research, mind is considered to be a wholly natural thing, whose investigation is a principal objective of the discipline of neurobiology. The findings of neurobiological studies leave no doubt that the overall function of the human brain, just like the overall function of all other organs of the human body, is governed by the principles of physics and chemistry. Accordingly, it ought to be feasible to ascertain whether mental states, including morally relevant volitions, can be accounted for in terms of physicochemical brain states, such as electrical activity patterns in the network of cerebral nerve cells. If they can be, then mental states would be subject to the natural laws of causal determination, just as are all other bodily functions, such as respiration or digestion.

During the just ended "Decade of the Brain" proclaimed by President George Bush in 1990, some important methodological progress was actually made in the study of mental states that did bring significant advances in our understanding of the biological bases of thoughts and feelings. Probably the most promising among these novel methods is brain imaging, which permits the observation of states of the very parts of the living human brain that are involved in the generation of mental phenomena. Thus many of the most mysterious functions of the human brain, such as language, emotions, and cognition, that cannot be studied in experimental animals recently became accessible to neurobiological investigations (Damasio et al., 1996).

Three Modern Proposals for a Monist Solution

Although these latter-day developments in brain research have not yet led to a detailed account of the mechanisms of many important mental phenomena (including volition), most neurobiologists confidently expect that all these recent technical breakthroughs will soon reveal the physical bases of mental states. They, as well as many contemporary philosophers—such as Gilbert Ryle (1949/1984), who lampooned dualism as invoking a "ghost in the machine"—believe that all being and phenomena can be explained as manifestations or results of matter. As materialists, they follow the Aristotelian monist tradition and consider the mind-body enigma to be a pseudoproblem while regarding dualism as a fantasy of wooly headed fabulists. Aristotelian monism is the only game in town. The mind is the brain (Churchland, 1986; Crick, 1994).

How is mind instantiated as an attribute of the brain? The following three theories represent different examples of modern monist proposals that were devised to explain the relation of mind and body:

1. Certain psychologists put forward behaviorism, which enjoyed some popularity in the first half of the twentieth century. It asserted that there is no mind-body problem because mental states are not even genuine attributes of the brain, but are mere figments of the imagination. Behaviorists simply deny the existence of mental states and hence reject the idea that such ethical concepts as moral responsibility play a significant role in human social relations (Skinner, 1971). Behaviorism no longer has many adherents because it not only turned out to be incompatible with any ontologically reasonable intuition about morality and justice, but it even denied the reality of our most undeniable subjective experiences, such as pleasure and pain.

2. Epiphenomenalism appears, on first sight, to be a kind of dualism in that it envisages mental states as being different from brain states (Broad, 1925/1962). Yet on second sight, especially when considered in a moral context, it is essentially a monist theory, since it considers mentalist states as causally ineffective and gratuitous by-products of physicalist brain states. In other words, mental states would have no influence on behavior. Like behaviorism, epiphenomenalism not only seems to be incompatible with any ontologically reasonable intuition about morality and justice but, in view of its alleged causal inefficacy of subjective experiences such as pleasure and pain, also seems to reduce people to zombies or automata.

3. The identity theory is a modification of epiphenomenalism. Like epiphenomenalism, but unlike behaviorism, it does admit the existence of mental states as attributes of brain states in living creatures that have a conscious mind. Unlike epiphenomenalism however, the identity theory does consider mental states to be causally effective and hence capable of influencing behavior. It attributes the causal efficacy of mental states to some kind of "identity" between certain mental states and certain brain states, in the sense that "evening star" and "morning star" are alternative names for the identical planet Venus. Just as the two popular names of Venus denote different aspects of the same planet, so do "mental states" and "brain states" denote different aspects of the same organ of our body. We happen to know about the mental-state aspect of that organ from its inside, while our theories about the brain-state aspect happen to describe the same thing from the outside (Macdonald, 1989). Thus the identity theory is even more obviously a monist theory than is epiphenomenalism, since it holds that mental states are brain states, albeit of the special kind that presents different aspects from inside and outside.

Are Psychological Theories about Mental States Reducible to Neurobiological Theories about Brain States?

While contemporary psychologists are, on the whole, as beholden to monism as are neurobiologists, many psychologists reject in principle the possibility of developing a physicalist account of mind that would reduce psychological theories about mental states to neurobiological theories about brain states. The reasons for their in-principle rejection of the possibility of a neurobiological reduction of psychological theories about mental states usually include the following claims:

1. The intentional character of mental states makes them "emergent" properties of brain states and hence not wholly reducible to brain states.
2. The introspective nature of the perception of mental states renders them categorically different from and hence refractory to explanations by theories about extrospectively perceived brain states.
3. Such mental states as feelings, beliefs, and desires are imaginary, ad hoc concepts that do not correspond to anything in the real world, any more than did the concepts of "vital force" of naïve biology or of "phlogiston" of naïve thermodynamics.

In my opinion, these claims by psychologists regarding the in-principle impossibility of reducing psychological theories about mental states to neurobiological theories about brain states can be, and have been, successfully refuted (Churchland, 1986). In any case, from the neuroscientific perspective, reductionism is all we have. As a neurobiologist, I must hold that if mental states are attributable to brain states, they have to be explainable in principle by neurobiological theories. This view, however, does not commit me to the belief that a total reduction of psychological theories to neurobiological theories is actually possible in practice. The reason for this caveat is that the brain belongs to a class of phenomena whose high degree of complexity limits the extent to which theories developed to explain them can be successfully reduced by theories developed to explain less complex phenomena. That is why the project of total reduction of psychological theories to neurobiological theories is probably utopian in practice, even though it ought to be possible in principle. It seems likely, therefore, that a significant residue of unreduced psychological theory will remain with us long into the future.

The Persistence of Dualism

Yet despite its general overt rejection by neurobiologists, psychologists, and philosophers, dualism has remained viable in modern secular societies, albeit surviving mainly underground as a tacitly held belief. How has dualism managed to persist through all these years as other myths and unscientific misconceptions have fallen by the wayside in the course of ever-growing, no-nonsense scientific sophistication? The answer is that dualism is more compatible than monism with the ancient theory of human nature according to which mankind is partly beast and partly divine—that mankind lives both in as well as out of nature. The Israelite version of this theory has been passed on to us via the Book of Genesis and its story about Adam and Eve's ejection from the Garden of Eden once they stopped being amoral beasts and turned into moral creatures who, like God, knew evil. As archeological records eventually revealed, this theory of bipartite human nature dates back at least to predynastic Egypt, long before the Bible was written.

As translated into modern idiom, the centerpiece of that ancient theory is the person, who is comprised of both a body and a mind. The person's body is endowed with naturalistic attributes, which it shares with the beasts, and which are amenable to study by scientific methods. But the person's mind is endowed with supernaturalistic properties, such as uniqueness, irreplaceability, sacredness (i.e., being an end in itself), and free will. The mind shares these supernaturalistic properties, which are beyond the reach of study by scientific methods, with God rather than with the beasts. They provide the metaphysical foundations of morality, because according to the old and still vigorous tradition of moral philosophy descended from Plato, moral values cannot be accounted for by Aristotelian considerations of mankind as natural beasts. Rather, moral value devolves from the supernaturalistic properties of persons as autonomous agents. It is because of the rational difficulty of rejecting that ancient theory of the person out of hand that philosophers and theologians have wrestled with the part-beast, part-divine theory of human nature and have kept on putting forward dualist solutions of the mind-body problem.

Thus the latter-day obituary notices of dualism are premature; they merely reflect the failure of modern devotees of monism to fathom the moral foundations of the mind-body problem. However incisive and illuminating may have been the neurobiological progress made in recent years, monism remains the ontologically unsatisfactory solution of the mind-body problem that it always has been. While monism may be an adequate or perhaps even the only way to deal with mind as a natural phenomenon, it cannot give a satisfactory account of mind as a moral phenomenon.

At the dawn of the Middle Ages, in the fourth century CE, the first Christian philosopher, St. Augustine, was beholden to the Platonic dualist solution of the mind-body problem. He regarded the mind not as an attribute of the body but as a substance endowed with reason that rules the body. Augustine epitomized his dualist view by characterizing a person as an immortal rational mind that invests a mortal body during the person's secular lifetime and discards that body after the person's death, at the onset of its eternal afterlife.

Descartes's Dualism

The most notorious dualist solution of the mind-body problem—substance dualism—was put forward by the French mathematician-philosopher René Descartes in the mid-seventeenth century. Following in Plato's and Augustine's footsteps,

Descartes maintained that persons represent an amalgam of two distinct substances, or *re*. One of them was the material body, or *res extensa*, which Descartes thought of as the kind of mechanical automaton in human or animal form that enjoyed great popularity in seventeenth-century France. But persons were also endowed with spiritual qualities that automata obviously lacked. These spiritual qualities were attributes of the other substance of the amalgam, namely, the nonmaterial mind, or *res cogitans*, which made persons more than mechanical automata. Though lacking extent in physical space, the mind was nevertheless a separate substance rather than an attribute of the body.

According to Descartes, it was from their nonmaterial *res cogitans* that persons derived both their freedom of will and the responsibility for their actions, without which there could be no morality. Absent morality, all that would be available for the regulation of human social relations would be the kind of mindless conditioning envisaged by behaviorist psychologists such as B.F. Skinner, which, as we previously noted, is incompatible with any ontologically acceptable intuitions.

In his treatise *Passions of the Soul* Descartes provided some details about his notions regarding the nature of the amalgam of body and mind. He stressed that the mind's role in the body is not that of a pilot in a ship, whose only contact with the vessel is via the steering apparatus. Rather, the mind is connected to all parts of the body, so that it *directly* feels the body's pains and other sensations. Descartes conjectured that this connection is mediated by the pineal gland, located in the human brain just above the optic chiasm. He selected the gland for this honor because it lies as a single organ in the vertical midplane of the brain, and he believed (incorrectly) that the natural distribution of the pineal gland was limited to the human brain. In fact, the pineal gland is present in the brains of all vertebrate animals and is now known to subserve the regulation of diurnal physiological rhythms set by the daily light-darkness cycle. The picture Descartes offered was one of the mind communicating with the pineal gland and thus intervening in and being affected by the interaction between sensory input channels and motor output channels. That interaction is mediated by nerves (whose function he thought was of a hydraulic rather than, as we now know, electrical nature).

Descartes's version of mind-body dualism differed, however, from the dualism of antiquity and early Christian dogma, which had envisaged that the body owed its very life to the mind. Hence the proximate cause of a person's death was generally attributed to the mind's departure from the body. But Descartes claimed that the death of the body was attributable to the mechanical breakdown of the automaton, and that live bodies differed from dead bodies as running clocks differ from stopped clocks. Therefore the mind was not the essence of life in the here and now. Rather, upon death the immortal mind left the body because the *res cogitans* could not inhabit a lifeless body. Hence, according to Descartes, the exit of the mind from the body was the consequence rather than the cause of death.

Today this distinction between the alternative causes of death may seem like trivial metaphysical hairsplitting. Yet Descartes's concept that the human body is an automaton, that it owes its life to the proper operation of its working components, and that death is to be understood as a breakdown of the automaton stimulated the great scientific and medical progress that would be made in the following three centuries. This concept entailed the heuristic notion, which had also inspired Descartes's English contemporary, William Harvey (who identified the heart as a blood pump), that to understand the function of the body, it is necessary to study its components and find out how they make the automaton work. This notion was to provide the conceptual basis for the eventual rise of physiology, to which Descartes made some fundamental contributions.

Kant's Epistemic Dualism

By the latter part of the eighteenth century, the explanatory success of Isaac Newton's physics in the natural world of material substances had discredited Descartes's concept of a nonmaterial *res cogitans*. So, rather than abandoning dualism, Immanuel Kant replaced Descartes's substance dualism by a radically different kind of dualism, based on Kant's own theory of knowledge that he called "critical idealism." Kant's dualism differs fundamentally from Aristotelian monism or from Augustinian and Cartesian dualisms in that it is not a descriptive theory meant to represent the world as it is. Rather, Kantian dualism is a metaphysical theory meant to relate the two branches of metaphysics, ontology (which deals with the nature of our existence in the world) and epistemology (which deals with processes by which we come to know the world in the first place). To distinguish it from its predecessor substance dualisms, I have named Kant's dualism "epistemic dualism" (Stent, 1998).

The point of departure of Kant's theory of critical idealism was his insight that we humans are creatures who are sensual as well as rational. Our direct contact with the world's things is limited to the appearances that we perceive via our sensual faculties, such as sight, smell, hearing, and touch, in a sensible world of phenomena. We are familiar with that sensible world thanks to our everyday experience, which we share with the beasts, especially with our kin in the class of mammals. Thus we can know the world's things only as they appear to us in the abstract forms in which they reach our mind, but not as they may be in themselves. Yet we manage to make sense of and orient ourselves in that sensible world of phenomena by taking it for granted that the sources of the appearances of the phenomenal world are real things-in-themselves, or *noumena*.

The noumena whose existence we take for granted are not actually knowable, since we cannot perceive them directly via our senses. But noumena at least are thinkable and thus can serve as the elements of an indirectly inferred intelligible world. To identify these elements in our mind, we interpret our perceptions of phenomena in terms of a priori concepts, or categories, such as space, time, causality, and object, that are innate in our rational faculty. These categories arise a priori in our intuition rather than being derived a posteriori from experience. In our interpretive effort we also make tacit resort to categorical propositions inherent in our rational faculty, whose validity we similarly accept a priori rather than infer a posteriori from experience. Examples of such a priori categorical propositions are "Some A are B; therefore all A are B" (induction), or "The occurrence of a set of conditions A is both necessary and sufficient for the occurrence of B" (causation by A of B). Rational use of these categories and of categorical propositions then allows our mind to construct an orderly intelligible world from our sensory perceptions of the phenomena of the sensible world. Indeed, it is only in the process of constructing the intelligible world that sensory perceptions of phenomena become experience, that is, gain meaning, after the mind has interpreted them in terms of its a priori categories and categorical propositions. Kant designated the part of our rational faculty whence spring our a priori categories and propositions as pure reason, because it is not corrupted by our sensory impressions of the sensible world of unreliable and possibly misleading appearances.

Characterization of the Kantian categories as a priori for the individual does not mean, however, that they are present already full-blown at the person's birth. Instead, as the cognitive developmental studies that Jean Piaget initiated in the 1920s have shown, the Kantian categories arise in our mind postnatally, as a result of a dialectic interaction between the genome-controlled development of the human nervous system and the sensible world. Thus the Kantian categories, though immanent in the mind, develop gradually during childhood via a succession of distinct developmental stages by a process that Piaget (1971) termed "genetic epistemology."

Kant called his revolutionary epistemological doctrine "critical idealism" because it shares with other forms of idealism the rejection of the materialist doctrine that physical matter is the only essential reality in the world, and that all being and phenomena can be explained as manifestations of matter. Thus in designating space and time as a priori categories existing only in the human mind, Kant rejected the realist views of these concepts as self-subsisting things, or as relations between self-subsisting things, held, respectively, by Isaac Newton and Gottfried Leibniz. But unlike its predecessor idealist theories, such as that advocated by Plato, critical idealism provides a coherent, closely reasoned account of how we come to construct the ontological reality in which we live our lives.

The gist of Kant's epistemic dualism is that it invokes two metaphysically distinct domains of the intelligible world. According to Kant, to be human means to live as a dualist in both domains of the intelligible world, with either domain having been constructed by us by use of the categories of pure reason.

One of these domains is the naturalistic, amoral domain that we construct by use of the part of pure reason that Kant designated as "theoretical reason." Theoretical reason resorts to value-neutral, naturalistic categories, such as space, time, causality, and object. The naturalistic domain's noumena are objects, as exemplified by the starry heavens above. They are governed by the natural laws of causal determination.

The other domain is the supernaturalistic, moral domain that we construct by use of the part of pure reason termed "practical reason" by Kant. Practical reason resorts to value-laden, supernaturalistic categories, such as good and evil, sacredness, free will, and person. The supernaturalistic domain's noumena are persons, as exemplified by Kant himself. They are governed by the moral laws of freedom within them.

Epistemic dualism entails the belief that our interpretation of a person's actions is fundamentally different, depending on whether we encounter that person in an amoral, naturalistic context or in a moral, supernaturalistic context. In a naturalistic context—especially in a scientific setting—we regard human beings as objects whose actions form part of the causally determined events of nature. But in a moral context we regard them as subjects whose actions are determined by freely willed decisions made autonomously in their minds rather than heteronomously determined by inflexible natural laws acting on their bodies.

Evolutionary Epistemology

How can it be that if our mind brings the Kantian categories to the sensible world of phenomena a priori, they happen to fit that world so well? In the mid-twentieth century, the Austrian ethologist Konrad Lorenz (1944) provided a Darwinist answer to that question. According to Lorenz, what is a priori for individuals is a posteriori for their species, because experience has as little to do with the matching of the Kantian categories with reality as has the fin structure of a fish with the properties of water. The success of our brain in constructing an intelligible world that is well matched with the phenomenal world is simply another product of the natural selection process that guided the development of our brain in the course of our evolutionary history. Any early hominids who happened to think that before is after, or that near is far, or who failed to apprehend that phenomenon A is the cause of phenomenon B left few descendants. Lorenz's evolutionary explanations of the origins of the Kantian categories gave rise to a discipline at the interface between biology and philosophy called evolutionary epistemology (Campbell, 1974).

Let us grant that, as the adherents of monism would have it, mental states are brain states. Then it would follow that, in line with the dogma of evolutionary epistemology, our brain is genetically endowed with some innate mental states. One set of mental states would include the value-neutral Kantian categories of theoretical reason, by means of which we deal with the natural, amoral domain of objects. But since our species, *Homo sapiens*, has always lived as a social animal, the dogma of evolutionary epistemology leads to the further conclusion, still fully in harmony with monism, that natural selection endowed our brain also with another set of mental states. That other set of innate mental states would correspond to the value-laden Kantian categories of practical reason, by means of which we deal with the supernaturalistic, moral domain of persons.

Some of the person's supernaturalistic properties, such as uniqueness, irreplaceability, and sacredness, are add-ons to the naturalistic properties of the person's body, with which they are not in rational conflict. But there is at least one supernaturalistic property that *is* in conflict, namely, free will.

In neuroscientific circles free will is generally considered as a pseudoproblem and its discussion as a waste of time, like arguing about extrasensory perception. For instance, Churchland (1986) argued that the recent advances in neurobiology are going to allow us soon to account for all naturalistic mental states in neuro-biological terms. Meanwhile she consigned the supernaturalistic attributes of the mind—free will foremost among them—along with dualism to the historical gar-bage heap of abandoned theories.

This expectation is unlikely to materialize in the near future, at least not before we abandon the traditional theory of the person as a moral agent whose free will is one of its indispensable supernaturalistic categories. To judge a person's action as morally praise- or blameworthy, we must presume that the person both willed it and was free not to will it. Thus Kantian ontology justifies the concept of free will as a logically necessary component of the theory of personhood that governs the interpersonal relations of moral agents. This simple truth is obvious in the law courts, the arenas of applied moral philosophy. To find anyone guilty of a crime and impose a punishment, a judge or jury must hold the criminal morally responsible, that is, posit that a person with free will committed the crime.

Interactionism

Perhaps it is not surprising that only a few contemporary neurobiologists or psy-chologists who profess an interest in the mind-body problem accept—or are even aware of—Kant's epistemic dualism. After all, most of them are beholden (tacitly or overtly) to materialism and seem to be unaware of the shortcomings of monism in the context of morality. But it does seem surprising that so many among even those contemporary philosophers who are aware of the ontological inadequacy of monism and who do favor some kind of dualism fail to mention Kant's epistemic dualism. Instead, they put forward various, in my view much less satisfactory so-lutions of the mind-body problem.

One of the best-known contemporary examples of a non-Kantian dualist the-ory was presented by two renowned scholars, the Austro-British philosopher Karl G. Popper and the Australian neurobiologist John C. Eccles. In their collaborative book *The Self and Its Brain*, they accepted the Kantian category of the person (to which they referred as a "self") as a morally responsible, autonomous agent with free will. Their aim was to reconcile the Kantian notion of personal autonomy with modern (mid-twentieth-century) neurobiological insights into brain states.

The solution of the mind-body problem offered by Popper and Eccles (1977) was a variant of Descartes's substance dualism in that their theory, which they designated "interactionism," envisaged that mental states were real and existed as entities distinct from brain states. Interactionism shares with Kantian critical ide-alism the ontological idea that we live in more than one world—according to Popper and Eccles's triune rather than dual theory, in three metaphysically distinct worlds. World 1 comprises the universe of physical objects that are the source of our sensory impressions. World 2 comprises the universe of mental states that include psychological dispositions and conscious as well as unconscious states. And World 3 comprises the contents of thought and, in particular, the intellectual products of the human mind.

The nub of Popper and Eccles's theory is that the mental states representing Worlds 2 and 3 interact reciprocally with the brain states that mediate the input sensations from World 1 and the motor outputs to it. On the one hand, the mental states of Worlds 2 and 3 are causally effective in governing behavior by interacting with the brain states responsible for the physical implementation in World 1 of the decisions made by mental states. On the other hand, the brain states responsible for the input sensations from World 1 are causally effective in influencing the mental states that represent Worlds 2 and 3. Interactionism thus provides for the autonomy essential for the exercise of free will by allowing for the possibility of an intervention by an autonomous self in the interaction between mental and brain states.

Popper and Eccles make no reference to Kantian dualism (except for a brief mention of Kant's assertion of the "unknowability" of things-in-themselves), nor do they consider how—or even whether—the three worlds of their theory relate to the sensible and intelligible (or to the phenomenal and noumenal) worlds of Kantian critical idealism. In a first approximation, Worlds 1 and 2 might correspond to Kant's sensible world, while World 3 might correspond to Kant's intelligible world. But if there is any conceptual match between interactionism and epistemic dualism, it is not very close. Popper and Eccles do refer to what they call "Kant's strange distinction" between theoretical and practical reason in the construction of the intelligible world. However, they do not comment on its possible relevance for their concept of World 3.

In his review of *The Self and Its Brain*, the cognitive scientist Donald MacKay (1978) found that

> what makes [Popper and Eccles's] joint effort so remarkable is that it seeks to reverse an all but universal trend in contemporary thinking about the relation of mind to brain. For a couple of decades at least, the great majority of brain scientists have proceeded on the working assumption that the central nervous system is a physically determined system in the same sense as the heart or lungs or any part of the body. . . . Yet here, in 1977, is a book in which two acknowledged leaders in scientific thought condemn this whole trend as misguided and obstructive of progress.

As MacKay observed, monism and all of its latter-day versions were fatally deficient because they could not give "the fullest recognition of the moral and spiritual dimensions of our human nature." Dualism, by contrast, "offers the only way to do justice to the data of experience." Yet MacKay concluded his review by saying that he did not believe that Popper and Eccles had established their case for an "interactionist" version of dualism. In particular, they failed to put forward any neurobiologically credible mechanism to account for the supposed interaction between mental and brain states or for the intervention in that interaction by the autonomous self in the service of free will. All the same, MacKay wished *The Self and Its Brain* (pp. 599–606), "whatever may be the fate of its more adventurous speculations, a long life as a spur to the theorist of cognitive functions." MacKay's good wishes did not materialize. Insofar as *The Self and Its Brain* is still known at all, it is remembered as a philosophical *folie-à-deux* of two *éminences grises*.

Complementarity

In putting forward his epistemic dualism in the latter part of the eighteenth century, Kant anticipated the concept of complementarity introduced into physics by Niels Bohr in the first part of the twentieth century. In his use of the term "complementarity" Bohr did not refer to its ordinary, everyday meaning—the aspects of two different parts that make them a whole. Rather, under Bohr's meaning, complementary aspects of the world give rise to rationally irreconcilable concepts whose inconsistency can never be demonstrated empirically (Bohr, 1933).

Bohr presented his complementarity concept upon the advent of quantum mechanics and its epistemological paradoxes, such as the incoherent description of the electron in terms of both a wave and a particle. According to Bohr, the wavelike mode of electron propagation, on the one hand, and the particulate nature of electron effects, on the other, both express important features of the phenomena associated with electrons. These features are complementary aspects of reality because, although they are irreconcilable from a conceptual point of view, there are no observational setups under which they can be shown to be in direct contradiction. The reason why no empirical contradiction is demonstrable is that a critical demonstration of either the wave or the particle nature of the electron demands mutually exclusive observational arrangements.

To illustrate this point, Bohr presented a thought experiment whose apparatus consisted of a gun that shoots an electron beam at a wall. The wall has two small holes through which some of the electrons impinging on it may pass and then hit a backstop at some distance behind the wall. Either hole can be opened or closed. When only one of the holes is open, the distribution of electrons hitting the backstop is characteristic of discrete particles that happened to go through the single open hole, but when both holes are open, the electron distribution hitting the backstop is not characteristic of discrete particles, but of a continuous wave of radiation impinging on the wall. This second result implies that when both holes are open, one and the same electron goes through both holes, as it would if it were propagated as a wave.

To check out this uncanny inference, the setup is modified to include also a monitor that can register directly whether a given electron went through hole 1 through hole 2, or through both holes. The monitor shows that when both holes are open, any given electron actually goes through only one of the two open holes, as it ought to if it were a particle. Under this modified setup, however, the distribution of electrons hitting the backstop is no longer that characteristic of a wave, even though both holes are open, but that of discrete particles impinging on the wall, some of which went through hole 1 and others through hole 2. This third result leads to the even more uncanny inference that a single electron goes through both holes only when we are not watching through which hole it actually went. It is uncanny, but not contradictory, as it would have been if the device had shown that any given electron goes through only one of the two open holes, yet the electron distribution at the backstop is still that characteristic of an electron wave.

The furthest-reaching epistemological consequence of Bohr's complementarity concept, however, is that far from having both properties of wave and particle, an electron takes on one or the other property only as we are watching it under one or the other of mutually exclusive observational setups. Thus, according to Bohr, in the drama of existence, we play the dual role of actor and observer. It seems ironical, indeed bizarre, that this conclusion should have been forced on us by physics, for it spells the end of naïve realism — the commonsensical belief that there exists a real world of things external to us and independent of our experience of it, and that this real world actually is as we see, hear, feel, and smell it.

Applying to the mind-body problem Bohr's insight that mutually exclusive observational arrangements are needed for the study of complementary aspects of the electron, we can see the reason that we cannot fathom mind from a single, coherent set of beliefs about the world. Mind has to be approached from the two mutually exclusive starting positions in the intelligible world of epistemic dualism: the naturalistic, amoral domain of objects and the supernaturalistic, moral domain of subjects. Just like complementarity, epistemic dualism turns out to be antithetical to the metaphysical foundations of science.

Coda

Thus the beastly and the divine, the natural and the supernatural, all appear to be complementary aspects of human nature. But how did mind, with its innate Kantian categories, arise in the course of organic evolution? Konrad Lorenz's argument that the human mind was no less subject to Darwinian natural selection than the human body provides the answer. Hominids who happened to carry a set of genes that evoke mental states corresponding to the Kantian categories were favored by a higher differential reproductive rate because their minds were able to construct a reality with a superior match with the world of natural objects and supernatural subjects.

There exists a specialized discipline, styled sociobiology, dedicated to the evolutionarily oriented study of the social behavior of animals (Wilson, 1975). Some of its practitioners also apply Darwinist principles to devising accounts of the origins of human social behavior. Working in the Aristotelian monist-naturalistic tradition, which considers *Homo sapiens* as just another species of social animals, sociobiologists extend the theories they have devised to account for the evolution of social behavior among the birds and the bees to the origins of human morality.

They have little trouble in arguing how a social animal acting in accord with a genetically determined, innate belief in the sacred, unique person endowed with autonomous free will would have been provided with a higher differential reproductive potential. That is, from the sociobiological perspective it is not difficult to put forward more or less plausible theories in support of the evolutionary fitness of a social animal carrying a brain with mental states corresponding to naturalistic and supernaturalistic Kantian categories.

So far, so good. But some sociobiologists proclaim that thanks to their insights into the evolutionary origins of supernaturalistic categories, we finally can rid ourselves of our paradoxical metaphysical hangups. After all, don't we believe that neurotics are able to rid themselves of disabling mental obsessions once psychoanalysis has uncovered their psychogenetic origins? Even if supernaturalistic categories did provide Darwinian fitness to our caveperson ancestors, so the sociobiological reasoning goes, we have no further need for them these days, when they just cause us no end of trouble.

I believe that this sociobiological prognosis is unlikely to be realized. Admittedly, our intuitive attribution of free will to the person is incompatible with our attribution of causal necessity to nature. Yet as rational beings, we do not seem to be able to abandon the idea of supernatural moral autonomy any more than we can abandon the idea of natural causal necessity. Indeed, those rare individuals who have abandoned either of these ideas are usually diagnosed as psychopaths, and most of them live in prisons or mental institutions. I doubt that philosophers will be able to develop a solution to the mind-body problem that is much of an improvement over Kant's internally incoherent epistemic dualism. Being the bizarre creatures that we are, we have no choice other than to consider the beastly and the divine, or the natural and the supernatural, as complementary aspects of the person. That is the deeply paradoxical nature of the mind that we drew in the lottery of organic evolution.

References

Bohr, N. 1933. "Light and Life." *Nature 131*, pp. 421–23, 457–59.

Broad, C.D. 1925/1962. *The Mind and Its Place in Nature*. London: Routledge and Kegan Paul.

Campbell, D.T. 1974. "Evolutionary Epistemology," in P.A. Schilppe (Ed.). *The Philosophy of Karl Popper*, The Library of Living Philosophers. Vol. 14. La Salle, IL: Open Court.

Churchland, P.S. 1986. *Neurophilosophy*. Cambridge, MA: MIT Press.

Crick, F.H.C. 1994. *The Astonishing Hypothesis: The Scientific Search for the Soul*. New York: Scribner.

Damasio, H., T.S. Grabowski, D. Tranel, R.D. Hichwa, and A. Damasio, 1996. "A Neural Basis for Lexical Retrieval." *Nature 380*, 499–506.

Kant, I. 1934. *Critique of Pure Reason*. Trans. N.K. Smith. London: Macmillan.

———. 1949. *Critique of Practical Reason*. Trans. L.W. Beck. Chicago: University of Chicago Press.

Lorenz, K. 1944. "Kant's Lehre vom Apriorischen im Lichte gegenwärtiger Biologie." *Blätter für deutsche Philosophie*, 18, pp. 94–125.

Macdonald, C. 1989. *Mind-Body Identity Theories*. London: Routledge.

MacKay, D.M. 1978. "Selves and Brains." *Neuroscience*, 3, pp. 599–606.

Piaget, J. 1971. *Genetic Epistemology*. Trans. E. Duckworth. New York: Norton.

Popper, K.G., and J.C. Eccles. 1977. *The Self and Its Brain*. Berlin: Springer International.

Ryle, G. 1949/1984. *The Concept of Mind*. London: Hutchinson.

Skinner, B.F. 1971. *Beyond Freedom and Dignity*. New York: Knopf.

Stent, G.S. 1998. "Epistemic Dualism of Mind and Body." *Proceedings of the American Philosophical Society*, 142(4), pp. 578–88.

Wilson, E.O. 1975. *Sociobiology: The New Synthesis*. Cambridge, MA: Belknap Press of Harvard University Press.

7

Mind, Brain, and Culture

David R. Olson

Ever since Descartes advanced his argument that the mind (what today we would call mental structures) is to be clearly distinguished from body (what today we would call neurological structures)—the famous doctrine of dualism—philosophers and psychologists have attempted to state just how mind and body are related (Cummins, 2000, p. 128). Some, the materialists, deny the literal existence of mind, claiming it to be epiphenomenal; others, phenomenologists, deny body, claiming that we live in a world as experienced. Still others deny that there is a problem, since mind is just one aspect of bodily function. Yet others claim that dualism is correct, if not exactly as Descartes set it out. Gunther Stent is in the last group.

Stent grants that monism, the view that there is only one type of substance, and that is material substance, may be the only way to deal with mind as a natural, biological system, but monism cannot give an account of mind as a moral, logical, or normative phenomenon. There are, as Nietzsche famously said, no laws of nature. Laws are of human invention, as are rules, conventions, definitions, and principles. How are we to account for these normative structures? Are we simply to set aside our concern with logic, truth, moral obligation, and the like?

To acknowledge the importance of these normative concerns, Stent suggests that dualism, however repugnant, must be invoked. But he is talking about a dualism of a different kind from that of Descartes. Descartes, driven to defend his mind-body distinction, appealed to two substances, a mental substance and a physical substance. We no longer have any patience with "mental substance" and hence little patience with Descartes. Kant's solution, as pointed out by Stent, was to set aside the hope of glimpsing things simply as they are and to acknowledge that human experience is always a product of human knowledge. As we now would say, we see the world in terms of our available models. The philosophical question we have to answer is how the mind goes about constructing knowledge of various kinds. As Stent points out, the gist of Kant's dualism was that we construct knowledge about two quite distinct worlds—the world of nature, which we construct by methods of pure reason directed at the formation of causal laws, and the world of human moral nature, which we construct by means of practical reason directed at the formation of norms and rules in the service of ideals and goals. Kantian dualism is therefore epistemic dualism directed not at two kinds of substance in the natural world but rather at two kinds of knowledge created and evaluated by human minds.

Stent acknowledges that epistemic dualism may capture a true or at least a valid distinction without solving the question posed by cognitive science about the nature of mind. Cognitive science is concerned with the natural science question, the first of Kant's categories, about the mind. Is mind a causal, biological mechanism, or is something else needed for a satisfactory account of mind? Is mind a natural object? (We know as well that it is a cultural object, but we can come back to that.) As Stent grants, following such writers as Dennett, in the attempt to provide a scientific explanation of intention, for example, "Reduction . . . is all we have (148)."

But Stent does not insist that the sciences of the mind confine their efforts to the reductionism program. His reason for embracing the normative or moral dimensions of mind is not that monism is false. Rather, it is that although this view is a possible one, in principle, it is not feasible for reasons of sheer complexity: "It seems likely . . . that a significant residue of unreduced psychological theory will remain with us long into the future." Meanwhile, Stent proposes that we have two other options that will help us to acknowledge in our theories what is simply inescapable in our social worlds—the existence of such normative factors as free will and responsibility. (I would add as well the inescapability of first-person conscious experience.) These options are, first, Bohr's concept of complementarity, the possibility of incommensurable but complementary descriptions of a single event. It may be that we cannot understand the mind from a single perspective, just as we cannot understand light as exclusively wave or particle. This option harks back to Kantian epistemological dualism.

The other option Stent offers is that of evolutionary epistemology—the possibility that evolution has selected humans to have ideas of a certain type. Persons holding dramatically false beliefs would be less likely to contribute their genes to the gene pool. Those contributing may have been more likely to entertain ideas about truth and goodness, as well as about space, time, and number. In my view, evolutionary epistemology may help to explain why some ideas are easily acquired. It may be easier to acquire the belief in the value of those sharing the same family or ethnic identity than the value of strangers; but that does not make the belief more valid. Some ideas may be difficult to acquire and yet may be valid or true or good. We may be predisposed evolutionarily to believe that we are motionless and the stars rotate around us, but that does not make the belief true. Closer to home, we may be predisposed to ascribe intentionality and responsibility to ourselves and others, but again the predisposition may be an illusion. With Stent, I believe that intentionality and responsibility are not illusory, but I fail to see how an evolutionary bias to believe so makes it so.

Let me be more specific. If evolution has selected us to be intentional creatures, prone to honor truth, goodness, and responsibility, we still have to answer the question how, by working with the purely causal mechanisms of the brain, that is achieved. How, in a word, could norms for truth and goodness arise in a purely causal system? If evolution merely has evolved a way of thinking, as in Kantian epistemology, to allow us to manage social behavior, including rules for truth telling and acting morally and responsibly, we may have an explanation of why we have the illusion of free will, but that will not allow us to achieve our scientific goal of explaining how such behavior is actually achieved. The cognitive science question is not only or even primarily about what is believed so much as about how a brain could form something like a belief in the first place. Again, I see no refuge in evolutionary epistemology.

How, then, are we to proceed? My suggestion, unsurprisingly, is that we may profitably take a developmental perspective on this. First, consider the issue of moral responsibility from the perspective of genetic psychology. Infants and young children, although possessing intact brains, have not yet reached what we call the "age of accountability." We ascribe neither free will nor responsibility to them. The same is true for our non-language-using primate cousins. We assign responsibility only to language-using creatures, and then only when they reach a certain, rather high, level of competence. For intentionality, responsibility, and accountability we need a language—and not a Fodorian "language of thought" (Fodor, 1975), but rather an acquired, full-scale ordinary language that, once acquired, can function as a language of thought. More than that, accountability and responsibility, including the ability to make judgments of truth and goodness, require a metalanguage, a language that allows one to formulate not only statements, but statements about statements. This metarepresentational development in children, a class of research that proceeds under the label of "children's theory of mind," has indicated quite clearly that such competencies fall into the child's reach only in the late preschool or early school years.

The primary focus of this research is on young children's understanding of the belief in themselves and others. Most parents recall with amusement the failed efforts of three- and four-year-olds to keep a secret, tell a lie, play hide-and-seek, and the like. In the past decade it has become clear that such failures reflect a general inability to think about the epistemic states of others, specifically, that someone could hold a belief that they themselves know to be false (Astington, Harris, and Olson, 1988). Interestingly, they also fail to acknowledge that they themselves could have held such beliefs. Their own as well as others' mental states, in particular those of belief, are not accessible to them. As Perner (1991) has suggested, children's models are models of situations taken to be true, not models of their own and others' minds. Such understandings of mind are said to be metarepresentational in that the difficulties the child faces are not so much in forming representational states such as beliefs as in representing such states as beliefs—that is, a consciousness of beliefs.

This metarepresentational development may also be seen in children's use of, and later, in their knowledge about the use of, language. Two-year-old children, in learning a language, learn to make statements, even using a single word. "Cat" while pointing at a cat can be taken as an elliptical form of the assertion "That is a cat." Such assertions may be true or false and may be accepted or corrected by parents: "No, that is a dog." However, making a statement about a statement such as "It is true that that is a cat" is a much more complex metarepresentational achievement tied to the management of complex clauses within or between sentences. Consequently, the ability to judge a negative statement as true is something that children manage only when they are about six or seven years of age, roughly the age of accountability.

How does this bear on the mind-body problem? I believe that Stent is correct in insisting that if a psychology is to be of any interest, let alone significance, it must center on judgments of truth and goodness and the ability to act intentionally in terms of these judgments. But we already have noted that such judgments are not to be seen in the early and hence basic functioning of the human nervous system, but only in the activities of a person with sophisticated linguistic powers — powers that are not only representational but also metarepresentational. I further agree with Stent that monism, the view that there is only one kind of material substance — the kind ultimately characterizable in terms of physical science — is correct. Is there a way to reconcile these two claims?

Perhaps, first, we have to reduce our ambitions by not looking for normative structures — judgments of truth and goodness — in the basic working of the brain. These are higher-order structures and processes dependent upon high-level cognitive, indeed cultural, resources. They are part of the systems or structures in the cultural world, analogous to the structures in the physical world that are mechanically detected by perceptual mechanisms, on which brain structures operate. There is some hope that current work employing connectionist models may model not only situations, but also language about situations. Models of relations between perceived situations and language about these situations are what allow judgments of truth and falsity and also may fall to that modeling game. What we call mind is the set of models or structures that this causal machine, the brain, has constructed for the management of action and interaction in a social world. The move to intentionality comes with the acquisition of language and the use of language to represent events. Responsibility and accountability come later with the ability to make statements about statements. Rather than finding intentionality and responsibility in the internal biological properties of the brain, we find them in the models and relations that the brain comes to represent as a consequence of a long period of learning and development. I have elsewhere (Olson, 1994) examined in some detail how writing allows for a somewhat distinctive representation of language, world, and mind.

Consequently, the processes of the biological brain used to construct these models remain much the same across development — they remain causal and computational — but the products they construct change as a function of type of representation. This is a view that is becoming more common in the cognitive sciences. Thus Clark (1997, p. 98) has made much the same point: "It remains possible that such [higher-order intentional action] does not involve the use of any fundamentally different kind of computational device in the brain so much as the use of the same old (essentially pattern-completing) resources to model the special kinds of behavior observed in the world of public language." Bechtel (1997, p. 189) goes further, suggesting that the basic cognitive processing mechanisms are networks of connections that themselves are not propositional and inferential, but that when these networks are supplemented by external symbols such as speech and writing, they can achieve the effects we recognize as inference and judgment: "To the degree that cognition is systematic, it is due to the ability of an embodied [connectionist] cognitive system to use symbols in the environment that afford syntactical structuring." It is in this sense that mind is a cultural product constructed by the biological brain; while the mind is recognized by its normative properties, the brain remains causal and computational. This, too, is a dualism, but neither one of substance nor one of epistemology, but rather one of development in a world of public symbols.

References

Astington, J., Harris, P., and Olson, D. 1988. *Developing Theories of Mind*. Cambridge: Cambridge University Press.

Bechtel, W. 1997. "Embodied Connectionism." Pp. 187–208 in D.M. Johnson and C.E. Erneling (Eds.), *The Future of the Cognitive Revolution*. New York: Oxford University Press.

Clark, A. 1997. *Being There: Putting Brain, Body, and World Together Again*. Cambridge, MA: MIT Press.

Cummins, R. 2000. " 'How Does It Work?' versus 'What Are the Laws?': Two Conceptions of Psychological Explanation." Pp. 117–144 in F. Keil and R. Wilson (Eds.), *Explanation and Cognition*. Cambridge, MA: MIT Press.

Dennett, D. 1978. *Brainstorms: Philosophical Essays on Mind and Psychology*. Sussex: Harvester.

Fodor, J. 1975. *The Language of Thought*. New York: Crowell.

Johnson, D.M., and Erneling, C.E. (Eds.). 1997. *The Future of the Cognitive Revolution*. New York: Oxford University Press.

Keil, F., and Wilson, R. (Eds.). 2000. *Explanation and Cognition*. Cambridge, MA: MIT Press.

Olson, D. 1994. *The World on Paper: The Conceptual and Cognitive Implications of Writing and Reading*. Cambridge, UK: Cambridge University Press.

Perner, J. 1991. *Understanding the Representational Mind*. Cambridge, MA: MIT Press.

8

Chalmers's Naturalistic Dualism: The Irrelevance of the Mind-Body Problem to the Scientific Study of Consciousness

Don Ross

If the scientific study of consciousness was once neglected—as almost every book published on the subject begins by reminding us—the opposite has been the case during the past decade. Shelves groan with recent books, articles, and new journals as cognitive scientists crowd into the space left vacant since the project of "scientific phenomenology," as Edmund Husserl imagined it, was abandoned by his closest but skeptical students. In 1991, Daniel Dennett published *Consciousness Explained*, which implied, in its bold title, that where Husserl had failed, the contemporary synthesis of cognitive scientific disciplines has already succeeded. Dennett's apparent hubris inevitably produced a backlash, a storm of claims to the effect that his story is satisfying only to the extent that it avoids the supposedly difficult problems. I have dealt elsewhere (Ross, 1994) with the objections raised by the first wave of critics. Dennett, I argued, has not so much produced a theory of consciousness, in the standard sense of the term, as a set of suggestions for reconceptualizing the subject so as to make it amenable to scientific study. It remains my view that this reconceptualization shows the way forward.

Meanwhile, however, the backlash has grown stronger, at least rhetorically. Where most of Dennett's initial critics, such as Block (1993), argued that his reconceptualization was incomplete, the most widely read of recent authors, David Chalmers (1996), argues that the very project of reconceptualizing consciousness is mistaken. In another recent and widely-ranging study, Norton Nelkin (1996) makes essentially the same point. Both Chalmers and Nelkin label their positions in ways that sound shockingly retrograde and (in the case of Chalmers) oxymoronic to the antirationalist and materialist spirit that has dominated the literature: Nelkin calls his view "scientific Cartesianism," and Chalmers, even more jarringly, dubs himself a "naturalistic dualist." There is, however, something peculiar in these revisionist accounts: When they depart from the space of the purely conceptual and offer suggestions as to how the scientific study of consciousness actually should proceed, both sound surprisingly like Dennett. How is it that such apparently strident rhetorical disagreements can make so little difference to the practical issues surrounding the methodology of consciousness studies?

In what follows, I will focus on the tension between Chalmers and Dennett, both because I have dealt with Nelkin's views elsewhere (Ross, 1999), and because Chalmers's is by far the more apparently radical of the two challenges. Chalmers is not, of course, merely reacting to Dennett: He claims to reject the entire approach he calls "reductive functionalism," of which he (like Nelkin) regards Dennett's as the most sophisticated particular expression. As we shall see, much philosophical heat begins to cool if we try to be careful in our use of charged adjectives such as "reductive." However, I will be arguing for a broader thesis, potentially more disturbing to philosophers of consciousness, namely, that traditional philosophical arguments over the ontological relationship between the mind and the body have become simply irrelevant to practical cognitive science. Nothing significant, I will argue, turns on whether a theorist chooses to call her or his position materialist, monist, dualist, epiphenomenalist, or whatnot. The fact that Chalmers could argue for dualism—the most heretical position of them all in the contemporary literature—without this making any methodological difference is, I will argue, the most revealing available indicator of my general point.

Before delving into the details of Chalmers's work, let us first canvass the general issues at stake between him and his "reductive functionalist" opponents, Dennett in particular. Dennett is at his most rhetorically shocking in denying (a) the possibility of phenomenology and (b) the existence of qualia. But as a careful reading of Dennett makes clear, (a) is not equivalent to the epistemological claim that first-person reports of sensations are irrelevant to the study of consciousness, and (b) is not equivalent to the ontological claim that people and other creatures do not have sensations at all. As Chalmers and others note with great force, the second claim would fly directly in the face of fundamental and universal experience, and the first would cut us off from the main source of evidence we have into the phenomena we are setting out to study. But this force is deployed against nonexistent opposition. All Dennett intends by claim (a) is that we shall not get far in our study of consciousness if we follow Husserl's recipe and simply compile subjects' reports of their sensations, mainly because subjects tend to deliver such reports in terms of categories that presuppose an almost certainly false folk theory of mind. Thus the Husserlian methodology would guarantee that progress toward an improved theory would be blocked. Dennett's claim (b) is largely semantic: His point is that "qualia" is a concept that has become loaded with a battery of associated properties—(1) ineffability, (2) intrinsicality, (3) privacy, and (4) direct accessibility—that, he argues, no general type over which cognitive-scientific theories might quantify satisfies. In place of Husserlian methodology and the Husserlian project of compiling a catalog of qualia, Dennett urges us to take subjects' introspective reports as corrigible data, which stand to be amended as we fill in the details of a unified functional theory of the mind/brain.

Chalmers essentially accepts Dennett's proposed methodology, since, he argues, our only means of studying consciousness is to search for "organizationally invariant features" in neural and information-processing architectures, which are linked by psychophysical laws with types of dispositions on the part of subjects to report that they are having particular sorts of qualitative experiences. Thus Chalmers agrees with Dennett's claim (*a*) so long as that claim is understood as Dennett intends it, as a claim about methodology. He disagrees with Dennett's claim (*b*), even on its proper, nonabsurd interpretation, but does so on the basis of no argument whatsoever. Instead, he merely asserts that we "know" that there are qualia bearing the traditional properties. However, the "we" here must be qualified, since Dennett (among others) is evidently in possession of no such knowledge, if one grants that one cannot know what one does not believe. Here Chalmers suggests that he and Dennett stand on opposite sides of a "Great Divide" (Chalmers, 1996, p. xiii) between, in effect, those who believe that the world contains qualia and those who do not. In response to Dennett's claim that introspection reveals nothing but judgments that one is in various particular experiential states at various times, Chalmers replies, "To this, all I can say is that Dennett's introspection is very different from mine" (Chalmers, 1996, p. 189). In fact, however, that is not all that Chalmers thinks that he can say, since he goes on to offer a diagnosis of Dennett's mistake, which does not involve the hypothesis that Dennett is a zombie: "In general when one starts from phenomenal judgments as the explananda of one's theory of consciousness, one will inevitably be led to a reductive view. But the ultimate explananda are not the judgments but experiences themselves. No mere explanation of dispositions to behave will explain why there is something it is like to be a conscious agent" (Chalmers, 1996, p. 191). This does not constitute an argument, however; it is merely a reiteration of Chalmers's basic intuition that phenomenal qualia are fundamental features of reality, independent of the psychological phenomena (reactions, judgments, dispositions to issue public and private reports, and so on) that, lawfully or not, accompany them.

It should not be supposed that I am accusing Chalmers of imagining that he has arguments where he does not. He is quite clear from the beginning that his strategy is to lighten the burden of argument carried by the dualist through showing that his intuitions fare as well in the face of the data as those held by "reductive functionalists." And this enterprise does involve arguments, of which Chalmers supplies many. I will not review most of these arguments, as my purpose here is not to try to drag Chalmers across his Great Divide. Rather, what I wish to do is shed some light on why so "great" a chasm can turn out to make so little difference to practical issues in cognitive science. My central claim will be that for all Chalmers's avowal of naturalism, he does not take it sufficiently seriously. The result is a prying apart of the gap that genuine naturalists, such as Quine, Churchland, and Dennett, have strenuously attempted to close — that between purely conceptual speculation and empirical study. My target, then, is larger than Chalmers's position itself: It is any sort of philosophical cognitive science that places too much weight on intuitions and questions of conceivability.

Let us begin by distinguishing two sorts of naturalism, which I shall label "weak" and "strong." A weak naturalist is someone who supposes that ontological and epistemological theses should be constrained by empirical evidence, in the sense that we are free to speculate within such constraints, but must not allow conceivability considerations to trump empirical ones. (Thus, for example, the weak naturalist must wrestle with the implications of Aspect's confirmation of the Einstein-Podolsky-Rosen prediction [see Mermin, 1985], rather than ignore or dismiss it on the grounds that it violates fundamental logical intuitions.) Chalmers is a sincere weak naturalist, and he takes this seriously when, in his book, he turns from his argument for dualism to practical suggestions for constructing a scientific theory of consciousness. There is, however, a stronger variety of naturalism. On this interpretation, what is conceivable is irrelevant to the probability of a speculative hypothesis being true, except in the negative and trivial sense that one cannot postulate what one cannot represent. (I use "represent" here because we can mathematically represent situations, especially in microphysics, of which we cannot conceive in any other way.) According to such naturalism, which perhaps finds its clearest and strongest expression in Churchland (1979), the true master of metaphysical speculation is induction on the history of science. Thus, to cite some notable examples, the argument for reductionism given by Oppenheim and Putnam (1958) is strongly naturalistic in that its argument is based strictly upon extrapolation of trends toward reduction across the suite of scientific disciplines; and if we now find its conclusion doubtful, as we should, this is because over the more than forty years since its publication, the specific extrapolations offered by its authors seem to have been, without exception, mistaken. The general argument for strong naturalism, as originally presented by Quine (1960, 1969), is itself a broad induction on the history of science: What empirical research has taught us, over and over again, is that what we have at various times found inconceivable in fact has turned out to be actual, and so our conceptions have been continuously revised. Of course, we cannot inquire at all outside of some conceptual framework or other, but no argument from conceivability to actuality, or from inconceivability to impossibility, should be regarded as persuasive.

Chalmers does not deny strong naturalism *tout court*. Nevertheless, his argument for his claim that qualia are basic elements of reality places enormous weight on conceivability. He can, he claims repeatedly, conceive of a possible world that is physically identical to the actual one but for the fact that his counterpart — ex hypothesi psychologically and behaviorally indistinguishable from himself — has no qualia. Therefore, he maintains, qualitative experience does not logically supervene on the physical. But materialist monism requires that everything logically supervene on the physical. Everything, Chalmers maintains, does so supervene — except qualitative experience. Therefore, a physical description of reality does not exhaust its properties, leaving out the qualitative ones. Hence, he concludes, dualism is true.

Chalmers may be correct to say that qualia do not logically supervene on the physical. Though he presents arguments for this claim and carefully considers and answers possible objections, I will not attempt to evaluate them. Logical space is vast; and the peculiar discoveries of twentieth-century physics suggest that it is much larger than "conceivability space." Therefore, I find all claims concerning its boundaries unpersuasive. Dennett (1991a) strenuously argues that the concept of a zombie is incoherent, so that Chalmers's sensationless counterpart falls outside of logical space. I shall not review Dennett's arguments for this opposing view either, since I think that even if Chalmers is correct concerning the topology of logical space, the appropriate response should be "So what?" In order to defend this response, we shall have to follow Chalmers's argument a stage deeper, into considerations of the relationship between logical necessity and reference.

Chalmers's argument for dualism is, obviously, an a priori one since, as he acknowledges, there is no empirical evidence for it. It is odd for a naturalist to present a priori arguments for a claim about what there is, such as dualism. Chalmers is aware of this and so addresses a great deal of space to the following argument: Referential terms, such as "sensation of type x" or "water," have both primary and secondary intensions. These correspond approximately to Frege's "sense" and "reference," except that primary intensions, unlike senses, are public meanings—that is, truths about language rather than truths about a mysterious "third realm," as they are for Frege. Thus, to take the literature's standard example, "water" has as its primary intension "watery stuff" and, as its secondary intension, "H_2O." The first is a conceptual truth, which can be determined a priori, while the second can only be determined a posteriori. Chalmers follows Kripke and Putnam in agreeing that discoveries about secondary intensions (references) can teach us new facts about primary intensions (senses). Thus we can know, where Aristotle could not, that "watery stuff" is H_2O in all possible worlds. However, he denies that this holds in the case of the referential terms used to describe sensations: If the primary intension of "sensation of type x" is "a feeling of the sort I am having at time t," then nothing we could discover about the world, such as law-like correlations between such sensations and types of physical states, could lead us to suppose that our primary intensions to refer to objects in the domain of the phenomenal in fact referred to objects in the domain of the physical. Where qualitative experiences are concerned, primary intensions determine meaning in all possible worlds. Thus if a zombie reports that she or he is having a sensation, then she or he is, as a matter of a priori fact, mistaken. This is, of course, trivially true given what Chalmers and other philosophers mean by "zombies." But now we have been led round in a circle, back to the question of whether zombies are logically possible. Let us grant, for purposes of argument, that they are. Would this establish Chalmers's conclusion?

For the strong naturalist, the answer must be "no." Before examining why this is so in general, we shall consider more closely what Dennett intends when he claims that the concept of a zombie is incoherent. For Dennett, the boundaries of the logically possible are not constrained by issues of conceivability; instead, they are mainly constrained by, as Dennett acknowledges, a mild verification principle. If there were zombies, then we could in principle never know it, since zombies would report sensations just as nonzombies do and would in all measurable respects be indistinguishable from them. This sort of reasoning, of course, offends realist intuitions to the effect that what there is, or could be, is not restricted by our epistemic limitations. But this is the point at which the principle of strong naturalism becomes relevant. "Can you show us a case from the history of science," asks the strong naturalist, "where any science postulated generalizations about objects or events to which we can in principle have no epistemic access? If there are no such cases, then philosophers have no business introducing such objects or events into a supposedly naturalistic ontology."

Consider an analogy. Suppose (as may or may not in fact be the case) that the big bang is a genuine singularity along the temporal dimension, such that no information could be retrieved from the other side of it. Then what possible point could there be in speculating about what being was like prior to the big bang? Of course, we *could* speculate if we wished: Perhaps there was energy but no matter. "No!" says *Chalmers, the inconsistently naturalistic physicist, "this violates the most famous postulate of general relativity; the secondary intensions associated with 'energy' and 'matter' tell us that this is not logically possible." *Chalmers admits that the situation is conceivable; we merely need conceive of the universe as classical physicists did. So conceivability is evidently a red herring. What matters here, emphasizes the strong naturalist, is that general relativity is based, ultimately, on data gathered from this side of the singularity. In the conceivable though (ex hypothesi) nonactual world where we could recover information from beyond it, who is to say that we might not develop a broader physics under which we would revise our concept of—that is, revise the secondary intensions associated with— "energy" and "matter"? Through all of this, the physicist goes on studying the actual world, perhaps slightly indignant that useful grant money is being squandered on such arguments among philosophers. This last fact is not just a bit of sociological color: The physicist, though a realist about the actual world, is also something of a verificationist. She or he may be willing to posit mysterious entities whose substance is beyond further immediate investigation—as Newton, with misgivings, was prepared to posit gravitational force—but she or he is not interested in speculations on which no evidence, however indirect, could bear in principle. If the physicist is a mild verificationist, then the strong naturalist must be one too. So just as the physicist is uninterested in informationally sealed spaces, so the cognitive scientist is not interested in zombies.

We can press the point further. Why would one even be tempted by weak naturalism if one had absolutely no verificationist intuitions? Why should the actual world be privileged as a determiner of referential meaning in logically possible but nonactual ones? Because here is where the available data are. The whiff of verificationism lies in the word "available." Realists about possible worlds—which Chalmers implies himself to be in doubting whether mere natural necessity is a strong enough conceptual basis for logical semantics—have no business privileging the actual world except on the basis of an epistemological thesis to the effect that our scientific generalizations are intended to support counterfactuals only across the domain of "nearby" possible worlds, where what counts as "nearby" is determined by the generalizations of the physics accepted at the time of measurement. Why should this be so? Again, because a science that failed to privilege readily available data over unavailable data would refrain, out of conservatism, from advancing most of the useful generalizations that science has obtained. If science proceeds in this fashion, as it does, then the strong naturalist—or, as I have just suggested, even the weak naturalist—should refrain from cluttering

scientific speculation with considerations drawn from worlds that are merely logically possible.

Before considering a response that Chalmers would likely make at this point
to the argument I have been pursuing, I should note another implication of strong
naturalism, with its accompanying element of mild verificationism, for Chalmers's
project. Cartwright (1983, 1989, and elsewhere) has argued vigorously, from premises derived from the practice of science, that even the purported "laws" of physics
are not taken by physicists as being strictly true, if by "law" we mean a statement
falling within the scope of a universal quantifier and unaccompanied by an indefinite set of ceteris paribus clauses. What pass in the textbooks as laws, Cartwright argues, are merely summaries of measurements of causal capacities of types,
taken perforce from within a limited range of space-time to which we have epistemic access. It would require a transcendental argument to elevate these generalizations into the status of known universal truths. But, for the strong naturalist,
there could be no such transcendental arguments, and neither physicists nor other
scientists pursue them. Now, Chalmers, throughout his book, takes for granted
that the project of science is to seek laws, and the project of a science of consciousness is to seek psychophysical laws linking the phenomenal with the physical
(at least indirectly, via invariant structures of functional organization). It is clear
that by "laws" Chalmers does not mean "summaries of measurements," since it is
the strongly nomic aspect of fundamental laws that, he argues, entitles us to know
a priori that in no possible world could laws that fail to refer to qualia as brute
elements explain consciousness. (Hence no such laws could explain consciousness
in the actual world.) But if such "fundamentalism," to use a pejorative term of
Cartwright's, violates the practice of scientists, then we again have grounds for
questioning Chalmers's professed naturalism.

Before expanding on the implications of my conclusion to this point that
Chalmers is not consistently naturalistic, it is time to consider an objection that
might be raised on his behalf, as alluded to earlier. His "reductive functionalist"
opponents, he might argue, no more derive their view from empirical data than
he does; Dennett's reconceptualization of consciousness as a set of dispositions to
render certain judgments about the conscious subject's mental states is as much
a piece of a priori reasoning as Chalmers's. However, Dennett, unlike Chalmers,
is primarily influenced by pragmatic considerations. If conscious states must be
presented to an internal homunculus, then an infinite regress faces those who
would seek to provide a complete picture of the mind's functional organization.
Dennett is driven by the need to break down conceptual barriers, which he views
as retarding the progress of cognitive science. I do not see that Chalmers can make
any such claim. A cognitive scientist who accepts his dualism will proceed exactly
as will one who accepts Dennett's "multiple-drafts" model, as Chalmers implicitly
concedes when he acknowledges that the task of the cognitive scientist remains
as it was: to study functional organization and search for neural correlates with
various specific aspects of experience (Chalmers, 1996, pp. 233–246). All Chalmers's dualism adds is the claim that no particular sort of functional organization
will *logically* determine properties of consciousness, from which he concludes that

the generalizations discovered by cognitive science concerning relationships between functional organization or neurological properties and properties of consciousness will not be "fundamental."

If I am right to claim that scientists are not, and have no reason to be, concerned with logical necessity, then what is novel in Chalmers's view of consciousness is irrelevant to the scientific study of the mind. Only a sort of dualism (or any other ontological hypothesis) that holds consciousness to be essentially and ultimately mysterious could have such implications. Such a view is famously defended by McGinn (1989), though not on the basis of dualist premises. But if the truth or falsity even of dualism is irrelevant to the scientific study of consciousness, then surely so is any other ontological thesis concerning the mind-body problem. (McGinn's view is excluded from this generalization, since it is an epistemological thesis, throwing up its hands at the possibility of defending any ontological thesis.) If one is persuaded by Cartwright's arguments that it is not the business of science to seek fundamental laws, then Chalmers's claim that a functionalist theory could not explain consciousness, but only serve as a step toward such an explanation, goes by the board also.

This does not quite finish matters, however, since the issue of reductionism remains outstanding. Even if we acknowledge that the goal of science is not to discover fundamental laws—that is, generalizations about empirical matters that are logically necessary—and even if one rejects the generic reductionism advocated by Oppenheim and Putnam on the basis of induction on the recent history of science (see Fodor, 1974; Garfinkel, 1981; Kitcher, 1984), it must nevertheless be acknowledged that science *sometimes* achieves explanation through reduction. I have questioned Chalmers's claim that consciousness cannot be explained reductionistically, but in the course of doing so, I have deliberately allowed him a hostage that I now wish to free: his claim that more typical functionalist accounts, such as Dennett's, are reductionistic. If this is not the case, as I will now argue, then the space between Chalmers's project and Dennett's is narrowed even further.

It is clear enough why Chalmers supposes that standard functionalist accounts are reductionistic: They seek to explain consciousness, as he sees it, by equating it with something else. But one must be rather more careful here. First, we should distinguish two sorts of explanation. One may explain a phenomenon by identifying it with a "lower-level" phenomenon (a usual example is "temperature is mean molecular kinetic energy"); or one may explain a phenomenon in terms of others, that is, by providing explanations that do not refer to the explanandum in their explanans. Fodor (1987) takes this to be a requirement of explanation, and Fodor's own program for explaining mental properties by identifying them with computational properties that supervene on physical ones is arguably reductionistic—especially if Kim (1989) is correct in his argument that supervenience implies reducibility in the sense of identification. (Interestingly, Fodor's position on consciousness is not dissimilar to McGinn's; see Fodor, 1992.) However, it is not clear that all explanations of the second sort deserve the label "reductionist." In particular, I question whether this adjective appropriately applies to Dennett's account.

Certainly, Dennett seeks to explain consciousness in terms of something else — namely, judgments made by parts of the mind/brain about what is going on in other parts of the mind/brain. But Dennett also bifurcates the traditional concept of consciousness into two further concepts — awareness and self-hood. Awareness, for Dennett, is simply the ability of a cognitive system to respond selectively to information. This he takes to be a necessary condition for consciousness, a point on which he and Chalmers are in agreement (Chalmers, 1996, pp. 219–229). Dennett notes, however, that what is often meant by consciousness is a stronger notion — *self-hood*, the capacity to unite past experiences into a coherent narrative. Self-spinning is a form of judgment, to be sure, but a highly complex one. Most important, it requires that the conscious subject assume the intentional stance toward himself, that is, describe, explain, and predict his behavior (and some of his internal states) in terms of propositional attitudes. Dennett (1991b) makes it clear that propositional-attitude states, such as believing that p, are not identical with internal states; Dennett is, implicitly if not explicitly, a semantic externalist about the contents of propositional attitudes. So this aspect of what is sometimes meant by "consciousness" does not, for Dennett, reduce in the sense of supervening locally. According to Chalmers, however, an account of consciousness is still reductionistic if it holds that consciousness supervenes globally, that is, if all of the physical facts there are determine all of the facts there are about the distribution and character of conscious states. Yet Dennett denies even this, arguing (1991b) that belief-desire psychology tracks "real patterns" in available data. Are "real patterns" supervenient?

To answer this question, let us first regiment Dennett's largely implicit definition of a "real pattern," based on the examples he provides. A pattern is real if (1) it is projectible under at least one physically possible perspective, and (2) it encodes information about at least one structure of events or entities S, where that encoding is more efficient, in information-theoretic terms, than the bit-map encoding of S, and where for at least one of the physically possible perspectives under which the pattern is projectible, there exists an aspect of S that cannot be tracked unless the encoding is recovered from the perspective in question.

Clause (1) here is necessary to avoid anthropocentric instrumentalism; we must allow for the existence of real patterns that happen to be contingently inaccessible to human perceivers. Clause (2) reformulates Ockham's razor in information-theoretic terms, blocking a Meinongian explosion by excluding pure semantic artifacts such as arbitrary conjunctions of real patterns. Are patterns so defined globally supervenient on the physical? By clause (1) a real pattern must be more than merely logically possible; it must exist in the set of possible worlds that are nearby according to physics. But this does not imply global supervenience on the physical, since, as Dennett (1991b) explicitly argues, two patterns that disagree in their predictions may be equally efficient in representing the data; thus there is room for indeterminacy in specifying the patterns, even given all of the physical facts. However, the information-theoretic restriction on existence implies a caveat to this claim — and a most interesting one in light of remarks made by Chalmers.

The work of Shannon (1948), which Chalmers discusses (Chalmers, 1996, pp. 276–310), has shown us how to measure information-flow as a physical process. Of equal interest is Schrödinger's (1944) principle of negentropy, which provides a basis for understanding information-storing systems (i.e., systems that, by Chalmers's admission, may meet both the necessary and sufficient conditions for being regarded as conscious [Chalmers, 1996, pp. 293–299]) in terms of their capacity for reducing entropy in their local environments (for expansion on the significance of this idea in cognitive science, see Ross and Zawidzki, 1994). If information is regarded in its physical aspect, then real patterns—and hence consciousness along with all other aspects of mind—may indeed globally supervene on the physical. But this is not a prospect that disturbs Chalmers at all. Indeed, in the most speculative portion of his book, he cautiously endorses the possibility that information may be more fundamental than consciousness itself (Chalmers, 1996, pp. 301–3). At this point, I submit, the gap between Chalmers and Dennett, at least with respect to ideas worthy of scientific study, as opposed to mere articulation of conceptual intuitions and semantic preferences, has closed completely, and Chalmers's willingness to embrace the possibility that information is fundamental undermines even such purely philosophical force as one would suppose that a defense of dualism must have.

This last part of my argument, on the issue of reductionism, is of course highly speculative. Here I have only been following both Chalmers and Dennett into deep metaphysical waters where neither fears to tread. This simply amounts to turning the screw slightly tighter on my central claim, which is that cognitive scientists have only one available strategy for studying consciousness: comparing subjects' reports of experience, taken as fallible, with such facts as they can unearth about functional and neurophysiological architectures. Philosophers of science should continue to study cognitive science, to be sure, as they study other sciences, but their time of hoping to guide it usefully by means of purely conceptual disputes on issues such as the mind-body problem has passed. It is consistent with naturalism to view philosophy, historically, as the mother of the sciences, though not as their queen. But in terms of this metaphor, it is time to let psychology, one of philosophy's last children, leave home.

Acknowledgments

I would like to thank Laurence Goldstein for his comments and suggestions on an earlier draft of this chapter. I also gratefully acknowledge the financial support of the University Research Fund of the University of Cape Town.

References

Block, N. 1993. "Review of Dennett, *Consciousness Explained.*" *Journal of Philosophy*, 90, pp. 181–93.

Cartwright, N. 1983. *How the Laws of Physics Lie.* New York: Oxford University Press.
———. 1989. *Nature's Capacities and Their Measurement.* New York: Oxford University Press.
Chalmers, D. 1996. *The Conscious Mind.* New York: Oxford University Press.
Churchland, P.M. 1979. *Scientific Realism and the Plasticity of Mind.* New York: Cambridge University Press.
Dennett, D. 1991a. *Consciousness Explained.* Boston: Little, Brown.
———. 1991b. "Real Patterns." *Journal of Philosophy,* 88, pp. 27–51.
Fodor, J. 1974. "Special Sciences." *Synthese,* 28, pp. 77–115.
———. 1987. *Psychosemantics.* Cambridge, MA: MIT Press/Bradford.
———. 1992. "The Big Idea: Can There Be a Science of Mind?" *Times Literary Supplement,* July 3, pp. 5–7.
Garfinkel, A. 1981. *Forms of Explanation.* New Haven, CT: Yale University Press.
Kim, J. 1989. "The Myth of Nonreductive Materialism." *Proceedings and Addresses of the American Philosophical Association,* 63, pp. 31–47.
Kitcher, P. 1984. "1953 and All That: A Tale of Two Sciences." *Philosophical Review,* 93, pp. 335–73.
McGinn, C. 1989. "Can We Solve the Mind–Body Problem?" *Mind,* 98, pp. 349–66.
Mermin, N.D. 1985. "Is the Moon There When Nobody Looks? Reality and the Quantum Theory." *Physics Today,* April, pp. 38–47.
Nelkin, N. 1996. *Consciousness and the Origins of Thought.* Cambridge and New York: Cambridge University Press.
Oppenheim, P., and Putnam, H. 1958. "Unity of Science as a Working Hypothesis." Pp. 3–36 in H. Feigl, M. Scriven, and G. Maxwell (Eds.), *Minnesota Studies in the Philosophy of Science.* Vol. 2. Minneapolis: University of Minnesota Press.
Quine, W.V.O. 1960. *Word and Object.* Cambridge, MA: MIT Press.
———. 1969. *Ontological Relativity and Other Essays.* New York: Columbia University Press.
Ross, D. 1994. "Dennett's Conceptual Reform." *Behavior and Philosophy,* 22, pp. 41–52.
———. 1999. "Review of Nelkin, *Consciousness and the Origins of Thought.*" *Dialogue,* 37, pp. 456–458.
Ross, D., and Zawidzki, T. 1994. "Information and Teleosemantics." *Southern Journal of Philosophy,* 32, pp. 393–419.
Schrödinger, E. 1944. *What Is Life?* Cambridge and New York: Cambridge University Press.
Shannon, C. 1948. "A Mathematical Theory of Communication." *Bell System Technical Journal,* 27, pp. 379–423.

9

Emergence and Efficacy

William Seager

Imagine the day when physics is complete. A theory is in place that unifies all the forces of nature in one self-consistent and empirically verified set of absolutely basic principles. There are some who see this day as perhaps not too distant (e.g., Hawking, 1988; Weinberg, 1992; Horgan, 1996). Of course, the mere possession of this theory of everything will not give us the ability to provide a complete explanation of everything: every event, process, occurrence, and structure. Most things will be too remote from the basic theory to admit of explanation in its terms; even relatively small and simple systems will be far too complex to be intelligibly described in the final theory.

But since as our imagined theory is fully developed and mathematically complete, it will enable us to set up detailed computer simulations of physical systems. The range of practicable simulations will in fact be subject to the same constraints facing the explanatory use of the theory; the modeling of even very simple systems will require impossibly large amounts of computational resources. Nonetheless, possession of a computational implementation of our final theory would be immensely useful. Real versions of something very like my imaginary scenario now exist and are already fruitful. For example, there are computer models of quantum chromodynamics that can compute the theoretically predicted masses of various quark-constituted subatomic particles (see Weingarten, 1996). The looming problem of computational intractability is all too evident, for realizing these calculations required the development of special mathematical techniques, the assembling of a dedicated, parallel supercomputer specially designed for the necessary sorts of calculations (a computer capable of 11 billion arithmetical operations per second), and roughly a year of continuous computing. Weingarten reports that a special two-year calculation revealed the existence of a previously unrecognized particle, whose existence could be verified by examining past records from particle-accelerator experiments. Modeling the interactions of particles would be a much more challenging task, suggesting to the imagination computational projects analogous to the construction of medieval cathedrals, involving thousands of workers for many decades.[1]

I want to introduce a thought experiment that flatly ignores the inevitably insuperable problems of computational reality. Imagine a computer model of the final physical theory that has no computational limits; imagine that detailed specifications of the basic physical configuration of any system, at any time, in terms appropriate for the final theory, are available, so that if the configuration of any physical system is specified as input, then the output configuration of the system, for any later time, can be calculated (and appropriately displayed) in a reasonable time. There is nothing incoherent in the idea of an absolutely perfect simulation. In fact, we have some of them in physics already. The Kerr equations for rotating black holes are (if the general theory of relativity is true) absolutely perfect models of these strange objects. The famous astrophysicist and mathematician Subrahmanyan Chandrasekhar confessed that "in my entire scientific life . . . the most shattering experience has been the realization that an exact solution of Einstein's equations of general relativity, discovered by the New Zealand mathematician Roy Kerr, provides the *absolutely exact representation* of untold numbers of massive black holes that populate the universe" (quoted in Begelman and Rees, 1996, p. 188).

However, we are not so lucky with the rest of the world; and so even within our dream, certain approximations in the input configurations will have to be allowed. We cannot input field values for every point of space-time, and it is conceivable that some configurations require an infinite amount of information for their specification if, to give one example, certain parameters take on irrational values that never cancel out during calculation. Let us therefore imagine that we can input specifications of whatever precision we like to allow for modeling the system for whatever time we like and to whatever level of accuracy we desire. Even though it is physically impossible, I think that the idea of such a computer program is perfectly well defined and, I will try to show, can starkly illuminate a problem about the efficacy of emergent properties (which is a much more serious problem than might appear from this bloodless preliminary description).[2]

Emergentism is not a single doctrine but rather a system of related views characterizable through a variety of distinctions.[3] It is common to distinguish a supposedly "benign" or acceptable emergentism from an unacceptably nonnaturalistic, "radical" emergentism. Within benign emergentism further divisions are possible. For example, John Searle (and also Paul Churchland, 1985, note 6) recognizes an emergence of "systems features" (or, in Churchland's phrase, "network properties"), which are properties that a system has but that no proper part of the system possesses (Searle's examples are particular weights of systems and their shapes), as distinct from (but encompassing) what he calls "causally emergent system features," (Searle, 1992, p. 112) which are not merely a matter of physical composition but rather "have to be explained in terms of the causal interactions among the elements" (Searle, 1992, p. 112) (examples are liquidity and transparency; see Searle, 1992, pp. 111 ff.).[4] Searle then explicates the notion of radical emergence as further demanding that the emergent property have its own causal powers, which "cannot be explained by the causal interactions of" (Searle, 1992, p. 112) the parts of the system.

I think that emergence is and should be a metaphysical (or perhaps it would be better to say ontological) doctrine, and so I regard the widespread reliance on the notion of explanation in the explication of emergentism as misplaced, a more or less subtle confusion of metaphysics with epistemology that is distressingly rampant in discussions of these problems. The fact that we cannot explain the causal powers of a property in terms of the basic constituents of a system might reflect no more than cognitive weakness, or perhaps an overwhelming complexity of the system at issue, rather than a metaphysical fact of radical emergence. But our computer-model thought experiment makes everything clear. A property F of a system S is radically causally emergent just in case S's behavior diverges from the behavior of our computer model of S, where it is the possession of F that causes the divergence. Otherwise, assuming, naturally, that F is not itself a basic physical property B, and so explicitly mentioned in the final theory as B, F is a benignly emergent property.

It is worth mentioning here that the indeterminism that we will likely find in the final physics can easily be accommodated by considering ensembles of identically prepared systems and measuring the telltale divergences of emergentism against the behavior of the ensemble. One can envisage the emergent properties revealing themselves in at least two distinct ways. First, the divergent behavior might be different from the behavior of all the members of the ensemble. Second, we could have a merely probabilistic case for emergence if the behavior of the real system was consistently like that of only a tiny fraction of our ensemble. That is, persistently improbable behavior would also be a mark of radically emergent properties at work. Thinking about indeterminism also suggests a new kind of emergentism: the emergence of indeterminism. We can imagine emergent properties that introduce indeterminate behavior into a system that the final physics claims to be deterministic; or, as in the second case, emergent properties could skew the probabilities that the final physics assigns to a system's possible behavior (sometimes free will is thought to introduce such indeterminacies). It is, however, rather more probable that determinism is an emergent property of systems constituted from fundamentally indeterministic elements. It is very likely that macroscopic systems will behave in essentially deterministic ways — that is, that the probabilities of their various possible macroscopic state transitions will approach 1 and 0.[5] Our imaginary computer model will naturally take all this into account.

Note also how this model nicely finesses another issue: the notorious oddity of quantum part-whole relations. In quantum mechanics, systems have causal properties that do not always smoothly reduce to the properties of their parts. For example, systems that are in superpositions of possible states are behaviorally distinct from systems that are in mixtures of these states; and individual systems can become "entangled" and thus form a new unified system with distinctive properties. (To see how strange this can get, consult Albert, 1992, or, for a particular example, Seager, 1996.) But the theory itself tells us how these superpositions and entanglements arise through particle creation, annihilation, and interaction, as

well as how they subsequently behave. Our computer program would naturally—
and by assumption successfully—include such features in its simulations. This
means that we shall not have to regard quantum mechanics as a theory propound-
ing the radical emergence of quantum mechanical properties (e.g., the properties
of superpositions). On the other hand, there may be some merit in the notion
that quantum mechanics is precisely the scientific appropriation and regimenta-
tion of the idea of radical emergence. This is an intriguing idea that I shall not
explore here, but I will remark that quantum mechanics is, due to its linearity, at
best a very nongeneral theory of emergence.

To see better how the thought experiment works, let us examine a classic case
from a naïve point of view that might briefly suggest that we have a case of radical
emergence. The mechanical model of gases allows us to deduce the perfect gas
law relating pressure (P), temperature (T), and volume (V): $PV = RT$. If we
plugged a specification of the initial state of a gas—recall that we are assuming
that we can somehow obtain appropriate descriptions of these states—into a computer simulation based on the idealizations of the simplest mechanical model
(which is, for all its conceptual simplicity, no less computationally intractable than
our envisaged computational implementation of final physics), the computer
would generate output states that provide a pretty fair representation of the gas
and that would, naturally, obey the perfect gas law. But under a variety of conditions the actual gas's behavior would exhibit greater or lesser divergences from the
behavior of the model gas. We might—rather too quickly—deduce that there are
radically emergent properties of gases at work, or we could deduce that the theoretical structure of our model is inaccurate. Of course, the latter is correct. A
better model of the parts of the gas (almost) eliminates the divergences. For example, a better model admits that there are some interactions between the microscopic parts of a gas, and that the parts must take up a little of the volume of the
gas. An intuitive appreciation of the microstructures involved in the model led
van der Waals to incorporate these features in a modified gas law: $(P + a/V^2)(V
- b) = RT$. As is common in the development of scientific theories, the appear-
ance of a possible radically emergent property disappears with a refined analysis
of the components of the system and their interactions. Pressure and temperature
remain as emergent properties of the gas: They are not properties deployed in the
computer model or the basic theory, but they are obviously benignly emergent.
They can be successfully applied to the gas as represented by the computer model,
with no aspect of the gas's behavior "left over." That is, the computer-generated
simulated gas "acts" just as if it had a temperature and exerted pressure, without
our having to write these into our program.

Any case of apparently radical emergence can (and usually should) be taken
as evidence of weakness in the underlying theory. Interesting methodological issues
are raised by the problem of determining under what conditions we should agree
that radical emergence has been empirically discovered. An extremely bizarre
possibility can be imagined in which radical emergence is true, but invisible,
because we are clever enough to develop a theory that, while it is actually false,
manages to generate all the empirical effects of the emergent properties from the

theory's hypothesized microproperties, entities, and processes. According to such a fantasy, it might be that the extremely complex devices employed by high-energy physicists are revealing radically emergent features (of complexes such as particle accelerators, detectors, and computers) that serve only to spur theorists' efforts at modifying their fundamental theories to incorporate them. (Theorists possess, after all, a notorious ability to account for any empirical result.)[6] But I am for now assuming that the final theory is true.

That old whipping horse, vitalism, can be regarded as involving radical emergence. Another distinction looms here that should be briefly mentioned. It seems possible to develop a theory of "substance emergence" as well as the more typical property emergence.[7] The former posits the appearance, if and whenever certain definite material configurations arise, of a new substance that then takes an active part in the causal commerce of the world. I suppose that the emergent substance is annihilated upon the destruction of its material base (but who knows?). Maybe vitalism ought best to be regarded as a kind of substance emergence (talk of the élan vital might suggest this interpretation), but this nicety need not worry us here. Either way, vitalism posits that living matter behaves differently than dead matter, but that is uncontroversial. The proper expression of the radical claim of vitalism is that our final computer model of the physical configuration of, say, a living cell or bacterium would fail to provide an accurate representation of the cell's behavior. Unlike simulated gases, computer-simulated cells will just not act like their real counterparts. So says vitalism.

I do not think that there is any evidence that life is a radical emergent property (let alone an emergent substance). But given the absence of our final computer program, what justifies amplifying the evidence into an outright denial of vitalism? It is what I call the "physical resolution" of living systems into basic physical parts that take an entirely normal place within the developing picture of the physical world.[8] Though not conclusive, it is highly suggestive that no strange, inexplicable processes have been found in living cells, and that a great many of the basic mechanisms of life have been explained in molecular terms. This is far from proof, of course, since we have examined only a tiny fraction of the mechanisms of life, and those the most elementary. After all, the emergentist, no less than the physicalist, positively expects that all systems will resolve into ordinary material subsystems and ultimately into the basic physical building blocks. It is only their complex combination in living systems that reveals the emergent properties. So perhaps it is a kind of faith that underpins the antivitalist, though it is a faith, unlike that of the unredeemed vitalist, that all of the still fragmentary evidence we do possess fully supports. Expressed in terms of our computer thought experiment, the faith is that a complete elementary final physics simulation of an entire organism (plus the requisite features of its environment) would successfully replicate the behavior of the real thing. That faith is supported by the piecemeal successes of resolving a range of very simple biochemical processes into their physical parts, which reveals how the nonliving properties of these processes produce them. (Here it is assumed that no radical emergence occurs in the gap between the elementary physical and the biochemical levels—presumably a reasonable assumption, for which we have still more evidence than for our antivitalism, and which is, as always, an excellent working hypothesis.) The faith is coupled with a parsimonious desire to understand the most with the least number of hypotheses, and so far, absolutely no vitalistic assumptions of radical emergence have been warranted.

But reflecting on this example and looking ahead to the case of the mind suggest yet another possible sort of emergence: a form of noncausal emergentism I shall label epiphenomenal emergence. The classic doctrine of mental epiphe-nomenalism is a doctrine of emergence, at least so long as it is not a form of panpsychism. (I take it that epiphenomenal panpsychism is almost equivalent to the Leibnizian doctrine of preestablished harmony, or a universal psychophysical parallelism. It adds only the idea that the physical side of the equation causes the psychical side.) Classical epiphenomenalism maintains that certain material con-figurations bring about instantiations of mental properties that were not exempli-fied prior to the appearance of that physical configuration, and these properties are not to be identified with the physical. Unfortunately (or not, depending upon one's viewpoint), these mental properties have no distinctive, observable causal influences on behavior. Noncausal emergentism is invisible.

Perhaps classical epiphenomenalism is not of much interest, but mixing ep-iphenomenalism with emergentism forces us to ask a very disturbing question: Is benign emergentism a kind of epiphenomenalism? Recall again the benign emer-gence of temperature and pressure. As we know, the pressure of a gas does not really cause anything; it has no efficacy of its own. Pressure is the mathematical average of the impact forces of the gas's constituents as they strike the gas's con-taining boundary; and mathematical averages do not cause anything. If one is inclined to think otherwise, consider this example: A demographer might say that wages will go up in the near future since the average family size fell twenty-odd years ago (and so now relatively fewer new workers are available). There is not the slightest reason to think that "average family size" can, let alone does, cause things, although I think that we easily understand the explanation to which such statistical shorthand points.[9] By its very nature, pressure is not one whit less a statistical fiction than is average family size. The ascription of causal efficacy to pressure is only a *façon de parler*, a useful shorthand for the genuine efficacy of the myriad of microevents that constitute "pressure phenomena." It is entirely correct to use the overworked phrase, and say that pressure is nothing but the concerted actions of the countless particles that make up a gas. In terms of our computational thought experiment, it is easy to tell whether some property has any causal efficacy of its own: Do we need to code that property into the simu-lation? If not, then the property has no efficacy of its own.

Benign emergence arises wherever we can find a descriptive and/or explan-atory scheme whose application to some class of systems provides a useful kind of shorthand notation for describing the behavior of these systems. The behavior is being orchestrated from below, as it were, in the details of these systems' physical constitution. The joint action of these constituents happens to form patterns that we can codify in terms of the benignly emergent properties deployed in our "high-level" description of the systems (an interesting discussion of this process can be found in Dennett, 1991b). Consider, for instance, the Coriolis force, which gunnery officers must take into account when computing the trajectory of long-range cannon shells. (A host of other activities require cognizance of the Coriolis force as well.) This is a benignly emergent property of the Earth or any other rotating system. But in the context of assessing causal efficacy and the proper physical basis of the world, it is highly misleading to say that the Coriolis force causes diversions in a shell's trajectory. At least, if we really thought that there was such a force — hence with its own causal efficacy — the world would end up being a much stranger place than we had imagined. Just think of it: Rotate a system, and a brand-new force magically appears out of nowhere; stop the rotation, and the force instantly disappears. That is radical emergence with a vengeance. Of course, there is no need to posit such a force. The Coriolis phenomena are related to the underlying physical processes in a reasonably simple way — in fact, simple enough for us to directly comprehend — but no matter the complexity, our imaginary computer model of any rotating system would naturally reveal the appearance of a Coriolis force.

Another extremely important example of presumably benignly emergent phenomena is found in evolutionary biology. The theory of evolution, with its profound use of the concept of natural selection, along with the now unravelled genetic basis of inheritance, is an undeniably deep insight into the nature of the world. Unlike the case of pressure in thermodynamics, there is no simple mathematical relation that connects, say, adaptedness (to environment X) to underlying physical structure. But given our knowledge of biochemistry and the molecular basis of genetics, it is very likely that adaptedness (along with all other evolutionary properties) is indeed benignly emergent. If so, we know that adaptedness itself adds nothing to the causal forces of the world. Evolutionary theory is a way of consciously apprehending certain abstract structures in the world that brilliantly highlights certain more or less enduring patterns to be found in the "dance of the atoms." We need the idea of evolution to understand the world, but the world has no need of it. The world — not even the biological parts of it — is not being driven by evolutionary properties. Predator-prey relations will be revealed in the final physics computer model of an environment in precisely the form they take in the world itself. The Hardy-Weinberg law will emerge from the quark/lepton/boson sea of our imaginary simulation with not a jot of evolutionary theory needed in the underlying program (unless, of course, evolutionary properties are more than just benignly emergent).

The basic problem is that, metaphysically speaking, benignly emergent properties are unnecessary hypotheses, even if they are parts of useful high-level explanatory schemes. The world can be described, predicted, and understood in terms of any number of interesting and useful explanatory schemes. But a reasonable principle of economy enjoins us not to multiply hypotheses beyond necessity; and manifestly, by definition, one might say, there is never any need to appeal to benignly emergent properties when we consider the metaphysical underpinnings of the world. They are nothing but artifacts of convenient ways of thinking and speaking. I am not saying that the benignly emergent properties are practically eliminable, or that there is any prospect of doing without these ways of organizing the world around us, or even that it would be abstractly desirable to do away with them. In fact, they are necessary for our understanding of the world and indispensable aids in the construction of the picture of the physical world that finally reveals them to be nothing but benignly emergent properties. But I am saying that they are metaphysically unnecessary and therefore cannot be counted among the "driving elements" or forces of the world.

It seems to me interesting that such an outlook would be entirely acceptable, and indeed possessed of a rather austere beauty, were it not for one recalcitrant phenomenon: consciousness. We understand perfectly how things like the Coriolis and centrifugal forces, or pressure and temperature, or adaptedness and natural selection "cause" things in the world through the action of a host of underlying genuine causes whose proper description does not require any appeal to these properties. Again I stress that this is not in any way to dismiss the importance of the high-level schemes. It is a remarkable and fascinating feature of the world that it can support such a wondrous hierarchy of high-level descriptive schemes, sometimes (especially in such cases as thermodynamics, evolutionary theory, and, perhaps, intentional psychology) in ways that utterly transcend the details of the systems so described.[10] But there is no discomfort in assigning the benignly emergent properties a metaphysically second-class status. This is true also for mental properties so long as we suppose that they are not conscious states (here it helps to consider them as states of beings other than oneself). For these mental states, the analogy with the Coriolis force can look quite good. (A well-developed treatment can be found in Dennett, 1987; I do not find the extension of the theory to consciousness in Dennett, 1991a, so plausible.)

But if consciousness turns out to be benignly emergent in the same way as the Coriolis force, then we have an extremely serious problem about the efficacy of the mental (see Kim, 1993, e.g., chapter 8, for more on explanatory exclusion[11] and efficacy, as well as emergentism). If the mental turns out to be benignly emergent in the way that pressure and temperature are, then the problem may appear to be less severe. This appearance has given false comfort. For in fact, with regard to their efficacy, there seems little to choose between the Coriolis force and the force of pressure (or any other benignly emergent property): They emerge from the concerted actions of the relevant physical systems' substructures in fundamentally the same way. Another example to nail the point down: Do centers of mass—say, their positions or the motions of these positions—really cause anything? Surely not. They are, we say, convenient fictions. They are very useful in calculation and as general aids to understanding, but they are not themselves efficacious. Now, notice that formally, the center of mass and the force of pressure are perfectly analogous. The center of mass is the average position of all the masses. The pressure is the average force of impact of all the particles. Such properties have no efficacy of their own. They are nothing but certain extremely useful ways of describing the observable effects of the joint action of the constituents of the system to which they apply.

It has often been remarked that if we try to imagine that the efficacy of, say, the painfulness of a consciously experienced pain is to be eliminated in the meta-physically correct view of the world, great discomfort ensues. Nonetheless, it looks very much as if the benign emergence of the mental is tantamount to epiphe-nomenalism. Note that if this argument is correct, then both reductive and non-reductive materialism fall victim to it, since they both subscribe to the complete-ness of physics as expressed in the imaginary computer thought experiment. There has been much work lately on the problem of mental efficacy within the context of nonreductive materialism, with results that remain controversial. The problem of benign emergence I am urging here threatens to make the problem much worse.

Because it is especially clear in, but not unique to, his position, let me illus-trate the problem as it arises for John Searle. Searle explicitly claims that con-sciousness is benignly emergent and is not epiphenomenal (see Searle, 1992, pp. 112, 126). He also notes that "first-person features are different from third-person features" (1992, p. 117). I take it that first-person features are the subjective properties of states of consciousness, whereas third-person features are the objective properties of the physical world. If we say that pain is not epiphenomenal, we are at least saying that pains cause some events. Let us suppose, to be definite, that a certain pain in subject S causes S to start sweating, trembling, and complaining. But now consider the idea that it is not the painfulness that causes these effects, but some nonmental features either of the pain or the subject in general. Since the painfulness is distinct from the third-person features of the pain, this is a possibility. (Searle in effect admits this during the development of his thought experiments in 1992, chapter 3.) Worse than that, since pain is benignly emergent, this possibility must be actual. Our perfect computer model of S would show S sweating and trembling and making certain sounds, without any need to code the "painfulness" into the program. So even if, in some attenuated sense, the pain is not epiphenomenal, the painfulness, at least, is epiphenomenal after all.

Contrary to what many think, the situation is not improved by trying to sup-pose, pace Searle, that we can identify first- and third-person features. Unless we adopt panpsychism, there is no hope of identifying consciousness with the ele-mentary physical features of the world. If subjective properties are benignly emer-gent, they are to be identified as high-level patterns or configurations of the basic elements, and as such they are themselves benignly emergent and hence meta-physically redundant.

Since the conclusion of this argument is likely to be hard to accept, let me make the point another way. Let us try to distinguish between benign emergence and epiphenomenalism. The difference we would like to find is that the benignly emergent properties retain a causal efficacy that their epiphenomenal surrogates lack. But how could this efficacy be defined? Epiphenomenal emergentism asserts that there is a lawlike connection between certain (sets of) physical states and their correlated emergent states, so the sorts of counterfactuals that typically attend and reveal causal efficacy remain true under the hypothesis of epiphenomenalism. In the nearest world where the emergent states are different, the underlying physical states will be different as well (none of the relevant physical states that ground the epiphenomenal state will obtain), and so the target caused event will also not occur.[12] So a counterfactual analysis of efficacy cannot distinguish between benign emergence and epiphenomenalism.

It is evident that epiphenomenal emergence entails a kind of benign emergence. The only thing we might consider unbenign about classical epiphenomenalism is the supposedly nonphysical nature of the epiphenomenal properties it posits. This is nothing to worry about: Let us simply define epiphenomenal physical emergentism (EPE) as the doctrine that the epiphenomenal properties brought into being upon the creation of certain basic physical configurations are, whatever else they might be, physical properties. Of course, there is also a more familiar form of epiphenomenalism that asserts that the epiphenomenal properties are nonphysical. But I am concerned here with EPE, and in particular with mental EPE—the doctrine that mental properties are (1) epiphenomenal and (2) physical as well as mental properties. I can be prevented from making this definition if it is impossible for a physical property to be epiphenomenal; and for this, I would like to see a proof. Any possible proof would seem to require the assumption that all physical properties are causally efficacious, which begs the question. In fact, I think that there are lots of epiphenomenal physical properties even within physics, but they are usually dismissed as "mathematical artifacts": properties that arise in the mathematical expression of the theory, but that do not do anything (and were not targets of reduction) and so are considered "unobservable" or "unphysical"— though they might be useful for calculation. But one is not entitled to take such a simple stance toward them, since sometimes these artifacts can bite. This is shown, for example, in the astonishing Bohm-Aharonov effect, in which a particle responds, if that is the right word, to a magnetic field that has value zero (where the particle is), the explanation of which appeals to the efficacy of what was thought to be a mathematical artifact of electromagnetic theory (the so-called vector potential). Note that our imaginary computer model would catch this effect. Of course, from the point of view I have been urging, pressure, temperature, the Coriolis and centrifugal forces, and so on are all epiphenomenal physical properties.

One might want to say that a physical property is a property that can be instantiated only by physical objects. (This is assuming that we also have some idea of what these are, apart from their instantiating just any physical property— perhaps we could say that objects are physical in virtue of possessing fundamental physical features such as mass, charge, and momentum.) If we allow that it is possible that there are nonphysical objects, perhaps in very distant possible worlds, that instantiate mental properties, then mental properties are, by this criterion, not physical, and mental EPE is ruled out. But then we have also rejected physicalism and adopted classical mental epiphenomenalism, for we are asserting that the actual world has honest-to-God nonphysical properties instantiated within it that do not do anything in this world. On this line, if you will not allow me to define mental EPE, then you are denying the truth of physicalism.

Some doubts may remain about the converse—whether benign emergentism implies epiphenomenalism—but I think that these doubts stem from the attractive but illicit assimilation of the explanatory to the causal order. I am not claiming that benignly emergent properties are explanatorily epiphenomenal. They are features of useful, utterly indispensable descriptive schemes by which we bring order and understanding into our picture of the world. But metaphysically they do not do anything; the efficacy of the benignly emergent properties is, by definition, an unnecessary hypothesis. So we have it that benign emergence is equivalent to epiphenomenalism. This places us in an unpleasant dilemma with regard to the mental: Either mental properties are epiphenomenal, or they are radically emergent properties.[13] This is a disturbing conclusion that I am sure will be resisted. One mode of resistance is once again to say something soothing like the following: A proper analysis will legitimate the claim that pressure causes things insofar as the concerted appropriate actions of the gas's constituents cause things. As I have said earlier, this is not really objectionable as a *façon de parler*. But it is obviously unsatisfactory with regard to the conscious mind. Consider the relevant gloss on a case of mental causation: Consciousness causes things insofar as a bunch of nonconscious events cause things. The way the mental property drops out of the picture is only too evident: This is a species of epiphenomenalism.

The problem can be approached from a slightly different angle. The world is made of basic physical constituents, all with their basic physical properties, arrayed and interacting in innumerable complex ways, but everything that happens happens because of properties and events at the basic level. The high-level descriptions we use to order and understand the world are products of consciousness, and they are apparent only to consciousness. The efficacy that high-level properties appear to possess is also only evident to consciousness. The high-level properties are like shadows cast in the mind by the action of the fundamental elements of physical reality upon the conscious mind. Imagine that I try to show that pressure is efficacious as such by getting you to squeeze a balloon—you can feel the pressure actively resisting your efforts, can't you? But obviously this does not tell us anything about pressure as such, but only about the conscious apprehension of the world as revealing "pressure phenomena." The question should be: Does the mathematical average of impact forces on your hand play an essential causal role in producing your apprehension of the balloon's resistance, or can the myriad of impact forces do this by themselves? Obviously, it is the latter question that gets the affirmative answer. Your apprehension is caused—in part, of course—by the myriads of impacts whose average force is codified as pressure. This average itself does not intervene in the causal process.[14] Metaphorically speaking, the world does not need to pay any attention to high-level properties, whereas, so to speak, the world is paying attention to the low-level properties described in the final physical theory. They, and only they, are driving the world forward. Metaphorically speaking, the world is running a perfect simulation of the final physics. Consciousness is, if benignly emergent, a feature of a high-level description, apparent only to consciousness itself. The world does not need to pay, and is not paying, any attention to it. It is, therefore, epiphenomenal.

Or else it is radically emergent (hopefully—I guess—a case of radical physical emergence). This would mean that the physical world itself is the home of radical emergence—and I mean here, as earlier, radical causal emergence, not explanatory emergence, the "disunity of science," theoretical nonreductionism, or some other weaker notion by which we might seek to salve our consciences. I think that this idea would be a stunning reversal of three hundred years of scientific progress and require a complete rethinking of the metaphysical basis of naturalism and the very nature of physical theory. For example, radical emergentism would seem to raise serious problems for some basic conservation laws (notably the conservation of energy), which form a part of the basic physical theory, which are evident at all levels of description, and which are all "implemented" in the most fundamental physical processes. If this is the cost of a scientific approach to consciousness, then it is a very high cost indeed.

It remains possible to say that although the metaphysical picture of physical resolution suggested by the approaching final physics has no alternative, we are simply incapable of understanding how consciousness can be fitted into the picture. If this is the correct response to the dilemma, then the argument of this chapter is another step in the development of "mysterianism" about consciousness.[15] Although it is seemingly evident that nature has managed to combine consistently a genuinely efficacious consciousness with a world that causally resolves itself into a system of nonconscious elementary units, how this has been accomplished is as deep a mystery as the production of consciousness itself.[16]

Notes

1. Would it ever make sense to start such a project? Not if computer technology progresses sufficiently quickly. Suppose that the original length of the computation is n years, and technology advances so quickly that after d years have passed the computation would take less than $n - d$ years. Then it would never make sense to start the computation. Of course, there are noncomputer technical constraints on the time required for such computations, and presumably the pace of progress in computer technology must eventually slow down rather than continue its heretofore exponential acceleration. For some n, the computations make sense, as evidenced by the real world examples given earlier; but the problem of this note is equally well illustrated (see Weingarten, 1996). Computers of the 1980s would have taken about one hundred years to perform the reported computations. The project was not worth starting.

2. Could we define physicalism in terms of this imaginary computer implementation of final physics? We might try something like this: Physicalism is the doctrine that everything that occurs/exists in the actual world would have its exact counterpart in a final physics computer simulation of the world, or that the simulation would be, in some appropriate sense, indistinguishable from the actual world. Such a formulation has the advantage of automatically including what Hellman and Thompson, 1977, call the principle of physical exhaustion, but it obviously requires a clearer specification.

3. The classical doctrine of radical mental emergence is associated with such authors as C.D. Broad, 1925 and C. Lloyd Morgan, 1923. A modern review of this material would be welcome. For a start, see Kim, 1993, chapter 8; and for more on emergence, see the collection edited by Beckermann, Flohr, and Kim, 1992.

4. Searle's example of weight really belongs in the category of causally emergent

features, since the binding energy between the constituents—a matter of their causal interaction—affects the mass of the total system.

5. Many deep issues lurk in this region, having to do with the emergence of the apparently classical macroworld from the nonclassical, quantum microworld; see Hughes, 1989.

6. One story goes like this: An experimentalist rushes to show the latest graph to a theorist, who proclaims, "This is easy to explain," and launches into a theoretical assessment. The experimentalist breaks in with "I'm sorry, this graph is upside down." The theoretician replies, "Ah, this is even easier to explain."

7. What is more, it is possible to add to property and substance emergence a notion of law emergence (in fact, this is the sort of emergence that writers like Broad and Morgan may have had in mind). Law emergence would posit that certain complex assemblies of matter exhibit novel behavior in virtue of obeying genuinely new laws of nature. In terms of our computational thought experiment, the behavior of such complex assemblies would diverge from the behavior of identical simulated assemblies because of the new, high-level laws of nature that govern emergent phenomena at the appropriate level of complexity. It may be, however, that law emergence is not a genuinely distinct sort of emergence if we take the view that it is the properties of things that explain why they obey the laws that they do. If there is a physical description of the conditions under which the new laws emerge and "take hold" (and presumably there is if they are laws), then perhaps we could regard systems that meet these descriptions as possessing an emergent property that causes the divergent behavior. It is not clear to me whether this is an alternative to law emergence or simply a different formulation of it.

8. For more on this idea and its relation to epistemic/explanatory matters, see Seager, 1991.

9. One possible snare: The conscious apprehension of "average family size" evidently can cause things, but examples like these are—if they are examples of efficacy of any kind—examples of the efficacy of representational states of mind, not of the efficacy of what is represented. Thoughts about unicorns have their effects, but admitting this does not concede any causal powers to unicorns.

10. It is one of the glories of physics that it often can show how the elementary transforms itself into complex systems that obey the laws of the high-level theories, as in the case of thermodynamics, but in many other places as well. For example, Newton famously showed how the gravitational force of a myriad of low-mass particles could act as a single high-mass object, and it is a set piece in physics texts how the angular momentum of the parts of a body is combined into the angular momentum of the whole (from which follows the law of the conservation of angular momentum). Nowadays, chaos theory is successfully entering this business. The way that thermodynamical properties emerge may have more relevance to psychology than mere metaphor. There are deep analogies between thermodynamics and the dynamics of neural networks (see, for example, Churchland and Sejnowski, 1992), and if the latter underlie psychology, then psychological properties may be surprisingly closely analogous to thermodynamical properties.

11. I think that this is misleadingly labeled by Kim. It should be termed something like "efficacy exclusion." Explanation is a matter of how we understand phenomena, and for that, the high-level schemes of benignly emergent properties are indispensable and do not exclude one another. But efficacy is a matter of what is driving the world

forward at its metaphysical roots, and there if the efficacy of the elementary parts, in all their conjunctions, suffices to produce every phenomenon in the world, then there is just no evidence for their being any other efficacious features in the world.

12. This is somewhat crude. For a more precise discussion of efficacy and counterfactuals, see Seager, 1991, chapter 6.

13. I note again that panpsychism should be allowed as a third, though I doubt any more welcome, disjunct.

14. This is almost evident from the way that talk of pressure will break down in conditions of extremely rarified gases. While we reduce the number of particles to very small numbers, pressure can be held constant in the sense that we can imagine increasing the velocity of the remaining particles of the gas, but with sufficient rarefaction we will no longer observe pressurelike phenomena.

15. The term "mysterianism" is Owen Flanagan's (1992, p. 9) dismissive label for the views of Colin McGinn, 1989, and certain aspects of Thomas Nagel's position on subjectivity (see Nagel, 1974).

16. Another possible response, but one I will not explore here, is the wholesale denial of the kind of scientific realism that underpins the whole argument given here. A nonrealist approach to science similar to that of Bas van Fraassen reduces all scientific theorizing to mere model constructing (see van Fraassen, 1980). The realm of efficacy can then be in the surface phenomena, where we found it in the first place. However, a problem analogous to the one urged earlier will emerge in the efforts to make the maximally unified model of the physical world. We may have to be content with a radically disunified science.

References

Albert, David. 1992. *Quantum Mechanics and Experience.* Cambridge, MA: Harvard University Press.

Beckermann, A., Flohr, H., and Kim, J. (Eds.). 1992. *Emergence or Reduction? Essays on the Prospects of Nonreductive Physicalism.* Berlin: W. de Gruyter.

Begelman, Mitchell, and Rees, Martin. 1996. *Gravity's Fatal Attraction: Black Holes in the Universe.* New York: Scientific American Library, distributed by W.H. Freeman.

Broad, C.D. 1925. *The Mind and Its Place in Nature.* London: Paul, Trench, Trubner.

Churchland, Patricia, and Sejnowski, Terrence. 1992. *The Computational Brain: Models and Methods on the Frontier of Computational Neuroscience.* Cambridge, MA: MIT Press.

Churchland, Paul. 1985. "Reduction, Qualia and the Direct Introspection of Brain States." *The Journal of Philosophy*, 82, pp. 8–28.

Dennett, Daniel. 1987. *The Intentional Stance.* Cambridge, MA: MIT Press.

———. 1991a. *Consciousness Explained.* Boston: Little, Brown.

———. 1991b. "Real Patterns." *Journal of Philosophy*, 88, pp. 27–51.

Flanagan, Owen. 1992. *Consciousness Reconsidered.* Cambridge, MA: MIT Press.

Hawking, Stephen. 1988. *A Brief History of Time.* New York: Bantam Books.

Hellman, Geoffrey, and Thompson, Frank. 1977. "Physicalist Materialism." *Noûs*, 11, pp. 309–45.

Horgan, John. 1996. *The End of Science: Facing the Limits of Knowledge in the Twilight of the Scientific Age*. Reading, MA: Addison-Wesley.

Hughes, R.I.G. 1989. *The Structure and Interpretation of Quantum Mechanics*. Cambridge, MA: Harvard University Press.

Kim, Jaegwon. 1993. *Supervenience and Mind*. Cambridge, UK: Cambridge University Press.

McGinn, Colin. 1989. "Can We Solve the Mind-Body Problem?" *Mind*, 98(391), pp. 349–66.

Morgan, Conwy Lloyd. 1923. *Emergent Evolution*. London: Routledge and Kegan Paul.

Nagel, Thomas. 1974. "What Is It Like to Be a Bat?" *Philosophical Review*, 83, pp. 435–50. Reprinted in Nagel, *Mortal Questions*. Cambridge: Cambridge University Press, 1979.

Seager, William. 1991. *Metaphysics of Consciousness*. London: Routledge.

————. 1996. "A Note on the Quantum Eraser." *Philosophy of Science*, 63(1), pp. 81–90.

Searle, John. 1992. *The Rediscovery of the Mind*. Cambridge, MA: MIT Press.

van Frassen, B. 1980. *The Scientific Image*. Oxford: Clarendon Press.

Weinberg, Steven. 1992. *Dreams of a Final Theory: The Search for the Fundamental Laws of Nature*. New York: Pantheon Books.

Weingarten, Donald. 1996. "Quarks by Computer." *Scientific American*, 274(2), pp. 116–20.

III

Eliminative Materialism:
Sound or Mistaken?

Introduction

David Martel Johnson

Those people we refer to as eliminative materialists maintain that the world is thoroughly material in nature, and, furthermore, that this implies that the informal theory about human beings' outer behavior and inner mental workings commonly called folk psychology must be wrong. To be more specific, these thinkers claim it follows from the facts that the world is material, and that material things behave and interact in certain ways, that there are not, never were, and never could be any such items as the beliefs, desires, emotions, sensations, moods, acts of choosing, and so on that ordinary people, some philosophers, and some philosophically inclined scientists think of as constituting the human mind.

This position has not proved popular. For example, the great majority of present-day theorists would answer the question posed in the title of this part by saying that eliminativism was mistaken. In fact, quite a few observers think that this view has roughly the same status as that associated, during the classical period of Greece, with the radical skepticism of Gorgias and with Zeno's paradoxical arguments against the possibility of motion. According to them, in other words, it is a position that (virtually) everybody knows is false, even though it is surprisingly difficult—perhaps even impossible—to say how and why it is false. All four of the chapters included in this part of the book fall into this same general pattern. That is, all the authors represented here agree that eliminativism is false, and merely disagree about what is the most basic error involved in that position, and how that error (the one each author chooses) needs to be remedied.

Thus in the first chapter (titled, a bit immodestly, "A Particularly Compelling Refutation of Eliminative Materialism"), William Lycan claims that the key to exposing the pretensions of eliminativists like the Churchlands and Stephen Stich is to revive a version of an argument that once played a central role in the "commonsense philosophy" of G.E Moore. It is important to see, Lycan says, that this argument takes the form of a "plausibility comparison." In particular, it boils down to the assertion that there is no abstractly formulated premise to which a philosopher might appeal, as part of an attempt to establish his or her conclusion that beliefs and desires do not exist, that could have as much evidential weight as any concrete instance of the contrary claim, with which we are acquainted from familiar contexts of ordinary life. Thus, in Lycan's opinion, the only thing necessary to show that eliminativism stands on an unsound foundation is to ask oneself, honestly, which of the following two propositions is more convincing: (1) "There are no beliefs, desires, or minds that exist anywhere in the universe"; or (2) a case proposed by Lycan, "Granny wants a beer, and believes there is one under the couch."

By contrast, Ausonio Marras ("Commonsense Refutations of Eliminativism") and also David Henderson and Terry Horgan ("What Does It Take to Be a True Believer? Against the Opulent Ideology of Eliminative Materialism") reject Lycan's proposed critical strategy on the grounds that it fails to take account of the nontrivial distinction between philosophical propositions, contexts, and procedures of confirmation, on one side, and those associated with common sense (and science), on the other. Because of this distinction, these last people say, theorists are only entitled to "fight fire with fire." In other words, they must employ all and only philosophical statements and arguments in attempts to mount an attack on a philosophical position like eliminativism.

Let me summarize this disagreement between Lycan and his critics still more completely, as follows. Lycan proposes to justify his Moore-like procedure of assessing philosophical claims by comparing their plausibility with that of parallel statements in everyday life, by invoking Willard Quine's doctrine that there are no reliable means of dividing a priori, philosophical propositions, on the one hand, from empirically known propositions of science and common sense, on the other. Evidently Marras, Henderson, and Horgan do not agree with this Quinean doctrine, or do not believe it carries the same implications Lycan says it does. And because of this, all these last people say it is necessary to refute eliminativism in another, more indirect fashion.

Barbara Von Eckardt's chapter is different from the other three, because it is the only one that does not take explicit account of Lycan's position. Instead, her concern is with another, related problem, derived from an earlier article by Ramsey, Stich, and Garon (1990). As indicated by the title of her chapter, "Connectionism and the Propositional Attitudes," it is the question of whether, on the hypothetical assumption that future experimental neuroscience showed that the brain was structurally organized along "connectionist" lines (so that, e.g., beliefs did not have localized positions in the brain but instead were widely distributed), that automatically would establish the truth of eliminative materialism and the falsity of folk psychology as well. According to Von Eckardt, the answer is no. Nevertheless, her strategy for defending this answer is at least roughly analogous to the one that Marras and Henderson and Horgan employ, as shown by the fact that she also considers it illegitimate and perhaps even nonsensical to appeal to commonsense statements as a means of judging the adequacy and truth of a philosophical thesis (e.g., one based on certain findings of brain science). Does she take this position because it seems to her that commonsense ways of thinking and talking about mental phenomena do not really amount to a theory at all, and therefore cannot compete either with philosophical claims or with discoveries made by scientists? Or is the reason that even though folk psychology has some kind of genuine theoretical import, she thinks that its theoretical force has nothing to do with either philosophical or scientific accounts of the human brain? As far as I can tell, these are questions that, at least in this chapter, do not receive answers.

Finally, let me expand the discussion to give readers a sense of the extremely wide, complex, and controversial context in which the philosophical position of eliminative materialism is set. To be specific, another possible problem with this view, of quite a different sort than those discussed by the five authors just mentioned, is this. Suppose that eliminativists at last realized their dream of convincing the great majority of their fellow theorists that beliefs, desires, and minds were merely mythical entities that had no legitimate standing in the body of scientifically confirmed knowledge. Would they then have to say exactly the same thing about all the theoretical entities scientists have posited, without exception? By parity of reasoning, for example, would they also be forced to deny that there were electrons, the element carbon, the Big Bang, the DNA molecule, the species bottle-nose dolphin, the genus of giant squids called *Architeuthis*, and so on? One reason for thinking that the answer is yes is that eliminativists propose to justify their claim that beliefs and other mental entities are bogus rather than real by pointing out how misleading all these entities are. According to them, in other words, anyone who maintained (falsely) that beliefs and desires were genuinely existing things eventually would be forced to accept an indeterminate, but progressively increasing, number of additional false propositions as well. But the trouble with this idea is that, as philosophers of science are fond of pointing out, absolutely all scientific theories—even those that are best confirmed and most widely accepted—either include or imply false statements. Accordingly, it seems to follow that eliminativists do not have any good means of deciding which theoretical entities exist and which do not. In fact, it is apparently the case that their program would involve the destruction of the whole ideal of objective, scientific knowledge, since it would introduce a kind of radical relativity, where that which exists would depend on the outlook and commitments of the person who happened to be considering the matter.

Nietzsche says (*Twilight of the Idols*, "Maxims and Arrows," "Maxim 36") that no prince sits on his throne securely, unless and until an anarchist tries to assassinate him. Similarly, even though eliminativism is beset on all sides by powerful objections, this does not prove that—similar to Zeno's arguments against motion—it is nothing more than a hopeless view that no one needs to take seriously. For example, one important result of eliminativists' attack on the notion of "mind" (parallel to the case of Nietzsche's anarchist) may be that it forces us to make that notion clearer and sharper than it was before. More concretely, eliminativism may have established the point that the idea of mind (at least as its past defenders understood it) was too weak, vague, and implicitly contradictory to be a useful guide for picking out real and existing items. But, encouraged by eliminativists' objections, we now have an opportunity to reconstruct this concept on a more adequate foundation. In particular, my own view is that eliminativists are right to locate the essence or center of what we now think of as mind in the propositional attitudes of belief and desire. But instead of implying that since brain science has shown that there are no beliefs, there also cannot be any such things as minds, this might only mean that, although there are minds that exist now, there were no such items in the relatively recent past. However, what I am talking about in these final, digressing sentences is, as they say, another story.[1]

Note

1. For a further account of this same story, see Johnson, 1997, 2000, and 2003.

References

Johnson, David Martel. 1997. "Taking the Past Seriously: How History Shows That Eliminativists' Account of Folk Psychology is Partly Right and Partly Wrong." Pp. 366–75 in D. M. Johnson and C. E. Erneling (Eds.), *The Future of the Cognitive Revolution*. New York: Oxford University Press.
———. 2000. "Aristotle's Curse of Non-existence against 'Barbarians.'" Pp. 126–35 in D. Sfendoni-Mentzou (Ed.), *Aristotle and Contemporary Science*. Vol. 1. New York: Peter Lang.
———. 2003. *How History Made the Mind: The Cultural Origins of Objective Thinking*. Chicago: Open Court Press.
Johnson, D.M., and Erneling, C.E. (Eds.). 1997. *The Future of the Cognitive Revolution*. New York: Oxford University Press.
Ramsey, W., Stich, S., and Garon, J. 1990. "Connectionism, Eliminativism, and the Future of Folk Psychology." *Philosophical Perspectives*, 4, pp. 499–533.
Sfendoni-Mentzou, D. (Ed.). 2000. *Aristotle and Contemporary Science*. Vol. 1. New York: Peter Lang.

10

A Particularly Compelling Refutation of Eliminative Materialism

William G. Lycan

The 1960s saw heated discussion of eliminative materialism in regard to *sensations* and their phenomenal features. Thus directed, eliminative materialism is materialism or physicalism plus the distinctive and truly radical thesis that there have never occurred any sensations; no one has ever experienced a sensation. This view attracted few adherents, though to this day some philosophers are eliminativists with respect to various alleged phenomenal features of sensations.

But in the 1980s the eliminativist focus shifted to the propositional attitudes. Eliminativism in regard to these is materialism plus the claim that no creature has ever had a belief, desire, intention, hope, wish, or the like. Though no one out-and-out accepts this startling doctrine without qualification, Paul Churchland, Patricia Churchland, Stephen Stich in some moods, and others have endorsed it as a plausible conjecture or good bet.[1]

Why would anyone take so outrageous an idea seriously for thirty seconds, much less consider it a good bet? There are arguments, and some of them seem fairly powerful. Each of the arguments presupposes the widely held "theory" theory of folk or commonsense psychological ascriptions. Each of the latter references needs explaining.

Folk psychology (cf. folk physics, folk meteorology) is the set of commonsense generalizations about the mind, "platitudes," as David Lewis calls them, at least tacitly accepted by almost everyone and expected by almost everyone to be accepted by almost everyone (e.g., "If a person wants X, believes that Y is a means of getting X, and has neither any better strategy nor any competing desire or motive, the person will try to obtain Y," or "People don't like having their toes stepped on"). According to the "theory" theory of folk psychology, the folk generalizations are at least roughly causal-explanatory in purport; we use them in the explanation and prediction of human behavior. The mental states and events that figure in them are the theoretical entities posited by the proponents of these explanatory hypotheses. Thus propositional attitudes are conceived as inner states of people that supposedly play characteristic roles in causing these people's behavior.

Here, in brief, are some of the eliminativist arguments against the reality of the attitudes (the arguments overlap somewhat):

E1. Folk psychology is a failed or at least bad theory, superseded by a better cognitive science or neuroscience, and so should be rejected as false.

E2. Folk psychology will not be vindicated by either cognitive science or neuroscience and so should be rejected as false.

E3. Folk psychology itself posits things of a kind that will simply not be found in human brains or anywhere else in nature.

E4. Folk psychology presupposes supervenient causation of propositional attitudes by perceptual and other states, and of behavior by the attitudes. But if the attitudes are supposed to do their causing by virtue of their propositional contents, then there is a problem of explanatory exclusion, leading to a charge of epiphenomenalism:[2] Suppose that a memory, say of singing a wrong note in public, causes me to wince in embarrassment. The memory presumably causes the wince by being identical with or at least supervening on a neurophysiological state N that (together with background conditions) guarantees the wince by biological law. But then N and the background conditions alone suffice to cause the wince; the object or content of the memory itself—my having sung the wrong note—plays no role and is in that sense epiphenomenal.

E5. Folk psychology characterizes propositional attitudes as "wide" features of cognizers—that is, as features that do not supervene on their subjects' molecular composition at the time; attitude contents are determined in part by causal, historical, and social factors outside the subjects' heads; and this makes the attitudes objectionably un- or contrascientific and possibly epiphenomenal again (cf. also the more recent problems of intentional causation).

E6. According to a competing line of attack, attitude contents are determined neither by what is in subjects' heads nor by causal, historical, and social factors; in fact, they are entirely indeterminate. Can we then still suppose that the attitude contents are genuine properties of the owner/subject?

Unsurprisingly, there are also a number of common arguments against eliminativism. I will list these too, in order to emphasize that my own antieliminativist case will rely on none of them.

F1. The "theory" theory itself is a false account of folk psychology. (That is not a direct argument against eliminativism, but it would undercut every known defense of the view. Also, I myself accept the "theory" theory, so I will have no truck with this argument.)

F2. We know that there are propositional attitudes because we introspect them in ourselves.

F3. The posited attitudes are indispensable to prediction, reasoning, deliberation and understanding, the capturing of important macroscopic generalizations, and/or various less cognitive pursuits.

F4. "Cognitive suicide" arguments show that eliminativism is somehow self-defeating or self-refuting.

I believe that both (F2) and (F3) can be fleshed out into powerful defenses of folk psychology; I think that (F4) is hopeless. But as I have said, my own antieliminativist argument is distinct from all these. It is a Moorean argument. Indeed, it is a fairly obvious Moorean argument, and I am surprised not to have heard it given by anyone previously. (Naturally, I have heard no rebuttal either.)

Remember how G.E. Moore used to argue against idealists and other anti-realists (as well as skeptics). In considering an antirealist view, he would first draw from it a very specific negative consequence regarding his own everyday experience. For example, take the idealist claim that there are no material objects, as defended by, among others, Bradley and McTaggart. From it, Moore would deduce that he, Moore, did not have hands at the ends of his arms—hands being near-paradigm cases of material objects. (Some scholarly work was put in, in order to assure us that the idealist claim was intended in such a sense as to have that consequence.)

Now, consider the idealist's defense of the antirealist claim about material objects. Let us charitably suppose that the defense has taken the form of a deductively valid argument. The argument must of course (on pain of regress) have had premises, themselves undefended, so it is an argument that looks schematically like this:

(P_1) . . .
(P_2) . . .

.
.

[steps]

.
.

∴ (C) There are no material objects. QED

To this we may add as a corollary:

∴ (C′) I do not have hands.

By hypothesis, the argument is valid. But that is to say only that each of the sets $\{P_1, \ldots P_n, \sim C\}$ and $\{P_1, \ldots P_n, \sim C'\}$ is inconsistent. The idealist of course wants us to accept P_1–P_n and therefore to accept C and reject $\sim C$ on the strength of them. But nothing in the argument itself forces us to do that, since if we wish to deny its conclusion we have only to reject one of the premises. Any argument can be turned on its head.

More generally—in fact, throughout philosophy and every other subject—a deductive "proof" can be no more than an invitation to compare plausibility: Of the propositions $P_1, \ldots P_n$, and $\sim C$, which is the least plausible?

Applying that crucial question to any specific argument for idealism concerning the external world, Moore thought that it scarcely left room for debate. Since ~C, the reality of material objects, is directly entailed by something Moore already knows to be true (~C', that he does have hands), the culprit must be one of the other members of the inconsistent set; it must be one of the premises that is false. It may be interesting to continue our plausibility survey and decide which of the P_i is less plausible than the rest; in fact, surely it will be instructive and illuminating to do that. But that is not necessary in order to vindicate our commonsense belief in the reality of material objects. For the latter philosophical purpose, it does not matter which of the P_i is false. In fact, we do not even have to know what the argument's premises are exactly; whatever they are, they cannot all be true. The idealist was doomed from the start.

I have deliberately made Moore sound closed-minded, dogmatic, and pig-headed. Many philosophers have rejected his style of argument on just that ground, finding it obvious that Moore is just begging the question against his opponent, and rather crassly too. But it is important to see that Moore is doing no such thing. He is only modestly inviting a plausibility comparison. The comparison is, in effect, between (a) "Here is one hand and here is another" and (b) a purely philosophical premise such as McTaggart's assumption that every existing thing has proper parts that are themselves substances.[3] How could a proposition like (b) be considered as plausible as (a)? How could I possibly be more certain or more confident that every existent thing has proper parts that are substances than that I have hands?

We may wonder where metaphysical premises (often called intuitions) come from. Are they deliverances of the *lumen naturale*? Does the Third Eye of the metaphysician's mind get a rare look at a Platonic Form? Perhaps they just articulate features of our ordinary ways of conceiving certain things. Whatever, their epistemic credentials are obscure, and more important, they are shoddy. A metaphysician who claims to "just know" that such an abstract premise is true ("This is a very deep intuition") cannot be taken very seriously. But Moore has excellent grounds for the competing proposition (a): He remembers seeing and feeling his hands on millions of occasions, and he can do so again at will. A forced choice between (a) and (b) has got to favor (a).

Even so, is Moore clinging to his humdrum commonsense beliefs come what may? Is common sense then sacred and utterly irrefutable? Is that not precisely what our founder, Socrates, taught us to leave behind, indeed, to snicker at? Remember, it used to be "common sense," as obvious as practically anything, that Earth is flat and motionless, and that the Sun rises and gradually travels westward to pass over our heads.

This is a second standard misinterpretation of Moore. Moore did not hold that common sense is irrefutable. Commonsense beliefs can be corrected, even trashed entirely, by careful empirical investigation and scientific theorizing. (Literal) exploration and astronomy have teamed up to show that despite appearances, the Earth is a spheroid that moves around the Sun and that "up" means only "away." Chemistry and physics have shown that the most "solid" granite boulder is actually a region of nearly completely empty space, populated only by some minuscule and invisible particles racing through it at unimaginable speeds.

But philosophers (especially idealist philosophers) are not explorers or scientists. McTaggart provided no evidence for his claim that every existent thing has proper parts that are substances; it just seemed true to him, for some reason. Common sense must yield to evidence, as I have said; but it need not yield to bare metaphysical pronouncement. Moreover, as is notorious, a priori metaphysical views historically have little staying power; one philosophical era's fundamental principles are often rejected in the next era as ludicrous superstition. No purely philosophical premise can ever (legitimately) have as strong a claim to our allegiance as can a humble commonsense proposition such as Moore's autobiographical one. Science can correct common sense; metaphysics and philosophical "intuition" can only throw spitballs.

This brings me (none too soon) back to the admittedly scientistic doctrine of eliminative materialism. I contend that the eliminativist is refuted by Moore's technique in just the same way as was the spatial or temporal idealist.

The argument will now be quite straightforward: Numerous commonsense mental ascriptions, such as that Granny wants a beer and believes there is one under the sofa, are individually more plausible, and always will be more plausible, than are the purely philosophical premises of any argument designed to convince us to the contrary. As Moore saw, purely philosophical assumptions have very weak epistemic credentials and cannot by themselves outweigh simple commonsense facts.

The eliminativist may protest that his/her case is not purely philosophical, but rests on scientific considerations of cognitive psychology, neuroscience, connectionist modeling, and the like. Indeed, that flaunted feature is what often makes eliminativism sound so hip. But this is to misunderstand the Moorean argument a third time. Moore would not deny that arguments for eliminativism contain premises that are endorsed, perhaps simply established, by science. The point is that each argument also contains at least one purely philosophical premise. Make no mistake: In order to reach the staggering conclusion that there has never been a belief, a desire, or any other propositional attitude, any argument for eliminativism will have to rest on one or more a priori principles connecting scientific truths to negative ontology. And it is terminally unlikely that any such principle could be more credible for me than that Granny wants beer. Come to think of it, I want beer.

Notice that my Moorean argument is immune to the customary Churchland-Churchland counterblow, a comparison to alchemy, witchcraft, and other folk but false theories. However beloved such theories were to their proponents, they do not qualify as Moorean common sense. To count as Moorean-commonsensical, a belief must be the sort of belief that every normal human being holds every day of his/her life, such as "Here is one hand and here is another," or "I had breakfast before I had lunch," or "The sun is shining." Thus, to address the topic of this book directly, whatever science can show about the mind, it cannot show that there is none.

I pause to deal with a trenchant objection offered by Ann Wilbur MacKenzie,[4] who reminded me that according to one school of linguistic theory, lexical semantics is an empirical science—in particular, it is claimed, there can be purely empirical evidence for propositions to the effect that a predicate F_1 analytically implies another predicate F_2.[5] Suppose we were to get empirical evidence that, say, "S believes that p" entails something dubious, say, "S's brain has a live turtle in it." Then we would have a compelling argument for eliminativism about beliefs, with no philosophical premises. (Until now I have tacitly been assuming that lexical semantics is not empirical but philosophical, and that any such entailment claim is a tendentious philosophical thesis.) The argument would run as follows:

(1) [Empirical data $e_1, \ldots e_n$]
∴ (2) "S believes that p" entails "S's brain has a live turtle in it." [Ampliative scientific inference from $e_1, \ldots e_n$]
∴ (3) "If S believes that p, then S's brain has a live turtle in it" is true. [From 2, by corresponding conditional theorem]
∴ (4) If S believes that p, then S's brain has a live turtle in it. [3, Disquotation]
(5) No one's brain has a live turtle in it. [Empirical fact]
∴ (6) S's brain does not have a live turtle in it. [5]
∴ (7) S does not believe that p. [4, 6]
∴ (8) No one has ever believed anything. [Universal generalization from 7, since "S" and "p" were arbitrary names] QED

None of this argument's premises is contentious in a distinctively philosophical way.

My own position is that lexical semantics is not empirical, at least not to the degree intended, that is, that there is no uncontroversial form of ampliative inference from any robust body of publicly observable data to semantic claims such as (2), and further, that such semantic claims are indeed philosophical in my somewhat pejorative sense. My reason is Quinean: I do not accept any principled distinction between allegedly analytic truths and merely widespread commonsense beliefs, or between purely lexical implications and material inferences.[6] There is no space here to rehearse the arguments for and against this skepticism. Instead, for the sake of discussion I shall abandon the Quinean position and grant the existence in principle of analytic lexical implications, but argue that eliminativism is in trouble nonetheless.

Suppose, then, that there are lexical implications that can be discovered empirically by linguists. But my example is obviously extreme, for surely "S believes that p" does not analytically imply "S's brain has a live turtle in it." I chose that example to illustrate how a well-established empirical fact could be used to support eliminativism without the aid of philosophical premises; the consequent of the eliminativist's corresponding conditional is supposed to be a proposition that science (unaided) can discover to be false. But at the same time it should not be so garishly false as "S's brain has a live turtle in it." The conditional will presumably have the form "If S believes that p, then S is in a state of type F," but the non-existence of F-states will not be so obvious or so easy for science to establish.

The trouble is that there is a tradeoff here, to wit, an inverse proportion between the scientific impeachability of the consequent and the apparent analyticity of the conditional itself. In my turtle example, the consequent is eminently impeachable, but the conditional is ludicrous. But at the other end of the spectrum, if we have a plausible candidate for an analytic conditional, the conditional's consequent will be pretty safe from science. Take "If S believes that p, then if other things are equal, S is disposed to assert that p," which I suppose would be analytic if any such conditional were. It is hard to imagine how science (alone) might falsify "If other things are equal, S is disposed to assert that p" — and remember that on MacKenzie's strategy, it is science alone that must falsify the consequent.

Consider an intermediate candidate: "If S believes that p, then some state of S's brain has the content that p." Though it is hard to see how science alone might impugn that conditional's consequent, perhaps it is possible. But the conditional is hardly analytic, for "S believes that p" does not mean anything about any brain. Let us move back along the spectrum toward analyticity by deleting the anatomical reference: "If S believes that p, then some inner state of S has the content that p." Now it is harder to imagine science's falsifying the consequent, because for all the conditional asserts, the "inner state" may be global and utterly diffuse or distributed. But at the same time, even this weaker conditional is not a plausible candidate for analyticity: Behaviorists, Wittgensteinians, and such who deny that beliefs are or require inner states were not simply contradicting themselves.

Thus a dilemma: For any conditional premise mobilized by the eliminativist, if that conditional is plausibly taken as analytic, its consequent seems immune to purely scientific refutation — and contrapositively, if its consequent risks such refutation, it is pretty plainly not analytic.

Of course, the believer in analyticity need not hold that all analyticities are obvious. Perhaps a conditional like "If S believes that p, then some inner state of S has the content that p" is indeed deeply analytic even though it does not seem so, and the behaviorists and such do not seem to be contradicting themselves. But this possibility is of no use to the eliminativist, for a deep, unobvious analyticity has no epistemic power, even if it makes for metaphysical necessity. Even if there is a hidden contradiction in the idea of someone's believing that p without being in an internal state of some scientifically vulnerable kind, that does not help the eliminativist use the relevant negative scientific discovery to overturn common-sense belief ascriptions. If we are to be convinced that we should give up on belief, the contradiction would have to be brought out by further argument. For these reasons, I do not think that MacKenzie's strategy can succeed.

My antieliminativist argument has one sobering feature: that of seeming to prove too much. If I am right, then it seems that there simply could not be any successful philosophical argument for eliminativism; and since there is unlikely to be any nonphilosophical argument for eliminativism at all, the doctrine is systematically indefensible. Yet (contra the "cognitive suicide" arguments [F4]) it is perfectly coherent, indeed empirical. How can a thesis be both empirical and seemingly impossible to defend?

Theoretically, commonsense views can conflict not just with philosophical assumptions but directly (neglecting the laws of logic) with each other. (A candidate triple might be "People autonomously perform many entirely free actions," "Actions are physical events," and "Every physical event has a determining, nomologically sufficient physical cause"—though I myself do not think that any of these three propositions qualifies as commonsensical.) So perhaps some commonsense views must face plausibility comparisons with each other, and one must lose, thus being defeated not by science but by philosophy plus other common sense.

But it seems unlikely that our folk psychological ascriptions would meet this unusual fate. Are we then stuck with the odd contention that folk psychology is an empirical but also irrefutable theory?

There is a halfway house. Recall "solid." Chemistry and physics showed us something very startling and contracommonsensical about our granite boulder, something that can fairly be expressed in eliminative style by saying that the boulder is not solid at all. Yet of course the boulder is solid: It is impenetrable, hard, and obdurate, and if one chips at it or splits it open, one finds only more boulder inside, without perceptible gaps. There is a difference between being solid in this operational sense and being solid in the sense of being filled through and through (to the real continuum) with stuff. Science has forced us to distinguish these two paronymous meanings of the word.[7] So too, perhaps, science will force us to distinguish a fairly superficial, operational sense of "believe" and the rest from a more commissive sense. But no eliminativist argument has yet been convincing enough to do that either.

Notes

1. E.g., P.M. Churchland, "Eliminative Materialism and the Propositional Attitudes," *Journal of Philosophy*, 78 (1981), pp. 67–90; P.M. Churchland and P.S. Churchland, "Stalking the Wild Epistemic Engine," *Noûs*, 17 (1983), pp. 5–18; S.P. Stich, *From Folk Psychology to Cognitive Science* (Cambridge, MA: MIT Press/Bradford Books, 1983); W. Ramsey, S. Stich, and J. Garon, "Connectionism, Eliminativism, and the Future of Folk Psychology," in J. Greenwood (Ed.), *The Future of Folk Psychology* (Cambridge, UK: Cambridge University Press, 1991).

2. See, e.g., Jaegwon Kim, "Mechanism, Purpose, and Explanatory Exclusion," in J.E. Tomberlin (Ed.), *Philosophy of Mind and Action Theory*, Philosophical Perspectives, 3 (Atascadero, CA: Ridgeview Publishing, 1989).

3. J. McTaggert, *The Nature of Existence*. Vol. 1 (Cambridge, UK: Cambridge University Press, 1921).

4. During the discussion of this chapter at the conference "The Mind as a Scientific Object," York University, 1996.

5. Jerrold J. Katz is perhaps the best-known remorseless defender of this position.

See, e.g., *The Philosophy of Language* (New York, Harper and Row, 1966), and "Where Things Now Stand with the Analytic-Synthetic Distinction," *Synthese*, 28 (1974), pp. 283–319.

6. See Chapters 11 and 12 of my *Modality and Meaning* (Dordrecht: Kluwer Academic Publishing, 1994). Someone might argue that even if such a conditional as "If S believes that *p*, then S's brain has a live turtle in it" is only a commonsense generalization rather than an analytic truth, then a fortiori it is a commonsense proposition; if it is a commonsense proposition, then it is at worst on all fours with a mental ascription such as "S believes that *p*," and so the eliminativist argument still eschews reliance on any tendentiously philosophical premise. Of course, no one could call my extreme example, "If S believes that *p*, then S's brain has a live turtle in it," a commonsensical proposition. But not even a vastly more cautious instance of "If S believes that *p*, then S is in a state of type F" would really qualify as commonsensical in Moore's strong sense; so long as F-states are themselves scientifically rather than commonsensically decidable, the relevant instance of our schema will hardly be the sort of thing that ordinary people believe every day of their lives (more on this later). In addition, it will still lose out in a direct plausibility comparison with "Granny believes there is a beer under the sofa."

7. There is at least one further halfway house: Sellars's solution to Eddington's problem, a relativizing of truth to conceptual framework, combined with a scientistic privileging of one of the frameworks. "Philosophy and the Scientific Image of Man," in R. Colodny (Ed.), *Frontiers of Science and Philosophy* (Pittsburgh, PA: University of Pittsburgh Press, 1962). As Sellars used to put it in conversation, "*Of course* the boulder is solid; but it isn't *really* solid!"

11

Commonsense Refutations
of Eliminativism

Ausonio Marras

Like William Lycan, I too believe that eliminative materialism, in any of its chief varieties, is a false doctrine, but I am skeptical that it is open to a direct, Moorean refutation, as Lycan supposes. Here are the reasons for my skepticism.

1. Eliminativism in regard to the propositional attitudes is, in Lycan's words, "materialism plus the claim that no creature has ever had a belief, desire, intention, hope, wish, or the like." This startling doctrine, endorsed by Churchland, (1981) Stich, (1983) and others as a plausible conjecture, is putatively established by its proponents by a number of arguments such as the ones that Lycan enumerates (E1–E6). But this doctrine, Lycan argues, is refuted by the fact that many commonsense mental ascriptions such as "Granny wants a beer and believes there is one under the sofa" are "individually more plausible . . . than are the purely philosophical premises of any arguments designed to convince us to the contrary." Since on his account the conclusion of eliminativist arguments entails that commonsense ascriptions are never true, the falsity of eliminativism is, he claims, directly entailed by something that he, Lycan, knows to be true (that his Granny wants beer), just as the falsity of McTaggart's claim that time is unreal is "directly entailed" by something that Moore knew to be true (that he had breakfast before he had lunch).

I certainly agree with Lycan that statements of the form "S wants *x*" or "S believes that *p*" have stronger epistemic credentials and are more likely to be true (and known to be true) than any purely philosophical proposition. But I doubt that the truth of such Moorean commonsensical statements directly entails the falsity of eliminativism, the philosophical doctrine that there are no beliefs, desires, and the like. Let me explain by first producing something like an ad hominem argument.

Stephen Stich—possibly the most clearheaded among the eliminativists— once said on this matter: "A question I have often encountered . . . is whether I think there are any such things as beliefs. But the question is less than clear. If it means: Are statements of the form 'S believes that *p*' or '*x* is the belief that p' ever true, the answer is plainly *yes*. . . . However, if the question is construed as asking whether there are belief state tokens or belief state types (i.e., *properties*), then the answer is negative" (Stich 1983, p. 226). Here is a champion of eliminativism who (at least in one of his moods) has no problem allowing that commonsense belief ascriptions are often "plainly true," but who is not prepared to accept (indeed, explicitly denies) what on Lycan's Moorean account they "directly entail"—namely, the thesis that there are such things as beliefs. How can Stich have it both ways? How can he claim both that commonsense belief ascriptions are often plainly true, and that nonetheless there are no belief states or properties? The answer, I think, is as follows.

The thesis that there are (or are not) such things as beliefs, desires, and so on is a philosophical thesis, and like most philosophical theses it does not wear its meaning on its sleeve. Until we are told what kinds of things beliefs are supposed to be, it is "less than clear," as Stich puts it, what we are asking when we ask whether there are any such things as beliefs. The point is that eliminativism, in any of its forms, is a philosophical thesis whose precise content is to be determined not by direct confrontation with commonsense statements, but only vis-à-vis some other philosophical thesis that tells us something about the nature of beliefs and desires, whose existence it affirms. As Lycan himself makes clear, the thesis that various forms of eliminativism oppose is folk psychology under the so-called "theory"theory interpretation; and that, by my lights, is some form or other of intentional realism—the thesis that there are inner states (types and tokens) that meet some such conditions as having determinate content (whether broad or narrow), as having causal efficacy, as having (perhaps) combinatorial structure, and the like. As the various standard arguments for eliminativism make plain, the conclusion they aim to establish is that there are no states or properties that satisfy all or any of these conditions, and depending on which conditions are claimed not to be satisfied, there are distinct brands or grades of eliminativism (including subtle blends of eliminativism and epiphenomenalism, as E4 types of arguments, in Lycan's listing, make plain).

So it is unsurprising that Stich should conclude: "In denying that believing that p is a property [a state type], we need not deny that statements of the form '*x* is a belief that p' are often unproblematically true" (1983, p. 226). For, he explains, "it is simply a mistake to assume that every meaningful predicate or open sentence corresponds to or expresses a property" (p. 225). The point is that while for Stich (at least in one of his moods) a sentence of the form "S believes that *p*" may be unproblematically true, its truth conditions are not unproblematic, or at any rate they are not what intentional realism takes them to be.

Stich holds that ascriptions of the form "S believes that *p*" are true just in case S is in a state similar to the state that would underlie our ordinary utterance of *p*. But for Stich there is no unique such state that all believers that *p* share; and so there is no belief property corresponding to "S believes that *p*"—certainly no belief property of the sort intentional realism claims there is. But still, Stich argues, different people may each be in some state or other that resembles, by diverse and even conflicting similarity measures, the state that would underlie our ordinary utterance of p; and, depending on a number of contextual considerations, people in one or another of these states may sometimes merit a true ascription of the belief predicate. I do not believe Stich's story for a moment; but my aim here is not to defend or refute eliminativism (Stich's or anyone's), but to illustrate how much more tortuous the route is from the acceptance of Moorean commonsense statements to the rejection of a philosophical thesis such as eliminative materialism, than Lycan makes it out to be.

2. Lycan might reasonably protest that I have represented Stich's position in one of his less-than-clearly eliminativist moods (for Stichean scholars, that is the "modified Panglossian" mood; cf. Stich, 1983, chapter 5). Recall that on Stich's "Syntactic Theory of the Mind" (STM), the scientifically relevant—the "real"—mental states are syntactic computational states, which (unlike folk psychological states) have no content essentially. Now as long as the STM theory, in Stich's words, *"cleaves reasonably close to the pattern presupposed by folk psychology,"* (p. 229) belief ascriptions can often be regarded as true, even though the states ascribed are not the belief states of folk theory but, rather, syntactic belief-*like* states (belief-like because they resemble folk-psychological beliefs in regard to their "causal profile" or functional role). If it should turn out (and for Stich, this is a "real possibility," p. 229) that the functional architecture of the mind is significantly different from that presupposed by folk psychology, then belief ascriptions would no longer be unproblematically true (in Stich's words: "We could no longer say that belief sentences stand a good shot at being true"; 1983, p. 229). In that eventuality, there will be nothing—no belief or belief-like state—to which the predicate "is a belief that p" applies. I am much more skeptical than Stich, that such a scenario will ever materialize, but I believe, with Stich, that it is a strictly empirical question whether it will or not: It is not a question to be decided a priori, by means of a Moorean argument.

This brings me to my second main point. As Lycan acknowledges, Moorean common-sense beliefs are not irrefutable. They can be refuted by scientific theorizing. That the earth is flat and motionless was refuted by science, and so was the belief that granite boulders are (literally) solid. So why is it exactly that our commonsense belief in the existence of such states as beliefs and desires is not open to an analogous sort of refutation by what may turn out to be our best scientific psychology? Lycan's answer is: "In order to reach the staggering conclusion that there has never been a belief, a desire, or any other propositional attitude, any argument for eliminativism will have to rest on one or more a priori principles connecting scientific truths to negative ontology. It is terminally unlikely that any such principle could be more credible for me than that Granny wants beer."

I suspect that the same is true of any commonsense empirical belief that stands to be refuted by scientific evidence. Scientific evidence by itself refutes nothing: One needs a complex inductive (or abductive) argument that relates evidence to theory, that confronts the proposed theory with competing theories, and that with the help of several assumptions (methodological, epistemological, and even metaphysical) chooses one theory over competing theories and thus "refutes" the targeted belief. I doubt that there is any real disanalogy between the style of argumentation that would refute our belief in folk psychological beliefs and the style of argumentation that would refute any other commonsensical belief. Eliminativist arguments that appeal to a (future) cognitive psychology to refute our belief in the propositional attitudes will be no more dependent on principles that "connect scientific truths to negative ontology" than are arguments that appeal to basic physics to refute our common-sense belief that the granite boulder is solid through and through.[1]

In the end, Lycan, I think, comes to much the same conclusion about the refutability of folk psychology by science. Chemistry and physics, he says, have shown us that the boulder is not solid after all. Yet in some "operational sense," the boulder is solid: It is impenetrable, hard, and so on. Perhaps—he goes on to say—"science will force us to distinguish a fairly superficial, operational sense of 'believe' and the rest from a more commissive sense." This "halfway house" for beliefs does not sound unlike Stich's first ("modified Panglossian") proposal that I described earlier: There really are no beliefs; but belief ascriptions are sometimes "plainly true." Indeed, depending on what the "operational" and the "commissive" senses exactly come to, even the more virulent Stich (and, to a degree, even Churchland, let alone such an exemplary halfway-house resident as Dennett, 1981) may feel vindicated.[2]

3. I would like to conclude with a metaphilosophical point. Suppose that the Moorean argument were valid, and that we thereby had all the "epistemic warrant" we need to be able to claim that there are such things as beliefs, and even that they have just the properties attributed to them by folk theory. Still, the really interesting and fundamental question remains: How is it possible for beliefs, so conceived, to exist—that is, to have the properties ascribed to them by folk theory? As Kant taught us, it is the question how, not the question whether, that is often the more philosophically interesting. Interesting philosophical theorizing, like all theorizing, often has a transcendental character: Granted that such and such is the case (that scientific knowledge is possible, that we are free agents, that our thoughts are causally efficacious, or whatever), how is it possible for this to be the case, given certain other (independently plausible but prima facie conflicting) beliefs, philosophical assumptions, and scientific commitments? The aim of this sort of transcendental theorizing is not to establish the truth of a belief (for which we may already have adequate warrant), but to accommodate the belief within a web of other beliefs. So granted (as Lycan and I cheerfully grant) that there are propositional attitudes folk theoretically conceived, how is it possible for them to have determinate intentional content, to be causally efficacious and be so in virtue of their content, and so on, given certain widely accepted assumptions about externalism, holism, the closure of the physical domain, supervenience, the principle of causal/explanatory exclusion, and so on? Many eliminativist (and epiphenomenalist) arguments have forced us to think about just these kinds of questions. A Moorean type of refutation of eliminativism need not, of course, blind us

to these questions, but may just invite a certain complacency in thinking that our folk-psychological beliefs are not only true but unproblematically true. If that happened, it would be a pity.[3]

Notes

1. In response to Ann MacKenzie's objection (which he discusses in his chapter), Lycan observes—correctly, I think—that for any lexical implication that can be discovered empirically by linguists there will be "an inverse proportion between the scientific impeachability of the consequent and the apparent analyticity of the conditional itself." So any moderately plausible ("nonludicrous") candidate in the spectrum for an analytic conditional of the form "If S believes that p, then Q" will be such that the "falsifiability" of its consequent by "science alone" will be far from obvious. But that is part of the scientific predicament. Providing inductive confirmation or disconfirmation for any moderately interesting scientific claim is always a rather complex matter, one in which considerations of a methodological and philosophical sort inevitably come into play. Notice that what goes for "falsification" goes for "verification," or validation: The sort of complexity that attaches to the falsification of the antecedent of the above conditional by modus tollens also attaches to its validation by the "abductive" method of confirmation of hypotheses. The eliminativist with respect to beliefs is in no different predicament than the "theory" theorist.

2. Stich has recently had second thoughts about the soundness of his earlier eliminativist arguments, suggesting that they presuppose a controversial and problematic "description theory" of reference. See Stich, 1996.

3. I wish to thank the Social Sciences and Humanities Research Council of Canada for support in this research.

References

Stich, Stephen. 1983. *From Folk Psychology to Cognitive Science.* Cambridge, MA: MIT Press.
———. 1996. *Deconstructing the Mind.* New York: Oxford University Press.
Churchland, Paul. 1981. "Eliminative Materialism and the Propositional Attitudes," *Journal of Philosophy* 78, pp. 67–90.
Dennett, Daniel. 1981. "True Believers: The Intentional Strategy and Why It Works," in A.F. Heath (Ed.), *Scientific Explanation.* New York: Oxford University Press, pp. 53–75.

12

What Does It Take to Be a True Believer? Against the Opulent Ideology of Eliminative Materialism

David Henderson and Terry Horgan

Eliminative materialism, as William Lycan tells us in this volume, tells us is materialism plus the claim that no creature has ever had a belief, desire, intention, hope, wish, or other "folk psychological" state. Some contemporary philosophers claim that eliminative materialism is very likely true. They sketch certain potential scenarios for the way theory might develop in cognitive science and neuroscience that they claim are fairly likely, and they maintain that if such scenarios turned out to be the truth about humans, then eliminative materialism would be true.

Broadly speaking, there are two ways for those who maintain that eliminative materialism is false (or that the likelihood of its being true is very low) to reply to such arguments. One way is to argue that the scenarios the eliminativists envision are themselves extremely unlikely—that we can be very confident, given what we now know (including nontendentious scientific knowledge), that those scenarios will not come to pass. The other is to argue that even if they did come to pass, this would not undermine commonsense psychology anyway. People would still have beliefs, desires, and other folk psychological states.

The two strategies are not incompatible; one could pursue them both. But the second strategy attacks eliminativism at a more fundamental level. If it can be successfully carried out, then the dialectical state of play will be strikingly secure for folk psychology, for it will turn out that folk psychology simply is not hostage to the kinds of potential empirical-theoretical developments that the eliminativists envision. It does not matter, as far as the integrity of folk psychology is concerned, whether or not such scenarios are likely to come to pass.

Eliminativist arguments inevitably rely, often only implicitly, on certain assumptions about what it takes for a creature to have beliefs, desires, and other folk psychological states—assumptions about some alleged necessary condition(s) for being a "true believer" (to adopt this colorful usage from Dennett, 1987b). With some such assumption in play, the eliminativist then envisions a scenario in which

211

the putative necessary condition is not satisfied. Since that scenario might very well come to pass, it is argued, eliminativism is very likely true.

To pursue the second strategy of reply against eliminativist arguments is to argue that the assumptions about putative necessary conditions for true believerhood that are operative in eliminativist arguments are themselves very likely false. We advocate the second strategy. Lycan, we take it, advocates this generic strategy too and offers an argument of his own in an effort to implement it—his "particularly compelling" Moorean argument. Our way of implementing the strategy differs from his in significant ways, however. In this chapter we will set forth our own antieliminativist argument in a way that highlights the differences between our approach and Lycan's.

What Eliminativist Arguments Need to Assume

For concreteness, let us focus on one common eliminativist argument. (The key points we make will generalize to others.) Eliminativists often assume that a necessary condition for being a true believer is possession of a so-called "language of thought" (LT)—that is, a system of internal mental representations that (1) possess languagelike syntactic structure and (2) possess the propositional content of putatively attributable beliefs, desires, and other folk psychological states. They then argue that it is entirely possible, or even likely, that mature cognitive science will not posit an LT. They conclude that it is entirely possible, or even likely, that humans are not true believers.

In what sense of "necessary condition" must the eliminativist claim that possession of an LT is a necessary condition for being a true believer? In considering this question, two distinct notions of necessary condition need to be distinguished. First is the idea of a conceptually grounded necessary condition—that is, one that, in some fairly robust sense, is built into the very concept of belief, or anyway the very concept of a true believer (a creature that has beliefs, desires, intentions, and other folk psychological states). Second is the idea of a de facto necessary condition—that is, one that, as a matter of scientific fact, is a prerequisite for having beliefs and for being a true believer.

Given this distinction, the question we are raising can be sharpened and reformulated this way: Does it suffice for the eliminativist's purposes to claim that possession of an LT is merely a de facto necessary condition for being a true believer, or must the eliminativist make the stronger claim that LT possession is a conceptually grounded necessary condition for true believerhood?

We will address this question by considering two different kinds of staunch advocates of the LT hypothesis, whom we will call Zenon and Jerry.[1] Zenon, let us suppose, has the following views. First, he holds that a conceptually grounded necessary condition for being a true believer is susceptibility to a "robust folk psychological interpretation"—that is, a coherent overall assignment of beliefs, desires, and so on that conforms to the generalizations of folk psychology, and that allows for systematic folk psychological explanations of a vast and diverse range of the creature's behaviors and behavioral capacities. (Robustness excludes creatures and systems whose behavioral capacities are too narrow, parochial, and constrained for such entities to count as true believers—e.g., chess-playing computers.) Prototypical true believers must actually possess and exercise the relevant behaviors and behavioral capacities, which we call "true-believer-indicating" capacities (TBI capacities). (Nonprototypical true believers, such as total paralytics, must have internal states that are sufficiently relevantly similar to prototypical ones—indeed, states that would subserve TBI capacities, were it not for the lack of a properly functioning body.)

Second is a conceptually grounded constraint on how beliefs are realized: They must be realized by autonomous internal states of the creature. Thus humanoid robot bodies who behave systematically just like ordinary humans, but whose behavior is completely remote-controlled by Martians who are deliberately causing these bodies to behave in a way that is susceptible to robust folk psychological interpretation, would not be true believers.[2]

Third, Zenon believes that it is a conceptually grounded sufficient condition for being a true believer that a creature satisfies, clearly and unequivocally, these conceptually grounded necessary conditions. Although there can be borderline true believers—creatures for whom there is no clear fact of the matter, whether or not they satisfy the requisite conditions—nevertheless those creatures who clearly do satisfy these conditions thereby qualify as full-fledged true believers.

Fourth, he holds that there is overwhelmingly strong evidence that humans satisfy all these conditions. Hence, he maintains, there is overwhelmingly strong evidence that humans are genuine true believers. His reasoning here is as follows: There is no serious doubt that humans have the relevant TBI capacities; indeed, the behavioral capacities of normal humans are paradigmatic. Nor is there any serious doubt that normal humans are susceptible to robust folk psychological interpretation (since we routinely interpret ourselves and one another as true believers). Moreover, we certainly know enough about the etiology of human behavior to be very confident that normal behavior is the product of autonomous inner states rather than the product of remote control by Martians, or anything of the sort.[3] So there are bound to be some states of ordinary humans that realize beliefs, desires, intentions, and so on; the realizing states are ones temporally coincident with the states assigned by folk psychological interpretation.

Fifth, he maintains that folk psychological states are realized in humans by states of the kind described in cognitive science, whose essence involves cognitive "functional architecture." We will call this "psychotectonic realization," borrowing from Colin McGinn (1989) the term "psychotectonic" for states and processes described at the level of cognitive "engineering." The states that psychotectonically realize beliefs, etc, desires, and so on are themselves realized physically in the brain.

Sixth, he holds that there is very good evidence, including evidence from cognitive science, that the psychotechtonic realizing states in humans involve languagelike mental representations; they are states in an LT cognitive architecture. Indeed, seventh, he holds that as a matter of scientific fact, the only way that beliefs could be psychotechtonically realized, at least in cre... s whose constitution is physical and whose range of entertainable beliefs a.. associated TBI capacities is as vast as that of humans, is by states in an LT cogni..e architecture. This seventh claim is the contention that having an LT is a de facto necessary condition for being a true believer.[4]

For Zenon, the LT hypothesis is no part of the concept of belief or the concept of a true believer. Although he is staunch and confident in his advocacy of the LT hypothesis, this is not because he thinks that the hypothesis is somehow built into the notion of belief itself. On the contrary, he would deny this. Rather, he holds that as a matter of scientific fact, the only kind of cognitive architecture that can subserve TBI capacities—at any rate, TBI capacities as extensive and subtle as those of humans—is an LT cognitive architecture. For him, then, possession of an LT is not a conceptually grounded necessary condition for true believerhood, even though he adamantly argues that it is a de facto necessary condition.

Let us suppose that Jerry, in contrast to Zenon, holds that possession of an LT is indeed a conceptually grounded necessary condition for true believerhood. That is, Jerry maintains that the LT requirement is built right into the concept of a belief (and into folk psychological concepts generally). Jerry also agrees with Zenon in these claims: (1) that mature cognitive science will certainly posit an LT cognitive architecture; (2) that beliefs and the like are psychotectonically realized in humans by states in this LT architecture; and (3) that as a matter of scientific fact, no non-LT cognitive architecture could subserve TBI capacities.

Both Zenon and Jerry would vigorously take issue with the eliminativist's premise that it is entirely possible, or even likely, that mature cognitive science will not posit an LT. In doing so, they would be pursuing the first kind of anti-eliminativist strategy we mentioned at the outset—arguing that the eliminativist's favored future-science scenario is simply not going to be a part of mature science and has no serious likelihood of being a part of it.

With this fact duly noted, however, it is crucial to appreciate that Zenon and Jerry would part company with respect to the following subjunctive claim:

> (S) If we were to obtain good evidence that humans do not possess an
>   LT, we would then have good evidence that humans are not true
>   believers.

For Zenon, this subjunctive conditional is simply false. Even in the envisioned hypothetical scenario, he says, there would still be enormously good evidence that all relevant conceptually grounded necessary conditions for true believerhood are satisfied; hence there would still be overwhelmingly strong evidence that humans are true believers. Thus the epistemically appropriate conclusion to draw would be, not that humans fail to be true believers, but rather that beliefs are psychotectonically realized in a way that does not involve languagelike representations. The evidence against an LT would point, not to eliminative materialism, but rather to the falsity of Zenon's erstwhile beliefs (1) that possessing an LT cognitive architecture is a de facto necessary condition for being a true believer, and (2) that humans possess an LT cognitive architecture.

For Jerry, however, having an LT is a conceptually grounded necessary condition for being a true believer. By virtue of the very concept of a belief, he maintains, beliefs can only be psychotechtonically realized by states in an LT cognitive architecture. Thus a putative psychotechtonic realization relation that satisfied all other conceptually grounded constraints, but did not involve an LT, would not be a genuine realization relation for beliefs and other folk psychological states; it would violate a conceptually grounded necessary condition for true believerhood. So for him, the subjunctive claim (S) is true.

This parable about Zenon and Jerry has two important morals concerning what the eliminativist needs to assume about the relation of the LT hypothesis to folk psychology. First, it is not enough to claim that possessing an LT is a de facto necessary condition for being a true believer, and that we have good evidence for this. Some who accept these claims could also maintain (with Zenon) that our evidence for them would simply dissolve in the hypothetical scenario where we obtain evidence that humans lack a language of thought. In that scenario, they contend, we would have evidence that beliefs are psychotechtonically realized some other way in humans. So the eliminativist must claim, in opposition to this, that even if we were to obtain good evidence that humans do not possess an LT, we would still have good evidence that possession of an LT is a prerequisite for being a true believer.

The second moral (and our main point in the present section) is this: The eliminativist must claim, with Jerry, that having an LT is a conceptually grounded necessary condition for being a true believer. In order for the hypothetical scenario to be one in which the evidence points toward eliminativism, rather than pointing (as Zenon maintains) toward the conclusion that beliefs are psychotectonically realized by non-LT states, there would have to be some reason why the non-LT states, despite satisfying all the other conceptually grounded constraints, would not qualify as legitimate psychotechtonic realizers of beliefs. But since non-LT states would be otherwise eligible as belief realizers (apart from the fact that they do not involve languagelike representations), evidently the only reason they could nonetheless fail to be genuine belief realizers is that the requirement of LT realization is built into the very concept of a belief.

Having thus clarified the assumption needed by the eliminativist argument, we should add some observations about what the argument is not necessarily presupposing. First, the eliminativist need not assume that there is a tenable distinction between analytic and nonanalytic truths. Many in contemporary philosophy think not. Lycan is among them, and we take it that various eliminativists are among them too. As far as we can tell, this is a matter about which the eliminativist can remain neutral. Nevertheless, there are some things one might say about belief that would be just plain wrong in virtue of how our concepts work—that would constitute changing the subject, rather than changing what one claims or believes about the original subject. Conditions of true believerhood whose denial would constitute changing the subject are conceptually grounded necessary conditions. Presumably there can be such conditions whether or not the analytic/synthetic distinction is viable.

Second, the eliminativist need not assume that the claim that being a true believer requires LT possession is a purely conceptually grounded truth, untinged by any empirical claims. Certain conceptually grounded truths might be conditional in form, with a conditional 'slot' filled by some empirical claim that is not itself conceptually grounded. Here is a plausible example:

Given that the stuff we call water on Earth is composed of H_2O molecules, superficially waterlike stuff can be real water only if it too is composed of H_2O molecules.

Likewise, the eliminativist could perhaps rely upon a putatively conceptually grounded truth of the following form:

Given that . . . , a creature can have beliefs only if it has an LT.

As long as " . . . " were filled in by some relatively nontendentious empirical claim, a conceptually grounded conditional statement of this form could still serve the eliminativist's dialectical purposes. Of course, this empirical claim, whatever it is, needs to be one whose epistemic warrant is not only very high, but would remain very high even if we were to obtain good evidence that humans do not possess an LT. Here is an example of a conditional statement containing such an empirical constituent that an eliminativist might rely upon as a putative conceptually grounded necessary truth:

Given that beliefs are realized by physicochemical processes, a creature can have beliefs only if it has an LT.

Finally, it need not be assumed that the relevant conceptually grounded truths are knowable a priori, where we understand "a priori" in the standard way, as a nonempirical way of knowing. Epistemic status is a different matter from semantic/modal status. This leads to our next section.

Philosophy and Ideological Inquiry

We will use the term "ideology" for inquiry into the workings of human concepts and into the semantics of the terms that express these concepts, and also for the facts that such inquiry seeks to discover (cf. Horgan, 1993; Graham and Horgan, 1994; Henderson and Horgan, 2000). Ideology as an area of inquiry is a broadly empirical, interdisciplinary enterprise encompassing such fields as psychology, linguistics, social anthropology, and philosophy. In our view, even the philosophical dimension of ideology is empirical, rather than being a priori in the traditional sense.[5] The data that philosophers employ are relatively close at hand—data that include, but need not be limited to, one's own conceptual/linguistic intuitions about how to describe various concrete scenarios, actual or hypothetical. Philosophical thought experiments really are experiments: They generate empirical data in the form of such intuitions. Such data constitute powerful, albeit defeasible, empirical evidence vis-à-vis questions of ideology because, ceteris paribus, the relevant intuitive judgments are likely to reflect the workings of one's own conceptual and semantic competence.

In order to appreciate that the kind of ideological inquiry typically pursued in philosophy is indeed a broadly empirical enterprise (even though the data employed are largely available from the armchair), it is illuminating to compare such inquiry to the methodology typically employed by linguists in constructing and evaluating theories of natural-language syntax. The empirical data for syntactic theory include certain judgments and judgment dispositions of competent language users—in particular, judgments and dispositions concerning the grammaticality or ungrammaticality of various sentencelike strings and concerning the grammatical ambiguity or nonambiguity of various sentences. Such judgments are relevant simultaneously to psychological theories of human language processing and to linguistic theories about the syntax of language itself. Native speakers, after all, can be expected to have judgment dispositions about these matters that reflect a solid mastery of their own language (or their own regional dialect, at any rate). When native speakers are intersubjectively consistent and also uniformly confident about such syntactic judgments, normally the best psychological explanation will be that these judgments reflect the natives' syntactic competence, their mastery of the syntactic norms or syntactic structures underlying their language. This psychological hypothesis, in turn, has a direct implication for linguistic theory—that under an adequate theory of syntax for the natives' language (or dialect), these syntactic judgments will turn out to be correct.

Similar observations hold with respect to hypotheses or theories concerning ideology. Certain robust patterns of judgment among competent users of concepts and language will be plausibly explained as manifesting the users' conceptual/semantic competence. Here too, as with grammaticality judgments, many of the relevant data are close at hand, some of them in the form of our own introspectively accessible linguistic intuitions about how to describe various actual and envisioned scenarios. Since the evidence these data provide is empirical, it is of course defeasible. Nevertheless, it can be very strong—comparable in epistemic weight to the empirical evidence that syntactic judgments provide for theories of syntax.

Consider, for instance, the thesis mentioned earlier about the ideology of our concept *water*:

> Given that the stuff we call water on Earth is composed of H_2O molecules, superficially waterlike stuff can be real water only if it too is composed of H_2O molecules.

Hilary Putnam (1975) convinced virtually the entire philosophical community of this thesis by asking us to consult our intuitions about how to describe his Twin Earth scenario. (The influential arguments of Saul Kripke, 1972, for related ideological theses work similarly.) We were right to be convinced, because the deliverances of our descriptive intuitions very likely reflect the proper workings of our own conceptual/semantic competence with the notion of water and hence are very likely correct.

Philosophers have not often been explicit about the nature of ideological investigation in philosophy. When they have been explicit, typically they have conceived it as a nonempirical enterprise, pursued by employing reason alone. But such inquiry is more credibly construed, especially within the framework of a broadly naturalistic approach to human cognition and to epistemology, as broadly empirical, as argued at greater length elsewhere (Graham and Horgan, 1991, 1994; Henderson and Horgan, 2000; Horgan, 1993).

The Ideology of Folk Psychology: Opulent or Austere?

Recall that Jerry and the eliminativists hold that possession of a language of thought is a conceptually grounded necessary condition for being a true believer. Zenon, on the other hand, claims that the conceptually grounded prerequisites for being a true believer are much more modest: The putative requirement of an LT cognitive architecture is not built into folk psychological concepts, nor are any other putative requirements that could turn out, under any remotely likely scenario for the future development of cognitive science or neuroscience, not to be satisfied by humans. Zenon's conception of the ideology of folk psychology we will call "austere;" competing conceptions that treat LT possession and/or various other scientifically tendentious features as conceptually grounded prerequisites for true believerhood we will call "opulent" (cf. Graham and Horgan, 1991, 1994; Horgan, 1993).

It is an empirical question whether the ideology of folk psychology is opulent or austere. Here are some broadly empirical arguments in defense of the austerity hypothesis against the opulence hypothesis. All involve data so close at hand that we can obtain them from our armchairs (*die vom Armchair aus zuhandenen Daten*). This fact does not, however, prevent them from being empirical and hence epistemically defeasible. (The arguments, as here formulated, will be directed explicitly against the claim that possessing an LT is a conceptually grounded necessary condition for being a true believer, but they are really broader in scope and apply, mutatis mutandis, against other putative conceptually grounded prerequisites for being a true believer sometimes embraced by eliminativists.)[6]

First is the argument from recalcitrant intuitions. When we envision a scenario in which the LT hypothesis turns out to be false and then ask ourselves whether it seems intuitively appropriate to describe this scenario by saying, "Humans turn out not to have beliefs and desires," the answer is negative. On the contrary, it seems natural to say things like the following about this hypothetical situation: "Humans will have acquired grounds to believe that the LT hypothesis is false." If the LT hypothesis is really built into the ideology of folk psychology, however, then this fact ought to reveal itself in our own descriptive intuitions about the envisioned scenario: Describing the people in this scenario as having beliefs and desires should seem semantically mistaken to us, just as it seems semantically mistaken to describe the stuff in the oceans and lakes of Putnam's Twin Earth as water. But it does not. So, since these judgments very probably emanate from our conceptual/semantic competence with respect to the concepts and terms of folk psychology, it is very likely that our descriptive intuitions about the envisioned scenarios are correct, and hence that the falsity of the LT hypothesis would not falsify folk psychology at all. That is, it is very likely that the ideology of folk psychology is austere vis-à-vis the LT hypothesis, not opulent.

Second is the argument from ideological conservatism. Notions like action, assertion, having reasons, and epistemic warrant all are folk psychological: They presuppose that humans are true believers.[7] These notions play certain essential roles in human life that would surely persist even if we discovered that the LT hypothesis was false. Hence if folk psychology were ideologically committed to an LT, this commitment would go directly contrary to certain central purposes for which folk psychology concepts and terms are employed. But since human concepts and terms evolve in a broadly pragmatic way, in general they are not likely to have conceptually grounded satisfaction conditions that are more severe or restrictive than is required by the purposes they serve. So folk psychology is not likely to exhibit any such gratuitous, counterpragmatic features. Hence the ideology of folk psychology is very likely austere vis-à-vis the LT hypothesis, rather than opulent.

Third is the argument from conceivability. Although we humans can readily conceive discovering that the LT hypothesis is false, we cannot even conceive of ourselves then dropping folk psychological notions like action, assertion, and epistemic warrant; thus we cannot conceive of ceasing to regard ourselves and one another as true believers. To drop these notions on these grounds—or even to try dropping them—would be actions, performed for a reason; and notions like action and having a reason are themselves thoroughly folk psychological. This conceivability mismatch between dropping the LT hypothesis, on the one hand, and dropping folk psychology on the other, is naturally accommodated under the ideological hypothesis that folk psychology is conceptually austere, for in that case, the envisioned scenario is one in which the folk psychological concepts still would apply to humans. But if folk psychology is ideologically committed to an LT cognitive architecture, however, then no such accommodation is possible. Instead, it remains a puzzle why we should find ourselves unable to conceive dropping concepts whose putative ideological commitments we can fairly easily conceive ourselves discovering to be false. So the conceivability mismatch provides evidence for the austere conception of folk psychology against the opulent conception vis-à-vis the LT hypothesis, since the former accommodates the mismatch whereas the latter renders it puzzling.[8]

We again emphasize that the arguments just set forth are empirical arguments and hence defeasible: In each case, the claim is that the austere conception of folk psychology's ideology accords better with the adduced empirical data than does the opulent conception. Here, as with abductive empirical reasoning in general, the fact that several distinct forms of evidence converge on the same conclusion means that their net epistemic import is even greater than the sum of their respective individual epistemic weights. In our view, the empirical case for the austere conception against an opulent conception that treats the folk psychology hypothesis or scientifically tendentious hypotheses as conceptually grounded prerequisites for true believerhood is overwhelmingly strong.

As remarked earlier, these arguments against the specific claim that LT possession is a conceptually grounded necessary condition for true believerhood can be readily adapted against the various other putative conceptually grounded necessary conditions that sometimes figure in eliminativist arguments. The arguments thus provide strong empirical support for the claim that folk psychology is ideologically austere *tout court* (and not merely austere vis-à-vis the LT hypothesis). The upshot is that it is highly unlikely that science can yield eliminativist results, for it is highly unlikely that any conceptually grounded necessary conditions for true believerhood would fail to be satisfied in any remotely plausible scenario for how future science would go.

This leaves it open whether or not various features that eliminativists treat as conceptually grounded necessary conditions for true believerhood are de facto necessary conditions for true believerhood. Perhaps some are. But debates about such matters do not threaten the integrity of folk psychology. The right way to look at it is this: No scenarios that are even remotely likely to be true of humans are ones under which any conceptually grounded necessary conditions for true believerhood would fail to be met. At most, what could reasonably be concluded, if we were to acquire good evidence that some such scenario were true for humans, would be that certain conditions thought to be de facto necessary for true believerhood are not really de facto necessary conditions after all.

Comments on Lycan

As we understand Lycan's antieliminativist argument, in effect he too construes eliminativists as needing, and implicitly relying upon, putative conceptually grounded necessary truths. He describes his own Moorean argument as at root a comparison of plausibilities: the plausibility of commonsense mental ascriptions (e.g., that Granny wants a beer and believes that there is one under the sofa) versus the plausibility of such eliminativist assumptions (e.g., that possession of a language of thought is a conceptually grounded necessary condition for being a true believer). In effect, the Moorean argument relies upon the contention that claims of the former kind will always seem intuitively more plausible than claims of the latter kind.

We are inclined to agree with this contention, but its dialectical force against eliminativism certainly can be questioned. Why, one might well wonder, should comparative intuitive plausibility have epistemic trumping power in the context of debates about eliminativism? After all, comparative intuitive plausibility can be a pretty shaky reed epistemically, especially when what is under comparison is a specific commonsense claim, on the one hand, versus a general theoretical hypothesis, on the other. It is not intuitively plausible that these hands I am looking at are mostly empty space, or that simultaneity is relative to a reference frame, but so much the worse for intuitive plausibility in these cases. When common-sense claims are being compared with theoretical hypotheses that call these very claims into question, defending the former by direct appeal to comparative intuitive plausibility excessively privileges common sense. Higher intuitive plausibility does not have automatic epistemic trumping power.

We take it that Lycan would agree. "Commonsense beliefs," he says, "can be corrected, even trashed entirely, by careful empirical investigation and scientific theorizing" (p. 8). But for him, such epistemic trumping power over common sense can only accrue to empirical scientific hypotheses, ones that are well supported by empirical evidence. They cannot accrue to the "purely philosophical" premises that he thinks eliminativist arguments invariably rely upon. He says:

> Philosophers . . . are not explorers or scientists. . . . Common sense must yield to evidence . . . but it need not yield to bare metaphysical pronouncement. . . . No purely philosophical premise can ever [legitimately] have as strong a claim to our allegiance as can a humble commonsense proposition such as Moore's autobiographical one. Science can correct common sense; metaphysics and philosophical "intuition" can only throw spitballs.

Thus Lycan's Moorean argument turns out to depend crucially upon the supposition that the eliminativists need premises that are nonempirical. These are the kind of premises that he claims can never epistemically trump commonsense beliefs.

One is tempted to become embroiled in arguments concerning whether any kind of allegedly nonempirical claim can trump commonsense beliefs (rather than being "bare metaphysical pronouncement"), and if so, which kinds can possess this privileged epistemic status, and why.[9] But we can set these issues aside here. From our own point of view, Lycan's argument is flawed at a more fundamental level: it falsely assumes that eliminativist arguments employ nonempirical premises. We claim, on the contrary, that although these arguments do need premises about putative conceptually grounded necessary conditions for true believerhood, such premises are empirical ideological hypotheses. In principle, these hypotheses could receive enough evidential support to become very well warranted—enough so to epistemically trump commonsense claims, like the claim that Granny wants a beer and believes that there is one under the sofa.[10] Lycan's Moorean argument therefore commits a straw-man fallacy, since it rests crucially upon a misconstrual of the eliminativist reasoning toward which it is directed.

Our own antieliminativist approach recognizes the eliminativist assumptions for what they are—broadly empirical contentions about the ideology of folk psychological concepts—and then gives broadly empirical arguments against these assumptions. Certain intuitive, commonsense judgments enter here too: for instance, judgments about what would be the right way to characterize various actual or hypothetical scenarios. But such commonsense judgments figure not as direct and automatic trumpers over putatively nonempirical philosophical claims, but in a different way, as data for ideological theorizing—data that defeasibly may be presumed to emanate from our conceptual/semantic competence, and thus defeasibly may be presumed to reflect the nature of the folk psychological concepts themselves.

Lycan's Moorean argument, despite its flaws, can be seen as gesturing toward the kind of reasoning we have offered here: a broadly empirical, albeit still philosophical, argument for the ideological austerity of folk psychology. We and Lycan share the goal of effectively implementing the second of the strategies we described at the outset. Our argument does so successfully, we submit, whereas his does not.

Notes

1. Jerry Fodor and Zenon Pylyshyn are perhaps the most prominent philosophical defenders of the LT hypothesis as one that cognitive science needs. It also figures centrally in their account of belief and other folk psychological states. But we do not mean to suggest that the actual Zenon Pylyshyn is the first kind of LT fan we will describe, or that Jerry Fodor is the second kind. As far as we can tell, it is not clear from their writings how to classify either of them on this matter (although the discussion of commonsense psychology in Pylyshyn [1984] perhaps suggests a tendency toward the first kind of position concerning LT, whereas the treatment of propositional attitudes in Fodor [1980a], and other writings of Fodor's perhaps suggests a tendency toward the second). We borrow their names mainly for vividness.

2. A possible third condition that Zenon might perhaps embrace as another conceptually grounded prerequisite for being a true believer is that the creature have a certain phenomenology, a certain "what it's like" of belief—for instance, a phenomenology that distinguishes believing "That's a rabbit" from believing "That's a collection of undetached rabbit parts."

3. Conceptually grounded phenomenological aspects of true belief, if any, are accessible through introspection, and so there is no serious doubt that any such aspects are also instantiated in humans.

4. An important mode of reasoning to support this kind of claim is what Horgan and Tienson (1996, chapter 5) call "inference to the only available explanation." They themselves employ it in defense of an LT cognitive architecture. The basic idea is this: The range of potential beliefs and the like that humans can possess is so vast that the only way to implement such states in a physical system with resources on the scale of a human brain is via a system of representations with languagelike syntactic compositionality.

5. A nontraditional, partially empirical notion of the a priori is described in Henderson and Horgan (2000), where it is argued that the philosophical dimension of ideology typically is a priori in this nontraditional sense (but not in the traditional sense).

6. See Graham and Horgan (1991) and Horgan (1993), where these arguments are given in more general form and also are applied explicitly against several other putative conceptually grounded prerequisites for true believerhood sometimes invoked by eliminativists. The next several paragraphs are slight modifications of the formulations in Horgan (1993).

7. Cf. Baker (1987) and Graham and Horgan (1988, 1991). It is widely accepted

in philosophy of mind that the concept of an action is the concept of an item of be-havior that is caused, in a certain characteristic way, by FP states like belief, desire, and intention; cf. Davidson (1963), Goldman (1970), and Brand (1984). Eliminativists, in our experience, tend to grant that action is a folk psychological notion.

8. It should be stressed that this argument is empirical, not transcendental. Maybe non-FP-tinged successors of FP concepts could be devised, even though we presently have virtually no idea what such replacement concepts would be like. But even those philosophers who, like us, do not buy transcendental arguments should acknowledge that conceivability considerations can constitute important empirical data about matters of ideology.

9. Such a challenge to Lycan might include the idea that nonempirical knowledge of conceptually grounded necessary truths is provided by a specific kind of intuitive apprehension that is a by-product of conceptual competence. It is ironic that Lycan so quickly dismisses intuition as a potential vehicle of a priori knowledge, given the central role of intuitive comparative-plausibility judgments in his own Moorean argument.

10. This is not to say, of course, that eliminativists have actually provided such evidence. On the contrary, often they do not even articulate their needed ideological premises explicitly, let alone argue for them.

References

Baker, L.R. 1987. *Saving Belief: A Critique of Physicalism*. Princeton, NJ: Princeton University Press.

Brand, M. 1984. *Intending and Acting: Toward a Naturalized Action Theory*. Cambridge, MA: MIT Press.

Davidson, D. 1963. "Actions, Reasons, and Causes." *Journal of Philosophy*, 60, pp. 685–700.

Davidson, D., and Harman, G. (Eds.). 1972. *Semantics of Natural Language*. Dordrecht: Reidel.

Dennett, D. 1987a. *The Intentional Stance*. Cambridge, MA: Bradford Books/MIT Press.

———. 1987b. "True Believers: The Intentional Strategy and Why It Works." Pp. 13–35 in D. Dennett, *The Intentional Stance*. Cambridge, MA: Bradford Books/MIT Press.

Fodor, J. 1980a. "Propositional Attitudes." Pp. 177–203 in J. Fodor, *Representations*. Cambridge, MA: Bradford Book/MIT Press.

———. 1980b. *Representations*. Cambridge, MA: Bradford Books/MIT Press.

Goldman, A. 1970. *A Theory of Human Action*. Englewood Cliffs, NJ: Prentice-Hall.

Graham, G., and Horgan, T. 1988. "How to Be Realistic about Folk Psychology." *Philosophical Psychology*, 1, pp. 69–81.

———. 1991. "In Defense of Southern Fundamentalism." *Philosophical Studies*, 62, pp. 107–34.

———. 1994. "Southern Fundamentalism and the End of Philosophy." *Philosophical Issues*, 5, pp. 219–47.

Gunderson, Keith (Ed.). 1975. *Language, Mind, and Knowledge*. Minnesota Studies in the Philosophy of Science. Vol. 7. Minneapolis: University of Minnesota Press.

Henderson, D., and Horgan, T. 2000. "What Is A Priori and What Is It Good For?"

Pp. 51–86 in *Southern Journal of Philosophy*, 38, Spindel Conference Supplement.

Horgan, T. 1993. "The Austere Ideology of Folk Psychology." *Mind and Language*, 8, pp. 282–97.

Horgan, T., and Tienson, J. 1996. *Connectionism and the Philosophy of Psychology.* Cambridge, MA: MIT Press.

Kripke, S. 1972. "Naming and Necessity." Pp. 253–355 in D. Davidson and G. Harman (Eds.), *Semantics of Natural Language.* Dordrecht Reided.

McGinn, C. 1989. *Mental Content.* Oxford: Basil Blackwell.

Putnam, H. 1975. "The Meaning of 'Meaning.'" Pp. 131–193 in Keith Gunderson (Ed.), *Language, Mind, and Knowledge*, Minnesota Studies in the Philosophy of Science. Vol. 7. Minneapolis: University of Minnesota Press.

Pylyshyn, Z. 1984. *Computation and Cognition: Toward a Foundation for Cognitive Science.* Cambridge, MA: Bradford Books/MIT Press.

13

Connectionism and the Propositional Attitudes

Barbara Von Eckardt

While it is generally agreed that if our future complete cognitive theory is classical, folk psychology stands a reasonable chance of being vindicated, there is much less agreement about the implications for folk psychology if connectionism wins the computational war. Much of the controversy has focused on Ramsey, Stich, and Garon (RS&G) (1990), who argue the following: "If connectionist hypotheses of the sort we will sketch turn out to be right, so too will eliminativism about propositional attitudes" (p. 500).

The "sort" they have in mind are distributed, superpositional networks intended as models at the psychological level—that is, models that explain psychological data at a level of description that abstracts away from the specific neuroanatomy or neurophysiology of the brain. To say that a network is "distributed" is to say that the information contained in a single proposition is stored in the connection strengths and biases of numerous units. To say that it is "superpositional" is to say that those very same connection strengths and unit biases store the information associated with more than one proposition.[1] For ease of discussion, let us refer to this sort of connectionist network as a "connectionist* network." By "eliminativism about propositional attitudes," RS&G mean, not that reference to the propositional attitudes will actually be dispensed with in our folk psychological practices, but that it will turn out that propositional attitudes do not exist. It is important to note that the conclusion RS&G are arguing for is a conditional one. They give no reasons to support the claim that our future complete cognitive theory will consist of a distributed, superpositional connectionist network (although they may think this). Rather, they are only interested in arguing that if cognitive science turns out in this way, then things look bleak for folk psychology.

What justifies this conditional, according to RS&G? Basically, their argument is this: According to folk psychology, propositional attitudes are characterized by a cluster of three features that RS&G call "propositional modularity." The problem is that if we examine the sort of connectionist* networks that might be expected to contain propositional attitude-like states, we do not find states with any of these features. Hence if our future complete cognitive theory turns out to be connectionist*, we will be forced to conclude that propositional attitudes do not exist. Although this is the argument at the most general level, the strategy is to focus on a more specific case and assume that the argument will generalize. In fact, RS&G discuss only one propositional attitude—belief—and two particular sample connectionist* networks.

Not everyone has been convinced. Some philosophers have questioned whether folk psychology is committed to the propositional attitudes being propositionally modular in all of the ways RS&G need for their argument (Bechtel and Abrahamsen, 1993; Bogdan, 1993; Botterill, 1994; Clark, 1995). Others have questioned the claim that connectionist* networks are not propositionally modular in the requisite ways (Forster and Saidel, 1994; Botterill, 1994; Clark, 1995; Smolensky, 1995). Still others have criticized some of the argument's inferential steps (Egan, 1995; Stich and Warfield, 1995). Although many of these replies contain legitimate points, there is room for an additional response. In the first place, with the exception of Clark (1995), the complexity of RS&G's argument has not generally been appreciated. Upon close examination, RS&G's overall argument turns out to be comprised of three subarguments, one for each of the features of propositional modularity. The argument reconstructions offered in the literature tend to focus on one or at most two of these subarguments. Second, because the three strands of the argument have not been kept sufficiently apart, there has been some confusion over exactly what the three features of propositional modularity are supposed to be. In particular, as we will see, with respect to the feature of semantic interpretability, not enough attention has been paid to the question of what kinds folk psychology assumes there to be, and what kinds connectionist* networks allow.

The purpose of this chapter is thus to present the case against RS&G in a systematic way, with attention to all three of the subarguments. In the course of building this systematic case, I will have occasion to sort through both the various critical points made to date and the responses to them by RS&G (where these exist). I will also be adding a few wrinkles of my own. The bottom line, however, will be that even though many of RS&G's critics have missed some of the subtleties of RS&G's argument, their assessment has been roughly correct. If our future cognitive theory turns out to be connectionist*, nothing follows regarding the existence of the propositional attitudes.

Setting the Stage

Let us then look at RS&G's argument more closely. To do so, we need to examine four things: (1) what the two sample connectionist* networks are like, (2) what it means to be a network that might be expected to contain belieflike states, (3) what propositional modularity comes to, and (4) why connectionist* networks that might be expected to contain belieflike states do not, in fact, contain them, according to RS&G.

1. To make their case, RS&G construct two sample connectionist* networks. Network A is designed to "judge" the truth or falsity of sixteen propositions such as *dogs have fur, dogs have paws, cats have paws, fish have eggs,* and so forth. It is a three-tiered, feed-forward network consisting of sixteen input units, four hidden units, and one output unit. The input coding for each proposition is a sequence of sixteen 0s and 1s. For example, the input coding for *dogs have fur* is 11000011 00001111. RS&G interpret an output close to 1 as meaning that the presented proposition was judged to be true and an output close to 0 as meaning that the proposition was judged to be false. The network was "trained up" by means of backwards propagation until it consistently gave an output greater than .9 for true propositions and an output of less than .1 for false propositions. The second network, Network B, is similar to Network A except that it encodes one additional proposition. Like Network A, B was designed to "judge" the truth or falsity of a presented proposition, contains four hidden units, and was trained up by backwards propagation.

2. RS&G's argument relies crucially on the idea that among the myriad possible distributed, superpositional connectionist networks, there is a class of networks in which it would be natural to find belieflike states, if such states exist. A belieflike state is a state that has the sort of propositional content and plays roughly the sort of functional role beliefs are generally taken to have. The latter is determined by the various folk psychological generalizations that involve beliefs (for example, that beliefs in combination with desires lead to the formation of intentions to act). RS&G do not really have much to say about this particular class of networks in general. Instead, they simply focus on their two sample networks that, in a crude way, model one of the capacities in which it would be natural to find belieflike states — the capacity to judge whether one or another of a specific group of propositions is true or false. Executing this capacity presumably involves beliefs (if beliefs exist), because the folk psychological explanation of how we are able to judge the truth or falsity of a presented proposition would typically be that we judge a proposition p to be true if we believe p, and we judge p to be false if we believe that it is not the case that p. Consider now the many cognitive capacities that, at the folk psychological level, we would explain, at least partly, by claiming that the subject had one or more beliefs. Call these our "belief capacities." We can then say that the networks RS&G are interested in consist of the class of connectionist* networks that purport to account for one or another of these belief capacities.

3. Another key component of RS&G's argument is the claim that propositional attitudes exhibit a cluster of features they call "propositional modularity." Propositional modularity comes to this: "Propositional attitudes are *functionally discrete, semantically interpretable,* states that play a *causal role* in the production of other propositional attitudes, and ultimately in the production of behavior" (RS&G, 1990, p. 504). Each of these components is initially characterized in fairly natural folk psychological terms, although, as we shall see, when RS&G proceed to give their argument, the notion of functional discreteness, at least, begins to take on certain architectural dimensions.

Here is what RS&G say initially about the components of propositional modularity:

Functional discreteness

It typically makes perfectly good sense to claim that a person has acquired (or lost) a single memory or belief. Thus, for example, on a given occasion it might plausibly be claimed that when Henry awoke from his nap he had completely forgotten that the car keys were hidden in the refrigerator, though he had forgotten nothing else. (1990, p. 504)

Semantic interpretability

[The] generalizations of common sense psychology are couched in terms of the *semantic* properties of the attitudes. It is in virtue of being the belief *that p* that a given belief has a given effect or cause. Thus common sense psychology treats the predicates expressing these semantic properties, predicates like *"believes that the train is late,"* as *projectable* predicates—the sort of predicates that are appropriately used in nomological or law-like generalizations. (1990, p. 504)

Independent causal role

On the common sense view, it may sometimes happen that a person has a number of belief clusters, any one of which might lead him to infer some further belief. When he actually does draw the inference, folk psychology assumes that it is an empirical question what he inferred it from, and that this question typically has a determinate answer. Suppose, for example, that Inspector Clouseau believes that the butler said he spent the evening at the village hotel, and that he said he arrived back on the morning train. Suppose Clouseau also believes that the village hotel is closed for the season, and that the morning train has been taken out of service. Given these beliefs, along with some widely shared background beliefs, Clouseau might well infer that the butler is lying. If he does, folk psychology presumes that the inference might be based either on his beliefs about the hotel, or on his beliefs about the train, or both. It is entirely possible, from the perspective of common sense psychology, that although Clouseau has long known that the hotel is closed for the season, this belief played no role in his inference on this particular occasion. Once again we see common sense psychology invoking a pair of distinct propositional attitudes, one of which is causally active on a particular occasion while the other is causally inert. (1990, p. 506)

RS&G also give an example of a case in which folk psychology explains why some action occurred on the basis of a particular set of beliefs and desires, where, however, the agent had more than one belief-desire set that could have resulted in the action.

4. RS&G's overall argument breaks down into a main argument and three subarguments, one corresponding to each of the three features of propositional

modularity. The main argument can be reconstructed as a conditional proof as follows:

*The Argument from Connectionism**

C1.   Suppose that according to our future complete cognitive science, our belief capacities are realized by connectionist* networks.

C2.   In particular, suppose that our belief capacity to judge the truth or falsity of a presented proposition is realized by a network similar to Network A or B.

C3.   Folk psychological belief states play a role in executing belief capacities only if there are belieflike states in the subpersonal systems realizing those capacities — namely, states that have the semantic and functional role characteristics of folk psychological belief states.

C4.   According to folk psychology, folk psychological belief states are propositionally modular — that is, they are functionally discrete, are semantically interpretable, and can play an independent causal role.

C5.   There are belieflike states in the subpersonal systems that realize belief capacities only if there are states in those systems that are also functionally discrete, are semantically interpretable, and can play an independent causal role.

C6.   But there are no states in Networks A and B with any of these properties.

C7.   Thus folk psychological belief states do not play a role in executing the belief capacity modeled by Networks A and B.

C8.   Thus, since Networks A and B are typical of connectionist* networks in general, folk psychological belief states do not play a role in executing any belief capacities.

C9.   Thus folk psychological belief states do not exist.

C10. Therefore, if our belief capacities are realized by connectionist* networks, then folk psychological belief states do not exist.

This is RS&G's main argument. The subarguments are required in order to support premise C6 and, hence, C7. The first subargument attempts to show that there are no states in Networks A and B that are functionally discrete; the second, that there are no states that are semantically interpretable; and the third, that there are no states that play a discrete causal role.

The Subargument for No Functional Discreteness

Here is how RS&G argue for the absence of functional discreteness at the subpersonal level:

The incompatibility between propositional modularity and connectionist models like ours can be made even more vivid by contrasting Network

A with a second network, we'll call it Network B . . . [that] encodes all the same propositions as Network A plus one more. In . . . traditional cognitive models, it would be an easy matter to say which states or features of the system encode the added proposition, and it would be a simple task to determine whether or not the representation of the added proposition played a role in a particular episode modeled by the system. But plainly in the connectionist network those questions are quite senseless. . . . Since information is encoded in a highly distributed manner, with each connection weight and bias embodying information salient to many propositions, and information regarding any given proposition scattered throughout the network, the system lacks functionally distinct, identifiable substructures that are semantically interpretable as representations of individual propositions. (1990, pp. 513–14)

At the capacity level, Network B differs from Network A only in the fact that it can "judge" the truth or falsity of one additional proposition, specifically, the proposition that fish have eggs. Network B thus seems tailor-made to determine whether connectionist* networks contain belieflike states that are functionally discrete. RS&G argue that Network B, and hence connectionist* networks generally, do not contain such states on the grounds that each connection weight and bias in the model embodies information relevant to many propositions, and therefore there is no distinct subset of connection weights and biases that contain just the information that fish have eggs. We can certainly grant that point, but does that show that there are no subpersonal belieflike states in Network B that are "functionally discrete"? It depends on what is meant by "functionally discrete." Recall the earlier characterization according to which beliefs are functionally discrete in the sense that it is meaningful to claim that a person has acquired or lost a single belief. In that ("cognitive") sense of functional discreteness, there is nothing about connectionist* networks that prevents them from having belieflike states that are functionally discrete. In fact, Networks A and B suggest just the opposite. Suppose that Network C, architecturally identical to Network B, is originally trained up on just the first sixteen propositions and then undergoes a second training session to add the proposition that fish have eggs. This would constitute a demonstration that connectionist* networks can have functionally discrete belieflike states in the cognitive sense because Network C, over time, would have acquired the subpersonal analogue of a single belief. Of course, after training, Network C might not have any belieflike, functionally discrete substructures in the sense of enduring computational structures that are physically isolable, but this is a different sense of functional discreteness—an "architectural" sense. In this sense of functional discreteness, it is doubtful whether folk psychology is committed to beliefs being functionally discrete.

The subargument is thus a fallacy of equivocation. (Bogdan, 1993, p. 192, seems to be suggesting a similar analysis, although his understanding of the three components of propositional modularity is different from mine.) To see this, let us reconstruct RS&G's first subargument thus:

The Argument for No Functional Discreteness

FD1. According to folk psychology, beliefs are functionally discrete.

FD2. Thus folk psychological belief states play a role in executing belief capacities, only if there are belieflike states in the subpersonal systems realizing those capacities that are also functionally discrete.

FD3. Network B differs from Network A in storing one additional proposition. However, because Network B is a distributed superpositional network, there is no physically isolable computational substructure that stores the information for just that or any other single proposition.

FD4. Thus there are no subpersonal belieflike states in networks like Networks A and B that are functionally discrete.

FD5. Thus folk psychological belief states do not play a role in executing the belief capacity modeled by networks like Networks A and B.

This argument commits a fallacy of equivocation because its apparent soundness rests on using the key term 'functionally discrete' in two senses. To make FD1 and FD2 true, we must use the term in the cognitive sense. That is also how RS&G explicitly characterize functional discreteness, as we saw earlier. But FD4 follows from FD3 only if 'functionally discrete' is understood in the architectural sense. The problem now is that the conclusion of the argument, FD5, is supposed to follow from both FD2 and FD4, but it can do so only if "functionally discrete" is used in the same sense in both lines, which it is not. So the argument is invalid. What happens if we disambiguate the problematic term? Suppose we read "functionally discrete" as meaning *functionally discrete in the cognitive sense*, throughout the argument. Then the argument will be invalid because FD4 will not follow from FD3. Alternatively, suppose we read "functionally discrete" as meaning *functionally discrete in the architectural sense*. Then the argument will be valid, but now FD1 will be false. So the argument is either invalid or has at least one false premise. In sum, however we understand "functionally discrete," the first subargument is unsound.

The Subargument for No Semantic Interpretability

Let us turn now to the second subargument, which concerns the semantic interpretability of beliefs. Again, it will be useful to begin our examination by looking at what RS&G have to say:

> Common sense psychology treats predicates expressing the semantic properties of propositional attitudes as projectable. Thus "believes that dogs have fur" or "remembers that dogs have fur" will be projectable predicates in common sense psychology. Now both Network A and Network B might serve as models for a cognitive agent who believes that dogs have fur; both networks store or represent the information that dogs

have fur. Nor are these the only two. If we were to train up a network on the 17 propositions . . . plus a few (or minus a few) we would get yet another system which is as different from Networks A and B as these two are from each other. The moral here is that though there are *indefinitely* many connectionist networks that represent the information that dogs have fur just as well as Network A does, these networks have no projectable features in common that are describable in the language of connectionist theory. From the point of view of the connectionist model builder, the class of networks that might model a cognitive agent who believes that dogs have fur is not a genuine kind at all, but simply a chaotically disjunctive set. Commonsense psychology treats the class of people who believe that dogs have fur as a psychologically natural kind; connectionist psychology does not. (1990, pp. 514–15)

The term 'semantic interpretability' or a careless reading of RS&G's initial characterization of semantic interpretability might suggest that the second problematic feature of propositional modularity is simply that beliefs have semantic properties. In fact, however, this quotation makes clear that RS&G have something stronger in mind. It is not simply being subject to a semantic interpretation that is problematic on their view (since they grant that it makes sense to say that Networks A and B encode various propositions), but rather that according to folk psychology, the properties that constitute beliefs having content are natural-kind properties, namely, properties that figure in lawlike generalizations, whereas there are no corresponding natural-kind properties "describable in the language of connectionist theory."

In order to reconstruct this second subargument, we need a name for the folk psychological natural-kind properties under discussion. Let us say that a "belief content property" is a property expressed by predicates of the form "believes that _____," with the blank filled in by some sentence. For example, the property of believing that dogs have fur is a belief content property according to this definition. We can then reconstruct RS&G's second subargument as follows:

The Argument for No Natural Kinds

NK1. According to folk psychology, beliefs are semantically interpretable. That is, they have content and belief-content properties that are natural-kind properties, namely, properties picked out by the lawlike generalizations of folk psychology.

NK2. Folk psychological belief states play a role in executing belief capacities only if connectionist* natural-kind properties exist that "correspond" to belief-content properties.

NK3. Correspondence between belief-content properties and connectionist* natural-kind properties requires that for each belief-content property B, there exists a connectionist* natural-kind property C such that a person will have B if and only if the connectionist* network that partially realizes that person (or that realizes that person's mind/brain) has C.

NK4. But there are no connectionist* natural-kind properties corresponding to belief-content properties in networks like Networks A and B.

NK5. Thus folk psychological belief states do not play a role in executing
the belief capacity modeled by networks like Networks A
and B.

Note that the structure of this argument is very similar to the structure of the
argument for no functional discreteness. In both arguments, there are three key
premises: (1) a premise claiming that folk psychology attributes some property to
beliefs ("the folk psychology premise"); (2) a premise requiring that folk psychology map onto connectionism* in a certain way in order for it to be true that folk
psychological belief states play a role in executing belief capacities ("the mapping
premise"); and (3) a premise claiming that this mapping condition is not satisfied
("the no-satisfaction premise").[2] In the argument for no functional discreteness,
the folk psychology premise is FD1, the mapping premise is FD2, and the no-
satisfaction premise is FD4. In the argument for no natural kinds the folk psychology premise is NK1, the mapping premise is NK2, and the no-satisfaction
premise is NK4.

My criticism of the argument for no functional discreteness was complicated
by the fact that the argument, as RS&G originally present it, uses the key term
'functional discreteness' equivocally. Once we disambiguated the term, critical
attention was focused on the interaction of the folk psychology premise and the
no-satisfaction premise. Specifically, it turned out that on the cognitive sense of
"functional discreteness," the folk psychology premise was acceptable but the no-
satisfaction premise was not (since it did not follow from facts about Networks A
and B); whereas on the architectural sense, the folk psychology premise was not
acceptable, while the no-satisfaction premise was.

The argument for no natural kinds is also problematic, but now we want to
begin by looking at the mapping premise. RS&G do not defend NK2 but, presumably, think that it follows from a general constraint on how a higher-level
theory must map onto a lower-level theory if the former is to be vindicated by the
latter: namely, that the objects that fall under a natural kind of the higher-level
theory exist only if this higher-level natural kind corresponds to a natural kind of
the lower-level theory. But this constraint is much too strong because it is unlikely
to be satisfied by other pairs of hierarchically related scientific theories for which
we take some sort of vindication for granted. Do the natural kinds in chemistry
correspond in the required sense to natural kinds in physics? Do the natural kinds
of anatomy correspond to the natural kinds of biochemistry? Do the natural kinds
of neuroscience correspond to the natural kinds of chemistry? It is highly unlikely
that in all cases such correspondences exist (Horgan and Woodward, 1985; Egan,
1995). There are two reasons for skepticism. The first is that the relationship
between entities and processes at higher levels and entities and processes at lower
levels is often a matter of multiple realization. That is, higher-level entities, often
defined in terms of their function, are realized by more than one kind of structure
at the lower level. Where this is the case, the correspondences RS&G are looking

for will be nonexistent. For example, the natural kinds of anatomy include such properties as being a knee or being a heart. Multiple realization occurs because there are differences in what hearts and knees are like at the cellular level from one species to another and because there are now such things as artificial (and hence nonorganic) knees and hearts. Second, the relationship between entities at the higher level and those at the lower level is typically a relationship of whole to parts, but that means that there may not be a kind at the lower level corresponding to just that configuration of parts that constitutes the whole. For example, cells consist of parts (the nucleus, mitochondria, cell wall, and so on) that themselves are made up of complex molecules in various kinds of arrangements. Is there a kind in biochemistry, that corresponds to the kind of being a cell or even being a cell nucleus? That seems very doubtful. Nevertheless, despite the fact that natural kinds at the higher and lower levels may not always correspond, insofar as higher-level entities and processes are realized in some fashion or other at the lower level, we will want to say that those higher-level entities and processes exist. So premise NK2 is clearly problematic.

Furthermore, even if we accept the mapping premise NK2 of the argument for no natural kinds, a question can also be raised about the no-satisfaction premise, NK4. RS&G rest their case on the fact that connectionist* networks that encode different numbers of propositions will differ at the level of weights and biases, even if they all encode one particular proposition — say, the proposition that dogs have fur. Some critics of RS&G's position (e.g., Clark, 1995; Smolensky, 1995) have suggested that there may nevertheless be more abstract computational properties that all the various networks in question share. We will investigate this possibility shortly in connection with the final subargument. For now, however, assume, with RS&G, that given that our mind/brains are connectionist* devices, there is no computational property such that a person will believe that dogs have fur if and only if the connectionist* network that partially realizes that person (or that realizes that person's mind/brain) has that property. But does that mean that there is no corresponding connectionist* property? Certainly not. If our final complete cognitive science theory turns out to be a connectionist* theory, then the networks this theory describes will have both computational and representational properties. RS&G themselves describe connectionist* networks this way. In particular, they describe Networks A and B as "encoding," "representing," and "storing" the information that dogs have fur. The point is that the predicate "encodes the proposition that dogs have fur" is just as much a predicate in the language of connectionist theory as the predicate "has four hidden units." Furthermore, such representational descriptions are not simply a matter of convenience, for insofar as theories in cognitive science seek to explain the intentionality and evaluability of our cognitive capacities (Von Eckardt, 1993), as well as how we execute those capacities, representational properties will play a role in the generalizations of cognitive science and hence will count as natural-kind properties. So even if there is no computational connectionist* property to correspond to the belief-content property of believing that dogs have fur in networks like Networks A and B, there is a representational connectionist* property — the property of encoding the proposition that dogs have fur. For purposes of satisfying the correspondence requirement (assuming it to be legitimate), a representational property will do just as well as a computational one. In sum, RS&G's second subargument, like their first, fails to be convincing.

The Subargument to No Independent Causal Role

Let us turn, finally, to the third subargument, which concerns the property of playing an independent causal role. Again, we will begin by letting RS&G make their own case. Contrasting a classical semantic network with the distributed, superpositional character of Network A, they write:

> In the connectionist network, by contrast, there is no distinct state or part of the network that serves to represent any particular proposition. The information encoded in Network A is stored holistically and distributed throughout the network. . . . It simply makes no sense to ask whether or not the representation of a particular proposition plays a causal role in the network's computation. It is in just this respect that our connectionist model of memory seems radically incongruent with the propositional modularity of common sense psychology. For . . . common sense psychology seems to presuppose that there is generally some answer to the question of whether a particular belief or memory played a causal role in a specific cognitive episode. But if belief and memory are subserved by a connectionist network like ours, such questions seem to have no clear meaning. (1990, p. 513)

Like the first two subarguments, the third has a folk psychology premise (CR1), a mapping premise (CR2), and a no satisfaction premise (CR4).

The Argument for No Independent Causal Role

CR1. According to folk psychology, different beliefs can play independent causal roles.

CR2. Folk psychological belief states play independent causal roles in executing belief capacities only if there are belieflike states in the subpersonal systems realizing those capacities that can also play independent causal roles.

CR3. Because networks like Networks A and B are distributed superpositional networks, there are no isolable computational states that store the information for just a single proposition.

CR4. Thus there are no subpersonal belieflike states in networks like Networks A and B that can play independent causal roles.

CR5. Thus folk psychological belief states cannot play a role in executing the belief capacity modeled by Networks A and B.

To begin our analysis of this argument, let us look more closely at CR1 and CR2 and ask what it means for a belief, on the one hand, and a computational belieflike state, on the other, to be capable of playing an independent causal role. For beliefs, let us say that the belief that p and the belief that q can play independent causal roles just in case the following scenario is possible:

Folk Psychological Independent Causal Role Scenario for Beliefs
At time t_1, a person S believes that p, believes that q, and does not believe that c (either S believes that not c or S believes neither c nor not c). Furthermore, both p and q entail c, so that S could infer c from either. In the interval from time t_1 to time t_2, S infers c on the basis of, say, p but does not infer c on the basis of q, so that at time t_2, S believes that p, that q, and that c.

Similarly, for a system to contain subpersonal belief states capable of playing an independent causal role means that in the system, there are subpersonal states and processes that realize each of the states and processes of the folk psychological independent role scenario. In other words, at time t_1, there is a subpersonal state corresponding to believing that p and another corresponding to believing that q, but none corresponding to believing that c; in the interval t_1 to t_2, there is a process corresponding to the inference from p to c but no process corresponding to the inference from q to c; and finally, at t_2, there is a subpersonal state corresponding respectively to believing that p, believing that q, and believing that c. Note that because of the possibility of multiple realizability, there is no need for there to be a subpersonal kind corresponding to each of these folk psychological kinds. In fact, however, as I suggested earlier, there probably will be such a kind (assuming that we are realized by connectionist* systems), although it will most likely involve a representational or semantic property rather than a narrowly computational one. If that turns out to be the case, then the following scenario will occur at the subpersonal level:

Subpersonal Independent Causal Role Scenario for Belieflike States
At time t_1, system S stores the information that p and the information that q, but does not store the information that c. Furthermore, both p and q entail c. In the interval from time t_1 to time t_2, S is changed so that at t_2, it stores the information that c; moreover, this change is caused by S's going into a state that corresponds, in some sense, with its actively entertaining the information that p rather than the information that q, although the change could have been caused by S's going into a state that corresponds with its actively entertaining the information that q rather than the information that p.

This subpersonal scenario clarifies what it means for a belieflike state to be capable of playing an independent causal role. We must now address the question of whether connectionist* systems can realize such a scenario. RS&G, of course, argue that they cannot. The first point to make about their argument concerns their strategy of arguing inductively on the basis of Networks A and B. The point is that it is logically amiss to be arguing over whether the independent causal role feature of propositional modularity can exist in a connectionist* network by pointing to Networks A and B. The reason is that these simple memory networks do not model the right sort of belief capacity. The sort of belief capacity that is required, if we take RS&G's gloss on the independent causal role feature of propositional modularity seriously, is one that involves inference and, in particular, one for which the folk psychological explanation would be that the subject had multiple sets of beliefs, only one of which was causally instrumental in his or her response (as, for example, in the Inspector Clouseau scenario). Let us call such a belief capacity an "ICR belief capacity." There is a crude analogy to this in Networks A and B. From a folk psychological point of view, Network A has a number of different beliefs that can be instrumental in responding "true," and on any particular occasion, folk psychology might want to say that it was only one of those beliefs (namely, the belief corresponding to the proposition being queried) that actually caused the response. But since, in the Network A case, the input differs whenever we are inclined to say that the internal state differs, Network A does not seem to capture the sort of thing going on in the Clouseau example. In that example, in contrast to Network A, the input to the process is presumably the same for both possible inferences. (We can think of that input as Clouseau putting a question to himself: "Did the butler lie?" or, perhaps, the more open-ended "What do you make of the butler's story?") But even though there is only one input and two possible inferential routes for arriving at the conclusion, we want to say that Clouseau actually took only one of those routes. (Of course, there will presumably be something that caused his mind/brain to take the inferential route it did.)

Having said all of that, let us return to RS&G's argument as it is framed, that is, in terms of Networks A and B. Even though the belief capacity realized by Networks A and B only crudely approximates an ICR belief capacity as characterized earlier, RS&G and most of their critics have assumed that the approximation is close enough in relevant respects so that inspection of Networks A and B will tell us something about whether connectionist* networks can have ICR belief states. In order to get on with the discussion, I will, for the moment, accept that assumption. The question then becomes whether reflection on Networks A and B suggests that CR4 is true, as RS&G suppose. Critics have questioned the truth of CR4 on two grounds. Egan (1995) seems to accept CR3 but argues that CR4 does not follow from it. Clark (1995) and others apparently accept the inference from CR3 to CR4 but argue that CR3 is false and that hence there are subpersonal belieflike states in networks like A and B that can play independent causal roles. Let us look at both of these responses to RS&G's third subargument in more detail.

Egan (1995) offers a reconstruction of RS&G's overall argument that, as I read her, actually amounts to a pared-down version of the argument for no independent causal role. Her take on that portion of the argument covered by CR3 and CR4 looks like this: "(1) the network lacks functionally discrete, identifiable substructures that are semantically interpretable as representations of individual propositions; (2) therefore, the representation of a particular proposition cannot plausibly be said to play a causal role in the network's computation" (Egan, 1995, p. 183). She then offers the following criticism:

Compelling though this argument may appear, it fails to establish its conclusion. (1) is true for a wide range of connectionist models—so-called "distributed" networks. (2) follows from (1) only if the representation of a particular proposition must be realized as a discrete, identifiable substructure to be causally efficacious. RSG do not offer an argument for this claim. To establish its truth, and hence to establish claim (2) of their argument, RSG need to argue that distributed representations are *epiphenomenal*—that they play no causal roles in the network's behavior—something they do not attempt. The growing literature on distributed representations does not construe them as epiphenomenal. . . . If distributed connectionist models are taken at their face, and in the absence of an argument to the contrary surely they should be, then claim (2) of RSG's argument appears to be false. (Egan, 1995, p. 183)

Egan is surely right that distributed representations can be causally efficacious, but that is not what is at issue in this subargument. Rather, what is at issue, and what is not adequately captured by her version of the argument, is whether two propositional representations that are realized in the same superpositional distributed network can play independent causal roles, that is, whether there can be occasions when one propositional representation rather than the other will have caused the outcome in question. The point is that the distributed representations of a network might not play independent causal roles even if we grant Egan's claim that in general, distributed representations can play causal roles *tout court*. In other words, the question is not whether being functionally discrete (presumably in the architectural sense) is necessary for playing a causal role *tout court* but whether it is necessary for playing an independent causal role in the sense captured by the subpersonal ICR scenario described earlier.

In fact, RS&G are correct on this point, for, as our subpersonal ICR scenario makes clear, if the folk psychological independent causal role story is correct, then, at the subpersonal level, the "inferential" change from t_1 to t_2 must be caused by a computational state associated with only one of the propositions rather than the other. But the claim that a state associated with the content *that p* caused the change, rather than a state associated with the content *that q*, implies that the p state can, in some sense, exist without the existence of the corresponding q state. But to say that is simply to say that the p and q states in question are, at least partly, functionally discrete in the architectural sense. I will take it, then, that the inference from CR3 to CR4 is unproblematic.

A second way to criticize the argument for no independent causal role lies with the truth of CR3 itself. A number of philosophers have argued that there are isolable computational states that store the information for just a single proposition, and hence that there are subpersonal belieflike states in networks like A and B that can play independent causal roles, namely, the pattern of activation of the hidden nodes when the proposition in question is presented to the network. (RS&G credit this suggestion to Adrian Cussins and Gary Cottrell. See also Botterill, 1994; and Clark, 1995.)

Note, first, that while finding a functionally discrete computational state in Networks A and B suffices to undermine the truth of CR3 and hence the soundness of RS&G's argument, it does not suffice to demonstrate that CR4 is false, that is, that there are subpersonal belieflike states in networks like A and B that can play independent causal roles. Being functionally discrete is only a necessary condition for being capable of playing an independent causal role, not a sufficient condition. To be sufficient, a state must not only be functionally discrete but also be an ICR state in the sense defined by our subpersonal ICR scenario.

Thus we cannot demonstrate the falsity of CR4 by pointing to patterns of activation in Networks A and B. But can we show the falsity of CR3? There are four hidden nodes in Networks A and B, and each is capable of different degrees of activation. Thus, according to RS&G, when Network A is presented with the encoded proposition *dogs have fur*, the relevant activation pattern is (21,75,73,12). Moreover, it turns out that there is a unique pattern in response to each presented proposition. RS&G, however, are not persuaded by this fact:

> What is being proposed is that the pattern of activation of the system on presentation of an encoding of the proposition p be identified with the belief that p. But this proposal is singularly implausible. Perhaps the best way to see this is to note that in common sense psychology beliefs and propositional memories are typically of substantial duration; and they are the sorts of things that cognitive agents generally have lots of even when they are not using them. . . . An activation pattern, however, is not an enduring state of a network; indeed, it is not a state of the network at all except when the network has had the relevant proposition as input. More-over, there is an enormous number of other beliefs that you've had for years. But it makes no sense to suppose that a network could have many activation patterns continuously over a long period of time. At any given time a network exhibits at most one pattern of activation. So activation patterns are just not the sort of things that can plausibly be identified with beliefs or their representations. (1990, p. 518)

RS&G are correct that according to folk psychology, people have specific beliefs for long periods of time and also have many beliefs simultaneously, so if patterns of activation last only for a short period of time and a network can have only one (or a few) at a time, then it is implausible to identify a network's having a particular pattern of activation with a person's having a particular belief. However, the critics have a response to this reply. Folk psychology not only assumes that people have beliefs, but also distinguishes between having a belief in the long-standing sense and having a belief play an active causal role in inference or in the processes leading to action. Obviously, simply having a belief is not enough for it to play a causal role. Otherwise, we would constantly be engaged in thousands of inferences. So, according to folk psychology, beliefs can be inactive or active. This distinction is sometimes marked by talking about beliefs in the dispositional sense versus beliefs in the occurrent sense. What the Clouseau scenario imagines is that after interrogating the butler, but before making his inference, Clouseau has two sets of inactive beliefs, both of which could lead to the conclusion that the butler is lying. At the moment when he engages in the reasoning process, one of these belief sets becomes active while the other remains inactive.

It is implausible to identify beliefs in the dispositional, long-standing sense with patterns of activation, as RS&G suggest, but it is not at all implausible to think of patterns of activation as the subpersonal realizers of beliefs in their occurrent sense. What, then, could count as a belieflike state in the dispositional sense? RS&G's critics have proposed that what realizes a network's dispositional belief that *p* is the network's disposition to produce the activation pattern that realizes the occurrent belief that *p*. (RS&G attribute this suggestion to Ned Block and Frank Jackson. See also O'Brien, 1993; Botterill, 1994; and Clark, 1995.) But, again, RS&G have a reply:

> Our reply to this suggestion is that while dispositions to produce activation patterns are indeed *enduring* states of the system, they are not the right sort of enduring states—they are not the discrete, independently causally active states that folk psychology requires. . . . The propositional modularity presupposed by common sense psychology requires that belief tokens be functionally discrete states capable of causally interacting with one another in some cognitive episodes and of remaining causally inert in other cognitive episodes. However, in a distributed connectionist system like Network A, the dispositional state which produces one activation pattern is functionally inseparable from the dispositional state which produces another. Thus it is impossible to isolate some propositions as causally active in certain cognitive episodes, while others are not. We conclude that reaction pattern dispositions won't do as belief tokens. (1990, p. 519)

RS&G's response here seems to be a combination of both the argument for no functional discreteness and the argument for no independent causal role with a special focus on dispositional states. If we separate the argumentative strands, we can see in what ways the response is problematic.

The first strand is that "the propositional modularity presupposed by common sense psychology requires that belief tokens be *functionally discrete* states" (my emphasis); however, according to RS&G, a network's disposition to produce an activation pattern is not functionally discrete in the requisite way. Therefore, "reaction pattern dispositions won't do as belief tokens." Clearly, here we are back to the architectural functional discreteness reading of the argument for no functional discreteness. Although we can agree that dispositions to produce an activation pattern are not functionally discrete in the architectural sense, we should reject the claim that folk psychology requires this (O'Brien, 1993; Botterill, 1994; Clark, 1995). As we noted earlier, folk psychology simply makes no assumptions whatsoever regarding how our ordinary mental states are computationally or biologically realized.

The second strand of RS&G's response relies on the connection between playing an independent causal role and functional discreteness. We can represent it like this:

The Independent Causal Role Argument against Activation Pattern Dispositions

APD1. According to folk psychology, belief states are enduring and can play independent causal roles.

APD2. Thus to be the subpersonal realizers of folk psychological belief states, connectionist* states must also be enduring and capable of playing an independent causal role.

APD3. Connectionist* belief states can play an independent causal role only if they are architecturally functionally discrete.

APD4. Therefore, to be the subpersonal realizers of folk psychological belief states, connectionist* states must be enduring and architecturally functionally discrete.

APD5. While activation pattern dispositions are enduring, they are not functionally discrete.

APD6. Therefore, activation pattern dispositions cannot be the subpersonal realizers of folk psychological belief states.

The difficulty with this argument is that it fails to take seriously the fact that folk psychological belief states come in two forms—occurrent and dispositional. When that fact is taken seriously, we see that there are several ways to read APD1: (1) as having the logical form "$(x)[(Bx \rightarrow (Ex \ \& \ Cx)]$" ("All belief states are both enduring and capable of playing an independent causal role."); (2) as having the logical form "$(\exists x)(Bx \ \& \ Ex \ \& \ Cx)$" ("Some belief states are both enduring and capable of playing an independent causal role."); or (3) as having the logical form "$[(\exists x)(Bx \ \& \ Ex) \ \& \ (\exists x)(Bx \ \& \ Cx)]$" ("Some belief states are enduring and some belief states can play an independent causal role").

I suggest that folk psychology is indifferent as between the second and the third. As a consequence, once the distinction between occurrent and dispositional belief states is made, it is perfectly in tune with the dictates of common sense to maintain that it is the dispositional belief states that are enduring, while it is the occurrent ones that are capable of an independent causal role, and hence that APD4 can be satisfied by identifying activation pattern dispositions as the subpersonal realizers of the folk psychological belief states that are enduring and the activation patterns themselves as the subpersonal realizers of the folk psychological belief states that are capable of an independent causal role. This is so even if we accept the claim of premise APD5 that activation pattern dispositions are not functionally discrete in the architectural sense (see Clark, 1995, for a similar point).

In sum, RS&G's final argument is no more successful than either of their first two. In the first place, networks like Networks A and B are not really complex enough to serve as representative networks for arguing in support of the no-satisfaction premise CR4. Second, even if one does examine such networks to see whether there are belieflike states approximating an independent causal role (where this means only that it is determinate which of several possible states actually played the role in question), premise CR4 seems to be false. RS&G only have a case with respect to the truth of CR4 if it is assumed that playing an independent causal role requires functional discreteness in the architectural sense, but, on this assumption, the folk psychology premise, CR1, is false. In either case, the argument is unsound.

Summary and Coda

RS&G's argument consists of a main argument, the argument from connectionism*, and three subarguments, the argument for no functional discreteness the argument for no natural kinds, and the argument for no independent causal role. The three subarguments are not independent arguments for particular premises of the main argument. Rather, each covers the same ground as the central portion of the main argument (C4 to C7), but only with respect to one of the three properties (being functionally discrete, being semantically interpretable, and playing independent causal roles) that make up the compound property mentioned in the main argument (being propositionally modular). Thus, insofar as there are problems with the subarguments, there are problems with this portion of the main argument.

Before bringing the discussion of RS&G's article to a close, we should note one additional questionable step in the argument (Stich and Warfield, 1995, pp. 395–411). C3 states that folk psychological belief states play a role in executing belief capacities only if there are belieflike states in the subpersonal systems realizing those capacities. C5 states that there are belieflike states in the subpersonal systems that realize belief capacities only if there are states in those systems that also are functionally discrete, are semantically interpretable, and can play independent causal roles. C3 seems reasonable enough, but what about C5? The questionable character of C5 becomes even more obvious when we combine it with C3 to get this:

> C3/5: Folk psychological belief states play a role in executing belief capacities only if there are states in the subpersonal systems realizing those capacities that are functionally discrete, are semantically interpretable, and can play independent causal roles.

In other words, C3/5 is claiming that being functionally discrete, being semantically interpretable, and playing an independent causal role are somehow constitutive of or essential to being a belief, that nothing could be a belief state unless it had these properties. Contemporary philosophers have questioned whether anything has constitutive or essential properties, but even if these general worries are set aside, questions can be raised about the specific properties at issue. Suppose that future cognitive science theory posited states that had all the properties we take beliefs to have except that (1) we could not acquire or lose such states one by one, (2) although the states had semantic properties, these properties did not figure in the theory's lawlike generalizations, and (3) when the states could have been psychologically generated in several alternative ways, it was indeterminate which way they were actually generated. Would it not be a serious option to say that beliefs exist, but we were mistaken about some of their properties? If so, then C5 of the main argument is also not acceptable.

Notes

I am grateful to Jeffrey Poland and David Pitt for helpful comments.

  1. Ramsey, Stich, and Garon say only that the models in question are ones in which the encoding of information is "widely distributed," but clearly that is not enough for their purposes. If the network were large and each proposition were stored distributively in its own subregion of the network, their argument would not even get off the ground.

  2. Clark (1995) also notes this structure when he suggests that there are three "ways out" of the sort of eliminativist arguments RS&G are putting forth:

> We might just *deny* that the folk care about propositional modularity. . . . Or we might try to show that propositional modularity is safe *whatever* turns up in the head. . . . Finally, we might argue that distributed, sub-symbolic, superpositional connectionist models are actually more structured than RS&G think, and hence visibly compatible with the requirements of propositional modularity. (Clark, 1995, p. 345)

References

Bechtel, W., and Abrahamsen, A. 1993. "Connectionism and the Future of Folk Psychology." Pp. 340–67 in S. Christensen and D. Turner (Eds.), *Folk Psychology and the Philosophy of Mind*. Hillsdale, NJ: Erlbaum.

Bogdan, R. 1993. "The Architectural Nonchalance of Commonsense Psychology." *Mind and Language*, 8(2) (Summer), pp. 189–205.

Botterill, G. 1994. "Beliefs, Functionally Discrete States, and Connectionist Networks: A Comment on Ramsey, Stich, and Garon." *British Journal for the Philosophy of Science*, 45(3) (September), pp. 899–906.

Christensen, S., and Turner, D. (Eds.). 1993. *Folk Psychology and the Philosophy of Mind*. Hillsdale, NJ: Erlbaum.

Clark, A. 1995. "Connectionist Minds." Pp. 339–56 in C. Macdonald and G. Macdonald (Eds.), *Connectionism: Debates on Psychological Explanation*. Oxford: Blackwell.

Egan, F. 1995. "Folk Psychology and Cognitive Architecture." *Philosophy of Science*, 62(2) (June), pp. 179–97.

Forster, M, and Saidel, E. 1994. "Connectionism and the Fate of Folk Psychology: A Reply to Ramsey, Stich, and Garon." *Philosophical Psychology*, 7, pp. 437–52.

Horgan, T., and Woodward, J. 1985. "Folk Psychology Is Here to Stay." *Philosophical Review*, 94, pp. 197–225.

Macdonald, C. 1995. "Introduction: Connectionism and Eliminativism." Pp. 293–310 in C. Macdonald and G. Macdonald (Eds.), *Connectionism: Debates on Psychological Explanation.* Oxford: Blackwell.

Macdonald, C, and Macdonald, G. (Eds.). 1995. *Connectionism: Debates on Psychological Explanation.* Oxford: Blackwell.

O'Brien, G. J. 1993. "The Connectionist Vindication of Folk Psychology." Pp. 368–87 in S. Christensen and D. Turner (Eds.), *Folk Psychology and the Philosophy of Mind.* Hillsdale, NJ: Erlbaum.

Ramsey, W. 1994. "Distributed Representation and Causal Modularity: A Rejoinder to Forster and Saidel." *Philosophical Psychology,* 7, pp. 453–60.

Ramsey, W., Stich, S., and Garon, J. 1990. "Connectionism, Eliminativism, and the Future of Folk Psychology." *Philosophical Perspectives,* 4, pp. 499–533.

Smolensky, P. 1995. "On the Projectable Predicates of Connectionist Psychology: A Case for Belief." Pp. 357–94 in C. Macdonald and G. Macdonald (Eds.), *Connectionism: Debates on Psychological Explanation.* Oxford: Blackwell.

Stich, S., and Warfield, T. 1995. "Reply to Clark and Smolensky: Do Connectionist Minds Have Beliefs?" Pp. 395–411 in C. Macdonald and G. Macdonald (Eds.), *Connectionism: Debates on Psychological Explanation.* Oxford: Blackwell.

Von Eckardt, B. 1993. *What Is Cognitive Science?* Cambridge, MA: MIT Press.

IV

Is "Mind" Just Another Name for the Brain and What the Brain Does?

Introduction

Christina E. Erneling

One of the chapters in this part (by Itiel Dror and Robin Thomas) presents two metaphors of different ways of approaching the study of the mind: the tales of Pinocchio and Frankenstein. In Carlo Collodi's 1883 book about Pinocchio, it is the fairy godmother who miraculously provides Pinocchio with a mind; but in Mary Shelley's book *Frankenstein; or, The Modern Prometheus* (1818), the monster's mind is a result of material design, or the successful combination of bodily parts. Itiel Dror and Thomas think that the Pinocchio tale in this respect expresses views similar to Descartes's dualism between the body and the mind. The body and mind consist of different substances; and only the body can be studied scientifically, since the mind is a mysterious, nonmaterial entity. The story about the monster that Frankenstein created out of pieces of cadavers, on the other hand, implies no such dualism. The mind and the body are of the same ontological kind, and consequently they can be studied in the same way, that is, with scientific methods.

Not only Itiel Dror and Thomas's chapter, but also the other three chapters in this part are in line with the assumptions expressed in Shelley's *Frankenstein; or, The Modern Prometheus*. All these chapters reject Cartesian dualism and more specifically argue that the interdisciplinary approach of cognitive neuroscience, consisting of a combination of neuroscience with behavioral and information-processing analyses of mental functions, eventually will lead us to understanding the mind scientifically. Neuroscience provides information about the physical machinery of the mind, and computational analysis of its computational architecture provides information about it as a processor of information. Since behavior is a result of the workings of the mind, analysis of it also plays an important part in deciphering the mind as well.

An important assumption found in all four chapters is that the mind is not a unitary entity, but a complex system that is divided into subsystems, or modules, each of which specializes in specific functions, and which, in many cases, can be divided into further subsystems (see Tadeusz Zawidzki and William Bechtel's chapter). Cognitive subsystems like memory, attention, vision, and reasoning are subsystems of the overall cognitive system. They interact with each other and also can be divided into further subsystems. Such horizontal faculties are individuated according to their function—for example, memory. But some neuropsychologists also speak of vertical faculties, which are individuated with reference to subject matter—for example, language or music. The assumption of modularity is central to all neuropsychological studies (see Vinod Goel's chapter for arguments for this). This point is also explored in detail in Goel's, Ingvar's, and Zawidzki and Bechtel's chapters.

Zawidzki and Bechtel trace the idea of modularity to Franz Joseph Gall (1758–1828) and point to several examples of likeness and difference between early nineteenth-century ideas and today's conceptions of modularity (e.g., Jerry Fodor's). They reject the top-down analysis favored by both Gall and many contemporary cognitive scientists—that is, the view that analysis begins with the cognitive task of analyzing a mental function and the behavior related to it and then proceeds to connect this with underlying neural mechanisms. It is more fruitful, they argue, to take an interdisciplinary approach that presupposes that there is a dynamic interplay between these methods, on one side, and neuroscience research, on the other. For example, neural evidence can help individuate, modify, and restrain cognitive models. To support their case, these authors provide a detailed and illuminating discussion of how the cognitive phenomenon of attention has undergone reconceptualization when it has been approached in this way. Further examples of similar reconceptualizations (the cases of vision and memory) are given in Itiel Dror's and Thomas's chapter.

Goel, instead of analyzing such examples, discusses and rejects two objections to cognitive neuroscience. The first objection has to do with the independence of computational level explanations—that is, the idea that psychological states can be realized in different brain states, indeed in any physical states whatsoever. The second objection is based on Fodor's argument that higher mental functions, like problem solving, cannot be accounted for in terms of modularity. Goel maintains that neuroscience is a valuable source for individuating and understanding human cognition even on a computational level, since we are interested not in just any model, but rather in a model that fits with the human brain. Furthermore, while modularity assumptions are crucial to neuroscience, he rejects Fodor's claim that higher mental processes are not modular, because he claims that the notion of modularity with which Fodor operates is too restricted a notion of modularity.

Martin Ingvar, who is a neurobiologist, also accepts the approach of modularity and focuses on how the brain handles the perception-action cycle of input and output. Discussing memory, learning, and emotion, he explains how the brain handles excessive information demands and time limitations by a parallel mode of cognitive processing. His discussion of emotions, a topic that until recently undeservedly has been neglected in neurobiology, is informative and suggests interesting topics of study. His paper, as well as the other, more philosophical papers, show that even if our understanding of the brain has increased greatly during the last decade, there is still much to learn.

To summarize, the general understanding of mental activity aimed at in these chapters goes beyond descriptions of the biological brain and its neural activity. The interdisciplinary approach outlined earlier distinguishes this way of understanding things from theoretical approaches that aim at abolishing all reference to the mind or behavior (e.g., eliminativism, as it is discussed in the previous part). All the authors propose a no-center view of the mind (see David Martel Johnson's introduction to this volume). No one discipline is able to capture the mind all by itself, at least not at the present time. (For example, in regard to this last suggestion, Itiel Dror and Thomas propose that the ultimate goal should be to understand the mind in computational terms alone.)

As mentioned before, the chapters in this part reject the dualistic ontology of the Cartesian approach. Nevertheless, they all embrace another Cartesian assumption, that of atomism, in the sense of claiming that all basic mental or cognitive entities count as individuatable states of mind stuff and, as such, are states of particular brains that belong to particular persons. For example, Itiel Dror and Thomas maintain that "the mind is a set of representations and their processing in the brain, which helps or allows us to explain and predict behavior," and in a partly similar way, Zawidzki and Bechtel discuss the decomposition of "individual mental activities." All three strands or parts of cognitive neuroscience—the computational, the behavioral, and the neuroscientific—share this assumption of atomism or individualism.

Of course, individual neurophysiological processes are the necessary substratum of mental phenomena. For example, we need the brain to act, think, perceive, speak, and feel envy and anger. But something more is also needed. We are not just brains interacting with other brains, but are human beings acting as social agents undertaking various projects in accordance with local conventions of appropriateness and correctness. Explaining anger is not just stating which cells are active in various parts of the brain or describing patterns of blood flow, but also involves accounting for the social conventions and rules that entitle people to become angry in some situations, but not in others. Explaining anger also involves the account of the "hidden" mechanisms that make up the complex social network and are constitutive of mental activities. Let me expand in order to explain what I mean.

One of the reasons Gall was justifiably ridiculed was that his list of faculties included such things as destructiveness, friendship, and language, and that he claimed to be able to find a location for each of them. Destructiveness, for example, was thought to be located just above the ear. One important thing that is wrong with this is that each of these psychological faculties actually decomposes into many different components or modules located in many different parts of the brain, as is shown by the example of attention discussed by Zawidzki and Bechtel.

But there is something else wrong with Gall's project besides his insensitivity to decomposition of complex mental phenomena. The trouble with his approach, as well as with that of much of contemporary cognitive neuroscience, is that they leave out the idea that to be destructive, or to be angry, or to speak a language involves more than the physiological activity in the brain and the behavior caused by it. It also involves a social context with other people and with rules of uptake, correctness, and other matters.

Acts of anger or linguistic competence are not individuated just by being events at one or another time t_i and locations l_{i-n}, but by being acts or activities that take place "at" some specific person who is part of a group of people within which interactions with one other are related through rules. Consider a short illustration from language acquisition: One, obviously too simple, way to decompose linguistic competence is to say that it involves the acquisition of speech-production skills, syntactical skills, and semantically communicative skills. This is enough for the point I want to make. Undoubtedly the acquisition of all such skills presupposes a functioning brain, and this fact needs to be studied. But to explain what happens here, we also need to look beyond this. For example, to learn to utter something meaningful—that is, to acquire semantically communicative skills—is not just to acquire the specific configuration of specific brain processes. It also involves having other people consider what one says as a piece of linguistic communication. If I promise you something verbally, it does not matter what the state of my brain is. The important thing, rather, is that my promise is taken as such by other people. This depends not just on my and your behavior and brain processes, but also on a social network of meanings and rules. To explain typically human mental phenomena only in terms of the brain is like trying to explain tennis as a competitive game by referring to the physics of ballistic trajectories.

If this is correct, then it is necessary to study the brain in the way the authors suggest. But in addition to analyzing mental capacities in terms of individual performances or brain structure, or computational architecture, one also has to take account of the social network that makes them possible. What I am proposing is to get rid of a lingering Cartesianism in understanding the mental—namely, the atomistic idea that assumes that mental capacities are essentially individual capacities.

How wide should we cast our interdisciplinary net in attempting to understand mental life? The chapters in this part suggest that a broadening is necessary, and the suggestions I have just made further widen the net. So do the chapters in the next few parts, which look to evolutionary biology, and then also to culture, for additional clues to a proper understanding of the mind. Is this a feasible approach, or does one run the risk, by pursuing such a no-center view, of losing sight of our proposed subject matter, the mind?

14

All in the Interest of Time: On the Problem of Speed and Cognition

Martin Ingvar

The Building Blocks

The brain has, with its weight of less than 1.5 kilograms, some 100 billion nerve cells. These cells have a surface area with a size somewhere on the order of a football field. The potential for handling and storing of ordered information in the brain is related to its architecture. The selective and energy-consuming processes by which cellular ionic gradients are upheld underlie most of the known mechanisms in the brain's information processing. The basic speed for transfer of information is below two hundred meters per second. The synaptic mechanisms also introduce a loss of time in the information processing. The need for synchronicity is limited as long as the need for inner representation is limited. In such primitive systems, many seemingly complicated behaviors can be elicited without the need of formally representing them in a neuronal system. Rather, sequences may be stored simply based on the local neural properties (figure 14.1).

In the course of development, reactive processing becomes a problem for two reasons. Both the increased demands of more elaborate responses and the consequential size increase of the brain reduce the speed of processing. The biological hardware is just too sluggish for sequential processing of fast events like human thought processing (Rumelhart and McClelland, 1986). Hence very early on the central nervous system (CNS) adopted a parallel mode of information processing. An intuitive addition to the nervous system agenda would be to use constraint in the information processing in order to gain speed. However, adding constraints in a process of handling information tends to slow the process even more, as constraints imply large-scale neuronal processing with synchronous processing in all units (Rumelhart and McClelland, 1986).

Consciousness has become a subject for scientific study (Churchland and Churchland, 1997). Some argue that consciousness is a mere by-product of any representative system, whereas others ascribe specific developmental advantages

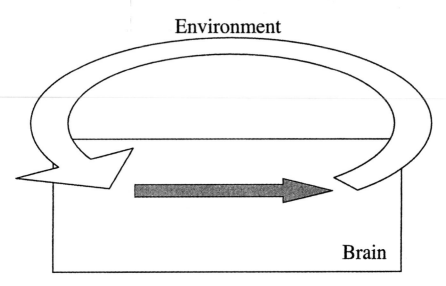

FIGURE 14.1. A simple drawing of a perception-action cycle. The small arrow represents the nervous system, whereas the large arrow symbolizes the extra-individual
feedback loop (James, 1894).

that explain this development. With the development of computational neuroscience, the former view seems to have gained impetus. The ultimate aim of
computational neuroscience is to explain how electrical and chemical signals are
used in the brain to represent and process information. Realistic brain computing
is still not a reality, but new insights are available from the study of simplified
models of large networks of neurons. Brain models are being used to connect the
microscopic level, accessible by molecular and cellular techniques, with the systems level, accessible by the study of behavior.

Modularity Revisited

With increased complexity, modularity becomes a real option for organizing the
brain. While the term "modularity" has been used both with specific meaning
and a more general descriptive meaning (Fodor, 1981), the context of this chapter
is the more general perspective. Several authors have adopted a hierarchical view,
which implies a modular view of the CNS organization (Sejnowski, Koch, and
Churchland, 1988) (figure 14.2).

Slicing the loaf another way, hierarchies based on other dimensions than
anatomy can be constructed, such as the dimension of information (e.g., bits/
bytes/words/sentences/concepts/knowledge/wisdom). As the predictive power is low
between distant levels of such hierarchies, their value as metaphors for the organization of the human brain is somewhat limited.

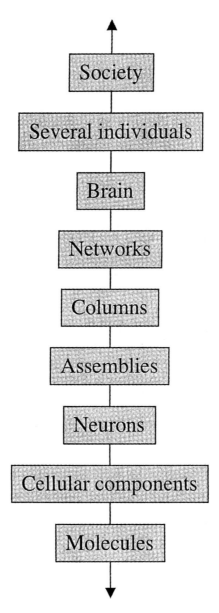

FIGURE 14.2. Information processing from a hierarchical point of view. It is possible to make reasonable extrapolations of the functional implication of changes in a level to adjacent levels. However, cross-level predictability decreases with distance between the levels. Hence computational neuroscience has a formidable task when brain-based models encompassing all levels are implemented. (Freely after Sejnowski, Koch, and Churchland, 1988.)

The perspective of parallel distributed processing (PDP) on cognition explic- itly states that different regions work in parallel, and with a much more intense computational capacity internally in a unit than between units (Rumelhart and McClelland, 1986). The PDP perspective has been very successful in conveying the view that general mechanisms may be found in the distributed processing units for learning, memory, and information extraction.

Multiple Representations of Time

An obvious effect of a parallel mode of processing is that the timing of the proc- essing becomes independent between different modules. Maintenance of syn- chronicity between modules has been demonstrated in vivo and even has been suggested as one way of conveying information from one module to the next (Rager and Singer, 1998). This view has been debated to some extent. It seems safe to conclude that the frequencies of this synchronous event are probably below 100 Hz, and hence any modulation of the signal can carry only limited amounts of information. While a parallel system benefits greatly from decreasing depen- dency between modules, the cost is that the results of the computations are re- ported independently in the time domain. This generates the need for specific modules that have a buffering capacity in the time domain and allow a continuous filling in of information as the processing results from different modules are pre- sented. Hence constructs that allow representation from sparse data are effective in such circumstances (Rumelhart and McClelland, 1986).

Adding Memory to the Perception-Action Cycle

A pure perception-action cycle has little need for representation, but also minor capacity for learning. Hence from a computational point of view it could be seen as a neuronal automaton where speed and consistency prevail over flexibility (Er- mentrout and Edelstein-Keshet, 1993). Adding a memory function means that information processing is continuously performed, both in response to perceptions from the outer world and from stored information (Grossberg, 1999) (figure 14.3). A memory function implies that the neuronal network changes its properties in response to its use, and that any information in the network is dynamically inter- acting with the memory. Several different mechanisms for such an interaction have been proposed, but the adaptive resonance theory (ART) in some instances stands out as very reasonable. It provides a plausible method for the use of memory in information reduction, thereby decreasing the computational demand in the assemblies (Grossberg, 1999). The ART model has a particularly nice feature in that it predicts that different actions and perceptions can be elicited in different regions depending on the state of learning (Grossberg, 1999). Hence psychological based models of bottom-up versus top-down processing have a clear substrate in the ART theory.

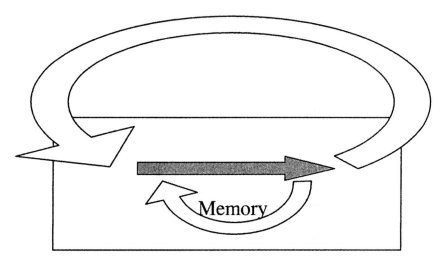

FIGURE 14.3. The addition of memory allows for processing that continuously allows for comparison between perception and memories (Grossberg, 1999).

PDP models do not imply a separation of the memory store from processing modules. Rather, memory should be seen as information processing changes, in response to the information processing itself, in the tissue (Petersson, Elfgren, and Ingvar, 1997). Such a view receives support from all kinds of memory research (Tulving and Markowitsch, 1997).

The now classic work on memory stratification separates phylogenetically old types of memories that require little representation while forming and newer forms of memory often referred to as episodic/semantic memory that require large representation and allow for cross-modal associations much more readily. William James suggested a dichotomy between short-term and long-term memory (James, 1890, 1894). Later Hebb suggested that short-term memory function was based on reverberating neuronal circuits and that such activity could be the explanation for the remake of the properties of the synaptic functional architecture—that is, long-term memory (Hebb, 1949).

The need for rapid processing and representation of large amounts of data is apparent in, for example, listening, where the information is presented serially and the extraction of the content cannot be made before the presentation is complete. Representational theories, such as the working-memory theory of Baddeley, have been extremely helpful in explaining the phenomenology on the behavioral level (Baddeley, 1998). Ongoing work has shown that language-learning capacity seems to be very closely related to the size of the phonological buffer capacity (Baddeley, Gathercole, and Pagagno, 1998). The insight that information buffering is a necessary means for information extraction has led to the further building of theory and now suggests that some episodic memories are dependent on a specific episodic buffer (Baddeley, 2000). The anatomical substrate has yet to be determined for this function, but it seems probable that higher-order cortices in the fronto-parietal system are important players.

Adding Emotion to the Perception-Action Cycle

The emotional regulation of information processing has attracted much interest lately as theories of emotion, as well as the understanding of the neural correlates of emotional regulation, have become better known. A practical separation of a feeling component, and the public manifestations thereof, was suggested early on by James (James, 1894), although he knew about the interaction between these two components that had been demonstrated by Darwin (Darwin, 1872). The odd separation of emotion from cognition has prevented the development of a proper theoretical framework to explain the relation between these entities. Emotions can be said to be the means by which a person appraises the significance of stimuli so as to prepare the body for an appropriate response (figure 14.4). Emotional

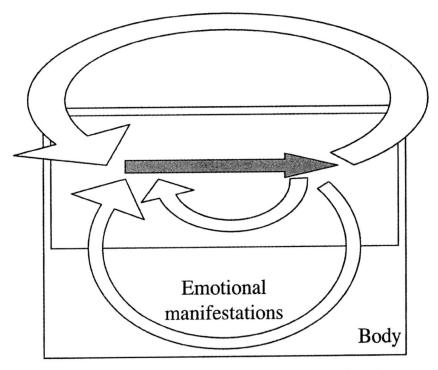

FIGURE 14.4. Adding emotional manifestations to brain processing allows the preparation of the body, as well as body feedback on the emotional setting (Darwin, 1872; James, 1894). Already Darwin noted that it was possible to influence the mood of a subject by electrically stimulating the facial muscles that create a smile.

manifestations also provide feedback to the brain, thereby providing modulation of cognitive processing. Whether or not the anatomical substrate for the generation of emotions is the limbic system is a disputed question, but some of the early theories hold up fairly well (MacLean, 1952).

Information Reduction

The brain has a limited capacity for processing, storing, and retrieval of information. Hence one central theme of the brain's functioning is information reduction. James suggested the existence of several mechanisms that could act as a filter in order to prevent information overflow of our perceptual networks (James, 1890). The mechanisms of attention provide one mechanism of reducing information. These neural systems involve both a network subserving top-down modulation (sources of attention) and the sites of modulation in areas that primarily and secondarily process the attended information (Frith and Dolan, 1997; Posner, 1994). The cortical correlates of the sources of attention have principally been assigned to the right posterior parietal cortex, the anterior cingulate cortex, and the prefrontal cortex (Mesulam, 1990). Attentional modulation of cerebral computational activity has been shown to be very sensitive to different contextual cues, supporting the concept of top-down modulation of cortical activity (Buchel et al., 1998; Ghatan et al., 1998).

Memory capacity is limited, and hence the brain needs to uphold a proper balance between stability (nonlearning mode) and plasticity (nonremembering mode). The stability-plasticity dilemma is a classic problem in studies of learning properties of artificial neuronal networks (Freeman, 1994).

Storing of memories is based on what relevance is assigned to the information. The regulation of relevance can be experimentally studied by explicitly manipulating that parameter. Indeed the emotional system plays an important role in this, but other factors as outlined in figure 14.5 also play an important role. Thus modulation of context, stress level, novelty, understanding, structure of information, and other factors each have an influence on the probability that information will be added into, for example, episodic memory.

Integrating Input-Output Function

A principal goal of perception is to learn to respond to coherent information across space, time, and modality. For example, we learn to associate different representations, sounds, and shapes with objects. These cross-modal associations can help considerably with identification in a noisy environment—for example, lip reading. These associations exist because of statistical dependencies between modalities in the external environment. Thus coherence in the time domain plays an important role in the forming of associative memory (LeDoux, 2000).

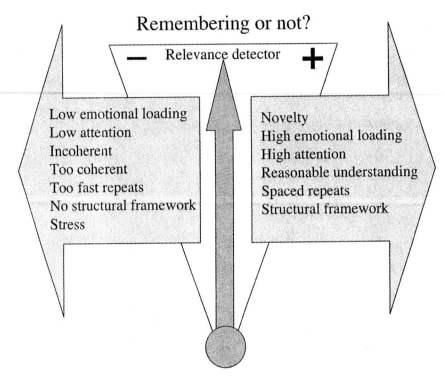

FIGURE 14.5. The principle of relevance detection: Relevance is a composite entity with several subparameters, and any neuronal network has relevance determination built into it as a means of protection for overflow.

The 500-Millisecond Jump

The handling of the temporal domain is a formidable task for any real time processing system. A simple touch of a finger on the nose will generate pieces of sensory information that diverge, simply because of the time difference of the signals of up to 500 ms that reach the central nervous system. While this may seem to be a trivial observation, the problem becomes much more elaborate when we reflect that we have multiple sensory channels. The sheer size of the cerebellum and other anatomical components involved reveals the computational demands involved. The conscious experience, which is the result of elaborate prospective and retrospective processing, most likely has a different time setting from the outer world (Gazzaniga, 1998). A crucial experiment is difficult to construct, but see the serious attempt made by Libet (Libet, 1991; Libet et al., 1979). His theory of a constant back-projection in time, for example, of a sensory experience, provides a possible explanation of how a very slow brain still can operate in real-time mode (Hesslow, 1994).

While such back-propagation would provide a solution to many of the real-time processing needs, the bandwidth is limited, and hence such a mechanism easily may be disturbed. An overflow of the input buffers can easily be attained by rapid presentation of images or by a sequential presentation of number series with more than ten objects. Working memory plays an important role in the conscious experience as the mechanism for representing both externally and internally generated information. The difference in timing between the output and the input is illustrated by Fuster when describing working memory of two classes: "If that, then now this" versus "If now this, then that" (Fuster, 1993). Fuster's formulation pinpoints the problem posed by a low bandwidth in transferring data from the input to the output, at least if the data representation is elaborate.

Automaticity Revisited

As stated earlier, information reduction, and thereby reduction of computational demands, are primary mechanisms in the nervous system during acquisition of knowledge or skills. Automatization of processing, either in its entirety or of subcomponents, is important for obtaining process modification. Both theoretical (Schneider and Shiffrin, 1977; Shiffrin and Schneider, 1984) and neuroimaging data (Petersson, Elfgren, and Ingvar, 1999) point to the possibility that development of automaticity is both a local and a global process. The argument for the global process with recruitment of different structures in the performance of a certain task depends on the level of automaticity that has developed during learning. Automaticity implies the transition from an unlearned processing state, which is characterized by large scale computations, flexibility in solutions, and imprecise timing that is both easily disturbed and highly attention grabbing (Raichle et al., 1994), toward a state of automaticity, which implies a substantially lower computational demand, rigid solutions, and precise timing that is not attention demanding and is resistant to interference from other processes. In figure 14.6, a schema for a systematic view of global automatization describes how the higher-order cortices with their abundance of processing and feedback loops require more time to process information as compared to lower-order cortices. With parallel processing in a multilevel organized structure, integration of different timings in different networks is a highly demanding task. When fewer layers are involved, there are more automatized processes and fewer computational demands. With increasing automaticity, less activity is seen in the higher-order cortices (Petersson Elfgren, and Ingvar, 1997, 1999; Raichle et al., 1994). However, automaticity does not seem to be hardwired, as it is overridden in functional failure (Odergren, Stone-Elander, and Ingvar, 1998). (See figure 14.7.)

Predictions for Effective Computations

The latest phylogenetic developments all go toward the development of prospective properties of the human brain. While associative memory allows for more

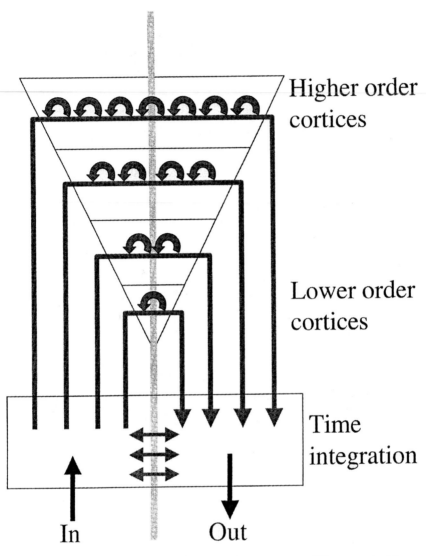

FIGURE 14.6. A schema for the organization of processing on different cortical levels as a parallel system where processing is handled at the lowest possible level. From the figure, it becomes apparent that phylogenetic development, with added layers of representational processing, must be followed by the addition of representational power in the input-output time-integrating zones.

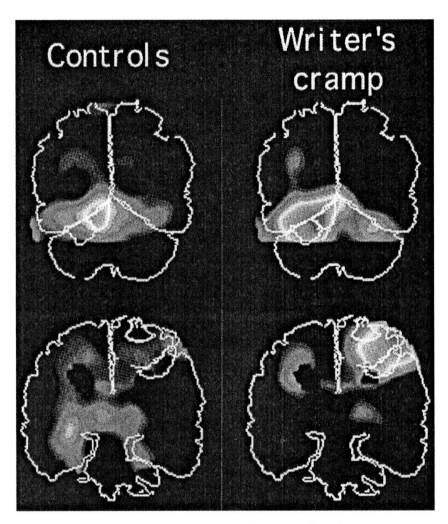

FIGURE 14.7. A proficient writer can maintain the writing of simple messages with only monitoring and comparison of forward information from the motor system and feedback information from the sensory system in the cerebellum. If this system is disturbed (in this case by dystonic symptoms), the "delegated processing" is recentralized, and neocortical processing is instigated. However, the result is writing that is formally correct, but with handwriting that carries evidence of poor automatization in the employed network (data from Odergren, Stone-Elander, and Ingvar, 1998).

effective perception-action, the later-developed phases of semantic memory forms supply the function of statistically based predictions of consequences of behavior (Marsh, Hicks, and Bryan, 1999). The prospective properties of memory are coupled to scenario building and guiding of intentions (Fuster, 2000). Obviously, prediction quality plays a central role in evolutionary survival. In the shorter term, any elicited motor behavior not only conveys information to the motor system, but also provides sensory feedback predictions in order to allow for an effective and rapid correction mechanism (Wolpert 1997; Wolpert, Ghahramani, and Jordan, 1995). This mechanism (termed forward modeling) allows elaborate and effective use of computational resources by removing on-line computational demand in the feedback process, yet allowing error correction within an intended motor behavior. Forward modeling seems not to be limited to the motor system. Prediction of sensory responses makes it possible to provide preprocessing of responses and thereby to regulate activity based on attention. A highly probable sensory input that is omitted will generate a response in the sensory cortex (Carlsson et al., 2000). Reciprocally, the highest of all predicted sensory inputs—namely, self-generated sensory input—can effectively be suppressed, thereby minimizing the computational load (Blakemore, Wolpert, and Frith, 1998).

Predictive processes also are coupled to coping mechanisms, where predictions are used in the choice of coping strategy. Expecting an unknown discomfort elicits one pattern, whereas expecting a known discomfort elicits the opposite (Hsieh, Stone-Elander, and Ingvar, 1999).

Consciousness?

The limited speed of brain networks has necessitated the development of a number of mechanisms to minimize computational demands by selective choice of information, predictive mechanisms, memory organization, and use of automatization. From the low speed of conscious processing and its restricted capacity of relatively low bandwidth, in conjunction with the very rapid and highly specialized parallel low-level systems, it provides a meaningful mechanism for internal simulations, for overall computations of the central executive function (attention), and for deductive reasoning in the process of information extraction and reduction. Thus we conclude that the main use of consciousness is for processing internal information in conditions where conscious processing of information from the outer world (on-line) would be demanding, and where this last sort of processing is therefore avoided due to timing problems that arise from the use of parallel processing in a piece of slow machinery.

Acknowledgments

The author's work is supported by the Swedish Medical Research Council (8276), Hedlunds stiftelse, Karolinska Institutet, and Stockholm County Council.

References

Baddeley, A. 1998. "Working Memory." *Comptes Rendus de l'Académie des Sciences*, series 3 (París) 321(2–3), pp. 167–73.

———. 2000. "The Episodic Buffer: A New Component of Working Memory?" *Trends in Cognitive Science*, 4(11), pp. 417–23.

Baddeley, A., Gathercole, S., and Papagno, C. 1998. "The Phonological Loop as a Language Learning Device." *Psychological Review*, 105(1), pp. 158–73.

Blakemore, S.J., Wolpert, M.W., and Frith, C.D. 1998. "Central Cancellation of Self-Produced Tickle Sensation." *Nature Neuroscience*, 1(7), pp. 635–40.

Buchel, C., Josephs, O., Rees, G., Turner, R., Frith, C.D., and Friston, K.J. 1998. "The Functional Anatomy of Attention to Visual Motion: A Functional MRI Study." *Brain*, 121(P7), pp. 1281–94.

Carlsson, K., Petrovic, P., Skare, S., Petersson, K.M., and Ingvar, M. 2000. "Tickling Expectations: Neural Processing in Anticipation of a Sensory Stimulus." *Journal of Cognitive Neuroscience*, 12(4), pp. 691–703.

Churchland, P.M., and Churchland, P.S. 1997. "Recent work on Consciousness: Philosophical, Theoretical, and Empirical." *Seminars in Neurology*, 17(2), pp. 179–186.

Darwin, C. 1872. *The Expression of the Emotions in Man and Animals*. London: Murray.

Ermentrout, G.B., and Edelstein-Keshet, L. 1993. "Cellular Automata: Approaches to Biological Modeling." *Journal of Theoretical Biology*, 160(1), pp. 97–133.

Fodor, J.A. 1981. "The Mind-Body Problem." *Scientific American*, January, 244(1), pp. 114–123.

Freeman, W.J. 1994. "The Role of Chaotic Dynamics in Neural Plasticity." *Progress in Brain Research*, 102, pp. 319–33.

Frith, C., and Dolan, R.J. 1997. "Brain Mechanisms Associated with Top-Down Processes in Perception." *Philosophical Transactions of the Royal Society of London: Series B: Biological Sciences*, 352(1358), pp. 1221–30.

Fuster, J.M. 1993. "Frontal Lobes." *Current Opinion in Neurobiology*, 3(2), pp. 160–65.

———. 2000. "Executive Frontal Functions." *Experimental Brain Research*, 133(1), pp. 66–70.

Gazzaniga, M.S. 1998. "Brain and Conscious Experience." *Advances in Neurology*, 77, pp. 181–92.

Ghatan, P.H., Hsieh, J.C., Petersson, K.M., Stone-Elander, S., and Ingvar, M. 1998. "Coexistence of Attention-Based Facilitation and Inhibition in the Human Cortex." *Neuroimage*, 7(1), pp. 23–9.

Grossberg, S. 1999. "The Link between Brain Learning, Attention, and Consciousness." *Consciousness and Cognition*, 8(1), pp. 1–44.

Hebb, D. 1949. *The Organization of Behavior*. New York: Wiley.

Hesslow, G. 1994. "Will Neuroscience Explain Consciousness?" *Journal of Theoretical Biology*, 171(1), pp. 29–39.

Hsieh, J.C., Stone-Elander, S., and Ingvar, M. 1999. "Anticipatory Coping of Pain Expressed in the Human Anterior Cingulate Cortex: A Positron Emission Tomography Study." *Neuroscience Letters*, 262(1), pp. 61–64.

James, W. 1890. *The Principles of Psychology*. New York: Holt.

———. 1894. "What Is Emotion?" *Mind*, 9, pp. 188–205.

LeDoux, J.E. 2000. "Emotion Circuits in the Brain." *Annual Review of Neuroscience,* 23, pp. 155–84.

Libet, B. 1991. "Conscious vs Neural Time" [Letter]. *Nature,* 352(6330), pp. 27–28.

Libet, B., Wright, E.W., Jr., Feinstein, B., and Pearl, D.K. 1979. "Subjective Referral of the Timing for a Conscious Sensory Experience: A Functional Role for the Somatosensory Specific Projection System in Man." *Brain,* 102, pp. 193–224.

MacLean, P. 1952. "Some Psychiatric Implications of Physiological Studies on Fronto-temporal Portion of the Limbic System (Visceral Brain)." *Electroencephalography and Clinical Neurophysiology,* 4, pp. 407–18.

Marsh, R.L., Hicks, J.L., and Bryan, E.S. 1999. "The Activation of Unrelated and Canceled Intentions." *Memory and Cognition,* 27(2), pp. 320–27.

Mesulam, M.M. 1990. "Large-Scale Neurocognitive Networks and Distributed Processing for Attention, Language, and Memory." *Annals of Neurology,* 28(5), pp. 597–613.

Odergren, T., Stone-Elander, S., and Ingvar, M. 1998. "Cerebral and Cerebellar Activation in Correlation to the Action-Induced Dystonia in Writer's Cramp." *Movement Disorders,* 13(3), pp. 497–508.

Petersson, K.M., Elfgren, C., and Ingvar, M. 1997. "A Dynamic Role of the Medial Temporal Lobe during Retrieval of Declarative Memory in Man." *Neuroimage,* 6(1), pp. 1–11.

———. 1999. "Dynamic Changes in the Functional Anatomy of the Human Brain during Recall of Abstract Designs Related to Practice." *Neuropsychologia,* 37(5), pp. 567–87.

Posner, M.I. 1994. "Attention: The Mechanisms of Consciousness." *Proceedings of the National Academy of Sciences of the United States of America,* 91(16), pp. 7398–403.

Rager, G., and Singer, W. 1998. "The Response of Cat Visual Cortex to Flicker Stimuli of Variable Frequency." *European Journal of Neuroscience,* 10(5), pp. 1856–77.

Raichle, M.E., Fiez, J.A., Videen, T.O., MacLeod, A.M., Pardo, J.V., Fox, P.T., and Petersen, S.E. 1994. "Practice-Related Changes in Human Brain Functional Anatomy during Nonmotor Learning." *Cerebral Cortex,* 4(1), pp. 8–26.

Rumelhart, D.E., and McClelland, J.L. 1986. *Parallel Distributed Processing: Explorations in the Microstructure of Cognition.* Cambridge, MA: MIT Press.

Schneider, W., and Shiffrin, R. 1977. "Controlled and Automatic Human Information Processing: I. Detection, Search, and Attention." *Psychological Review,* 84(1), pp. 1–66.

Sejnowski, T.J., Koch, C., and Churchland, P.S. 1988. "Computational Neuroscience." *Science,* 241(4871), pp. 1299–1306.

Shiffrin, R.M. and Schneider, W. 1984. "Automatic and Controlled Processing Revisited." *Psychological Review,* 91(2), pp. 269–76.

Tulving, E., and Markowitsch, H.J. 1997. "Memory beyond the Hippocampus." *Current Opinion in Neurobiology,* 7(2), pp. 209–16.

Wolpert, D.M. 1997. "Computational Approaches to Motor Control." *Trends in Cognitive Sciences,* 1(6), pp. 209–16.

Wolpert, D.M., Ghahramani, Z., and Jordan, M.I. 1995. "An Internal Model for Sensorimotor Integration." *Science,* 269(5232), pp. 1880–82.

15

Can There Be a Cognitive Neuroscience of Central Cognitive Systems?

Vinod Goel

Neuropsychology has been an active field of study for at least 150 years. During this period it has been concerned with clinical diagnosis, rehabilitation, and research. In terms of research, its primary objective has been to induce the functional architecture of the normal mind by examining the behavioral consequences of neurological pathologies. The primary strategies used are localization and dissociation of function. During the course of the past century researchers have described and cataloged a number of behavioral deficits and in some cases have successfully mapped them onto localized cortical regions. Some notable areas of success include disorders of language, memory, and visual perception. Boller and Grafman (1988, 1989a, 1989b, 1990, 1991, 1992a, 1992b) offer an extensive review of much of this literature.

Cognitive science has more recent origins, usually dating itself from the late 1950s (Chomsky, 1957; Miller, Galanter, and Pribram, 1960; Newell and Simon, 1956). It is also concerned with articulating functional architecture, though by examining normal human behavior. It has two driving forces. First, there is the conviction that the human cognitive system is an information-processing system such that only explanations that appeal to and causally implicate the content of mental states (i.e., beliefs and desires) will capture the right generalizations of human behavior (Fodor, 1975, 1987; Pylyshyn, 1984). Second, there is the tantalizing prospect that we may be able to understand cognitive information processing in terms of computational information processing (Cummins, 1989; Fodor, 1975; Goel, 1991; Newell, 1980; Pylyshyn, 1984). During the last few decades cognitive science has pushed this line of research and has developed computational models that simulate various cognitive processes with varying degrees of success.

The last two decades have seen growing interaction between these two disciplines to the benefit of a number of cognitive domains, including vision (Marr, 1982), object recognition (Farah, McMullen, and Meyer, 1991; Warrington,

1982), visual imagery (Kosslyn, Thompson, and Alpert, 1997), memory organization (Dolan and Fletcher, 1997; Jonides, Smith, Koeppe, Awh, and Minoshima, 1993; Tulving, Kapur, Craik, Moscovitch, and Houle, 1994), organization of spatial concepts (Banich and Federmeier, 1999; Kosslyn, Maljkovic, Hamilton, Horwitz, and Thompson, 1995; Laeng, 1994), and the processing of language (Caplan and Hildebrandt, 1988; Price, 2000). This interaction has also had a radical impact on the structure of computational architectures (Rumelhart and McClelland, 1986a, 1986b) and even the philosophy of mind (Churchland, 1986; Searle, 1992).

There is consensus that this interaction has given rise to a new field, variously called "cognitive neuroscience" (Gazzaniga, 2000; Lister and Weingartner, 1991; Shallice, 1988) or "cognitive neuropsychology" (McCarthy and Warrington, 1990) and characterized by a commitment to neuroimaging and patient data and computational explanations. As we will see later, this dual commitment has methodological implications that set cognitive neuroscience apart from both traditional neuropsychology and cognitive science.

The interaction has proceeded in both directions. Neuropsychology has contributed to the individuation of cognitive functions, and cognitive science has contributed to our understanding of how these functions might be computed. A classic example is offered by the work of Marr, whose early work on three-dimensional shape representation influenced Warrington's conceptualization of why her patient failed to correctly categorize rotated objects. Warrington's neuropsychological findings in turn influenced Marr's (1982) computational model of visual recognition.

However, the central domains of reasoning and human problem solving largely have failed to participate in, and benefit from, this interaction. In fact, two arguments—generally advanced by cognitive scientists—lead one to question the relevance of neuropsychological evidence to cognitive theories. The first has to do with the independence of computational processes and the mechanism in which they are realized, and the second has to do with the implausibility (in the case of high-level central processes) of the strong modularity assumptions that neuropsychology seems to require. Neither argument can be rejected out of hand. Both are substantive enough that they need to be considered and responded to seriously. Both are considered here, in turn. The conclusion for which I will argue is that they do not preclude a fruitful interaction between cognitive science and neuropsychology in the domain of reasoning and human problem solving.

The Argument for Independence of Computational Level

The argument for independence of computational level is not actually specific to neuropsychology or the domain of problem solving. It is a general argument against the necessity of appealing to neurophysiology to capture the generalizations necessary to explain human mental life. The general idea is that liberation from neurophysiology is one of the great virtues of the cognitive/computational revolution. It gives us the best of both worlds. It allows us to use an intentional/ semantic vocabulary in our psychological theories; and if this vocabulary meets certain (computational) constraints, we get a guarantee (via the Church-Turing hypothesis) of physical realizability of the postulated process/mechanism.[1] Beyond this we do not have to worry about the physical. The cognitive/psychological vocabulary will map onto the computational vocabulary, and it is mental/computational structure, not physical structure, that we are interested in. More strictly, the argument takes the following form:

(P1) There are good reasons to believe that the laws of psychology need to be stated in intentional vocabulary (Fodor, 1975; Pylyshyn, 1984).

(P2) Computation (sort of) gives us such a vocabulary (Cummins, 1989; Fodor, 1975; Goel, 1991, 1995; Newell, 1980; Pylyshyn, 1984).

(P3) Our theory construction is motivated by computational concepts/ considerations and constrained by behavioral data.

(P4) Computational processes are specified independently of physics and can be realized in any physical system.

(C1) Therefore, there is no way, in principle, that neurological data can constrain our computational/cognitive theories.

A closer examination will reveal at least two flaws in the argument. First, premise P4 is not strictly true. Computational processes cannot be realized in any and every system (Giunti, 1997; Goel, 1991, 1992, 1995). If it were true, then computational explanations would be vacuous (Searle, 1990), and our problems would be much more serious. It is true that computational processes can be realized in multiple systems, but that is far removed from universal realizability. The former gives computational theorizing much of its power; the latter would drain computational explanations of much of their substantive content.

Second, the conclusion C1 depends on what "computational/cognitive theories" will be theories of. It is true that the organization of a computing mechanism (for example, whether a Turing machine has one head or two) is irrelevant, when we are interested in specifying what function is being computed and are concerned only with the mappings of inputs to outputs. This is a typical concern for mathematicians and logicians. If cognitive theories only enumerate the functions being computed, then the argument would seem to hold. However, cognitive scientists (and often computer scientists) have little interest in computation under the aspect of functions. Our primary concern is with the procedures that compute the functions. Real-time computation is a function of architectural considerations and resource availability and allocation. It is real-time computation—the study of the behavioral consequences of different resource allocation and organization models—that must be of interest to cognitive science, because it is only with respect to specific architectures that algorithms can be specified and compared (to the extent that they can be). If we are interested in the computational architecture of the mind—and we clearly are (Newell, 1990; Pylyshyn, 1984)—then the constraints provided by the mechanism that realizes the computational process become very relevant. Presumably neuroscience is where we learn about the architectural constraints imposed on the human cognitive/computational system. As such, it can hardly be ignored.

But this whole line of argument and counterargument makes the unwarranted assumption that the only contribution that neuroscience can make is in terms of specifying mechanisms. However, a glance through any neuroscience text (e.g., Kandel, Schwartz, and Jessell, 1995) will show that neuroscience is still far from making substantive contributions to our understanding of the computational architecture of the central nervous system. It may, however, have something immediate and interesting to say about the individuation of cognitive functions. Neuropsychological studies catalog the breakdown of cognitive processes. Lesion studies identify cortical regions necessary for various cognitive processes, while imaging studies identify cortical regions sufficient for those cognitive processes. Both are sources of knowledge regarding dissociation of cognitive functions. Recurrent patterns of dissociation may be a much better indication of joints in the system than uninterrupted normal behavioral measures (Shallice, 1988). So rather than exposing the computational architecture of the mechanisms that are computing the functions, lesion and imaging studies are helping to identify the functions that are actually being computed.

For example, a key question for cognitive theories of reasoning is whether logical reasoning is inherently a sentential linguistic process or a process requiring spatial manipulation and search. Mental logic theories (Rips, 1994) (should) predict that the language (syntactic) system is both necessary and sufficient for deductive reasoning, while mental model theories (Johnson-Laird, 1994) predict that the visuospatial system is necessary and sufficient. Contrary to these theories, neuroimaging studies are providing evidence for the engagement of both systems (Goel, 2003; Goel and Dolan, 2003; Goel, Buchel, Frith, and Dolan, 2000; Goel, Gold, Kapur, and Houle, 1997, 1998; Goel, Grafman, Sadato, and Hallet, 1995). The presence of semantic content engages the language system in the reasoning process. The absence of semantic content engages the spatial system in the identical reasoning task. This unexpected dissociation calls for a reorganization of cognitive concepts and theory. Similarly, dissociations emerging in problem-solving studies of patient populations are causing us to rethink and reconceptualize aspects of information-processing theory (Goel and Grafman, 2000; Goel, Grafman, Tajik, Gana, and Danto, 1997).

In summary, the response to the argument for independence of computational level would seem to be twofold. First, cognitive science needs to be interested in the architecture of the human computational/cognitive system, and, in the long run, neuroscience may be our best source for such information. Second, and more immediately, neuropsychology, by studying the patterns of dissociations, may help us individuate the functions that the cognitive system is computing. The issue of dissociations leads us to the second anti-interaction argument.

Modularity Requirements

"Modularity" is a popular word in the neuropsychology literature. There is considerable consensus (McCarthy and Warrington, 1990; Shallice, 1988; Vallar, 1991) that it is presupposed by the logic of inferring cognitive structure from deficits. Jerry Fodor (1983) has argued that there are compelling reasons to expect perceptual input and language systems to be modular, and equally compelling reasons to expect the central systems involved in higher cognitive functions like problem solving not to be modular. This latter part of the argument led Fodor to a rather gloomy conclusion about the prospects of a cognitive neuroscience of central systems.

The task of evaluating the necessity of modularity for inferences from deficits to cognitive structure, and the validity of Fodor's argument that higher cognitive functions like problem solving will not be modular is complicated by the fact that there are several distinct claims one can make with respect to modularity, and the literature is not always careful to distinguish them (for an example, see Farah, 1994). I will begin by making some general remarks about modularity, independent of neuropsychology, and then turn to neuropsychology's specific claims. We will see that there are not one, but three distinct claims of modularity, associated with three distinct mappings of functions to structures and resulting in three distinct enterprises, which I will call traditional neuropsychology, weak cognitive neuropsychology, and strong cognitive neuropsychology. At this point, the distinction between neuropsychology and cognitive neuropsychology will take on more importance than it has thus far. I will then introduce a further complication in terms of alternative methods of individuating functions, which will further increase the number of distinct claims associated with modularity. Once I have laid out this space of possibilities, we will be in a position to respond to Fodor and comment on the necessity of modularity for neuropsychology.

What Is Modularity?

Setting neuropsychology aside for a moment and just examining only the notion of modularity, we find that there exist two very different views about the structure of the world. The first is that of a highly integrated, nondecomposable system where everything is connected to everything else. It is eloquently expressed by the poet Francis Thompson (1859–1907) in the following words:

> All things by immortal power,
> Near or far,
> Hiddenly,
> To each other linked are,
> That thou canst not stir a flower
> Without troubling of a star.

The second view holds that while this may be true, the degree, intensity, and number of "links" among "things" vary. This heterogeneity in the distribution of links or relations results in stable clusters that we recognize as subsystems or modules. The idea is that the world is constructed of complex systems that can be decomposed, to some extent, into stable subsystems, such that intrasystem interactions are stronger (more robust, abundant, coherent, and so on) than intersystem interactions. In fact, it is this varying degree of relations/interactions—along with our goals and interests—that allows us to individuate systems/subsystems in the first place. Individuated as such, systems correspond to modules. How pervasive a phenomenon decomposability, or modularity, turns out to be is an open empirical question, but there is converging evidence from at least three sources, the natural sciences, design/engineering practice, and arguments about the evolution of complex systems (Simon, 1962, 1973), that suggests that it is a deep fact about the world.

The main problem that is typically encountered in the individuation of systems is that relations/interactions among components can be of many types, including spatial, temporal, logical, conceptual, causal, and so on. In fact, relations are downright cheap, making the notion of systems (and thus modules) equally cheap. But for the purposes of natural science, we generally restrict ourselves to a subset of all possible relations, namely, the ones that are causally efficacious in the functioning of the system, under the aspect of the system in which we are interested. There is generally just one such aspect, and the causal properties involved are of a pedestrian sort. This is usually sufficient to render the notion of systems and modules substantive and useful.

Psychological Claims of Modularity

In the psychological disciplines, the issue of modularity generally surfaces as the issue of the relationship of behaviorally individuated functions and causally individuated structures. In the most trivial case, we could individuate one function—say, human intelligence—and map it onto one structure, the human central nervous system. However, when we claim that the cognitive system is modular, we are claiming that (1) there are multiple behaviorally individuated subfunctions and multiple causally individuated substructures, and (2) there is a unique one-to-one mapping between disjoint sets of behaviorally individuated functions and causally individuated structures. This one-to-one mapping is crucial, because it provides causal constraints on the individuation of functions. Without such constraints, functional individuation is too cheap to be of any scientific value.

By way of an example, suppose that we individuate the following three functions on the basis of behavioral data: ($f1$) raise left arm, ($f2$) raise left foot, and ($f3$) wiggle right ear. If these functions can be mapped onto three causally differentiated structures in a one-to-one fashion, we would be justified in claiming to have discovered three modules. If, however, all three of our behaviorally individuated functions mapped onto one causally differentiated structure in a many-to-one fashion, we would say that our functional individuation was too fine grained, and we would collapse the distinctions until we achieved a one-to-one mapping. That is, raising the left arm does not constitute a module, but the conjunction of the three does constitute a module. If we encountered the reverse problem, where one function mapped onto several causally distinct structures, we would conclude that our individuation was too coarse grained, and we would refine it until we achieved a one-to-one mapping. One final possibility is a many-to-many mapping between our functional individuation and causally individuated structures. Here we would have a total cross-classification, would have to assume that our functional individuations were simply wrong, and would start over.

Both neuropsychology and cognitive neuropsychology are committed to articulating the functional architecture of the mind and individuating behavioral functions and causal structures in such a way that the one-to-one mapping is satisfied. However, there are interesting differences between what each means by "functional architecture," and thus what each considers the relevant causal structures and mappings to be. For early traditional neuropsychologists, like Franz Joseph Gall, articulating the functional architecture meant carving up the neurophysiological mechanism at its physical-causal joints. Their claim of modularity was that one could individuate behaviorally distinct cognitive functions and map them onto causally distinct neurophysiological subsystems without cross-classification.[2] Thus it was a commitment to mapping A in figure 15.1.

Suppose, however, that we take the cognitive conception of the world seriously and believe that any generalizations that do justice to human behavior will have to causally implicate the semantic or information content of our mental states

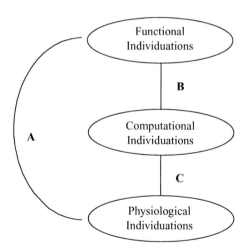

FIGURE 15.1. Traditional neuropsychology is committed to mapping A, weak cognitive neuropsychology to mapping B, and strong cognitive neuropsychology to mapping B and C. The claim of modularity is that such mappings can be accomplished without cross-classification.

(Fodor, 1987; Pylyshyn, 1984). In that case, we are oblig... d to map our behaviorally individuated functions onto computational structures and procedures individuated along what one might call "flow of information" lines (as opposed to the "flow of physical effect"). This is the level and notion of modularity captured by information encapsulation (Fodor, 1983). Information encapsulation constrains the flow of information throughout the system by denying any significant interaction among procedures that compute different functions. A crude but effective way of understanding it is in terms of local versus global variables in computer programming. Information encapsulation requires locally defined variables. The resulting claim of modularity is that one can map behaviorally individuated cognitive functions onto informationally encapsulated computational procedures without cross-classification. This is a commitment to mapping B in figure 15.1. Notice that this is a quite distinct claim from mapping A, associated with traditional neuropsychology. I will refer to a commitment to mapping B as a commitment to weak cognitive neuropsychology. It is believed to constitute a perfectly coherent and interesting enterprise (McCarthy and Warrington, 1990; Shallice, 1988), though most researchers opt for what I shall later call strong cognitive neuropsychology

In addition to mapping cognitive functions onto computational procedures, one may also desire to map the computational procedures onto causally individuated neurophysiological subsystems. This is mapping C in figure 15.1 It is associated with the claim that computational structures individuated along the lines of information flow/encapsulation can be mapped onto causally individuated neurophysiological structures without cross-classification. Together, mappings B and C constitute what I will call strong cognitive neuropsychology.

I call it the strong version of cognitive neuropsychology, because it is actually making a much more substantive and more easily falsifiable claim with respect to modularity than traditional neuropsychology (mapping A) or weak cognitive neuropsychology (mapping B). In some sense, the general neuropsychological claim of modularity and the weak cognitive neuropsychological claim of modularity are not as substantive as one might think. Given that there are causal or informational joints in the system (which is bound to be true), it is always possible to reindividuate the behavioral functions such that there is a one-to-one mapping. (There can, of course, be substantive empirical claims of modularity with respect to specific behavioral functions.) However, in strong cognitive neuropsychology, where an additional mapping from computational to physiological structure is required (mapping C), both the computational and neurophysiological levels are causally individuated (by the flow of information and physical-causal effect, respectively), so in the case of cross-classification, there are limited degrees of freedom for reclassification.

Thus far we have identified three distinct claims of modularity—a commitment to mapping A, mapping B, or mapping B and C—and associated them with three enterprises, traditional neuropsychology, weak cognitive neuropsychology, and strong cognitive neuropsychology. However, before we can understand and respond to Fodor's argument we need to introduce one more dimension into the discussion — that of the method of individuating functions. Fodor notes that the literature individuates functions in two distinct ways, "horizontally" and "vertically." Accordingly, he suggests that talk of modules or faculties divides up, at a first instance, into two categories, horizontal faculties and vertical faculties.

Horizontal faculties are individuated functionally by their effects. Typical examples of such faculties would be memory and attention. It is important to note that this individuation is independent of the content of the input to the faculty, so horizontal faculties are invariant across domains (e.g., the same memory faculty gets exercised in remembering your mother's face as in remembering the third movement of Brahms's *German Requiem*), and each horizontal faculty can, in principle, have access to every mental content at some point in time. Different cognitive processes are explained by varying degrees of interactions among horizontal faculties. It would be a mistake, on this account, to look for a language faculty or a music faculty. These are simply different manifestations/interactions of the same horizontal faculties. The substantive claim associated with horizontal faculties is that an individuation of cognitive functions along horizontal lines maps onto causally individuated structures without cross-classification. These structures can be either neurophysiological or computational.

Vertical faculties, on the other hand, are individuated by reference to subject matter, or the domain of content of the input information (as opposed to the operations that are performed on this content). On a vertical individuation, one would expect to find language and music faculties, because they are generally taken to constitute different domains. Whether one would also expect to find a memory or attention faculty depends on the brand of vertical faculties being evoked.

What Fodor is calling vertical faculties are again a specification of cognitive functions, except this time the functions are more complex and are individuated by the input or domain. Again, the substantive claim is that the cognitive functions map onto causally differentiated structures without cross-classification.

The method of individuating functions is orthogonal to the commitment to specific mappings, resulting in the six distinct claims of cognitive modularity summarized in table 15.1. The important point for our present purposes is that Fodor's notion of *cognitive modules* is a commitment to (1) vertical individuation, (2) mapping B from behavioral functions to computational procedures, and perhaps also (3) mapping C from computational procedures to the implementing mech-

TABLE 15.1. Dimensions of Modularity

Method of Individuating Functions	Weak Cognitive Neuropsychology (Mapping **B**)	Strong Cognitive Neuropsychology (Mapping **B & C**)	Traditional Neuropsychology (Mapping **A**)
Horizontal			
Vertical	Fodor	Fodor?	Gall

anisms.[3] It occupies one, perhaps two, of the six cells. We now turn to Fodor's argument that central systems, such as those involved in problem solving, will not be modular in his sense of the term.

Fodor's Argument against the Modularity of Central Systems

Fodor's argument for the nonmodularity of central, higher cognitive functions is rather straightforward. However, it does use some specialized vocabulary and is illustrated with an example of belief fixation in science (as modeled by philosophers of science). In a nutshell, the argument is that belief fixation in science is (1) isotropic (i.e., everything we know is relevant to determining what else we should believe) and (2) Quinean (i.e., the degree to which we believe a proposition is a function of all our other beliefs). These are conceptual/logical claims about the structure of scientific reasoning. From these premises, he concludes that the central processes that mediate such reasoning cannot be encapsulated. The conclusion is a claim about human psychology. It does not follow as a point of logic from the premises,[4] but given what we know of how the world works, it is certainly very plausible.

Fodor's use of the example from the philosophy of science seems to have misled some commentators in the cognitive neuroscience community into thinking that the argument is based upon some special properties (actual or putative) of scientific reasoning. This is an unfortunate misconception. Fodor is using belief fixation in science as an example of nondemonstrative inference. The point is that in any nondemonstrative inference, one can not a priori exclude any information as irrelevant. There is no way of determining a priori what may or may not be relevant; anything goes. Nondemonstrative inference is perhaps the most ubiquitous operation of higher-level central systems. It is hard to imagine how such processes could be encapsulated.

Response to Fodor

Fodor's argument is a good one and it has taxed researchers in the cognitive neuroscience community (Marshall, 1984; Shallice, 1984). Critics have largely failed to appreciate both the power and the limitations of Fodor's argument. Shallice (1988, p. 20), for example, dismisses Fodor's view because "the criteria he suggests may well be too specific" and opts for a view of modularity that is "less explicit and more useful for neuropsychological purposes." Shallice endorses a notion of "functional subsystem" or "isolable subsystem" along the lines of Tulving (Tulving, quoted in Shallice, 1988, p. 21):

> [O]ne system can operate independently of the other, although not necessarily as efficiently as it could with the support of the other intact system. The operations of one system could be enhanced without a similar effect on the operations of the other; similarly the operations of one system could be suppressed without a comparable effect on the activity

of the other. The functional difference also implies that in important, or at least in non-negligible ways, the systems operate differently; that is, their function is governed at least partially by different principles.

While there is something to be said for vagueness at times, this move conflates the question of dimensions or lines of individuation with the question of whether the resulting categories are binary or graded. The two are independent issues. Shallice is endorsing graded categories (or degrees of modularity); but so is Fodor. The difference is that Fodor specifies what constitutes the category, whereas Shallice's specification of "functional subsystems" does not.

It seems to me that the proper response to Fodor is to note the limited scope of his argument. It is an argument only against information encapsulation of domain-individuated subsystems, engaged in nondemonstrative inference. Of the various notions of modules reviewed, only Fodor's notion was both domain individuated and dependent on information encapsulation.

Traditional neuropsychology individuates functions by domain, but the claim of modularity concerns mapping A, where the issue is one of mapping onto causally individuated neurophysiological structures, not informationally encapsulated computational structures. The resulting claims of modularity are untouched by the argument. The horizontal faculties, individuated by effect or output, can claim modularity of both computational procedures and mechanisms without worrying about the argument.

The upshot would seem to be something like the following: If you think that cognitive functions must be individuated by domain, and that the only or most relevant notion of modularity for cognitive neuroscience needs to be based on information encapsulation of computational procedures, then Fodor's argument should give you reason to worry. If you are so worried, some of your options are (1) to deny the central role of nondemonstrative reasoning in higher-level cognitive functions, (2) to argue that one can place a priori limits on the propositions that may be relevant to a given nondemonstrative inference, or (3) to argue that no conclusion about psychological mechanisms follows from the logical structure of nondemonstrative argument forms. Good luck.

There is, however, no reason to take this position. A more promising move would seem to be to question whether the conjunction of individuation by domain and modularity of computational procedures is necessary (or sufficient) for cognitive neuroscience inferences. An examination of the logic of inferring cognitive structure from deficits reveals it to be neither. I conclude this section by examining and commenting on the logic of neuropsychological inference.

The Logic of Inferring Structure from Deficits

I have said several times that neuropsychology is in the business of trying to articulate the functional architecture of the normal mind. It is, of course, not alone in this endeavor. This is also the goal of cognitive psychology; and it can generally pursue it without worrying a great deal about modularity. So why is modularity a special concern for neuropsychology? The answer lies in what the disciplines recognize as independent variables. Cognitive psychology is primarily committed to inducing the causal structure by manipulating environmental factors in normal populations and measuring behavioral responses. Neuropsychology also measures behavioral responses of environmental manipulations, and in addition, it is also prepared to accept the direct manipulations of neurophysiological structures (i.e., lesions) as an independent variable. These two factors require some special methodological assumptions that psychology, in general, is free of.

To begin with, the involvement of pathological populations seems to require at least the following assumptions:

A1. The cognitive system must be nonchaotic, in the sense that introduction of arbitrary perturbations (i.e., lesions) must not lead to radical and unpredictable change in its dynamics (i.e., behavior). That is, the behavior of a lesioned system must be explainable in terms of the dynamics of the original system plus the damage. It must continue to be the same type of dynamical system.

A2. The cognitive system must be such that arbitrary damage does not turn it completely off. There must be variable degrees of performances to evaluate.

A3. Damage to the system should result in selective impairment, as opposed to uniform degradation.

Conditions A1 and A2 seem to carry the force of logical necessity. If it is the case that perturbations change the dynamics of the system in truly unpredictable ways, then introducing perturbations is not going to give one any predictive power or insights into the original system. Similarly, if every disturbance results in a complete absence of performance (i.e., shuts off the system), then one cannot infer the structure of the system by examining variability in performance. Condition A3 is the modularity requirement. While not logically necessary in the strict sense, it gives the methodology scope and power. Without it, neuropsychology would not be very interesting. I will return to this issue later.

The acceptance of neurological manipulations (lesions) as an independent variable introduces the issue of localization and requires additional assumptions. Since lesions have a specific location in space, one can measure both the extent and the location of damage, as well as behavioral consequences. Of course, one is not interested in spatial location per se, but in the causal joints. However, on the assumption that

A4. causal contiguity corresponds to spatial contiguity and locality,

the traditional neuropsychological project of mapping behavioral deficits onto localized neurophysiological structures can go forward. Notice that while causal contiguity neither implies nor is implied by spatial contiguity and locality, it is not an unreasonable assumption on a nineteenth-century conception of how the world works.[5]

Life is a little more complicated for contemporary cognitive neuropsychologists who want to utilize localization data. The complicating factor is that while the computational structures and processes are underwritten by the neurophysiological structures, the well-known multiple-realizability results regarding computational systems are widely interpreted as allowing few (if any) inferences from the structure of computational procedures to the structure of the mechanism that realizes the procedures, or vice versa (Fodor, 1975; Newell, 1980; Pylyshyn, 1984).[6] To associate computational procedures with spatial location, we need to make the following additional strong assumption:

A5. The computational functions are directly implemented in special-purpose hardware.

We also need to retain assumption A4 that causal contiguity corresponds to spatial contiguity in these subsystems.

Assumptions A1–A3 underwrite weak cognitive neuropsychology. Assumptions A1–A4 are required by traditional neuropsychology. All five assumptions, A1–A5, are required by strong cognitive neuropsychology. Notice also that each of the assumptions is independent in the sense that none implies or is implied by any of the others.

One certainly cannot make any claims of completeness for this set of conditions. As the inferences involved are inductive, it is not possible to specify a sufficient set. However, notice that the list does not include the conjunction of individuation by domain and modularity of computational procedures, and it is not obvious that it needs to do so. Therefore, the conclusion would seem to follow that cognitive neuroscience has no methodological reasons to require both individuation by domain and modularity of computational processes. One may have other theoretical reasons for insisting on both, but nothing about the logic of the methodology requires that one do this.

Oddly enough, members of the cognitive neuroscience community who have responded to Fodor have granted him both domain individuation and information encapsulation. With respect to the latter, the literature's agreement with Fodor on the importance of information encapsulation is understandable. Given a commitment to an intentional/computational psychology, one needs to insist that functional individuation respect computational individuation. (Notice, however, that traditional neuropsychology, having no commitment to a computational level, is under no such compulsion.)

With respect to the former, the literature seems to agree that individuation of functions by effect is insufficient for the purposes of cognitive neuroscience and that individuation by domain is required. This is less understandable. The underlying assumption seems to be that a horizontal individuation of functions will be incompatible with the presence of conditions A2 and A3. If these conditions are violated, lesions will result in (1) total nonperformance or breakdown, or (2) degraded performance in all or many areas. So in the absence of the domain-specific modularity, cognitive neuroscience would be a study of the correlation of volume of cortical tissue loss and degradation of performance along some metric, and of course, the search for a general-purpose mechanism. Shallice (1988, p. 18) for example, writes:

> If Lashley's (1929) idea of mass action were valid, then neuropsychology would be of little relevance for understanding normal function. Any form of neurological damage would deplete by a greater or lesser degree the available amount of some general resource, say the mythical g. Knowing which tasks a patient could or could not perform would enable us to partition tasks on a difficulty scale. It would tell us little, if anything, about how the system operated.

I think that this conclusion is overly pessimistic. Conditions A2 and A3 are independent of horizontal and vertical individuation. One can get perfectly good selective impairments with horizontal faculties. A nice illustration of this is provided by several computational models (Goel, Pullara, and Grafman, 2001; Kimberg and Farah, 1993). Kimberg and Farah (1993) describe a production-system model to simulate certain tasks given to frontal lobe patients. The model is "lesioned" by reducing the sensitivity of the conflict-resolution strategy that controls the firing of productions. The result is not a general degradation in performance, as predicted earlier, but a series of selective impairments of relevant cognitive functions. Similarly, Goel, Pullara, and Grafman (2001) demonstrate how a general impairment of working memory can selectively impact patients' ability to solve Tower of Hanoi problems.

Conclusion

To summarize, I have articulated and responded to two arguments that question the feasibility of developing a cognitive neuroscience of central systems. My response to the argument for independence of computational level was twofold: (1) Insofar as cognitive science is interested in the architecture of the cognitive computational system, over the long run, evidence from neuroscience may be a valuable source of information. (2) More immediately, dissociation data from lesion and neuroimaging studies are providing clues to assist in the individuation of the cognitive functions that are actually being computed. With respect to modularity, I have argued that while modularity assumptions are indeed required by neuropsychology, Fodor's antimodularity arguments concerning central systems are predicated on just one of several notions of modularity and thus have limited scope. In particular, the notion of horizontal modules may do much more work for neuropsychology than is currently believed. If there are insurmountable obstacles facing a cognitive neuroscience of central systems, these two objections are not among them.

Notes

1. The Church-Turing hypothesis makes the conjecture that all computable functions belong to the class of functions computable by a Turing machine. If we constrain the class of functions called for by our psychological theories to the class of computable functions, then there will be some Turing machine that can compute the function.

2. Fodor (1983) talks of this in terms of no sharing of resources or mechanisms across functions.

3. Though this is less than certain from Fodor's discussion.

4. Fodor, of course, does not claim that it does.

5. On a twentieth-century conception of the world (indeterminism, chaos theory, and the like) this is a much less secure assumption.

6. Elsewhere (Goel, 1991, 1992, 1995) I have argued that there are some minimal inferences one can draw from the structure of computational systems to the structure of the implementing mechanisms, but this is very much a minority position.

References

Banich, M.T., and Federmeier, K.D. 1999. "Categorical and Metric Spatial Processes Distinguished by Task Demands and Practice." *Journal of Cognitive Neuroscience*, 11(2), pp. 153–66.

Boller, F., and Grafman, J. (Eds.). 1988. *Handbook of Neuropsychology*. Vol. 1. Amsterdam: Elsevier.

———. (Eds.). 1989a. *Handbook of Neuropsychology*. Vol. 2. Amsterdam: Elsevier.

———. (Eds.). 1989b. *Handbook of Neuropsychology*. Vol. 3. Amsterdam: Elsevier.

———. (Eds.). 1990. *Handbook of Neuropsychology*. Vol. 4. Amsterdam: Elsevier.

———. (Eds.). 1991. *Handbook of Neuropsychology*. Vol. 5. Amsterdam: Elsevier.

———. (Eds.). 1992a. *Handbook of Neuropsycholgy*. Vol. 6. Amsterdam: Elsevier.

———. (Eds.). 1992b. *Handbook of Neuropsychology*. Vol. 7. Amsterdam: Elsevier.

Caplan, D., and Hildebrandt, N. 1988. *Disorders of Syntactic Comprehension*. Cambridge, MA: MIT Press.

Chomsky, N. 1957. *Syntactic Structures*. The Hague: Mouton.

Churchland, P.S. 1986. *Neurophilosophy*. Cambridge, MA: MIT Press.

Cummins, R. 1989. *Meaning and Mental Representation*. Cambridge, MA: MIT Press.

Dolan, R.J., and Fletcher, P.C. 1997. "Dissociating Prefrontal and Hippocampal Function in Episodic Memory Encoding." *Nature*, 388, pp. 582–85.

Farah, M.J. 1994. "Neuropsychological Inference with an Interactive Brain: A Critique of the Locality Assumption." *Behavioral and Brain Sciences*.

Farah, M.J., McMullen, P.A., and Meyer, M.M. 1991. "Can Recognition of Living Things Be Selectively Impaired?" *Neuropsychologia*, 29(2), pp. 185–93.

Fodor, J.A. 1975. *The Language of Thought*. Cambridge, MA: Harvard University Press.

———. 1983. *The Modularity of Mind: An Essay on Faculty Psychology*. Cambridge, MA: MIT Press.

————. 1987. *Psychosemantics: The Problem of Meaning in the Philosophy of Mind*. Cambridge, MA: MIT Press.

Gazzaniga, M.S. (Ed.). 1994. *The Cognitive Neurosciences*. Cambridge, MA: MIT Press.

————. (Ed.). 2000. *The New Cognitive Neurosciences*. Cambridge, MA: MIT Press.

Giunti, M. 1997. *Computation, Dynamics, and Cognition*. New York: Oxford University Press.

Goel, V. 1991. "Notationality and the Information Processing Mind." *Minds and Machines*, 1(2), pp. 129–65.

————. 1992. "Are Computational Explanations Vacuous?" in *Proceedings of the Fourteenth Annual Conference of the Cognitive Science Society*. Hillsdale, NJ: Lawrence Erlbaum.

————. 1995. *Sketches of Thought*. Cambridge, MA: MIT Press.

————. 2003. "Evidence for Dual Neural Pathways for Syllogistic Reasoning." *Psychologica*, 32, pp. 301–309.

Goel, V., Buchel, C., Frith, C., and Dolan, R.J. 2000. "Dissociation of Mechanisms Underlying Syllogistic Reasoning." *Neuroimage*, 12(5), pp. 504–14.

Goel, V., and Dolan, R.J. (2003). "Explaining modulation of reasoning by belief." *Cognition*, 87(1), B11–22.

Goel, V., Gold, B., Kapur, S., and Houle, S. 1997. "The Seats of Reason: A Localization Study of Deductive and Inductive Reasoning Using PET (O15) Blood Flow Technique." *NeuroReport*, 8(5), pp. 1305–10.

————. 1998. "Neuroanatomical Correlates of Human Reasoning." *Journal of Cognitive Neuroscience*, 10(3), pp. 293–302.

Goel, V., and Grafman, J. 2000. "The Role of the Right Prefrontal Cortex in Ill-Structured Problem Solving." *Cognitive Neuropsychology*, 17(5), pp. 415–36.

Goel, V., Grafman, J., Sadato, N., and Hallet, M. 1995. "Modelling Other Minds." *NeuroReport*, 6(13), pp. 1741–46.

Goel, V., Grafman, J., Tajik, J., Gana, S., and Danto, D. 1997. "A Study of the Performance of Patients with Frontal Lobe Lesions in a Financial Planning Task." *Brain*, 120, pp. 1805–22.

Goel, V., Pullara, S.D., and Grafman, J. 2001. "A Computational Model of Frontal Lobe Dysfunction: Working Memory and the Tower of Hanoi." *Cognitive Science*, 25(2) pp. 287–313.

Johnson-Laird, P.N. 1994. "Mental Models, Deductive Reasoning, and the Brain." Pp. 999–1008 in M.S. Gazzaniga (Ed.), *The Cognitive Neurosciences*. Cambridge, MA: MIT Press.

Jonides, J., Smith, E.E., Koeppe, R.A., Awh, E., and Minoshima, S. 1993. "Spatial Working Memory in Humans as Revealed by PET." *Nature*, 363, pp. 623–25.

Kandel, E.R., Schwartz, J.H., and Jessell, T.M. (Eds.). 1995. *Essentials of Neural Science and Behavior*. Norwalk, CT: Appleton and Lange.

Kimberg, D.Y., and Farah, M.J. 1993. "A Unified Account of Cognitive Impairments Following Frontal Lobe Damage: The Role of Working Memory in Complex, Organized Behavior." *Journal of Experimental Psychology: General*, 122(4), pp. 411–28.

Kosslyn, S.M., Maljkovic, V., Hamilton, S.E., Horwitz, G., and Thompson, W.L. 1995. "Two Types of Image Generation: Evidence for Left and Right Hemisphere Processes." *Neuropsychologia*, 33(11), pp. 1485–510.

Kosslyn, S.M., Thompson, W.L., and Alpert, N.M. 1997. "Neural Systems Shared by Visual Imagery and Visual Perception: A Positron Emission Tomography Study." *Neuroimage*, 6(4), pp. 320–34.

Laeng, B. 1994. "Lateralization of Categorical and Coordinate Spatial Functions: A Study of Unilateral Stroke Patients." *Journal of Cognitive Neuroscience*, 6(3), pp. 189–203.

Lashley, K.S. (1992). *Brain Mechanisms and Intelligence: a Quatitative Study of Injuries to the Brain*. Chicago: University of Chicago Press.

Lister, R.G., and Weingartner, H.J. (Eds.). 1991. *Perspectives on Cognitive Neuroscience*. New York: Oxford University Press.

Marr, D. 1982. *Vision: A Computational Investigation into the Human Representation and Processing of Visual Information*. San Francisco: W.H. Freeman.

Marshall, J.C. 1984. "Multiple Perspectives on Modularity." *Cognition*, 17, pp. 209–42.

McCarthy, R.A., and Warrington, E.K. 1990. *Cognitive Neuropsychology: A Clinical Introduction*. San Diego: Academic Press.

Miller, G.A., Galanter, E., and Pribram, K.H. 1960. *Plans and the Structure of Behavior*, New York: Holt.

Newell, A. 1980. "Physical Symbol Systems." *Cognitive Science*, 4, pp. 135–83.

———. 1990. *Unified Theories of Cognition*. Cambridge, MA: Harvard University Press.

Newell, A., and Simon, H.A. 1956. "The Logic Theory Machine: A Complex Information Processing System." *IRE Transactions on Information Theory*, IT-2(3), pp. 61–79.

Pattee, H.H. (Ed.). 1973. *Hierarchy Theory*. New York: G. Braziller.

Price, C.J. 2000. "The Anatomy of Language: Contributions from Functional Neuroimaging." *Journal of Anatomy*, 197(3), pp. 335–59.

Pylyshyn, Z.W. 1984. *Computation and Cognition: Toward a Foundation for Cognitive Science*. Cambridge, MA: MIT Press.

Rips, L.J. 1994. *The Psychology of Proof: Deductive Reasoning in Human Thinking*. Cambridge, MA: MIT Press.

Rumelhart, D.E., and McClelland, J.L. (Eds.). 1986a. *Parallel Distributed Processing: Explorations in the Microstructure of Cognition*. Vol. 1, *Foundations*. Cambridge, MA: MIT Press.

———. 1986b. "PDP Models and General Issues in Cognitive Science," in D.E. Rumelhart and J.L. McClelland (Eds.), *Parallel Distributed Processing: Explorations in the Microstructure of Cognition*. Vol. 1, *Foundations*, Cambridge, MA: MIT Press.

Searle, J.R. 1990. "Is the Brain a Digital Computer?" Pp. 21–37 in *Sixty-fourth Annual Pacific Division Meeting for the American Philosophical Association*. Los Angeles, CA, March 30, pp. 21–37.

———. 1992. *The Rediscovery of the Mind*. Cambridge, MA: MIT Press.

Shallice, T. 1984. "More Functionally Isolable Subsystems but Fewer 'Modules'?" *Cognition*, 17, pp. 243–52.

———. 1988. *From Neuropsychology to Mental Structure*. Cambridge, UK: Cambridge University Press.

Simon, H.A. 1962. "The Architecture of Complexity." *Proceedings of the American Philosophical Society*, 106, pp. 467–82.

————. 1973. "The Organization of Complex Systems," in H.H. Pattee (Ed.), *Hierarchy Theory*. New York: G. Braziller.

Tulving, E., Kapur, S., Craik, F.I.M., Moscovitch, M., and Houle, S. 1994. "Hemispheric Encoding/Retrieval Asymmetry in Episodic Memory: Positron Emission Tomography Findings." *Proceedings of the National Academy of Sciences of the United States of America*, 91(March), pp. 2016–20.

Vallar, G. 1991. "Current Methodological Issues in Human Neuropsychology," in F. Boller and J. Grafman (Eds.), *Handbook of Neuropsychology*. Vol. 5. Amsterdam: Elsevier.

Warrington, E.K. 1982. "Neuropsychological Studies of Object Recognition." *Philosophical Transactions of the Royal Society of London*, B298, pp. 15–33.

16

The Cognitive Neuroscience Laboratory: A Framework for the Science of Mind

Itiel E. Dror and Robin D. Thomas

Researching the mind as a scientific object raises two momentous questions: first, whether the mind exists as a scientific object to begin with; and second, whether, even if the mind is a scientific object, it can be studied scientifically, and if so, how. In this chapter we attempt to answer both these questions. Before we embark on each question separately, we want to consider their interrelations and dependencies.

One can view the first question as a prerequisite for the second. Obviously, if the mind is not a scientific object to begin with, then the question of how it can be studied scientifically becomes irrelevant and dissolves. It may be, however, that although the mind is not a scientific object in the extreme sense, it still may have some aspects that are scientific. In other words, stating that the mind is not entirely and completely an object of scientific investigation is not to say that some of its aspects may not be scientific. In fact, no scientific object is entirely scientific. Even the most scientific of objects are based on the supposed purity of mathematics and logic, which in reality contain contradictions and paradoxes. Hence even if the mind is not entirely a scientific object, just as in the case of other scientific objects, it still is possible to view it as such, as long as at least some of its aspects are scientific. All of this discussion depends on one's notion of what constitutes an object as being "scientific"—a critical question that requires a discussion in its own right. For our purposes, we will adopt the common notion that involves investigation of empirical regularities that characterize other accepted "sciences."

An alternative to thinking of the first question as a prerequisite to the second is to reverse the order of inquiry. In this second case, the investigator puts on hold the concerns of whether or not the mind is a scientific object and attempts to address the issue of how the mind can be studied scientifically. Obviously, if one finds a way to study the mind scientifically and can pursue it successfully, then the question of whether the mind is a scientific object has been answered.

283

Criteria from other scientific domains can be used to determine whether the mind has been successfully studied as a scientific object (e.g., making and testing predictions in an observable and replicable framework). In this case, the mind would count as a scientific object as much as an object in any other area of scientific inquiry. If one continues to insist that the mind still is not a scientific object, then that would entail a skeptical attitude—i.e., the idea that not all so-called sciences are really scientific, and therefore that there are no scientific objects at all. However, if this avenue fails to uncover a means of studying the mind as a scientific object, that does not itself prove that the mind is not a scientific object. It may be the result only of the incompetence of researchers or of some obstacle in studying the mind that it is not possible to resolve or avoid.

It seems, then, that the questions of whether the mind is a scientific object and, if so, how it can be studied depend on each other, but only in a partial and weak sense. Given these weaknesses and limited dependencies, we pursue each of these questions separately. We will argue both that the mind is a scientific object and that it can be studied scientifically. Furthermore, we will point out what we think is the path for studying it scientifically and illustrate the first few steps that we and others have taken on that path.

Is the Mind a Scientific Object?

The framework of the controversies about the scientific nature of the mind depends on one's stance on the mind-body problem and, more specifically, on one's views about dualism.[1] Adopting a dualist position does not necessarily rule out a scientific approach to mind, since noncorporeal aspects of the mind might be theoretically governed by rules and principles in just the same way as other scientific objects. Similarly, rejection of dualism does not necessarily lead to a deterministic, scientific conception of mind. Nevertheless, dualism introduces a different frame of discourse about the nature of mind, a frame that should be rejected. To illustrate this point, we propose to contrast the underlying views of minds implicit in the tales of Pinocchio and Frankenstein.

In 1818 Mary Shelley published her book *Frankenstein*, the underlying view in her story is that the mind is a scientific object. That is, if you "put it together" correctly, you can create a sentient being with a mind. A very different view of mind emerges from the story *Pinocchio*. Carlo Collodi's 1883 book is an antithesis to Mary Shelley's *Frankenstein*, since here the fairy godmother provides Pinocchio with a mind. Contrary to Frankenstein's monster, who has a mind by material design, Pinocchio has to acquire a mind through the fairy godmother's gracious miracle.

The story about Frankenstein's monster encompasses a scientific framework to examine whether the mind is a scientific object or not. What is a mind made of? What are the essential components of a mind? How would one go about constructing a mind? In contrast, the story about Pinocchio rules out any meaningful discussion about the mind and also, needless to say, any scientific examination of it. Pinocchio reflects Gilbert Ryle's dogma of the ghost in the machine. Such a mind can only be portrayed by saying what it is not:

> The working of minds had to be described by the mere negatives of the specific descriptions given to bodies; they are not in space, they are not motions, they are not modifications of matter, they are not accessible to public observation. Minds are not bits of clockwork, they are just bits of not-clockwork. (Ryle, 1949, p. 21)

We support Ryle's assertion that such a dogma is "entirely false, and false not in detail but in principle. It is not merely an assemblage of particular mistakes. It is one big mistake and a mistake of a special kind. It is, namely a category-mistake. It represents the facts of mental life as if they belonged to one logical type or category, when they actually belong to another. The dogma is therefore a philosopher's myth" (Ryle, 1949, p. 17).

Eliminating the mind as an ontological ghost not only achieves an important Ockhamist ontology, but it clears the path to a scientific investigation of mind. As stated earlier, the existence of a ghost in the machine does not necessarily rule out a scientific mind, because such a ghost may be governed by scientific principles. However, such a claim immediately raises two concerns: First, although it provides the existence of the mind as a scientific object, it excludes any scientific exploration of it. The mind is not accessible to public observation, and furthermore, it can only be described by mere negatives. Second, the scientific ghost is a self-defeating concept. The ghost is a ticket taking one away from the rest of the physical universe and thus is also an attempted escape from the trivialization of our existence. The appeal of having a ghost in the first place is fictitiously to differentiate ourselves from the rest of the world and hence to elevate ourselves to a higher form of existence (compare, e.g., Descartes). A scientific ghost—one that is governed by rules and principles, like any other physical and scientific object—is self-defeating and no better than not having a ghost altogether.

The question remains, What then is the mind? We propose that the mind is a set of representations and their processing in the brain, which helps or allows us to explain and predict behavior. The mind is a complex set of functions and their relations, which are realized in the biological brain. On the one hand, the mind is not a ghost that is free to come and go, but on the other hand, nor is it reducible to mere biological descriptions.

Can the Mind Be Studied Scientifically, and If So, How?

Rescuing the mind from a category mistake provides a ghost-free mind that is an appropriate object for scientific scrutiny. However, freeing the mind from the ghost does not, by itself, pave the path for such a scientific venture. What is the correct scientific framework for examining the mind? What methodology and conceptual terms would best serve as tools for such an investigation? What levels of description and what types of description can capture the essence of the mind?

The answers to these questions will determine the success or failure of investigating the mind as a scientific object. The existence of the mind as a scientific object is scientifically void if one cannot study it in a scientific manner. If we cannot reveal the principles and regularities that govern the mind, then the fact that they exist may remain important at a metaphysical level, but it is a death for any empirical scientist who is looking for an object for inquiry.

A central objection to the scientific study of the mind is that its private nature prevents any scientific exploration of it. This view characterizes certain early schools of psychology that adopted the method of introspection. According to Freud, such methods of studying the mind had "no objective verification . . . , and no possibility of demonstrating it" (Freud, 1966, p. 22). This lack of scientific quality prompted the behaviorists' rejection of introspection techniques. However, in their attempt to make psychology a scientific inquiry, it was necessary for behaviorists to do away with the mind and any mental life altogether.

As we now shall try to show, there is a way to study the mind scientifically—namely, the interdisciplinary approach of cognitive neuroscience. This approach views the mind as an information-processing machine that can be deciphered by integrating knowledge from behavior, neuroscience, and computational analyses. Such a tripartite investigation is essential for a full scientific understanding of mind.

The brain is the machinery of the mind and thus obviously plays a critical role in the investigation of it. However, if our goal is to understand the mind, then the biological brain is not, by itself, the object of inquiry. The level and type of understanding we seek need to go beyond the mere biological descriptions of neuronal activity and brain structures. Again, behavior is an end result of the working of the mind, and thus it too plays a critical role in the investigation of the mind. Because of their focus on the nature of the process, computational analyses bridge the two factors just mentioned, revealing the essential underpinning of the mind.

Marr (1982) laid down a framework for understanding complex information-processing machines (for a discussion of his contribution and its effect on the "new way" of studying the mind, as well as its limitations and drawbacks, see Dror and Gallogly, 1999). Marr suggests studying complex information-processing machines at three different levels: (1) the level of computational theory, which deals with the appropriateness and goals of the entire computation, (2) the representation and algorithm level, which deals with the specific computations that underlie the computational theory, and (3) the hardware-implementation level, which deals with the neuronal structures that encode the representations and carry out the algorithms.

Marr's approach builds on the existing notion of modularity. There is a system—for our purposes, the mind—that exists as some higher level of description and can be characterized and generalized at this overall level. This system, however, is not a unitary entity; it is a complex system that is divided into subcomponents. Each subcomponent is a module that specializes in specific functions.

Each module is physically realized as a neural substrate—that is, a population of neurons that work together.

Marr's contribution was that the modules are computational modules. The functions that the modules specialize in are systematic mappings of input to output, which are distinct in terms of computations and mathematical descriptions. Prior to Marr, the notion of modularity existed in a different form. For example, phrenology theory suggested that the mind was composed of thirty-seven "powers" and "organs," such as self-esteem, desire to live, and so on. Fodor's (1983) notion of modularity follows in the footsteps of phrenology, as they both propose strong modularity, a notion in which modules are independent and domain specific.

The cognitive neuroscience approach proposes weak modularity, whereby modules are computationally distinct but are neither independent nor necessarily domain specific. Any given module is characterized computationally and works together with other modules in performing complex processes. That is, the working of the mind is comprised of groups of modules that work and interact together. Specific modules may take part in various compositions and configurations of modules that underlie different domains, and thus may contribute to a variety of different domains of the mind.

The workings of the modules can be characterized in at least three different forms: First, there is the symbolic computational form, which is based on rules and production systems. Second, there is the neural network form (also known as connectionism and parallel distributed processing). Both of these have made considerable contributions to examination of the modules and their underlying computations (for a comparison of the two approaches, their compatibility, and their possible role in cognitive science and philosophy, see Dror and Dascal, 1997; Dror and Young, 1994). Third, there is the mathematical form, in which a description is a complete abstraction of the physical operations of the modules and captures their essence in the purest possible way. Although the final computational characterization of the modules in any form must be biologically realized, the process of learning and deciphering them computationally can also include biologically implausible analyses (Dror and Gallogly, 1999).

The transition brought about by the cognitive neuroscience approach is that deciphering the modules is conceived as accomplished by integrating behavior, neuroscience, and computational analyses. As they merge together, these three factors move toward a unified and scientific explanation of the mind. Probably one of the most intense areas of investigation that illustrates the interactions within the tripartite approach of cognitive neuroscience is how the mind organizes information in terms of memory systems and processes. The central issue here concerns the division into distinct subsystems. One way of analyzing the overall memory system is according to the length of time information is stored (see Atkinson and Shiffrin, 1968, pp. 89–195). Findings from list-learning memory paradigms suggested that there were different mechanisms for temporary and permanent storage of information. In a typical list-learning paradigm, one is presented with a list of items to be remembered. When the participant is required to recall the list, a common finding is that early and late list items are almost always correctly retrieved, whereas items in the middle of the list are forgotten. Based on this behavior, it has been postulated that there are a short-term store (working memory) from which the last few items are retrieved and a long-term store from which the first few items are retrieved. This division of the mind into distinct modules not only should be able to account for behavioral data that already have been collected, but also should be able to make testable predictions. An example of such a case in memory is the fact that processes that use different modules may operate without interfering with each other (the dual-task experimental paradigm) and can be selectively damaged, as will be illustrated shortly.

Even with such scientific criteria, given the complexity of the mind, one can theoretically postulate other modular architectures that can account for behavior. That is why the construction of the modularity of the mind must be further constrained by the machinery of the mind, i.e., the brain. This additional support needed to investigate the mind scientifically can refute and dismiss incorrect hypothesized architectures.

With recent advances in brain-scanning technologies, this possibility is now a reality. Scientists can observe the activity of the brain during behavior. For example, positron emission tomography (PET) is a functional scan that shows what specific brain structures operate during a given cognitive task. In the case of memory, PET studies indicate that the frontal cortex is the locus of working memory processes, whereas the medial temporal lobes are involved with long-term memory processes. Hence the organization of the biological brain corroborates the modularity architecture suggested by behavior.

Furthermore, brain research suggests that there is a module dedicated to transferring and integrating recurring patterns into long-term store, specifically, the hippocampal complex. In a well known case of memory pathology, the patient H.M., having had his hippocampus removed, could not store new information about events occurring in his life, even though his memories of events occurring prior to the removal of the hippocampus were intact and retrievable. Furthermore, his ability to interact in normal conversation was also not affected by the operation, indicating that his working memory system was functioning normally. This illustrates how studies about the organization of the brain can constrain and guide the postulation of modules in the attempt to provide a scientific account of the mind.

The relation between the hippocampus and the neocortex was further established by computational analyses. These analyses showed that there is a basic tradeoff between remembering rapidly learned material and material that is gradually consolidated into preexisting knowledge structures (McClelland, McNaughton, and O'Reilly, 1995). This further accounts for the modularity of the mind and explains why it is divided into these components, and what their specific computational roles are.

Other intriguing memory modules of the mind have been emerging from the cognitive neuroscience approach. For example, personal autobiographical events that are stored as episodic histories recruit different modules than factual impersonal semantic knowledge about the world (Tulving, 1983). Another example pertains to modules that deal with unconscious memories, namely, implicit memories that are distinct from modules of conscious memories (see Schacter, 1989, for a discussion of implicit memory and for an overall summary of memory from a cognitive neuroscience perspective).

Another domain of researching the mind that has demonstrated the scientific power of converging evidence and interrelatedness of the different perspectives of the cognitive neuroscience approach is mental imagery. The mind's use of mental images has been a point of many speculations throughout history; and mental imagery is often referred to as the "mind's eye." Modern cognitive psychology began a systematic investigation into the representation and processing of this mental phenomenon. The nature of mental imagery and of its underlying computational modular architecture is dependent on and derived from their representations. (Computer models have demonstrated the critical role that representations have in determining which computational modules are needed for subsequent processing. See, for example, Dror, Zagaeski, and Moss, 1995; Dror, Florer, Rios, and Zagaeski, 1996.) Based on behavior, two competing speculations were made. One was that mental images were actually propositional representations that described the images (Pylyshyn, 1973); the other was that images were indeed pictorial representations (Kosslyn, 1980; see Dror, Ivey, and Rogus, 1997; Smith and Dror, 2001 for a discussion about the representations used in mental transformations).

Brain research resolved this debate, demonstrating that mental images are indeed pictorial representations (Kosslyn et al., 1993; Kosslyn, Thompson, Kim, and Alpert, 1995). Brain research also has aided in revealing the different modules involved in imagery (for behavioral experiments that selectively tap into different imagery subprocesses, see Dror and Kosslyn, 1994). Furthermore, neuroscience researchers have shown that perceptual vision and visual imagery use the same computational modules. The difference between the two is that in perceptual vision, the input to the modules comes from the outside world via the eyes and the peripheral visual system, whereas in mental imagery, the input to these same modules originates from memory components described earlier. This has been shown by numerous brain-scan studies (e.g., Farah, 1988) in which activations of the same brain structures occur during visual perception and visual imagery. Brain damage also shows similar selective behavioral deficits in perception and imagery (for a review, see Farah, 1988). For example, patients with visual neglect ignore half of their perceptual and imagined space.

The images, whether they originated from the eyes or from memory, are initially processed in the primary visual area in the calcarine cortex (Kosslyn et al., 1993, Kosslyn, Thompson, Kim, and Alpert, 1995). Thereafter, further processing is divided into two different visual pathways. One goes dorsally to the parietal lobes and processes spatial information, and the other ventrally to the temporal lobes and processes object information. Although brain research has demonstrated this distinction in a variety of ways, it was not clear why this division occurs. A computational analysis revealed that recognizing objects and processing their spatial locations are computationally distinct. Modular and split neural network techniques demonstrated that when the two processes are computed by a single undifferentiated mechanism, they interfere with each other. In contrast, when they are allowed to differentiate, they specialize in their respective computations and perform much better (Jacobs, Jordan, and Barto, 1991; Rueckl, Cave, and Kosslyn, 1989). Here again, we see how computational analyses play an important role in figuring out the modular architecture of the mind. Similarly, Kosslyn, Chabris, Marsolik, and Koenig (1992) have shown that computing metric spatial relations (exact distances) is computationally distinct from computing categorical spatial relations (such as above/below, in/out). The computational distinctions between "what" and "where" processes, or metric and categorical spatial relations, have been utilized in behavioral experimentation (see, for example, Dror, Kosslyn, and Waag, 1993).

As our two examples illustrate, adopting a cognitive neuroscience approach is needed in order to achieve a full understanding of the mind. The connections made in cognitive neuroscience are essential in figuring out the complex machinery of the mind. There are two ways to conceptualize how the different domains of cognitive neuroscience interact. According to one of them, each domain (behavior, neuroscience, and computational analyses) contributes its respective part. None of these domains, by itself, can complete the full puzzle of the mind; each domain fulfills part of the puzzle, and only together can the puzzle be completed.

An alternative conceptualization, the one we hold, is that eventually understanding of the mind will be achieved in computational terms alone. However, making sense of these terms requires cooperation with the other domains. The other domains constrain and guide the computational analyses and hence are essential to the scientific enterprise of researching the mind. Nevertheless, computations are the essence of the mind. Once we have such an understanding, it would enable us in principle to determine whether alien life (if and when we encountered it) had a mind like ours. The fact that their machinery (i.e., brain) was built differently from ours would not exclude the possibility that they might have a mind very similar to ours. The crucial factor would not be whether it was built from the same material in the same way, but what computational architecture arose from their brain, and the functional way that it computed and processed information. In a similar fashion, a computational understanding of the mind could help us figure out whether a robot had a mind or not. Its humanlike behavior, by itself, would be a limited source for making such a determination, but examining whether its behavior emerged from the critical computational components of a mind could settle the question of whether it had a mind or not. In the same way, one can examine whether animals have, and to what extent they have, a mind similar to ours. Furthermore, it could be used to address the problem of "other minds," that is, determining if, and how much, we humans have minds that are similar to one another.

Summary

Researching the mind is undoubtedly a complex and long-lasting endeavor since there are many obstacles to pursuing a scientific inquiry of mind. First, by admitting that the mind is a scientific object, we humans join the rest of the physical universe and, in this sense, trivialize our existence. Second, given the complexity and many facets of the mind, we cannot conduct a scientific investigation of it by looking at it from a single direction. We need to adopt a multidisciplinary approach that attacks this scientific object from various perspectives, namely, the cognitive neuroscience approach that looks for converging, guiding, and constraining knowledge from behavior, neuroscience, and computational analyses. The ultimate goal of understanding the mind is revealing its functional architectures, that is, its computational components and how they interact.

Acknowledgment

We would like to thank Sandra Holley for very useful and valuable comments and suggestions.

Note

1. These sections are taken, in part, from Itiel Dror's master's thesis in philosophy, "Artificial Intelligence in the Mirror of Language, Logic, and Cognition."

References

Atkinson, R.C., and Shiffrin, R.M. 1968. "Human Memory: A Proposed System and Its Control Processes." Pp. 89–195 in K.W. Spence and J.T. Spence (Eds.), *The Psychology of Learning and Motivation*. Vol. 2. New York: Academic Press.

Dror, I.E., and Dascal, M. 1997. "Can Wittgenstein Help Free the Mind from Rules? The Philosophical Foundations of Connectionism." Pp. 293–305 in D.M. Johnson and C.E. Erneling (Eds.), *The Future of the Cognitive Revolution*. New York: Oxford University Press.

Dror, I.E., Florer, F.L., Rios, D., and Zagaeski, M. 1996. "Using Artificial Bat Sonar Neural Network for Complex Pattern Recognition: Recognizing Faces and the Speed of a Moving Target." *Biological Cybernetics*, 74, pp. 331–38.

Dror, I.E., and Gallogly, D.P. 1999. "Computational Analyses in Cognitive Neuroscience: In Defense of Biological Implausibility." *Psychonomic Bulletin and Review*, 6(2), pp. 173–82.

Dror, I.E., Ivey, C., and Rogus, C. 1997. "Visual Mental Rotation of Possible and Impossible Objects." *Psychonomic Bulletin and Review*, 4(2), pp. 242–47.

Dror, I.E., and Kosslyn, S.M. 1994. "Mental Imagery and Aging." *Psychology and Aging*, 9, pp. 90–102.

Dror, I.E., Kosslyn, S.M., and Waag, W. 1993. "Visual-Spatial Abilities of Pilots." *Journal of Applied Psychology*, 78, pp. 763–73.

Dror, I.E., and Young, M.J. 1994. "The Role of Neural Networks in Cognitive Science: Evolution or Revolution?" *Psycoloquy*, 5(79).

Dror, I.E., Zagaeski, M., and Moss, C.F. 1995. "Three-Dimensional Target Recognition via Sonar: A Neural Network Model." *Neural Networks*, 8, pp. 149–60.

Farah, M.J. 1988. "Is Visual Imagery Really Visual? Overlooked Evidence from Neuropsychology." *Psychological Review*, 95, pp. 307–17.

Fodor, J.A. 1983. *The Modularity of Mind*. Cambridge, MA: MIT Press.

Freud, S. 1966. *Introductory Lectures on Psycho-Analysis*. New York: Norton.

Jacobs, R.A., Jordan, M.I., and Barto, A.G. 1991. "Task Decomposition through Competition in a Modular Connectionist Architecture: The What and Where Vision Tasks." *Cognitive Science*, 15, pp. 219–50.

Johnson, D.M., and Erneling, C.E. (Eds.). 1997. *The Future of the Cognitive Revolution*. New York: Oxford University Press.

Kosslyn, S.M. 1980. *Image and Mind*. Cambridge, MA: Harvard University Press.

———. 1994. *Image and Brain: The Resolution of the Imagery Debate*. Cambridge, MA: MIT Press.

Kosslyn, S.M., Alpert, N.M., Thompson, W.L., Maljkovic, V., Weise, S.B., Chabris, C.F., Hamilton, S.E., Rauch, S.L., and Buonanno, F.S. 1993. "Visual Mental Imagery Activates Topographically Organized Visual Cortex: PET Investigations." *Journal of Cognitive Neuroscience*, 5, pp. 263–87.

Kosslyn, S.M., Chabris, C.F., Marsolek, C.M., and Koenig, O. 1992. "Categorical versus Coordinate Spatial Representations: Computational Analyses and Computer Simulations." *Journal of Experimental Psychology: Human Perception and Performance*, 18, pp. 562–77.

Kosslyn, S.M., Thompson, W.L., Kim, I.J., and Alpert, N.M. 1995. "Topographical Representation of Mental Images in Primary Visual Cortex." *Nature*, 378, pp. 496–98.

Marr, D. 1982. *Vision*. San Francisco: W.H. Freeman.

McClelland, J.L., McNaughton, B.L., and O'Reilly, R.C. 1995. "Why There Are Complementary Learning Systems in the Hippocampus and Neocortex: Insights from the Successes and Failures of Connectionist Models of Learning and Memory." *Psychological Review*, 102, pp. 419–57.

Posner, M.I. (Ed.). 1989. *Foundations of Cognitive Science*. Cambridge, MA: MIT Press.

Pylyshyn, Z.W. 1973. "The Imagery Debate: Analogue Media versus Tacit Knowledge." *Psychological Review*, 87, pp. 16–45.

Rueckl, J.G., Cave, K.R., and Kosslyn, S.M. 1989. "Why Are 'What' and 'Where' Processed by Separate Cortical Visual Systems? A Computational Investigation." *Journal of Cognitive Neuroscience*, 2, pp. 171–86.

Ryle, G. 1949. *The Concept of Mind*. London: Hutchinson.

Schacter. 1989. "Memory." in M.J. Posner (Ed.), *Foundations of Cognitive Science*. Cambridge, MA: MIT Press.

Smith, W. and Dror, I.E. 2001. "The Role of Meaning and Familiarity in Mental Transformations." *Psychonomic Bulletin and Review* 8(4), pp. 732–741.

Spence, K.W., and Spence, J.T. (Eds.). 1968. *The Psychology of Learning and Motivation*. Vol. 2. New York: Academic Press.

Tulving, E. 1983. *Elements of Episodic Memory*. Oxford: Clarendon Press.

17

Gall's Legacy Revisited: Decomposition and Localization in Cognitive Neuroscience

Tadeusz Zawidzki and William Bechtel

The standard philosophical account of explanation—the deductive nomological model in which a phenomenon is explained when a description of it is derived from statements of laws and initial conditions—does not do justice to the explanations generally offered in the life sciences. There, instead, explanations often take the form of specifications of mechanisms, wherein an overall activity of a system is decomposed into subfunctions, and these are then localized to components of the system (Bechtel and Richardson, 1993; Machamer, Darden, and Craver, 2000). Mental activities have been no exception. The brain (including the central nervous system) has long been taken to be the bodily organ responsible for mental activities, and the task has been to decompose mental functions and identify the resulting component functions with parts of the brain. In many respects, this effort embodies the vision of Franz Joseph Gall (1758–1828).

Modern cognitive neuroscience, the most sophisticated attempt yet to link mental functions with neural structures, has embraced the quest for mechanistic explanation through decomposition and localization (Bechtel, 2000). Thus part of the legacy of Gall is very much still alive. However, there are different strands in this legacy. Part of our goal is to differentiate three of these strands. One, which we link with Jerry Fodor's proposal for modularity, follows Gall himself in seeking direct neural instantiation of whole mental functions such as language (or at least syntactic processing). The second and third strands both go beyond Gall in decomposing individual mental activities into component processes. It is then component processes at some level in the decomposition that are linked to brain structures. The second strand, prevalent in philosophical accounts of mind-brain relations and in psychological research that is cut off from neuroscience, recognizes the need to decompose overall activities into constituent activities, but adopts a top-down perspective in which decomposition precedes localization. The third strand construes decomposition and localization as each informing the other. One element of this view is the claim that brain regions are not demarcated in structural terms alone, but are in part identified through the process of assigning functions to them. The second element of the third strand, and the one to which we will devote primary attention, is that information gleaned from neural studies of component structures often leads to fundamental revisions in functional decompositions of cognitive performance. It is this (neo-)Gallean theme that we see as most common in cognitive neuroscience, and that we will be principally concerned to explicate through a case study of research on attention.

Strand 1: Gall and the Program of Direct Localization

Gall is best known, and ridiculed, for his program of organology (more widely known as "phrenology," the term supplied by his collaborator Johann Gosped Spurzheim in 1818)—the claim that different mental faculties such as memory for verbal material, memory for people, reproductive instinct, affection, religious sentiment, and sense of metaphysics are each localized in distinct parts of the brain, and that these capacities are revealed by bumps on the overlying skull (see figure 17.1). The overall program of using bumps on the skull to identify mental faculties initially attracted much positive attention, both in the lay public and in scientific circles, but it soon fell into disrepute in both. In France, where Gall was working after having been driven out of Vienna in 1802 as a result of opposition by ecclesiastical authorities, Marie Jean Pierre Flourens led the opposition. Employing ablation studies on a number of lower vertebrates such as pigeons, Flourens (1824) argued that there was no differentiation of function between parts of the cortex, and that all parts of the cortex had equal potential for any mental capacity.

Gall based his claims about localization of particular functions on a vast number of cases of skulls, both human and animal, that he collected and examined, and on correlations he drew between the skulls and the characters the individuals exhibited or were reported to have exhibited. His analysis of cases was critically flawed—he made much of cases that fit his proposed localization of functions and paid insufficient attention to contrary cases. But it is not his repudiated empirical claims that are of contemporary interest, but rather the assumptions that underlay his inquiry, of which we will distinguish four. The first of these is that the skull fit closely to the cortex so that bumps on the skull were reliable indicators of how much the underlying brain area had expanded. This was an empirical contention that simply turned out to be false. The second assumption was that an enlargement in a brain area corresponded to greater development in the function associated with that brain area. While again this is false, it was certainly not implausible and, moreover, is not conceptually all that different from the idea that greater activity in a brain area corresponds to greater metabolism and thus blood flow, an assumption that underlies contemporary neuroimaging.

Gall's third and in many ways most interesting assumption was that different mental processes were localized in different parts of the brain. By making this assumption, Gall set himself against the dominant antilocalizationist tradition of

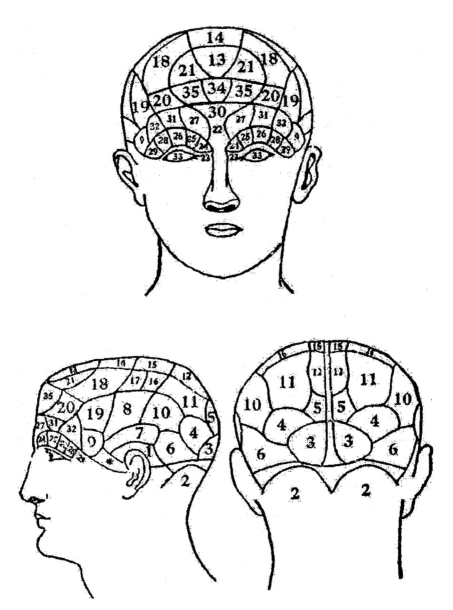

FIGURE 17.1. Phrenological map of the human skull. From G. Spurzheim, *Phrenology or The Doctrine of the Human Mind*, Third American Edition (Boston: Marsh, Capen and Lyon, 1834).

the eighteenth century, especially the legac of Albrecht von Haller, who contended that all neural tissue was highly i le and thus provided a *sensorium commune*, and rejected any attempt at localization of specific functions in the brain (see Clarke and Jacyna, 1987). It was Gall's endorsement of localization that led many brain scientists later in the nineteenth century, who also sought to identify the neural location of particular functions, to adopt the label *neophrenologist*. The fourth assumption is what leads us to classify Gall as a direct localizationist. His decomposition of function into faculties, each solely responsible for a mental trait, upon which j   h trait on which Gall noted individual differences was memory for verbal material. If people differed on this trait, then they differed in the development of the faculty. This is an approach that still plays an important role in cognitive science, although generally it is not based on degrees of development of an ability, but on whether the ability can be lost (e.g., through brain damage) without loss of other abilities. Thus the fact that an individual might lose the capacity to remember new facts or new episodes, but retain the ability to learn new procedures, supports the distinction in the psychological literature between explicit and implicit memory (Squire, 1987). (Contemporary neuropsychologists often emphasize the importance of showing that each capacity can be separately impaired—thus a double dissociation—in establishing that they are really separate cognitive abilities. See Shallice, 1988.) Simply dissociating cognitive abilities does not constitute direct localization. Rather, it is the idea that this capacity is to be directly assigned to a module. The third and fourth of these assumptions comprise what is philosophically interesting in Gall's view—the idea that specific brain regions are responsible for specific psychological capacities:

> When we see that nature follows such a course, how can it still be doubted that each part of the brain has different functions to fulfill, and that as a consequence, the brain of man and animals must be composed of as many special organs as the man or animal has distinct moral or intellectual faculties, inclinations, and aptitudes for work? (Gall and Spurzheim, 1812, p. 254)

While we attribute direct localization to Gall, the view is hardly unique to him. It is exhibited today, for example, in Chomsky's claim that there is a language module (Chomsky, 1980; Pinker, 1994). The linkage between Gall and Chomsky was clearly recognized by Fodor (1983) when he "rehabilitated" Gall. Fodor contended that a good part of the mind had the character of Gall's faculties; he identified these areas as modules and claimed that they were responsible for processing particular contents. Fodor even went far beyond Gall in emphasizing the encapsulation of these modules—each module had to rely on its own internal resources, and its operation could not be penetrated by other information the subject possessed. Fodor's account departs from Gall's in that he only identified such modules in specific sensory input domains and in language processing, and he viewed these modules not as directly controlling particular behaviors, but as supplying input to more central cognitive processes that are responsible for higher-level reasoning and operate in a more holistic manner. Fodor also identified a number of other characteristics of information processing within modules: for example, that such processing is very fast, automatic, and mandatory (i.e., as soon as the input is received, it is processed). He also contended that such modules are likely to be hardwired into the cognitive system. Accordingly, they presumably would be systems that are physically identifiable in the brain, although Fodor did not emphasize identifying their physical localization.

One important point to note about both Gall and Fodor is that for both of them, the decomposition of the mind into faculties or modules comes prior to linking those faculties with physical parts of the brain. This is done by determining what distinct functions the mind performs. Gall (using *physiology* to refer to function) wrote:

> The physiology of the brain need not be contradictory to the anatomy of the brain; its anatomy must become the support of its physiology. But physiology has been found independently of anatomy. Nothing whatever in brain physiology has conflicted with an anatomical fact; nothing has been interpreted by structure or by the arrangement of parts of the brain; brain anatomy has served only to confirm physiological discoveries. (1825, p. 118)

For Fodor, likewise, modules are identified independently of their brain realization. The primary criteria for identifying modules are their functions—each module is specific to a given sense or to language. Accordingly, for neither Gall nor Fodor does study of the brain contribute to the decomposition into modules.

Vertical versus Horizontal Modules

In linking his modularity thesis to Gall's organology, Fodor characterizes the faculties or modules as vertical so as to distinguish them from another sort of module that often appears in cognitive theories, which he calls horizontal. The difference lies in the fact that Gall's and Fodor's faculties are responsible for all mental processes in a specific domain (e.g., visual processing), whereas horizontal faculties operate across content domains. Short-term memory, if there turns out to be such a system, stores different types of information and so would be a horizontal module. Moreover, in carrying out any given task, it is assumed to interact with other cognitive capacities. Figure 17.2, for example, shows Atkinson and Shiffrin's (1968) classical model, in which the short-term store receives inputs from the echoic store and supplies inputs to the long-term store, all the while being operated on by attentional processes. In Fodor's perspective, these horizontal faculties belong to central cognition, and he is deeply pessimistic about the ability of cognitive science to make any progress in understanding the precise operations involved. Cognitive science nonetheless has generally taken such horizontal faculties to be its principal focus and has tried to develop a number of tools for demonstrating the existence of particular processing components (modules) and determining how they interact

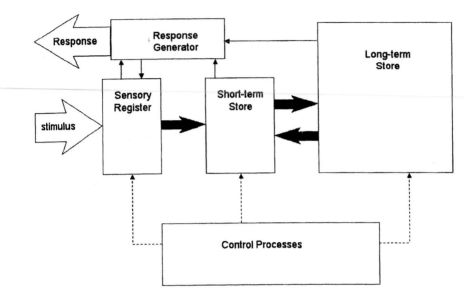

FIGURE 17.2. Atkinson and Shiffrin's (1968) memory model.

with each other. (As we shall see, cognitive neuroscience offers consolation to the worry that we shall not be able to determine what physical brain components perform these mechanistic operations.)

What makes horizontal modules conceptually interesting is not just that they operate across domains, but that they are identified by decomposing mental activity into multiple processing steps. It is mechanisms responsible for these steps in mental processing that one then might attempt to localize in the brain. An investigator who begins with a vertical decomposition could go on to propose a further decomposition into multiple processing stages within a vertical module. What would then distinguish the person adopting the vertical approach would be commitment to the idea that the component modules identified would only figure in performing the one overall task (e.g., visual perception), whereas a theorist adopting the horizontal conception of modules would be open to a module performing a certain operation (e.g., short-term retention of information) in the context of quite different tasks.

A common route to discovering multiple interactive components is the recognition that the module one initially associated with a task is insufficient to perform the whole task. For example, Broca (1861) identified a region in the left frontal cortex that, when damaged, left patients unable to speak articulately. Broca, though, determined that they still could comprehend speech, and so he did not propose this as the locus of an overall language module. A decade later, Wernicke (1874) identified a second brain region that, when damaged, produced deficits in comprehension while leaving the ability to produce articulate speech (albeit speech lacking in coherent semantic interpretation) intact. Wernicke also proposed a way that the two areas might be linked together to enable people to repeat speech they had just heard. He further proposed centers for reading and writing and how these centers might be related in reading aloud, writing from dictation, or copying written text. Wernicke's differentiation of tasks was a step toward developing a horizontal functional decomposition of an overall language function into subtasks or component functions, which then together performed various language tasks.

If the goal of functional decomposition is to understand how a physical, mechanical system carries out a task, then decomposition into centers for reading, articulating, and so on is only a minimal first step, since these are not tasks that can be carried out by simple machines. The goal is to continue the decomposition into smaller and smaller tasks (e.g., recognizing the form of a word, accessing its phonetics). It is the simple functions remaining at the end of such a series of decompositions that can be linked with specific machinery one might find in the brain, and that then provide the components for an explanatorily adequate mechanistic model (Lycan, 1981; Bechtel, Mandik, and Mundale, 2001).

What we shall distinguish as the second and third strands in Gall's legacy both emphasize the quest for horizontal modules and the need for decomposition, ultimately into components carrying out simple cognitive operations. What distinguish the strands are the methodologies for identifying the modules. In Wernicke's case (and in the case of Geschwind, 1974, who revived the legacy of Wernicke), the deficits resulting from brain lesions played a critical role in generating the functional decomposition. Strand 3 will likewise emphasize this approach. But brain lesions and other information about brain processes have played only a minor role in the decompositions developed in cognitive science. Instead, the decompositions have been directed either by analysis of how overall tasks might be performed or behavioral evidence about decomposition. Since these start on purely the mental side, we term them *top-down* decompositions; they comprise what we are distinguishing as the second strand in Gall's legacy.

Strand 2: Top-Down Complex Localization

One approach to functional decomposition is to proceed in an a priori manner, by asking what activities could together suffice for performing the overall task. Such an approach is common in engineering: One designs a machine to carry out a task by first identifying component tasks, then identifying component tasks within these tasks, and so on, until one reaches a point where the tasks invoked in the analysis correspond to the capabilities of known physical devices (Dennett, 1978). Then one arranges the devices so that they interact appropriately to perform the task. This approach is exemplified in designing computer programs: The programmer must analyze the overall performance that is sought into component activities until these activities correspond to the primitive operations of one's programming language or to already developed programming modules. Such an approach has been followed by many investigators in artificial intelligence. A common result is that initial proposals as to how a given task should be decomposed turn out to be inadequate to account for the way the task is usually performed. Therefore, researchers need to develop alternative models, including new modeling tools (e.g., scripts and frames) and new modeling frameworks (e.g., production systems and case-based reasoning systems). In all these cases, though, the guide to developing new tools and frameworks has come from considerations of the task that needs to be performed (e.g., making a medical diagnosis or reading a newspaper story) and means-end reasoning about that task.

Another approach to identifying functional components is through behavioral experimentation. The goal here is to find evidence in the behavior of the mind/brain about how it breaks down tasks. The challenge in such research is to find a variable to measure that might point to the differentiation of tasks. Two of the most widely invoked dependent variables are reaction times and error patterns. In reaction-time studies one measures the amount of time it takes a subject to perform a given task. The problem is that one must measure a whole activity, which involves sensory processing, whatever central activities are involved, and motor processing. To determine the amount of time involved in a specific cognitive operation, one generally has to compare the reaction times required for different overall activities. One of the first approaches to using reaction times to identify cognitive processes was Donders's (1868/1969) subtraction method, in which the researcher devised two tasks, one of which was thought to involve all of the operations required by the first task, plus an additional step that would require additional time. The time difference in the performance of the two tasks was then a measure of how long the additional task required.

There are at least two problems with this approach. First, it requires a proposal for determining a task decomposition before one can set up the subtraction. Second, it assumes that performing the additional task simply adds to the other operations and does not occur simultaneously with them. Saul Sternberg (1967) developed a procedure known as the additive factors method to overcome the latter problem. In this procedure, one devises procedures to alter different variables that are presumed to affect different component tasks. If the changes in reaction times resulting from manipulating two variables are additive, then the affected component tasks are revealed to be independent, even if they occur simultaneously. If, on the other hand, the change in reaction time from manipulating two variables is not equal to the sum of changes for manipulating the variables independently (this is called an interaction), then the component tasks are not independent. A related way of demonstrating whether two components are independent is the interference paradigm. If requiring a subject to perform a second task while performing an initial task leads to increased reaction times, this provides evidence that a common component is employed in both tasks.

While all of these methods begin with a hypothesis about the decomposition of the task, it should be emphasized that the additive factors method and the interference paradigm provide a means for possibly falsifying the initial hypothesis and so guiding the quest for a more adequate decomposition. What is important for our purposes, though, is to note that they start on the behavioral side, using behavioral data to propose and revise task decompositions. The task decomposition is set, therefore, before one might begin to consider neural evidence.

So far we have focused on top-down decomposition in artificial intelligence (AI) and cognitive psychology, but the program has also been endorsed in philosophy of mind. The dominant philosophical account of mind of the past thirty years is functionalism, which holds that mental activities are to be understood in terms of their interaction with other mental activities, not their physical realization. One strand of functionalism, homuncular functionalism, advocates a multistage decomposition of cognitive performance, usually first framed in intentional terms, but eventually reaching a point at which a task is sufficiently simple that one can envisage a mechanistic system performing it. Dennett (1978, p. 80) characterizes this as the approach of AI researchers:

> The AI researcher *starts* with an intentionally characterized problem (e.g., how can I get a computer to *understand* questions of English?), breaks it down into sub-problems that are also intentionally characterized (e.g., how do I get the computer to *recognize* questions, *distinguish* subjects from predicates, *ignore* irrelevant parsings?) and then breaks these problems down still further until he reaches problem or task descriptions that are obviously mechanistic.

One stream of functionalism takes the emphasis on function to show that reduction of psychological states to brain states is not possible, largely because psychological states can be realized in very different types of brain states (Putnam, 1975b; Fodor, 1987). Accordingly, that strand of functionalism often denies that knowledge of the brain can shed light on psychological processes. Homuncular functionalism, as Lycan (1981) makes clear, does not endorse such a chasm between mind and brain and indeed is compatible with the classical theory of the identity of mind and brain.

Closely identified with the identity theory is a model of reduction according to which psychological processes are identified with neural processes, and psychological laws are derived from laws of neuroscience. The resulting picture is nicely described by Chalmers:

> The paradigm of reductive explanation via functional analysis works beautifully in most areas of cognitive science, at least in principle. . . . [M]ost nonphenomenal mental concepts can be analyzed functionally. Psychological states are characterizable in terms of the causal role they play. To explain these states, we explain how the relevant causation is performed. . . . In principle, one can do this by giving an account of the underlying neurophysiology. If we explain how certain neurophysiological states are responsible for the performance of the functions in question, then we have explained the psychological state. We need not always descend to the neurophysiological level, however. We can frequently explain some aspect of mentality by exhibiting an appropriate cognitive

model—that is, by exhibiting the details of the abstract causal organization of a system whose mechanisms are sufficient to perform the relevant functions, without specifying the physicochemical substrate in which this causal organization is implemented. In this way, we give a how-possibly explanation of a given aspect of psychology, in that we have shown how the appropriate causal mechanisms might support the relevant mental processes. If we are interested in explaining the mental states of an actual organism or type of organism (e.g., learning in humans, as opposed to the possibility of learning in general), this sort of explanation must be supplemented with a demonstration that the causal organization of the model mirrors the causal organization of the organism in question. (Chalmers, 1996, p. 46)

The approach of AI, cognitive psychology, and homuncular functionalism in philosophy, which we have characterized in this section, emphasizes a top-down direction to the development of mechanistic theories of mind: The decomposition is first developed by analyzing behavior and perhaps subsequently connected to underlying neural processes. There are some vocal opponents of the picture of functional decomposition first, structural localization second, such as Paul and Patricia Churchland (Churchland and Churchland, 1990). In their extreme eliminativist mode, they recommend ignoring the functional decomposition of cognitive capacities in favor of an approach that focuses solely on the brain. (As McCauley, 1996b, argues, based on a number of texts, this is not the only position that the Churchlands adopt. In other contexts, they embrace the sort of interactive approach that we discuss in the next section.) Insofar as they endorse eliminating not just folk psychology, but also the functional analyses of cognitive psychology and cognitive science, the Churchlands seem to endorse the view that if such functional analyses are to play any role in a proper science, it must be that of providing a prior decomposition that is to be completed before neuroscience takes over to localize functions. The eliminativist claim is that neuroscience will not find any components carrying out these functions, and that the whole functional analysis will be eliminated.

Strand 3: Interactive Decomposition and Localization

Cognitive neuroscience, both in its late-nineteenth- and early-twentieth-century anticipations and in its current more mature development, supports a different perspective on the functional decomposition and neural localization of mental function. Structure and function are intimately linked. The identification of neural structures, the very "carving" of the brain, does not proceed independently of an assumed functional decomposition of cognitive capacity; conversely, the functional decomposition of cognitive capacity is informed by neuroanatomical and neurophysiological evidence (Bechtel and Mundale, 1999; Mundale and Bechtel, 1996). These features of the methodology of contemporary cognitive neuroscience, exemplified in the case we discuss later, set it apart from the direct localizationist tradition of Gall and the top-down approach to reductionism found in much contemporary philosophy of mind. The complex interplay between cognitive, functional decomposition and neural localization that we highlight suggests that the study of complex systems like the brain is an inherently interdisciplinary endeavor involving the close cooperation of many different theoretical perspectives, rather than their independence in a strict division of labor.

To illustrate the nature of this dynamic interaction between behavioral and neuroscientific research that strand 3 advocates, we will focus in the rest of this chapter on cognitive neuroscience research on attention. (Much the same process of interaction has occurred in other cognitive domains. For an analysis of how it has developed in the case of vision, see Bechtel, 2001.)

Case Study: Decomposition and Localization of Attentional Mechanisms

To illustrate how behavioral and neuroscientific investigations interact dynamically in attention research, we will focus on three models of attention. The first was introduced by Broadbent (1958) and others primarily on the basis of behavioral evidence that suggested the existence of a limited cognitive resource, or "bottleneck," that stimulus information competes for, somewhere between perception and motoric response. The second model was introduced by Michael Posner (1992) on the basis of both behavioral and neural evidence. According to the second model, there are three attentional systems, a visuospatial, posterior network; a non-modality-specific, top-down, anterior network; and a vigilance network. The posterior system is conceptualized as a "spotlight" that illuminates different locations in the visual field. As we will see, this neurally inspired account brought the whole notion of a bottleneck into question. The third model is Desimone and Duncan's (1995) attentional-template, biased-competition model, in which different processing streams compete for the control of overt behavioral response and receive biases from an attentional template according to their relevance to the demands of a task. Part of the appeal of Desimone and Duncan's model is that it accounts for behavioral features that Posner's model does not. Thus, through the evolution of these three approaches, we will see how cognitive neuroscience is developing improved decompositions of attention through a fruitful interplay of behavioral and neuroscientific research.

Attentional effects are measured behaviorally by comparing reaction times and error scores on tasks under different conditions. Differences in performance are taken to indicate that under certain conditions human information-processing resources are more taxed than under other conditions. Thus in one type of task, the visual search task, two conditions are compared. In both conditions, there is an array of objects or shapes that must be searched in order to discover some target that is prespecified in terms of a unique feature or set of features. In the first condition (the obvious condition), the target is prespecified in terms of an obviously distinguishing feature. For example, the array may consist of a set of grey shapes and one black shape, and the subject may be asked to identify the black shape (figure 17.3). Reaction time in this condition does not increase with the number of grey shapes, or distractors, in the array. In the second (nonobvious) condition, the target is prespecified in terms of a nonobvious feature or set of features, such as a conjunction of features. For example, the array may consist of different shapes of various colors, and the subject may be asked to identify the grey triangle (figure 17.4). Relative to this array, this conjunction of properties is nonobvious. The subject must engage in controlled or attention-demanding processing to discover the target. It is for this reason that reaction time in this condition increases with the number of distractors in the array.

The limited-capacity model explains the different performance in these two conditions in the following way: In the first condition, a relatively unlimited, preattentive perceptual capacity scans the array in parallel and selects the target automatically for further processing by the limited attentional resource and eventually for motoric response. Because the array is scanned in parallel by a relatively unlimited, preattentive cognitive resource, the number of distractors has little or no effect on reaction time. In the second condition, the limited attentional resource must be used in a controlled, serial search for the target. Each item in the array must be selected for processing by the limited attentional resource, in se-

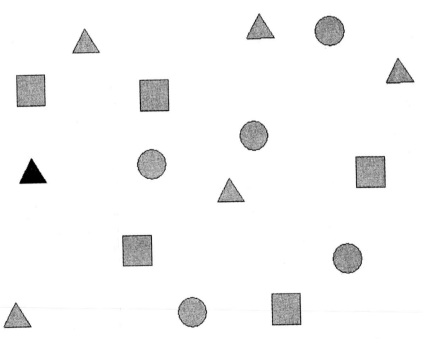

FIGURE 17.3. Stimuli for which picking out the black triangle does not require attention-demanding processing.

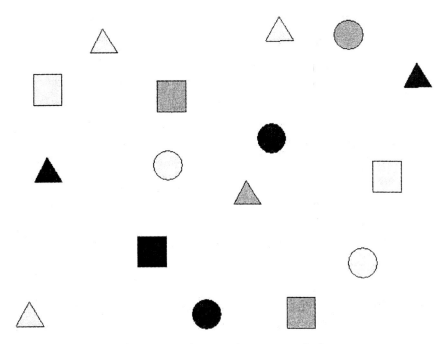

FIGURE 17.4. Stimuli for which picking out the gray triangle does require attention-demanding serial search.

quence, until the target is found. It is for this reason that reaction time increases with the number of items to be processed.

The understanding of such results in terms of selection by a limited attentional resource suggests a very definite research program. Attention is functionally analyzed as a processing bottleneck or limited-capacity resource that selects from competing stimulus information represented automatically and in parallel with preattentive perceptual resources. Such a model raises the following questions: When in the processing of perceptual input, and on what basis, is information selected for processing by the limited attentional resource? What type of processing, for example, semantic or formal, is the limited attentional resource required for? What are the relationships and differences between controlled and automatic processing? These functional questions about the types of processing that distinguish the limited attentional resource from less limited preattentive resources suggest corresponding questions about the localization of the relevant cognitive functions. Where in the brain are limited attentional resources found? Where in the brain does preattentive, automatic, parallel processing occur? How does selection among information competing for attention occur in the brain?

Michael Posner is one of the first cognitive psychologists to bring brain research to bear on the study of attention, and, as we shall see, in his hands, brain studies do not answer these questions, but rather lead to their replacement. His work concentrates on visuospatial attention, which he defines in terms of the following experimental paradigm: Posner studies covert attentional effects in visual processing, that is, attentional effects that are not facilitated by overt eye movements. A typical experiment involves three locations on a screen facing an alert subject (figure 17.5). In the middle of the screen is a fixation point on which the subject must focus his or her vision. There is a square on each side of the fixation point, separated by some angle of eccentricity. The subject first fixates on the fixation point. Next, the subject is cued by a luminance increment in one of the boxes. The subject is trained not to respond to this luminance increment with a saccade or any other motoric response. Finally, a target, like an asterisk, appears in one of the boxes. The subject's task is to respond to the target, for example, with a key press, as quickly as possible. Posner has obtained the following results with this experimental paradigm: If the target appears in the cued location within one hundred milliseconds after the cue, then the subject's processing of that information is facilitated in comparison with the condition where the target appears at an uncued location. This facilitation is measured in terms of reaction time. Thus the subject takes longer to respond when the target appears at an uncued location than when it appears at the cued location.

Prima facie, such results can be accounted for using the classical model of limited attentional resources. Visual space is represented by an automatic, preattentive, parallel cognitive resource. The representations of the different locations in this space compete for further processing by the limited attentional resource. The cueing of a particular location in visual space leads to the selection of the representation of that location for further processing. Assuming that a response to the target requires processing by the limited attentional resource, it is not surprising that responses to targets appearing in cued locations are facilitated. The cue has already led to the selection of that location for further attentional processing, so when the target appears there, it can be processed more rapidly than when it

FIGURE 17.5. Setup for Posner attention task. The subject is instructed to fixate on the cross throughout the experiment. A luminance cue appears for one of the boxes surrounding the fixation point (left panel). Subsequently, a target appears in one of the boxes (right panel). From M.I. Posner and M.E. Raichle, *Images of Mind* (New York: Scientific American Library, 1994).

appears at a location that has not been cued and is not already being processed by the limited attentional resource.

Despite its prima facie compatibility with the classical cognitive analysis of attention in terms of selection for processing by a limited resource, Posner develops a different and more complicated model of visuospatial attention, based on more fine-grained evidence obtained from experiments with subjects with brain lesions and from position emission tomography (PET) studies. This work constitutes an early example of neural evidence modifying and constraining the development of a cognitive model. The PET studies show that a massively distributed network of brain areas involving the parietal cortex, the midbrain, and the thalamus is active during performance of the covert, visuospatial attention task, and the lesion studies show that different deficits in the performance of this task result from lesions in different areas of this network (Posner, Grossenbacher, and Compton, 1994, p. 221). Posner uses such evidence to argue for the claim that visuospatial attention is realized by elementary cognitive operations, each of which is localized in a specific neural structure (Posner, 1992, p. 12). Because parietal lesions only affect the capacity to shift attention from the ipsi- to the contralesional side, and not vice versa, Posner argues that the posterior parietal lobe must be responsible for disengaging attention to a location in the ipsilesional visual hemifield. Because damage to midbrain structures (especially the superior colliculus) affects the capacity to shift attention in both directions, Posner argues that these midbrain structures must be responsible for the actual move from one attended location to another. Analogous lesion evidence and similar argumentation lead Posner to conclude that parts of the thalamus (the pulvinar) are responsible for an engage operation, whereby attention to a new location is engaged after a shift from an old location (Posner, 1992, p. 12) (figure 17.6)

It is clear that Posner's fine-grained analysis of the role of specific neural structures in the performance of the covert, visuospatial attention task constitutes a radical reconceptualization of the cognitive role of attention. The metaphor of the limited processing bottleneck is replaced by a "spotlight" metaphor (Posner, Grossenbacher, and Compton, 1994, p. 224). These metaphors differ along several interesting dimensions. Posner's work suggests that attentional deficits are not deficits in types of processing, but rather deficits in efficiency of processing. Victims of lesions with attentional deficits still have the capacity to process information from every sensory modality, as well as semantic information and high-level information about visual form (Posner et al., 1984, p. 1873). Their problem is that they cannot enhance this processing to the requisite degree when it is required for the purposes of some task. The spotlight metaphor is a more appropriate way of thinking about these deficits. It is not that some information cannot make it into a limited-capacity bottleneck. Rather, the system responsible for enhancing processing in primary sensory areas, as demanded by some task, is disabled with respect to one of these areas. The spotlight has trouble reaching some areas of visual space.

Along with this reconceptualization comes a cognitive/functional distinction

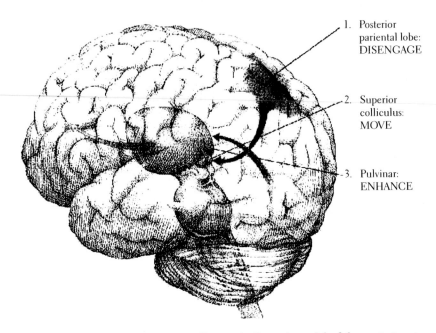

1. Posterior
   pariental lobe:
   DISENGAGE

2. Superior
   colliculus:
   MOVE

3. Pulvinar:
   ENHANCE

FIGURE 17.6. The three brain areas figuring in Posner's model of the posterior attention system. From M.I. Posner and M.E. Raichle, *Images of Mind* (New York: Scientific American Library, 1994).

that makes little sense on the traditional processing bottleneck model of attention. When we reconceptualize attention as a spotlight, it makes sense to distinguish between the "site" and the "source" of attention (Corbetta et al., 1991, p. 2384). The site of attention is the neural area whose activity is enhanced for the purposes of some task. The source of attention is the neural area that effects this enhancement. Thus where the traditional bottleneck model of attention makes a distinction between two types of processing, that is, preattentive versus attentive, that take place at different sites, the spotlight model of attention sees attention as the enhancement of processing at various preattentive sites, caused by sources of enhancement like the posterior attention network.

The site/source distinction emerges quite naturally in the neurally informed study of attention. When one studies brain anatomy, no obvious candidates suggest themselves as locations of the processing bottleneck that defines attention in the classical model. All one sees is massively parallel, distributed processing. For the neurally informed student of attention, attention is not a separate, limited-capacity processing module. Rather, it is the activity of coordinating parallel processing streams through selective enhancement. As Allport (1989, pp. 648–52) argues, the only limited resource that parallel, preattentive processing streams compete for is the control of behavior. Coherent, coordinated behavior inevitably involves selectivity. Only a small number of overt actions can be performed at the same time.

For example, one cannot both raise one's arm and lower it at the same time. The temptation to treat attention as a limited-capacity processing module is an artifact of the fact that the tasks used to measure attention involve coordinated, overt responses and thus the inevitable selection of some processing streams over others. Thus to speak of competition for a limited processing resource is less an explanation of attention than a description of what needs to be explained—the fact that in the type of coordinated activity that is required in tasks used to measure attention, only one processing stream can control overt behavior at a time (Allport, 1989, p. 640). The "spotlight" metaphor and the site/source distinction, on the other hand, suggest a functional analysis of attention that is much more explanatory relative to facts about the brain.

Despite the reconceptualization of attention as a spotlight, many of the questions suggested by the bottleneck model remain. It is still not obvious how selection works. On what basis does the spotlight select a specific neural area to enhance? Posner's work suggests that low-level cues, like luminance changes at specific locations in the visual field, may lead to the enhancement of relevant neural areas. This seems to be an example of "stimulus-driven attentional capture" (see Yantis, 1993). In both Posner's covert attention shift task and the obvious condition of the visual search task described earlier, attention is the product of a preattentive process. However, performance on the nonobvious condition of the visual search task suggests a very different attentional effect. Here the actual search seems to demand attention. Attention is part of the controlled, sequential processing that is necessary to locate the target. Posner tries to localize the division between the kind of attention that is automatically captured by luminance changes at locations in the visual field and the kind of controlled attentional processing required for serial search in an anatomical division between what he calls the anterior and posterior attention networks.

As we have seen, the posterior attention network explains the capture of attention by luminance changes at specific locations in the visual field. Posner argues that the anterior attention network, and especially a neural area called the anterior cingulate, is responsible for the kind of controlled, attention-demanding processing that we see in tasks involving search for nonobvious targets. He hypothesizes that the anterior attention network (figure 17.7) is where non-modality-specific, linguistically conveyed information is brought to bear on the control of attention (Posner, Grossenbacher, and Compton, 1994, p. 219). Such information permits the controlled, attention-demanding search for targets that are not distinguished from distractors by obvious, modality-specific cues.

However, matters are not quite so straightforward. In their PET study, Corbetta et al. (1991) examined the neural activation that accompanies performance on a visual search task involving two frames representing an array of moving objects. The subjects were asked to report if the two frames were the same or different with respect to certain visual features, such as color, shape, and speed. There were two conditions. In the divided-attention condition, subjects were asked to report if they noticed a difference in any of the object features—color, shape, or speed. In the selective-attention condition, subjects were asked to report

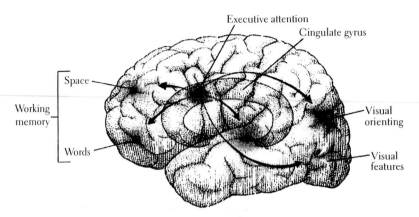

FIGURE 17.7. Posner's proposal for an anterior attention system. From M.I. Posner and M.E. Raichle, *Images of Mind* (New York: Scientific American Library, 1994).

if they noticed a difference in a specific object feature, either color, shape, or speed. These two conditions yielded dramatic differences in the pattern of neural activation. Where the selective-attention condition involved primarily the enhancement of early visual areas responsible for the detection of the relevant feature, the more attention-demanding, divided-attention condition involved additional activation of the anterior cingulate (Corbetta et al., 1991). This seems to confirm that the anterior cingulate is involved in controlled, attention-demanding processing. However, the experiment also seems to suggest that Posner's characterization of the difference between anterior attentional function and posterior attentional function is misleading, for in both the divided-attention and the selective-attention conditions, non-modality-specific, linguistic instructions play a role in the control of attention. In the selective-attention condition, which does not result in activation of the anterior cingulate, the instruction to detect changes in color as opposed to shape or motion, for example, activates the appropriate automatic selection for attention.

The results of Corbetta et al. (1991) are consistent with increasing evidence from behavioral studies of attention that there are very few examples of stimulus information that can capture attention from the bottom up. In other words, it is hard to specify what captures attention in a task-neutral way. Many high-level features, like word form or even semantic properties, can capture attention automatically (Duncan, 1980, p. 291). Conversely, attention to supposedly compelling low-level cues, like luminance changes, can be successfully and automatically inhibited if the task requires attention to properties that vary independently of such low-level cues (Yantis, 1993). Such evidence leads Yantis to argue that Posner's studies are not examples of bottom-up attentional capture by luminance changes, since the requirement of the task—reaction to target onset—necessitates the detection of luminance changes (Yantis, 1993, p. 159). Given this argument,

Posner's division of attention into a posterior system that is driven by visual stimuli and an anterior system that is driven by top-down, task-specific information seems ill motivated.

If attentional capture by luminance increments at locations in the visual field is just a special case of automatic attentional capture by stimulus information that is most relevant to successful performance on the specific task the subject is engaged in, then it may be better to think of such automatic attentional capture as a general phenomenon that can affect many different processing dimensions, rather than as a specific attentional system that scans visual space for inherently salient cues, like a spotlight (see Chelazzi and Corbetta, 2000, pp. 670–71). Such a reconceptualization still retains many features of the spotlight model. It still makes sense to make a distinction between the site and the source of attentional enhancement of processing. The difference is that there are many possible sites of such attentional enhancement besides the processing centers that represent visual space, and there may be correspondingly many sources of such attentional enhancement. Something like this model is suggested by Desimone and Duncan (1995, pp. 199–200). They argue that attentional selection involves biased competition among different processing streams for the control of behavioral response. The competitive bias comes from an attentional template that is formed in conformity with task demands. In this model, the attentional template is the source of attentional enhancement, and visual areas that meet the requirements of the templates are the sites of attentional enhancement.

Desimone and Duncan's model has the advantage of offering both an explanation of automatic attentional capture by task-relevant features and an explanation of why certain tasks require controlled, attention-demanding processing: When targets and distractors are not distinct along some obvious perceptual dimension, both representations of targets and of distractors get an equivalent competitive bias (Desimone and Duncan, 1995). However, this model raises many new questions. Where exactly are attentional templates located? Are the attentional templates appropriate for different tasks located in distinct brain areas, or in the same brain area? How exactly is the weak competitive bias propagated from attentional templates to sensory processing areas? How are instructions translated into attentional templates? When targets and distractors are insufficiently distinct to yield automatic attentional capture, how and where does controlled, attention-demanding processing take place, and what is the role of templates in such processing? If attentional templates play no role in such controlled processing, then how do instructions yield appropriate sequences of controlled, attention-demanding processing?

Thus there have been at least three cognitive/functional conceptualizations of attention, and both neural and cognitive psychological evidence have contributed to their articulation. Based primarily on behavioral evidence, attention was first conceptualized as a processing bottleneck located somewhere between perception and motor response. Neural evidence threw doubt on this conceptualization. The brain's massively parallel processing makes the existence of such a bottleneck unlikely. This led some to reconceptualize the limited resource that stimulus information seems to compete for as the control of overt behavioral response, and the selectivity that adjudicates such competition as the result of enhancement and amplification of specific processing sites. The sources of such enhancement and amplification were thought to be multiple. Some involved top-down task-specific information, while others seemed to involve low-level visuospatial cues. Posner identified these sources of attentional enhancement as the anterior and posterior attentional networks, respectively. However, behavioral evidence suggests that Posner's division is ill motivated. Most, if not all, automatic, attentional capture by supposedly obvious visual and sensory cues is determined by top-down influences — that is, by task-specific information. Thus the distinction between a visual-cue-based posterior attentional network and a top-down task-specific anterior attentional network seems spurious. However, the distinction between automatic attentional capture and target detection that requires controlled, attentional processing still seems robust. It is reasonable to suggest that the anterior attentional network, and especially the anterior cingulate, is crucial to the latter, while the former is performed by a diversity of attentional systems associated with relevant sensory areas in something like the way proposed by Desimone and Duncan's attentional-template biased-competition theory.

Besides influencing the functional decomposition of attention, neuroscientific investigation also has influenced theories of the role of attention in the overall functional decomposition of the human cognitive system. Decomposition operates on at least two different levels in this case. The overall cognitive system is decomposed into major, component subsystems, like memory, attention, vision, reasoning, and so on. These subsystems interact in specific ways to yield the functionality of the overall system. However, these subsystems can themselves be decomposed into component operations. For example, as discussed earlier, Posner decomposes visuospatial attention into "disengage," "move," and "engage" operations. Such elementary cognitive operations need not be restricted to specific subsystems. For example, the "move" operation might contribute both to attention and to control of motoric response. In another example, very similar left dorsolateral prefrontal areas are activated in semantic encoding tasks in memory studies and in lexical processing tasks in language studies (Gabrieli, Poldrack, and Desmond, 1998). Subsystems that share component operations might, for this reason, engage in unanticipated interactions. Thus discovering that two subsystems share component operations may lead to a reconceptualization of the higher-level decomposition of the entire cognitive system.

Precisely such a reconceptualization is the topic of considerable controversy in contemporary discussions of attention. Some researchers argue that visuospatial attention actually uses many of the same component operations as the control of oculomotor response. For example, Rizzolatti and Craighero (1998) argue that there is little difference between attending to some part of the visual field and intending to focus one's eyes on it. Snyder, Batista, and Andersen (1998) dispute this. Similar questions arise about the relation between attention and spatial working memory (see Chelazzi and Corbetta, 2000). In fact, the whole question of how task demands influence attention, broached earlier, requires an investigation of the interaction between attention and working memory. Such questions can only be addressed through neuroscientifically informed research. These examples of crucial research programs in cognitive science are further evidence of the need for bottom-up constraints in the functional analysis not just of subsystems of the brain, but of the entire mind-brain.

The study and modeling of attentional processing constitute a nascent field in cognitive science. The voluminous experimental literature does not yet support a unified theory capable of garnering significant consensus among researchers. The foregoing gives a brief idea of the direction in which such research seems to be tending. The conclusions about the mechanisms of attention that we highlight are at best suggestive. However, for the purposes of this chapter, clearer and more substantial philosophical conclusions can be drawn. The functional analysis of attention qua cognitive phenomenon has undergone substantial and useful reconceptualizations as the result of neuroscientific investigation. Furthermore, such reconceptualizations would be impossible without neuroscientific investigation. A decomposition of attention based solely on an a priori, top-down task analysis could not motivate the site/source distinction, nor could it reveal that attention is more a matter of how information is processed than of what information is processed. It could not call into question the distinction between stimulus-driven and task-influenced attentional effects, nor could it suggest functional overlap between visual attention and control of oculomotor response. Such insights into the phenomenon of attention have been made possible by a complex and dynamic dialogue between neuroscientific investigation, fine-grained behavioral experimentation, and computational modeling. The traditional picture of the methodology of cognitive science, in which cognitive, functional decomposition precedes and guides neuroscientific investigation, completely uninformed by work in the neurosciences, stands revealed as an exceedingly unsophisticated framework for guiding and describing actual research on attention.

Conclusion

Gall's legacy is very much alive in the efforts in contemporary cognitive neuroscience to link cognitive functions to the brain. We have differentiated three strands in this legacy. Gall and some contemporary modularists decompose cognitive function into large-scale cognitive capacities. The second and third strands emphasize the decomposition of cognitive capacities into component information-processing operations and only seek to localize these in the brain. They differ, though, in their procedures. The second strand emphasizes a top-down approach, first using behavioral tools to decompose cognitive operations, assuming that these functions are what must be localized in the brain. The third is far more interactive, moving back and forth between behavioral tools and information about brain organization and function. Decomposition and localization are collaborators in the effort to discover the mechanism of cognition. It is the third strand that is making the greatest progress in contemporary cognitive neuroscience. We use a case study of research on attention to reveal how this dynamic interplay operates. Although the mechanisms of attention are far from being fully understood today, the progress that has been made would have been impossible without drawing on both behavioral and neuroscientific investigations.

References

Allport, D.A. 1989. "Visual Attention." Pp. 631–82 in M.I. Posner (Ed.), *Foundations of Cognitive Science*. Cambridge, MA: MIT Press.

Atkinson, R.C., and Shiffrin, R.M. 1968. "Human Memory: A Proposed System and Its Control Processes." Pp. 89–195 in K.W. Spence and J.T. Spence (Eds.), *The Psychology of Learning and Motivation*. Vol. 2, *Advances in Research and Theory*. New York: Academic Press.

Bechtel, W. Forthcoming. "Cognitive Neuroscience: Relating Neural Mechanisms and Cognition," in P. Machamer, P. McLaughlin, and R. Grush, *Philosophical Reflections on the Methods of Neuroscience*. Pittsburgh, PA: University of Pittsburgh Press.

———. 2001. "Decomposing and Localizing Vision: An Exemplar for Cognitive Neuroscience," in W. Bechtel, P. Mandik, J. Mundale, and R.S. Stufflebeam (Eds.), *Philosophy and the Neurosciences: A Reader*.

Bechtel, W., Mandik, P., and Mundale, J. Forthcoming. "Philosophy Meets the Neurosciences," in W. Bechtel, P. Mandik, J. Mundale, and R.S. Stufflebeam (Eds.), *Philosophy and the Neurosciences: A Reader*.

Bechtel, W., Mandik, P., Mundale, J., and Stufflebeam, R.S. (Eds.). 2001. *Philosophy and the Neurosciences: A Reader*. Oxford: Basil Blackwell.

Bechtel, W., and Mundale, J. 1999. "Multiple Realizability Revisited: Linking Cognitive and Neural States." *Philosophy of Science*, 66, pp. 175–207.

Bechtel, W., and Richardson, R.C. 1993. *Discovering Complexity: Decomposition and Localization as Strategies in Scientific Research*. Princeton, NJ: Princeton University Press.

Broadbent, D.E. 1958. *Perception and Communication*. London: Pergamon Press.

Broca, P.P. 1861. "Remarques sur le siège de la faculté du langage articulé; suivies d'une observation d'aphémie (perte de la parole)." *Bulletin de la Société de l'Anatomque de Paris*, 36, pp. 330–57.

Chalmers, D. 1996. *The Conscious Mind*. Oxford: Oxford University Press.

Chelazzi, L., and Corbetta, M. 2000. "Cortical Mechanisms of Visuospatial Attention in the Primate Brain." Pp. 667–86 in M.S. Gazzaniga (Ed.), *The New Cognitive Neurosciences*. Cambridge, MA: MIT Press.

Chomsky, N. 1980. "Rules and Representations." *Behavioral and Brain Sciences*, 3, pp. 1–15.

Churchland, P.M., and Churchland, P.S. 1990. "Intertheoretic Reduction: A Neuroscientist's Field Guide." *Seminars in the Neurosciences*, 2, pp. 249–56.

Clarke, E., and Jacyna, L.S. 1987. *Nineteenth-century Origins of Neuroscientific Concepts*. Berkeley: University of California Press.

Corbetta, M., Miezin, F.M., Dobmeyer, S., Shulman, G.L., and Petersen, S.E. 1991. "Selective and Divided Attention during Visual Discriminations of Shape, Color, and Speed: Functional Anatomy by Positron Emission Tomography." *Journal of Neuroscience*, 11 (8), pp. 2383–402.

Dennett, D.C. 1978. *Brainstorms*. Cambridge, MA: MIT Press.

Desimone, R., and Duncan, J. 1995. "Neural Mechanisms of Selective Visual Attention." *Annual Review of Neuroscience*, 18, pp. 193–222.

Donders, F.C. 1868/1969. "On the Speed of Mental Processes." *Acta Psychologica*, 30, pp. 412–31.

Duncan, J. 1980. "The Locus of Interference in the Perception of Simultaneous Stimuli." *Psychological Review*, 87(3), pp. 272–300.

Farah, M., and Ratcliff, G. (Eds.). 1994. *The Neuropsychology of High–Level Vision: Collected Tutorial Essays*. Hillsdale, NJ: Erlbaum.

Flourens, M.J.P. 1824. *Recherches expérimentales sur les propriétés et les fonctions du système nerveux dans les animaux vertébrés*. Paris: Crevot.

Fodor, J.A. 1974. "Special Sciences (Or: The Disunity of Science as a Working Hypothesis)." *Synthese*, 28, pp. 97–115.

———. 1983. *The Modularity of Mind*. Cambridge, MA: MIT Press.

Gabrieli, J.D.E., Poldrack, R.A., and Desmond, J.E. 1998. "The Role of Left Prefrontal Cortex in Language and Memory." *Proceedings of the National Academy of Sciences of the United States of America*, 95, pp. 906–13.

Gall, F.J., and Spurzheim, J.C. 1812. *Anatomie et physiologie du système nerveux en général, et du cerveau en particulier, avec des observations sur la possibilité de reconnaître plusieurs dispositions intellectuelles et morales de l'homme et des animaux, par la configuration de leurs têtes*. Vol. 2. Paris: F. Schoell.

———. 1825. *Revue critique de quelques ouvrages anatomico-physiologiques, et exposition d'une nouvelle philosophie des qualités morales et des facultés intellectuelles*. Vol. 6 of *Sur les fonctions du cerveau et celles de chacune de ses parties, avec des observations sur la possibilité de reconnaître les instincts, les penchans, les talens, ou les dispositions morales et intellectuelles des hommes et des animaux, par la configuration de leur cerveaux et de leurs têtes*. Paris: J.B. Baillière. English translation by Winslow Lewis, Jr. Boston: Marsh, Capen, and Lyon, 1835. [On the functions of the brain and of each of its parts. With observations on the possibility of determining the instincts, propensities, and talents, or the moral and intellectual dispositions of men and animals by the configuration of the head.]

Geschwind, N. 1974. *Selected Papers on Language and the Brain*. Dordrecht: Reidel.

Lycan, W.G. 1981. "Form, Function, Feel." *Journal of Philosophy*, 78, pp. 24–49.

Machamer, P., Darden, L., and Craver, C.F. 2000. "Thinking about Mechanisms." *Philosophy of Science*, 67, pp. 1–25.

Machamer, P., McLaughlin, P., and Grush, R. (Eds.). 2001. *Philosophical Reflections on the Methods of Neuroscience*. Pittsburgh, PA: University of Pittsburgh Press.

McCauley, R.N. (Ed.). 1996a. *The Churchlands and Their Critics*. Oxford: Basil Blackwell.

———. 1996b. "Explanatory Pluralism and the Co-evolution of Theories in Science," in R.N. McCauley (Ed.), pp. 14–47, *The Churchlands and Their Critics*. Oxford: Basil Blackwell.

Mundale, J., and Bechtel, W. 1996. "Integrating Neuroscience, Psychology, and Evolutionary Biology through a Teleological Conception of Function." *Minds and Machines*, 6, pp. 481–505.

Pinker, S. 1994. *The Language Instinct*. New York: W. Morrow and Co.

Posner, M.I. (Ed.). 1989. *Foundations of Cognitive Science.* Cambridge, MA: MIT Press.

———. 1992. "Attention as a Cognitive and Neural System." *Current Directions in Psychological Science,* 1(1), pp. 11–14.

Posner, M.I., Grossenbacher, P.G., and Compton, P.E. 1994. "Visual Attention." Pp. 217–39 in M. Farah and G. Ratcliff (Eds.), *The Neuropsychology of High-Level Vision: Collected Tutorial Essays.* Hillsdale, NJ: Erlbaum.

Posner, M.I., Walker, J.A., Friedrich, E.F., and Rafal, R.D. 1984. "Effects of Parietal Injury on Covert Orienting of Attention." *Journal of Neuroscience,* 4, pp. 1863–74.

Putnam, H. (Ed.). 1975a. *Mind, Language, and Reality: Philosophical Papers of Hilary Putnam.* Vol. 2. Cambridge: Cambridge University Press.

———. 1975b. "Philosophy and our Mental Life." Pp. 215–71 in H. Putnam (Ed.), *Mind, Language, and Reality: Philosophical Papers of Hillary Putnam.* Vol. 2. Cambridge, UK: Cambridge University Press.

Rizzolatti, G., and Craighero, L. 1998. "Spatial Attention: Mechanisms and Theories." Pp. 171–98 in M. Sabourin, F. Craik, and M. Robert (Eds.), *Advances in Psychological Science.* Vol. 2. *Biological and Cognitive Aspects.* Hove: Psychology Press.

Sabourin, M., Craik, F., and Robert, M. (Eds.). 1998. *Advances in Psychological Science.* Vol. 2, *Biological and Cognitive Aspects.* Hove, UK: Psychology Press.

Shallice, T. 1988. *From Neuropsychology to Mental Structure.* New York: Cambridge University Press.

Snyder, L.H., Batista, A.P., and Andersen, R.A. 1998. "Change in Motor Plan, without a Change in the Spatial Locus of Attention, Modulates Activity in Posterior Parietal Cortex." *Journal of Neurophysiology,* 79, pp. 2814–19.

Spence, K.W., and Spence, J.T. (Eds.). 1968. *The Psychology of Learning and Motivation: Advances in Research and Theory.* Vol. 2. New York: Academic Press.

Spurzheim, J.C. 1818. *Observations sur la phraenologie, ou la connaissance de l'homme moral et intellectuel, fondée sur les fonctions du système nerveux,* Paris: Treuttel et Wurtz.

Squire, L.R. 1987. *Memory and Brain.* New York: Oxford University Press.

Sternberg, S. 1967. "Two Operations in Character Recognition: Some Evidence from Reaction Time Experiments." *Perception and Psychophysics,* 2, pp. 45–53.

Wernicke, C. 1874. *Der aphasische Symptomcomplex: Eine psychologische Studie auf anatomischer Basis.* Breslau: Cohen und Weigert.

Yantis, Steven. 1993. "Stimulus-Driven Attentional Capture." *Current Directions in Psychological Science,* 2(5), pp. 156–61.

V

Does Evolution Provide a Key to the Scientific Study of Mind?

Introduction

Christina E. Erneling

The philosopher René Descartes claimed that human cognition was different from animal cognition because humans, but not animals, possessed thought (see Thomas Leahey's chapter in part I). Specific features of human experiences and behavior and the fact that humans were able to use language were the basis for this bifurcation between animals and humans. Descartes never denied that animals were aware of their surroundings, and that they had experiences, but he argued that they lacked reflective, thoughtful awareness of their own awareness. Furthermore, in his opinion human behavior was more flexible and creative than animal behavior. Descartes saw animals as machines that responded to their environment with reflexes. Humans, on the other hand, were able to respond creatively to novel situations by thinking about them. Finally, another reason that animals could not think as we do was that they could not think with linguistically stated propositions. This linguistic ability was, according to Descartes, innate, and it also was the basis for the acquisition of any particular language. Human cognition was unique in its self-reflection, in its creativity, and in its linguistic nature, and it could not be studied in the same way as things in the natural world.

The four chapters in this part all challenge these ideas. Stuart G. Shanker and Talbot J. Taylor argue that at least some nonhuman animals, in particular, certain sorts of apes, are also able to communicate by means of language, just like human infants. Charles Lumsden appeals to theoretical and empirical advances in evolutionary biology, especially sociobiology, to present hypotheses about how it might be possible to study subjective experience objectively. Peter Gärdenfors outlines his view of how self-awareness, free will, and linguistic communication emerged from animal cognition. Jagdish Hattiangadi goes back even further in time and traces the origin of mind from evolutionary organic changes—in particular, in the forerunners of vertebrates.

In addition, the chapters in this part (especially those of Shanker and Taylor and of Lumsden) challenge the usual dichotomy people tend to recognize today between the study of culture, on one side, and of nature, on the other. (See Rom Harré's discussion of the supposed conflict between psychology-as-one-of-the-sciences and the idea that psychology is one of the humanities in part I.) These authors argue that cultural and natural aspects of the environment have interacted in the past and continue to interact now in a dynamic way to channel the development of typically human characteristics. Nevertheless, interactions of this sort are not essentially different from activities and influences of many purely natural phenomena. Therefore, a fortiori, it is neither necessary nor appropriate for theorists and researchers to try to draw a sharp distinction between these sorts of things.

Shanker and Taylor challenge another deep-seated assumption both of the Cartesian tradition and of most of Western philosophy and psychology—the assumption of individualism. Descartes sanctified the individual, the "I" and the "I think," in his search for ultimate certainty and argued that all knowledge of the world and of the mind must begin with awareness of one's own experience as a thinking being. Influenced by views of this kind, philosophers and psychologists often have conceived of humans as isolated subjects set up against the world. For example, many of them say that language acquisition is not a social achievement, but a process in which an individual's internal and innate linguistic capacity unfolds as a result of experience, as contrasted with this capacity's being shaped by such experience. Such a view of language acquisition and human mentality is disputed by Shanker and Taylor and also to some extent by Lumsden.

Shanker and Taylor disagree with the modern version of Descartes's preformism and of individualistic-genetic determinism. Even more fundamentally, they argue that this view operates with a mistaken conception of what language is and how it is acquired. According to them, language comprehension and production are not based on an innate knowledge of the underlying structures of all human languages embedded in humans' genetic code. Instead, they are essentially interactive skills. The child—and also, in some instances, the ape—picks up communication techniques in the social and normative settings of close dyadic, interactive situations. This requires analysis not only of individual physical and biological capacities but also, most importantly, of social factors, all of which interact during development. Rejecting the bifurcation of nature and nurture— that is, between what is innate and what is learned, between animals and humans, between the individual and the environment, and between nature and culture— they reinterpret what we know both about how children learn language and about how language skills are acquired by apes like Kanzi. Thus their chapter not only is a criticism of Cartesian conceptions of mentality, but also provides an alternative starting point for answering the question of how we should approach the mind scientifically.

Similarly, Lumsden also rejects the Cartesian bifurcation between humans and animals and between the individual and the environment, especially the sociocultural aspects of such a division. He focuses his discussion on a particular aspect of the human mind that so far has eluded any scientific (i.e., objective and intersubjective) treatment, namely, subjective experience or consciousness. Although he thinks that we never will be able, as it were, to experience another individual's private subjective experience, this does not rule out the possibility that we might come up with intersubjectively testable hypotheses of how members of a particular species typically experience the world. We obtain clues for formulating such hypotheses from an understanding of the evolution of that species, because "subjectivity is considered to express the net consequences of the organism's biological history just as much as any neural, biochemical, or physiological facet of its being in the world as that individual in that species at that moment in history."

Generating hypotheses about the content of conscious experience, of subjectivity, is not easy. The conscious experience has to be objectively described and also must be consistent with what we know about biology and neurophysiology, yet be able to capture what it is to be a creature, one that has a special point of view on the universe. In cases of more complex mental activity, as in humans, the issue is complicated by what Lumsden and Wilson have termed the circuit of gene-culture coevolution, that is, the chain of reciprocal causation running from the genome through mental development to the mind and culture and back again.

Gärdenfors, like the authors just discussed, rejects the bifurcation between animal and human cognition. However, he retains and focuses on one crucial aspect of the Cartesian conception of the mind, namely, the idea that all cognition essentially involves representation. Typical forms of human cognitive activities like the exercise of free will, self-awareness, and linguistic communication have evolved in a series of small steps of increases in the power to represent the environment, each building on the previous ones. He distinguishes between what he calls cued representations, which stand for things that are present in the current external environment of the organism, and detached representations, which stand for objects and events that are neither present in the current environment nor triggered by something in it. The differences between cued and detached representations are a matter of degree, not of kind. The ability to detach representations from the current environment increases the chances of survival of the organism. Instead of slow and sometimes fatal trial-and-error processes to deal with the environment, the organism can try out various alternative actions in advance and benefit from past experience. Based on this, Gärdenfors outlines an account that links cued representations to increasingly powerful forms of detached representations as they occur in typically human forms of cognition like self-awareness, the exercise of free will, and linguistic communication.

Hattiangadi, like Lumsden and Gärdenfors, traces the evolution of subjective consciousness and representation. Instead of focusing on higher mental cognitive faculties or on sociobiological aspects, he tells a story about how physiological changes in certain forerunners of vertebrates led to their development of inner representations or maps of the environment. His hypothesis is that the mind is a combination of perception and of awareness (or dreaming, or inventing illusory moving pictures), which have different evolutionary origins. All animals possess the faculty of perception, but only a certain group—vertebrates and their forerunners—have evolved the physiological preconditions for consciousness or subjective experience. Compensating for a loss of flexibility of movement and loss of the control of neurological development, some early animals developed an internal organ that made up an internal map of the environment, enabling them to locate food to consume. His chapter is quite technical and presents evidence for this hypothesis from different biological disciplines like zoology, comparative physiology, comparative neurology, and evolutionary biology. His account is not incompatible with the approaches taken by the other authors, and ultimately a description of physiological changes will have to accompany stories told about changes on other levels.

In light of recent substantial and methodological scientific advances, it is not surprising that the chapters in this part all reject Cartesian bifurcation of the animal and human mind and also the various methodological restrictions associated with Descartes. Approaching the mind historically by looking for evolutionary roots of the mind and using new evidence from psychology, neurology, biology, and related sciences, they present hypotheses that provide new approaches to the mind as a scientific object. Unrestrained by the limitations of Cartesian assumptions, they try to account for what is central to both the scientific and our commonsense or folk psychological views of the mental—self-awareness or subjective experience, flexibility of behavior, and linguistic communication. These chapters open up exciting vistas for further research and show how many different approaches might be fruitful. They also point to ways of overcoming the bifurcation between nature and culture, or nature and convention (see also parts II, VI, and VII).

18

The Detachment of Thought

Peter Gärdenfors

The Ladder to Human Thinking

When comparing the human mind to that of other animals, several properties have been proposed as being uniquely characteristic of human thinking. We are said to be alone in having a symbolic language, a free will, self-consciousness, and a sense of humor. I do not believe, however, that a sharp border line can be drawn between human and animal cognition. Rather, human thinking has evolved away from that of our common ancestors among the primates in a series of small steps.

The main thesis in this chapter is that what characterizes the evolution of human thinking is that it shows a successively greater detachment from the current environment. In contrast, animal cognition is more entrained with the external world as it is presented to the sensory organs. I will outline the detachment of thought in a series of steps. My objective is to analyze the functions of certain aspects of cognition rather than to study their neurophysiological foundations or their behavioral correlates.

My analysis builds on distinguishing between two kinds of mental representations: cued and detached. On the basis of this distinction, I will argue that as a result of an increasing detachment of representations, a ladder of cognitive functions can be perceived. The main steps, in the order they will be presented here, are planning, deception, self-awareness, free will, and linguistic communication.

Cued versus Detached Representations

I will argue that in order to understand the functions of most of the higher forms of cognition, one must rely on an analysis of how animals represent various things, in particular, the surrounding world and its possibilities. There is an extensive debate in the literature on what is the appropriate meaning of "representation" in this context (see, e.g., Roitblat, 1982; Vauclair, 1990; Gärdenfors, 1996; and Grush, 1997). Here I will not go into the intricacies of the debate, but only point out that there are different kinds of representations. The central idea of this chapter is that in order to give an accurate analysis of many phenomena in animal and human cognition, it is necessary to distinguish between two kinds of representations: cued and detached.

A cued representation stands for something that is present in the current external situation of the representing organism. In general, the represented object need not be actually present in the actual situation, but it must have been triggered by something in a recent situation. Delayed responses, in the behaviorist's sense, are based on cued representations according to this characterization.

When, for example, a particular object is categorized as food, the animal will then act differently than if the same object had been categorized as a potential mate. I am not assuming that the animal is, in any sense, aware of the representation, only that there is some generalizing factor that determines its behavior.

In contrast, detached representations may stand for objects or events that are neither present in the current situation nor triggered by some recent situation. A memory of something that can be evoked independently of the context where the memory was created would be an example of a detached representation. Similarly, consider a chimpanzee who performs the following sequence of actions: He walks away from a termite hill, breaks a twig, peels its leaves off to make a stick, returns to the termite hill, and uses the stick to "fish" for termites. This behavior seems impossible to explain unless it is assumed that the chimpanzee has a detached representation of a stick and its use.

A distinction that is similar to that between cued and detached representations has been made by Leslie (1987), who argues that "decoupled" representations are necessary for an organism to engage in pretense. When a child pretends that a banana is a telephone, Leslie (1987, p. 415) says that the pretend representation must be "quarantined" from some of the sensory information. The perception of the banana must be complemented with information about telephones that is evoked from the child's memory. Leslie (1987, p. 416) claims that the emergence of pretense "is an early symptom of the human mind's ability to characterize and manipulate its own attitudes to information."

I am not claiming that it is possible to draw a sharp line between cued and detached representations. There are degrees of detachment, and, as will be seen later, there are different types of detachment. However, I still believe that the rough distinction between the two major kinds of representations is instrumental in that it directs our attention to key features of the representational forms.

Another caveat concerning my use of the notion of representation is that I am not making any ontological claims: I am not proposing that representations are entities with some kind of reality status.[1] Rather, I view representations as theoretical terms in the way standardly conceived of in philosophy of science (e.g., Sneed, 1971). Representations are theoretical idealizations, similar to 'forces' in Newtonian mechanics, that are introduced to predict and explain empirical generalizations (cf. Lachman and Lachman, 1982).

The Inner World

What is the main advantage of detached representations in comparison to cued ones? In order to answer this question, I will elaborate an idea introduced by Craik (1943, p. 61):

> If the organism carries a "small-scale model" of external reality and of its own possible actions within its head, it is able to try out various alternatives, conclude which are the best of them, react to future situations before they arise, utilize the knowledge of past events in dealing with the present and future, and in every way to react on a much fuller, safer and more competent manner to the emergencies which face it.

Under the heading of the inner environment, this kind of "small-scale model" has been made popular by Dennett (1986, p. 79): "The inner environment is simply any internal region that can affect and be affected by features of potential behavioral control systems." Such an environment is necessary for representing objects (like food and predators), places (where food or shelter can be found), actions (and their consequences), and so on even when these things are not perceptually present. The evolution of this kind of representational power will clearly increase the survival values of the animal. As Dennett (1981, p. 77) puts it:[2]

> Mutations equipped with such benign inner environments would have a distinct survival advantage over merely Skinnerian creatures in any exiguous environment, since they could learn faster and *more safely* (for trial and error learning is not only tedious; it can be dangerous). The advantage provided by such a benign inner environment has been elegantly expressed in a phrase of Karl Popper's: it "permits our hypotheses to die in our stead."

As a tentative definition, the inner world of an animal will be identified in this chapter with the collection of all detached representations of the animal and their interrelations. Again, I am not assuming that the animal is aware of its inner world or of the processes utilizing this construct.

It seems that many species of animals have inner worlds. For example, the searching behavior of rats is best explained if it is assumed that they have some form of "spatial maps" in their heads. Evidence for this, based on rats' abilities to find optimal paths in mazes, was collected by Tolman already in the 1930s (Tolman, 1948). However, his results were swept under the carpet for many years, since they were clear anomalies for the behaviorist paradigm. Vauclair (1987) provides a more recent analysis of the notion of a "cognitive mapping."

It is difficult to assess when detached representations first appeared in the animal kingdom, but a wild speculation is that their appearance was coordinated with the development of the neocortex, that is, roughly with the appearance of mammals. However, it is only with the development of cross-modal representations that we obtain advanced forms of an inner world (Davenport, 1976; Murray, 1990;

Allott, 1991).[3] It is interesting to note that the human language function does not reside in the same places in the brain as the call systems of the other apes (Deacon, 1992). The call systems are automatic reactions that cannot be suppressed. The development of the areas in the frontal lobes allowed language to develop as a voluntary, that is, detached, system (Barber and Peters, 1992, p. 316).

In support of the general speculation concerning the correlation between detached representations and the neocortex, one can note that mammals play, but reptiles do not (Sjölander, 1993). Playing is a way of building up a repertoire of behaviors that can be used on later occasions. However, this mechanism presupposes that the behaviors are represented in a detached way (see Gulz, 1991). Only among the mammals does one find evidence of dreaming in the form of rapid eye movements during sleep. Dreaming apparently presumes an inner world.

My aim in the remainder of this chapter is to establish that existence of an inner world is a prerequisite for the evolution of many higher cognitive functions. The functions I will consider are planning, deception, self-awareness, free will, and linguistic communication.

Immediate and Anticipatory Planning

One of the main evolutionary advantages of an inner world is that it frees an animal who is seeking a solution to a problem from dangerous trial-and-error behavior. Jeannerod (1994, p. 187) says that his general position is that "actions are driven by an internally represented goal rather than directly by the external world." By exploiting its inner world, the animal can simulate a number of different actions in order to "see" their consequences and evaluate them (also compare Grush, 1997, and Barsalou, 2000). After these simulations, it can choose the most appropriate action to perform in the outer environment. Of course, the success of the simulations depends on how well the inner world is matched to the outer. Evolutionary selection pressures will, in the long run, result in a sufficient correspondence between the two environments. As the Norwegian poet Olav Haugen writes: "Reality is a hard shore against which the wave-borne dreamer strands."

The ability to envision various actions and their consequences is a necessary requirement for an animal to be capable of planning. Following Gulz (1991, p. 46), I will use the following criterion: An animal is planning its actions if it has a representation of a goal and a start situation and is capable of generating a representation of partially ordered sets of actions for itself for getting from start to goal. This criterion presupposes representations of (1) goal and start situations, (2) sequences of actions, and (3) the outcomes of actions. The representations of the actions must be detached, otherwise the animal has no choice. In brief, planning presupposes an inner world.

There are several clear cases of planning among primates, and less clear cases in other species (see, e.g., Ellen and Thinus-Blanc, 1987, chapters 5, 7, 8, and 9, and Gulz, 1991, pp. 58–61). The termite-fishing chimpanzee mentioned earlier is one such example. By the way, this is an example of planned toolmaking.

However, as Gulz (1991) emphasizes, all evidence for planning in nonhuman animals concerns planning for present needs. Apes and other animals plan because they are hungry or thirsty, tired or frightened. Oakley (1961, p. 187) notes that "Sultan, the chimpanzee observed by Kohler, was capable of improvising tools in certain situations. Tool-making occurred only in the presence of a visible reward, and never without it. In the chimpanzee the mental range seems to be limited to present situations, with little conception of past or future."

Man seems to be the only animal that can plan for future needs. Gulz (1991, p. 55) calls planning for present needs immediate planning, while planning for the future is called anticipatory planning. Humans can predict that they will be hungry tomorrow and save some food; we realize that the winter will be cold, so we start building a shelter already in the summer. The crucial distinction is that for an animal to be capable of anticipatory planning, it must have a detached representation of its future needs. In contrast, immediate planning only requires a cued representation of the current need. There is nothing in the available evidence concerning animal planning, notwithstanding all its methodological problems, that suggests that any other species than Homo has detached representations of its desires (see Gulz, 1991, chapter 10).[4] The awareness of other animals concerns the here and now, while we are both here and in the future.

For example, apes and some other species manufacture tools for various purposes, but it seems to be only humans who transport tools over long distances. Bringing tools along is a clear indication of anticipatory planning. The carrier realizes that there may be a future need for the tool. Based on the distribution of early stone tools found in Tanzania and Kenya, Toth (1985) argues that already members of the species Homo habilis, who lived between 2.5 and 1.7 million years ago, transported their tools several kilometers. In contrast, studies of chimpanzees show that they carried their tools at most a few hundred meters, and the longest observed time lapse between the manufacturing of a tool and its use was seventeen minutes. There are thus no signs that the chimpanzees have the cognitive capacities for anticipatory planning, while already Homo habilis seems to have planned for the future.

The Human Dilemma

Why is it cognitively more difficult to plan for future needs than for present ones? When you are planning to satisfy current needs, it is necessary that you represent possible actions and their consequences in your inner world, and that the value of the consequences be determined in relation to your present need, but no separate representation of this need is required. To plan for future needs, however, it is also necessary to represent these potential needs (and realize that some of them will arise). Furthermore, the consequences of the actions you are planning to perform now must be evaluated in relation to these future needs.

From an evolutionary perspective, it appears obvious that the ability to plan for future needs is valuable. When the ability once has arisen, it will therefore spread in the population. The modern human cannot but plan for the future. The French poet Paul Valéry says in one of his aphorisms: "Man throws an arrow, tied to a rope, toward the future. It sticks in an *image* and he hauls himself toward this object."

I believe that this foresight results in a fundamental human predicament. The problem is that the actions that are appropriate for fulfilling future needs are often in conflict with those that satisfy present desires. For example, if I do not want to get cold later in the night, I should go out into the forest to look for more firewood, but right now I am warm and cozy and have no desire to leave the campfire. We must choose between acting for the present or for the future, while other animals, who presumably are not aware of their future needs, only choose for the present moment. The conflict I am presenting here is similar to the conflict between the ego and the superego in psychoanalytic theory.

There are great individual differences in how this dilemma is handled that are well illustrated by the fable about the cricket and the ant. Some people, like the ant in the fable, have difficulties living in the present, and they obtain their greatest satisfaction by planning for the future. These people set up retirement plans at the age of twenty-five. Other people have hardly any foresight at all. Like the cricket in the fable, they live from hand to mouth and do not worry about tomorrow. This disposition appears to be common among drug addicts. Using the stern terminology of economists, one could say that people of this kind are discounting the future very rapidly.

The conflict between the present and the future self is closely related to what Kirkegaard calls "despair" in his book *The Sickness unto Death*. He describes the unavoidable human dilemma in the following way:

> However much . . . the despairer has succeeded in altogether losing his self, and in such a way that the loss is not in the least way noticeable, eternity will nevertheless make it evident that this condition is that of despair, and will nail him to his self so that the torment will still be that he cannot be rid of his self, and it will be evident that he cannot be rid of his self, and it will be evident that his success was an illusion. And this eternity must do, because having a self, being a self, is the greatest, the infinite, concession that has been made to man, but also eternity's claim on him. (Kirkegaard, 1849/1989, p. 51)

Kirkegaard also points out that the kind of "sickness" that despair constitutes is unique for human beings:

> The possibility of this sickness is man's advantage over the beast, and it is an advantage which characterizes him quite otherwise than the upright posture, for it bespeaks the infinite erectness or loftiness of his being spirit. (Kirkegaard, 1849/1989, pp. 44–45)

Deception

I want to analyze the evolution of self-consciousness as a series of comparatively small steps. A good planner must consider the actions of other individuals (in particular, if the planner belongs to a social species). A special case of representations in the inner world concerns the minds of other individuals. In my opinion, the first step in the evolution of self-awareness is *you-awareness*, that is, when other agents are not only seen as acting things, but as having an inner world of their own, with beliefs, desires, and so on.

It is only when this representational capacity is accomplished that deliberate deception becomes possible. Deception, in its intentional sense, presumes a representation of other minds. To see this, let us turn to the worthwhile survey of tactical deception in primates written by Whiten and Byrne (1988). After their initial attempt to define "tactical deception" was criticized in the commentary, they ended up with the following definition: "Acts from the normal repertoire of the AGENT, deployed such that another individual is likely to misinterpret what the acts signify, to the advantage of the AGENT" (1988, p. 271). The key word in this definition is "deployed." When this word refers to human behavior, it refers to an intentional act. I submit that this use of deception presupposes that the deceiver has some representation of how the individual to be deceived will interpret the deceiving act. In other words, deception presupposes that the inner world of the deceiver contains some form of representation of the inner world of the target individual. This is a special case of having what is called a "theory of mind." Note that deception presumes all the cognitive functions of (immediate) planning and some more, that is, an inner world containing a model of the inner world of other individuals. Thus this analysis predicts that deception will occur later than planning in the evolution of cognitive functions.[5]

Most of the examples in Whiten and Byrne's survey come from field observations of chimpanzees and baboons. For instance, Byrne (1995, p. 124) presents the following case concerning the foraging of baboons, where a juvenile uses a special tactic to obtain food from an adult animal:

> The juvenile, named Paul, came across an adult female, Mel, just finishing the laborious process of digging up a corm. These were major sources of nutrition at that very dry, cold time of the year, but difficult to obtain from the hard ground; Paul was probably unable to dig his own. He looked around, seeing no other baboon, and screamed loudly. His mother, who was higher ranking than Mel, ran into view grunting aggressively and immediately pursued Mel. When they had both left the immediate area, Paul ate the corm.

One interpretation of this behavior is that Paul imagines that if he screams, his mother will think that Mel has hurt Paul and then chase Mel away so that Paul can eat the corm. If this interpretation is correct, Paul's behavior will be a case of intentional deception involving a model of the inner world of another animal. However, there is another, weaker interpretation where Paul's behavior is seen as a case of trial and error, and thus not intentional deception. If this kind of behavior is successful the first time it is tried, Paul will be more likely to repeat it in the future. If this interpretation is the correct one, his behavior is an example of conditioning that does not involve any representation of the inner world of another individual.

Unfortunately, almost all evidence concerning potential deception is based on more or less anecdotal material. Without controlled experiments, it is therefore strongly debatable whether the evidence can establish that deception in the intentional sense occurs among other animals than humans.[6] Heyes (1998) has criticized the strong interpretations and claims that there is no clear-cut evidence that apes or monkeys have any "theory of mind," but the debate is still going on. Primatologists have countered Heyes's analysis. Byrne (1995, pp. 132–34) claims, for example, that there are cases of counter-deception that cannot be explained unless intentional deception is involved.

Self-Awareness

Deception in the full intentional sense presupposes that the deceiver has a representation of the dupe's inner world. On this level, an animal can have goals concerning the intentions of other individuals, for example, can want somebody to believe that an attack would fail. This is an example of a second-order intention.

But a smart agent will not be duped: He will realize that somebody is trying to deceive him and will counteract. Hence the really smart deceiver will foresee the reasoning of such a smart agent (cf. Dennett, 1988). The important aspect of this escalation in smartness is that it can only work if the deceiver-to-be realizes that the agent he wants to deceive not only has his or her own representations of the external world, but his or her inner world contains a representation of the deceiver himself.

Do animals other than humans have self-awareness? Gallup's (1977) experiments show that chimpanzees and orangutans, but no other primates, can recognize themselves in mirrors.[7] When it comes to recognizing oneself in a photograph, only chimpanzees have been successful.

But recognizing oneself in a mirror or in a photograph only requires awareness of one's own body, not of one's own mind. The final step in the evolution of higher-level inner representation is small but crucial for self-awareness in its proper sense: I must realize that the inner world of my opponent contains a representation of myself not only as a bodily agent, but as an agent with inner representations as well. I believe that it is only after this insight that the agent can become self-conscious in the sense that it can form representations of its own representations.

In other words, self-awareness can then develop as a shortcut in the representations involved in the deception game: In my inner world, I can have a detached representation of my own inner world. The most important aspect of this form of detachment is that I can attend to different aspects of my inner world and use this attention in my planning. Other animals can only attend to the external world as it is represented to them. In particular, I can attend to my own feelings and desires and form a representation of how these feelings could be different.

However, I submit that this kind of self-awareness never could develop without the previous establishment of a representation of the inner world of other individuals. In other words, I claim that an "I" experience must be preceded by a "you" experience.

Free Will

There is a strong connection between the possibility of a free will and the capability to plan for future needs. Harry Frankfurt (1971) proposes in a classic article with the title "Freedom of the Will and the Concept of a Person" that a necessary condition for an individual to be a person is that he or she not only wants something, but also wants to want it. Frankfurt calls such wishes "second order wants."

When we reflect upon our choices, we are often, but not always, satisfied with them. For example, a smoker frequently wishes that he or she did not want to smoke. In such a case, a (first-order) wish to smoke is in conflict with a second-order wish not to smoke. What is called akrasia or weakness of the will is precisely a conflict where the first-order desire wins. Many animals have a will, but presumably only humans can ponder on their wishes and want them to be different. It is essential to note that such reflections presume that agents have detached representations of their own wishes.

Animals who plan can choose, in the sense that they can image different actions and their consequences in their inner worlds and then perform the action that is judged to lead to the best consequences, but this does not entail that they have a free will. In his analysis, Frankfurt demands that to have a free will, it is not sufficient that one can choose, but it must also be the case that one should be capable of choosing one's will, that is, be able to fulfill one's second-order desires. In other words, one is free to have the will one wants. A drug addict who repeatedly succumbs to his cravings does not have a free will in this sense.

Having a free will presupposes a form of self-awareness in the sense that one must be aware of one's desires to be capable of wanting to have another desire. Kirkegaard expresses the connection in the following way: "In general, what is decisive with regard to the self is consciousness, that is to say self-consciousness. The more consciousness, the more will; the more will, the more self. Someone who has no will at all is no self. But the more will he has, the more self-consciousness he has too." (1849/1989, p. 59).

The question now is: What is the evolutionary value of being able to choose one's own will, of being able to abstain from what you currently want? The answer, as always, is that a free will increases our fitness. Our desires have been molded during an extended evolutionary process, where many of the ecological conditions were different from what they are nowadays. If we can choose our will, we can better adjust to the new circumstances. To take an everyday example, food rich in sugar content has been scarce during most of the time humans have existed.

Since such food is rich in energy, we have developed a craving for ripe fruits and other things rich in sugar. In our modern world, we are rather confronted with a profusion of sugar, and in the long run overconsumption of it is detrimental to our health. People who can let a second-order want control their behavior and choose not to consume excessive amounts of sugar presumably will have a slightly higher evolutionary fitness than those who succumb to the temptations. In this way, one can, for good or for bad, let one's wisdom take power over one's desires.

Free will is necessary for responsibility. Being responsible means that one can realize the potential consequences of the actions one chooses and can realize that one can behave differently. Small children and animals are not responsible, since they do not have this capability. (This does not mean that they cannot learn to avoid undesirable behavior.) Similarly, morality presupposes a free will. Formulating and obeying a moral rule require that one has detached representations of one's goals and desires, and that one can let the detached goal of the moral rule override one's current desires.

Linguistic Communication

Thinking does not presume a language. Humans, as well as animals, can simulate sequences of actions in their inner worlds. Such simulations are, among other things, necessary for planning. Language is, in my opinion, a very late phenomenon on the evolutionary scene. As I have tried to show in the previous sections, an individual can have a great many cognitive functions, including self-awareness and free will, without having a symbolic language.[8]

Against this position, it can be argued that we all have the experience of something like an omnipresent inner monologue (or dialogue) while we are engaged in thinking. I believe, however, that this experience is deceptive. First, we can "think" without language. Consider, for example, the mental simulation of a slalom skier or a high jumper. Second, and more important, the inner speech is best interpreted as just parts of the simulations in the inner environment. The inner soliloquy is part of what we perceive in the inner environment (see Gärdenfors, 1995).

In contrast, I believe that language presumes the existence of an intricate inner world. In order to make this clear, I will introduce a distinction between signals and symbols. Both signals and symbols are tools of communication. The fundamental difference between them is that the reference of a symbol is a detached representation, while a signal refers to a cued representation. In other words, a signal refers to something in the outer environment, while a symbol refers to the inner world. Language consists of symbols — it can be used to talk about things not present in the current situation. This idea can be traced back to Hockett's (1960) notion of "displacement." Glasersfeld (1977, p. 64) expresses the point as follows:

> We can talk not only about things that are spatially or temporally remote,
> but also about things that have no location in space and never happen

at all. . . . [I]n order to become a symbol, the sign must be detached from input. What the sign signifies, i.e., its meaning, has to be available, regardless of the contextual situation.

With few exceptions, linguistic communication is achieved with the aid of symbols. Sjölander (1993, pp. 5–6) explains elegantly what is missing in animal communication:

> The predominant function of language is to communicate about that which is not here and not now. A dog can "say": I am angry, I want water, I want to go out, I like you, etc. But it has no communicative means enabling it to "say": I was angry yesterday, nor can it "say": I will be angry if you lock me up tonight again, and I will chew up the carpet. Likewise, the dog can "say": There is a rat here! but it cannot "say": There is a rat in the next room. . . .
>
> Clearly, if you live in the present, communicating mainly about how you feel and what you want to do in the moment, the biological signals inherent in each species are sufficient. A language is needed only to communicate your internal representation of what could be, what has been, and of those things and happenings that are not present in the vicinity.

A similar characterization can be found in Glasersfeld (1977, pp. 63–65), who traces the idea back to Langer (1948). This last author clearly distinguishes symbols from signals:

> A term which is used symbolically and not signally does *not* evoke action appropriate to the presence of its object. . . . Symbols are not proxy for their objects, but are *vehicles for the conception of objects.* To conceive a thing or a situation is not the same as to "react toward it" overtly, or to be aware of its presence. In talking about things we have conceptions of them, not the things themselves; and *it is the conceptions, not the things, that symbols directly "mean."* Behavior toward conceptions is what words normally evoke: this is the typical process of thinking. (Langer, 1948, p. 61)

Symbols referring to something in one person's inner world can be used to communicate as soon as the listeners have, or are prepared to add, the corresponding references in their inner worlds.[9] The actual conditions of the outer situation need not play any role for the communication to take place: Two prisoners can talk fervently about life on a sunny Pacific island in the pitch dark of their cell.

Following Peirce's (1931) trichotomy of signs (which he calls indices, icons, and symbols where indices correspond to what is called signals here), the role of icons can be characterized as follows: Like symbols, icons refer to detached representations, but unlike symbols, the choice of representation is not arbitrary. On the contrary, an icon in some aspects resembles the thing it represents.

Many animals have intricate systems of signals, for example, the dances of bees. However, even if their dances seem to have a kind of gr_____ ___r, it still consists only of signals. The bees categorize, in a sophisticated way, __ ____ where nectar can be found. The crucial point is that they only use their da___ s in a situated manner, and thus the dances are not symbols according to my crite___n. The same point is made by Glasersfeld (1976, p. 222): "In my terms, the ____s do not qualify for symbolicity, because they have never been observed to communicate about distances, directions, food sources, etc., without actually coming from, or going to, a specific location."

In spite of all attempts to teach apes various forms of symbolic codes (see, e.g., Savage-Rumbaugh, Shanker, and Taylor, 1998), humans seem to be the only animals that use language in a fully detached way. Even though the pygmy chimpanzee Kanzi's performance is quite impressive, his use of symbols is dependent on the context: They mainly express requests to "direct teacher's attention to places, things and activities" (Savage-Rumbaugh, Rumbaugh, and Macdonald, 1985, p. 658). Human children, in contrast, very early use language outside the context of request. Vauclair (1990, p. 319) notes that "the use of symbols by apes is closely tied to the achievement of immediate goals, because the referents occur in the context of behavior on their objects." This is congenial with Gulz' (1991) conclusion that only humans are anticipatory planners. My conjecture is that this capability is required for the complete detachment of language. We are still waiting for Kanzi to tell us a story by the campfire.

The fact that a language consists of symbols referring to detached representations is a necessary, but far from sufficient, condition to separate language from other forms of communication. I next turn to what needs to be added to this condition.

The first thing to notice is that human linguistic communication presumes an advanced kind of inner world. To see this, let us turn to Grice's (1957, 1969) theory of meaning. His initial definition in the second article reads as follows (1969, p. 151):[10]

"U meant something by uttering x" is true if, for some audience A, U uttered x intending

(1) A to produce a particular response r.
(2) A to think (recognize) that U intends (1).
(3) A to fulfill (1) on the basis of his fulfillment of (2).

Although Grice defines "meaning," I am more interested in applying the definition to linguistic communication in general. The feature I want to focus on here is that condition 2 expresses a third-order intention (Dennett, 1981, pp. 277–78): U intends A to think that U intends something. Gomez (1994, p. 68) claims that a truly requestive situation like "May I have some salt, please?" even involves a fifth-order level of intentionality: U wants A to understand that she wants him to understand that she wants the salt.[11] The upshot is, if I am correct, that a full-blown linguistic communication presumes a mind that is capable of you-awareness as well as self-awareness. A consequence of this is that language, in the normal sense, is most likely a very recent phenomenon in the evolution of thinking.

The Role of Grammar

There are forms of communication that do not involve a grammatical structure. Bickerton (1990, p. 122) calls such a simplified mode of language a protolanguage and argues that "there is a mode of linguistic expression that is quite separate from normal human language and is shared by four classes of speakers: trained apes, children under two, adults who have been deprived of language in their early years, and speakers of pidgin." However, he never defines what constitutes protolanguage, but only characterizes it negatively by comparing it to ordinary language. He presents five types of differences: Protolanguage is less ordered than ordinary language; it contains no null elements;[12] it does not always respect the valence relations of verbs; it does not allow expansion of utterances; and it contains hardly any grammatical items (Bickerton, 1990, pp. 122–26).

As regards the evolutionary timing of the transition from protolanguage to language, several authors (Bickerton, 1990; Donald, 1991; Lieberman, 1992) speculate that this is essentially concurrent with the transition from *Homo erectus* to *Homo sapiens* (on the order of 200,000 years ago). One of the anatomical changes that occur in this transition between the two species is the lowering of the larynx, which clearly is connected with the development of a spoken language (Lieberman, 1992).

So whence grammar? As human societies grew more complex, speed and efficiency in communication were rewarded. Barber and Peters (1992, p. 311) argue that

> [t]he need for fast and efficient processing is thus a major force that drives language away from iconicity and toward systematicity — and this in turn drives language toward arbitrariness . . . , for the following reason. In the long run it is less effort to deal with a tightly patterned system with a small number of reusable parts (both items and rules) than to deal with a sprawling system with many, many unique parts. But the reduction to reusable parts and patterns destroys most of the iconicity . . . , and at the same time compresses a great deal more information into a small number of rules: it radically increases the "depth" of the system while decreasing the algorithmic complexity.[13]

A similar point is made by Savage-Rumbaugh and Rumbaugh (1993, pp. 86–87), who note the need for communication that is independent of context as one of the evolutionary forces behind the development of grammar:

> It will also be argued that syntax, rather than being biologically predetermined, is a skill which arises naturally from the need to process se-

quences of words rapidly. As overall intelligence increased, spurred by the ever-increasing use of language for planning future activities, communications became increasingly complex and increasingly independent of context. When complex ideas began to require groups of words for their expression, it became essential to devise a means to specify which of the words in a group modified (or were related to) which other words. Syntactical rules were developed to solve this dilemma. Such rules were the inevitable outgrowth of complex symbolic communication involving multiple symbols.

Adding grammar to a communication system thus increases its efficiency. For a neuroscientist, the question is in what way the brain must change in order to achieve this capacity. It seems that the grammaticality of language has probably not evolved as an independent cognitive ability (in contrast to Chomsky's claims concerning a "language acquisition device"). Rather, it could build on already existing structures, since it seems to be tied to a more general capability of combining actions into sequences. Neurologically, sequencing is typically lateralized to the left hemisphere in humans. Corballis (1989) argues that in the course of evolution, sequencing emerged in the left hemisphere and was essential for tool-making and other practical skills.[14] In order to reproduce or create a tool, a sequence of actions had to be performed, and old elements of action sequences had to be recombined to produce something new. This practical, mainly manual ability forms the basis for all kinds of sequencing and was extended to sequencing of symbols, which then resulted in a grammatical language. Also, playing involves sequences of motor actions performed on symbolically used objects (see Vauclair and Vidal, 1994). Remember that Jean Piaget has always emphasized that play and imitation are cardinal for the development of symbolic capacities. Apes seem to lack the sequencing capability, which could explain why they are bad at imitating action sequences and why they never invent new forms of play, as well as why they cannot learn more than a protolanguage.[15]

Conclusion

In this chapter, I have outlined the evolution of human thinking as a series of steps, where each step has been characterized in terms of the representational capacities of the organism. My presentation has been based on the distinction between cued and detached representations.

The inner world of an animal has been defined as the collection of all its detached representations. I have argued that the notion of an inner world must serve as a basis for all higher cognitive functions like planning, deception, self-awareness, free will, and language. My main thesis is that the general trend in the evolution of cognition is that more and more representations become detached. In other words, I view the evolution of cognition as the story of the detachment of thought.

Let me conclude with an analogy. When the early humans learned to carry water with them in vessels, their freedom to explore and to occupy new territories was greatly expanded and they could spread around the world. In the same way, when humans learned to carry the environment with them in their inner worlds, their freedom was further extended and with the aid of anticipatory planning they could, to some extent, occupy the future. This has led to increasing cognitive flexibility, but also to the human dilemma involved in weighing one's present desires against the needs that are predicted for the future.

Notes

1. Roitblat (1982, p. 359) seems to make this kind of claim in his response to the commentary: "Representations have exactly the same ontological status as genes. . . . Genes, though not 'observed,' were proposed as *things*; their status was, and remains, that of a theoretical construct."

2. For further arguments on the evolutionary value of the inner environment, see Sjölander, 1993, pp. 4–6.

3. Murray (1990) argues that the amygdala is crucial for cross-modal sensory-sensory associations.

4. But isn't the squirrel who is gathering and storing food for the winter engaged in anticipatory planning? No, it is not planning at all. It has no representation of the winter, in spite of its needs at that time.

5. This thesis is most naturally interpreted as a statement about phylogeny, but can also be given an ontogenetic meaning.

6. However, there are cases when it is clear that deception is not taking place: The partridge feigning a broken wing to lure away the fox from her chickens is not fooling the fox. "Fooling" presumes an intention to make somebody else misinterpret the fooling act. There is no evidence that the partridge has any representation of what the fox thinks. She merely acts instinctively when the fox approaches, and hence cannot have any intention to fool.

7. Epstein, Lanza, and Skinner (1980) performed a similar experiment intending to show that pigeons also can learn the same kind of behavior. Davis (1989) argues, in my opinion convincingly, that their experiment does not show that pigeons have any form of self-awareness.

8. A similar point is made by Donald (1991).

9. For a model theoretic account of how such communication can be established, see Gärdenfors, 1993.

10. This definition is revised several times in the second article, but the more complicated versions have the same general structure as the definition given here.

11. However, he also claims that the mutuality of intentional communication can be achieved by "attention contact" without metarepresentations of the inner environment of the other (Gomez, 1994, p. 73).

12. "Null element" is a syntactic notion referring to places in a sentence where one can infer (using government and binding theory) that some constituent should be present, but where there is no explicit constituent.

13. Ellegård (1979, p. 142) speaks about the "double articulation" of language and remarks concerning the evolution of grammar: "My hypothesis is thus that the double

articulation of human speech emerged as a necessary consequence of the increasing number of signs, and the increasing demands for fast and more or less automatized production. The reaction of the brain toward these demands was the double articulation in phonemes and morphemes" (my translation).

14. See also Allott, 1991, and Tomasello, 1991.

15. See also Barber and Peters, 1992, p. 344 and Donald, 1991, pp. 70–75. On the other hand, Bickerton (1990, p. 139) argues that "it is tool-making and *protolanguage* that share the same processes."

References

Allott, R. 1991. "The Motor Theory of Language." Pp. 123–57 in W. von Raffler-Engel, J. Wind, and A. Jonker (Eds.), *Studies in Language Origins*. Vol. 2. Amsterdam: John Benjamins.

Barber, E.J.W., and Peters, A.M.W. 1992. "Ontogeny and Phylogeny: What Child Language and Archeology Have to Say to Each Other." Pp. 305–51 in J.A. Hawkins and M. Gell-Mann (Eds.), *The Evolution of Human Languages*. Redwood City, CA: Addison-Wesley.

Barsalou, L.W. 2000. "Perceptual Symbol Systems." *Behavioral and Brain Sciences*, 22(4), pp. 577–660.

Bickerton, D. 1990. *Language and Species*. Chicago: University of Chicago Press.

Byrne, R. 1995. *The Thinking Ape: Evolutionary Origins of Intelligence*. Oxford: Oxford University Press.

Corballis, M.C. 1989. "Laterality and Human Evolution." *Psychological Review* 96, pp. 492–505.

Craik, K. 1943. *The Nature of Explanation*. Cambridge, UK: Cambridge University Press.

Davenport, R.K. 1976. "Cross-Modal Perception in Apes." Pp. 143–49 in S.R. Harnad, H.D. Staklis, and J. Lancaster (Eds.), *Origins and Evolution of Language and Speech*, 280. New York: New York Academy of Sciences.

Davis, L.H. 1989. "Selfconsciousness in Chimps and Pigeons." *Philosophical Psychology*, 2, pp. 249–59.

Deacon, T.W. 1992. "Brain-Language Coevolution." Pp. 49–83 in J.A. Hawkins and M. Gell-Mann (Eds.), *The Evolution of Human Languages*. Redwood City, CA: Addison-Wesley.

Dennett, D. 1981. *Brainstorms: Philosophical Essays on Mind and Psychology*. Cambridge, MA: MIT Press.

———. 1988. "Why Creative Intelligence Is Hard to Find." *Behavioral and Brain Sciences*, 11, p. 253.

Donald, M. 1991. *Origins of the Modern Mind*. Cambridge, MA: Harvard University Press.

Ellegård, A. 1979. "Om det mänskliga språkets ursprung." Pp. 131–47 in *Kungliga Vitterhets, Historie, och Antikvitets Akademiens Årsbok*. Stockholm.

Ellen, P., and Thinus-Blanc, C. (Eds.). 1987. *Cognitive Processes and Spatial Orientation in Animal and Man*. Vol. 1, *Experimental Animal Psychology and Ethology*. Dordrecht: Martinus Nijhoff.

Epstein, R., Lanza, R.P., and Skinner, B.F. 1980. "Self-Awareness in the Pigeon." *Science, 212*, pp. 695–96.

Frankfurt, H. 1971. "Freedom of the Will and the Concept of a Person." *Journal of Philosophy, 68*, pp. 5–20.

Gallup, G.G. 1977. "Self-Recognition in Primates." *American Psychologist, 32*, pp. 329–38.

Gärdenfors, P. 1992. "Medvetandets Evolution" [The evolution of consciousness]. Chapter 5 in Gärdenfors, *Blotta tanken*. Nora: Doxa.

———. 1993. "The Emergence of Meaning." *Linguistics and Philosophy, 16*, pp. 285–309.

———. 1995. "Speaking about the Inner Environment," in S. Allén (Ed.), *Of Thoughts and Words*, London: Imperial College Press, pp. 143–151.

———. 1996. "Cued and Detached Representations in Animal Cognition." *Behavioural Processes, 36*, pp. 263–73.

Gibson, K.R., and Ingold, T. (Eds.). 1993. *Tools, Language, and Cognition in Human Evolution*. Cambridge, UK: Cambridge University Press.

Glasersfeld, E. von. 1976. "The Development of Language as Purposive Behavior." Pp. 212–26 in S.R. Harnad, H.D. Steklis, and J. Lancaster (Eds.), *Origins and Evolution of Language and Speech*. New York: New York Academy of Sciences.

———. 1977. "Linguistic Communication: Theory and Definition." Pp. 55–71 in D.M. Rumbaugh (Ed.), *Language Learning by a Chimpanzee: The LANA Project.* New York: Academic Press.

Gomez, J.C. 1994. "Mutual Awareness in Primate Communication: A Gricean Approach." Pp. 61–80 in S.T. Parker, R.W. Mitchell, and M.L. Boccia (Eds.), *Self-Awareness in Animals and Humans*. Cambridge, UK: Cambridge University Press.

Grice, H.P. 1957. "Meaning." *Philosophical Review, 66*, pp. 377–88.

———. 1969. "Utterer's Meaning and Intentions." *Philosophical Review, 78*, pp. 147–77.

Grush, R. 1997. "The Architecture of Representation." *Philosophical Psychology, 10*, pp. 5–23.

Gulz, A. 1991. *The Planning of Action as a Cognitive and Biological Phenomenon.* Lund: Lund University Cognitive Studies.

Harnad, S.R., Steklis, H.D., and Lancaster, J. (Eds.). 1976. *Origins and Evolution of Language and Speech*. New York: New York Academy of Sciences.

Hawkins, J.A., and Gell-Mann, M. (Eds.). 1992. *The Evolution of Human Languages.* Redwood City, CA: Addison-Wesley.

Heyes, C. 1998. "Theory of Mind in Nonhuman Primates." *Behavioral and Brain Sciences, 21*, pp. 101–15.

Hockett, C.F. 1960. "The Origin of Speech." *Scientific American, 203*(3), pp. 88–96.

Jeannerod, M. 1994. "The Representing Brain, Neural Correlates of Motor Intention, and Imagery." *Behavioral and Brain Sciences, 17*, pp. 187–202.

Kesner, R.P., and Olton, D.S. (Eds.). 1990. *Neurobiology of Comparative Cognition.* Hilldale, NJ: Lawrence Erlbaum Associates.

Kirkegaard, S. 1849/1989. *The Sickness unto Death.* London: Penguin Classics.

Lachman, R., and Lachman, J.L. 1982. "Memory Representations in Animals: Some Metatheoretical Issues." *Behavioral and Brain Sciences, 5*, pp. 380–81.

Langer, Susanne, K. 1948. *Philosophy in a New Key: A Study in the Symbolism of Reason, Rite, and Art.* Cambridge, MA: Harvard University Press.

Leslie, A.M. 1987. "Pretense and Representation: The Origins of 'Theory of Mind.'" *Psychological Review,* 94, pp. 412–26.

Lieberman, P. 1992. "On the Evolution of Human Language." Pp. 21–47 in J.A. Hawkins and M. Gell-Mann (Eds.), *The Evolution of Human Languages.* Redwood City, CA: Addison-Wesley.

Murray, E.A. 1990. "Representational Memory in Nonhuman Primates." Pp. 127–55 in R.P. Kesner and D.S Olton (Eds.), *Neurobiology of Comparative Cognition.* Hillsdale, NJ: Lawrence Erlbaum Associates.

Oakley, K.P. 1961. "On Man's Use of Fire, with comments on Tool-making and Hunting." Pp. 176–93 in S.L. Washburn (Ed.), *Social Life of Early Man.* Chicago: Aldine Publishing Co.

Parker, S.T., and Gibson, K.R. (Eds.). 1990. *"Language" and Intelligence in Monkeys and Apes.* Cambridge, UK: Cambridge University Press.

Parker, S.T., Mitchell, R.W., and Boccia, M.L. (Eds.). 1994. *Self-Awareness in Animals and Humans.* Cambridge, UK: Cambridge University Press.

Peirce, C.S. 1931. *Collected Papers of Charles Sanders Peirce.* Edited by Hartshorne, Weiss, and Burks. Cambridge, MA: Harvard University Press.

Roitblat, H.L. 1982. "The Meaning of Representation in Animal Memory." *Behavioral and Brain Sciences,* 5, pp. 353–72.

Rumbaugh, D.M. (Ed.). 1977. *Language Learning by a Chimpanzee: The LANA Project.* New York: Academic Press.

Savage-Rumbaugh, E.S., and Rumbaugh, D.M. 1993. "The Emergence of Language." Pp. 86–108 in K.R. Gibson and T. Ingold (Eds.), *Tools, Language, and Cognition in Human Evolution.* Cambridge, UK: Cambridge University Press.

Savage-Rumbaugh, E.S., Rumbaugh, D.M, and McDonald, K. 1985. "Language Learning in Two Species of Apes." *Neuroscience and Biobehavioral Reviews* 9, pp. 653–65.

Savage-Rumbaugh, E.S., Shanker, S.G., and Taylor, T.J. 1998. *Apes, Language, and the Human Mind.* New York: Oxford University Press.

Sjölander, S. 1993. "Some Cognitive Breakthroughs in the Evolution of Cognition and Consciousness, and Their Impact on the Biology of Language." *Evolution and Cognition,* 3, pp. 1–10.

Sneed, J. 1971. *The Logical Structure of Mathematical Physics.* Dordrecht: Reidel.

Stadler, M. 1989. "On Learning Complex Procedural Knowledge." *Journal of Experimental Psychology: Learning, Memory, and Cognition,* 15, pp. 1061–69.

Tolman, E.C. 1948. "Cognitive Maps in Rats and Men." *Psychological Review,* 55, pp. 189–208.

Tomasello, M. 1991. "Processes of Communication in the Origins of Language." Pp. 85–97 in W. von Raffler-Engel, J. Wind, and A. Jonker (Eds.), *Studies in Language Origins,* Vol. 2. Amsterdam: John Benjamins.

Toth, N.S. 1985. "Oldowan Reassessed: A Close Look at Early Stone Artifacts." *Journal of Archaeological Science,* 12, pp. 101–20.

Vauclair, J. 1987. "A Comparative Approach to Cognitive Mapping." Pp. 89–96 in P. Ellen and C. Thinus-Blanc, (Eds.) *Cognitive Processes and Spatial Orientation in Animal and Man,* Vol. 1, *Experimental Animal Psychology and Ethology.* Dordrecht: Martinus Nijhoff.

———. 1990. "Primate Cognition: From Representation to Language." Pp. 312–29 in

S.T. Parker and K.R. Gibson (Eds.), *"Language" and Intelligence in Monkeys and Apes*. Cambridge, UK: Cambridge University Press.

Vauclair, J., and Vidal, J.-M. Forthcoming. "Discontinuities in the Mind between Animals and Humans." Paper presented at the conference on "Cognition and Evolution," Berder, March, 1994.

von Raffler-Engel, W., Wind, J., and Jonker, A. (Eds.). 1991. *Studies in Language Origins*. Vol. 2. Amsterdam: John Benjamins.

Washburn, S.L. (Ed.). 1961. *Social Life of Early Man*. Chicago: Aldine Publishing Co.

Whiten, A., and Byrne, R.W. 1988. "Tactical Deception in Primates." *Behavioral and Brain Sciences*, 11, pp. 233–73.

19

The Mind as an Object
of Scientific Study

Jagdish Hattiangadi

This chapter is an attempt to study qualia and to show that some factual issues arising in biology are relevant to it. This very claim gives the project an unhealthy air of paradox. After all, one may say, the word *quale* and its plural *qualia* were introduced into philosophy as technical terms precisely in order to capture that aspect of an experience that escapes the scrutiny of any natural science. A quale picks out a first-person aspect of an experience whereas any natural science deals with third-person descriptions of its objects of study. How can there be a scientific study of qualia?

The general strategy of this chapter is not to focus on the ontic status of qualia so much as on the person or the animal having the experience at first hand. These, you will allow, can be studied physically, chemically, and biologically. I suggest that such a study will shed some light on metaphysics in what may seem antecedently to be an unlikely way.

Thomas Nagel (1974), in a famous article, suggests that after natural science has described bats as exhaustively as you like, there remains an unanswered question, "What is it like to be a bat?" There are two aspects to the world, mysteriously coexistent, an internal aspect, to be described in the first person ("the bat's perspective of the world"), and an external aspect, to be described in the third person ("the natural science of bats"). This dualism is reminiscent of Kant's conclusions along the same lines. Kant thought that if we were to study the world under the Principle of Causality, we would have nothing left to know about the mechanism of nature, that is, everything would be fully predictable. The possibility of human freedom and the possibility of acting for reasons and purposes, however, would not be found in the universe as described there (Kant, 1781, "Third Antinomy"). But Kant thought that this only left us with the most difficult problem we face, "Why is the world intelligible?" Why do we understand each other and act in accordance with reasons and ends if we are physical things (Kant, 1790)?

Other solutions are also possible that can evade Kant's and Nagel's mystery, though each seems to most philosophers to be unlikely to be right. I will be pursuing one of them. The difficulty that we need to avoid is the following (in deference to Nagel's spirited and thoughtful defense of Kant's dualism, in the following summary argument, I have let the word "bats" stand for any being that supports conscious experience):

1. Qualia presuppose that bats exist as irreducible wholes, as their possessors.
2. Bats are wholly realized as physical structures.
3. All physically realized things are fully physically reducible to their respective elements.

These claims are not tenable together. Let us first reject the Cartesian option. If one rules out two bats in one spot, whereby one bat is reducible to microphysical structure, but the other bat, which is presupposed by the qualia possessed by bats, is irreducible (or ghostlike, thereby denying lemma 2), the following courses are left open for us to pursue:

A. Find qualia among, or as properties of, the elements (i.e., deny lemma 1).
B. Show how irreducible wholes may emerge from the elements (i.e., deny lemma 3).

I will be exploring B in my account, a doctrine I will call "emergent scientific realism."

If we pursue the first strategy, then we are stuck with the enigmatic ontological status of qualia because the query "If qualia presuppose whole bats, but bats have no properties that are not reducible to properties of its parts, then where are qualia found among the bat's neurons?" becomes an insoluble problem, since qualia are not properties of parts of bats at all, but of the whole bat. By taking up the second route to the problem in what follows we can avoid having to deal with that kind of ontological difficulty.

Kant, Nagel, Jaegwon Kim, and many others share a view that was perhaps the best eighteenth-century thesis about the nature of the physical universe, but our estimates have changed since then in two respects. Chance and time have come to play a different part in our recent understanding of the world. A new function for time gradually entered into the mainstream of our ideas about the universe in the nineteenth century, perhaps under the influence of the anti-Enlightenment philosophers. At about the same time, and independently of that development, chance became much more influential after it had received careful mathematical scrutiny in the nineteenth century. In recent years, chance and time have become more and more prominent in our understanding of the world.

Physical equations, or laws, are designed to be very general, applying to all motions wherever and whenever they occur. They succeed in achieving this level of generality only because they are conditional in form. This is why considerations of symmetry and invariance are so important in physics. The laws of physics apply specifically to the conditions that obtain at a location at a time. These are needed to apply the equations of physics to the world. In the eighteenth century it was believed, for good but not conclusive reasons, that if all the physical conditions were assumed to be given at a certain moment of time, then all the conditions at any other time, before or after, would thereby be completely determined by the conditional laws governing the universe. This implies that chance has no part to play in the universe. Time is treated here as merely one axis in a coordinate system in which the equations of physics are interpreted. In such a physical world, we could (for all the laws of physics) travel either backward or forward in time, as we may in space.

Today, statistics and irreversible temporality feature prominently in some of the most basic laws of physics. Our best cosmological models for these equations, the big bang theories, incorporate chance and unidirectional time into the evolutionary account. It has been suggested that the very existence of the universe, beginning with the big bang, is the result of a chancy quantum event. Biology also makes chance and time fundamental to its account in Darwin's theory of small variations in offspring (chance) and evolution by natural selection (time).

Chance and time have more than an inconsequential part to play in the universe. The doctrine of emergence, as developed among the sciences, accidentally may have provided the solution to what David Chalmers, reflecting on Nagel's perspectival theory ("the bat's point of view"), calls the "hard problem" of consciousness (Chalmers, 1995). The following model, inspired by Niels Bohr, suggests itself to us, and therefore I will adopt it (Bohr, 1972).

At a given time and location,[1] the state of the world is not determined fully by any prior states, except in a purely statistical way. In a world of chance, the conditions themselves, in accordance with conditional laws, make preexistent structures tend to break up and dissipate (this is a consequence of the second law of thermodynamics). But if these conditional laws allow for chance, then they are compatible with accidental configurations of conditions (remotely possible, but which do happen, very rarely) that make for stable structures. Stable structures perpetuate themselves as stable structures by utilizing the prevailing natural conditions to perpetuate their stable existence. The inspiration for this metaphysics is Bohr's model of the atom.

We notice that a stable structure needs an explanation in terms of a unique event in time for its emergence, but thereafter the structure itself contributes toward the explanation of its own continued existence. On the basis of general laws as we know them, the likelihood that components of a certain kind of structure will come together are negligible, but once the structure comes into existence, the likelihood that its components will be found together increases, precisely because the structure is stable. A living cell, for instance, brings together nucleic acids and hydrocarbon compounds in a certain specific configuration. If we scan the universe randomly, this is an unlikely combination to find. We are safe in predicting that the next spacecraft that looks into space will not see this combination, nor the next spacecraft after that, nor the next. If we find these components together, that will be an important and unusual event. However, we can predict the existence of such cells in a very wide variety of environments on the surface of the Earth. The reason is that living cells, once they are born, use metabolism to keep themselves alive and to reproduce more of themselves. They spread into other stable environments, even where these environments would seem to us to be extremely inhospitable. Living cells keep evolving, using free energy from the environment. The mode of their evolution is unpredictable on the basis of the antecedent conditional properties of the universe, such as those describable in geometry, physics, or chemistry, but once they are born, new conditional laws arise that apply to them as living systems, and that are not reducible to, even though they are compatible with, the preexisting conditional laws. Consider, for instance, the Mendelian laws of inheritance, which presuppose some very partic- ular genomic structures. These reproductive structures are not likely to have been randomly generated. The Mendelian laws of genetics that are applicable to or- ganisms that inherit this unusual reproductive structure are, however, general and conditional in their form.

These preliminary remarks set up my task, to give a substantive picture of the evolution of organisms that possess qualia. We will be looking for an emergence of a new kind of organism in a local evolutionary setting, rather than studying the difference between conscious and nonconscious structures in a timeless compar- ison, which is the alternative strategy that has been abandoned in this essay chap- ter. Let me begin with the question that must be answered sooner or later: What are the necessary and sufficient conditions for a being's possession of qualia? I will state the desideratum as generally as possible, thereby incurring the risk of being vague, because the mechanism proposed here is only one possible way in which this desideratum can be met. It is not part of my claim that this mechanism is the only possible way in which consciousness can exist.

Nagel's 1974 article would not be nearly as interesting if he had asked, "What is it like to be an asteroid?" or "What is it like to be a fern, or a mushroom, or a bacterium?" The fact that a bat is a living organism, that it is an animal, that it has hormones, muscles, and nerve tissue—these are all necessary conditions for the fact that it is the kind of thing of which we can ask what it is like to be it. (Those who pursue the first, or reductive, strategy, which I have abandoned in this chapter, may be tempted to consider as one possible solution that mind is ubiquitous, as Leibniz did.) Let us say that animals that can perceive have all these other things. What more do they need?

Sufficient conditions for an organism to be conscious would have to include some general organizing principle for perception among these animals. Let me begin by stating this vaguely: An organism must possess perceptions and whatever they entail, for which there must also exist what Kant called a "unity of apper- ception." When I have a stream of consciousness, we will want to know what the unity is that holds these perceptions together, which determines for the organism how it will react as a unitary being, or as a whole, to the environment. This unity of mind speaks for the animal as a whole in some matters, or is, in such matters, a "self."

I have laid emphasis on this aspect of awareness because, under the influence of various forms of behaviorism, people have supposed that the distinguishing mark of the mind is that it is capable of allowing its possessor to do certain very clever things. While there is a place for emphasizing the publicly observable character of what organisms can do, in matters concerning conscious awareness this only confuses the issue. The reason is that no complexity or cleverness of action is by itself a mark of consciousness. Given the state of the philosophical discussion concerning the Turing test today, we are not surprised when someone maintains that anything that can be done by a human being can also be done by a computer or a finite-state Turing machine. I will not be challenging that claim, but in fact supporting it. We do not even need to postulate perceptions in a mechanical zombie in order for us to imagine that it can be programmed to do whatever it is that we can do (provided only that the actions to be mimicked can be described sufficiently precisely).[2]

Kant's idea of the unity of the apperception involved transcendental analysis, but William James, who was more pragmatically inclined, called it the "binding" problem, as it is now known to psychologists and neurobiologists (see James, 1983). The form of organization of perceptual awareness we are seeking is one that, if found, solves the binding problem. If we begin with a particular case of the binding problem, which arises in the study of certain specialized cortical neural cells, we find that a solution suggests itself. Suitably generalized, it will get us on our way.

Hubel and Wiesel (1974) discovered that if one stimulates certain neural cells, one by one, in the visual cortex, where these cells lie on the surface of the brain, at the very ends of the columns that constitute that part of the brain, one can isolate a particular kind of perception for each cell stimulated. They were able to locate the cells that tracked perceived motions. What was astonishing about some of these specialized perceptual cells in the cortex, which they described in their celebrated articles, was that no cells recorded the whole of a movement perceived. Each cell, when stimulated by a complex perceived movement, gave the patient only portions or aspects of it. There are more than twenty-five different cells of this kind that could be involved in the tracking of a single possible motion. One cell may record an aspect of a movement away from the eye, one at one angle, one horizontal, and so on. During the time when a smooth and continuous movement is perceived, an appropriate number of cells fire; thereafter, attention turns elsewhere. "The moving finger writes, and having writ, moves on." There is no neuron for a replay, in which the different firings are summed up. How and where do we see the composite motion?

This subsidiary binding problem from neurophysiology, concerning perceptions of motions, is useful because it contains within it the seeds of the solution to the whole problem. Motions have been studied mathematically for a long time, and we can make use of this resource to launch our investigation. It is well known that if one begins with a finite number of points, and if one needs to find a unique curve passing through them, representing a trajectory through these points, it is impossible to perform this task in general. It is only under very special circumstances that a curve will fit a finite number of points uniquely. If one is given three points not on a straight line and is told that a circle passes through them, then there is only one circle that meets the criterion. If one is given four points and is told that they define an ellipse, then they will uniquely determine a particular ellipse. So the curve-fitting problem is soluble, provided that there is an adequate instruction or a constraint that must also be observed. In the absence of a constraint of any kind, there are always an infinite number of curves that can fit any finite number of points. But is curve fitting really the same thing as computing a unique smooth curve from the twenty-odd components?

Perhaps, one may conjecture, the twenty-five or more motion detectors give just the information analytically needed to be able to compute the real curve. We could try to "reverse-engineer" the structure of the perceived motions in each type of specialized cell (by working out what information in the different cells would be sufficient to analytically determine an arbitrary curve). But this possibility seems far-fetched for two reasons. First, if there are three or four motions being observed (imagine a child running around two puppies that are playing as we move our head to watch them play), then the information in the perceptual cells that are specialized for parts of movements would not provide us with any means of judging how many different smooth motions there are, and how they are composed. Second, we note that the information involved in perceiving motions is much more complicated than that, involving different sensory modalities and many features of our own posture and movements, too. If, therefore, we look at the entire binding problem, then there is no longer any temptation to find an analytic solution by reverse engineering for this particular subproblem. The solution must lie elsewhere.

It would seem that we can compute a whole, continuous, smooth movement out of the parts, but only when there is an instruction that is hardwired into the brain that guarantees that the result is unique. There is only one way this can be done finitely. The perceptions must activate preformed images, giving them at most some more detail and more content. In other words, we can have a unique solution to the problem of forming images of motion only if we give up the claim that the unique solution must also correspond exactly to the reality being perceived.

When we perceive anything, what we perceive has two components to it: One is that the imaging must be derived from a preformed set of images or by combining preformed images; the other is that the choice of images from a gallery must be determined in some way by features of the perceived thing. When David Hume and Thomas Reid disagreed on whether perceptions are direct or whether we see things by way of images, they were both right, up to a point, and both wrong. We do have direct perception, as Reid observed, and we have images, too, as Hume knew. Perceiving and becoming aware are two different processes. They are both real and somewhat independent of each other, though related. The two processes interact whenever we are consciously aware of anything. Perceptions by themselves do not give us qualia, until the imaging system incorporates features of them into the inner representation.

There is evidence of perception without awareness and of awareness without perception. Evidence of the former has been brought to our attention by the work of Nicholas Humphrey (1992) and Lawrence Weiskrantz (1986), who have demonstrated an amazing phenomenon called "blindsight." First observed in a monkey and later confirmed painstakingly by Weiskrantz among human patients, it involves perceptions without awareness. Patients with damage to the striate cortex, but the rest of whose visual apparatus is functioning normally, complain of blindness. They have no visual field or any awareness of objects from which light enters their eyes. Nevertheless, these patients have the ability to preform the shape of their hands in order to grasp objects (Milner and Goodale, 1995). The information about the shape of the grasped object, which is gathered visually, seems to be able to guide the patient's actions without the mediation of conscious images. This extraordinary phenomenon clearly shows that there is perception without awareness. We are certainly also aware of dreaming while our senses are at rest when we sleep, which demonstrates the existence of awareness without perceptions.

In what follows, therefore, I will assume that the first conscious beings, with their "awareness" superimposed on their perceptions, emerged out of a group of animals that could already perceive. I will study this as a process of natural selection as this is understood by biologists. Here are the three main questions I will take up:

1. What kind of mechanism allows an animal to have an image-producing organ?
2. Which were the original animals to acquire this form of awareness?
3. What possible advantage for surviving as a stable life form could there be for an animal to create illusions when it could already perceive what is out there?

In brief, the answers that I will sketch to these questions are the following:

1. Mechanism: Aberrant central pattern generators.
2. Origins: Chordate ancestors of vertebrates.
3. Advantage for stability: A new niche found by swimming.

The Mechanism of the Unity of the Apperception as It Is Found among Humans and Related Animals

Let us look at animals in general to see how a mechanism for supporting qualia could have come about. Before we get to the mind of the vertebrates, we have to look at the structures that preexisted in their ancestors, which structures are shared by other animals generally. It is only then that we can see how the mechanism works, for it must originate within these kinds of preexisting structures, as we saw in the introductory remarks about emergence in evolution. I will therefore describe this in the following six stages:

1. Animal tissue
2. Hormones
3. Nerves
4. Perceptions

5. Central pattern generators (CPGs)
6. Aberrant CPGs in the brain

1. Animals are multicellular eukaryotes with differentiated cells. They differ from fungi and plants, also multicellular eukaryotes, in that animals have muscles, nerves, and hormones, and this gives them an advantage in the rapidity and control of their movement. The basic communicative system governing movements among the cells in animals is by way of hormonal secretions in the body fluids. Many animals survive with rudimentary nervous systems, using only the endocrine system of communications, of which I will say a few more things later. Nerves are a specialized part of this system. Hormones can initiate, slow down, speed up, and stop muscular movements. This is done in animals chemically by a process called ligation, whose function is much more general than the control of muscles. There are fewer than thirty hormones, which have very different structures. The endocrine system is so fundamental to animal communication that all the major phyla have it, and animals' taxa differ comparatively little in the mode of its action in them. Even some very simple animals like unicellular protozoans show responses of speeding up when fed adrenaline and slowing down when doused with acetylcholine. They have no organs, being unicellular, but possess a characteristic reaction that is similar to an adrenaline "rush" in an animal.

2. Hormones basically work like this: Each animal cell has molecules floating on its lipid bilayer surface called receptor molecules, which extend, at their submersed end, deep into the cell. A hormone molecule floating in the fluids surrounding the cell will fit the exposed region of a corresponding receptor molecule like a key and lock mechanism. When a hormone attaches to it, some changes are triggered in the receptor molecule that in turn activate or inhibit a stereotyped pattern of activity that is stored in the cell. Hormones that are secreted into the body fluids of animals can in this manner control the "mood" of an animal, as well as the coordination of localized movements.

Calling these molecules "molecules of emotion," as Candace Pert (1997) has done, is quite appropriate because the basis for moods, feelings, and emotions in us is primarily hormonal in origin, even though it is only in the nervous system of the vertebrates that one finds a clear central structure or organ that is in some respects "in charge of the body" and within which emotions can actually be experienced. If moods linger, but thoughts are fleeting, this is because chemicals are slow to dissipate in body fluids, whereas electrical signals can be more rapidly turned on or off.

3. Nerves form a subsystem of communication that is much faster and more local than the hormonal system, even though the secretions between nerves, or neurotransmitters and neuromodulators, are also particular hormones. We may think of nerves as an optional telegraphic system in a country served by a postal service (by the slower endocrine system) as well. Of course, while speedy nerves may seem to be optional for animals considered as a group, they are obligate for those animals whose prospects for continued survival depend heavily upon rapid and controlled responses to the environment.

Nervous arrangements vary widely among animals. There are some species of animals that have no nervous system to speak of at all. For instance, the sea squirt, a taxon that is hypothetically cast by some as ancestral to our own, exhibits none in its adult form, though it possesses one in its tadpole state, for about a day. There are also other very intricately neurulated forms, for instance, among the insects and some cephalopods. Nervous organization, therefore, is very varied. Hormones are, as compared to this, the building blocks of most animal cell communication. Hormonal communication does not differ as drastically among the different animal taxa, whether in their general mode of action or in their chemical composition. The reason for emphasizing this is that, as we will see later, some of our ancestors had, compared to other contemporaneous animals, very rudimentary nervous systems—and that is an important part of the story of consciousness. It is important to note that animals can survive using intercellular communication that depends exclusively, or almost exclusively, on the endocrine system.

The basic arrangement of nerves in the annelid worms and insects, which is also shared by the central nervous system of vertebrates, is called "segmentation" or "metamerism." A pattern of nervous organization is repeated along a line. In the annelid worm, for instance, locomotion is effected by means of muscle contractions in rings of muscles found around it, iterated along the length of its body. Along its length are also nerves arranged in clusters, called ganglia, one in each nervous segment. If we pay attention to the ganglia, we can see why neither worms nor insects, which have a more developed form of this organization, can be credited with having qualia. To learn this, we need to look at the ability to perceive.

4. Among humans, perceptions and awareness are very closely linked in normal circumstances, so that we colloquially speak of perceptual awareness as if it were one thing. But it is easy to show that though the worm has perceptions, it cannot be credited with awareness. We cannot ask what it is like to be a worm, as we did with the bat. The reason is that perceptual signals go to the worm's various peripheral ganglia just as readily as they go to its head ganglion. In the case of the worm, each ganglion is a bit like a brain, but none is sufficiently centralized to compare with ours. So if one cuts off its head, the worm will grow a new one, and its locomotion will not be arrested while it accomplishes this feat. When nervous processing is more evenly distributed, it is clear that there are no qualia to report, because there is no one thing to being like such a worm.

We could devise a test for the possession of qualia in the case in question, namely, that one should expect an answer to our question, "What is it like to be that?" But if we adopt this test (the Nagel test), then we presume that there must be some one thing to be like it, not several. When there are several ganglia acting like brains, we cannot ask what it is like to be a collection of them. Insects cannot count as having qualia, though they are very much better neurulated and much more versatile in their patterns of behavior than worms, because they, too, do not have a centralized enough nervous system. To see this point more clearly, we can conduct a thought experiment. Suppose I am lying unconscious on a bed, and you show with an electromyogram that some of my muscles are still firing. Am I then experiencing this activity in the ganglia related to the nerves in that muscle?

Since we think that an unconscious person is not aware of anything, we must conclude that the activity that takes place in the ganglion of an unconscious human is not evidence of consciousness. This is exactly analogous to neural activity in the ganglia of a comparatively decentralized worm or insect. There is no awareness in active ganglia without a further mechanism in place, and they lack that additional mechanism, as far as we can tell.

Insects are very well neurulated and exhibit very complex adaptive behavior, and some of them show very startling abilities. But as we have noted already, a Turing machine can do anything a human can. This does not tempt us to ascribe consciousness to a Turing machine. No more should we be tempted to say of insects that they are conscious, at least on the basis of their very intelligent and very complex adaptive behavior. The function of the head ganglion among insects remains much less centralized than we would require for a conscious being. Compare the activity of one of our own peripheral ganglia when they are active. We associate no sense of awareness with the processing of information in the ganglia in our spinal chord. If our brain were also to function like one of these ganglia, then we would have no need to postulate consciousness in our brain either.

5. Central pattern generators are cells, often found within the ganglia of an animal, that control specific rhythmic movements of the muscles. To be more explicit, two or sometimes three cells in a complex interactive array, a complex known as the central pattern generator (CPG), have the ability to erupt spontaneously, or to erupt when one of them receives the right signal from another cell. Typically, the CPG will send a signal via a nerve to a muscle cell, and then the muscle cells will react, generating a spike in a nerve that comes back with a signal to the ganglionic CPG, which then continues the cycle. Many CPGs are organized in such a way that they continue their cycles indefinitely, and if the cycle of signals comes to a temporary halt, then they will erupt spontaneously to perpetuate the cycle. Other cycles can have a limited number of turns before they are programmed to stop. In crickets, the motion of the wings is controlled by a CPG, but it is a cycle that continues only for a while before it halts. The pacemaker in the human heart is a CPG that controls the heartbeat, but it is designed not to stop too readily. Our walking and breathing are also controlled in this manner, though in these cases we also can override the CPG signals by sending messages from the brain—for instance, when the medical practitioner asks us to say "Aah!" or asks us to breathe deeply.

Since a great many movements in animals are rhythmic, central pattern generators are very common in all animals. It is just one such CPG that, we speculate, became aberrant and gave us our mind.

6. The hypothesis of an aberrant CPG being proposed is this: A central pattern generator that began in the ganglion in the head of one of our chordate ancestors, by a mistake in its genetic programming, strayed and kept cycling inside that ganglion instead of going to the muscles and back. It went from perceptual cell to perceptual cell to perceptual cell and back, endlessly. The CPG that lost its way became an organ for conscious experience.

This CPG would keep perceptual cells firing regularly in the brain, so that it would perceive imaginary objects steadily. If an object is normally perceived, it stops exciting the nerves after a while and disappears from our senses. But with the aberrant CPG working, a perceptual cell that once fires in response to a sensory input will then continue firing in response to CPG prompting even after the object has stopped exciting the perceptual organ. By firing a number of such cells simultaneously, the cycle generated by the aberrant CPG gives the animal that has inherited it the illusion that it is in a certain steady environment, like a movie of the world around it. When it perceives a new object of special interest, say, some food when it is getting hungry, the perceptual signal from the food will be written over the steady (but fictional) perceptual pattern of images that is CPG generated. The food will then appear as an object intruding as an image within the cinematic scene.[3] In a steady inner perception of a number of object images, the newly overlaid food image will now appear as having a spatial relation to the other object images. This intrusion of a perceptually recorded reality into a fictional setting gives this cinema verité a purchase on verité that is based on more than formal similarity. In effect, the steady state of perceptions of the imaginary objects would be like an internal space, telling the animal where, in relation to its internal environment, it could find the food.

In simpler terms, the mechanism for representation within the aberrant CPG would give the animal the continuous monitoring of things as images in phenomenal space and time. By locating perceptual cues in given directions, it could navigate its way to the real object, which is perceived. Conscious awareness is, in effect, a navigational device (Gibson, 1950).

Aberrant CPG rhythms in the brain give us qualia because of the persistence of an object image as it is perceived in the foreground against a steadily perceived background. Take away the background, or take away the perceptual focus, and there is no perceptual awareness.[4] Hence it is the rhythm of the animal's aberrant CPG cycle that gives it conscious awareness. It is this rhythm that also predisposes us to be aware of and appreciate a beat. Without it, our sense of conscious timing in many activities would be inexplicable. The CPG-generated rhythm refreshes the perceptual cell (gets it to fire) quickly enough, one after the next, that the perceptual cell cannot find a gap between firings.[5] The rate at which this happens is not much less than 60 Hz, because we know from the design of computer monitors that when the "refresh rate" of pixels in a cathode ray monitor falls below this rate, we begin to see a definite flicker. It is not unlikely that the 40-Hz cycle associated with conscious processes is related to the lower limit of this rhythm (see Crick, 1994).

Even if a perception does not feed into the perceptual cells of the CPG-generated rhythm, it still can excite very complicated and even remarkably intelligent activity for the animal concerned.[6] A musician playing the piano, if proficient, does not pay any attention to the keys, but concentrates on the music (Schrödinger, 1992). There will be no awareness associated with all perceptual cues involved in this very complicated activity. Whenever a perception is not held steadily for long enough, it will be passed by in consciousness, but it may still affect us without our conscious awareness of it. Consider, for instance, subliminal signals, for which there is ample experimental evidence, and even laws banning their use in advertising. There are also interesting experiments showing up errors from threshold effects just below the level of awareness, when unexpected objects are flashed before the eyes of subjects. Perceptions must be held in a field together with other images, steadily, in order to be fully present before the mind's eye. It is just this that the rhythm of the mind contributes to the defeasible illusion that we create for ourselves with its aid.

The Origins of Vertebrate Conscious Experience among the Chordates

There is a strong temptation for philosophers to suppose that the difference between animals endowed with consciousness and those not so endowed is this: Those that have more advanced circuitry than others, in terms of complexity, have conscious minds. On this account, the line for an animal's having a mind at all is drawn horizontally across the temporal path of evolution, at a certain level of complexity.

But to think that the conscious mind is fundamentally a complex structure is only to say, in other words, that we do not understand it as yet. If we look at anything at all in enough detail, it will seem to be complex. Whenever we understand something, however, we understand it as a simple thing. This allows us to filter out the "noise," if we wish, in the ever-complex real world around us. In this spirit, I suggest that the mind, or conscious awareness, is a simple imaging organ. Animals possessing it are not separated from those that lack it by a horizontal line across a level of complexity, but rather by a vertical line that separates some animal taxa from others. To insist that the mind is "understood" by noting that its very complexity makes it unfathomable is simply to support Kant's view, with a "scientific"-sounding reason, that there is something mysteriously beyond our ken about the seat of reason itself.

In the original animal in which it arose, the brain that supported conscious awareness must have been quite primitive. It would grow complex over the years if, however simple its origin, it proved to be a successful experiment. In that case, the increasing complexity that is evident in it now would just be the result of additional functions it acquired over time. These additional functions, piled one on top of another and across each other in an enormously jumbled heap, would certainly make it complex as it evolved in the process of the exploitation of new niches by its possessors.

If I am right that an aberrant CPG mechanism gave us our imaging organ, which in turn gave us qualia, then the rhythm that defines the mind must be a measurable one, and it is. If we put electrodes on the head of any vertebrate, we find that it has characteristic electroencephalogram (EEG) patterns from which we can tell whether the animal is asleep or awake, and if it is awake, whether it is alert or resting. It is an astonishing fact about vertebrates that every one of them, when studied, exhibits physiological patterns of waking and sleeping combined with the familiar associated EEG patterns. I.G. Karmanova (1982) has compiled a very extensive record of all the studies of wakefulness and sleep and the associated EEG patterns in vertebrates, which she summarizes in the form of a diagram (figure 19.1).

It is quite different with invertebrates. We find that while every muscle and nerve in any animal sends out an electromyogram reading when it is active, there is no dominant rhythm in the "head ganglion" or brain of the invertebrate, such as one finds in every vertebrate form.

The hypothesis that conscious experience is a vertebrate phenomenon was

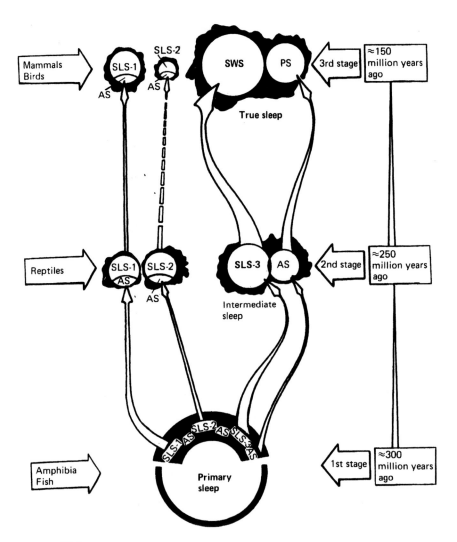

FIGURE 19.1.

proposed by C. Savory more than forty years ago on the basis of plain physiological evidence (Savory, 1959). Savory was an arachnologist and noted in his remarks on the comparative account of animal behavior provided by Konrad Lorenz and Nikolaas Tinbergen that they failed to note some fundamental differences between the behavior of vertebrates and invertebrates. He was unaware of the data from EEG patterns, but he suggested on the basis of behavioral evidence alone that invertebrate action patterns are both more automated and more locally generated in the ganglia than vertebrate patterns of behavior. He also pointed out that insects do not sleep in the sense of having their external perceptual organs disabled for the purpose of resting.

Finally, there is ample evidence for the claim that vertebrates have in common some very unusual features of nervous organization. A few are mentioned here in passing: The peripheral nerves of vertebrates have an extremely orderly myelination of their processes, which speeds up the passage of information in nerves. This helps large animals remain competitively organized, compared to smaller animals, in their overall response. This myelinated organization is lacking in invertebrates and is found fully developed in all vertebrates after the very earliest forms (hagfishes and lampreys have very rudimentary myelination). The retina of the vertebrate eye is enervated backward, which is unusual in animals generally, but universal among vertebrates. In fact, the vertebrate eye shows a single plan (Walls, 1942). Certain smooth muscle types have evolved especially among vertebrates that aid in rapid movement and that are adapted for this kind of centralized locomotive ability of large bodies that the mind of the vertebrate provides the vertebrate form. The brain of vertebrates exhibits a form of metabolic organization that is very different, in which the blood is kept out, with nutrients being distributed in a secondary internal system. When blood goes across the blood-brain barrier, losses of normal function result (e.g., from stroke). Finally, almost all vertebrates inhabit a special niche in their respective environments: They are several orders of size bigger than the invertebrates, with very few exceptions. In this way they can push aside the invertebrates from food that they wish to appropriate; they can avoid being ingested by the smaller animals; and they can eat the smaller invertebrates if their digestive habits allow for it. These facts are not conclusive, but they do show a strong correlation between vertebrates and the rhythmic mind that emerged to be exploited. But the full force of these observations, and more evidence of the mindedness of vertebrates, can only be appreciated when we inquire into the advantage that an animal has in dreaming when it could just as well perceive its surroundings.

An intriguing question that comes up concerns the identification of the particular chordate form in which the mindful animal first originated. This is a fascinating issue, of course, but not an easy one to study. There is a particular complication here because there is no general agreement among experts concerning the path by which vertebrates evolved from the chordates, or even where to place the chordates among the taxa related to them. The best account of the ancestry of vertebrates, as well as the most thoroughly worked out, seems to be that developed by Richard P.S. Jefferies, (1986) which I have adopted in its recently improved form in the light of newly found facts concerning DNA sequencing. Since the study of the stable advantage of its form provides some clues as to which was the first mindful chordate, I will add a few words on the first animal that was consciously aware of its environment in the next section.

Advantage

In summary, the advantage that the conscious mind gave us is this: The ancestors of the first vertebrates had the ill fortune of inheriting very poor neural programming, due to a glitch in their genetic endowment. This all but hobbled their locomotive ability, which is the main advantage enjoyed by animals in competition with the eukaryotes in the kingdoms of plants and fungi. In spite of poor nervous programming, the chordate that inherited an aberrant central pattern generator, and therefore an organ for consciousness, was able to learn to navigate in a way that allowed it to find a safe niche away from its competition. By avoiding competing too closely with their closest-related invertebrates, many of which had superior programming of their nervous systems, the vertebrates were more successful than any other of their closest chordate relatives. In brief, the conscious mind is not the only way to do what we do, nor even the best out of many, but it was just our ancestors' way of doing it in order to eke out a precarious existence.

There is strong evidence that insects and vertebrates have comparatively recently diverged from a common ancestor. A very particular cluster of genes for development was found in the fruit fly *Drosophila*. A similar cluster is also found among the vertebrates. This is the HOM family of genes in flies, similar to what was identified as the HOX family of genes first found among mice. But the common ancestor of insects and humans was still a primitive animal several hundred million years ago.

Very soon after diverging from the ancestor common to the insect heritage, our line of the ancestry lost a fundamental developmental pattern that almost all animals possess. In animals, the embryo develops by dividing in very predictable patterns, which can be used to classify them into taxa. One of the fundamental differences in form of embryonic development is between protostome and deuterostome development, with the insects falling into the former and vertebrates into the latter. We can see a difference of pattern emerging between the two within the first few cell divisions of each, with the cells in a protostome arranged spirally and in a deuterostome (or ours) arranged radially. The spiral form of cell growth is lapped, like bricks in a well-built wall, whereas the radial form piles up one over the other.

After a number of divisions, the cells form a structure called a blastula, with a fluid cavity in the middle (figure 19.2) and the cells in a layer around it. The blastula then gastrulates by a process of indentation in the blastula, as in figure 19.2. From the side, the newly forming gastrula looks like the letter C (see figure 19.2). This is the first opening of the animal, and when a protostome animal forms a through gut from mouth to anus, this first opening will become the mouth.

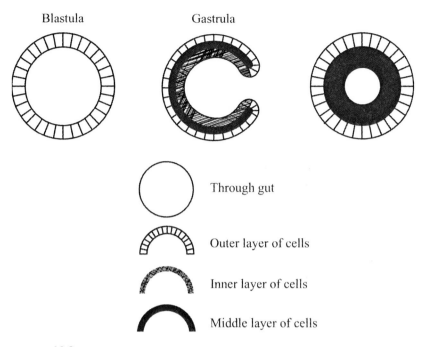

Blastula   Gastrula

Through gut

Outer layer of cells

Inner layer of cells

Middle layer of cells

FIGURE 19.2.

While this is happening, a middle layer of tissue begins to form (see figure 19.2). This mesodermal tissue develops into the various organs of the adult body, whereas the inner layer becomes the lining of the gut, and the outer layer the skin. At the mouth of the opening, where the middle and the outer layer rub against each other, the first neural cells appear. These neuroblasts divide and migrate from that position to other adjacent ones, going on to occupy their eventual positions in the adult nervous system. In the original protostome plan, the nerves begin where the mouth and the head ganglion will be. In the deuterostome form, however, the nerves develop close to the future site of the anus, far from the head. It would seem that the well-laid-out spatial program for nervous development that expresses itself in protostome species became garbled in the expression of the altered heritage of deuterostome species.

The effect of this is a fundamental difference in development, particularly in the protostome form of neurulation and that found among the deuterostomes, whose taxon, we recall, includes the vertebrates. Among the protostomes, the nerves develop with great specificity. The first sixteen neuroblasts in any protostome animal can be labeled by their initial position and followed during development to adulthood. It is found that the eventual destination of each labeled neuroblast within the adult nervous system is highly predictable. Among vertebrates this is not so. The nerves grow in a much more random fashion, with about half of them dying before they make their final connections. The neural connections that are made seem to be guided by pathways among the glial cells, but only those neurons that are in much use survive, and the others atrophy and die. Gerald Edelman and Vernon Mountcastle (1978) have called this form of trial-and-error development "neural Darwinism."

There are many arguments to show that deuterostome nervous development was a handicap for an animal in competition with animals from other taxa. Of many facts, I pick the three most salient.

1. None of the deuterostome species other than the vertebrate species are capable of free locomotion or swimming. Their very appearance shows that they are very poor in their locomotive ability. There are three main classifications of deuterostome species; the echinoderms, the hemichordates, and the chordates. Of these, the echinoderms that have survived today have all lost their bilateral symmetry. Losing bilateral symmetry makes it impossible to swim freely in a straight line. One can see how much of a handicap this must be because they have consequently reverted to a five-pointed or pentameric symmetry and have become relatively stationary, like the starfish. The hemichordates have some locomotion, but it is very local, not very perceptually guided, and rather sluggish. The chordates at one stage lost almost all their nerves. They lost their bilateral symmetry and regained it secondarily, a fact that has been painstakingly and brilliantly demonstrated by Richard P.S. Jefferies (1986). The emergence of the CPG-based mind among the chordates was probably closely followed in time by the secondary recovery of bilateral symmetry among them. Jefferies has identified the fossil animals that, if his account is right, must have been key intermediates in the rise of the chordates from the benthic floor to the wide waters of the ocean above (see figure 19.3). Indeed, there is a touch of genius in his writings, in which the remarkable story of the locomotion of vertebrates, which is very important to the emergence of the mind, is recounted by reading it from the detailed study of the fossil record alone.

2. The second fact showing how poorly the nerves of deuterostome species are organized comes from comparative neurophysiology. The nerves of insects are arranged in a very finely programmed way. Each ganglion is arranged into neuropiles, into which the neural axons send their dendrites, like wires into a telephone exchange. In vertebrates, we find that the nerves are all over the place, with axons and dendrites going hither and thither in no predictable spatial arrangement. A comparative neurophysiological study that correlates how much nervous tissue is needed to provide a particular function, however this is quantified, shows us that the insect form of nervous organization is much more efficient in the sense that much more is done by insects with fewer neurons than by vertebrates of equivalent levels of functional complexity.

3. The most telling feature of the deficit in the deuterostome form of development is a criterion used by biologists to study the success of certain traits. They count how widespread a trait is by determining the number of known species that possess a certain trait. They can also do the same thing by estimating how much

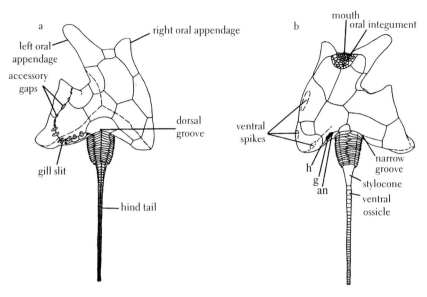

FIGURE 19.3.

biomass the possessors of a certain trait have in comparison with another trait. The estimated number of known species in the deuterostome form of development in comparison with the number in protostome form of development is roughly one to ninety-nine. That is, deuterostome species are about 1 percent of all the species of animals that have survived, and the other 99 percent are protostome species. If we think this an unfair comparison, we could compare just the number of known insect species that have survived with the number of all surviving known deuterostome forms. The numbers are equally startling. There are about fifty-five thousand known species of deuterostomes, but about ten million known species of insects.

Among the struggling deuterostome species, however, if we count the proportion of the vertebrate forms, the results are equally striking. The vertebrate species constitute about 95 percent of all the deuterostome species that have survived. Clearly, this is the story of a developmental loss that has since been regained among the chordate ancestors of vertebrates.

We come at last to the question of the paradoxical advantage of minds that can dream. What was the gain to the chordate from the ability to dream about its surroundings when it could perceive it instead?

The main answer is that it gave the chordate a substitute form of navigation that made up for the loss of nervous programming. The chordates were generally to be found at the bottom of the ocean floor, struggling through mud, with poor perceptual organs, and living off small bits of food left over around them. If a chordate bred successfully in any patch of the ocean floor, it would multiply, but since it could not travel very far, many of its offspring soon starved. Its success was therefore limited. It had the genetic ability to generate nerves, but the genetic spatial program for arranging them most usefully in the body was lost, and with it the ability to compete with successful and motile invertebrates.

The aberrant CPG gave the chordate ancestor of the vertebrate a form of illusion. How could illusion prove better than perceiving reality? The CPG organ for creating illusions was useful because it gave it a steady internal space in which it could locate the objects that it needed. This internal space may lack realism in some respects, but where it was useful, it was so useful that being deluded was a cost that was well worth bearing.[7] What it lacked in genetic programming was made up for by its makeshift navigational monitor. Using its organ for dreaming, the sluggish, poorly neurulated chordate could navigate in the free water above the ocean floor. It was at about this time that it had regained its bilateral symmetry, so that it could both swim and navigate. It could locate food at a distance when its own patch had lost its yield. Above all, by swimming freely, it could rise above the competition on the ocean floor, where it was handicapped, competing there, as it was, with better-neurulated protostome species. The freely swimming fish developed its vertebrae to take advantage of its superior navigation and eventually became bigger by developing its special form of myelinated nerves that allowed signals to travel rapidly in a long, flexible body.

The story of motility lost and then regained among the chordates is that of Richard P.S. Jefferies, whose representation of the cornutes from the fossil record shows us how dramatic was the loss of bilateral symmetry among them. Some cornute species appear to have lost their sight altogether. The mitrates, which evolved later, regained their eyes and their bilateral symmetry, suggesting that they were more prone to free movement.

If we now ask who was the star of the show, the first animal that woke up to the universe, we would have to pick an unlikely creature, a little bit like an echinoderm and a bit like a modern chordate, with a calcite skin, called the mitrate (see figures 19.4 and 19.5 for a particular specimen that has been studied by Jefferies; for example, Jefferies, 1986). It had a head cum body and a tail, and its brain lay near the anus, controlling that locomotive organ. The tail was structured to move the creature backward, its external skeletal skin protected it from attack, and it probably rose a bit above the ocean floor to float upon the surface, far from its competitors, before its descendants exchanged the hard skin for size and the benthic life for pelagic freedom. It is very likely that the first mitrate to dream up the environment used it for a very particular local purpose, as a guess, perhaps something as simple as this: It was not restricted to food in its immediate neighborhood if it could image an environment and locate patches of food that were far away, as signaled within that monitor. It would need a monitor because its peculiar manner of locomotion (backward) would need a method of turning around slowly and moving backward in the direction of the food, which it could not then see until it came close enough so that its chemical sensors near the mouth could identify the food. Whatever the initial advantage of the mind, it

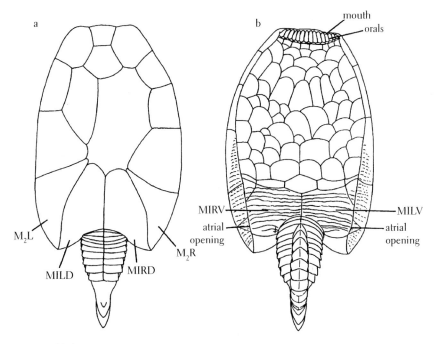

FIGURE 19.4.

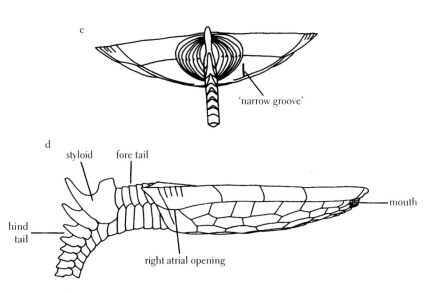

FIGURE 19.5.

was likely very local. The eventual advantage of the trait probably depended on other functions that were derived from its form. Before long, the animal was able to locate objects and, soon thereafter, conspecifics at a distance. This allowed a freely swimming fish to find mates. The better the navigational system, the better its success at reproduction. Once a mechanism invented for metabolic purposes, with continuing foraging functions, gets implicated in competitive reproductive success, the result is a proliferation of progeny with that trait. Metabolism and reproduction are two very fundamental processes in all of life. This is how the chordate mind radiated adaptively as the vertebrate in all its forms, occupying all the niches in which its various forms could survive.

The mind of the vertebrate is not an epiphenomenon or a causally irrelevant kind of "froth," a merely functionless appendage to the vertebrate body. Rather, we may wish to say that the very form of the vertebrate body evolved to exploit the system of spatial navigation that was afforded by the conscious mind. The vertebrate form or body plan is manifest as the adaptive radiation of a lucky chordate's mind. The advantage that it found for them was a niche in which they were not in such close competition with the marine arthropods and, later, the insects.

I should nevertheless emphasize here that we cannot distinguish the mind of the vertebrate in terms of something that vertebrates can do but insects cannot. Behavioral criteria are beside the point, because the Turing test tells us that even a mechanical zombie can, in principle, duplicate any behavior that can be described accurately. Conscious awareness is only our way of doing the same things that insects do better and more efficiently. As far as we can tell, insects fail the Nagel test for consciousness. If we had to choose a candidate for the Nagel test among invertebrate animals, then the cephalopods (cuttlefish, squid, octopuses) come to mind as prime candidates. If they qualify, then there is at least the possibility that the vertebrate account of the mind has been misdirected.[8] Octopuses are indeed very intelligent and, like vertebrates, have an origin among comparatively poorly neurulated ancestors (bivalves). Like vertebrates, they are much larger than the animals around them. Could they be thought to have minds? Perhaps.

They do exhibit remarkable intelligence and problem-solving abilities. We must be careful, however, not to confuse problem-solving ability or intelligence with the Nagel test for the mind. We have no reason to think that any animal, however clever, must have a mind because of its cleverness. We have Turing to thank for that insight. It is reasonable to take machines to be the very antithesis of conscious minds. Turing argued that anything we can do, however clever it is, if it can be stated precisely enough, can be done by a computer (a finite-state machine) that is programmed appropriately. If so, we have no reason to think that an animal without a mind cannot duplicate anything that is done by an animal with one. Hence my account of the mind has been making the case that the vertebrate mind is merely the chordate's way of surviving, not that this mind can do something that insects cannot do better in their own way.

The question, therefore, is whether octopuses pass the Nagel test, not how clever they are. Here the evidence is equivocal. There is evidence that whatever an octopus learns by the use of its optic lobe of the brain, and whatever it learns with its chemotactic lobe, do not seem to transfer from one to the other. When these lobes are severed, the optic lobe acts independently of chemotactically learned actions, and vice versa. Does this suggest a lack of unity? Such evidence is not conclusive. A person with good eyesight who suddenly loses all vision will seem at first to have lost spatial sense, too, when he or she is found groping around. But after a while, the inner spatial sense will manifest itself even in blind navigation. When an octopus is similarly handicapped by severed lobes, or due to loss of vision, it is not enough to note how it reacts immediately; it is necessary to see if it can regain its spatial sense in some other way, in time. If it were able to do that, then we would know that it has spatial intuition over and above the physiological knowledge of space that its body has embedded in its responses. The octopus would pass the Nagel test if there were a second spatial organization, providing it with a "unity of apperception" that can reestablish itself in its behavior in time. This would convince us that it has a mind. The evidence at hand is not conclusive as yet. Much work will need to be done along the lines of the pioneering studies of J.Z. Young (1964) in order to see whether some mollusks have minds, and if they do, in what way their mind is similar to our own, or how it differs from ours.

Our mind, therefore, did not emerge to engage in the performance of anything unique. It allowed our ancestors to do what other animals also could do, but in allowing us to do that, it gave our otherwise unlucky ancestors a lifeline to survival. Of course, over hundreds of millions of years, as function upon function has been piled onto this successful organ of our unlucky ancestry, our mind has acquired a complex beauty that we should pause and admire. In this chapter I have dealt only with some aspects of the origin of the mind, and not at all with its evolution into an organ that continues to fascinate us. In particular, it remains to understand how this mind could one day give human beings all the things that Kant found enigmatic: that freedom combined with bondage, those moral imperatives, those exalted thoughts of divinity, that ability to pursue good and evil, and above all that reason, in whatever manner we possess it, that seemed to Kant to lie entirely beyond the world that can be understood by natural science and even, in some respects, beyond its own ability to comprehend itself (Kant, 1790).

Notes

1. The state of the world includes all locations, of course, but in accordance with the relativity principle, one has to allow that for any coordinate system, there are many that fall outside the "light cone" in which several locally simultaneous events will correlate with distinct events in time in the distal coordinates. This relativistic possibility need not hamper our consideration of determinism. From our location in our own coordinate system, we can choose any point in time out of the set of equivalent points in a distal coordinate system (i.e., beyond the light cone) as a conventionally equivalent "now." If we establish a class of compatible conventional moments in time as the conventional "same time" for the universe, then the discussion of determinism in Laplace's sense carries over into the special theory of relativity.

2. This point was made very engagingly and forcefully by Ronald de Sousa Canadian Philosophical Association meetings in June 2000, where we spoke at the same session.

3. Cinema, video, television, and photography are but external projections of our mental structures. I am grateful to Ian Jarvie for his intriguing discussion of issues in a number of books concerning the epistemology, the metaphysics, and (though this is not here under consideration) the sociology of cinema.

4. This and the remarks on the importance of rhythm to perception that follow in the text are contributed by and very well supported experimentally by Gestalt psychologists.

5. Nerves fire by an exchange of chemicals with the surrounding fluids, and when they have fired, their electrochemical state needs to return to the earlier state before it can fire again. The constancy of percept is therefore felt whenever neural processes are called upon to fire as soon as they are ready to fire again. It is part of this model of perceptual cells in the brain that the electrical signal cycling through perceptual cells in the brain has a strong tendency to stay its course until it is overridden by external information like perceptual overrides or sleep CPGs.

6. One question that arises is how far the rhythm defines the mind. The cessation of rhythm may be described as "brain death," and we know that brain-dead people can be artificially kept alive. Jeanette Bicknell, who recently completed a doctoral degree studying the philosophy of film, has pursued an interesting question about the place of rhythm in the mind, namely, whether there is any known case of lack of appreciation of rhythm, as there is ample evidence of atonality. She reports that the literature seems to support little by way of this kind of arrhythmic deficit, and the one case she found reported is equivocal. Nicholas Ashby has also developed a very interesting neutral monist account of mind that was awarded a doctoral degree (2000) at York University, titled "A Musical Theory of Experience."

7. Konrad Lorenz provided the clue to this idea in his "Kant's Doctrine of the A Priori in the Light of Contemporary Biology" (1962) when he pointed out that the question Kant asks, whether noumenal objects have spatial characteristics just as phenomenal objects do, must be answered in the affirmative. We live and die in the noumenal world. Our survival, through evolution by natural selection, allows us to be adapted to things as they are, to the extent that we survive. This suggested to Lorenz that in the light of Darwinian biology, a priori features of the world, as interpreted by Kant, can be considered to be genetically a posteriori. We can conclude that the original dreamer, *Mitrocystites mitra*, which we suppose acquired that ability to be deluded, that is, to be appeared to, would have had progeny whose delusions would imitate "noumenal space" more and more accurately in all those respects that are relevant in each species to its special mode of survival.

8. I am grateful to David Martel Johnson for pressing this point in 1995 when I read an early version of this chapter to the Department of Philosophy at York University. Several members of the department also raised interesting objections, not all of which have been answered in this chapter. I also wish to thank members of the Department of Biology and the Cognitive Science Group, in 1996–97 for their criticism. Finally, I would like to thank a number of distinguished colleagues who have joined me in unsuccessful attempts to find funding for the purpose of instituting research along the lines set forth in this chapter, in particular, a core group of four out of seventeen distinguished colleagues who gave much time and effort over many years, the

late Professor Robert Haynes and Professors Michael Ruse, Ronald de Sousa, and Ronald Paul Thompson.

References

Bohr, Niels. 1972. *Collected Works.* L. Rosenfeld (Ed.). Vol. 6, *The Foundations of Quantum Physics.* J. Kalckar (Ed.). Amsterdam: North-Holland.

Chalmers, David. 1995. "Facing the Problem of Consciousness." *Journal of Consciousness Studies.* This may be read on the Internet at http://www.u.arizona.edu/~chalmers/papers/facing.html.

Crick, Francis. 1994. *The Astonishing Hypothesis: The Scientific Search for the Soul.* New York: Scribner.

Drager, U.C., and Hubel, David H. 1975. "Responses to Visual Stimulation and Relationship between Visual, Auditory, and Somatosensory Inputs in Mouse Superior Colliculus." *Journal of Neurophysiology,* 38, pp. 690–713.

Edelman, Gerald, and Mountcastle, Vernon B. 1978. *The Mindful Brain: Cortical Organization and the Group-Selective Theory of Higher Brain Function.* Cambridge, MA: MIT Press.

Gibson, James J. 1950. *The Perception of the Visual World.* Boston: Houghton Mifflin.

Hattiangadi, Jadish N. 1998. "On Interacting Systems of Space: Or Coefficient Fields," in G. Hunter, S. Jeffers, and J.-P. Vigier (Eds.), *Causality and Locality in Modern Physics.* Dondrecht: Kluwer.

———. 2000. "Meditations on Substance in Aristotle, Descartes, and Bohr," in Demetra Sfendoni-Mentzou (Ed.), *Aristotle and Contemporary Science.* Vol. 1. New York: Peter Lang.

Hobson, J. Allan, and Brazier, Mary A.B. (Eds.). 1980. *The Reticular Formation Revisited: Specifying Function for a Nonspecific System.* International Brain Research Organization Monograph Series. New York: Raven Press.

Hubel, David H., and Wiesel, Torsten N. 1974. "Sequence Regularity and Geometry of Orientation Columns in the Monkey Striate Cortex." *Journal of Comparative Neurology,* 158, pp. 267–94.

Humphrey, Nicholas. 1992. *A History of the Mind.* London: Chatto and Windus.

Hunter, G., Jeffers, S., and Vigier, J.-P. (Eds.). 1998. *Causality and Locality in Modern Physics.* Dordrecht: Kluwer.

James, William. 1983. *The Principles of Psychology.* Cambridge, MA: Harvard University Press.

Jefferies, Richard P.S. 1986. *The Ancestry of the Vertebrates.* Cambridge, UK: Cambridge University Press.

Kant, Immanuel. 1781. *Immanuel Kant's Critique of Pure Reason.* Trans. Norman Kemp Smith. London: Macmillan, 1963.

———. 1790. "On the Form and Principles of the Sensible and Intelligible Worlds," in *Kant's Inaugural Dissertation and Early Writings on Space.* Trans. John Handyside. Chicago: Open Court, 1929.

Karmanova, Ida Gavrilovna. 1982. *Evolution of Sleep: Stages of the Formation of the "Wakefulness-Sleep" Cycle in Vertebrates.* Trans. A.I. Koryushkin, O.P. Uchastkin, and Werner P. Koella. New York: Karger.

Kim, Jaegwon. 1993. *Supervenience and Mind*. New York: Cambridge University Press.

Lorenz, Konrad. 1962. "Kant's Doctrine of the *A Priori* in the Light of Contemporary Biology." *General Systems Yearbook of the Society for General Systems Research*. II.

Milner, A. David, and Goodale, Melvyn. 1995. *The Visual Brain in Action*. Oxford: Oxford University Press.

Nagel, Thomas. 1974. "What Is It Like to Be a Bat?" *Philosophical Review*, V. 813, pp. 435–50.

Pert, Candace B. 1997. *Molecules of Emotion: Why You Feel the Way You Feel*. New York: Scribner.

Savory, Theodore H. 1959. *Instinctive Living: A Study of Invertebrate Behaviour*. London: Pergamon Press.

Schrödinger, Erwin. 1992. "Mind and Matter," in *What Is Life? The Physical Aspect of the Living Cell; with, Mind and Matter: and Autobiographical Sketches*. Cambridge, UK: Cambridge University Press.

Sfendoni-Mentzou, Demetra (Ed.). 2000. *Aristotle and Contemporary Science*. Vol. 1. New York: Peter Lang.

Walls, Gordon. 1942. *The Vertebrate Eye and Its Adaptive Radiation*. Bloomfield Hills, MI: Cranbrooke Institute of Science.

Weiskrantz, Lawrence. 1986. *Blindsight: A Case Study and Implications*. Oxford: Clarendon Press.

Young, J.Z. 1964. *A Model of the Brain: The William Withering Lectures, 1960*. Oxford: Clarendon Press.

20

The Significance of Ape Language Research

Stuart G. Shanker and Talbot J. Taylor

No supposition seems to me more natural than that certain kinds
of plants multiply by seed, so that a seed always produces a plant
of the same kind as that from which it was produced, but *nothing*
in the seed corresponds to the plant which comes from it; so that
it is impossible to infer the properties or structure of the plant
from those of the seed that comes out of it; this can only be done
from the *history* of the seed. So an organism might come into being even out of something quite amorphous, as it were causelessly;
and there is no reason why this should not really hold for our
thoughts, and hence for our speaking and writing.

(Wittgenstein, *Zettel*, §608)

Has molecular genetics proven Wittgenstein wrong? Scientists can now produce
a field of plants that are all the identical height and that all have the same amount
of fruit on them, each one the same diameter, the same weight, even the same
sweetness. What is more, we are well on the way to having a fairly complete
understanding of the chain of biochemical events leading from the transcription
of DNA to the plant structures that emerge. Why is it not equally conceivable
that molecular geneticists should one day understand how our genome causes us
to think and speak and write the way we do?

The genetic engineering analogy has seemed particularly apt to those who
construe language development as a purely biological phenomenon: a matura-
tional process akin to the growth of a plant, rather than a skill that a child must
master, like learning how to add and subtract. Part of the reasoning behind this
genetic determinist thesis is that all languages have the same abstract structure;
all ("normal") children go through the same milestones when acquiring language;
and children who acquire language do so automatically, effortlessly, and without
any explicit instruction from their caregivers. The determinist concludes that the
capacity to speak must therefore lie in the genetic program that controls the maturation of this species-typical phenotypic trait. That is, like the growth of a plant,

the "growth of language" (Chomsky, 1980, p. 134) is governed by unitary timing constraints that are genetically encoded (Petitto, 1997).

One obvious objection to this scenario is that the genetically engineered plant is a special case: one in which environmental factors are highly controlled and genetic structure extremely simple. But if the same seeds are planted in a different soil, or if the amount of sunlight and daytime temperature is significantly varied, the plants will change in a myriad of unexpected ways. Indeed, it now appears that developmental outcome may be essentially unpredictable, as the parameters of a developmental system vary in unexpected ways in even the most highly controlled situations, let alone in a nonlaboratory setting. For example, on April 20, 1998 scientists in New York, Oregon, and Alberta ran the same battery of tests on inbred mice.[1] Somewhat surprisingly, despite the most stringent efforts to conduct the tests under identical conditions, the mice in Edmonton confidently sped through the mazes, while the mice in Portland and New York cowered anxiously in corners and narrow passages. The study shows just how cautious one must be before one concludes that a certain gene causes a certain behavior, for the most subtle environmental factors — such as handling, air quality, chemicals in the water, and even the appearance and smell of the lab technicians — can have a profound effect on the behavior of genetically identical mice (see Crabbe, Wahlsten, and Dudek, 1999).

As far as the genetic determinist is concerned, this objection merely signifies that the outcome of gene-environment interactions is exceedingly variable, but that does not mean that each of these factors cannot in principle be experimentally isolated and manipulated. There is, however, a much deeper problem with this argument. Suppose that the environment actually influences the expression of an organism's structural genes. That is, suppose that genes do not produce differentiated phenotypic traits by themselves, but rather that at each level of the developmental system, the effect of any level of influence is dependent on the rest of the system, making all factors potentially interdependent and mutually constraining (Gottlieb, Wahlsten, and Lickliter, 1998, p. 260). According to the latter, dynamic systems approach, even simple "fixed traits," like eye color, are not solely caused by genes, but rather are a consequence of horizontal and vertical coactions among the various levels of a developmental system (Gottlieb, 1997).

When we apply these rival schools of genetic theory to the case of language acquisition, we arrive at two fundamentally different conceptions of what is involved in a child's capacity to speak. On the one hand, the genetic determinist sees this capacity as residing in a genetic code that contains the blueprint for the construction of one or more neural modules that regulate language comprehension and production. The environment may influence how well a child speaks, but not the maturation of the child's capacity to speak. The dynamic systems theorist, on the other hand, insists that the minimum unit for developmental analysis must be the developmental system, comprised of both the organism and the set of physical, biological, and social factors with which it interacts over the course of development (Gottlieb, Wahlsten, and Lickliter, 1998, p. 260). Thus a child does indeed have certain biological capacities that enable him or her to learn how to speak, but unless the child is exposed to the appropriate type of environment—namely, nurturing interactions with primary caregivers—he or she will not develop linguistic skills that, as we shall see later, are themselves shaped by that nurturing environment.

In short, we are confronted here with the latest version of the nature/nurture debate. Herein lies the reason ape language research has generated so much controversy. If it could be shown that apes are capable of acquiring the linguistic skills typically exhibited by a two-year-old child—that is, comprehension and production skills that were once thought to lie irrevocably beyond the scope of nonhuman primate capacities—this would immeasurably strengthen the empiricist case for seeing language development as a complex phenomenon that only can develop in a nurturing environment. That is, if nonhuman primates were able to develop primitive linguistic abilities, this not only would significantly weaken the nativist thesis that language is a uniquely human birthright, but much more important, it also would significantly weaken the genetic determinist thesis that a child's capacity to acquire language resides in a genetic blueprint that is potentiated by appropriate environmental inputs. Hence there is tremendous impetus for the genetic determinist to establish that language proper does not come "on line" until just after the age of two years, and thus that none of the communicative skills that apes hitherto have demonstrated can be described in linguistic terms, but instead must be seen merely as the result of advanced cognitive abilities.

The strategy operating here reflects the overall importance of language in the genetic determinist scheme and the lengths to which the genetic determinist must go to preserve this paradigm. The reasoning here is that there can be no denying the importance of environmental factors in the complex behaviors displayed, for example, by bonobos, but the startling communicative skills attained by such captive bonobos as Kanzi and Panbanisha pose no threat to nativism, for according to classical genetic theory, a gene predetermines the limits of a character's development. A "good" environment will allow the full potential contained in the gene to be expressed, and a "poor" environment only partial expression (think, e.g., of the role of nutrition in height). But the environment does not affect the actual content of the "information" that is "contained" in the gene; it only affects the extent to which that information can be released. Hence what we see in the case of Kanzi and Panbanisha is how a stimulus-rich environment allowed for the full cognitive potential contained in their genes to be realized. But language is set apart from all this as the quintessential canalized trait: a species-specific human behavior that is not only highly resistant to environmental perturbations, but also cannot be acquired without the requisite genetic substrate.

To say that what we are dealing with here is the latest version of the nature/nurture debate is somewhat misleading, however, insofar as this might lead one to suppose that the resolution of this conflict will simply lie in the weighting that is ultimately assigned to genetic and environmental factors. The problem here is that this latter line of reasoning accepts the genetic determinist version of the nature/nurture debate, which holds that since both nature and nurture must be involved in the development of complex behaviors, the problem that confronts the behavioral scientist is that of establishing how much influence should be accorded to each separate factor. We have already seen how dynamic systems theory challenges the very assumption that the genetic and environmental factors involved in development can be treated as separable and quantifiable components. At a still deeper level, however, the problem here is that, as often is the case in scientific polemics, these rival schools of thought not only present us with alternative causal hypotheses about the development of a complex behavior, they actually present us with different conceptions of the very behavior—in this case, language—that each seeks to explain.

Our principal concern in this chapter is with this latter issue. One cannot address the question of whether ape language studies have gathered sufficient evidence to quell the objections raised by the skeptics of ape language research (ALR) without considering the prior question of whether these objections stem from a conception of language acquisition that invites the sort of preformationist thesis afforded by genetic determinism. That is, the question whether apes have demonstrated linguistic skills comparable to those of a two-year-old child cannot be separated from the question of what the two-year-old has learned in learning how to speak, and how he or she has learned this. Hitherto the debate over the significance of ape language research has been dominated by the generativist view of the formal (e.g., morphosyntactic) features that establish a categorical distinction between communicative and linguistic behavior. But when we explore the interactionist view that a child's linguistic development only can be understood within the overall context of the physical, biological, and social factors affecting the child, we arrive, not just at a different explanation of the development of the child's language skills, but, indeed, at a different understanding of the very nature of these language skills.

Biology Times Environment

The nativist maintains that children are able to acquire the specific natural language to which they are exposed at birth because they are born with innate knowledge of the underlying structural principles of that language and, indeed, of all possible languages. The interactionist responds that the appeal of this sort of nebulous Platonist thinking will begin to wane once we have learned more about the interplay of the biological and environmental factors involved in language development. All of the great advances in psycholinguistics during the past generation have been in respect to the latter issue.

One of the most significant areas of research for our current understanding of the biological factors that are crucial for language acquisition has been the studies conducted with children suffering from developmental disorders. In general, we have learned that a child is unlikely to develop rudimentary linguistic skills unless he or she first has developed the abilities (1) to self-regulate, (2) to take in and respond to the world (which is primarily a function of the child's reactivity to stimuli, his or her ability to process stimuli, and his or her ability to control the movements of his body), and (3) to engage in sustained dyadic inter-actions (Greenspan, 1997). In addition to these basic biological functions, it is becoming increasingly clear that a majority of the cases of language deficits are the result of problems in the child's attentional control and/or his or her ability to inhibit nonsalient information, memory problems (both short-term and long-term), and—perhaps most important of all, and intimately tied to the foregoing factors—problems in auditory processing (Leonard, 1997). A child suffering from a severe auditory-processing problem, who does not understand most of what is said to him, may experience great problems with interaction. For this kind of child, the world may be a hostile place, filled with sounds that make demands on him but to which he cannot respond. He may come to feel shut out from the world of people, or, worse, people may seem frightening—always yelling because he so often angers and disappoints them (Greenspan, 1997, p. 42).

Such a child is likely to adopt behaviors that will only serve to exacerbate his or her communicational and attentional deficits. Conversely, the more such a child develops communicational skills, the more motivated he or she becomes to attend to subtle aspects of language use, such as inflections. According to the nativist view of language acquisition, there must be an implicit (i.e., embodied) rule in the child's "mind/brain" that extracts morphological rules for regular in-flectional endings (Pinker, 1999). But what we have learned by studying children suffering from "grammatical SLI (Specific Language Impairment)" is that speech language therapy is most effective when it works on developing the child's com-municational skills rather than trying to instill specific linguistic constructions through drill and reinforcement (Leonard, 1997), for this brings the child naturally to attend to, and thus master, the use of inflectional endings (Tallal, 1976). Ac-cordingly, when one talks about the biological factors that are involved in language development, one should not ignore the central role played by affect.

When one talks about the characteristics of the environment that are crucial to language development, one immediately thinks of all the work that has been done on the impact of motherese, or infant-directed speech (Gallaway and Rich-ards, 1994; Golinkoff and Hirsh-Pasek, 1999). But it is no longer quite so clear whether dyadic interaction with a primary caregiver belongs to the environmental or the biological side of the equation. That is, as Lock (2001) points out, it is no longer clear whether the unit of analysis in developmental psycholinguistics should be the infant or the dyad (cf. note 3). This is a result of the biological significance of secondary altriciality.[2]

What goes missing in the genetic determinist account of human development is the element of the typical or normal experiences that are essential for the emer-gence of species-specific traits and behaviors and, indeed, for the timing of critical neurobiological events. Since the inception of our species, the human infant has been exposed to a highly stable and uniform environment, first in the womb, which provides the fetus with surroundings that are highly (but not totally) buf-fered from external shocks,[3] and then in close dyadic relationships with primary caregivers. That is, the secondary altriciality of our species helps to ensure that children experience remarkably similar rearing conditions during the first few years of their lives. Indeed, one of the most important lessons we have learned from the study of developmental disorders is just how serious are the consequences for a child's cognitive and linguistic development if he or she is unable to undergo the typical emotional experiences involved in these early dyadic interactions with a primary caregiver (Goldstein and Hockenberger, 1991).

Thus, as important as biological factors are in the explanation of a child's development of language skills, they are not the full story nor even the main protagonists in the story, for the child's social environment is no less essential for his or her development of species-typical behaviors. Indeed, even to phrase the issue in this manner is misleading, insofar as it encourages the genetic determinist view that development is the outcome of "biology times environment," where the genetic side of the equation can in principle be separated from the experiential. But the various elements of the social environment are so intimately and intricately interconnected with biological factors that they cannot be meaningfully separated out in a straightforward additive manner. Rather, all of the elements in this complex matrix interact with and are modified by the others, so that the child's ability to speak emerges in a way that is similar to the emergence of a new compound from a chemical reaction, and not to the way a computer program processes data.

The Child's Entry into Language

It is not just how a child acquires language that is at issue here, but also what a child is acquiring when he or she develops language skills. If one adopts a telementational view of language — namely, as an articulated system that is used to communicate epistemically private thoughts from one mind to another — one is led to see the acquisition of language as an epistemological problem that the child's "mind/ brain" must be equipped to solve. But if one adopts an interactionist approach, language development is seen as the result of the gradual accretion of a set of practical techniques whereby the child engages with those in his or her social environment. The child initially learns that his or her wishes and desires may be satisfied by means of certain of his or her own behaviors and vocalizations, for example, shifts of gaze, turns of the head, crying, pointing, facial expressions, and phonetically consistent forms. The child is then led to develop these communicative behaviors into more and more "adultlike" forms of participation and, at the same time, more effective means of securing his or her interactional ends. The development of linguistic techniques emerges partly as a result of the child's seemingly natural fascination with language itself (Karmiloff-Smith, 1992) and partly in response to the ever more demanding techniques that those in his or her environment require or encourage for the realization of his or her goals (Briggs, 1998).

Thus, rather than postulating a neuromechanical device — a "mind/brain" — that is genetically programmed to acquire a formal system of communication, the interactionist focuses on the child as a developing social agent who actively and intentionally picks up and makes use of the communicational techniques that he or she already possesses, as well as those that are displayed in the behavior of the agents in his or her environment. The child is highly motivated to use and develop these communicational tools so that he or she may achieve his or her context-dependent interactional goals. These goals in turn develop as a function of the child's developing interactional environment and his or her own growing abilities and increasingly differentiated affects.

Furthermore, children's behavior, as well as other people's behavior, is constantly being subjected to normative assessment, rephrasing, explanation, further embellishment, characterization and comparison, and other responses. Their behavior (and others' behavior), both verbal and nonverbal, is a constant discursive subject even long before the children are themselves at all verbal: "What's that you've got? That's your rattle, isn't it?" "That's a funny face—I'd better burp you again." "Yes, I know you don't want your diaper changed, but we have to, don't we?" "What a loud noise! Daddy must be home." Reflexive discourse, of countless different flavors and varieties, is constantly at work constructing, giving verbal form to, making sense of, and giving importance and value and color to the child's sociocultural and communicational world.

Not only is it the case that dyadic interaction is essential for a child's linguistic development, therefore, but equally important, the child's language skills are essentially interactive. What the child comes to acquire is not an abstract system, but cultural techniques: ways of behaving that count as the performance of particular, culturally conceived acts. That is, the child learns how to perform such and such a linguistic act as that linguistic act is conceived of and spoken of in his or her cultural environment—that is, in what Michael Agar (1994) terms his or her languaculture. Language development is thus a matter of learning "how to do things with words"; and what those "things" consist in—what behavior counts as an instance of any one of them—are matters determined by the reflexive practices of the cultural environment in which the child is raised (Taylor, 1997).

Why Are Bonobos Able to Learn the Rudiments of Language, and Why Only So Much?

When he was two years old, Kanzi, a male bonobo that was born and raised at the Language Research Center at Georgia State University, spontaneously began to use the symbols on a lexigram board to request various food items. By the time he was eight, he had mastered the productive use of more than 250 symbols. He uses these signs purposefully, without any cuing or imitation. He is able to use these signs to refer both to objects and locations in the immediate, present surroundings and to others that are "absent," and even to comment on events that occurred in the past, to ask questions, or simply to provide information (both requested and unsolicited).

Even more significant than his use of signs on the lexigram keyboard is Kanzi's ability to understand spoken English sentences. When he was eight years old, Kanzi was extensively tested on the same data set as Alia, a two-year-old child

(Savage-Rumbaugh et al., 1993). The sentences on which they were tested involved such requests as to put something on or in something; to give or show something to someone; to do something to someone; to take something to a distal location; to fetch an object or objects from a distal location; or to engage in some make-believe sequence. Almost all of the sentences were new to Kanzi, and many involved somewhat bizarre requests in order to ensure that he was not able to derive their meaning on the basis of semantic predictability—that is, without really understanding the grammatical relationships involved.

The results of this comparative study are fascinating. Kanzi was correct on 72 percent of the 650 sentences on which they were tested, while Alia was correct on 66 percent. Even in the cases that were classified as errors, Kanzi was usually partially correct. For example, if he was asked to fetch two objects from some location, he might return with only one, or he might give the right item to the wrong person or the wrong item to the right person. In those cases where both Kanzi and Alia were completely mistaken in their responses, it was generally either because of inattention or because they responded to some atypical request (e.g., "Put the knife in the hat") with a customary action (Kanzi attempted to cut a bar of soap with the knife, while Alia attempted to cut an apple).

Perhaps the most striking difference between Kanzi and Alia was in respect to their memory abilities: Alia could tolerate fairly long delays before executing the task that had been requested, whereas Kanzi needed to act fairly promptly if he was to perform the requested task. Yet Kanzi actually performed better than Alia when asked to go to a distal location to fetch an object. Interestingly, both experienced difficulty when confronted with what, in effect, were conversational implicatures. For example, they were asked to "go outdoors and get an orange" while seated in front of an array of objects that included an orange. Half of the time Kanzi would pick up the object immediately in front of him and then go to the location named, while Alia responded in a similar fashion 25 percent of the time. But when the ambiguity was removed and Kanzi was asked, for example, to "go get the orange that's outdoors," he responded appropriately 91 percent of the time.

These controlled studies confirmed Kanzi's ability to understand English sentences exhibiting a variety of syntactic patterns. Some of these sentences exhibited a degree of syntactic complexity, including the use of embedded constructions. Many of the sentences were paired with their semantic inversion so as to ensure that Kanzi was responding to the syntactic structure and not simply to semantic cues. For example, Kanzi had no difficulty with such sentence pairs as "Put the raisins in the refrigerator" and "Go get the raisins that are in the refrigerator"; "Can you put some oil on our ball?" and "Put the ball in the oil"; and "Pour the Coke in the lemonade" and "Pour the lemonade in the Coke."

The testing conditions were so rigorous that even longtime critics of ALR were forced to acknowledge that Kanzi's behavior was free from the kind of characteristics whose presence in the behavior of the first generation of signing apes had been so telling. Thus the debate over the research with Kanzi and his sister

Panbanisha has concerned, not the legitimacy of the data, but rather their inter-pretation. The nativist critic of ALR objects that insofar as Kanzi and Panbanisha, like the chimpanzees before them, have not demonstrated the capacity to acquire the "subcomponents" of language, which only emerge in the human child after around the age of two—such as the mastery of regular inflectional forms—there is no reason to construe their behaviors in linguistic terms rather than as sophisti-cated communicational skills that are the result of advanced cognitive abilities. This objection turns on the genetic determinist conception of the child's linguistic capacity as residing in a genetic code that contains the blueprint for a language ac-quisition device, for it is thought that without this "innate capacity," bonobos can-not ("automatically" or "implicitly") extract morphological rules for regular inflec-tional endings. If it seems otherwise, this must be because they have memorized inflectional forms (without recognizing them as such) on a case-by-case basis.

When Kanzi's behavior is viewed on its own merits, however, rather than through this genetic determinist lens, one is most forcefully struck by the fact that it satisfies the same criteria that license our description of the two-year-old child as understanding the meaning of the various words and sentences on which he or she was tested. There was nothing in Kanzi's behavior to suggest that the findings should have been couched in mechanomorphic terms (Crist, 1999). That is, Kanzi did not seem to understand what the words or sentences he was tested on meant, any more than Alia did. Rather, both demonstrated through their actions that most of the time, they clearly had understood what they were being asked to do, even if it was not always clear to them why they were being asked to do this. The fact that there are certain more advanced linguistic constructions that Kanzi has not mastered no more vitiates the fact that he has mastered these simpler operations than the fact that a child has not learned how to solve algebraic equations vitiates the fact that she has learned how to add and subtract.

Hence the real question we are confronted with here is not "How should such behavior be (scientifically) described?" but rather "How was Kanzi able to learn the rudiments of human language skills?" Our hypothesis is that this was possible because (1) bonobos share some of the required biological factors nec-essary to benefit (verbally) from being brought up in a language-enriched envi-ronment, and (2) Kanzi (and his sister Panbanisha) were brought up in an inter-actional environment that was partially similar to that in which human children are brought up.

We now know that apes share the same basic perceptual capacities as humans (Snowdon and Hausberger, 1997). Indeed, in some respects, some of their capac-ities—for example, hearing—may far exceed our own (both in terms of the dis-tances and the range of sounds they can detect). Moreover, as Kanzi's history makes clear, bonobos appear to share what has been described as a "general au-ditory processing mechanism" in humans, namely, the ability to draw categorical distinctions between phonemes and to adjust to whatever is the phonemic system of the culture to which they are exposed at, or possibly even before, birth. We also see the phenomenon of "talker normalization" in both Kanzi and Panbanisha (they have no problem identifying different vowels as the same despite significant acoustic differences, which include listening to speech on headphones and even on the telephone).[4]

As far as the environment in which they were raised is concerned, what is perhaps most significant about Kanzi's and Panbanisha's upbringing is precisely the fact that they were not "language trained." On the contrary, Kanzi and Panbanisha were raised in a human environment in which they received the type of enriched attention that a child with biological challenges receives if he or she is fortunate enough to be diagnosed early. Like such a child, Kanzi and Panbanisha have developed linguistic and cognitive skills that far surpass anything our initial preconceptions about their capacities might have led us to expect. In this respect, Kanzi and Panbanisha do not represent the end of a story in animal language research that began with the work of the Kelloggs and the Gardners (Kellog and Kellog, 1933; Gardner, Gardner, and Van Cantfort, 1989). Rather, they represent a beginning in our understanding of the importance and the complexity of the interplay between biological and environmental factors in primate development.

They also demonstrate the overall importance of the reflexive character of the interactional environment in which they were raised for the acquisition of rudimentary linguistic skills. Kanzi's and Panbanisha's uses of the lexigram symbols and their responses to what others had said were constantly being discussed, corrected, evaluated, embellished, and so on. That is, Kanzi and Panbanisha were not being drilled in the use of a formal system: They were being naturally raised, or enculturated, in reflexive linguistic practices. The reason Kanzi's and Panbanisha's communicative behaviors are properly described in linguistic terms is precisely that they have themselves acquired these reflexive skills.

In other words, the crux of this debate does not turn on the number of symbols that Kanzi and Panbanisha can use productively, or the fact that they can use these symbols spontaneously, in an informative, noninstrumental, and obviously intentional manner. Nor does the issue turn on the different types of sentential constructions they can understand. Rather, the crux of this issue turns on the fact that Kanzi and Panbanisha can be observed to perform all these feats in a truly normative fashion. They do not simply respond to spoken utterances by doing such and such or press a button because they associate it with some specific reward. Rather, they frequently perform such acts as asking for clarification; they can be seen trying to explain to an infant or to one of the non-language-trained apes at the Language Research Center what a symbol means or what someone is requesting; they can even be observed trying to justify their actions or to clear up misunderstandings. For example, on one occasion when he was asked to "put the paint in the potty," Kanzi responded by putting the clay—which he often confused with "paint"—in the potty. Even after the sentence was repeated, he was so certain that he had responded to it properly that he dragged the supposedly nontransportable potty over to the one-way mirror and pointed to the clay within it to indicate to the experimenter that he had completed the request correctly (Savage-Rumbaugh et al., 1993, p. 82).

Equally important here are the kinds of activities in which these normative behaviors are situated. It is hardly the case that Kanzi and Panbanisha have spent their lives sequestered in a laboratory working away at a lexigram board. Rather, the board was incorporated in the day-to-day activities in which the bonobos were raised, in much the same way that speech is used with young infants. Thus we see Kanzi and Panbanisha behaving in very humanlike ways to do humanlike things. They enjoy going for hikes and outdoor cookouts; they like to play games, including fairly sophisticated video games, and perhaps even more surprising, they seem to relish engaging in make-believe games; they like to paint and to play musical instruments; one of their favorite activities is to watch videos of themselves or other apes at the compound; they enjoy human company and share human emotions; and they maintain fairly rigid standards about how humans and bonobos should behave with one another. Thus Kanzi and Panbanisha were not simply learning what certain lexigram symbols "refer to"; they were learning how to do things with these symbols, how to make use of them to participate interactionally in more and more sophisticated (and satisfying) ways—and, in turn, enabling themselves to take an active part in the reflexive construction of more such interactional activities.

Without reflexivity, there are no meanings, no truths, no understanding, no language. To be sure, there are interactionally useful gestures and vocalizations. But language as we know it—with meanings, truth/falsity, words, and other such features—requires that there be ways of communicating about communication itself, and so of fashioning it into these languaculturally constructed phenomena. What Kanzi and Panbanisha have come to inhabit is a reflexively constructed world: our communicational world, but also our emotional world, our moral world, our social world, and our psychological world. This was acquired by means of learning to participate in reflexive language games; to do this in turn required the right kind of nurturing environment and the right kinds of biological characteristics to mesh with and benefit from that environment.

When we come to reflect, then, on the reasons bonobos in the wild have not developed comparable linguistic skills, the factor that primarily should occupy our attention is the absence of this sort of interactional, language-nurturing environment, and not the issue of innate capacities. That is not to say that there are not important biological differences between bonobos and humans. Perhaps the most striking differences to have emerged so far relate to their short-term memory limitations and their somewhat reduced ability to inhibit nonsalient information (which seems to be comparable to that of a young infant). What we do not yet know is the extent to which these biological characteristics can be influenced by environmental measures that are tailored to their existing attentional capacities and designed to enhance their planning abilities and their abilities to control their impulses, to inhibit prepotent responses, and to engage in more flexible thought and action patterns. The research with Kanzi and Panbanisha certainly suggests that these so-called executive functions (see Ozonoff, Pennington, and Rogers, 1991) are the result of a complex developmental interplay between biological and environmental factors,[5] and not, as had hitherto been held in some quarters, genetically predetermined (see Baron-Cohen, 1995).

The implications of this research for our understanding of language development in general are threefold:

1. Language learning does indeed depend on biological capacities, but not specifically linguistic ones. Rather, the biological capacities involved relate to low-level processes—for example, attention, inhibition, memory, motor control, and audiological processing—that are shared by bonobos.
2. Language learning also depends on the sociocultural interactional environment, not simply as a facilitative, scaffolding factor, but also as a reflexive-constructing factor.
3. Language learning is an integral component in all other aspects of a child's development, not just socioaffective and cognitive, but physical[6] and even biological[7] as well.

The child's—or bonobo's—behavior and natural abilities are shaped by the reflexive characteristics of the environment into languacultural phenomena, that is, into utterances, meanings, words, understandings, truths and falsities, names, apologies, acts of reference, and the like. The child or bonobo has to have the requisite biological capacities in order to be able to learn to participate in the reflexive language games in which this shaping occurs. These reflexive practices in turn are crucial for the continuing development of the child's (or the bonobo's) biological capacities. The various elements of the child's (or the bonobo's) developmental manifold are so intimately and intricately interconnected that they cannot be meaningfully separated out in an additive manner. Rather, all of the factors in this complex biological/environmental matrix interact with and are modified by the others. Just as the environments in which children are raised differ in myriad ways, so too do the skills that children develop and the manner in which they acquire these skills.

The ultimate significance of ape language research, therefore, may be that it considerably strengthens the argument that human beings are not at all like genetically engineered plants. We do not all possess the same "mind/brain" that "processes information" according to a "program" that we selected in the Pleistocene, nor do we all "grow" an identical telementational code that enables us to "encode" and "decode" this "information." Most important of all, there is no "genetic seed" that contains the structure of complex behaviors and abilities. What the child learns when he or she learns how to think, speak, and write, and accordingly, the explanation of how a child learns how to think, speak, and write, cannot be divorced from the sociocultural environment in which these skills and abilities are constituted and nurtured. Thus ape language research not only has overturned archetypal Western views about the bifurcation between animals and humans, it has fundamentally altered our understanding of the nature of human capacities and how typical human skills and abilities are nurtured (see Savage-Rumbaugh, Shanker, and Taylor, 1998).

Notes

1. These are brother-sister pairings that have been inbred for twenty generations, thereby producing genetically identical populations.

2. Adolf Portmann coined the term "secondary altriciality" in the 1940s, but it was Stephen Jay Gould who made it famous in his chapter "Human Babies as Embryos" in Gould, 1980. Portmann described mammals that have large litters of undeveloped and helpless offspring as altricial. Opposed to this are precocial mammals—those that give birth to a few, well-developed offspring that are capable of taking care of themselves at birth. In many respects humans would appear to be precocial—for example, we have long lifespans, large brains, and fairly well developed senses at birth and engage in complex social behavior. Yet the human infant can be said to be born approximately nine months prematurely (in order, perhaps, to preserve bipedality in the mother) and thus is helpless at birth. It was for this reason that Portmann described human babies as "secondarily altricial."

3. It should be noted here that these "shocks" can come from the uterine environment as well as external sources. For example, if a mother with two copies of the mutant form of the PAH gene stops using her special diet, this may have no effect on her own brain, but her rising phenylalanine level can seriously impair the brain development of her fetus.

4. There is also evidence that Kanzi may even be able to recognize the difference between his own attempts at replicating vowel sounds and what he is trying to imitate (personal communication from E.S. Savage-Rumbaugh).

5. In human as well as nonhuman primates (see Griffith, Wehner, and Rogers, 1999).

6. For example, Monnot has established that there is a significant positive correlation between the use of motherese and an infant's growth (see Monnot, 1999).

7. An interesting comparison here is with the various cases of so-called feral and abused children. In addition to the fact that in all such cases, the child is said to communicate by grunts (which is most likely the origin of the various myths about these children having been raised by animals), they are also all said to be insensitive to cold and pain, to be hypo- or hypersensitive to loud noises and bright lights, and never to laugh or smile (Curtiss, 1977; Gill, 1997).

References

Agar, M. 1994. *Language Shock: Understanding the Culture of Conversation.* New York: William Morrow.

Baron-Cohen, S. 1995. *Mindblindness.* Cambridge, MA: MIT Press.

Bremner, J.G., and Fogel, A. (Eds.). 2001. *Blackwell Handbook of Infant Development.* Oxford: Blackwell.

Briggs, J.L. 1998. *Inuit Morality Play.* New Haven, CT: Yale University Press.

Chomsky, N. 1980. *Rules and Representations.* New York: Columbia University Press.

Crabbe, J.C., Wahlsten, D., and Dudek, B.C. 1999. "Genetics of Mouse Behavior: Interactions with Lab Environment." *Science,* 284, pp. 1670–74.

Crist, E. 1999. *Images of Animals.* Philadelpia: Temple University Press.

Curtiss, S. 1977. *Genie.* New York: Academic Press.

Gallaway, C., and Richards, B.J. (Eds.) 1994. *Input and Interaction in Language Acquisition.* Cambridge: Cambridge University Press.

Gardner, R.A., Gardner, B.T., and Van Cantfort, T.E. (Eds.). 1989. *Teaching Sign Language to Chimpanzees*. Albany: SUNY Press.

Gill, J.H. 1997. *If a Chimpanzee Could Talk*. Tucson: University of Arizona Press.

Goldstein, H., and Hockenberger, E.H. 1991. "Significant Progress in Child Language Intervention: An 11-Year Retrospective." *Research in Developmental Disabilities,* 12(4), pp. 401–24.

Golinkoff, R.M., and Hirsh-Pasek, K. 1999. *How Babies Talk*. New York: Dutton.

Gopnik, M. (Ed.). 1997. *The Inheritance and Innateness of Grammars*. New York: Oxford University Press.

Gottlieb, G. 1997. *Synthesizing Nature-Nurture: Prenatal Roots of Instinctive Behavior*. Mahwah, NJ: Erlbaum.

Gottlieb, G., Wahlsten, D., and Lickliter, R. 1998. "The Significance of Biology for Human Development: A Developmental Psychobiological Systems View." Pp. 233–273 in R. Lerner (Ed.), *Handbook of Child Psychology*. Vol. 1, *Theoretical Models of Human Development*. New York: Wiley.

Gould, S.J. 1980. *Ever since Darwin*. New York: W.W. Norton.

Greenspan, S.I. 1997. *The Growth of the Mind*. Reading, MA: Addison-Wesley.

Griffith, E.M., Wehner, E.A., and Rogers, S.J. 1999. "Executive Functions in Young Children with Autism." *Child Development,* 70, pp. 817–32.

Karmiloff-Smith, A. 1992. *Beyond Modularity: A Developmental Perspective on Cognitive Science*. Cambridge, MA: MIT Press.

Kellog, W.N., and Kellog, L.A. 1933. *The Ape and the Child*. New York: Hafner Publishing.

Leonard, L. 1997. *Children with Specific Language Impairment*. Cambridge, MA: MIT Press.

Lerner, R. (Ed.). 1998. *Handbook of Child Psychology*. Vol. 1, *Theoretical Models of Human Development*. New York: Wiley.

Lock, A. 2001. "Preverbal Communication," in J.G. Bremner and A. Fogel (Eds.), *Blackwell Handbook of Infant Development*.

Monnot, M. 1999. "The Adaptive Function of Infant-directed Speech." *Human Nature.*

Ozonoff, S., Pennington, B.F., and Rogers, S.J. 1991. "Executive Function Deficits in High-Functioning Autistic Individuals." *Journal of Child Psychology and Psychiatry,* 32, pp. 1081–105.

Petitto, L. 1997. "In the Beginning: On the Genetic and Environmental Factors that Make Early Language Acquisition Possible." Pp. 45–69 in M. Gopnik (Ed.), *The Inheritance and Innateness of Grammars*. New York: Oxford University Press.

Pinker, S. 1999. *Words and Rules*. New York: Basic Books.

Savage-Rumbaugh, S., Murphy, J., Sevcik, R., Brakke, K., Williams S., and Rumbaugh, D. 1993. *Language Comprehension in Ape and Child*. Monographs of the Society for Research in Child Development, serial no. 233. Vol. 58, nos. 3–4. Chicago: University of Chicago Press.

Savage-Rumbaugh, S., Shanker, S., and Taylor, T. 1998. *Apes, Language, and the Human Mind*. New York: Oxford University Press.

Snowdon, C.T., and Hausberger, M. (Eds.). 1997. *Social Influences on Vocal Development*. Cambridge, UK: Cambridge University Press.

Tallal, P. 1976. "Rapid Auditory Processing in Normal and Disordered Language Development." *Journal of Speech and Hearing Research,* 19, pp. 561–71.

Taylor, T.J. 1997. *Theorizing Language*. Oxford: Pergamon Press.

21

I Object: Mind and Brain as Darwinian Things

Charles J. Lumsden

There have, roughly speaking, been four great watersheds or turning points in the biological history of life on our planet, a history that spans more than four billion years, or some 20 percent of the history of our universe itself. Edward O. Wilson and I have termed these the megaevolutionary steps behind the emergence of our conscious mind in order to distinguish their ecological scope and historical impact from the more familiar, but no less remarkable, events and mechanisms of micro-evolution (within species) and macroevolution (creating species) (Lumsden and Wilson, 1983). Although the recent outcome of these great turning points, each occurring about a billion years apart, is us, it would be a complete mistake to see them, on the basis of our current understanding, as in any way predestined or ordained to cause our appearance. That we are here seems indisputable, at least since Descartes: an upstart primate species taking its self-reflective turn gazing at the stars. Why we are here remains a subject of lively debate, at least among academics and parents of postmodern adolescents.

The first huge evolutionary twist in the road to human consciousness (Lumsden and Wilson, 1983; Wilson, 1993) seems to have passed through some becalmed tidal pool about three billion years ago, when the prebiotic dance of primitive self-replicating polymers hit a cusp: the assembly of multiple polymer replicators into the first one-cell microorganisms. A billion years later, multiple microorganisms had invented a form of symbiosis that produced the first complex or eukaryotic cells through the assembly of the cellular nucleus, mitochondrial energy organelles, and other complex membrane-bound intercellular compartments. Following a billion years of experimentation with cell-membrane proteins allowing increasingly complex forms of cell-cell adhesion and intercellular communication, the eukaryotes went on to form the basis of all advanced multicellular life of Earth, including the brain tissue on which your mind supervenes. Then, about a billion years ago, from the initial primitive multicellular agglomerations diverged the first organisms (initially in the form of flatworms and crustaceans) built according to well-defined body plans (Raff, 1996). The oceans, lands, and skies exploded with a diversity of organisms as complex, tightly interlocked eco-systems blanketed the globe amid the slow, unstoppable drift of the continents. Oceans opened and closed, and a billion years after the first metazoan life, some-where in Africa, the ancestral form of the conscious awareness you and I possess woke up.

What, then, are we, and what systems of thought must we create in order to comprehend our origins, meaning, and future? Are we gene machines pro-grammed for the expansive replication of nucleic acid, to be understood through the tenets of Darwinism and molecular biology? Perhaps instead we are carbon-based Turing machines awash in a language of thought that will be mapped by the algorithms and theorems of computer science. (In my parents' day the analogy was the cable-festooned switchboard of the harried telephone operator. Voice-mail systems need not apply: Press zero to reach something human.) On the other hand, we could be texts that read and deconstruct one another while being written by our overculture and edited by ourselves, comprehensible primarily through the deftly circuitous ploys of literary analysis. Or maybe it is dualism all the way, with our brain a transient home for a spirit knowable only in theological terms, a destiny grander than we ever will know without being there.

Serious, essential exploration of the mind today encompasses all these options and more. In keeping with the perspective set for this volume, my concern here will be primarily with alternatives and metaphors like the first two in the preceding paragraph, in other words, with mind, science, and the march of scientism—evolutionary science and scientism in particular. My purpose is simple. I intend to note, as others have noted, that in a period of stunning progress in the science of brain and mental activity, third-person descriptions of psychological processes do not suffice. In fact, they are radically insufficient because they do not in them-selves make intelligible the subjectivity of conscious existence. We can count syn-apses on nerve cells, map blood flow and metabolic activity in living brains, mea-sure cranial volumes of our hominid ancestors, chart rules and heuristics by which we stumble through the tough personal choices in our lives, and trace the natural history of brain anatomy and development, learning strategies, and complex be-havior across many species, including our own. But none of these analyses of neural and mental structure and function are, in themselves, telling us what con-scious states are.

They fail to reveal the answer to this question because, as Thomas Nagel famously pointed out (1974, 1986, 1997), disciplines like our current sciences, which objectively systematize existence from the third-person perspective, do not automatically systematize it from the first person perspective. In the matter of consciousness, the first-person perspective is essential. Thus for a creature to be conscious, to have any kind of conscious experience, is at least for that creature to have a point of view on the universe, to be in a state in which there is something it is like to be that creature. How do we describe and come to terms with this? Nagel has, I think appropriately, asked us to consider how far short our sciences fall of being able to answer questions such as what it is like to be a bat (or a dolphin or a soaring eagle) and, correctly, asks for the development of objective ways of understanding existence that will provide such answers. My second purpose here is to suggest that, perhaps unexpectedly, evolutionary theory may help to found this new discipline.

Before proceeding, I must note that there is a fairly traditional response to Nagel's position by scholars working within third-person, functionalist scientific approaches to mind and behavior. It is a sort of semantic version of the "hopeful-monster" scenario in evolutionary thinking. "Hopeful monsters" (HMs) are imaginary constructs used as foils in various deflationary critiques of adaptationist thinking in population biology. The classical HM is a one-of-a-kind mutant that springs from its sires into a population facing hard times; vastly improved by genetic mutation to deal with the harsh rigors of survival and reproduction, the HM casts its seed before the wind, so to speak, so that its lucky descendants will benefit from the "improved" mutant genes it passes on to them.

Nagel's thesis has been met by a number of epistemological HMs, all of which are more or less of the causal-residuum type. They come in two variants or flavors that begin with a scientific commonplace: Neuroscience and cognitive science are, after all, making inroads in the causal explanation of brain, thinking, and behavior. So (the reasoning goes) the unknown is in some genuine sense receding, leaving a smaller and smaller residuum that we do not understand in terms of structure-function relationships. Properly continued (this is where the first sort of HM comes in), it can be hoped that this process of experiment and theorizing will create a unified science spanning all the scholarly disciplines, with no causal residuum left at all. Or perhaps ultimately we will be left holding a residuum that no amount of causal ingenuity can reduce, but its boundaries will be sufficiently circumscribed so that, through our imaginations working in novel modes like that of "heterophenomenological narrative" (Dennett, 1991, 1996), we will penetrate the final unknown.

Unfortunately for these HMs, causal consilience is not the issue, because no amount of structure-function explanation is going to tell us what a conscious state is like to have. It is, however, also a mistake to interpret the priority of the subjective as a call for ways of knowing that are in themselves at most subjective, or that continue to rely only on our intrinsic potential for sympathetic imagination to put ourselves into the viewpoint of another conscious being. Instead, the challenge is twofold. First, we must begin more fully to understand what it is objectively to describe and objectively to know the first-person subjective. Nagel has argued extensively that the first-person subjectivity at issue here is not some phantasmal nuance knowable only to that person himself or herself; rather, it is a mode of being that admits of public comprehension, in part because it is expressed in the world through a body whose design is shared by others. Second, this form of understanding must itself be fully consistent and, if possible, integrated with the third-person causal perspectives of the physical, biological, and social sciences. It is not to be gotten, if it can be gotten at all, through acts of imagination (this we already can do), but through new ways of knowing that allow objective discourse about the first person.

The program outlined by Nagel itself wavers back and forth between two objectives: the call for objective facts about what it is like to occupy a particular conscious viewpoint, and the call for procedures or ways of being that would allow us to slip out of our own subjectivity and live at least momentarily in that of another—not to know what it is like for you to be the bat, but for the bat to be the bat. There is also a sliding scale of specificity in this type of thinking about which we have to be very careful. Given our current state of understanding, the difficulty of the anticipated project increases very rapidly as the focus narrows from facts common to the subjectivity of a group or species of embodied beings to the facts unique to one individual. I will be primarily concerned with the middle ground in this range. Before discussing the relevance to it of modern ideas about human evolution, let us briefly consider the implications of what we might call the standard view of biosocial evolution.

The Standard View

In this section I am going to be talking about classical sociobiology, the discipline launched by Edward O. Wilson's remarkable book *Sociobiology: The New Synthesis* in 1975. The subject is important both as a step to the modern evolutionary treatment of the human mind and as a means of bridging treatments of the human mind with those of nonhuman species.

I have colleagues who have given up using the term "sociobiology" except in circumstances that require a faintly pejorative allusion to what, supposedly, Darwinism is not good for. This may be due to the fact that sociobiology, with its ambitious goals of providing a science that could help unify the study of all forms of social existence, emerged at a time in which intellectual life, at least on some American campuses, was torn by post-Vietnam era debates that pitted middle-class, neoradical leftism against the presumed hegemony of so-called totalizing discourses, as if our freedom in some way were threatened by unities in our understanding. (A brief history of this episode in American intellectual history, recorded by two participants, is presented in Lumsden and Wilson, 1983.) It may also be due to the (at the time) inflammatory view that activity in the human genome helps shape the human mind and human behavior, as if individual liberty were threatened by an organic as well as a cultural-heritage component in our individual identity and uniqueness—a view astonishingly dated as we stand on the threshold of mapping the entire human genome and its manifold established effects on brain development and function.

Sociobiology, however, is neither a political doctrine about human determinism nor a series of tales about how Darwinism explains everything on the subject of humankind. It is, rather, a part of evolutionary science concerned with the large-scale patterns and organizational properties of all forms of social existence. This makes sociobiology quite distinct from ethology and evolutionary psychology, both of which focus on the biology and behavior of individual organisms within their natural environments. In a rough way, sociobiology is to ethology and evolutionary psychology as cognitive science is to neurophysiology. Sociobiology's concern is with social populations considered as organized wholes, including the question of how the interactions of the individuals in the population fit together to form its observed patterns of communication, dominance, resource acquisition, and other activities. A novel contribution of sociobiology has been to suggest that these large-scale properties not only can be characterized and studied objectively, but can be explained as natural phenomena rooted in biological evolution. The intellectual charm of sociobiology is to understand how the material process of biological evolution can establish self-organizing social patterns that supervene on the complex flux of individual birth, growth, reproduction, and death.

Sociobiology, together with its allied disciplines of ethology and evolutionary biology, has been quite successful in illuminating the principal regularities of animal social existence and in tendering explanatory hypotheses based on the concept of kin selection or genetic altruism. (The classic presentation of kin selection and allied ideas is Wilson, 1975; for recent summaries, see Frank, 1998, and Hofbauer and Sigmund, 1998.) This concept will be of relevance in our examination of subjectivity, so let us consider it in some detail. Organisms, of course, do not pass themselves on to future generations. They pass on their genes; and over the course of time genes that cause an increased number of copies of themselves to be transmitted will automatically increase in abundance. In a social population, in which parents and offspring live in proximity, a gene may affect identical copies of itself not only through effects on the direct offspring of the organism in which it is contained, but also through effects on its kin. Parents, brothers, sisters, and other kin share genes in common. Thus, under the appropriate circumstances, a social population can be a fertile ground for the spread of genes that, through their effects on neural circuits for kin identification, increase the likelihood that individuals will engage in behaviors that assist not only themselves, but kin as well. This is altruism through kin selection. In a more cognitively complex species, with appropriate territoriality behavior individual learning, and long-term memory capacity, this kin selection can be paralleled by complex agendas of reciprocated assistance and favor giving between nonkin—a type of sociality called reciprocal altruism.

Sociobiology did not itself invent the ideas of kin selection, reciprocal altruism, and other mechanisms such as group selection. These (at the time) radical evolutionary theses were very much in the air three decades ago and became part of the synthesized framework devised by Wilson (1975) to argue for a unified science of animal social behavior. In doing so, Wilson proposed four major organizational modes, or "pinnacles," around which all social life on our planet seems to be arrayed, and he pointed out that the ideas of individual and kin selection, together with reciprocal altruism, provided a means of understanding them. (Group selection, the action of natural selection on assemblages of organisms taken as a whole, was also a contender, though it enjoyed exceptionally bad press at the time as evolutionary science worked its way though a period of extreme reductionism. The situation today is somewhat improved; see Sober and D.S. Wilson, 1998.) These pinnacles are the colonial invertebrates such as the corals and sponges; the social insects (the ants, the termites, and the social bees and wasps); the social mammals (except us); and humankind.

In the colonial invertebrates, the myriad individual organisms constituting the complex whole generally derive from the same fertilized egg and reproduce by simple budding and fissioning. In other words, they are clones of one another, each possessing the same genetic makeup. From the standpoint of the reasoning sketched earlier, behaviors that benefit other members of such a colonial assembly will therefore be closely similar or identical in their effect on a member's genetic replication to behaviors that benefit itself, and they may in fact be superior if this cooperation gives "returns to scale" that increase safety or nourishment through working together. Since every organism in such a colony shares the same genetic makeup, every one of them has the same agenda when it comes to boosting gene replication. A potential for a high degree of cooperation among the members of such assemblages is thus predicted and in fact is consistent with the tight integration observed in the more complex forms of these colonies, which become superorganisms with a physiological cohesion rivaling that of a single multicellular organism. My favorite example is the Portuguese man-of-war, which to the casual gaze looks like a kind of exotic jellyfish, but in fact is a colony of many specialized individuals working for the benefit of the few charged with forming and releasing the sex cells that will seed the new colonies.

Heavy benefits to kin also appear to have dominated the organization of social life among the ants, wasps, and bees, although the degree of integration observed in these societies does not quite rival that found among the advanced colonial invertebrates. Unlike us, sexual reproduction in these insects occurs by means of the so-called haplodiploid mode of gene transmission, with the result that sisters are more closely related to each other than they are to their mothers. They share some three-quarters of their genes by common descent. (In organisms like ourselves, siblings on average share just one-half of their genes by common descent, thanks to our diploid mode of gene transmission, in which a full nuclear gene complement is passed into the fertilized egg by both the mother and the father.) This close kinship again sets the stage for the evolution of enhanced cooperation among colony members, often involving sterile females organized into physically differentiated castes that carry out specialized tasks such as colony defense, food retrieval, and brood maintenance. Since the members of these colonies are not genetic clones, however, integration is not expected to rival that found in the colonial invertebrates; indeed, behaviors consistent with the pursuit of an individual reproductive agenda are observed. The nervous systems of these insects, while meticulously crafted, do not appear to be complex enough to support the more advanced features of individual recognition and autobiographical memory needed to engage in the kind of reciprocity of favors active in reciprocal altruism.

This is not the case in the social mammals, however, where large, complex brains sustain individual recognition and long-term memory for specific events. With diploid inheritance and some one-half of the genome shared among siblings by common descent, kin selection is weaker in these animal societies than it is in the colonial invertebrates and in the social insects, with greater strife and more focus on benefits to oneself, one's immediate kin, and perhaps one's current social allies. In this mode of existence, social life is a resource to exploit, rather than to serve and protect.

The ideas of individual and kin selection and of reciprocal altruism begin to make intelligible, at least in general terms, an otherwise paradoxical trend that cuts across the first three of the four pinnacles: As the complexities of brain and behavior go up, the cohesion and integration of the animal societies go down. Social evolution in human beings has dramatically reversed this trend, making possible huge societies based on diverse role specialization and highly complex forms of communication and information exchange. Before turning to the human case, however, I would like to pause and ask what the mode of reasoning we have sampled in this section, which connects propositions about genetic transmission to predicates about social form, might tell us about understanding the first-person perspective.

The Subjectivity Hypothesis: Darwinian Supervenience

It is appropriate to return to subjectivity at this point because, while not yet in sight of the sociobiological pinnacle representing human evolution, we at least have reached the bats (somewhere in the foothills of pinnacle three). Even though these nocturnal flyers have not much occupied the attention of sociobiologists as a paragon of animal sociality, ever since Thomas Nagel (1974) asked, "What is it like to be a bat?" they have been as entrenched in the debates about subjectivity as Erwin Schrödinger's legendary cat has been in the debates swirling around the meaning of quantum theory. (A congenial introduction to the quantum feline is Penrose et al., 1997.) Yet, properly grounded, the kind of sociobiological discourse we examined in the preceding section may provide new insight into what, objectively, it is like to be (for instance) a bat.

Why is this so? It is because, through sociobiology, we can talk about subjective experience without getting bogged down in the perils of perception. There is more to subjective experience than the way the world "looks," and sociobiology has something to say about this. Discussions of, for example, batness or bat subjectivity all too readily grind to a halt over the ineffable, scarcely imaginable strangeness of knowing how the world is when it is lived through sonar rather than sight. While the technology of virtual reality may eventually tear through these barriers to our imagination by allowing us more easily to slip out of our usual perceptual modes and into other, very alien modes, in the meantime, the ground covered by the subjectivity discussion can be productively expanded and linked to sociobiology and the rest of evolutionary science. There are four steps. The first three are already contained in the position staked out by Nagel, at least as I read him from my perspective as a working scientist. The first of these is subjective realism: Subjectivity exists and is essential to conscious experience as it is. The second is materialism: Our assertions about the first-person viewpoint and about the content of conscious experience must be entirely consistent with, and also perhaps must be able eventually to predict new things about, what we know of neurophysiology and psychology. The third step is objective synthesis in two different senses: One, we want an objective, public discourse about the subjective; and two, we can dream of a new mode of understanding the world in which the objective, third-person path to the conscious mind will be joined and integrated with the subjective, first-person path.

The fourth and final step is something different and incorporates the first three while going beyond them. I think that it is possible to state it simply, but properly developed, it has significant implications for helping us understand the conscious state. By step two, we require consistency with material cause and effect. Suppose, then, that we consider the mind of a creature like a bat, whose brain and behavior have been molded by the sociobiological processes we outlined earlier. Since that first person perspective is expressed through and enacted via the material embodiment of the organism, we can expect its nature and content to align with predictions made on the basis of the appropriate evolutionary forces, such as (for animal minds especially) kin selection, reciprocal altruism, and group selection. (I am not interested here in the view that the conscious mind is an epiphenomenon uncoupled from the organism's actions. The bankruptcy of such a stance, at least for science, if not for all the positive human disciplines, is self-evident.) Thus subjectivity is considered to express the net consequences of the organism's biological history just as much as any neural, biochemical, or physiological facet of its being in the world as that individual in that species at that moment in history.

I am suggesting this subjectivity hypothesis from the standpoint of theoretical understanding, rather than as an a priori assertion. In other words, from the hypothesis, objective predictions (possible-fact predicates) follow. We then may concentrate on positive work: strong procedures for inference making and stringent methods for inference testing. I will have little further to say about either of the points just mentioned, aside from noting that their importance is not diminished one whit by the evolutionary direction I have given them. I will return to them more fully in the final "Discussion" section. Rather, what we should note at once is that in contrast to stipulations about perceptual experience, these predicates are rich in content that describe the focus or center of conscious experience—that is, they express the shaping of subjectivity by the lived experience of the organism's values, motives, and desires. Thus, to list only the simplest assertions that already will be familiar from our treatment of classical sociobiology in the last section: To be a bat is to value one's own reproductive interests over that of strangers. To be a bat is to concentrate on the needs of at most one's immediate kin (almost always one's offspring). To be a bat is to have a brain specialized for high-speed aerial navigation and prey detection, and, with strict payload demands, sparing no neural matter for the complexities of elaborate alliance building and maintenance. So to be a bat is to be minimally interested in animal politics.

What is immediately interesting about these propositions is not, I think, so much their putative truth or falsity, but that we at once can identify ourselves with them, pro or con (true primates, our fascination with animal politics is comparatively insatiable alongside that of diminutive bat). Mammals ourselves, with a billion-plus years of diploid genetic evolution preceding the African burst of hominids, we shared much evolutionary history with the bat before our paths, deep in geological time, diverged, so we feel the pull of these perspectives, however much our subsequent evolutionary journey may have affected us. In matters of survival and reproduction, we tune into the bat more readily than we tune into the ant or the coral.

Us

While classical sociobiology has been notably successful in treating animal social existence, its application to human society has proven much more problematic. There is little surprise in this, since it is in animals rather than humans that we find more direct linkages between genetic activity during development and the final structure of brain and behavior — that is, animal minds sufficiently hardwired by the genes to be influenced by evolutionary forces. No similar kind of hardwired genetic pattern seems evident in the human mind; indeed, until the early 1980s, the question of how sociobiological thinking might be properly extended to humanity remained unclear. Although the bulk of Wilson's original sociobiological synthesis, which drew together the principles and data pertinent to animal sociality, provoked widespread attention, it was the chapter in which he applied adaptationist thinking to human societies that provoked howls of outrage (Lumsden and Wilson, 1983). These intensified a few years later when Wilson broadened the sociobiological analysis of humankind in his Pulitzer Prize–winning book *On Human Nature* (Wilson, 1978). But despite the controversy and the progress, clear limitations in the classical sociobiological approach were by then evident. The relation of culture to biological evolution could be treated in only the most cursory of terms, and, confined by the traditional focus of ethology and comparative psychology on behavior rather than inner processes, extensions to issues concerning the human mind were virtually impossible.

In 1981 Wilson and I presented a major generalization of sociobiological theory intended to clear the way for an evolutionary science of social existence in organisms with a complex mental life and a history based on the transmission of both genetic and cultural information between generations (Lumsden and Wilson, 1981). Advanced and refined during the past two decades, this theory of gene-culture coevolution forms the basis of our current treatments of the human mind and its connection to the sciences (e.g., Wilson, 1998; Lumsden, 1999; Lumsden, Brandts, and Trainor, 1997). As a means of reasoning about human nature, the gene-culture theory (GCT) has several notable differences when compared to classical sociobiology, evolutionary psychology, and ethology. First, GCT is not a priori adaptationist; in other words, it does not assume that well-understood forces of natural selection dominate the evolution of mind, and that, as a consequence, the principal scientific task is to explain what feature of a mental state adapts the organism to its environment, and why. Instead, GCT is based on a general quantitative treatment, expressed in mathematical form, of the dynamics of genetic, mental, and cultural information states characterizing a population. Although natural selection forces can be present, they are only one element in a web of interacting effects that include learning, teaching, innovation, social trends, and the random wash of mutation and individual happenstance. Under some circumstances, the genetic history of the population unfolds in a manner analogous to one controlled by the familiar adaptationist effects of kin selection and reciprocal altruism. More often, however, the evolution is different, at times strikingly so: Opportunities for group selection effects can, for instance, be enhanced; culturally transmitted codes for true altruism can spread through a population, even in the absence of kin selection or reciprocal altruism effects; and the interlocking reciprocal action of genetic and cultural change also can destabilize the biocultural history of such a population, so that instead of occupying a well-defined adaptive pinnacle, it pursues a complex, chaotic path of continual biocultural change.

What causes these differences? On the basis of current evidence, they are explained by the fact that the human mind is positioned midway in a network of reciprocal cause and effect, connecting genome to culture and back again. In human development, gene expression does not hardwire mental characteristics in any but the simplest cases of primitive reflexes. It is in the shaping of our mental development, not in the setting of final mental states, that human genome activity appears to exert its strongest action. It provides the basic neural competence for socialization and enculturation across the vast diversity of human social life, but it also makes some, rather than other, pathways or directions in our mental development more likely. We have termed the patterns of genome expression regulating these pathways the epigenetic rules and have divided them into two provisional classes: the primary epigenetic rules serving initial sensory processing and perception and the secondary epigenetic rules mediating the central processes of learning, memory, choice, and decision. Both classes are central to the emergence of consciousness in its uniquely human form.

Gene activity via the epigenetic rules thus instantiates a feed forward from the human genome through neural development to the mind. The myriad decisions we must all make, our choices about our styles of embodied existence and their expression in action, form the raw material of collective social life, from which there is a dual feedback that affects both mind and genome. The first is the flow of experience — socialization, teaching, learning, hanging out — through the epigenetic rules and thus into our individual life histories of mental growth and change. The second is the impact of these experiences on choices affecting our survival and reproduction. This chain of reciprocal causation running from the genome through mental development to the mind and culture and back again we have termed the circuit of gene-culture coevolution. The coevolutionary circuit, in the form it has acted on and through a succession of hominid populations over the past several million years, appears to be fundamental to understanding what, in contrast to the forces shaping animal social evolution, has made us human.

The epigenetic rules are also, I believe, keys to further unlocking the mysteries of human subjectivity. Their shaping action may be anticipated to leave its mark on our first-person viewpoints just as much as, if not more than, on the vast hidden realm of unconscious processing that sees to the cognitive housekeeping, because it is within these viewpoints that we make the choices and decisions that propel gene-culture coevolution from generation to generation. Because evolutionary science has just begun its analysis of coevolution, we must be even more tentative and provisional at this stage than we were earlier in making contact with the bat's perspective on its world by means of classical sociobiology. Part of the epigenetic pattern is, however, already somewhat clarified. Thus to be human is to have a subjective awareness limited to considering about three to seven chunks of experience at the same time; to be human is to experience the world as conceptual saliences organized as semantic clusters with prototypical members and often vague, overlapping boundaries; to be human is to need several seconds to link ideas in a new way, and yet to much more quickly recall this linkage once we have brought it into existence; and, perhaps paradoxically, since we are epigenetically conscious yet still diploid in our genetic aspect of our embodiment, to be human is, like the bat, to feel the pull of allegiances to self, kin, and our social allies while asking ourselves if these are right, and if their normative demands are worthy of us.

Discussion

There are serious objections to a subjectivity hypothesis of the form I have treated here. I will discuss three of these objections: scope, "skinning," and checking. The first two are, I believe, a product of the flexibility built into current arguments about subjectivity, while the third follows at once from any pretensions that a method might have to achieve some degree of objectivity.

Regarding scope, it can easily be objected that the inferences I have tendered are too broad because they are applicable (in the simplest instances) to an entire species. But this is, I think, a natural place to start such a treatment, since it is at the species level that we find a commonality of embodiment—a similarity in sensory, perceptual, and motor experience—and a shared evolutionary history consistent with mutually intelligible expressions of subjectivity. The application of an epigenetic approach, in which the particulars affecting the unique development of specific groups or individuals are taken into account, may then afford a means of narrowing the focus to increasingly singular modes of conscious experience. This is a crucial step, but in taking it, we must not lose touch with the positive intent of the founding program: After all, the question that was asked of us was what it is like to be *a* bat, not what it is like to be *that* bat over there.

"Skinning" is the subjectivity analog of the fact-value confusion in ethics. In calling for (objective) facts about the first-person perspective, we must not confuse fact finding—even exhaustive fact finding—with a procedure that lets us slip out of our skin and into that of another to possess that creature's first-person viewpoint on the universe. As Nagel argues (1974, 1986), even lacking an objective treatment of subjectivity, we can, via our gift of sympathetic imagination, partially adopt the viewpoint of another, provided that that other can be imaginatively "read." There is no reason to doubt that sets of objective facts will assist this perspective shifting, but there seems little reason at present to believe that such sets are either necessary or sufficient for the process to be completed successfully. Indeed, at the present time, the matter of transforming ourselves so that each of us may know what it is like to be *that* bat over *there* seems much less secure than, through Darwinian supervenience and its extensions to the gene-culture setting, beginning to articulate potentially objective facts about *a* bat.

Finally, there is the matter of checking or testing. Hypotheses about subjective experience need to be checkable if we are to achieve even a minimal measure of objectivity in our search for understanding. This counts as one of the principal challenges in the subjectivity program. Among possible options, I would like to draw attention to the ideas of Stephen Burwood, Paul Gilbert, and Kathleen Lennon (1999; BGL hereafter) as to how we might meet it. Drawing on a sustained critique of current functionalist and interpretationalist models in cognitive science, BGL consider the modern phenomenological tradition and argue strongly for the irreducible role of expressive embodiment both in conscious experience and in the public understanding of the subjectivity it incorporates. Although the importance of embodiment to mind is now widely appreciated (e.g., Damasio, 1999; Lakoff and Johnson, 1999; McClamrock, 1995; Nagel, 1986; Varela, Thompson, and Rosch, 1991), BGL go further. While space does not permit an adequate description of their reason-based formulation of subjective action, the idea, roughly, is that a subjective viewpoint is what makes an individual's action in an environment suited to it, and through our public knowledge about these actions and their suitability, we may come, at least in part, to some objective conclusions about the subjective viewpoint therein expressed. I suggest that the vigorous elaboration of ideas like these may lead to rapid progress in our understanding of what, in fact, a checkable treatment of objective facts about subjectivity is going to be like, and thus, also, what it will mean to treat a hypothesis like Darwinian supervenience with them.

Recently, both philosophers and scientists concerned with the mind have cautioned about the uncritical use of evolutionary ideas to explain human nature (among the more outspoken have been Nagel, 1997; Taylor, 1989; Wilson, 1998; and Lumsden, 1999). Some of the concerns are better founded than others. Objections based on excess incredulity are ill founded. In such cases, the relationship between evolutionary adaptive value and some characteristic of mental existence (such as our ability to do abstract mathematics) is noted to be hard to see. That our scientific imagination falls short at such times in itself, of course, proves nothing about the veracity of the conjectured connection between mind trait and evolutionary process. Only further investigation will suffice. More relevant are concerns about the back-to-front style used in (too) much adaptationist thinking about human mental evolution, which too frequently is written out as though we know for sure that a specific natural selection principle (such as kin selection) actually moved the human mind to an adaptive pinnacle. This sounds good; if we take such a proposal seriously, all we must do is say what it is about the specific mental characteristic (e.g., the real-time capacity of short-term memory) that optimizes the adaptive principle (e.g., maximizes inclusive fitness).

Alas, it is just not so. As my discussion of gene-culture coevolution earlier was intended to note, we are early in the period of rigorously understanding the mechanisms underlying the mind's evolution in a species like ours. Much further work will be needed before handy rules of thumb are established telling us what, if anything is optimized or maximized during gene-culture coevolution. If they are so established, the next step will be to use them right way round, shifting from the current fashion of post hoc storytelling over to prediction testing. In the current fashion, it is all too easy to wrap a general qualitative notion about kin selection or reciprocal altruism around a puzzle like brain size or the appearance of language and thereby concoct one of those notorious just-so evolutionary stories about why our brains just had to be big or language just the way it is. This is at most protoscience.

The reader may have noted that our approach to bat subjectivity did not run back to front, in the manner of just-so storytelling. We did not begin with the facts about bat subjectivity (none, apparently, are yet in hand) and then build a soft apology about why they had to evolve that way. Instead, for the bat, we began with the general principles of kin selection and then used the hypothesis of Darwinian supervenience to make predictions about principal characteristics of the bat's subjective viewpoint. The resulting inferences may or may not be true, but that is, I think, just the point.

It is also the case that I have approached subjectivity and Nagel's question by stressing similarities rather than differences. Because we share much evolutionary history with the bat, and because, like the bat, we are mammals that sire offspring through diploid genetic transmission, sociobiology suggests that we share more common ground than we at first might think, including subjective ground. This is not to deny differences, nor is it to suggest that the facts and experiences of these differences are less significant than are the similarities we share. (I for one would be first in line to spend a moment or two in the skin of a bat.) But I do mean to suggest that a full treatment of subjective experience must include both, and that similarities may prove a basis for coming to terms with the differences. In fact, it is from within this enlarged viewpoint—of ranges of similarities and differences—that we can appreciate one of sociobiology's principal contributions to this subject: the unity of life. To some, questions about our conscious experience lead inevitably to concerns about the singularity of the self, its place and meaning in a world teeming with other subjectivities. Can we ever hope to reach them? Sociobiology, an evolutionary science, reminds us of the common ancestry we share with all living things on Earth and beyond (Bylinsky, 1981; Dixon, 1981, 1990), bat to dolphin to exoterran life forms yet unknown. Shaped by common evolutionary forces, yet each a species with its own unique history, those endowed with conscious experience inevitably confront each other with a shared heritage of mind as well as body. Pristine solitude? Perhaps in other worlds, but at least in Darwin's universe, one is never truly alone.

References

Burwood, Stephen, Gilbert, Paul, and Lennon, Kathleen. 1999. *Philosophy of Mind.* Montreal: McGill–Queen's University Press.

Bylinsky, Gene. 1981. *Life in Darwin's Universe: Evolution and the Cosmos.* Garden City, NY: Doubleday.

Damasio, Antonio. 1999. *The Feeling of What Happens: Body and Emotion in the Making of Consciousness.* New York: Harcourt Brace.

Deacon, Terrence W. 1997. *The Symbolic Species: The Co-evolution of Language and the Brain.* New York: W.W. Norton.

Dennett, Daniel C. 1991. *Consciousness Explained.* Boston: Little, Brown.

———. 1996. *Kinds of Minds: Toward an Understanding of Consciousness.* New York: Basic Books/HarperCollins.

Dixon, Dougal. 1981. *After Man: A Zoology of the Future.* New York: St. Martin's Press.

———. 1990. *Man after Man: An Anthropology of the Future.* New York: St. Martin's Press.

Frank, Steven A. 1998. *Foundations of Social Evolution.* Princeton, NJ: Princeton University Press.

Hofbauer, Josef, and Sigmund, Karl. 1998. *Evolutionary Games and Population Dynamics.* New York: Cambridge University Press.

Lakoff, George, and Johnson, Mark. 1999. *Philosophy in the Flesh: The Embodied Mind and Its Challenge to Western Thought.* New York: Basic Books/Perseus Books Group.

Lumsden, Charles J. 1999. "Evolving Creative Minds: Stories and Mechanisms." Pp. 153–69 in Robert J. Sternberg (Ed.), *Handbook of Creativity.* New York: Cambridge University Press.

Lumsden, Charles J., Brandts, Wendy A., and Trainor, Lynn E.H. (Eds.). 1997. *Physical Theory in Biology: Foundations and Exploration.* London: World Scientific.

Lumsden, Charles J., and Wilson, Edward O. 1981. *Genes, Mind, and Culture: The Coevolutionary Process.* Cambridge, MA: Harvard University Press.

———. 1983. *Promethean Fire: Reflections on the Origin of Mind.* Cambridge, MA: Harvard University Press.

McClamrock, Ron. 1995. *Existential Cognition: Computational Minds in the World.* Chicago: University of Chicago Press.

Nagel, Thomas. 1974. "What Is It Like to Be a Bat?" *Philosophical Review,* 83, pp. 435–50.

———. 1986. *The View from Nowhere.* New York: Oxford University Press.

———. 1997. *The Last Word.* New York: Oxford University Press.

Penrose, Roger, with Shimony, Abner, Cartwright, Nancy, and Hawking, Stephen. 1997. *The Large, the Small, and the Human Mind.* New York: Cambridge University Press.

Raff, Rudolf. 1996. *The Shape of Life: Genes, Development, and the Evolution of Animal Form.* Chicago: University of Chicago Press.

Sober, Elliott, and Wilson, David S. 1998. *Unto Others: The Evolution and Psychology of Unselfish Behavior.* Cambridge, MA: Harvard University Press.

Sternberg, Robert J. (Ed.). 1999. *Handbook of Creativity.* New York: Cambridge University Press.

Taylor, Charles. 1989. *Sources of the Self: The Making of the Modern Identity*. Cambridge, MA: Harvard University Press.

Varela, Francisco J., Thompson, Evan, and Rosch, Eleanor. 1991. *The Embodied Mind: Cognitive Science and Human Experience*. Cambridge, MA: MIT Press.

Wilson, Edward O. 1975. *Sociobiology: The New Synthesis*. Cambridge, MA: Belknap Press of Harvard University Press.

————. 1978. *On Human Nature*. Cambridge, MA: Harvard University Press.

————. 1993. *The Diversity of Life*. New York: W.W. Norton.

————. 1998. *Consilience: The Unity of Knowledge*. New York: Alfred A. Knopf.

VI

Is the Mind a Cultural Entity?

Introduction

David Martel Johnson

All three of the chapters in this part take the form of commentaries on the work of other authors. Jerome Bruner's chapter comments on the French philosopher Ignace Meyerson. David Bakhurst's chapter criticizes certain ideas proposed by Bruner himself and then—in an attempt to "straighten the teeth" of Bruner's position—compares these ideas with corresponding themes in the work of the Russian thinker Evald Ilyenkov. Finally, the chapter by Jens Brockmeier is a series of observations about still another Russian, the linguist, semiotician, and literary and cultural scholar Mikhail Bakhtin. One reason these chapters take the form they do is that their authors share a certain conviction, that the founders of present-day cognitive science conceived of this field (one that grew out of nineteenth-century German roots and is now largely centered in Anglo-Saxon countries) in such a narrow and prejudiced way as to make it difficult for their intellectual descendants to make realistic sense of human mentality. Furthermore, according to these authors, this unsatisfactory situation would be improved if we could open that discipline to influences from other, relatively independent intellectual traditions associated with parts of the world that cognitive scientists neglected in the past.

Another shared theme of the three chapters brought together here is a concern with the link between mind and culture. To be more precise, they ask: How, why, and to what extent can invented and learned skills, programs, intellectual movements, and the like determine characteristics we traditionally think of as belonging to the human mind? Most present-day cognitive scientists have an ambivalent attitude toward this question. On the one hand, they—like everyone else—are familiar with the obvious fact that cultural factors have important effects on the thoughts and actions of individual humans. For example, both scientific investigation and ordinary experience show that members of distinguishable cultural groups tend to behave, assess, choose, and think in systematically different ways. On the other hand, cognitive scientists are also inclined to believe it is difficult or impossible to account for such cultural influences in a legitimately scientific manner—that is, in dispassionate, objective, and measurable terms that allow one to relate those influences to other, more established areas of scientific concern. In fact, many of the people in question suppose, in the style of Wilhelm Wundt, that cultural influences do not count as ordinary scientific factors that are capable of being analyzed explicitly and methodically, but instead are parts of a vague "background of life" that one must approach through the use of metaphor. In other words, adapting a phrase Bruner uses in a chapter in another book (1997, p. 287), getting a grip on the slippery subject of cultural influences on mentality seems to require the antiscientific procedure of "going literary."

However, one principal theme, not just of the chapters here, but of this whole volume, is that this idea is mistaken. For instance, anyone who encountered the third chapter, Jens Brockmeier's "The Text of the Mind," in another context, where it appeared just by itself, might be justified in supposing that it was a literary essay rather than one relevant to science, because it argues (through the author's interpretation of Bakhtin) that the human mind is a set of linguistic entities—for example, assertions, sentences, and texts. What else could this be, readers might ask, except a poetic image like those that occur in Lewis Carroll's *Alice in Wonderland*? In this context, however, the fact that Brockmeier's chapter is preceded by Bruner's "Ignace Meyerson and Cultural Psychology" and Bakhurst's "Strong Culturalism" throws a different light on things. Reading the chapters in this order shows that the claims of Brockmeier (and Bakhtin) need not be irrelevant to science after all, because—despite what some have supposed—it is both possible and legitimate for sciences like psychology, linguistics, and biology to take account of cultural factors like meaning, language, obligation, past experience, and history.

Let me bring this introduction to a close by mentioning just one illustration of the preceding point (a case based on certain remarks Bruner makes in his chapter). The means by which the nineteenth-century German psychologist Hermann Ebbinghaus proposed to challenge Wundt's assertion that "higher processes" like thought and memory could not be studied experimentally was by setting forth the following procedure: Experimenters could test the strength of any given instance of memory, Ebbinghaus argued, by first having their subject learn a list of nonsense syllables and then measuring how long it took him or her to relearn (and in this sense, recall) that same list later (see Boring, 1957, pp. 386–89; and Fancher, 1990, pp. 177–78). Furthermore, even today, many psychologists continue to think of Ebbinghaus's method of testing memory as an implicit proof that their discipline amounts to "real science." But even though, in some respects, this approach represented a step in the right direction, it also was misleading in other respects, for the following reason: The more discoveries experimenters made about the way human memory operates, the plainer it became to them that, generally speaking, the power and effectiveness of this mental ability, as measured by its success or failure in well-defined circumstances, depends on the scope, richness, and meaningfulness of the context within which subjects are able to set the item or material they are attempting to remember. For instance, what allows a good bridge player to recall all the cards that have been played so far in a game (and thus infer those that have not yet been played)? The answer is that this seemingly remarkable feat of memory results from the fact that the player organizes the game in terms of, for example, a distinction between the good or potentially winning cards that still remain in circulation at any given stage of play, as opposed to the cards that do not fall into that same category (see Baddeley, 1982, especially chapter 3). At least in this respect, then, attempts to illuminate the dynamics of a person's memory by referring to experimental results that involve "neutral" and "simple" elements like nonsense syllables point us in precisely the wrong direction.[1] Generalizing from this case, the lesson we should learn is that it is unhelpful and unrealistic for psychologists to follow a policy of appealing to observations that are as meaningless, brief, and context free as they are able to make them. Instead, practitioners of this and also of the other cognitive sciences need to find means of taking careful, systematic, and experimental account of sophisticated expressions of culture. For example, at least some of the empirical data they recognize should be richly patterned, should be closely connected with the rules, traditions, and institutions of their subjects' society, and should extend over nontrivial amounts of time.[2]

Notes

1. As Bruner mentions, one relatively early researcher who grasped this point was F.C. Bartlett (see Bartlett, 1967).

2. On this last point, see what Edward Reed (1997) says about "stimuli."

References

Baddeley, Alan. 1982. *Your Memory: A User's Guide.* New York: Macmillan.

Bartlett, F.C. 1967. *Remembering: A Study in Experimental and Social Psychology.* London and New York: Cambridge University Press.

Boring, Edwin G. 1957. *A History of Experimental Psychology.* 2nd ed. New York: Appleton-Century-Crofts.

Bruner, Jerome. 1997. "Will Cognitive Revolutions Ever Stop?" Pp. 279–92 in D.M. Johnson and C.E. Erneling (Eds.), *The Future of the Cognitive Revolution.* New York: Oxford University Press.

Fancher, Raymond E. 1990. *Pioneers of Psychology.* 2nd ed. New York: W.W. Norton.

Johnson, D.M., and Erneling, C.E. (Eds.). 1997. *The Future of the Cognitive Revolution.* New York: Oxford University Press

Reed, Edward. 1997. "The Cognitive Revolution from an Ecological Point of View." Pp. 261–73 in D.M. Johnson and C.E. Erneling (Eds.), *The Future of the Cognitive Revolution.* New York: Oxford University Press.

22

Ignace Meyerson and Cultural Psychology

Jerome Bruner

Mainstream psychology is just at the close of its first century of scientific "respectability." Respectability, even scientific respectability, always comes at a price, and so it is with psychology's new academic respectability. To qualify, the new discipline was to conduct itself with all the decorum and the caution befitting a nineteenth-century positivist science. It was to be factual and objective, and it was to eschew the subjective and insubstantial. How people interpreted the world, how they made sense of it, and how they constructed meanings were not fit topics for the new science unless they could be reduced to manageable centimeters, grams, seconds, and probabilities.

In taking on this Faustian bargain, psychology cut itself off from both historical and cultural scholarship. The humanities, what Wilhelm Dilthey had called the *Geisteswissenschaften*, became the "poor relations"—sometimes admired for their brio, but not to be taken seriously as a source of reliable knowledge about the real world. Psychology threw in its lot with the natural sciences.

This new "respectable" discipline duly dedicated itself to the study of behavior—what organisms do in the natural world, and never mind the context of historical, cultural meanings in which the doing occurred. We psychologists became intrigued with causal models that were immediate in their operations, virtually synchronic—reaction times, recognition times, the interval between the conditioned and unconditioned stimulus. Telos, history, collective tradition, and institutionalization became increasingly marginalized in the new psychology unless they could be given some biological reading as "evolutionary." Millisecond immediacy was plainly winning out against history and diachronicity. The only respectable diachronicity was social Darwinism, at least in the English-speaking positivist world. Besides, the new psychologists could easily translate Darwin into some version of "learning theory": What survived was what better adapted organisms to their environments. The study of adaptation could be as easily carried out in the controlled laboratory setting, without much heed for the messy historical detail of the real world.

The emphasis in the early years of the twentieth century grew increasingly individualistic, preoccupied with individual adaptation—although this was far more so in the anglophone than in the francophone intellectual world. There were vicious attacks in the first quarter of the twentieth century against all so-called mystical efforts to characterize collective aspects of mental functioning. Polemics against collective mentality, against the so-called Group Mind, were especially bitter, particularly in America—the hounding of William McDougall[1] for example, who many years later introduced me to psychology. It was the New Psychology's rejection of history and cultural tradition as relevant to the explanation or understanding of mind. As for a psychology of history, ordinary psychological theory would reduce it all to uniform principles of individual functioning.

Respectability is rarely a robust virtue; indeed, it is more a parody than a virtue. It soon becomes tiresome, often suffocating, to those who embrace it. Eventually it breeds rebellion among those raised under its chilling shadow. It is not surprising, then, that a new generation of psychologists has now become restless, increasingly eager to probe beyond man's kinship to the animal kingdom and to consider man's place in a cultural, historical, symbolic world—indeed, to consider how man constructs that symbolic world. Today, younger psychologists all over the world are preoccupied with what has now come to be called cultural-historical psychology. Its central premise is that our species has evolved into one that makes its world rather than simply finding it, and that this making is a collective act mediated by the complex instrumentality of human culture.

The new generation is discovering, of course, that there were always psychologists among us, even in the days of highest respectability, who were likewise in revolt against narrow positivism. Indeed, from the very start of our official existence, psychology's own founding fathers had mixed loyalties toward the exclusively positivist program of psychology—notably William James, but even Wilhelm Wundt, who abandoned the psychological laboratory to found a *Völkerpsychologie* dedicated to investigating the products of human endeavor in man's history. Their work has often been marginalized, treated by our forebears as a diversion from the positivist mainstream. I never knew until quite recently, for example, that the great Bronislaw Malinowski, a founding figure of modern anthropology, had actually studied with Wundt in Leipzig and had been influenced by his "folk psychology." But things are changing. We are rediscovering our past. Indeed, we are reinventing it. The Russian Lev Vygotsky, for example, is now being virtually canonized by some anglophone psychologists as an antipositivist, antibehaviorist icon—rather like a biblical David pitted against Ivan Pavlovich Pavlov's reductionist Goliath. Since reductionist behaviorism was as powerful in the United States (even without state support) as it ever was in Russia under the sheltering wing of the Communist Party, it is small wonder that Vygotsky's cultural-historical method has been given hungry attention in America. Surely Vygotsky merits the attention, but it is only a beginning, for we are still much in need of models who not only symbolize antibehaviorism, but who can lead us back into fruitful collaboration with the other human, cultural sciences—our former poor relations.

Until very recently, Ignace Meyerson was, to all intents and purposes, France's most closely guarded secret, his writing scarcely known to psychologists outside that country. Yet despite that, and by indirect means, the influence of Meyerson came to be felt, for even in France, Meyerson's thought had its major impact outside psychology. It reached psychology's humanist neighbors before it ever reached the consciousness of mainstream psychology—among historians, among students of autobiography, and among classicists and classical archeologists. There was his influence on the founding *Annales* historians, Febvre and Bloch, whose emphasis on man's constructed world(s) is typically Meyersonian. The message of the *Annales* school, ironically, soon came to be heard by psychologists. Indeed, it was *Annales* thinking that began to wean psychoanalysts (like Daniel Stern, for example) from their preoccupation with critical dramatic crises as the major formative factors in the life of the child.[2] Psychoanalysts like Stern are beginning to study the child's everyday construction of meaning in the ordinary routines of family living. The forming of mentalities is now a matter of psychological concern. Then there is Meyerson's voice in the writings of Philippe Lejeune,[3] focusing our attention on the implicit and conventional "contract" that governs the autobiographer's construction of his self and "life."[4] My own work on "narratives of self-making" owes much to the writings of Lejeune. Meyerson's voice is also to be heard in the classical scholarship of Jean-Pierre Vernant. I offer this quotation from his book with Pierre Vidal-Naquet. Citing Meyerson, these authors remark:

> The will is not a datum of human nature. It is a complex construction whose history appears to be as difficult, multiple, and incomplete as that of the self, of which it is to a great extent an integral part. . . . We must try to see how, through various forms of social practice (religious, political, legal, aesthetic, and technical), certain relations between the human subject and his actions come to be established. (Vernant and Vidant-Naquet, 1988, pp. 50–51)

Let me only note in passing that there was (in 1998) a new social psychology course being prepared at Britain's Open University that is virtually organized around the program implied in that quotation. I happen to know about it because I served in the interesting role of what the British call the "course assessor," a title virtually untranslatable even into American English. Up to now, Meyerson's influence on psychology (at least overseas) has come through the writings of the humanists he has so strongly influenced. But I see that changing.

Let me turn now to Meyerson's work itself—to the rich heritage of ideas that he has bequeathed us. I quickly confess that I am not an expert on Meyerson, but rather an ardent beginner. It was only in 1996 that I began my real acquaintance with him. Within an hour of beginning my reading of his collected papers, I felt my first pang: If only I had read these papers before writing my . . . , *car la culture donne forme à Esprit!* Indeed, I had already been reading Jean Pierre Vernant, Philippe Lejeune, and *Annales* historians like Georges Duby, Furet, and Françoise Philippe Aries for years—but why had I never read the master himself? Now let me come to the particulars.

There is one key programmatic Meyerson paper whose scope is so broad and so daring that it captured my attention immediately and has held it ever since. It was written for a *Festschrift* honoring the great phenomenological psychologist of figure-ground fame, David Katz. It is titled, "L'entree dans l'humain" and was first published in 1951. In it, Meyerson sets out about a dozen characteristics of "being human." The first four of them distinguish man from the rest of the animal kingdom; the remaining eight characterize what is distinctively human about human beings in their uniquely cultural-historical setting. I want to concentrate upon the latter of these uniquely human characteristics. But before I turn to these, let me remind you of the first four he chooses for distinguishing man from his evolutionary predecessors. They tell much about Meyerson's programma—and much about contemporary psychology.

Most of human conduct, in contrast to animal behavior, he begins, is "non directement necessaire à la conservation de la vie de l'individu ou de l'espèce" (Meyerson, 1987, p. 73). Law, art, religion, war, magic, technology—none is indispensable for life, or only very indirectly so; indeed, these activities sometimes work against biological adaptation. Yet these are the things that man most highly values in life. Second, man not only makes tools and instruments, adapting them to local conditions as necessary, but he takes collective measures to assure that the knowledge needed to do so is conserved and transmitted. It is this basic fact that makes "civilization" possible. We shall encounter this idea again in Meyerson's idea of *les oeuvres*. Human conduct, third, is virtually unlimited in its variability, only loosely tied to the species genome. Constraints on human variability, rather, are determined almost entirely by the stylizations imposed by social convention or by individual response to convention. Fourth, man uses a communally organized system of signs not only for communicating, but also for translating experience into symbolic forms. Thereby, man's world becomes a symbolically mediated one: "On peut dire que l'homme est un animal qui n'a pas de donnes immediates."

I could not help but think what a difference it would have made had we psychologists more closely heeded Meyerson's first four points about human life. Had we done so, first, psychology would never have become so exclusively preoccupied with a theory of motivation based on the model of animal drive, or on a notion of reinforcement based on drive satisfaction. We would have examined instead how human beings become committed to constructing shared realities that guide our actions toward each other and toward the world.[5] Second, had we heeded Meyerson, psychology would have looked at group behavior extending over long time spans, even over generations, rather than turning exclusively to laboratory studies of small groups of volunteer strangers assembled in a laboratory for an hour or two at the convenience of the experimenter[6]; and we would have been much more mindful of "collective invention," its conservation, and its transmission.[7] Third, psychological studies of human variability would not have been so closely linked to the normal, bell-shaped curve, but would have examined how the statistical distribution of human action is also shaped by cultural-historical constraints.[8] Indeed, it is probably when human response ceases to be normally distributed that it becomes uniquely interesting as human action. Fourth, psychology would have appreciated earlier and elaborated further the view that perception is, as it were, always social perception, and would have been suspicious earlier of such concepts as "the stimulus" as a direct impingement of the natural world. Even today, some philosophers of mind, like Dennett (1991) and Stich (1989), insist upon the "illusionary" quality of "meaning" in consciousness.

But that is only a start, for it is in his remaining guidelines that Meyerson makes his most original suggestions. Let me go through these one at a time and comment briefly on their significance for contemporary psychology.

1. His first principle emphasizes the *systematicity of human action*. In Meyerson's words, man's acts are formed in a fashion that subordinates them to goals, to social norms, and to perceived imperatives. It is this that embeds human acts into the culture's symbolic systems—language, religion, social hierarchies, and the rest. Action, in a word, cannot be understood without reference to the symbolic system to which it is subordinated. "Going to school" does not have the same meaning for inner-city black children in America as it does for whites. For black ghetto children it means getting caught in a system of failure controlled by race discrimination. It is this cultural construal that matters; if it can be changed, then school behavior changes. The proof is in community action changing self-definition through joint action within the broader community. Korean children in Japan (where Koreans suffer social and job discrimination) perform below the national level; in North America (where they do not suffer discrimination) children from the same kinds of backgrounds perform above the national level. When school is seen as "leading nowhere," Black children turn elsewhere: in America, to street culture and the petty crime that it promotes.

Is this just "common sense"? If it were only that, why is it not embodied in social policy? Why instead do we (at least in America) mandate better curricula, national standards, and a longer school year, especially when we know from social-educational experiments that locally inspired "job opportunity/job training" programs can be effective in changing the meaning of "going to school" among marginalized minority children?

2. This brings me to Meyerson's second principle, that human action is principally directed toward *work*—work that creates objects or services deemed useful or desirable for the group with whom one identifies himself or herself, and in whose symbolic world one lives. In human society, all else being equal, the meaning of work becomes transformed from a burden into a virtue. Meyerson saw this transformation as one of the most profound steps in human evolution. It is, in one sense, an incomplete, even a rather utopian, view of the division of labor and the meaning of work in human society. I take Meyerson to mean that it is within the power of human society to define work in such a way as to provide meaning and identity to those who perform it. When a culture fails to do this, alienation

follows. We know from Broadbent's investigations, for example, that job dissatis-faction produces not only absenteeism but bad health, low self-esteem, marital discord, accident-prone habits, and other negative effects. I want only to empha-size, with Meyerson, the centrality of work, that most human of phenomena, in organizing the human sense of self-worth.

3. Human action is not passive or reactive, but active and experimental in the sense of being tuned to the relation of means and ends. Man is attuned not only to the effects achieved by his own acts, but to the effects achieved by the acts of others. He is as sensitive to what acts are intended for as to what they actually achieve. Meyerson would not have been surprised by an experiment reported by Andrew Meltzoff (1995). Even eighteen-month-old infants imitate not what an adult actually does (simple imitation) but what the adult is seen as trying to do, even though the adult may have been interrupted. In a word, from very early on we are highly sensitive to the means-end structure of what we do and what others do. This point is further adumbrated in Meyerson's next one.

4. Human activity is directed toward the construction of a work, an *oeuvre*, to use the more appropriate French word. "L'homme est fabricateur et incarna-teur" (Meyerson, 1987, p. 76). Consequently, "L'esprit est d'autant plus esprit qu'il est plus réalisé." Finally, "L'esprit crée l'oeuvre, en même temps qu'elle l'exprime" (p. 76). It is in his works, then, that man is most formed, most authentic. The broader significance of this principle is spelled out in Meyerson's fifth point.

5. Man, as it were, bathes in a *world of works*: languages, religions, laws, sciences, modes of production. These shape him. This world of works, which constitutes the history of civilization, also forms the history of human psychological functioning. For example, concepts like "responsibility" or "accountability" have their origin not just in psychological processes, but in the historical oeuvre that constitutes our legal system. Law shapes mind, however true it may also be that law is a product of mind. Psychological functioning is not understandable without reference to its shaping by the world of works.

Raw intellectual capacity rarely limits how well we can function psychologi-cally. Limits are much more likely to be imposed by our history.[9] It may well be that our immediate memory capacity is limited by seven slots in which to store what we encounter, but the history of civilization determines whether we fill these slots with gold or with dross. Indeed, memory is the perfect example of a psycho-logical function shaped by the human world of works. The nature and uses of human memory changed with literacy — even the law changed. What will human memory look like in a half century with the advent of computerized information-retrieval systems?

6. Oeuvres are differentiated into a variety of domains, both within a culture and between cultures. Each is constrained within its own language and symbol system. These systems change and converge with history and with the intervention of human ingenuity. To trace continuities and changes in these systems over time is, of course, one of the central missions of psychologically sensitive historical studies, but these continuities and changes have been enormously complicated by the increased flow of information in the world, as well as by migration and human

mobility. So while Meyerson could properly say that human variety is one aspect of human richness, it also has become, under conditions of mobility, a central aspect of human challenge and trouble in today's world. The goods, services, and knowledge we exchange in return for distinctions (to use Bourdieu's terminology) are changing so rapidly that they create new problems of defining elites and even of defining cultures.

7. Man's history, conserved in shared oeuvres, shapes not only events but men's minds as well. History, in consequence, is "toujours une histoire de l'esprit" (Meyerson, 1987, p. 79). Indeed, it is hard to resist saying simply, "L'homme c'est histoire."

8. Man is future oriented, always in process of doing something. His constructions are built with a future product in mind, for example, not the stones he is using, but the house they will become in the future. Collective action serves to reinforce that future orientation by its grand designs. But there is always a tension that exists between competing conceptions of futurity — personal, communal, mondial, family, whatever. The orchestrating of different visions of the future is a central human problem as well as a central problem of history.

I would prefer to read Meyerson's characterization of what it means to "enter humanity" not simply as a guide to understanding a psychology of history. It was intended as a guide to understanding human psychology; and I conclude by remarking on its challenge to contemporary conceptions of "cultural psychology."

I find his conception of *oeuvres* particularly challenging. He speaks of the oeuvre as providing structure and continuity within individual human lives, but within a culture, and within history. He is touching upon a grossly neglected aspect of human life and human culture. Indeed, Meyerson thinks of the construction of reality as in support of these oeuvres and made possible by them.

An oeuvre is a more or less systematically encoded body of knowledge and technique. To assure its conservation and transmission, it is typically institutionalized in some way, and it is through its institutionalization that it "contains" the history of a civilization. Institutionalization implies some form of profession or guild, a method of managing memory, a way of delimiting identity.

What is particularly interesting about the concept of oeuvre is what I want to characterize as its *unitas multiplex*. "Science" and "the law" are both oeuvres in the grand sense. They both have a grand historical sweep, a form of accessible memory, supporting professions, and characteristics of grand oeuvres. In the large, they give meaning to what individuals do in the small. I can see my own work on the "New Look" in perception, for example, as relating to Aristotle's rejection of the *eidolon* theory in the *De sensu* when he asks how we know that it is Cleon's son who is descending the steps of the Parthenon. Once I sense the power of Aristotle's argument about a *sensus communis* as needed to construct the realities of my daily world, I find myself to be part of an oeuvre that has been two millennia in the building. I seem, as it were, both to have become a creature situated in history, a creature of history, and, at the same time, to have transcended history. If you will not think me too eccentric, I will even admit that when I go back to the *De sensu* now, after half a century of continuous encounter with it, it is not that different from having lunch with a colleague down the corridor who has a quite good sense of the general picture of things, though he may need some filling in about this detail or that. I even find myself telling Aristotle some rather revealing stories when it comes to those details.

I have had a very revealing experience these past few years. I have been serving as a working member of the Faculty of Law of my university. I was invited there on an extravagant act of faith. Scholars concerned with jurisprudence the world over have become newly interested in human cognition: how human beings think, how they categorize experience, how they construct stories to be convincing, how they decide among alternative versions of reality, how they justify themselves when accused, and so on. If I would share with them what I knew as a psychologist about such matters, they would share with me what they knew about the law, and perhaps we could find an intersection. Quite inadvertently, then, and by good fortune, I was to have an opportunity to extend my life or identity or soul by participating in a new oeuvre.

The first discovery that I made was shocking in its simplicity. Law is not only a profession, a set of statutes, a collection of procedures, a body of precedents, a legitimized way of exercising power, and a lucrative system of economic compensation. It is a culture—a way of constructing meanings, a way of relating to people, a mode of thinking, a style of telling stories and expressing trust in one's interlocutors, and a way of being in the present and yet in history. One cannot study "the psychology of law" by first studying psychology in a dark room, then studying law in the courts, and then adding the two together. Acting and thinking in terms of the law are becoming part of a collective oeuvre and operating in congruence with it.

I have been principally occupied with civil rights law and have been studying the record of cases relating to slavery (the word does not appear in the United States Constitution), to the emancipation of slaves, and to the restoration of civil rights since then. As one might well imagine, I have been enormously concerned with the history of meaning as it is expressed in major Supreme Court rulings. Let me finally, and all too briefly, sum up some major points that I see as relating to my previous discussion of Meyerson.

In any system of law, as in any cultural system, he who has the power to define reality controls the subsequent action. But reality cannot be arbitrary or be seen to be so. Reality must be justified and legitimized. In Anglo-Saxon law, justification and legitimization rest on the principle of precedent, *stare decisis*, by which one demonstrates that a decision now being made by the Court is governed by the same norms as comparable decisions made in the past. "The mind of man runneth not to the contrary." When the Supreme Court (*Prigg v. Pennsylvania*, 1836) struck down a Pennsylvania statute that would protect Blacks (freedmen or slaves) from arbitrary seizure and removal without a hearing by "slave snatchers" from the southern states, the reality evoked was the exclusive right of the federal courts to treat of such matters. Justice Joseph Story was at great pains to justify the property rights of southern slave owners and the preservation of peace between slave and free states as a condition for preserving the Union. The slave whose

abduction precipitated the case is mentioned only once in his extensive holding—
"one Margaret Morgan"—and blacks rarely, and then highly impersonally. It is
widely believed today that *Prigg v. Pennsylvania*, by legitimizing a right of seizure
assured in the infamous Fugitive Slave Law of 1793, laid the groundwork for the
Dred Scott case that helped to precipitate the bloody American Civil War three
decades later.

Each major case since then hangs on a precedent of meanings, an oeuvre,
either historically justified or implied. The famous *Brown v. Board of Education*
decision in 1954, mandating the desegregation of schools, was based upon the so-
called Equal Protection Clause of the Constitution. Its core argument was that
separate schools for Blacks and Whites implied discrimination against Blacks, however equal the facilities for the two races might be. As such, as tests showed, it
damaged the self-image and learning capacity of black children. It has been argued
that such a psychological principle would not have been invoked but for America's
being less than a decade removed from its part in the war against Hitler's racism.
But in 1992 the Supreme Court ruled in *Freeman v. Pitts* that if a racial imbalance
developed between White and Black schools within a county (De Kalb County,
Georgia), and the imbalance could be shown to be caused by "demographic factors," then a court order requiring rebalancing of the schools no longer could be
enforced. It was sufficient that the county authorities had shown "good faith" in
trying to keep the schools racially balanced. In fact, the imbalance had been
produced by White flight—White families moving out of racially mixed districts.
Now (and still) demographic factors achieve the reigning reality. The principle of
"psychic damage" in *Brown v. Board of Education* is honored by lip service, but,
alas, it is no longer realistic.

Such is the oeuvre of the law. It is formed by practice and forms practice. Its
symbolic system, for all its deep historical roots, is current: as real and as compelling as this morning's report from the Meteorological Office. Psychology is now
seeking to create a cultural psychology that takes the power of such symbolic
systems into account. Ignace Meyerson insisted from the start that psychology
follow this path, and damn the positivist respectability. I believe that his influence
is only beginning to be felt.

Notes

This chapter is a version, revised by David Martel Johnson, of an address Jerome Bruner delivered at the "Colloque Ignace Meyerson" held at the University of Paris XII,
March 9–10, 1995, titled "Meyerson Today: Reflections on Cultural Psychology."

1. His book *The Group Mind* became the prototypical "negative icon" among
American behaviorists like Knight Dunlap, Floyd Allport, and others, who insisted that
all explanations of human behavior be allocated to the individual and his individual
history of encounters with the environment—a very narrowly defined environment
consisting of "impinging stimuli" that were followed or not followed by reinforce-
ments.

2. See Stern, 1985.

3. See *Le Pacte autobiographique* (1975).

4. See, for example, U. Neisser (Ed.), *The Perceived Self* (Cambridge: Cambridge University Press, 1993).

5. See, for example, the discussion of "commitment" contrasted with "reinforcement" in Taylor, 1989, chapter 10.

6. I even include in this category such classics of social psychology as the Lewin, Lippett, and White study of "democracy, autocracy, and laissez faire,'" as well as Milgram's work (1974) on obedience to authority.

7. Aside from Bartlett's classic study of serial recall (1932), there are virtually no studies in psychology dealing with how group inventions are made, conserved, and passed on to successors. We are only now at the beginning of work on how, for example, "laws," social tools for the adjudication of conflict, are formulated and conserved and their invariant intergenerational transmission assured. These have mostly been undertaken by anthropologists (e.g., Gluckman, 1955; Geertz, 1983; Conley and O'Barr, 1990; and Merry, 1990) or by students of jurisprudence (e.g., Cover, 1975).

8. A clumsy effort to embrace this idea is contained in F.H. Allport's (1924) famous J-curve of conforming behavior, but Allport was so caught up in the then fashionable condemnation of "the group mind" that he insisted that all collective behavior be reduced to the behavior of individuals.

9. The famous *Einstellung* effect in problem solving, where problem solution is hindered by a priori, established ways of "structuring" the problem, expresses this same truth at a microtemporal level. Boyle's discovery of the "spring of the air" was hindered by an a priori belief in the insubstantiality of the air, just as Lavoisier's discovery of oxygen found its chief deterrent in the more ancient phlogiston theory. See Kuhn, 1962; Wertheimer, 1945; and O Sacks, 1995.

References

Allport, F.H. 1924. *Social Psychology*. Boston: Houghton Mifflin.

The Works of Aristotle. Vol. 3, *The Soul*. Oxford: Oxford University Press, 1930.

Bartlett, F.C. 1932. *Remembering*. Cambridge, UK: Cambridge University Press.

Bruner, J. 1987. "Life as Narrative." *Social Research*. Chicago: University of Chicago Press. 545–3, 1–17.

Conley, J.M., and William O'Barr. 1990. *Rules versus Relationships: The Ethnography of Legal Discourse*.

Cover, Robert. 1975. *Justice Accused*. New Haven: Yale University Press.

Dennett, D. 1993. *Consciousness Explained*. New York: Penguin.

Geertz, C. 1983. *Local Knowledge: Further Essays in Interpretive Anthropology*. New York: Basic Books.

Gluckman, M. 1955. *The Judicial Process among the Barotse of Northern Rhodesia*. Manchester: Manchester University Press.

Kuhn, T. 1962. *The Structure of Scientific Revolutions*. Chicago: University of Chicago Press.

Lejeune, P. 1975. *Le Pacte autobiographique*. Paris: Editions du Seuil.

McDougall, W. 1973. *The Group Mind*. New York: Arno Press.

Meltzoff, Andrew. 1995. "Understanding the Intention of Others: Re-enactment of Intended Actions by 18-Month-Old Children." *Developmental Psychology*, 3, pp. 838–50.

Merry, Sally Engle. 1990. *Getting Justice and Getting Even: Legal Consciousness Among Working-Class Americans.* Chicago: University of Chicago Press.

Meyerson, I. 1987. *Écrits.* Paris: Presses Universitaires de France.

Milgram, S. 1974. *Obedience to Authority: An Experimental View.* New York: Harper and Row.

Neisser, U. (Ed.). 1993. *The Perceived Self.* Cambridge, UK: Cambridge University Press.

Sacks, O. 1995. "Scotoma: Forgetting and Neglect in Science," in R. Silvers (Ed.), *Hidden Histories of Science.* New York: New York Review of Books.

Silvers, R. (Ed.). 1995. *Hidden Histories of Science.* New York: New York Review of Books.

Stern, D. 1985. *The Interpersonal World of the Infant.* New York: Basic Books.

Stevenson, H.W., and Stigler, J.W. 1992. *The Learning Gap.* New York: Summit Books.

Stich, S. 1989. *From Folk Psychology to Cognitive Science.* Cambridge, MA: MIT Press.

Taylor, C. 1989. *Sources of the Self.* Cambridge, MA: Harvard University Press.

Vernant, J.-P., and Vidal-Naquet, P. 1988. *Myth and Tragedy in Ancient Greece.* New York: Zone Books.

Wertheimer, M. 1945. *Productive Thinking.* New York: Harper.

23

Strong Culturalism

David Bakhurst

It is a familiar complaint that the models of the mind that predominate in psychology, philosophy of mind, and cognitive science typically pay insufficient attention to the fact that human beings are social animals, and that human psychological functioning occurs in a cultural setting (e.g., Shotter, 1975, esp. p. 136, Harré and Gillett, 1994). The protest is sometimes designed to undermine the supposed objectivity of psychological research that ignores the sociopolitical context in which it is conducted (e.g., Sarason, 1981). But more often, and more radically, the complaint is made in the course of arguing that to disregard the social or cultural context of our mental lives is to misrepresent the very nature of the mind itself, for mind is an essentially social phenomenon.

Those who lament the neglect of the social often see themselves as speaking from the margins, but they can take heart from recent changes of mood within academia. Throughout the humanities and social sciences there is a burgeoning interest in culture, stimulated in part by the rise of the "politics of identity" and the influence of constructionist and postmodern ideas on the intellectual scene. Even in Anglo-American philosophy there is greater willingness to countenance the relevance of social factors to the treatment of epistemological and metaphysical issues, no doubt due in part to the widespread disavowal of the broadly Cartesian assumptions that influenced much philosophizing in this tradition. Moreover, it appears that culture now has forced its way onto the agenda of cognitive science itself. The complaint that cognitive scientists are notorious for their hostility to matters sociocultural is outdated. So the time is ripe for some serious reflection on what is at stake in the debate over culture and mind.

My subject here is what I shall call strong cultural theories of mind: those that invoke the slogans that mind is "constructed," "distributed," "relational," "situated," or "socially constituted" to maintain that culture is in some sense constitutive of mind, and that therefore the nature and content of an individual's mental life cannot be understood independently of the culture of which that individual

413

is a part. Strong culturalism can take various, more or less radical forms. The version I shall explore starts from the old intuition that reductionism (or eliminativism) about the mental leaves out something crucial. For the strong culturalist, however, the missing ingredient is not primarily consciousness or phenomenology, but the sociocultural context of mind. Two intuitions often lie behind this claim. The first is that meaning is the medium of the mental, and meaning is (in some sense) an essentially social phenomenon. The second is that the human mind, and the forms of talk in which human beings explain and predict behavior, should be understood on the model of tools; and, like all artifacts, we cannot make sense of them independently of the social processes that make them what they are.

Presently I shall look in more detail at a view that incorporates these intuitions, but first let me raise the question of how we might argue for strong culturalism. One strategy is to press the case piecemeal and empirically. We might claim that the best theory of the development of some psychological function—say, long-term memory—makes essential reference to cultural phenomena like artifacts, rituals, and shared symbolic systems. Or we might propose that the most pleasing model of how a group deploys some body of knowledge represents that knowledge as socially distributed and/or externalized in the environment and argue that the relevant senses of distribution and externalization are best explained by the concept of culture. In both cases the appeal to culture is an argument from best explanation, and everything depends on how explanatory the culture-invoking theories and models are. If we can amass enough explanatory theories and models, and if they fit together, then we will have a general picture of mind in which culture plays a crucial role.

However, to make the case for culture in this piecemeal way can be frustrating. The "atomist" (as I shall call the despiser of culture) has a nasty habit of redescribing the events depicted in the culture-invoking model in a way that locates everything of psychological interest in the heads of individuals and portrays the cultural context as the merely empirical setting of mind, which in no way is constitutive of the phenomena our model was trying to capture. That the atomist should be able to turn this trick is not surprising, given the force of individualistic intuitions in our culture. Moreover, culturalists have to contend with the fact that the atomist's versions of events do have a certain prima facie plausibility. Atomists have going for them one powerful idea: If we identify mental activity with brain functioning, we have a chance of rendering the mental intelligible, because the operations of the brain will ultimately yield to scientific analysis. What could possibly be gained by spreading the mind out into social space, as culturalism seems intent to do?[1]

Faced with this opposition, it is tempting for the culturalist to forsake the piecemeal approach and look for a general, global argument to defeat atomism. Perhaps by reflecting on the concept of mind, we can establish that atomism is incoherent or otherwise misconceived. Here it seems natural that the culturalist should turn to the philosopher for inspiration. This in turn raises the question of whether the philosopher can deliver the goods: To what extent can culturalists aspire to find philosophical arguments that will compel us to take culture seriously as constitutive of mind?

Bruner's Critique of Cognitivism

Let us now examine in detail the position of one particular advocate of strong culturalism, American psychologist Jerome Bruner. Bruner's erudite defense of cultural psychology deserves attention for a number of reasons. Bruner has a special authority, since he was one of the originators of the cognitive revolution itself. He knows intimately the cast of mind he now attacks. Moreover, Bruner is an influential, even inspirational, writer: The humanism and antiscientism of his work speak to a certain widely felt need in our intellectual culture. Thus, whether or not one is persuaded by Bruner's culturalism, it is certainly important to consider why it has such appeal.

After I have set out Bruner's position, I shall consider how it might be developed and enhanced by the work of Russian philosopher Evald Ilyenkov, the central figure in my book *Consciousness and Revolution in Soviet Philosophy* (1991). Ilyenkov is, of course, by no means the only philosopher one might invoke to strengthen Bruner's hand. However, whatever the differences in their respective idioms, there are striking parallels between Bruner and Ilyenkov. This is not as surprising as it might seem. Russian psychologist Lev Vygotsky is an important influence on Bruner; Ilyenkov, perhaps better than anyone, makes explicit the philosophical ideas that informed Vygotsky and subsequent Russian thinkers of the sociohistorical school.[2] It is interesting to consider whether Ilyenkov can be cast as the underlaborer for the cultural psychologist.

At the beginning of *Acts of Meaning* (1990), Bruner argues that the cognitive revolution has gone the way of most political revolutions. The forces it unleashed have undermined the revolution's original intent. That intent was, Bruner avows, to return the concept of meaning to the center of psychology after the long winter of behaviorism. The end was

> to discover and to describe formally the meanings that human beings created out of their encounters with the world, and then to propose hypotheses about what meaning-making processes were implicated. [The cognitive revolution] focused upon the symbolic activities that human beings employed in constructing and making sense not only of the world, but of themselves. Its aim was to prompt psychology to join forces with its sister interpretative disciplines in the humanities and in the social sciences. (Bruner, 1990, p. 2)

However, Bruner opines, enraptured by computer models of mind, cognitive psychology became obsessed with the formal manipulation of symbols. Issues of our agency in the creation of meaning were eclipsed as psychologists assumed that all there is to understanding minds was understanding how physical systems manipulate representations. The behaviorist image of man was succeeded by one no less impoverished: man as information processor. Inevitably, the behaviorists' thirst to replace mental talk with a scientifically more respectable idiom was reborn as the contemporary critique of folk psychology.

To return us to the original ethos of the cognitive revolution, Bruner proposes a contextual revolution focused on the concept of culture. He asserts, as many have asserted, that the development of the psychological prowess of human beings qua species cannot be explained without appeal to culture, and that each human child only acquires mental powers through the appropriation of culture. Bruner approvingly quotes Geertz's remark that nature leaves us "unworkable monstrosities ... incomplete or unfinished animals who complete or finish ourselves through culture" (Bruner, 1990, p. 12; Geertz, 1973, p. 49). But there is more to Bruner's position than this. Culture, he suggests, is the habitat of the mental. As children, we are born into culture or, we might say, into "cultural worlds," complex symbolically structured normative environments. These worlds are "already there," confronting us "objectively"; they represent the environment we must learn to negotiate. By the same token, cultures themselves contain the means the appropriation of which enables us to find our way in the world. Culture is thus "the world to which we [have] to adapt and the tool kit for doing so" (Bruner, 1990, p. 12). Our minds take shape as we learn to use these tools, and hence the character of our mental lives is an expression of the culture in which we reside. It is in this sense that Bruner declares culture to be "constitutive of mind" (p. 33). Mind and self are aspects of a social world, which is neither "in the head" nor "out there" (pp. 105–6), but is fundamentally "transactional."

There is an important reflexivity in Bruner's position. It is not just that the powers we describe as exercises of mind are culturally constituted; so too are our modes of psychological description. Every culture contains its "folk psychology," its ways of understanding and explaining behavior. Bruner construes "folk psychology" more broadly than many writers, supplementing the idea of explanation in terms of propositional attitudes with considerations about the centrality of narrative in psychological discourse. For Bruner, narrative provides the crucial background to explanation in propositional attitude terms. Moreover, our understanding of our cultural environment is organized in "scripts" (and other devices) that have a narrative or protonarrative structure. Finally, we make sense of our lives, and the lives of others, through narrative. What hold me together as a subject of psychological explanation are the stories that give shape to my deeds as aspects of a single life. For Bruner, the "self" exists as a focus of narrative or as a "center of narrative gravity," to co-opt Dennett's term (Dennett, 1991a, p. 418). Selves have a soi-disant reality, hence, Bruner's interest in "self-accounting" in autobiography.[3]

It is crucial to Bruner's position that folk psychological explanation is ineliminable. As he wrote in his controversial Spencer lecture, "Psychology and the Image of Man": "A theory of human behavior that fails to make contact with man's conceptions of his world and his way of knowing, that sets these aside as epiphenomena, will neither be an adequate theory of human behavior nor will it prevail in common sense" (Bruner 1979, p. 189). Bruner seems to have in mind the following kind of argument: The subject of psychological explanation is the person. But psychological phenomena, like "selves," are constituted by our understanding of ourselves as agents. Thus if we drop folk psychological descriptions, we cannot individuate the entities that we look to psychology to explain. Further, to explain a piece of human behavior, we must see it as action in a context and the relevant contexts are fundamentally symbolic and normative. These contexts are made for folk psychological explanation, since they are seen as reason conferring. Our criterion of success in psychological explanation is the extent to which it renders actions intelligible from the agent's perspective, but that perspective is constituted by folk psychological notions. Psychology is thus an interpretative discipline that necessarily draws its terms of interpretation from folk psychology.

One final feature of cultural psychology we should note is its educational, and even political, dimension. Interpretative psychology is an exercise in self-understanding, and heightened self-understanding is a precondition of improving the human condition. Cultural psychology aspires to render perspicuous the structure of social life as it pertains to the emergence and flourishing of mind. If we can learn how culture makes mind, perhaps we can make cultures that make better, or at least more fulfilled, minds (Bruner, 1990, pp. 31–32).[4]

Ambiguity in Bruner's Position

For some, Bruner's position is illuminating and uplifting; for others, his "cultural revolution" in psychology is just that: an ideological redescription of the purposes and aims of psychological research that is fundamentally unscientific. But before one lauds or dismisses Bruner, it is wise to establish what he is actually saying. It is clear that for all its references to empirical research, the point of *Acts of Meaning* is to secure a conceptual reorientation. Bruner urges us to reflect upon what it is that psychology aspires to explain in a way that elucidates the terms in which those explanations must be cast. Less clear, however, is exactly what the desired conceptual reorientation amounts to, for Bruner's words invite at least three readings that differ in significant ways about the nature of the mental and its relation to the physical, and also accordingly, on the question of whether a science of the mind is possible. Although Bruner usually writes as someone asking us to rethink what a scientific psychology should be like, he sometimes commits himself to views that seem to undermine the very idea of a science of cognition.

Least Radical Reading (*Intentional Realism*)

Sometimes Bruner writes as if the recognition that psychological phenomena are "constituted in culture" is perfectly compatible with the idea of a scientific study of the mind. The culturalist simply urges us to recognize that in the domain of the psychological we do not encounter the same distinction between subject and object of inquiry, theorist and theorized, as that found in natural science. Our conception of ourselves as thinking beings influences the kind of beings that we are. We are, in Charles Taylor's phrase, "self-interpr̲e̲t̲i̲n̲g̲ ̲a̲nimals," whose status as minded beings depends on our relations to othe̲r̲ ̲s̲u̲c̲h̲ ̲animals. However, to admit that the objects of psychological research ar̲e̲ ̲"̲c̲o̲n̲s̲t̲ructions" is not to deny that they are real constituents of the world that can̲ ̲b̲e̲ ̲a̲nalyzed by rigorous and systematic methods.[5] Social institutions are also constructions, Bruner points out, but they are real: No account of human behavior could fail to make reference to them (1990, p. 38). Moreover, we can study these institutions in rigorous ways, just so long as we employ principles of explanation appropriate to the phenomena under study. Though what goes on in an economy or a legal system is, from a certain perspective, just a matter of the movement of matter or the processing of information, no sensible person thinks that the happenings in the institution, qua economic and legal phenomena, can be explained by laws relating events described in physical or computational terms. Likewise, it may be that psychological phenomena have to be explained with reference to normative principles constitutive of rationality, but explanation is nonetheless possible. We can establish, perhaps even codify, the norms by which cultural institutions operate and the rules by which individuals construct their identities, and so on. Thus, though cultural psychology is at odds with much cognitive science as presently practiced, it does not hold that "cognitive science" is an oxymoron.

More Radical Reading *(Intentional Irrealism)*

Sometimes, however, Bruner does seem to deny that psychological phenomena are "real" in a sense that would make them candidates for scientific inquiry, however understood. In arguing that the self is nothing more than a "discursive effect"—a product of our ways of talking—Bruner is not, like David Hume, portraying the self as a philosopher's fiction. On the contrary, Bruner fictionalizes selves in order to discuss them as they "really" are, namely, as what we say they are. But if the self is a "discursive effect," then should not the same be said of persons and their psychological states (beliefs, desires, and so on)? If such things are artifacts of our modes of interpretation, should we not declare, with Davidson (1987, p. 46), that the mental is "not an ontological, but a conceptual category"?

To suppose that phenomena of interpretation, narrative, and discourse, as Bruner understands them, might be objects of scientific inquiry is absurd. We can no more find laws governing the construction of narrative than we can establish strict norms by which novels are written or symphonies composed. Bruner sometimes entertains such ideas, but he really knows better. Thus when he analyzes the autobiographical material in the final chapter of *Acts of Meaning*, he simply tries to tell a good story. Such generalizations as emerge help us get a feel for the character of narrative "self-accounting," but they have little predictive power. They merely nudge us in the direction of understanding in the way that, say, reflecting on norms of symphonic composition might facilitate an appreciation of Beethoven's Fifth Symphony; but these norms hardly constitute even the basis of an understanding of the work (whatever that might mean). Understanding persons is like understanding fictional characters. Interpretations may be better or worse, more or less illuminating, but they are radically underdetermined by the evidence.

Read this way, however, Bruner's position might be open to a rapprochement with cognitive science of a Dennettian or eliminativist bent, for Bruner would concede that one can continue to study the physical systems that underlie the behavior we interpret in intentionalistic ways. It is just that we cannot reduce the mental to the physical, for what we interpret is not physically instantiated in a way that will allow us to theorize about it in physical terms. Where Bruner differs from the eliminativist is in his claim that folk psychology is an indispensable instrument of self-understanding, and hence that there always will be room for a closed interpretative psychology employing intentional notions.

Downright Bohemian Reading *(Global Irrealism)*

Sometimes, however, Bruner's denial that there is a "real" mind to study appears to be part of a wholesale critique of the notion of reality. Bruner rejects the idea that there is a ready-made world, or an "aboriginal reality," and when he uses the term "real," he often puts it in scare quotes. This suggests a full-blown constructionism, where what is "real" is a consequence of our modes of conceptualization. The relation between cognitive scientist and cultural psychologist cannot therefore be that the former deals with the real mechanisms that underlie the virtual reality constituted by intentional discourse. Science is just another social institution in the business of narrative construction. It is true that we can credit science with greater authority than other modes of inquiry and hence can take its deliverances as revealing "reality," but science itself can be understood only from the perspective of intelligence, and that perspective is to be illuminated from the interpretative stance of cultural psychology. We must accept that cognitive science and interpretative psychology are different "discourses." There is no independent standard of truth by which to establish the claims of the one over the other. All we can say is that cultural psychology understands its own character in a way that cognitive science does not.

Bruner is nervous about embracing so strong a constructionism. It is interesting that when he attacks the idea of an aboriginal reality, he usually invokes examples of phenomena the ontological status of which is controversial on everybody's view (e.g., the concept of intelligence). But there are certainly elements of radical constructionism in Bruner's work. It emerges in his interest in postmodernism, though its source, I think, is his view of the mind as "organizing experience." Bruner works with a dualism of conceptual scheme and empirical content that would have made the logical positivists proud. In *On Knowing*, Bruner writes: "Knowledge is a model we construct to give meaning to regularities in experience. The organizing ideas of any body of knowledge are inventions for rendering experience economical and connected. . . . The history of culture is the history of the development of great organizing ideas" (1979, p. 120). In *Acts of Meaning*, narrative is described as a mode "of organizing experience" (1990, p. 43). Such scheme-content dualism easily collapses into antirealism unless some philosophical scaffolding is quickly constructed. So far, Bruner has not done much to prevent the collapse (though cf. 1990, pp. 24–29).[6]

I do not see in Bruner's writings a way to resolve the conflicts between these readings. I propose now to introduce Ilyenkov into the picture; perhaps we can use his work to straighten the teeth of Bruner's position.

Ilyenkov: Ideality, Culture, and Mind

Our focus is Ilyenkov's work on "the problem of the ideal." Ilyenkov first addressed this issue in 1962 when he published his controversial article "Ideal'noe" in the multivolume Soviet *Filosofskaya entsiklopediya*. This piece simultaneously consolidated his reputation as one of the most creative of the younger generation of critical Russian Marxists and provoked considerable suspicion and distrust among the old guard of the Soviet philosophical establishment. Ilyenkov returned to "the problem of the ideal" throughout his career and produced another substantial article on the subject just before his suicide in 1979.[7]

In these writings, Ilyenkov is concerned with the status of nonmaterial phenomena. What account is a materialist to give of the place of the nonmaterial in the natural world? Many of Ilyenkov's Soviet contemporaries argued that all ideal phenomena are ultimately reducible to the mental states of individuals, and all mental states are realized in the brain.[8] Ilyenkov, in contrast, takes a radically different line. To understand our mental powers, we must first understand the nature of normativity, because our mindedness is primarily manifested in our capacity to respond to reasons. The thoughts, deeds, and words of thinking beings issue not, or not just, from causal influences upon them, but from their recognition that they ought to believe such and such or do so and so. The necessity acknowledged in this "ought" is rational in kind; it is grounded in objective reasons. Ilyenkov argues that we cannot understand the objectivity of reasons, and hence the normative constraints constitutive of thought and action, unless we suppose that certain ideal phenomena exist as aspects of the world, independent of the consciousness and will of human individuals.

Ilyenkov maintains that to understand this aright, we must return to themes in Hegel and, ultimately, Plato (a contention naturally resisted by cruder Soviet materialists), for the writings of these philosophers contain, albeit in distorted form, the recognition of the power that objectively existing ideal forms exercise over the individual:

> The classical systems of objective idealism were founded on the basic fact of the independence of the totality of social culture, and the forms of its organization, from particular individuals and, more broadly, the fact of the general transformation of the universal products of social production (both material and spiritual) into particular social forces con-

fronting the individual and dictating his consciousness and will. (Ilyen-kov, 1984, pp. 66)

Idealism, Ilyenkov argues, misconstrues this fact, giving it an excessively meta-physical (and mystagogical) interpretation, but the appropriate response to the follies of idealism is not to neutralize the ideal by putting it into the head. Rather, we should embrace Hegel's idea of social consciousness as the vehicle of objective ideality—as "a historically formed and historically developing system of 'objective representations' (Ilyenkov, 1991, p. 247; 1997, p. 77)"—and give that idea a broadly naturalistic interpretation.[9]

Social consciousness, so conceived, embodies the normative structure of our common life: It comprises "the general moral norms regulating people's daily life, legal structures, forms of government and political organization, ritually estab-lished patterns of activity of all kinds, rules of life which must be obeyed by everyone . . . up to and including the grammatical and syntactical structures of speech and language and the logical norms of reasoning" (Ilyenkov, 1991, p. 247; 1977, p. 77). These norms confront individuals with the authority of an external reality to which they must conform. It is crucial that for Ilyenkov, social con-sciousness exists not as some kind of ethereal collective "spirit" or *Weltgeist*, but as culture, and, in turn, culture exists only in and through the activity of the community. The ideal forms that constitute the normative constraints on thought and action are "forms of human social culture embodied (objectified, substantial-ized, reified) in matter, that is, [a quality] of the historically formed modes of the life activity of social beings, modes of activity which confront individual conscious-ness and will as a special non-natural [*sverkhprirodnaya*] objective reality, as a special object, on a par with material reality, and situated in one and the same space as it (and hence often confused with it)" (Ilyenkov, 1991, p. 249; 1977, p. 79). Moreover, as the quotation suggests, ideal forms are expressed not just in the practices of the community, but in the form that material things take on in virtue of that practice. Activity transforms the natural world, lending it significance and value, and ideal properties are thereby "objectified" in nature itself:

> "Ideality" is like a peculiar stamp impressed on the substance of nature by social human life activity; it is the form of the functioning of physical things in the process of social human life activity. (Ilyenkov, 1991, p. 256; 1977, p. 86)

> The ideal form is the form of a thing created by social human labor. Or conversely, it is the form of labor expressed in the substance of nature, "embodied" in it, "alienated" in it, "realized" in it, and thereby confront-ing its very creator as the form of a thing or as a relation between things, which are placed in this relation . . . by human beings, by their labor. (Ilyenkov, 1991, p. 268; 1977, p. 97)

Ilyenkov's point is not just that certain objects—artifacts, for example—represent embodiments of human activity and therefore have a special significance. All objects brought within "human spiritual culture" are lent an ideal form (Ilyenkov, 1964, pp. 41–42). Our world is replete with meaning: It is a world in which the material has been "idealized" through its incorporation into culture, and to respond to the world in a way appropriate to that meaning is to behave as a minded being and to give expression to one's humanity.

Before turning to the psychological significance of Ilyenkov's position, I want to stress its dynamism. First, this is a vision of human beings creating themselves through the creation of culture. Nature molded by activity confronts us as rich with significance. In light of this, we act, thereby further transforming nature, creating new significance, and calling forth further action. We must constantly adapt to our changing world and acquire the capacities necessary to inhabit it; there is no end to this dialectic of adaptation and further transformation so long as humanity survives.

Second, notwithstanding Ilyenkov's talk of culture as the "reification" or "objectification" of activity, his intention is not to represent the ideal as some kind of static presence. It exists only in relation to human activity, though in turn such activity is what it is because it is a response to ideality:

> The ideal form is the form of a thing, but outside this thing, in human beings as the form of their dynamic life activity, as aims and desires. Or conversely, it is the form of the dynamic life activity of human beings, but outside them, in the form of a created thing. "Ideality" in itself exists only in the constant succession and replacement of these two forms of "external embodiment" and does not coincide with either of them taken separately. It exists only through the unceasing transformation of a form of activity into the form of a thing and back—the form of a thing into a form of activity. (Ilyenkov, 1991, p. 269; 1977, p. 98)[10]

We should thus be cautious about identifying the ideal with any particular mode of its embodiment—whether in the material environment, in activity, or in the mind. It comes into view, as it were, as an aspect of the relation of agent and world, as the aspect in virtue of which an agent can exhibit a thinking response to a world whose character warrants and elicits the exercise of thought.

The consequences of Ilyenkov's position for psychology are significant. First, he advances a radical conception of thought in which the dominant metaphors in our depiction of the mind shift from representation and depiction to activity and movement. To be a thinking thing is to possess the capacity to inhabit an idealized environment, to respond to the ideal forms embodied in our culture, and to conform to and manipulate meanings as they are formed and transformed in the flux of social being. Second, Ilyenkov argues that it follows from his position that the higher psychological functions cannot be innate. On the contrary, they are as socially mediated as the environment that thinking beings inhabit. Through the objectification of activity, our forms of thought are written into the environment into which human children are born, and they become thinking beings as they acquire the capacity to orientate themselves in this environment by appropriating and internalizing (in Vygotsky's often-misunderstood sense) the forms of activity of the community.

> All the schemas Kant defined as "transcendentally inborn" forms of the work of particular minds, as the "internal mechanisms" present a priori in each mind, in fact represent the forms of self-consciousness of social beings (understood as the historically developing "ensemble of social relations"), assimilated from without (and confronting them from the very beginning as "external" patterns of the movement of culture, independent of their consciousness and will). (Ilyenkov, 1991, p. 250; 1977, p. 80)

The child does not, of course, assimilate these forms of thought by hypothesis formation or any other form of ratiocination. They emerge through enculturation as preconditions of the exercise of the child's cognitive capacities. For Ilyenkov, the child's entrance into culture, or *Bildung*, is always conceived as a social process, and before the child can be an active participant in its own becoming, there is much he or she must simply absorb.

Ilyenkov to the Defense of Cultural Psychology

Ilyenkov's idiom will be obscure to many of Bruner's readers, so before we consider how his position might complement Bruner's, let me restate it as straightforwardly as I can. Ilyenkov holds the following:

1. To understand our distinctively human mental powers, we must comprehend the nature of normativity: The defining characteristic of human minded behavior is that it is guided by reasons, rather than (merely) dictated by causes.
2. These reasons are objective; that is, they express requirements on thought and action that have their authority independent of the consciousness and will of thinking subjects.
3. To understand such rational requirements, we must admit that the world objectively contains "ideal" (nonmaterial) properties, such as value, significance, and meaning. These features are constitutive of reasons; to act for a reason is to respond to such features in a way their presence makes (or appears to make) appropriate.
4. This can be seen as a form of Platonism, but a benign one. Objectively existing ideal properties do not constitute a supersensible reality or group mind. Rather, they are elements of culture that must be understood in their essential relation to human activity.
5. Cultural phenomena are embodied in human practices and in the form the world takes on by virtue of human activity.
6. Adopting a "genetic" perspective—that is, one concerned with the origin of

the ideal—we can say that ideal properties are "objectifications" of human activity. By virtue of our active engagement with the world, nature is lent significance and value; it is "enculturated."

7. Artifacts are a prime example of objects that have significance by virtue of the objectification of activity. But all objects brought within the compass of our "spiritual culture" are made meaningful, and our relation to them engages our rational, conceptual powers.

8. To be a thinking thing is just to have the capacity to engage with the world normatively, that is, to inhabit an idealized environment. We must orient epistemology away from its preoccupation with the representation or picturing of reality and toward a conception of mind as a specific mode of active engagement with the world. (This is not a concession to behaviorism, at least as traditionally conceived, as the mode of engagement is irreducibly normative.)

9. Our distinctively human mental capacities are not innate but are acquired through enculturation (*Bildung*). We become rational animals—persons in the full sense—as we appropriate the distinctively human forms of activity that manifest mindedness.

10. Thus this position aspires to explain both the nature of the world as a possible object of thought (of rational engagement) and the nature and origin of the powers that constitute our relation to the world as such an object. There is a sense in which it is a deduction of the very distinction between subject and object, mind and world.

We can now see how Ilyenkov's philosophy might enhance Bruner's position. First, Ilyenkov's conception of humanity's spiritual culture as a mode of externalized activity augments Bruner's idea of culture as a socially constructed order of meanings and a vehicle of social memory. Second, Ilyenkov's claim that what it is to be a thinking thing is to inhabit an idealized environment lends substance to the idea that culture is constitutive of thought. Third, Ilyenkov fortifies Bruner's objections to reductionism. For Ilyenkov, thoughts are states, not of brains, but of persons, and moreover, of persons situated in an environment that influences them not just causally but normatively. From this it follows, Ilyenkov thinks, that talk of states and dispositions of the brain will not suffice to capture the character of our mental capacities. Fourth, the distinction between causal and rational influences upon behavior (which Ilyenkov inherits from Kant and his successors in the German classical tradition) complements Bruner's contrast between scientific and interpretative modes of explanation. (Indeed, the Kantian distinction is superior, since the idea of rational requirements does not, at least immediately, have the kind of subjective connotations frequently conveyed by the notion of interpretation.) Fifth, Ilyenkov's anti-innatism reinforces Bruner's view of the relation of culture and biology, where "the biological substrate, the so-called universals of human nature, is not a cause of action but, at most, a *constraint* upon it or a *condition* for it" (Bruner, 1990, pp. 20–21). Finally, we might observe that Ilyenkov, like Bruner, sees his position as educationally and politically significant. Ilyenkov and Bruner share a vision of the primacy of agency: There is a sense in which we are made by culture; but by the same token, cultures are our creation. A proper appreciation of the cultural mediation of our mental powers is vital if we are to create the conditions in which human beings can flourish.[11]

Introducing Ilyenkov can also help us decide which of the three readings of Bruner's position to privilege. Ilyenkov was a philosophical realist who would have had no sympathy for the "downright bohemian" elements in Bruner's work. Since Ilyenkov's mission is to assert that cultural and mental phenomena are genuine constituents of the furniture of the world, he also would have rejected the intentional irrealism of our second interpretation. Ilyenkov's realism about culture, together with his insistence that culture and mind are genuine objects of scientific investigation properly understood, suggest that if we enlist Ilyenkov in the service of cultural psychology, we must take the first, least radical, reading of Bruner's stance.

Having said this, we should observe one significant difference between our two thinkers. Unlike Bruner, Ilyenkov does not treat narrative as central to our modes of psychological explanation. Indeed, I think that Ilyenkov would dismiss Bruner's preoccupation with narrative as an overreaction to the apparent consequences of the more radical dimensions of Bruner's view. Bruner perceives that if he insists that psychology concern itself with persons, and then "fictionalizes" the self and its states, he risks losing an object of theoretical investigation altogether, so he reaches for narrative to restore an object of research. Narrative appears to be something cultural psychology can get its teeth into. We can present our forms of representation, interpretation, and discourse as structured by narrative constraints: This gives us norms, rules, and such to discover, describe, and codify. Thus Bruner invokes notions like scripts (see Bruner, 1979, p. 36). Ilyenkov, however, would say that such notions, as Bruner deploys them, make for bad science. For example, the script metaphor, despite its pedigree in artificial intelligence, has almost no explanatory force: Representing human social behavior as scripted neither enriches our powers of prediction nor facilitates understanding. So, from Ilyenkov's perspective, this talk of narrative is a placeholder for a genuine explanatory framework.

Yet despite this and other differences, Ilyenkov's philosophy seems made for Bruner's culturalism. We should be cautious, however, before we represent Ilyenkov as a source of philosophical arguments that promise to unhinge atomism and force cognitive science to take culture seriously. For one thing, Ilyenkov's position needs a great deal more development if we are really to understand his claim that Kantian categories are "forms of the self-consciousness of social beings" (Ilyenkov, 1991, p. 250), or that thought is "the mode of activity of a thinking body" (Ilyenkov, 1984, p. 37). How these views might be theorized further (if they should be theorized at all) is a question that remains open.[12]

It might be argued that although Ilyenkov's position is undeveloped, it does at least provide the core of a telling argument for strong culturalism, for Ilyenkov's account of the idealization of nature by human activity is really a transcendental argument designed to address the question of the very possibility of intentionality.

Ilyenkov is concerned with the issue of how the natural world can contain normativity, meaning, and reasons. He thinks that it begs the question to represent the mind as the source of meaning and intentionality, so he looks to human activity for the explanation. His solution to the problem of the ideal is—as we put it in proposition 10 earlier—an attempt to explain the very possibility of the relation of subject and object, of a thinking mind standing in relation to the world as a possible object of thought. While much cognitive science either treats intentionality as primitive or somehow endeavors to explain it away, Ilyenkov's strategy places our social being at the heart of its possibility, thus vindicating a strong culturalist's stance.

Ilyenkov would, I think, have liked this rendition of his strategy. It is unlikely, however, that his arguments will move opponents of culturalism. Some people reject such transcendental arguments out of hand, suspicious of the way they aspire to constrain empirical inquiry. Admittedly, such arguments do not always age well: Yesterday's transcendental insights into necessity sometimes turn out to be today's empirical falsehoods. Genuine though such concerns are, it would be rash to suppose that such arguments can never be effective. Yet if Ilyenkov's transcendental derivation of the subject-object relation is to be remotely illuminating, it must be carefully purged of any hint of a speculative, quasi-empirical account of how intentionality "got into the world" via the objectification of action.

We should be cautious, then, about making exaggerated claims on behalf of Ilyenkov's philosophy. It can hardly be portrayed as a knockdown argument against atomism. Nevertheless, even if we set aside the seemingly transcendental aspirations of Ilyenkov's philosophy, there remains much of interest that complements and extends Bruner's vision: (1) the claim that philosophical puzzles about the nature of meaning are resolved by appeal to considerations about human activity— the life of the sign is its use; (2) the view that the intentional cannot be subsumed in the net of (mechanistic) causal explanation; (3) the insistence that the subject of thought is the person, not some subpersonal system (e.g., the brain), hence Ilyenkov's frequently reiterated slogan "The brain does not think, the person thinks with the help of his brain" (a position interestingly endorsed by McDowell; see 1994a); and (4) the view that human mental functioning must be seen in its social context because culture is the medium of thought. All these ideas (which are developed in different ways in the work of the later Wittgenstein) at least represent a fertile source of powerful metaphors, intuitions, and suggestions that can give shape to culturalist research programs.

In addition, Ilyenkov and philosophers like him are important because they encourage us to interrogate the images of the relation of mind and world that predominate in our intellectual culture, and that often tacitly influence our empirical inquiries into the nature of mind. Let me close with two examples.

First, one intriguing, though undeveloped, aspect of Ilyenkov's thought is his hostility to representational models of the mind. As I mentioned, Ilyenkov writes as a philosophical realist: Our minds put us in contact with an objectively existing world independent of thought. This might seem strange, since Ilyenkov's anthropocentric conception of activity structuring the world could be taken to suggest a radical constructionism where we are never in contact with reality "in itself." It is possible that Ilyenkov was really a closet idealist who was sensibly reluctant to admit this to his Soviet peers. It is more likely, I think, that Ilyenkov believed that the anthropocentricity of his view could be reconciled with realism, so long as we reject the models of the mind that dominate the Cartesian, empiricist, and Kantian traditions in epistemology. On Cartesian and empiricist views, our access to reality is always via mental intermediaries: Our ideas, beliefs, concepts, and so on are often depicted as coming between us and reality as it is. Hence the specter of skepticism is always a threat, and idealism a temptation. On (vulgar) Kantian versions, our conception of the world is construed as the outcome of the filtering of experience through our "conceptual scheme," theories, or language. Hence we lose touch with "things as they are in themselves," for we have access only to the world as conceptualized. But this filtering metaphor has no place in Ilyenkov's philosophy (unlike Bruner's, where the dualism of scheme and content is, as we saw, influential). Indeed, the significance of Ilyenkov's stress on action and his construal of concepts as tools, instruments, or means of acting on nature is precisely to challenge the fundamental metaphors that have dominated so much epistemology. Tools may change the objects on which they are put to work, but they do not put us in touch with a different kind of object. If we drop mental intermediaries from the epistemological picture, then we can recognize the anthropocentricity of our concepts without fear of skepticism, or so Ilyenkov thinks.[13]

My second example concerns the discussion of the cons and pros of folk psychology. Many of the major participants in this debate (Bruner included) share the basic assumption that folk psychology is a species of theory for the explanation and prediction of behavior. Ilyenkov would have been astonished by this idea and would, I suspect, have attributed it to the positivist presupposition that the principal epistemic relation of mind and world is the relation of theory and evidence.[14] Ilyenkov would agree with Bruner that when we try to make contact with the mental lives of others, it is not bodily movement we seek to understand, but the behavior of a minded being. The entities identified by folk psychology are constitutive of the object of explanation. But Ilyenkov also would insist that when I use psychological terms to articulate my own thoughts, desires, and intentions, I am expressing my mental life, not theorizing about my behavior. The defense of folk psychology should proceed not by insisting that it is the best theory we have, but by denying that it is a theory at all.[15]

I conclude that even if Ilyenkov's ideas fall short of a conclusive defense of strong culturalism, they provide numerous penetrating and challenging insights that we would do well to heed. The task for the culturalist is to find a philosophically satisfying account of our nature as social beings that does not make psychology impossible. I do not think that Bruner has yet achieved this, though perhaps with the help of Ilyenkov and others I have only mentioned here, the end Bruner is striving for can be attained.

Notes

An earlier version of this chapter appeared in *Mind, Culture, and Activity*, 2(3), 1995, pp. 158–71. I am grateful to the publisher for permission to revise that article for this volume. The article was originally written for the Cognitive Science Seminar at the University of California, San Diego, and was subsequently presented at the University of Reading, Sheffield-Hallam University, and Loughborough University. I thank my audiences on those occasions for their insightful comments and criticisms. Thanks are also due to the Social Sciences and Humanities Research Council of Canada for supporting my research.

1. One important rationale for atomism is what Stephen Stich calls "the principle of autonomy," according to which psychology should concern itself only with phenomena that are, or that supervene upon, internal, physical states of the subject, since only such states can be causally relevant to behavior (see Stich, 1983, p. 164). When this principle, which has seemed so plausible to so many, is combined with (arguably equally plausible) externalist views about the determination of mental content, it appears to entail that psychology cannot legitimately invoke intentional states at all. Naturally, many find this eliminativist conclusion intolerable (for a good basic discussion, see Heil, 1992, esp. pp. 42–57).

2. One should, however, be cautious about portraying the sociohistorical school as a unitary movement with a single philosophical credo (as, for example, Levitin, 1982, does). I discuss complicating factors in Bakhurst, 1986, pp. 123–24 (n. 4), and 1990.

3. Bruner's position on the self has parallels with, on the one hand, the work of Alasdair MacIntyre (1981, chapter 15) and, on the other, themes in the writings of Daniel Dennett (see, e.g., 1991a). Bruner has much more to say about narrative in both *Acts of Meaning* and its predecessor, *Actual Minds, Possible Worlds* (1986). Much of it is thought-provoking (such as the remarks about language acquisition [1990, chapter 3; though cf. Shanker, 1992, pp. 65–71, discussed in note 6 below]); all of it is contentious. I include some critical remarks on Bruner's use of narrative in the final section of this chapter.

4. Bruner has, of course, written extensively on education. See Bruner, 1962, 1966, and 1996.

5. By "intentional realism" I mean only that intentional states are (in some sense) constituents of the furniture of the world, and not the much stronger position (of, e.g., Jerry Fodor) that the states individuated by folk psychology are discrete, semantically interpretable states that enter causal relations through their physical instantiation in the brain.

6. The roots of Bruner's commitment to this dualism of scheme and content are interesting. Stuart Shanker (1992, 1993) has argued that Bruner's recent work is haunted by a residual Cartesianism; that is, Bruner continues to work with a traditional epistemological dualism between subject and object even though he stresses the "transactional" nature of their interrelations. This dualism leads Bruner to continue to pose the fundamental questions of psychology in terms of the relation between the "inner world" of the individual mind, populated by the states picked out by folk psychology, and the external world of "autonomous of experience" (Bruner, 1990, p. 40). Thus Bruner focuses on questions like these: How does the child forge a conception of the world out of the mass of material (information) he or she is given? How does the child construct a theory of the minds of others? How do individuals calibrate and

coordinate their mental worlds? Bruner's distinctive contribution is to stress that to make progress with these questions, we must acknowledge that the individual's environment is structured by culture. Thus in *Child's Talk*, Bruner emphasizes that there is no chance of explaining how a Chomskian language acquisition device (LAD) might work unless we recognize that the environment provides a language acquisition support system (LASS) that antecedently organizes the information the child receives (see Bruner, 1983, chapter 2). But this way of seeing things keeps the fundamental structure of the Chomskian picture intact (which, according to Shanker, persists even in Bruner's most recent writings [Shanker, 1992, pp. 65–71]). A dualism of scheme and content clearly suits the wider epistemic dualism in Bruner's position; moreover, it facilitates the transactional model, since the conceptual scheme can be presented as something that subjects bring to cognition, although it in turn is inherited, at least in part, from their culture. (I discuss Bruner's commitment to scheme-content dualism in more detail in Bakhurst, 2001.)

Shanker argues that if Bruner fully understood the implications of his own position, he would see that it serves to undermine the dualistic framework in which he continues to operate. The appeal to culture should not be seen as a way of supplementing the resources we have to answer the traditional questions of cognitive psychology. Rather, our reasons to heed the significance of culture in psychology are also reasons to change our understanding of what it is that psychology needs to explain. I agree with Shanker on this. Shanker's inspiration, we should note, is the later Wittgenstein (see Bakhurst, 1995b, for a discussion of the relevance of Wittgenstein's thought to strong culturalist positions).

7. For a discussion of Ilyenkov's life and work, see Bakhurst, 1995a, pp. 157–64. I give a fuller treatment of his philosophical views and their consequences in Bakhurst, 1991, chapters 5–7, and 1997.

8. This is, of course, also the contemporary wisdom in the West, at least among most philosophers, psychologists, and cognitive scientists. For an elegant argument for a mentalistic construal of culture see Sperber, 1996, especially chapter 4.

9. Ilyenkov shares the early Marx's conception of naturalism rather than the view endorsed in contemporary epistemology and philosophy of mind, where a position is "naturalistic" if it is consistent with the causal-explanatory theories of the natural sciences. For a recent plea to broaden the notion of naturalism, to which Ilyenkov would have been sympathetic, see McDowell, 1994b, especially lectures 4–6, and 1996.

10. A sparkling passage in Ilyenkov's original 1962 article develops this idea further; see Ilyenkov, 1962, p. 222 (1984, pp. 172–73). (A partial translation is given in Bakhurst, 1991, pp. 184–85, n. 5.)

11. Such thoughts were an important ingredient of Ilyenkov's conception of communism.

12. Elsewhere I have argued that important parallels exist between Ilyenkov's ideas and recent writings of John McDowell's, but much remains to be done if these parallels are to be exploited in the service of cultural psychology (Bakhurst, 1997, pp. 46–49, and 2004; see esp. McDowell, 1994b).

13. This suggests fruitful parallels between Ilyenkov and figures like Davidson (1974, 1986) and Wittgenstein, as well as McDowell (1994b). My view of Ilyenkov's realism has evolved over the years; cf. Bakhurst, 1991, pp. 200–12, 1995a, pp. 166–72, and 1997, pp. 39–45.

14. We should observe that some thinkers deny that folk psychology is best seen as a theory, on the grounds that unlike a scientific theory, its principles are not explicitly

articulated by those who use it. It is thus sometimes urged (e.g., by Dennett, 1991b) that we should construe folk psychology as a craft rather than a theory. Nevertheless, this revision continues to portray folk psychology primarily as a device for the prediction and explanation of behavior, and it is this presupposition that would have confounded Ilyenkov.

15. For Western views sympathetic to this point, and to culturalist critiques of reductionism and eliminativism, see the chapters by McDonough and Margolis in Greenwood, 1991. In both his articles on *Acts of Meaning*, Shanker (1992, 1993) chides Bruner for his allegiance to the idea that folk psychology is a theory, and ties this to Bruner's Cartesianism.

References

Bakhurst, D. 1986. "Thought, Speech, and the Genesis of Meaning: On the 50th Anniversary of Vygotsky's *Myshlenie i rech'*." *Studies in Soviet Thought, 31*, pp. 103–29.

———. 1990. "Social Memory in Soviet Thought." Pp. 203–26 in D. Middleton and D. Edwards (Eds.), *Collective Remembering*. London: Sage.

———. 1991. *Consciousness and Revolution in Soviet Philosophy: From the Bolsheviks to Evald Ilyenkov*. Cambridge, UK: Cambridge University Press.

———. 1995a. "Lessons from Ilyenkov." *Communication Review, 1*(2), pp. 155–78.

———. 1995b. "Wittgenstein and Social Being." Pp. 30–46 in D. Bakhurst and C. Sypnowich (Eds.), *The Social Self*. London: Sage.

———. 1997. "Meaning, Normativity, and the Life of the Mind." *Language and Communication, 17*(1), pp. 33–51.

———. 2001. "Memory, Identity, and the Future of Cultural Psychology," in D. Bakhurst and S. Shanker (Eds.), 2001. *Jerome Bruner: Language, Culture, Self*. London: Sage, pp. 184–98.

Bakhurst, D., and Padden, C. 1991. "The Meshcheryakov Experiment: Soviet Work on the Education of the Blind-Deaf." *Learning and Instruction, 1*, pp. 201–15.

Bruner, J. 1962. *The Process of Education*. New York: Vintage.

———. 1966. *Toward a Theory of Instruction*. Cambridge, MA: Belknap Press of Harvard University Press.

———. 1979. *On Knowing: Essays for the Left Hand*. 2nd ed. Cambridge, MA: Belknap Press of Harvard University Press.

———. 1983. *Child's Talk*. Oxford: Oxford University Press.

———. 1986. *Actual Minds, Possible Worlds*. Cambridge, MA: Harvard University Press.

———. 1990. *Acts of Meaning*. Cambridge, MA: Harvard University Press.

———. 1996. *The Culture of Education*. Cambridge, MA: Harvard University Press.

Davidson, D. 1974. "On the Very Idea of a Conceptual Scheme." *Proceedings and Addresses of the American Philosophical Association, 47*. Reprinted in Davidson, *Inquiries into Truth and Interpretation*. Oxford: Clarendon Press, 1984.

———. 1986. "A Coherence Theory of Truth and Knowledge." Pp. 307–19 in E. LePore (Ed.), *Truth and Interpretation: Perspectives on the Philosophy of Donald Davidson*. Oxford: Blackwell.

———. 1987. "Problems in the Explanation of Action." Pp. 35–49 in P. Pettit, R. Sylvan, and J. Norman (Eds.), *Metaphysics and Morality: Essays in Honour of J.C.C. Smart*. Oxford: Blackwell.

Dennett, D. 1991a. *Consciousness Explained*. Boston: Little, Brown.

———. 1991b. "Two Contrasts: Folk Craft versus Folk Science, and Belief versus Opinion." Pp. 135–48 in J. Greenwood (Ed.), *The Future of Folk Psychology: Intentionality and Cognitive Science*. Cambridge, UK: University Press.

Geertz, C. 1973. *The Interpretation of Cultures*. New York: Basic Books.

Greenwood, J. (Ed.). 1991. *The Future of Folk Psychology: Intentionality and Cognitive Science*. Cambridge, UK: Cambridge University Press.

Harré, R., and Gillett, G. 1994. *The Discursive Mind*. London: Sage.

Heil, J. 1992. *The Nature of True Minds*. Cambridge, UK: Cambridge University Press.

Ilyenkov, E. 1962. "Ideal'noe" [The ideal]. Pp. 219–27 in *Filosofskaya entsiklopediya* [Philosophical encyclopedia]. Vol. 2. Moscow: Sovetskaya entsiklopediya.

———. 1964. "Vopros o tozhdestve myshleniya i bytiya v domarksistskoi filosofii" [The question of the identity of thinking and being in pre-Marxist philosophy]. Pp. 21–54 in *Dialektika—Teoriya poznaniya* [Dialectics—the theory of knowledge]. Moscow: Nauka.

———. 1977. "The Concept of the Ideal." Pp. 71–99 in *Philosophy in the USSR: Problems of Dialectical Materialism*. Trans. R. Daglish. Moscow: Progress.

———1984. *Dialekticheskaya logika* [*Dailectical Logic*]. Moscow: Nauka.

———. 1991. "Dialektika ideal'nogo" [The dialectic of the ideal]. Pp. 229–70 in his Ilyenkov, *Filosofiya i kul'tura* [Philosophy and culture]. Moscow: Politizdat. Originally published as "Problema ideal'nogo" [The problem of the ideal]. *Voprosy filosofii*, 1979, no. 6, pp. 145–58; no. 7, pp. 128–40.

Levitin, K. 1982. *One Is Not Born a Personality*. Trans. Yevgeny Filippov. Moscow: Progress.

MacIntyre, A. 1981. *After Virtue*. London: Duckworth.

Margolis, J. 1991. "The Autonomy of Folk Psychology." Pp. 242–62 in J. Greenwood (Ed.), *The Future of Folk Psychology: Intentionality and Cognitive Science*. Cambridge, UK: Cambridge University Press.

McDonough, R. 1991. "A Culturalist Account of Folk Psychology." Pp. 263–88 in J. Greenwood (Ed.), *The Future of Folk Psychology: Intentionality and Cognitive Science*. Cambridge, UK: Cambridge University Press.

McDowell, J. 1994a. "The Content of Perceptual Experience." *Philosophical Quarterly*, 44, 190–205. Reprinted in J. McDowell, *Mind, Value, and Reality*. Cambridge, MA: Harvard University Press, 1998, pp. 341–58.

———. 1994b. *Mind and World*. Cambridge, MA: Harvard University Press.

———. 1996. "Two Sorts of Naturalism." Pp. 149–79 in R. Hursthouse, G. Lawrence, and W. Quinn (Eds.), *Virtues and Reasons: Philippa Foot and Moral Theory*. Oxford: Clarendon Press. Reprinted in J. McDowell, *Mind, Value, and Reality*. Cambridge, MA: Harvard University Press, 1998, pp. 167–97.

———. 1998. *Mind, Value, and Reality*. Cambridge, MA: Harvard University Press.

Sarason, S. 1981. *Psychology Misdirected*. London: Macmillan.

Shanker, S. 1992. "In Search of Bruner." *Language and Communication*, 12(1), pp. 53–74.

———. 1993. "Locating Bruner." *Language and Communication*, 13(4), pp. 239–63.

Shotter, J. 1975. *Images of Man in Psychological Research*. London: Methuen.

Sperber, D. 1996. *Explaining Culture*. Oxford: Blackwell.

Stich, S. 1983. *From Folk Psychology to Cognitive Science*. Cambridge, MA: MIT Press.

24

The Text of the Mind

Jens Brockmeier

In his 1980 essay "Blurred Genres: The Refiguration of Social Thought," Clifford Geertz (1983) set out to give an account of a series of new developments in the human sciences. Viewed in the light of today's debates on the relations between mind, language, and culture, Geertz's account proves to have been amazingly predictive. Geertz understood the genre blurring of academic and literary discourses as part of the advent of a new postpositivist orientation. In outlining the beginning of an intellectual culture shift, he drew attention to the rise of a new attitude, a new outlook on the study of human nature. More and more human (or behavioral or social or cultural) scientists had become free, both epistemologically and sociologically, to shape their work in terms of its necessities rather than according to established borderlines and disciplinary constraints.

A striking case in point that Geertz observed was the recourse to the humanities for explanatory analogies. Since the 1960s, the organizing analogies in the social sciences had been increasingly coming from the contrivances of cultural performance, rather than from natural processes and physical manipulation. Beginning in those years, new models from literature, grammar, theater, painting, law, and play became widely used and accepted. For example, various theoretical discourses adopted the analogies of "game," "drama," and "text," demonstrating in this way not only the dispersion of traditional genres (reflecting the lack of a clear-cut borderline between the sciences and the humanities, the "two cultures" of knowledge), but also the outset of what soon would become known as the *interpretive turn*.

In this chapter, I shall look at the "text analogue," as Geertz dubbed it, as one of the novel explanatory analogies that have emerged in the wake of the interpretive turn. The text analogue has been used not only in describing social behavior, societal dynamics, and other cultural phenomena, but also to explain the mind. In order to point out how the mind can be understood as a text, I shall take a closer look at Mikhail Bakhtin's idea of the "dialogical" organization of the mind, an idea that has become an influential model of textual thought in the human sciences. In my view, Bakhtin's idea suggests understanding the mind like—and, to a degree, as—a linguistic text, which is akin to other linguistic and textual approaches to the mind that have emerged during the last third of the twentieth century, such as discourse theory and linguistic philosophy in the wake of Wittgenstein, poststructuralist theory of text, sociocultural psychology in the wake of Vygotsky, and narrative psychology. In one way or another, all these approaches conceive of the mind as a text interwoven with the fabric of culture.

Within the traditional disciplinary matrix, the turn to interpretive, hermeneutic ways of understanding the mind could at first appear to be merely an extension of the traditional methodological repertoire, an attempt to add qualitative and "soft" techniques to quantitative and "hard" methods of data collection. Yet, again in a strikingly predictive manner, Geertz (1973) had already pointed out in his book *The Interpretation of Cultures* what would become, and not only in anthropology, one of the most challenging implications of the interpretive approach: the inner connection between the interpretive, hermeneutic methodology (in terms of techniques of research) and the hermeneutic model (in terms of content, or subject of research).

Today it seems obvious that it has been this connection, or, perhaps better, these two halves of the interpretive penny, that have caused such an earthquake, at least in those parts of the human sciences that have defined themselves in terms of the modernist episteme. At stake has been not just a new method, but a new vision, a novel notion of what the human mind is all about. To be sure, in the light of the history of thought, this notion has not been as new as it has seemed to many who have spent most of their intellectual life in positivist and scientistic academic environments. What has been noticed, for example, in some quarters of cognitive science today is a tradition of hermeneutic thought that can be traced back to Aristotle's studies on the poetic and rhetorical fabric of human consciousness.

Geertz's remarks about the shift toward interpretation, both as methodology and model, not only seem more true now than when he wrote them, but seem true of a lot more than those debates in the social sciences to which he primarily was referring. In fact, all approaches to the mind as a text that I have mentioned have this twofold orientation: In highlighting human beings as social agents who try to make sense of their cultural world, they also bring to the fore the "ways of worldmaking" of science and philosophy themselves, to use a concept coined by Nelson Goodman (1978). This view has become emblematic of the new constructivist outlook upon human reality. In the process of worldmaking, the essential cognitive potential of the mind is based on its ability to use a great variety of differentiated strategies of constructing and understanding meaning. All of them entail both interpretive and explanatory processes. Therefore, it has been argued that causal explanation and interpretive understanding, rather than being seen as opposed to one another, are better understood as different, but complementary, aspects of the process of making sense of the human world. They are positions on one hermeneutic continuum of understanding that underlies all our cognitive activities. Differently put, there is no such thing as a natural or otherwise given distinction between interpretive and explanatory-scientific principles of knowing (Brockmeier, 1996), nor is there any difference of principle between the applied epistemology of ordinary discourse, the texts of everyday life, and the epistemology used by human or cultural scientists, the texts of the intellectual attempts to understand that discourse.

If it is thus only through various forms of interpretive understanding (which include specially defined forms, or modes, of causal-explanatory interpretation) that we do justice to the cultural nature of the mind, then it is only a small step to understand the mind itself as an essentially hermeneutic process. This is precisely what takes place in Bakhtin's works. I thus would like to expand this idea by offering a reading of Bakhtin's "dialogical mind" as a fundamentally interpretive domain, a domain of texts, genres, and narrative imagination.

Dialogical Models and Metaphors of the Mind

Dialogical models have been used in several areas of the human sciences to explain a spectrum of phenomena traditionally referred to as self, consciousness, and the mind. Instead of models, we can also speak of dialogical metaphors, since both terms denote the same construct, even if they locate it within different epistemological and linguistic coordinates. Upon closer inspection, however, it is difficult to define these models or metaphors precisely and to distinguish, for example, the meaning of the "dialogical mind" from that of the "discursive mind," the "social mind," or the "transactional mind," to name a few concepts frequently used in the literature. In one way or another, all these ideas are bound into broader enterprises like social constructivism; linguistic anthropology; the ethnography of speaking; discursive, narrative, and cultural psychology; discourse and conversational analysis; and communication and cultural studies. Furthermore, the vocabulary of dialogue is widespread in contexts of clinical psychology and psychoanalysis. Not surprisingly, then, dialogical models and metaphors refer to a variety of rather different phenomena (see, e.g., Anderson, Baxter, and Cissna, 2003; Dervin, Grossberg, O'Keefe, and Wartella, 1989; Hermans, 1996; Hermans and Kempen, 1993; Marková and Foppa, 1990; Rommetveit, 1992; Schafer, 1992; Shotter, 1995; Taylor, 1991; Wertsch, 1991).

Against this backdrop, I suggest that it is helpful to distinguish two different levels of meaning on which these expressions are used. On the one hand, they can be understood as indicating a specific area of analysis that embraces empirical phenomena of interaction and communication between two (or more) persons, especially in sociolinguistic, sociopsychological, (inter)cultural, clinical, and neuropsychological contexts of investigation. Here these expressions often refer to psychological entities and functions that, in contrast with traditionally individualistic and monological notions of the mind, are essentially dialogical. On the other hand, the use of dialogical models can represent a more general theoretical and methodological approach, a style of thought and investigation. Here we are not talking about any empirical entity, "dialogue," but about a paradigmatic orientation on the basis of what could be called the dialogical principle, using a key concept of Bakhtin (1981, 1984, 1986). This paradigmatic orientation has taken shape in a number of projects associated with the interpretive turn.

The fact that more and more human scientists have started to study the forms and modes of interpretive understanding and to conceive of human action and interaction as a domain to which we only have access through interpretive understanding can be seen as a side effect, if not a consequence, of another recent "discovery": that humans live in worlds of culture. That is, human behavior is not the lawful result of biological, economic, social, or other forms of causal determinations; rather, it is laid out within a matrix of life forms in which agency and intentionality play a central role. The idea of this cultural matrix brings into play a further fundamental quality of human existence: It is mediated by various symbol systems, or, put differently, it is embedded in the symbolic space of culture. Language is the hub in this symbolic space, endowing the human mind with its rich capacity to create and discover meaning.

In locating the use of dialogical models and metaphors on two levels of meaning—one indicating a specific area of analysis, the other a more general theoretical and methodological approach—I draw on the works of Bakhtin for three reasons. First, the Russian linguist, semiotician, and literary and cultural scholar is one of the great twentieth-century theorists of dialogue or, as he terms it, of "dialogism" as a model of the mind. Second, Bakhtin's thought has been a central point of reference in most of the new literature on textual models, on both the paradigmatic and empirical levels. Third, his writings on the dialogical principle demonstrate that there is no such thing as an empirical dialogue that can be taken as a given unit of analysis. Rather than representing a well-defined phenomenon, a specific area of human reality, or a particular method of analyzing situations of communication, the dialogical framework is a theoretical construction, an epistemic model. It draws a boundary, to borrow an expression from Wittgenstein, where none has so far been drawn. That is, it is as artificial and arbitrary a categorical abstraction imposed upon the manifold processes of human communication and reflection as the "monological framework" of the Cartesian notion of the mind as an individual, mental, and substantial *res cogitans*. Indeed, what Bakhtin describes as dialogical principle—I shall spell out this argument in a moment—is a way of demonstrating that the mind can neither be captured within a monological nor, alternatively, within a dialogical framework.

Instead, the concept of the dialogical principle highlights a dynamic that continuously unravels the fabric of such categories and their implicit ontological definitions of the singular noun "mind." The dialogical principle, as I understand it, is not the answer to the question of the mind; rather, it keeps the answer open. Aiming to conceive of the mind as a continuous process, it reflects the fact that our mental activities, inextricably embedded in the fluid orders of discourse and culture, remain a fleeting subject, a subject for which, as Bakhtin (1981, p. 37) writes, "all existing clothes are always too tight."

Dialogism and Discourse

The starting point of Bakhtin's conception of the mind was his theory of the utterance. Both written and oral forms of utterance were a central subject of investigation for the Russian language thinker. Studying the manifold linguistic and psychological functions of utterances, Bakhtin dealt with the entire gamut of language forms from literary prose to everyday discourse. He came to see that a common feature of all utterances, whatever their genre and context of use, is their inherent intersubjective or dialogical nature. Language, Bakhtin found, first of all refers to language; utterances reply to utterances; words link to words.

From this point of view, his theoretical thought developed more and more into a transdisciplinary enterprise or, perhaps better, into an intellectual project that simply ignored disciplinary borderlines. His studies became, as it were, investigations into linguistic, psychological, and philosophical anthropology, adopting an intellectual focus that echoes what Charles Taylor (1985) has called the "romantic tradition" of linguistic and philosophical thought, a tradition that can be traced back to Johann Gottfried Herder, Wilhelm von Humboldt, and Johann Georg Hamann. The underlying conviction of the romantic tradition is that the referential function of language as a representational system — the view of language as a lexicon, a system of terms linked to designata — is secondary. What is primary, as Taylor (1985, p. 256) writes, "is the activity of speaking, within which this [representational] system is constantly being made and modified." As Humboldt (1836) put it, language must be understood as *energeia*, not just *ergon*.

Bakhtin's theory is one of several modern approaches to understanding human behavior and the mind through the interpretive use humans make of language — of language as interpretive activity, as *energeia*. Tzvetan Todorov (1984) noted that Bakhtin, in examining linguistic utterances in general and text and discourse in particular, saw himself forced by the need to shore up his thoughts to make extensive forays into psychology, sociology, and the history of culture. He returned from them, as Todorov (1984, p. ix) stated, "with a unitary view of the entire area of the human sciences, based on the identity of their materials: texts, and of their method: interpretation." It is this view that connects Bakhtin's thought with the hermeneutic outlook of the Humboldt tradition.

The connecting link between Bakhtin's interpretive theory of text and his idea of the interpretive mind is his understanding of the utterance. The most important feature of the utterance is its inherent "dialogism" (some authors prefer the translation, "dialogicity" or "dialogicality"). By this term, Bakhtin designated the relation of every utterance to other utterances. As opposed to grammatical sentences, logical relations, and objectal semantic propositions, there is a potential or actual human subject behind every utterance, its author. This distinguishes an utterance (a unit of speech communication) from a sentence (a unit of language). In contrast to a sentence, every utterance is authored by someone; that is, it is personal, it has a voice, the voice of someone's mind. Whereas the proposition is part of a logical, semantic, and grammatical order, the utterance enters another "sphere of being" that includes a speaking subject's subjectivity, his or her intentions, beliefs, and world view. Bakhtin calls this sphere "discourse." Discourse is fundamentally characterized by dialogical relations—that is, by mutual reactions between utterances and their authors. These mutual reactions endow each utterance with a personal profile, with "personhood." That is, in discourse all linguistic communication and, in a broader sense, all sign-mediated interactions are to be understood within an order that is at the same time linguistic, psychological, and social.

By examining the dialogical nature of the utterance, we enter the intersubjective architectonics of the mind. To pick up on the metaphor of architectonic space, we also might say that Bakhtin's dialogical relations represent intersubjective microstructures of the symbolic space of culture. They highlight the basic elements of a discursive space that consists of grammatical forms and narrative schemes, idioms and commonplaces, names and proverbs, and modes of conversation ("speech genres") and of commemoration.

Dialogism thus is a concept that brings to the fore two facts—one that linguistic relations including meanings (which only come into existence when two or more voices "meet") are always relations between human agents, the other that human interactions are always sign-mediated, discursive relations. Bakhtin put much emphasis on this reciprocal relation between psychological and discursive processes. He saw them as being interconnected as are text and context. This view clearly distinguishes him from twentieth-century mainstream (psycho)linguistics in the wake of Ferdinand de Saussure and Noam Chomsky, who both systematically excluded language use (be it *parole* or be it performance) from linguistic inquiry. For Bakhtin, language as such, as an abstract system of rules that is detached from ourselves, from the "living impulse," was nothing but the "naked corpse of the word." For this reason he was not particularly interested in traditional linguistic thought. Here, he remarked (1981, p. 292), "we can learn nothing at all about the social situation or the fate of a given word in life." He went on: "To study the word as such, ignoring the impulses that reach out beyond it, is just as senseless as to study psychological experience outside the context of that real life toward which it was directed."

In this view, the linguistic and the psychological appear as inseparable aspects of the study of that kind of situated experience that Bakhtin called "real-life experience." Sometimes he used a new vocabulary to express this idea, intermingling two semantics that traditionally are kept distinct—for example, when he referred to the dialogical orientation as a "natural orientation of any living discourse" (1981, p. 279). In its fusion of life and language, of a biological and a linguistic vocabulary, this perspective suggests a strong similarity to Wittgenstein's idea of forms of life. Indeed, if discourse is not just to be limited to linguistic phenomena in the narrow sense, but rather captures the interactive, sign-mediated nature of the mind—that is, the semiotic "architecture of human life"—then Bakhtin's "discourse" and "dialogism" can be seen as describing the same phenomena to which Wittgenstein referred as forms of life and language games. All these concepts are meant to cover what in poststructuralist theory of text—to bring still another perspective into play—is seen as mutual interrelatedness of text and context, with context being conceived of as still another text or ensemble of texts. The point of text theory is helpful here because it also sets out the idea of the mind as a text, even if it is based on a different understanding of text. Let me explain.

Dialogism and Intertextuality

Although, as we have seen, Bakhtin laid much emphasis on the structural fusion of mind and language, Bakhtin scholars and theorists of text like Julia Kristeva (1980) and Tzvetan Todorov (1984) have suggested distinguishing the linguistic and psychological dimensions of dialogism, and that one should use for the first and more inclusive meaning the term "intertextuality." Intertextuality is a quality of all discourse. All utterances are in dialogue with prior utterances on the same subject, as well as with utterances yet to come, whose possible reactions they foresee and anticipate. Any text, in Kristeva's formulation, is ultimately an intertext. It is the site of an intersection of countless other texts, present, past, and future. Thus the idea appears illusory that a text, or any discursive sign system that in poststructuralist theory, following Jacques Derrida (1967), is often called *écriture*, has determinately fixed meanings. Rather, in all *écriture* the meaning disperses among innumerable alternatives. It disseminates, to use another concept introduced in this context by Derrida (1978). To reveal this fleeting nature of discourse—and this, to my mind, is precisely what the term *écriture* aims to capture—is the very aim of the practices of reading that characterize so-called deconstruction.

According to Kristeva, it was Bakhtin who first suggested this point of view on language; he was the one who first systematically examined texts as intertexts. Meanings, he argued, are negotiated in the dialogues between different texts and different voices. Even the apparently most self-referential utterance, concentrating on a particular object, cannot but be a response to what has already been said (or could have been said) about the object. At the same time, this utterance is the addressee of possible future voices on the same object as well as on its previous authors.

Ultimately, Bakhtin's concept of "addressivity," the idea that every utterance and every voice is addressed to someone, implies that there is no meaning without being addressed to someone. Differently put, there is no "voiceless" meaning. Because a single voice can make itself heard only by blending into the polyphonic choir already in place, there is no discourse, and not even a word, that is a transparent medium, passing freely or easily into the private property of a speaker. As language is always already occupied with the meanings of its earlier use, it is always already filled with possible alternative, even opposing and contradictory, meanings. Filled with a variety of "responsive reactions" to other utterances, it is populated or, as Bakhtin (1981, p. 294) says, even "overpopulated" with intentions and expectations. In this sense, language is both individual and social; it lies "on the borderline between oneself and the other." As Bakhtin goes on to explain:

The word in language is half someone else's. It becomes "one's own" only when the speaker populates it with his own intentions, his own accent, when he appropriates the word, adapting it to his own semantic and expressive intention. Prior to this moment of appropriation, the word does not exist in a neutral and impersonal language (it is not, after all, out of a dictionary that the speaker gets his words!), but rather it exists in other people's mouths, in other people's contexts, serving other people's intentions: It is from there that one must take the word, and make it one's own. (Bakhtin, 1981, pp. 293–94)

According to Kristeva and Todorov, this universal quality of discourse, its multi-voicedness and polyphony, is to be designated by the term *intertextuality*, whereas the term *dialogism* is set aside for a specific instance of intertextuality. This instance is the exchange of responses by two (or more) speakers, which, for Bakhtin, provide the very essence of human consciousness—conciousness, indeed, ultimately of human existence. Bakhtin shared this belief in the existential deep structure of the dialogic principle with other twentieth-century thinkers (most notably, Martin Buber; see Perlina, 1983). It is the activity of mutual exchanges between utterances and their voices that underlies the concept of the dialogical mind.

In the wake of Kristeva's and Todorov's distinction, concepts like the dialogical mind and the dialogical self, though referring to the same feature of intertextuality/ dialogism that belongs to all discourse, have obtained a certain prominence in the literature, the sometimes ambivalent prominence of a suggestive label. This label has been attached to a great many phenomena; for example, in the study of literary and philosophical texts, as Paul de Man (1993) pointed out, the notion of dialogue and dialogism can serve, and has served, both as a formal and descriptive method and as a translinguistic, anthropological principle of otherness. It is important, however, not to confuse the intertextual meaning, so to speak, of the dialogical mind with that of dialogical in the narrow sense. Bakhtin's approach to the relationship of language and the mind is a case in point of the "dialogical principle" that, as I have suggested, does not represent any empirically given entity.

Deconstructing Dialogue

To be sure, there is also the discourse genre of dialogue in the narrow and literal sense: two speakers involved in a dyadic exchange. We easily find instances of empirical dialogues thematized in Bakhtin's work, too. For example, he lists various types of utterance and rejoinder, such as question and answer, assertion and objection, assertion and agreement, suggestions and acceptance, and order and execution (Bakhtin, 1986, p. 72). "In all these cases," as Wertsch (1991, p. 55) noted, "the emphasis was on the ways in which one concrete voice and set of utterances could come into contact with others." Yet the more we view Bakhtin's ideas within the context of a psychological and philosophical anthropology of discourse, the more the dialogical principle manifests itself as a principle of textual deconstruction. That is, it appears in a fundamental sense critical of, and finally dissolving, every notion of dialogue in the empirical sense.

As already mentioned, in poststructuralist theory of text, deconstruction is the name of a theory and practice of reading that critically analyzes and finally undermines the assumption that language (or any semiotic text or sign system) provides grounds that permit one to determine *the* meaning of a text. The term *deconstruction*, a hybrid between "construction" and "destruction," designates a strategy to dismantle obsolete notions that claim to refer to, to denote, or to "have" such substantial meaning (such as the Cartesian concept of the mind). Instead of attempting to define or establish the boundaries, the unity, and the propositional semantic of a text, a deconstructive reading sets out to show that meaning inevitably dissipates into an indefinite, fluid, and meandering array of semantic possibilities. Meaning is an always emergent and always dissolving constellation. It can no longer be located in the text proper, nor can it be identified in mental representation nor in the relation of reference. Meaning arises, as Wolfgang Iser (1997, pp. xvi–xvii) describes the rationale of intertextuality, "out of the points of intersection at which different contexts clash, collide, overlap, interpenetrate, or are telescoped into one another. Thus meaning appears as something intangible; at best it can only be pinpointed as an operation that feeds a recall of other texts into a semantic project that is in the making." Consequently, in the deconstructive view, meaning dissolves into a movement that never comes to rest and that never manifests itself in an actual presence. For Derrida—and for Bakhtin—what has been called meaning, upon close examination, turns into an endless (and beginningless) regress, a movement or play of differences that opens up an indeterminable multiplicity of possible readings.

Derrida has developed his philosophy of intertextuality under the heading *différance*. The argument I wish to offer here is that Bakhtin's dialogical principle serves the same strategic aim as Derrida's *différance*. Both suggest a deconstructive reading of texts; both understand text in a broad sense, that is, not just as a linguistic entity but as a semiotic and semantic order, as a way of organizing signs and meanings. This enables them to apply the deconstructive reading to traditional concepts of consciousness and the mind. Finally, both conceive of the mind itself as operating according to these textual principles. (I already mentioned the shift from "method" to "model" characteristic of hermeneutic approaches.) Not surprisingly, then, both Derrida and Bakhtin repudiate the idea of a substantial, antonomous, and exclusively mental or spiritual mind, the mind as *reines Denken* (pure thought), an assumption essential to the Western metaphysical tradition (Brockmeier, 1992). Since I want to argue that the significance of the dialogical principle as a model of the mind lies exactly in the shift from the traditional hermeneutic belief in the defining-determining force of categories such as dialogue or monologue to this kind of deconstructive reading, I shall briefly outline how Bakhtin came to view the dialogical principle as a strategy to dissolve every notion of monologue and dialogue in an empirical, substantial, or metaphysical sense.

From Dialogue to the Dialogical Principle

In various writings from the 1920s, Bakhtin tried to identify what can count as the basic unit of discourse. Since he always rejected the notion of a merely individual mind—as implied in philosophical, psychological, and religious concepts of I, self, consciousness, and soul—all his thought and study were oriented toward the idea of a differential, interactional, social relation. Because he made it clear, particularly in his literary studies, that this relation was fundamentally a discursive process, some authors have gone so far as to conceive of the relationship between the individual mind and the other as the most elementary form of Bakhtin's vision of dialogue. For Holquist (1990, p. 18), for example, "in dialogism, the very capacity of consciousness is based on otherness."

In more linguistic terms, Bakhtin specified this basic relation as embracing several elements: the theme or object of an enunciation, the time and space of the concrete situation, and the relations of the interlocutors to each other and to what is happening. These elements constitute the common horizon of the interlocutors, the "we" or the "we-experience." As Bakhtin (1926/Todorov, 1984, p. 42) also put it: " 'I' can actualize itself in discourse only by relying upon 'we.' "[1] In remarks like this one, Bakhtin's view of sociability is, I suspect, still influenced by an obviously dual or dyadic model of the dialogue. Apparently, Todorov (1984, p. 43) comments, the idea that every utterance is addressed to someone meant "that we have at the very end the microsociety formed by two persons, the speaker and the receiver." Wertsch (1991, p. 54) writes, "[t]his is the form of communicative activity that typically comes to mind when one thinks of dialogue, and it played a fundamental role in much of Bakhtin's thinking."

At this point, then, Bakhtin considered every utterance as part of a dialogue, where dialogue is understood in its empirical, not paradigmatic, meaning, that is, as a form of conversation between two persons. Yet even in this context, we already find the outline of another meaning of dialogue, which later will turn into the dialogical principle:

> Verbal interaction is the fundamental reality of language. Dialogue, in the narrow sense of the term, is but one form, albeit the most important to be sure, of verbal interaction. But dialogue can be understood in a broader sense, meaning by it not only direct and *viva voce* verbal communication between two persons, but also all verbal communication, whatever its form. (Bakhtin, 1926/Todorov, 1984, p. 44)

Shortly after that, Bakhtin wrote: "It could be said that all verbal communication, all verbal interaction takes place in the form of an exchange of utterances, that is, in the form of a dialogue" (1930/Todorov, 1984, p. 44). Similarly, in an article from 1927 we find a description of discourse as the "scenario" of a certain event. In this view, even the simplest utterance takes on the appearance of a little drama, whose minimal roles are played by the speaker, the object, and the listener. Even though Holquist (1990, p. 18) is right in stressing the "simple yet all-important fact ... that they always enact a drama containing more than one actor," there too the whole scenario is about the setting of empirical dialogues.

How Bakhtin's understanding of dialogue expanded and transformed toward the dialogical principle becomes evident in a text written in 1959–61. Again, it is about discourse as drama. However, now the main roles are no longer played by the dyad of speaker and listener of an utterance. Instead, the whole metaphor shifts from the grounds of an empirical dialogue to a thought picture. This picture includes various roles that here are called voices, suggesting a form of interindividuality that contains more than one, two, or any specific number of interlocuters.

> Discourse (as all signs generally) is interindividual. All that is said, expressed, is outside of the "soul" of the speaker, and does not belong to him only. But discourse cannot be attributed to the speaker alone. The author (the speaker) may have inalienable rights upon the discourse, but so does the listener, as do those voices that resonate in the words found by the author (since there are no words that do not belong to someone). (Bakhtin, 1959–61/Todorov, 1984, p. 52)

The idea of interindividuality outlined in this text is based on the assumption that there is not just one particular subject, neither individual nor dialogical, to give intention and meaning to discourse. Especially in his analyses of the novel, but also in his studies of nonliterary everyday discourse, Bakhtin demonstrated that the dialogical principle is inherent not only in all forms of linguistic communication, but also in basic functions of the mind, like thought and imagination. In referring to linguistic and psychological conceptions of the speech dyad, these analyses ultimately questioned the idea of the dialogue as an empirically existing unit in itself. Every word, expression, or utterance used in an apparently closed exchange bears the traces not only of two but of all subjects, possible and real, who ever used or will use this word, expression, or meaning.

> [L]anguage has been completely taken over, shot through with intentions and accents. For any individual consciousness living in it, language is not an abstract system of normative forms but rather a concrete heteroglot conception of the world. All words have the "taste" of a profession, a genre, a tendency, a party, a particular work, a particular person, a generation, an age group, the day and hour. Each word tastes of the context and contexts in which it has lived its socially charged life; all words and forms are populated by intentions. (Bakhtin, 1981, p. 293)

Evidently, the picture of the word and its "social life" that Bakhtin draws in this extract from his essay "Discourse in the Novel," (one of the four essays in "The Dialogic Imagination") differs in several respects from that of the dyadic exchange. Now the term "dialogue" seems to have taken on the "taste" of one of those concepts that open up more insights than they actually entail. It provides new points of view upon the mind that are only conceivable beyond the epistemic framework of monological and dialogical models.

To sum up my line of argument, I have proposed to understand the dialogical

THE TEXT OF THE MIND

principle in a paradigmatic, not a dialogical, sense. Distinguishing between an ontological and an epistemological aspect of this concept, I have argued that on the one hand, the dialogical principle refers to intertextuality as the universal reality of discourse and thought. It is an ontological marker, so to speak. Immersed into language, the mind shares the dialogical fabric of discourse irrespective of the number of speakers or interlocutors involved in a specific discursive setting. On the other hand, the dialogical principle refers to a way of thought and analysis, an intellectual method, that can be likened to the practice of deconstructive reading as developed in poststructuralist text theory. The focus of this reading is on the inherent dialogical movement of discourse, which is to say that the strategy of investigation is oriented toward the sign-mediated, pragmatic, and interactional dimensions of the mind, as suggested in a similar way by Wittgenstein's concept of language game (for this similarity between Bakhtin and Wittgenstein, see Wertsch, 1991, pp. 105–6). In fact, insofar as, for Bakhtin, language does not exist but in its social use, as a form of human activity, he might be read as a Russian Wittgenstein.

Understanding Bakhtin from what I have suggested as a paradigmatic point of view links his thought to several textual models of the mind—from poststructuralist text theory to Wittgensteinian approaches to discourse and mind, as well as to other recent theory developments that stress, along similarly "dialogical" lines, the "discursive" (e.g., Edwards, 1997; Harré and Gillett, 1994), the "multivoiced" (e.g., Wertsch, 1991; Hermans, 1996); the "narrative" (Brockmeier and Harré, 2001; Bruner, 1991); the "transactional" (e.g., Bruner, 1987), the "distributed" (e.g., Hutchins, 1995; Salomon, 1993), the "social" (e.g., Bakhurst and Sypnowich, 1995) and the "sociocultural" (e.g., Wertsch, 1998) character of the mind.

The Heterogeneity of the Mind

Let me conclude with one further implication of the dialogical principle that I believe is essential for a textual (or intertextual) concept of the mind and its cultural situatedness. There are some aspects of Bakhtin's dialogical principle that highlight a feature of the mind that has been almost entirely neglected in psychological and philosophical studies: its internal diversity and heterogeneity. In psychology, diversity has been addressed, if at all, as a developmental phenomenon. Traditionally it has been thematized in the form of genetic hierarchies or developmental stages (as Wertsch observed; see 1991, chapter 5). Jean Piaget's genetic epistemology is a case in point, as it exclusively depicts cognitive diversity along a diachronic scale, without taking into account any interindividual or inner-individual diversity.

In contrast, Bakhtin is concerned with the fact that the mind, at all stages of its development and in all cultural settings, is a most heterogeneous ensemble of different orders with regard to practices, abilities, knowledge, intentions, and emotions. These different orders constitute a type of heterogeneity that does not just manifest itself over the course of time, in a diachronic perspective, but also at one and the same moment, in a synchronic perspective. To capture the synchronic diversity, Bakhtin's analyses of the dialogical mind aim to uncover both the puzzling multitude of voices, accents, and "overtones" present in every utterance, every expression, every word, and the irreducible diversity of these voices, accents, and overtones (which often includes, or leads to, oppositions and contradictions). This cotemporal heterogeneity of the mind is an issue Bakhtin remained fascinated with all his life. He coined a specific term for this multivoicedness: *heterophony*, a concept meant to reflect the simultaneous existence of various voices and positions (including discordant ones) in one mind.

Yet this kind of "orchestration" of the mind—which, as we remember, is inherent even to an isolated monologue, indeed, even to a single thought—is only one form of diversity. There is a second form of heterogeneity that Bakhtin termed *heteroglossia*. In a first, narrow reading, heteroglossia can be understood as the inner diversity of language as a whole. In the Bakhtinian scheme of things, there are many different "social speech types" that mark the internal stratification of any single national language into countless social dialects, professional jargons, generic languages, languages of generations and age groups, tendentious languages, languages of the authorities and institutions, and languages of various cultural circles and subcultural milieus. All of them coexist spatiotemporally in discourse and thus in mind, each with its own vocabulary, its own slogans, its own style. Heteroglossia thus can be seen as a particular fabric of the inner dialogism of the mind, a specific (as Bakhtin, 1981, p. 278, expresses the point) "multiplicity of social voices and a wide variety of their links and interrelationships (always more or less dialogized)."

We see here once more that it is the internal organization of language that ensures the primacy of context over text. In terms of text theory, every text carries the burden of a variety of other texts overlapping each other, forming thick palimpsests. Every discourse about an object is interwoven with both the history of the "contradictory acts of verbal recognition" of the object and the social heteroglossia that defines in a given moment the symbolic space within which the object exists, the space within which it becomes visible and intelligible as a subject of discourse (Brockmeier, 2001). In Bakhtin's words (1981, p. 278), we witness a "Tower-of-Babel mixing of languages that goes on around any object," a mixing that interweaves the "dialect of the object" with the social dialogues surrounding it.

Bakhtin primarily investigated heteroglossia in novelistic discourse. The novel, he remarked (1981, p. 263), "orchestrates all its themes, the totality of the world of objects and ideas depicted and expressed, by means of the social diversity of speech types [heteroglossia] and by the differing individual voices [heterophony] that flourish under such conditions." Yet he often pointed out that this "heteroglot orchestration" is not specific to literary texts but is a universal quality of every discourse, every thought, every discursive operation of the mind. Holquist (1990, p. 428) argues that heteroglossia was for Bakhtin the "base condition governing the operation of meaning" in an inclusive and fundamental sense. In studying the mind—which means examining the way that we construct and understand meaning—we cannot but investigate such heteroglot orchestration.

Besides heterophony (the diversity of individual voices) and heteroglossia (the internal social diversity of a discourse), there is a third form of diversity of the mind that inserts itself between these two forms. This is the diversity of discursive types or speech genres. To name this kind of heterogeneity, Bakhtin introduced a neologism that Todorov (1984, p. 56) translated as *heterology*. The great variety of discourse genres in a given culture arises spontaneously from social diversity. There are genres, for instance, that originated in the communication of professions and business (in factories, shops, offices, and the like), in the communication of public institutions (such as the university, the church, and the military), in everyday discourse (as in conversations in the street on in restaurants, jokes, and so on), and finally in what (in the Russian meaning of the word) is ideological communication, that is, the official discourse that particularly takes place in politics, history, the media, and the like. Of course, these public discourses do not have clear-cut boundary lines. Generic forms that originated in one public sphere can easily move into another sphere. They also can enter the sphere of familiar and private communication, where they might be used with an ironic or parodying accent. As a consequence, there is a permanent mix of genres from different social and cultural spheres.

In Bakhtin's writings there are different typologies of heterology. In his "Discourse in the Novel," for example, he recognizes and employs up to five types of inner stratification of language: by profession, social stratum, age, region (dialects and accents), and genre. Ultimately, all these forms of heterology translate into forms or structures of the individual mind. The more we understand the mind in this light, the more, we might say, do we become aware of the inappropriateness of the single-noun category of the mind.

It seems that—not least for this reason—Bakhtin became particularly interested in the role that speech genres play for the organization of the mind. Traditionally, "genre" is used as a term for a more or less normative literary category, but Bakhtin came to see that it is not only in fiction and drama that genres organize thought, memory, and imagination. Throughout the centuries, genres of both literature and speech have accumulated "forms of seeing and interpreting particular aspects of the world" (Bakhtin, 1986, p. 5). As he goes on to explain (p. 78):

> Even in the most free, the most unconstrained conversation, we cast our speech in definite generic forms, sometimes rigid and trite ones, sometimes more flexible, plastic, and creative ones (everyday communication also has creative genres at its disposal). We are given these speech genres in almost the same way we are given our native language, which we master fluently long before we begin to study grammar. We know our native language—its lexical composition and grammatical structure—not from dictionaries and grammars but from concrete utterances that we hear and that we ourselves reproduce in live speech communication with people around us.

Speech genres, then, are relatively stable patterns of discourse. At the same time, they are more changeable and plastic than grammatically defined language forms.

This makes them flexible in adapting to specific discursive contexts and particular experiences of the individual. That is, genres are not simply external constraints of thought, but internal, expressive forms of individuality. The more freely we employ them, the more fully and distinctively we reveal our particular subjectivity in them. It is for this reason, as Bakhtin remarks, that we have such a rich repertoire of oral and written speech genres. They are just as diverse as the forms of human activity (material and symbolic, practical and mental) in which they are involved. As a consequence, "no list of oral speech genres yet exists, or even a principle on which such a list might be based" (Bakhtin, 1986, p. 80).

Speech genres organize not only the production and composition but also the reception and understanding of language. They are crucial in making possible any act of social interpretation, for examle, reading other minds, as in other forms of mastering the puzzling web of "dialogue" we live in.

> Speech genres organize our speech in almost the same way as grammatical (syntactical) forms do. We learn to cast our speech in generic forms and, when hearing others' speech, we guess its genre from the very first words; we predict a certain length (that is, the approximate length of the speech whole) and a certain compositional structure; we foresee the end; that is, from the very beginning we have a sense of the speech whole. If speech genres did not exist and we had not mastered them, if we had to originate them during the speech process and construct each utterance at will for the first time, speech communication would be almost impossible. (Bakhtin, 1986, pp. 78–79)

Being themselves combinations of different forms and structures of language, speech genres offer culturally normative models for specific individual experiences, thoughts, and imaginations. In doing so, they assimilate the particular experience of the individual, including the most personal and intimate, to the normative canon of culture. All this usually escapes our attention. Growing up within a universe of speech genres, we learn to use them confidently and skillfully in practice, which may partly explain why it is quite possible for us to suspect their existence in theory. Bakhtin refers to Molière's Monsieur Jourdan, who, when speaking in prose, had no idea of what he was speaking and doing. Like Monsieur Jourdan, we use, whenever we think and communicate, countless genres without noting or suspecting that they exist at all. They are like the air we breathe.

Genres, then, serve an essential mediating function. They mediate between the mind and culture, between the self and the other, between language and thought, between the normative and the imaginative. They combine the canonical and the (cotemporal) diversity of the individual mind. They balance the rule and its break.

In summary, in drawing attention to several forms of internal diversity of discourse and the mind—heterophony, heteroglossia, and heterology—Bakhtin offers a point of view on the mind (if, after all, we still are ready to use this singular noun form) that has been widely neglected in traditional theories. I have described this point of view as the dialogical principle, as a critical reading of textual structures. In this strategy of dialogical, discursive, or deconstructive reading, the mind figures in a twofold sense as text—or "text analogue," to use Geertz's term. It can be understood as a text to be read and interpreted, and as the hermeneutic subject who interprets the world, including the mind itself, in the same way that a reader reads a text.

Note

1. This and some of the following extracts from Bakhtin's earlier writings are quoted from the English translations in Todorov (1984). The quoted year of publication of the Russian text refers to the "Chronological List of the Writings by Bakhtin and His Circle" in Todorov's book (pp. 121–123).

References

Anderson, R., Baxter, L.A., and Cissna, K.N. (Eds.). 2003. *Dialogue: Theorizing Difference in Communication Studies.* Thousand Oaks, CA: Sage.

Ammaniti, M., and Stern, D.N. (Eds.). 1994. *Psychoanalysis and Development: Representations and Narratives.* New York: New York University Press.

Bakhtin, M. 1981. *The Dialogic Imagination.* M. Holquist (Ed.). Trans. C. Emerson and M. Holquist. Austin: University of Texas Press.

———. 1984. *Problems of Dostoevsky's Poetics.* Ed. and trans. by C. Emerson. Minneapolis: University of Minnesota Press.

———. 1986. *Speech Genres and Other Late Essays.* C. Emerson and M. Holquist (Ed.). Trans. V. McGee. Austin: University of Texas Press.

Bakhurst, D., and Sypnowich, C. (Eds.). 1995. *The Social Self.* London: Sage.

Brockmeier, J. 1992. *"Reines Denken": Zur Kritik der teleologischen Denkform* ["Pure thought": A critique of the teleological form of thinking]. Amsterdam and Philadelphia: B.R. Grüner–John Benjamins.

———. 1996. "Explaining the Interpretive Mind." *Human Development,* 39, pp. 287–95.

———. 2001. "Texts and Other Symbolic Spaces." *Mind, Culture, and Activity,* 8, pp. 215–231.

Brockmeier, J., and Harré, R. 2001. "Narrative: Problems and Promises of an Alternative Paradigm." Pp. 39–58 in J. Brockmeier, and D. Carbaugh (Eds.), *Narrative and Identity: Studies in Autobiography, Self and Culture.* Philadelphia: John Benjamins.

Bruner, J.S. 1987. "The Transactional Self." Pp. 81–96 in J.S. Bruner and H. Haste (Eds.), *Making Sense: The Child's Construction of the World.* New York: Methuen.

Bruner, J. S., 1991. "The Narrative Construction of Reality." *Critical Inquiry,* 17 (Autumn), 1–21.

Bruner, J.S. and Haste, H. (Eds.). 1987. *Making Sense: The Child's Construction of the World.* New York: Methuen.

de Man, P. (1983). "Dialogue and Dialogism." *Poetics Today*, 4, pp. 99–107; also pp. 340–347 in M. E. Gardiner (Ed.), *Michail Bakhtin, 4 vols.*, Vol 3.

Dervin, B., Grossberg, L., O'Keefe, B. J., and Wartella, E. (Eds.). 1989. *Rethinking Communication. Vol. 2: Paradigm Dialogues*. Newbury Park: Sage.

Derrida, J. 1967. *De la grammatologie*. Paris: Editions de Minuit. English translation, *Of Grammatology*. Baltimore: Johns Hopkins University Press, 1976.

———. 1978. "Structure, Sign and Discourse in the Human Sciences." Pp. 278–95 in Derrida, *Writing and Difference*. London: Routledge and Kegan Paul.

Edwards, D. 1997. *Discourse and Cognition*. London: Sage.

Geertz, C. 1973. *The Interpretation of Cultures*. New York: Basic Books.

———. 1983. *Local Knowledge: Further Essays in Interpretive Anthropology*. New York: Basic Books.

Goodman, N. 1978. *Ways of Worldmaking*. Indianapolis, IN: Hackett.

Harré, R., and Gillett, G. 1994. *The Discursive Mind*. Thousand Oaks, CA: Sage.

Hermans, H.J.M. 1996. "Voicing the Self: From Information Processing to Dialogical Interchange." *Psychological Bulletin*, 119, pp. 31–50.

Hermans, H.J.M., and Kempen, H.J.G. 1993. *The Dialogical Self: Meaning as Movement*. San Diego: Academic Press.

Holquist, M. 1990. *Dialogism: Bakhtin and His World*. New York: Routledge.

Humboldt, Wilhelm von. 1836. *Über die Verschiedenheit des menschlichen Sprachbaues und ihren Einfluss auf die geistige Entwickelung des Menschengeschlechts*. Berlin: Dümmler.

Hutchins, E. 1995. *Cognition in the Wild*. Cambridge, MA: MIT Press.

Iser, W. 1997. "Intertextuality: The Epitome of Culture." Foreword to R. Lachenmann, *Memory and Literature: Intertextuality in Russian Modernism*. Minneapolis: University of Minnesota Press.

Kristeva, J. 1980. *Desire in Language: A Semiotic Approach to Literature and Art*. New York: Columbia University Press.

Lachenmann, R. 1997. *Memory and Literature: Intertextuality in Russian Modernism*. Minneapolis: University of Minnesota Press.

Marková, I., and Foppa, K. (Eds.). 1990. *The Dynamics of Dialogue*. London: Harvester Wheatsheaf.

Perlina, N. 1983. "Michail Bakhtin and Martin Buber: Problems of dialogic imagination." *Studies in Twentieth Century Literature*, 9, pp. 3–28; also pp. 104–116 in M. E. Gardiner (Ed.), *Michail Bakhtin, 4 vols.*, Vol. 1.

Rommetveit, R. 1992. "Outlines of a Dialogically based Social-Cognitive Approach to Human Cognition and Communication." Pp. 19–44 in A.H. Wold (Ed.), *The Dialogical Alternative: Towards a Theory of Language and Mind*. Oslo: Scandinavian University Press.

Salomon, G. (Ed.). 1993. *Distributed Cognitions: Psychological and Educational Considerations*. Cambridge, UK: Cambridge University Press.

Schafer, R. 1992. *Retelling a Life: Narration and Dialogue in Psychoanalysis*. New York: Basic Books.

Shotter, J. 1995. "Dialogical Psychology." Pp. 160–78 in J.A. Smith, R. Harré, and L. Van Langenhove (Eds.), *Rethinking Psychology*. London: Sage.

Taylor, C. 1985. *Human Agency and Language*. Cambridge, UK: Cambridge University Press.

———. 1991. "The Dialogial Self." Pp. 304–314 in D.R. Hiley, J.F. Bohman, and

R.M. Shusterman (Eds.), *The Interpretive Turn: Philosophy, Science, Culture.* Ithaca, NY: Cornell University Press.

Todorov, T. 1984. *Mikhail Bakhtin: The Dialogical Principle.* Minneapolis: University of Minnesota Press (French original published 1981).

Wertsch, J.V. 1991. *Voices of the Mind.* London: Harvester Wheatsheaf.

———. 1998. *Mind as Action.* New York: Oxford University Press.

VII

Rationality: Cultural or Natural?

Introduction

Christina E. Erneling

Although the authors in this part focus on different aspects of rationality (beliefs, the development of reason in children, the law of contradiction, and scientific rationality), they all stress the complexity and diversity of what people commonly refer to as a paradigmatic case of individual mental activity. In particular, they argue that the social and normative aspects of rationality are crucial, and that this implies that understanding rationality involves more than understanding how individual brains and cognitive processes work. The authors all go beyond the atomistic or individualistic assumptions of the Cartesian framework as discussed in the introductions to parts IV and V.

Timothy van Gelder argues that most classical as well as contemporary mind-body debates are based on four mistaken assumptions that, if rejected, allow one to dissolve the problem of relating the mental to the physical. (For a discussion of the mind-body problem, also see part II.) The basic mistake, as I read his chapter, is that those who take this wrong approach treat the mind as ontologically homogeneous and simple; that is, all mental phenomena, such as sensations, beliefs, and reasoning, are taken to belong to the same ontological kind—the mental as opposed to the physical. As a consequence, it is assumed that the relationship between mental and physical things is always the same, regardless of what mental phenomena one takes as a focus of attention (e.g., they are related either by identity, by realization, by supervenience, or by causation—all depending on the theory one holds).

The focus of van Gelder's discussion is beliefs. He argues that in contrast to, for example, sensations, beliefs are ontologically complex in a way that matters for how they are related to physical objects. Believing that *p*, according to van Gelder, is a complex behavioral, causal, and social situation. For a person to believe that *p*, that person has to have a complex physical inner constitution (most important, a brain), must have certain typical behavioral dispositions, and must be part of a social and normative institution of commitments. In the classical mind-body controversy, there are three views about what beliefs are: states or modifications of an inherently private and nonphysical mental substance, states of the brain, and behavioral dispositions. In addition to all these, van Gelder argues, beliefs also involve commitments and as such are normative entities, judged according to whether they are proper or improper. Thus at least one aspect of beliefs is not part of the causal order, but is metaphysically distinct.

The mistake of philosophers of mind, psychologists, neurophysiologists, and others is to assume that only one of these ontologically distinct parts or aspects of the mind is the mind. They assume that the mind is either the brain, computational or dynamic processes, behavior, or socially constructed linguistic practices. The truth is that the mind is all these things—a multiple of ontological kinds. Philosophers, scientists, and users of folk psychology are partly right, but each group restricts itself to only one aspect of the mind. Thus van Gelder calls for ontological pluralism. The mind is more than cognitive processes, more than the causal underpinnings that are studied by cognitive science, and more than the brain states studied by neurophysiologists. Scientists, whether they adhere to a computational or dynamic model of cognition or the brain, are operating correctly when they study cognitive processes and the brain, but they are not thereby studying the mind, which also involves complex normative systems or institutions, which are not physical systems. This reconceptualization of the mind's ontology also has consequences for the mind-body problem, which is, as mentioned, the starting point for van Gelder's chapter.

Ian Jarvie's chapter, which is about theories of rationality in science, nevertheless underlines the point made by van Gelder in different terms: Rationality, or, to use van Gelder's term, mind, involves more than individual cognitive activity and requires a mixed metaphysics. Most philosophers discussing rationality have interpreted rationality as a matter of individual beliefs, but according to Jarvie, it is a public and social activity that sometimes is internalized, rather than a state or process of individual cognition. Building on Karl Popper's analysis of scientific rationality, Jarvie generalizes it to cover all instances of rational activity, including magical thinking and practices. Rationality is neither a natural faculty of individual human beings nor simply a set of social conventions, but a socially instituted method that humans use to solve problems and to engage in criticism aimed at learning how the world is. The most rational method, as compared both to dogmatism and skepticism, is best characterized as a workshop where different actors are trying to solve problems in an open and critical way.

In other words, rationality, both in the individual and in collectives of individuals, as in science, involves more than cognitive and neurophysiological processes. Furthermore, it cannot be reduced to symbolic and conventional patterns of social interaction, since rationality is at the same time both natural and conventional. Thus the upshot of Jarvie's chapter is to show how this nature-convention distinction, which has dominated both philosophy of mind and philosophy of science for a long time, can be overcome.

Christina Erneling, in her chapter, focuses on a specific example of this mistake of seeing the mind and rationality as exclusively a matter of cognitive processes.

She discusses Alison Gopnik's and Andrew Meltzoff's (1997) theory of cognitive development and argues that it is based on a mistaken conception of the mind of the kind van Gelder has pointed out. She claims that this has led the authors to operate with a mistaken conception of science and scientific change—that is, of scientific rationality—since Gopnik and Meltzoff claim that cognitive development in children is similar to cognitive change in science. Erneling's main criticism of this idea is that these authors ignore the social aspect of both individual and collective conceptual change. Among other things, cognitive development in children, as well as change in science, involves beliefs, which are socially constituted.

David Martel Johnson has argued in previous publications that, strictly speaking, it is appropriate to think of both the mind in general and beliefs and desires in particular as more or less ordinary intellectual inventions. Furthermore, according to him, the invention of (strict) mind probably was made by various now unknown individuals who lived in mainland Greece during the time of Homer—the so-called Greek Middle Ages, from about 1100 to 750 BCE. Nevertheless, that is not the topic he proposes to discuss in his chapter here. Instead, he now focuses on the idea that there is also another, wider sense of the word "mind" that refers to something much more widely shared among humans (including many who lived before what he calls "the Greek revolution"). But according to him, even mind in this second, wider sense needs to be thought of as something that is social and cultural rather than narrowly physical in nature. In particular, it is not correct to suppose that it is a set of functions that simply and automatically arise out of a particular sort of brains.

Johnson's way of showing this is to criticize those theorists (e.g., Steven Pinker, George Lakoff, Mark Johnson, and Noam Chomsky) who maintain that (1) the brain is always of more explanatory significance than the mind on the grounds that (2) the first is capable—in principle—of accounting for every property of and fact about the second, but not vice versa. This view is wrong, according to Johnson, for at least three reasons. First, it fails to take account of the empirical fact that the human brain is a very pliable organ whose structures and functions can be influenced, not just by narrowly physical causal factors like temperature, atmospheric pressure, alcohol, or testosterone in the blood, but also by "meaningful" factors like newly invented ideas and ways of thinking. Second, he argues that this view cannot make adequate sense of Charles Darwin's influence on modern philosophy and science. Third, he claims that this conception of things is incompatible with neglected but important facts about our species that have been brought to light in relatively recent times by the cognitive sciences of paleontology and archeology. In particular, it is now clear that human thinking was radically transformed at the beginning of the Upper Paleolithic period, between approximately 60,000 and 40,000 years ago. But the evidence also indicates that this was a cultural rather than just a physical transformation because, for example, it was not accomplished by the replacement of one population of humans by another.

Three of the four chapters in this part—the ones by van Gelder, Jarvie, and Erneling—affirm a kind of "combination" view. According to that view, it has become both possible and necessary today to reconceptualize the mind's ontology because of the fact (overlooked by most previous thinkers) that social, cultural, and historical factors—and with them normative aspects—are part of what we mean whenever we talk about the mind in general, and more particularly about rationality (understood as applying to scientific practice as a whole and to individual cases of rational thinking). This approach does not rule out the brain or cognitive processes understood as either computational or dynamic in nature. On the contrary, it condones pluralism, even though it does not advocate the interdisciplinary study of the mind, conceived as consisting of different approaches to an ontologically homogeneous object. In fact, this approach endorses a multidisciplinary study of different and distinct aspects of what, in everyday life and in most philosophical and scientific contexts, we lump together as the same thing. This implies that different methodological and disciplinary approaches are needed, but these approaches are not all studying the same thing, since the mind, as a scientific object, is ontologically complex.

On the other hand, consistent with what he said in the introduction to this volume—in particular, his rejection of the no-center view and his claim that cognitive scientists finally must choose between just two possible alternatives—Johnson does not subscribe to the view that the mind generally or beliefs in particular are complex. Rather, he thinks that even though a person's having a mind or holding a belief presupposes certain facts about the physical world (and more especially about the structure and powers of the brain), the mind and belief are nothing more nor less, in themselves, than an intellectual invention. Therefore, like any other such invention (e.g., double-entry bookkeeping, the game of basketball, constitutional government), it is entirely cultural and not at all physical in its ontological nature. Of course, Johnson sees nothing wrong with cognitive scientists proposing to study the structure and processes of the human brain, but he does not interpret this as their uncovering and describing one or another "part" of the mind itself, but rather as the endeavor of trying to get a better grasp of some of the physical conditions that had to be present before it became possible for people to make the invention we now have come to think of as the mind.

Thus the authors in this part agree that the mind is in essential aspects cultural, but their chapters also show that the issue of the mind's ontology is far from a closed question. Equally open is the question of what relationship there is between the cultural aspects of the mind (or the mind as an invention) and the body.

Reference

Gopnik, A., and Meltzoff, A.N. 1997. *Words, Thoughts, and Theories*. Cambridge, MA: MIT Press.

25

Beyond the Mind-Body Problem

Timothy van Gelder

Wilfrid Sellars once famously described philosophy as aiming to understand how things, in the broadest possible sense of the term hang together in the broadest possible sense of the term (Sellars, 1962, p. 37). In the spirit of that suggestion, we can think of philosophy of mind as the attempt to say how minds hang together—how things fit to form minds, and how minds fit with other things. It can hardly be disputed that there are these kinds of fit; in that respect, at least, the world is a coherent place. The philosophical challenge is to understand and elucidate the nature of the fit, such as it is.

The mind-body debate in contemporary Anglo-American analytic philosophy is one among many discourses addressing this challenge. The mind-body debate reduces the general problem of fit to a very specific question: What is the ontological relationship between mental entities, on the one hand, and physical entities, on the other? It has developed a range of candidate answers to this question. These are the official "isms" familiar to any student of the debate: Cartesian dualism, central-state materialism, functionalism, and so forth. A great deal of effort within the debate is taken up with detailed argument over the merits of these various positions as solutions to the problem of how mental and physical entities relate.

In this chapter, I will argue that the classical mind-body debate is propped up by four deep assumptions. These assumptions are false, and for this reason the orthodox mind-body debate cannot hope to solve its central problem. The falsity of the assumptions entails dissolution of the classical problem and a pluralist orientation concerning the relationship between the mental and the physical. I will briefly describe this pluralism and some implications for the relationship between mind and science.

"Isms" and Assumptions

Consider the various standard positions available within the contemporary debate solely insofar as they purport to specify the ontological relationship of such mental entities as they deem actually to exist, on one hand, to the physical entities, on the other, as shown in table 25.1. Rows correspond to the basic kinds of metaphysical relation mental entities might bear to physical entities. Columns correspond to generic positions on the mind-body relationship. Thus baseline physicalism is the generic stance that mental entities are identical with, reducible to, realized by, supervenient upon, and in causal interaction with physical entities. The official isms of the debate are either generic positions or more specific positions obtained by adding further detail. For example, anomalous monism is a form of nonreductive physicalism that supplements that basic position with various theses such as (1) that the identity is token rather than type, (2) that the entities in question are events, and (3) that there are no psychophysical laws.

The four assumptions pervading the debate can now be read off the form of the table. The first, implicit in the fact that the table has only five main rows, is that the relations of identity, reduction, realization, supervenience, and causation are collectively adequate for a metaphysical account of the mind-body relationship. No other metaphysical relation enters into the debate, and it is assumed that this does not hamper the discussion. Indeed, the question of the collective adequacy of these five relations never even arises.

The second assumption is implicit in the fact that a generic position is specified by placing ticks ($\checkmark$) or crosses (x) in appropriate boxes. A tick indicates that a given relation obtains between mental and physical entities; a cross, that it does not obtain. The assumption is that a given relation obtains in the case of all mental entities or none of them; that in other words, the mental is relationally homogeneous with respect to the physical. One or another of the generic positions is true for all mental entities.

TABLE 25.1. Generic Positions in the Contemporary Mind-Body Debate

Relation of mental to physical:	Baseline Dualism/Idealism (inc. Parallelism)	Causal Dualism (inc. Cartesian Dualism, Epiphenomenalism, Occasionalism)	Baseline Physicalism (inc. Australian Materialism, Behaviorism, Neuroscientific Eliminativism)	Non-Reductive Physicalism (inc. Anomalous Monism, Functionalism, Biological Naturalism)	Weak Supervenience
Identity	x	x	$\checkmark$	$\checkmark$	x
Reduction	x	x	$\checkmark$	x	x
Realization (Constitution)	x	x	$\checkmark$	$\checkmark$	$\checkmark$
Supervenience	x	x	$\checkmark$	$\checkmark$	$\checkmark$
Causal Interaction	x	$\checkmark$	$\checkmark$	$\checkmark$	$\checkmark$

The third assumption is closely related. Mental entities are taken to be relationally homogeneous because they are also taken to be ontologically homogeneous. That is, mental entities are assumed to all belong to a single ontological kind for the purposes of understanding their relationship to the physical. They are taken to be all essentially modifications of mental substance, or all essentially causal role players, or all essentially "first person," and so on. This explains why a single account of the ontological relationship is taken to be sufficient for all mental entities. Note that the claim here is not that the debate recognizes no ontological differences among mental entities whatsoever. Indeed it does. However, such differences as it does recognize generally make no difference to how mental entities of these various sorts relate to the physical.

The fourth assumption is also implicit in the fact that the table specifies generic positions by means of ticks and crosses in relevant squares. To place a tick in a square of the table is to indicate that any given mental entity stands in that relation to the physical. The assumption is that mental entities are ontological simples as far as the mind-body problem is concerned. When we are describing how mental entities relate to the physical, we do not have to look inside these entities; we can just specify the relations that the mental entity as a whole bears to the physical. We do not have to first articulate the internal ontological structure of mental entities and then ask how the various ontological components relate to the physical. Mental entities might have internal ontological structure, but that structure is of no direct relevance for the mind-body problem.

The claim is that these four assumptions pervade the debate. They are largely responsible for its basic structure. The fact that the official isms are the standard reference points indicates that the assumptions are widely shared. Subscribing to all four assumptions makes it inevitable that the standard positions will be considered plausible accounts of the mind-body relationship.

It is not being claimed that all actual participants in the contemporary debate make all these assumptions in naïve and unqualified form. Indeed, it is easy to think of exceptions. For example, in a famous paper Frank Jackson (Jackson, 1982) argued that qualia cannot be subsumed within a broadly physicalist approach to the ontology of mind. Unlike other aspects of mind, qualia are epiphenomenal. Implicit in this position was the claim that there is no single solution to the mind-body problem. Qualia deserve one account; other aspects of mind deserve another. This amounts to rejection of the ontological (3) and relational homogeneity assumptions (2).

The existence of such counterexamples does not disprove the generalization that the assumptions are widely shared in the debate. If anything, they illustrate the extent to which the generalization is valid. Jackson's case is interesting precisely because it goes against the grain. Jackson himself only reluctantly conceded that qualia were exceptions to the general truth of physicalism. Critics of Jackson's position were overwhelmingly those who believed that no such exception need be made—that, in other words, the ontological and relational homogeneity assumptions can be maintained.

Why should we believe that all four assumptions are false? The argument proceeds as follows. Mental entities of at least one kind, namely, beliefs, are on-tologically complex in a way that is relevant to their relationship to the physical. Therefore, the simplicity assumption (4) is false. Describing the fit between beliefs and the physical requires reference to the metaphysical relation of institution; therefore, the assumption of sufficiency (1), or that the five standard relations suffice, is false. At least some mental entities are relevantly dissimilar to beliefs; therefore, the two homogeneity assumptions (2 and 3) are false.

The Nature of Belief

What are beliefs? Within the classical mind-body debate, there are basically three kinds of answers. The first, given by dualists and idealists, is that beliefs are states (modifications) of some inherently nonphysical mental substance. The second, given in various ways by physicalists, is that beliefs are states of the body, and of the brain in particular. Both these answers usually maintain that beliefs are rep-resentations (capable of) causing the believer to behave in certain ways. The third kind of answer, given by behaviorists, is that beliefs are not inner representational/ causal states of any kind. Rather, they are dispositions to behavior.

These answers are examples of what Arthur Collins has called "constitutive analyses" (Collins, 1994). They are attempts to specify what beliefs are, in the sense of providing an account of the ontological nature of beliefs. Collins has advanced a powerful argument purporting to demonstrate that all constitutive anal-yses are misguided.[1]

Beliefs are not things standing in need of any kind of ontological description. If this is right, every position in the standard mind-body debate has from the outset misconceived the nature of belief and the ontology of mind more generally. The argument begins with a version of Moore's paradox. Utterances of the form "I believe that p, but p's truth is an open question" are incoherent, even though the two components are compatible (they could both be true). The apparent contra-diction is resolved by recognizing that in saying, "I believe that p," you are asserting or taking a stand on p, and you therefore cannot also maintain that p is an open question.

Constitutive analyses identify a belief with some thing (brain state, disposition, or whatever). Call this thing B. Clearly, the existence of B and the truth of p are separate issues. Therefore, one might report the existence of B without asserting p. However, since B is the belief, to report the existence of B is to claim to believe p—and that, as we just saw, is a way of asserting p. One cannot assert p without asserting p. It seems that something has to give. According to Collins, we must surrender the constitutive analysis:

> The state of believing that p can be explicated as an epistemic state, that of being at risk about p. A person who believes that p is a person who stands to the right or wrong as p is true or false. But this "state" cannot

be given a constitution, mental or physical, internal or external, because, if it were, we would immediately be able to report that the state is present without taking a stand on p. (Collins, 1994, p. 943)

Beliefs are not to be given constitutive analyses but rather what Collins calls "logical" analyses. A logical analysis explains the logic of belief ascriptions rather than the ontological nature of beliefs. "I believe that p" is not a report of the existence of some entity, the belief; rather, it is equivalent to a disjunction: "p, or I am much mistaken."

There is room for debate over the proper lesson to be drawn from Collins's argument. I take it to have demonstrated that whatever the belief that p is, it cannot be something that might exist independently of the believer's taking a stand on p. In other words, believing that p essentially involves commitment to p. This is why claiming to believe p is a way of asserting p. Any adequate ontology of belief must respect this fact. Collins's argument establishes a problem, not for any constitutive analysis whatsoever, but for any constitutive analysis that separates the belief that p from commitment to p, such that it is then possible that the belief could exist without the commitment.

What, more precisely, is the relationship between believing that p and being committed to p? The most sophisticated discussion of these issues is that provided by Robert Brandom in his book *Making it Explicit* (Brandom, 1994). Much that he says there suggests that beliefs simply are commitments of a certain sort. For example:

> The inferentially articulated commitments expressed by assertional speech acts are doxastic commitments. Much of the theoretical work done by the concept of belief can be done instead by appeal to this sort of deontic status, and to the practical scorekeeping attitudes of acknowledging or undertaking such commitments. (Brandom, 1994, p. xv)

The "theoretical and explanatory work" done by the concept of belief includes playing central roles in theoretical accounts of phenomena such as knowledge, perception, and action. In order to know that p, for example, one must believe that p. Brandom's case for a close relationship between belief and doxastic (assertional) commitment is based on his success in two projects. The first is elaboration of the notion of doxastic commitment. The second is demonstrating that doxastic commitments can be called upon to do the theoretical work of beliefs. Brandom provides illuminating accounts of a wide range of belief-related phenomena within a single integrated framework by invoking doxastic commitments and attitudes toward them wherever one might be tempted to invoke the ordinary notion of belief.

These considerations suggest that belief should be identified with commitments on much the same basis as, say, lightning was identified with electrical discharges. Somewhat surprisingly, Brandom avoids this move. His statements of the relationship between beliefs and commitments always delicately avoid outright identification because, in Brandom's opinion, the fit between beliefs and commitments is, in a variety of ways, not close enough to warrant identification. For example:

> "[B]elief" may simply be *ambiguous* between a sense in which one believes what one is prepared to avow and a sense in which one also believes what one *ought* rationally to believe, as a consequence of what one is prepared to avow. . . . An unambiguous, univocal technical term "doxastic *commitment*" is introduced, which comprises both commitments one is prepared to avow and commitments that follow from those one acknowledges. But attention to the attitudes in terms of which those deontic statuses are explained makes it possible also to distinguish clearly between these two *kinds* of commitment, as "belief"-talk does not. (Brandom, 1994, p. 196)

Since talk of commitments and attitudes toward them actually provides superior accounts of belief-related phenomena, belief talk is eliminable in favor of commitment talk: "The proposal is accordingly not to *analyze* belief in terms of commitment, but to discard that concept as insufficiently precise and replace it with clearer talk about different sorts of commitment" (p. 196). But if beliefs are not to be identified with commitments, and talk of commitments is theoretically superior to talk of beliefs, we have a theoretical case for eliminating beliefs from our ontology, a case that directly parallels the infamous neuroscientific case. The lack of fit between beliefs and their theoretically superior counterparts provides, as Brandom puts it, reason "not to believe in beliefs" (p. 508).

On the other hand, there is also considerable evidence in *Making It Explicit* that Brandom has not joined the eliminativist camp. In dozens of places he seems to take for granted that there are such things as beliefs, and he often appears to be in the business of providing a philosophical account of the nature of beliefs.[2]

Collins's argument established that believing that *p* essentially involves commitment to *p*. If both identification and elimination are out of the question, there seems to be only one alternative: Commitments are constituents of beliefs. That is, beliefs are ontologically complex structures whose components include commitments, among other things. As we will see, this ontological complexity is relevant to how beliefs relate to the physical.

Institution

Commitments are a kind of deontic status, and deontic statuses are a kind of normative status. Possessing a normative status is a matter of having what one does count as (im)proper or (in)correct in relevant ways. Brandom is a social pragmatist about normative statuses. Such statuses arise only because people are in the business of treating each other as having those statuses: "The natural world does not come with commitments and entitlements in it; they are products of human activity. In particular, they are creatures of the *attitudes* of taking, treating, or responding to someone in practice *as* committed or entitled (for instance, to various further performances" (Brandom, 1994, p. xiv). In other words, commitments are instituted by human practices. They only exist and are what they are because certain practices take the shape they do. To understand why or how it is that there are deontic statuses in the world, one must understand how things can be brought into being as what they are by what we do.

Some instituted entities are physically realized. A church, for example, is a building, but not merely a building; it is a building made into a church by the community treating it as a church. However, some instituted entities are not physically realized; they lack material embodiment. Commitments are prime examples. As Brandom puts it:

> Norms (in the sense of normative statuses) are not objects in the causal order. Natural science, eschewing categories of social practice, will never run across *commitments* in its cataloguing of the furniture of the world; they are not by themselves causally efficacious—any more than strikes or outs are in baseball. Nonetheless . . . there are norms, and their existence is neither supernatural nor mysterious. Normative statuses are domesticated by being understood in terms of normative attitudes, which are in the causal order. (p. 626)

In the language of the debate, we would say that commitments are not identical with, reducible to, in causal interaction with, or even realized by physical entities. In at least one sense, they are abstract objects. Nevertheless, they are real, countable, temporal things, and it is plausible that they supervene on the physical. It is only because the physical is the way it is that we exhibit the practices we do, and it is our practices that institute commitments. If we stopped treating each other in the right kinds of ways, all commitments would vanish without a trace.

Institution is a metaphysical relation. It is not the same as identity, reduction, realization, supervenience, or causation. If one tried to account for the place of instituted entities in the world just in terms of these five relations, a large and essential part of the story would simply be missing. It would be like trying to understand how the president of the United States is related to the citizenry without talking about voting. Since commitments are instituted entities, and commitments are essential to beliefs, institution must enter into any adequate solution of the mind-body problem. The first of the four assumptions—that the five major relations suffice—is false.

Beliefs as Complexes

Thus far it has been argued that beliefs are ontological complexes involving commitments, which are abstract instituted objects. What else is involved?

Suppose Sheila believes that her name derives from that of a pre-Christian fertility symbol, the Celtic Sheela-nu-gig. Then Sheila stands committed to the claim that her name is derived from that of a fertility symbol. This is an interesting claim about Sheila. It is not true of my left shoe, even though my shoe exists in the same social milieu. What is it about Sheila such that she has this belief, and my shoe does not? The answer, at least in broadest outline, is obvious enough. Sheila does the right kinds of things, whereas my left shoe does not. That is, Sheila behaves in ways such that she and others correctly take her to be committed to the claim that her name has a certain origin. She behaves in these ways because her brain is wired in a certain very complex way. My shoe does not even have a brain.

Believing that p is thus a rather complex social/behavioral/causal situation. For something to believe that p, it must have a very complex internal constitution, such that it behaves in certain characteristic ways, and such that it is treated as standing in a web of deontic statuses, one of which is the doxastic commitment that p. The ontological constituents of belief include commitments, behavioral dispositions, and internal causal (possibly representational) states.

This is what is required for belief in the fullest sense. If any of these ontological ingredients are missing, what is left over is, at best, a degenerate case. A brain in a vat might be wired the right way, but unless that brain is situated appropriately in a body and social context, it is ontologically deficient. Call what it has "belief" if you like; nobody owns the term. The deep point is that you and I are possessed of much richer ontological structures. Much the same goes for a zombie remote-controlled by aliens. It behaves the right way and has the commitments, but has less than full-blooded belief, for the zombie is not causally responsible for its p-appropriate behaviors.

We can now see that the standard ontological analyses of belief offered within the mind-body debate are all partly right and partly wrong. They each latch onto an important ingredient of the total situation, but mistake it for the whole. Physicalists are right that believing that p, in the full sense, essentially involves having one's brain configured in an appropriate way. Their mistake is to identify beliefs with these brain states. Behaviorists are right that believing that p, in the full sense, essentially involves having the right behavioral dispositions. Their mistake, as physicalists often have pointed out, is to identify beliefs with behavioral dispositions. Even dualists were half right in believing that p essentially involves commitments, which are abstract instituted objects, located in time but not in space, lacking material constitution. Having understood that beliefs cannot be identified with material objects, Descartes's mistake was to identify them with nonmaterial objects.

Beliefs and the Physical

How do beliefs relate to the physical? This divides into three subsidiary questions:

1. What are the ontological constituents of beliefs?
2. How do these constituents fit together to form beliefs?
3. How do these constituents themselves relate to the physical?

TABLE 25.2. Relating Ontological Constituents of Beliefs to the Physical

	Doxastic Commitments	Behavioral Dispositions	Brain states
Identity	x	√	√
Reduction	x	x	√
Realization (Con-stitution)	x	√	√
Supervenience	√	√	√
Causal Interaction	x	x	√
Institution	√	x	x

Sketches of answers to the first two questions were provided earlier. The answer to the third is perhaps most easily conveyed in a table (table 25.2). The important thing to note here is the difference between the columns. The various constituents of beliefs relate to the physical in different ways. No one of the standard isms accounts for how all constituents of beliefs relate to the physical—and this is not only because the standard isms ignore the metaphysical relation of institution.

Once the three subsidiary questions have been answered, we have said all there is to be said about the ontological relationship of beliefs to the physical. It makes little sense to ask whether beliefs themselves are identical with, reducible to, and so on to the physical. They partly are and partly are not.

Pluralism

I shall take for granted that whatever sensations are, they do not have propositional content. They are unlike beliefs in that they do not essentially involve socially instituted doxastic commitments. The relevant ontological breakdown of sensations, if any, is unlike that of beliefs. Therefore, sensations are ontologically different in kind from beliefs and demand a different relational story. The second and third deep assumptions—those of relational and ontological homogeneity—are false.

Since all four assumptions are false, the solution to the mind-body problem cannot be anything like the standard isms of the debate. It cannot be entered in any one column of any table like table 25.1. All the standard answers in the official mind-body debate are wrong in their basic form. The general question of the ontological fit between mind and the physical world cannot be simplified in quite the way the tradition has always imagined.

The true solution to the mind-body problem is nothing less than a long story, only a small portion of which has been sketched here. We can, however, describe a kind of metaposition that captures the general form of the solution. If the orthodox mind-body debate has been characterized by a drive to monism, or at most dualism, the metaposition is a kind of pluralism. Pluralism acknowledges a multiplicity of ontological kinds in the general vicinity of mind, and a multiplicity of relational stories, and rejects as ill conceived questions about how high-level mental entities such as "beliefs themselves" relate to the physical.

This pluralism is not "dualism and more." As we have seen, orthodox dualism, corresponding to some selection of columns of table 25.1, is deeply misconceived. If dualism is the position that the mental and the physical are two wholly distinct substances, then the pluralism recommended here has nothing at all to do with dualism. Philosophers have for decades, indeed, centuries, been attempting to slay the dualist monster. It is time we recognized that the dualist monster is just a kind of philosophical hallucination arising as a by-product of an inadequate conceptual framework.

The pluralist framework recommended here is not a "discourse pluralism" of the kind recommended by Rorty and Price and criticised by Cussins.[3] It simply allows for a multiplicity of entities in the vicinity of the mental and is not committed in advance to any theses about the number of different discourses, the connection between discourse and reality (between how we talk and what there is), or any form of antirealism. Indeed, pluralism is perfectly consistent with a hard-nosed realism that divorces the question of what kinds of mental entities in fact exist from the question of how we talk about people, and what concepts we may have. A realist pluralism of this kind does not try to read ontological commitments off language or concepts. In particular, it is perfectly willing to allow that folk discourses and folk concepts are inadequate to the ontological structure of mental reality. Distinctions built into ordinary ways of talking need not reflect deep ontological distinctions, and there may be ontological differences among kinds of mental entities to which folk talk is entirely oblivious.

Cognition as Physical

What are the implications of a pluralism of this kind for our understanding of mind as a scientific object?

Cognition, as I use the term, is the entirety of states and processes that form the causal underpinnings of our sophisticated behaviors, from wine tasting to mental arithmetic and basketball. The most complex and critical component of the cognitive system is the brain; that is where most cognitive activity takes place. Cognition is thus largely inner, that is, internal to the skull. Cognition, as one aspect of the causal organization of the universe, is just another part of the subject matter of science. The relevant science is, of course, cognitive science (in the broadest sense).

Some decades ago, it was seen as an important task for philosophers of mind to defend the idea that cognitive science is a respectable form of science. That was when cognitive science was dominated by what has been called Good Old Fashioned Artificial Intelligence (GOFAI) (Haugeland, 1985). Cognition was described as the operation of a digital computer. GOFAI explanation was unique in science, and so its legitimacy as a form of science had to be established.

There is currently a powerful trend in cognitive science away from orthodox computational forms of explanation. Increasing numbers of cognitive scientists are applying the mathematical tools of dynamics—dynamical modeling and dynamical systems theory—to the study of cognition. Dynamical accounts of cognition are very different from computational accounts. Dynamical systems and computers are very different kinds of systems, and the tools of dynamics are very different from those of computer science. The gulf between computationalists and dynamicists currently constitutes the single most important theoretical chasm in cognitive science.[4]

The scientific credentials of this new kind of cognitive science do not stand in need of any defense. Dynamical explanation in cognitive science takes much the same form as dynamical explanation in many other branches of natural science. Insofar as dynamicists are successful, cognition is a scientific domain in a perfectly straightforward sense.

Dynamical cognitive science has even deeper implications. A sufficient condition for counting as physical, in a broad sense, has always been amenability to a certain kind of mathematical account—namely, explanation in dynamical terms. Any phenomenon that can be rigorously described in terms of the coupled interaction of a range of quantitative variables is automatically counted as physical, whatever else might be known or not known about its relationship to subatomic particles or anything else in the inventory of respectable physical entities.

Therefore, dynamical cognitive science is in the process of demonstrating that cognition is a physical phenomenon in the most substantial and direct sense. If the dynamical approach succeeds, then cognition is not physical because it is somehow built up from, or supervenient upon, physical stuff. Cognition is already as physical as quarks and gravity. In short, current developments in cognitive science suggest not merely that cognition is a scientific subject, but also that it is a physical phenomenon. We are already more thoroughly physical than most philosophers realize—and that includes those who loudly trumpet their physicalist allegiances.

Mind Is Not Cognition

An assumption that has dominated our philosophical and scientific tradition is that mind and cognition are the same thing. Almost everyone, from dualists to functionalists to redneck neurobiologists, subscribes to the idea that mind is that inner realm of states and processes that are causally responsible for our sophisticated behaviors. In this, Descartes, Jerry Fodor, and Paul Churchland are merry bedfellows; they just disagree over how best to describe that inner causal stuff.

If mind is cognition, then cognitive science is the science of the mind. If cognition is a scientific domain, then so is mind. Dynamical cognitive science would then be establishing that mind is inherently physical. The classical mind-body problem would have been effectively abolished, for the relation of the physical to itself is not an interesting metaphysical or philosophical issue.

However, it seems that the ultimate price of the doctrine of mind as cognition is elimination of mind as we ordinarily conceive it. If mind is cognition, and cognition is a matter for scientific investigation, then the concept of mind is held hostage to the outcome of these investigations. As the Churchlands have been pointing out, cognitive science is increasingly demonstrating that cognition bears little direct resemblance to mind as described in our everyday or "folk" vocabulary. They have bravely bitten the metaphysical bullet and embraced the idea that science is showing that all of us have been thoroughly deluded all our lives about the real nature of our own minds.

Gilbert Ryle argued valiantly against the ontological identification of mind and cognition (Ryle, 1949/1984). Unfortunately, his powers of persuasion did no justice to his powers of insight. His arguments were dismissed from a distance, and subsequent generations of philosophers returned to embrace the ghost in the machine.

From the pluralist perspective defended here, Ryle was essentially correct. Mind is not the same thing as cognition. They differ in ontological kind. One reason is that minds include beliefs, beliefs include commitments, and commitments are not, as Brandom puts it, part of the causal order. This is not to downplay the importance of cognition. Cognition is an essential ontological constituent of mind. Rather than thinking of mind as the inner engine of behavior, we should think of cognition as the inner engine of mind.

Two fundamental insights drive the rejection of the doctrine of mind as cognition. The first, owing to Ryle, is that having a mind is as much behaving in appropriate ways as it is having the right kind of internal states. The second, owing to Heidegger, is that in behaving the way we do, we ontologically constitute ourselves as having minds. We are ontologically self-constituting. For example, we only have commitments, and hence beliefs in the full sense, and hence minds in the full sense, because we have practices of treating each other as committed in certain ways.

There are two important consequences for our understanding of mind in relation to science. First, cognitive science is the science, not of mind as such, but of one major constituent of mind. Cognitive science cannot be the whole story about mind, for cognitive science studies causal mechanisms, and there is more to mind than causal mechanisms. Mind itself cannot be counted as a scientific object just because there is a successful science of cognition.

Second, mind as ordinarily conceived is under no direct threat of elimination from cognitive science. Cognitive science would have complete authority over the nature of mind only if mind were equal to cognition. Since there is much more to mind, there are limits to the impact cognitive science can have on our understanding of what minds are.

Consider again Brandom's analogy between doxastic commitments and strikes and outs in baseball. There are strikes and outs because people make it that way by playing baseball, that is, by behaving in certain cooperative ways. Science can tell us a great deal about baseball—about the physics of pitching and batting, the physiology of muscles, and so forth. The science of baseball might even come up with some surprises. What it could not do is reveal that there are, in fact, no strikes or outs. Our talk about baseball is not theoretical conjecture as to the way reality might be. It is perspicuous description of the way we make reality actually to be.

Similarly with beliefs. We institute ourselves as believers by taking part in the discursive game. As Brandom says, "Sapience of the sort distinctive of us is a status achieved within a structure of mutual recognition: of holding and being held responsible, of acknowledging and exercising authority" (Brandom, 1994, p. 276). We could not scientifically discover that there are no beliefs any more than we could scientifically discover that there are no strikes or outs in baseball. The most cognitive science could tell us is that the internal causal mechanisms that partly constitute our beliefs are rather different than we might have supposed on the basis of a misunderstanding of the ontology of belief. It could come to be the case that there are no beliefs, but only if we stop playing the discursive game.

Conclusion

The classical mind-body problem, as I have been discussing it, takes as its central issue the question of the ontological relationship between mental entities, on one hand, and physical entities, on the other. It specifies a range of possible answers to that question—that is, the standard isms—and proceeds to debate the relative merits of those answers. We can now see that the classical discourse is founded on false assumptions of homogeneity and simplicity. The central question is a bad one; there is no answer expressible in the terms in which the question is framed. Rejecting the homogeneity and simplicity assumptions entails embracing a pluralist orientation on the question of the fit between mind and physical world. Pluralism is not another position alongside the standard isms; it is simply the denial that the form of the standard isms is adequate to the issues. To adopt pluralism is to go beyond the classical mind-body problem.[5]

Notes

1. The central reference is *The Nature of Mental Things*, Collins, 1987; see also Collins, 1994, 1996.

2. For example: "The idea pursued here is that the state or status of *believing* is essentially, and not merely accidentally, related to the linguistic performance of *claiming*. Beliefs are essentially the sort of thing that can be expressed by making an assertion. . . . [S]peech acts having the pragmatic significance of assertions play an essential role in (social) functional systems within which states or statuses can be understood as propositionally contentful in the way beliefs are" (Brandom, 1994, pp. 153–54).

3. See Cussins, 1992; Price, 1992; Rorty, 1991a.

4. For overviews of dynamical cognitive science, see Port and van Gelder, 1995; van Gelder, 1995.

5. Acknowledgments are due to Arthur Collins, Tony Chemero, Brian Garrett,

Chris Gauker, John Haugeland, Beth Preston, Andrew Melnyk, Daniel Stoljar, Barry Smith, David Smith, and Amie Thomasson.

References

Brandom, R. 1994. *Making It Explicit*. Cambridge, MA: Harvard University Press.

Charles, D., and Lennon, K. (Eds.). 1992. *Reduction, Explanation, and Realism*. Oxford: Clarendon Press.

Collins, A.W. 1987. *The Nature of Mental Things*. Notre Dame, IN: University of Notre Dame Press.

————. 1994. "Reply to Commentators." *Philosophy and Phenomenological Research*, 54, pp. 929–45.

————. 1996. "Moore's Paradox and Epistemic Risk." *Philosophical Quarterly*, 46, pp. 308–19.

Colodny, R.G. (Ed.). 1962. *Frontiers of Science and Philosophy*. Pittsburgh: University of Pittsburgh Press.

Cussins, A. 1992. "The Limitations of Pluralism," in D. Charles and K. Lennon (Eds.), *Reduction, Explanation, and Realism*. Oxford: Clarendon Press.

Jackson, F. (1982) "Epiphenomenal Qualia." *Philosophical Quarterly*, 32, pp. 127–36.

Haugeland, J. 1985. *Artificial Intelligence: The Very Idea*. Cambridge, MA: MIT Press.

Port, R., and van Gelder, T.J. (Eds.). 1995. *Mind as Motion: Explorations in the Dynamics of Cognition*. Cambridge, MA: MIT Press.

Price, H. 1992. "Metaphysical Pluralism." *Journal of Philosophy*, 89(8), pp. 387–409.

Rorty, R. 1991a. "Non-reductive Physicalism," in R. Rorty, *Objectivity, Relativism, and Truth*. Cambridge, UK: Cambridge University Press.

————. 1991b. *Objectivity, Relativism, and Truth*. Cambridge, UK: Cambridge University Press.

Ryle, G. 1949/1984. *The Concept of Mind*. Chicago: University of Chicago Press.

Sellars, W. 1962. "Philosophy and the Scientific Image of Man." Pp. 35–78 in R.G. Colodny (Ed.), *Frontiers of Science and Philosophy*. Pittsburgh: University of Pittsburgh Press.

van Gelder, T.J. 1995. "What Might Cognition Be, If Not Computation?" *Journal of Philosophy*, 91, pp. 345–81.

26

Workshop Rationality, Dogmatism, and Models of the Mind

I.C. Jarvie

Current philosophy of mind polarizes around a choice between naturalistic reduction, on the one hand (mind equals brain), and conventionalist construction of mind (mind equals a site or node in culture), on the other. If we deny that the choice between nature and convention is exclusive and exhaustive, then a mixed metaphysic of the mind becomes possible. Karl Popper decisively criticized the exclusive dichotomy between provable truth by nature, *episteme*, and arbitrary truth by convention, *doxa*. His critique is sufficient to show that scientific truth in general and in the social sciences in particular is situated between truth by nature and truth by convention in nontrivial ways: Scientific truths are neither proven nor arbitrary. Traditionally, rationality is closely connected to truth by nature. If he was to account for the rationality of science, Popper had to break with tradition. This he did by identifying rationality with criticism aimed at getting closer to truth about nature.

Work on the problem of rationality by Joseph Agassi and myself utilized and extended that view. We made two distinct points: (1) Rationality is a social achievement that is sometimes internalized rather than a state of mind that allows access to the truths of nature; (2) without privileged access, it follows that all ideas should be approached rationally, that is, critically, since neither the discussants nor the forum of discussion need endorse any. This reversal of the approach that treats minds as prior to social organization may be applicable to other aspects of mind and possibly to the mind in general. What follows is a general overview of our results and some hints for their extended applicability.

Our work was developed out of the following argument in *The Logic of Scientific Discovery* (Popper, 1959):

(1N) A naturalistic account of science fails [is too narrow], because there are theories which are incontestably scientific but not true. (They are putative truths, or approximations to putative truths, or falsified putative truths.)

(2C)   A purely conventionalist account of science fails [is too wide] because it allows any statement to be scientific provided we adopt the convention to treat it so. Conventionalism does not recognize any scientific truths by nature, not even putative ones—which is incontestably untrue.

(3)   An account of science as a social institution that fosters use of a method responsive to the way the world seems to be escapes the exclusive dichotomy of truth by nature/truth by convention. Consequently, the conventionalism is methodological, not ontological; the naturalism is tentative, not dogmatic.

Popper later extended this social line of argument from science and experience to reason in general, taking reason to be the use of social conventions that function to encourage criticism as a means to search for truth (about nature). In attempting to account for experience, we employ institutions developed in a tradition of successive efforts to capture the way the natural world is. This account of reason is between the natural and the conventional, and so it is exclusively neither.

Agassi and I applied a variant of Popper's approach to the problem of the rationality of magic and other nonscientific ideas.[1] Thus we extended Popper's social line of argument from science in particular to the rationality of thought in general. Reason, on our Popperian view, is neither a natural faculty of the mind nor simply a way of talking (a set of social conventions). Rather, it is a socially instituted method of handling ideas and criticism directed toward the goal of learning how the world is. A paradigm general case of such social organization is to be found in the workshop.[2]

I will try to show that our workshop model of rationality mediates and resolves all the most significant disputes in the theory of rationality. I leave it for others to draw out the implications for philosophy of mind generally.

To begin with, I present a sketch of rationality, then a sketch of the workshop. The standard sociological notion of rationality is that we act rationally when means are well suited to realizing ends, aims, or goals. Agassi and I add the enriching assumption that institutional settings have a major effect on the possibilities for acting rationally. For example, the existence and accessibility of information can affect how well means can be suited to the achievement of ends. Our enriched conception enables us to solve all the usual problems of rationality while allowing for divergent assessments of the rationality of attitudes and mentalities, including dogmatism and skepticism, which for the traditional approaches to rationality remain inexplicable. So our approach generalizes in a striking way that has both theoretical and practical value.

Consider an egalitarian workshop, where workshops are deemed to be social institutions. "Workshop" as an ideal type can designate either an intellectual space that houses cooperation and exploration or a physical space for face-to-face practical problem solving. In both spaces a workshop is an institution that facilitates rational action, especially action aimed at solving problems. Hence rationality can be treated as a relative quality varying by action and situation in the workshop, not a particular mentality that is acquired and exercised by individuals. This ideal type simplifies and beautifies real existing workshops, no doubt, but we hope that it captures what the best intellectual (and practical) workshops aim at. Rationality in a workshop is a quality of action and context, not of mentality; the same, we propose, goes for rationality *tout court*. Rationality is dependent upon action and context, which allows that actions can be more or less rational. Treating rationality as a scale for measuring the match between action-means and achieved aims or goals disposes of mentalist discussions twice over. Rationality understood as a mode or feature of actions makes explanatorily redundant the conception of rationality as a state or faculty of mind, without denying its manifestations. This result may be generalized. It is a rational action to balance one's checkbook. It is the direct-edness of the action that renders mental arithmetic (or the use of a calculator) rational not the other way round.

The scale of rational actions is strange, since it peters out at both ends. That is, for our model to work, we need not assume that the scale has at one pole the purely irrational action against which all others are measured, and we definitely do not assume that there is some perfectly rational action compared to which all others fall short (pace rational choice theorists). Rather, the view offered is boot-strapping: We can only start where the actors are, develop ideas of how the ra-tionality of current action could be improved, try these ideas out, and then cali-brate the scale outwards from that point. Similarly with rationality in the workshop: A workshop is only one social institution among others, and those others set limits to rationality within it. Hence a workshop is a model for Popper's Open Society; it needs continuously to attend to improving its own openness and hence ration-ality at the same time as it undertakes first-order inquiry.

The Reasonable and the Rational

In efforts to act rationally, especially trying to solve problems by the use of reason, people often make mistakes. Is every mistake a failure to be rational? Not if com-mon sense is anywhere near the truth. A mistake involves failure to be rational only where (1) truth is manifest and (2) reason properly deployed is an unerring means of apprehending it. When truth is hidden, or when reason is not easy to employ properly, then mistakes are not necessarily failures to be rational. Let us call this the skeptical view (S). Against the tenor of this view is a classical presup-position that

(CP) truth is always manifest and reason always unproblematic. This also involves the further presupposition that there are reliable means of apprehending truth, otherwise (CP) is empty. It follows that all and only what is discovered by reliable means should be taken as true—that is, as scientific knowledge—and that when it comes to action, we should rely only upon such knowledge.

Sextus Empiricus (c. 160–c. 210 CE; 1967) classified the (CP) position as a form of dogmatism; more recent labels are justificationism, reliabilism, and found-herentism (Haack, 1993). Opposed to dogmatism is the position that truth is elu-sive and reason fallible (S). Possibly Sextus would classify that view as a form of skepticism; more recent labels are fallibilism, pancritical rationalism, and critical rationalism. Of course, neither dogmatists nor skeptics perfectly conform to our narrow characterizations of their positions (CP) and (S). Justificationist dogmatists often want to go beyond what can be discovered by reason to be true: They often want to justify the categories of what reason shows to be likely, plausible, reliably arrived at, the best available, and so on. Similarly, skeptical fallibilists are unin-terested in belief or in its suspension, and they often want to generalize. According to them, all assertions should be made tentatively; that is, all assertions should be implicitly bracketed by the metaidea of tentativity.

The received view, by contrast, holds that either there is a way (an ideal method) to force truth to manifest itself or the search for truth is pointless. Exten-sive criticism of the received view, along with its consequences, dogmatic justifi-cationism or discouragement, has not resulted in any noticeable increase in in-terest in robust fallibilism. Most philosophers continue to argue that there is no choice, and one must seek the ideal method, since any alternative to it is skeptical, and, they allege, skepticism leaves us helpless before irrationality. Hence the con-tinuing persistence of dogmatism among rationalists.

Workshop Rationality

A workshop—practical or intellectual—is a site where people undertake collabo-rative endeavor to figure something out. They employ all and any strategies at hand and others newly devised: tryouts, explorations, episodes of debate, closing questions, opening others, setting still others aside, models, analogies, metaphors, varying previous successes, cobbling together makeshift compromises, prototypes, stabs in the dark, and so on. Role structures of master and apprentice, teacher and student, may shift in the play of discussion. The apprentice can easily become more adept at a move than the master; the master will sometimes accept the strategy proposed by the apprentice. All such matters are fluid, as are the chal-lenges that the workshop takes up from time to time. Closed debates may be reopened as readily as current ones may be ignored.[3]

A workshop is structured, and so it is an institution, but its institutional char-acter is easily overlooked. It is important to note that a workshop, while structured, is flexible enough to permit an egalitarian atmosphere, such as that cultivated in the best laboratories, think tanks, schools, universities, seminars, and conferences— workshops all. A workshop need not have a location (it could exist as an e-mail discussion list or a conference telephone call) or a permanent population.

How does the workshop capture the middle ground between nature and con-vention of Popper's critical rationalism, and why should it recommend itself to the student of rationality or of mind? One reason it recommends itself is that both dogmatists and skeptics acknowledge its rational effectiveness. Dogmatists, such as fideists, simply limit the scope of workshop critical discussion, while skeptics allow falling back on it as a game, not necessarily a position to be taken seriously. In what, then, consists the workshop critical rationalism that we recommend over both dogmatism and skepticism? It is the position that rationality at its best is open-mindedness, and that we do well to think of open-mindedness socially. Open-mindedness shows itself in critical debate about open questions, utilizing tentative answers that are sufficient for action, or as stimulus to further debate, or both. It is commonplace to compare the critical rationalist position to the standard view of formal, legal, or parliamentary debate. This comparison has an advantage in that it highlights the role of formal procedures aimed at decision, even if tentatively and even if not always (remember tie votes and hung juries). Yet the comparison also has a disadvantage, because in formal debate, more often than not, initially fixed views engage in ritual combat that seldom has any impact upon the initial fixed positions. We think that the workshop is a better model: The problem is always to the fore; and while fixed positions and ritual combat can be part of a workshop's operations, they neither constitute nor detract from its rationality.

To clarify, let me say a few more words on debate. In debate, or in verbal combat, including legal procedure, views are expressed, defended, and attacked. Prior to debate or, more so, between debates (when courts or parliaments are recessed, for example), views are proposed, defended, attacked, and examined this and that way, much as a weapon is tested in the lab before use on the battlefield. For the skeptic, the painful question becomes, how is a view sustained and tempered between debates? But in a workshop the question of who proposes which view and when is not pressing, even though whoever does so may—if and when he or she wishes—bring it before the workshop and challenge members to examine it.

Background

In our studies of rationality Agassi and I distinguished, for purposes of cross-cultural analysis, three degrees of logical strength in the rules governing the workshop. First and weakest (rationality$_1$) is a model that attributes to workshop actors no more than goal-directed action with given aims and circumstances, where circumstances include the actor's knowledge and opinions about circumstances. At this strength, the magician's treatment of illness by incantation is as rational as any early doctor's use of suction cups and bloodletting or any modern one's use of antibiotics. At the second strength (rationality$_2$), we add to the workshop the element of rational thinking, or thinking obedient to explicit rules—a strength not found in magic in general, though it is sometimes given to specific details of magical thinking within the magical thought system.[4] It was the social anthropologist Sir Edward Evans-Pritchard who observed that when considering magic in detail, we may find the magician as consistent or as critical as anyone else; but when considering magic in general, or even any system of thought in general, we may find that the magically inclined could not be critical or even comprehend the criticism. Evans-Pritchard went still further: He was skeptical in fideist fashion as to whether it was possible to be critical of one's own system in a consistent manner—whatever that system might be (1937, 1951). On this level of discussion (rationality$_2$) magic in general is pseudorational because it lacks articulate standards of rational thinking (Jarvie and Agassi, 1967).

The third and strongest model of rationality analyzed was that where goal-directed action in the workshop (rationality$_1$), is subject to thinking that conforms not just to some rule or standard of rational thinking (rationality$_2$), but to the highest available standards of rational thinking (rationality$_3$). Once a standard is articulated, it can be subjected to criticism, and from that criticism desiderata and criteria can be developed for its further improvement. We advocate what we think of as the very highest standards available—the norm of the workshop in the scientific community. This is a variant of Popper's critical rationalism. Yet in our characterization of the highest level of rationality (rationality$_3$), there is a vagueness in the term "available." We mean nothing esoteric, just "fairly readily available." Yet this is vague still; it is not always clear what is, much less what was, fairly readily available. If workshop critical rationalism was not available outside science, what was? Two philosophers, Richard Popkin and Paul Feyerabend, articulate plausible answers. Popkin argues that the ancient tradition of skepticism was available to workshops; Feyerabend finds critical philosophy everywhere, most strikingly in theological commentary and discussions of witchcraft (e.g., *Malleus Maleficarum*), as well as John Stuart Mill's *On Liberty*.[5] However, is either Popkin's or Feyerabend's philosophy critical enough for science or to ground rationality? Both views can be shown to be too one sided and so less than fully rational (rationality$_3$). Moreover, they are philosophies of individual belief that lack a sense of the social and of the process of bootstrapping. Compared to the workshop model, both are wanting. What I shall argue is that these philosophies are transcended by the workshop, which can incorporate them while neutralizing the irrationality to which they are hostage.

Justificationist Rationality

First we need to set up a contrast between dogmatism, that is, what Bartley (1961) called "justificationism" (reliabilism, foundherentism), and skepticism or critical rationalism. Dogmatism (or justificationism, or uncritical rationalism) is the view that

(D) opinions are held rationally if and only if it can be shown that (in the present circumstances) holding these opinions is (rationally) obligatory or imperative.

An obvious corollary of (D) is that dissent, disagreement, and schism, indeed, the very existence of schools of thought in the workshop, detract from its rationality. This corollary is widely rejected (although it was forcefully advocated by Sir Francis Bacon, the leading justificationist father of the "modern" period), for even the strictest justificationism allows a period of transition characterizable by the examination of diverse opinion, usually involving dissent and disagreement in and by diverse schools of thought.[6] A justificationist workshop would rule out not schools of thought and disagreement *tout court*, but perennial schools of thought and irresoluble disagreements; not dissent on open issues so much as reopening already closed issues.[7] Open-mindedness is rational, the justificationist can allow, but avoiding all conclusions is not.

Skepticism is not necessarily identical with the view that all dogmatists are unreasonable (Popkin, 1960). The ancient writer Sextus Empiricus uses "dogmatism" to denote simply the opposite of skeptical noncommitment, namely, readiness to assert something categorically and without qualification. Of course, some dogmatists in this sense are also dogmatic in the sense of refusing, in an opinionated fashion, to examine other views. But the opponents Sextus took to task were not the irrationalists, the fanatics, the opinionated. Rather, he criticized those people we call "the justificationists." He used this term to denote two closely related positions that we find it helpful to separate: One of them might be termed dogmatism or justificationism in general; the other, dogmatism or justificationism in particular. Our proposal is to replace Sextus's noncommitment with the intellectual challenge brought before a workshop.

Dogmatism in general asserts no more than that the workshop may rest assured that on some (unspecified) occasion some (unspecified) position is true, or, to put it another way, some questions eventually get closed. Dogmatism in particular is more familiar, namely, the assertion that certain given positions are justified and true; that certain specific questions are closed in the workshop. Both Popper and Popkin fail to separate general dogmatism from particular dogmatism, since both seem to share Sextus's view that dogmatism implies that rational discussion (which is largely negative and destructive) has value mainly when it results in a question being closed. This collapses dogmatism into general dogmatism (rational debate helps close questions) and misses particular dogmatism (this question is closed; further debate on it is irrational). Both Popkin and Popper, being open-minded by temperament and conviction, want a philosophy of open-mindedness, with no closure; and so each rejects dogmatism. Popkin opts for one form of skepticism (fideism), Popper for another (critical rationalism), and the question immediately arises as to whether a distinction can usefully be made between the two as to their relative merits.

Mentalities and Indecision

I have alluded to differences of temperament, both psychological and sociological. Before venturing to reopen a closed question, the workshop can anticipate various possible outcomes: successful, promising, sensible, wild, and so on. The difference that temperament makes is very simple: Some people are delighted at the prospect of reopening and are quite disappointed if it ultimately fails. Others are dismayed by it. I make this point as an empirical observation subject to test. Anyone can test it when encountering specialists in a given field by offering an observation or a theory that clashes with received opinion. The normal reaction will be defensive, but on occasion the reaction will be quite amicable: Persons holding the received opinion will invite one to make the case as best one can. Defensiveness, I take it, is less rational than open-mindedness.

So far the temperaments have not been characterized sharply enough, for even those of a most dogmatic disposition delight in reopening some questions on some occasions. Even those of a most undogmatic disposition get bored by obviously lame attempts to reopen reasonably well closed questions. No less significant is the fact that opinions change radically more often than is admitted: The most temperamentally dogmatic discourager of the reopening of old issues may experience a change of heart on one specific issue (and on nothing else). A workshop facilitates switching roles.

Nevertheless, there are people of dogmatic character, or temperament, or disposition, and there are people of skeptical or open-minded disposition. Moreover, they often do not mix well—at least outside workshops. Is the difference one of a capacity or mental faculty to be rational, to think critically? Is it possible to choose rationally between these two temperaments or dispositions? If so, which of the two should be rationally chosen? Moreover, can there be more than two temperaments to choose from?

If the problem of choice ever arises, we need more than these two temperaments, for it has been shown that one of them, skepticism, can be a justification for avoiding choice and decision as such. This is the achievement of Walter Kaufmann, whose *Without Guilt and Justice* bears the subtitle *From Decidophobia to Autonomy*. The decidophobe, Kaufmann argues, can choose several strategies, one of which is to demand a very high standard of proof prior to any decision (Kaufmann, 1973). No one would knowingly advocate decidophobic skepticism—set impossibly high standards—not even the decidophobe. Would anyone want to choose the theory of rationality of the decidophobe, and how different is it from that of the dogmatist? Or is it not the case that, as Kaufmann suggests, dogmatism is also a version of decidophobia? That is, reopening issues calls for new decisions, which is precisely what the decidophobe wishes to avoid. The extreme decidophobe will normally prefer to avoid the workshop altogether; lesser decidophobes can be neutralized by the institutional rules.

Opinion and Temperament

The workshop can make the best of three dogmatisms: (1) justificationism or dogmatism as the general view that we may and ought to close certain debates once and for all; alternatively, (2) justificationism or dogmatism as the particular view that certain given opinions are obligatory, that certain specific debates must remain closed; and (3) the dogmatic temperament that finds certainty more agreeable than open questions. Clearly, all three are almost independent: Logic permits six out of the eight combinations (see tables 26.1 and 26.2 in the appendix to this chapter). It is logically impossible to hold specific dogmatism and reject general dogmatism: If this question is closed, then, logically, some question is capable of being closed.

Can we identify dogmatism, both general and specific, with the opposite of skepticism? The case of general dogmatism seems obvious; not so the case of specific dogmatism, since general dogmatism may allow specific dogmatism in one case and specific skepticism in another, whereas general skepticism forbids any dogmatism whatsoever. This can be remedied by introducing a replacement for specific dogmatism, namely, dogmatism pro tem, a category invented by Popper. He applied it to attested statements of observable fact ("basic statements"), but we wish to apply it much more generally. This removes any inconsistency between denying general dogmatism and asserting a specific one: The specific one is only pro tem. Note the power of tentativity.

Asymmetry between Skepticism and Dogmatism

Nevertheless, there is one profound asymmetry between general dogmatism and general skepticism, and it is unbridgeable. Moreover, the asymmetry is strongly reflected in the standards of rationality involved. Symmetry was made possible not so much by the Popperian ploy of dogmatism pro tem, but by what made this ploy necessary. The symmetry is one that treats assent and dissent on a par, despite the asymmetry between refutation and verification, whose implication for rational belief was stressed by Bacon and Popper alike.[8] On the one side we have the fact that criticism is logically binding; one cannot both admit the counterexample and yet stick to the thesis it contradicts without thereby being inconsistent. On the other side we have the fact that one may logically give up theories no matter how well verified they are. Refutation forces a choice on the workshop; verification does not. This fact looks like strong support for the claim that skepticism is a better philosophy for the workshop than dogmatism. But the claim can be contested. That verification is not binding by the canons of logic does not mean that it is not binding by some other canons—perhaps even some other logical canons.

Furthermore, it would be ironical to attribute greater rationality to the traditional variant of skepticism, which effectively abandons rationality by counseling that since no issue can ever get resolved, we should lie back and enjoy our *ataraxia*. None of the best workshops (or minds) operate under this philosophy. Dogmatism and skepticism agree that rationality is closure; the one holds it to be feasible, the other holds it to be unattainable.[9] Agassi and I, to the contrary, identify rationality not with closure but with process or at least with readiness for it: with openness, exchange, criticism, debate. At times, when a debate is bogged down, we may turn away from it and call it closed pro tem; at other times, a debate may need reopening, even though the issue appeared settled. A critical rationalist philosophy can coexist with both dogmatists and skeptics in the workshop, because each allows the necessary loophole for opening and closing debate, as follows.

General dogmatism is the idea that all debates should sooner or later be closed. The critical rationalist can fall back on the argument, in any particular case before the workshop, that the time for closure is not yet ripe. Specific dogmatism declares a particular debate closed. The critical rationalist can argue, "But this (new fact, situation, development) changes things." General skepticism keeps debates endlessly prolonged by demanding impossibly high standards for closure. The critical rationalist can argue that a specific idea produced in the workshop meets high-enough standards. Specific skepticism declares a particular position to have many weaknesses. All that the critical rationalist needs to say to the workshop is that even if this position has weaknesses, under some specific conditions we should accept it—in some sense of acceptance—as the best we have to hand: The critical rationalist may at times be more eager to avoid decidophobia than to reach any other specific goal. Hence the fact that scientific skepticism is invariably specific, not general.

The Rationality of Dogmatism

Reasonable people adopt dogmatism not as a temperament, but as a policy. Indeed, justificationist dogmatism is almost universal among professional philosophers. How can it be rational to opt for dogmatism when more critical positions are available? This seemingly insoluble question is soluble in the workshop model. First and foremost, Agassi and I treat dogmatism as an error, but a reasonable one. On general grounds, as long as the alternatives seemed to be dogmatism and skepticism, with skepticism seemingly leading to either nihilism or fideism, there was a case for preferring general dogmatism. Even Popper's ploy of specific dogmatism pro tem, which is ad hoc, concedes this in admitting, even stressing, its ad hoc nature. Further, as long as general dogmatism did not preclude specific skepticism, it was harmless and so all the more rational: It did some good and no harm, at least to all those who were not dedicated to philosophic questions alone. What seems irrational about dogmatism, that is, its vagueness, is thus transformed into an asset.[10] Consider why so many philosophers believe in inductive probability when they cannot estimate it. Just their inability to estimate is what makes it tolerable, since, were they able to estimate probabilities, they would find themselves committed to the probable hypothesis and thus obliged not to continue to debate it critically.

Yet as philosophies for the workshop and as models for the inquiring mind, both general dogmatism and general skepticism are wanting, and even when they are modified, they are still not very satisfactory. Workshops can, however, temper dogmatism with skepticism and vice versa; this is often done in the workshop by changing roles—playing devil's advocate, for example. For the working scientist, engineer, and social thinker, this is quite satisfactory. Not so for the philosopher, especially the epistemologist, but he counts for relatively little so long as the workshop is productive.

Given all this, how then is the balance maintained in the workshop if the philosopher is called in only on occasion? The answer seems to be: Not by dogmatism, but by those who maintain (or feign) a dogmatic temperament. Holding on to an idea gives stability, continuity, and challenge. This may explain the virtue of the tension many thinkers display between opinion and temperament. It also goes against Lewis Feuer's thesis about progress along isoemotional lines.[11] Often it is parallel conflict between both opinions and temperaments that produces spectacular results. The conflict in individuals is only a subjective psychological mirror of the sociological conflict between policies in the workshop; one carries on an inner dialogue rather than a public one. There are all kinds of reasons for regarding the public dialogue as prior (Mead, 1934). Be that as it may, the workshop clarifies issues of various kinds. Workshops can be of benefit to almost everyone, even to those who insist on a single policy. Benefits increase, however, as one becomes as pragmatic about temperament as one is about policy, as one more and more detaches one's work in the workshop from personal or private conviction and plays whatever role seems needed at the time.

The Upshot

Specific cases of dogmatism, I hope the present study indicates, may be better or worse, depending on the specific situations at the workshop. Certainly I advocate and note the benefits of flexibility in specific cases—we may try more dogmatism and more openness in this or that specific case. To go into the logic of this flexibility will take us into the methodology of research and of research programs. Yet one can ask about general dogmatism, in what sense is it rational? Obviously, it is rational$_1$ within dogmatic communities, no less than magic within magically minded communities. Also, I have shown, I hope, that it is rational$_2$ since it permits specific criticisms, much more so than magic ever does, and at times even fosters radical criticism, as magic never does. Finally, it was, as I argued, rational$_3$, as long as it was the only alternative known to nihilism or fideism. Now, of course, it is no longer rational$_3$ in the face of better alternatives.

Thus, quite commonsensically, it was reasonable in the past to hold to general dogmatism, especially if no specific dogma was endorsed. This explains its past prevalence. Yet what was good enough for the past is no longer good enough. Contrary to justificationism, which condemns all opponents equally, except for some unspecified transition period, critical rationalists do not condemn all opponents equally, and thus we do not condemn equally all justificationism: The workshop governed by it when a better alternative is known, we think, is the poorer for it.

Does this lead to any recommendations? Perhaps the best one can offer is this: An investigator can study the workshop atmosphere and its trappings and

TABLE 26.1. Varieties of Dogmatism

General dogmatism	yes	yes	yes	yes	no	no	no	no
Specific dogmatism	yes	yes	no	no	yes	yes	no	no
Dogmatic temperament	yes	no	yes	no	yes	no	yes	no

logically
impossible

learn to emulate it with ease. This should encourage the proliferation of workshops, permanent or casual, public ones and private inner ones, on all sorts of occasions. Such reforms will foster intellectual progress by increasing opportunities to alter temperamental givens, opportunities to learn from peers and juniors, and opportunities to appreciate newcomers. Above all, it should foster that sense of fulfillment derived from immersion in the task at hand without regard for ego or status. The mind may not be simply like a workshop but may actually be an internalized workshop rather more structured, goal directed, and improvable than Mead's "inner dialogue."

Appendix: Permutations of Dogmatism and Skepticism

Table 26.1 can be presented differently, with the terms replaced by means of the following set of rules of substitution, where an arrow requires us to replace the term on the left by the term on the right:

General dogmatism $\longrightarrow$ General skepticism
Specific dogmatism $\longrightarrow$ Specific skepticism
Dogmatic temperament $\longrightarrow$ Skeptical temperament
Yes $\longrightarrow$ No
No $\longrightarrow$ Yes

The resultant reformulation is shown in table 26.2:

TABLE 26.2. Varieties of Skepticism

General skepticism	no	no	no	no	yes	yes	yes	yes
Specific skepticism	no	no	yes	yes	no	no	yes	yes
Skeptical temperament	no	yes	no	yes	no	yes	no	yes

logically
impossible

Notes

1. Our approach is thus cognitive rather than symbolic, expressive, or aesthetic. Interesting as these approaches are, we believe that only a cognitive account can be explanatory.

2. The present chapter is a reworking by Jarvie alone of Jarvie and Agassi, 1979. See also Jarvie and Agassi, 1967, 1980, and 1996. The first three papers are reprinted in truncated form in Agassi and Jarvie, 1987.

3. Rationality on this model, then, resembles the practice hinted at in Plato's early dialogues, which may actually have been that of the historical Socrates. However, in some dialogues Plato depicts a Socrates who knows the answer before he starts, rather than the more engaging figure of the early dialogues who pursued inquiry in a genuine spirit of open-mindedness and workshop rationality. We suggest that it was the workshop atmosphere around Socrates that attracted pupils; if he had been the kind of teacher the later dialogues paint him to be, our image of his martyrdom would be very different.

4. Only if the rules are explicit can they be subject to rational discussion and assessment.

5. See Popkin, 1960, 1963, 1974; Feyerabend, 1970, 1975. See also reviews of the latter by Gellner, 1975; Agassi, 1976; and Tibbetts, Kulka, and Hattiangadi, 1977.

6. See Agassi, 1973. See also Toulmin, 1957, and Agassi's discussion of it in Agassi, 1963, pp. 45–6, as well as Born, 1949 and 1953.

7. The principle of verification, which is common to all positivists, when understood as of verification in principle—and, when cornered, positivists always put the stress on the qualifier—really amounts to just this: A problem that cannot be solved in principle is a mere pseudoproblem, for example, the perennial problems of philosophy. See Carnap, 1967, and the discussion in Agassi, 1975, pp. 446–47.

8. Philosophers keep rediscovering that Bacon made the asymmetry between verification and refutation central to his system. His judgment was sharp on the matter: Induction by enumeration (generalization) is puerile (childish), he wrote (*Novum Organum*, I, Aph. xlvi), since it does nothing to prevent an instance to the contrary appearing around the corner next year. Bacon illustrates the asymmetry with the story of the temple and the man who was shown the votive tablets of all those who fulfilled their vows after escaping from shipwreck and was asked if he acknowledged the will of the gods. In reply, he asked, "But where are the pictures of those who have perished, notwithstanding their vows?" Bacon's doctrine of idola is based on the psychological claim that people refuse to recognize the force of the asymmetry. So is Bacon's claim that he has a new method of demonstration—a method, writes R.L. Ellis, that he never described. (See Ellis's general preface to Bacon's philosophical works (vol. 1, pp. 61–127) and to Bacon's *Novum Organum* (vol. 1, pp. 131–93 in Bacon, 1857–74.) Modern writers who discover Bacon's stress on the asymmetry conveniently ignore Bacon's promise to offer a new method of proof.

9. We were anticipated in our discovery of the ground common to all parties in the dispute by E. Gellner in his remarkable 1976 book chapter. On p. 175 he writes, "[I]f the central idea . . . is paradoxically the a priori substantive exclusion of certain worlds . . . then the view that philosophy is, could be or ought to be 'neutral' is absurd." For the exclusion, see Popper, 1959, section 67.

10. Elusive, vague, and even absurd ideas can have great attraction, provided they also appear to give some insight into things. The combination of illumination plus

deeper mystery is a potent one. In Gellner's classic chapter on the function of absurd concepts (Gellner, 1973, chapter 2 of), he shows that their successful functioning can turn on the delicious ambivalence of the striking and of the absurd. The concept of functionalism itself and the functionalist school are susceptible to such an analysis. The principles of simplicity of nature, or of limited variety, or of the possibility of induction, and others are as useful as the claim that a preferred direction exists may be to one who lost his way. The vagueness of the principle is an encouragement, neither a guide nor an imposition.

11. Feuer's book (1974), nonetheless, is one of the few that incidentally offer a glimpse or two at the workshop in operation. Others are Jungk, 1958, and Sakharov, 1990. Mario Bunge (1987) and many others claim that the Copenhagen school does not exist, since it has no doctrine and since the doctrinal fragments offered by, say, Niels Bohr and Werner Heisenberg are incompatible with one another. This claim is true only in part: Copenhagen was a school not so much in the sense of offering a doctrine or even a single guideline (regulative principle) as in the sense of being a veritable workshop and famous as such. All writings on Niels Bohr's Copenhagen suggest this, as well as writings — especially biographical — concerning other quantum physicists and their laboratories, such as Enrico Fermi and E.O. Lawrence.

References

Agassi, J. 1963. *Towards an Historiography of Science.* History and Theory, Beiheft 2. Facsimile reprint, Middletown, CT: Wesleyan University Press, 1967.

————. 1971. "On Explaining the Trial of Galileo." *Organon,* 8, pp. 138–66.

————. 1973. "Continuity and Discontinuity in the History of Ideas." *Journal of the History of Ideas,* 34, pp. 609–26.

————. 1975. *Science in Flux.* Dordrecht: Reidel.

————. 1976. "Review of Paul Feyerabend *Against Method.*" *Philosophia,* 6, pp. 165–91.

Agassi, J. and Jarvie, I.C. (Eds.). 1987. *Rationality: The Critical View.* The Hague: Martinus Nijhoff.

Ayer, A.J. 1956. *The Problem of Knowledge.* London: Macmillan.

Bacon, F. 1857–74. J. Spedding, R.L. Ellis, and D.D. Heath (Eds.), *The Works of Francis Bacon.* Vols. 1–14. London: Longmans. Reprint, 1968. New York: Garrett Press.

Barnard, Alan, and Spencer, Jonathan (Eds.). 1996. *Encyclopedia of Social and Cultural Anthropology.* London: Routledge.

Bartley, W.W., III. 1961. *The Retreat to Commitment.* New York: Knopf.

Born, Max. 1949. *Natural Philosophy of Cause and Chance.* Oxford: Oxford University Press.

————. 1953. "The Interpretation of Quantum Mechanics." *British Journal for the Philosophy of Science,* 4, pp. 95–106.

Bunge, Mario. 1987. "Seven Desiderata for Rationality." Pp. 5–15 in Joseph Agassi and I.C. Jarvie (Eds.), *Rationality: The Critical View.* The Hague: Martinus Nijhoff.

Carnap, R. 1967. *The Logical Structure of the World, Pseudo-problems in Philosophy.* Berkeley: University of California Press.

Cohen, R.S., Feyerabend, P.K., and Wartofsky, M.W. (Eds.). 1976. *Essays in Memory of Imre Lakatos.* Boston Studies in the Philosophy of Science. Vol. 39. Dordrecht: Reidel.

Cohen, R.S., and Wartofsky, M.W. (Eds.). 1974. *Methodological and Historical Essays in the Natural and Social Sciences.* Boston Studies in the Philosophy of Science. Vol. 14. Dordrecht: Reidel.

Evans-Pritchard, E.E. 1937. *Witchcraft, Oracles, and Magic among the Azande.* Oxford: Clarendon Press.

———. 1951. *Social Anthropology.* London: Cohen and West.

Feuer, Lewis. 1974. *Einstein and the Generations of Science.* New York: Basic Books.

Feyerabend, P.K. 1970. "Against Method." Pp. 17–130, *Minnesota Studies in the Philosophy of Science.* Vol. 4. Minneapolis: University of Minneapolis Press.

———. 1975. *Against Method.* London: New Left Books.

Geraets, T.F. (Ed.). 1979. *Rationality To-day.* Ottawa: University of Ottawa Press.

Gellner, Ernest. 1973. *Cause and Meaning in the Social Sciences.* London: Routledge and Kegan Paul. Republished as *The Concept of Kinship.* Oxford: Blackwell, 1987.

———. 1975. "Beyond Truth and Falsehood." *British Journal for the Philosophy of Science, 26,* pp. 331–42.

———. 1976. "An Ethic of Cognition." Pp. 161–77 in R.S. Cohen, P.K. Feyerabend, and M.W. Wartofsky (Eds.), *Essays in memory of Imre Lakatos.* Boston Studies in the Philosophy of Science. Vol. 39. Dordrecht: Reidel.

Haack, Susan. 1993. *Evidence and Inquiry.* Oxford: Blackwell.

Jarvie, I.C., and Joseph Agassi. 1967. "The Problem of the Rationality of Magic." *British Journal of Sociology, 18,* pp. 55–74.

———. 1979. "The Rationality of Dogmatism." Pp. 354–62 in T.F. Geraets (Ed.), *Rationality To-day.* Ottawa: University of Ottawa Press.

———. 1980. "The Rationality of Irrationalism." *Metaphilosophy, 11,* pp. 127–33. Also reprinted in Joseph Agassi and I.C. Jarvie (Eds.), *Rationality: The Critical View.* The Hague: Martinus Nijhoff, 1987, pp. 445–51.

———. 1996. "Rationality." Pp. 467–70 in Alan Barnard and Jonathan Spencer (Eds.), *Encyclopedia of Social and Cultural Anthropology.* London: Routledge.

Jungk, Robert. 1958. *Brighter Than a Thousand Suns.* Harmondsworth: Penguin.

Kaufmann, Walter. 1973. *Without Guilt and Justice.* New York: Wyden.

Leach, E.R. 1970. *Lévi-Strauss.* London: Fontana.

Mead, G.H. 1934. *Mind, Self, and Society.* C.W. Morris (Ed.). Chicago: University of Chicago Press.

Popkin, R.H. 1960. *The History of Scepticism from Erasmus to Descartes.* Assen: Van Gorcum.

———. 1963. "Scepticism in the Enlightenment." *Studies on Voltaire and the Eighteenth Century, 24–27,* pp. 1321–45.

———. 1974. "Bible Criticism and Social Science." Pp. 339–60 in R.S. Cohen and M.W. Wartofsky (Eds.), *Methodological and Historical Essays in the Natural and Social Sciences,* Boston Studies in the Philosophy of Science. Vol. 14. Dordrecht: Reidel.

Popper, K.R. 1959. *The Logic of Scientific Discovery.* London: Hutchinson.

Sakharov, Andrei. 1990. *Memoirs*. New York: Knopf.
Sextus Empiricus. 1967. *Outlines of Pyrrhonism*. Cambridge, MA: Harvard University Press.
Tibbetts, Paul, Kulka, Tomas, and Hattiangadi, J.N. 1977. "Review Symposium on Feyerabend." *Philosophy of the Social Sciences*, 7, pp. 265–302.
Toulmin, S.E. 1957. "Critical Experiments: Priestley and Lavoisier." *Journal of the History of Ideas*, 18, pp. 205–20.

27

Is Cognitive Development Equivalent to Scientific Development?

Christina E. Erneling

One of Jean Piaget's strongest motivations, if not the strongest, for studying intellectual development in children was to get a better grasp of scientific reasoning (see, for example, Piaget, 1970, p. 1). In their book *Words, Thoughts, and Theories* (1997) Alison Gopnik and Andrew N. Meltzoff take the opposite approach and argue that scientific reasoning provides a model that helps us understand infants' and young children's reasoning and cognitive development. According to these authors, the child is not only actively and intelligently exploring its world, as Piaget claimed, but is thinking and acting just like a scientist. The child, like the scientist, creates, tests, and revises theories. In fact, the child in this respect surpasses the normal adult, who is portrayed as a much duller creature.

Although they differ from Piaget in their view of how scientific and child reasoning are related, their fundamental problem is the same as his. Like Piaget, they attempt to answer two of the most central problems in any philosophical and empirical attempt to account for the acquisition of knowledge and rationality: (1) to account for the learner's ability to go beyond information given, that is, in particular, to extract abstract concepts from concrete experience, and (2) to explain how a learner can be creative inside a rational framework. These were problems for Plato and St. Augustine, as the authors rightly point out in their introduction, and still are problems in contemporary cognitive science, as is evidenced by Noam Chomsky's 1950s revolt against behaviorism and by subsequent developments in cognitive science.

Furthermore, the book and its more general approach remain in the same tradition as that shared by Piaget and many early psychologists, as is shown by the fact that these, as well as many other authors, see psychology as a continuation of and replacement for philosophy (see, for example, Berkson and Wettersten, 1984). This tradition is based on a fundamental assumption made by academic psychology considered as a particular development of Western philosophy in general — that knowledge acquisition and conceptual change in all areas of science as well as in individual cognitive development are processes internal to the individual and not social achievements. Other people and social institutions are interpreted as aspects of the environment, in principle having the same type of effects on the learner (either a scientist or a child) as the physical environment. The problem of knowledge (and of how knowledge changes) is seen as one that exists for the individual mind in relation to the external world, and other people and social interactions are not supposed to be conditions for knowledge. The growth of knowledge is explained and justified in terms of individual activities such as having experiences, ideas, and hypotheses, and testing and rejecting them. Although both scientists and children typically interact with other people, this is merely a contingent fact and is not essential to the activity. The learner is like Robinson Crusoe: "Given resources, longevity, ingenuity and ability, no achievement of science as we know it would, 'in principle,' be beyond his powers" (Gellner, 1985, p. 107).

In this chapter, I first discuss Gopnik and Meltzoff's comparison between scientific activity and cognitive activity in children and argue that it is a misleading comparison, based on a confusion of two different conceptions of knowledge. Second, I discuss the substantive claim that infants and young children create, test, and revise theories. Here I argue that not only is it problematic to ascribe theories to preverbal infants, but, more seriously, such ascriptions seem to lack explanatory value in that they presuppose what they attempt to explain, namely, rationality.

More generally, the authors operate with an unnecessarily limited conception of knowledge and of the subject matter of psychology, and consequently also of the mind as a scientific object. As a result, the authors fail to provide a satisfactory account of the growth of knowledge both in science and in the child. Their failure is not primarily a result of inadequate empirical studies or lack of them, but is the result, I think, of conceptual confusion about what science, knowledge, and cognition involve.

This conceptual confusion is related to the more fundamental issue of the ontological commitments of the authors, which in fundamental respects are Cartesian. The Cartesian ontology of the mental rests on two main assumptions. The first is that the body and mind are different substances, and the second is the atomistic assumption that the basic entities or unities of cognition are individuatable states of mind stuff and, as such, are states of particular persons. They assume that cognitive representations and rules, both in science and in children, are atomic states of individuals. I think that this is the basic problem with their theory of cognitive development. The trouble is that, as van Gelder argues in this volume, there is a large class of mental states, for example, beliefs, that cannot be individuated as occurring in individual human beings, but only as "immanent" in normatively ordered and dynamic public contexts.

The Growth of Knowledge in Children and in Science

The authors' basic claim is that infants as young as nine months of age are miniature scientists, creating, testing, and changing theories about the world and other people's mentality. Children have and use theories of objects, of actions, and of how other people think and feel. The authors call their theory the "theory theory," because it is a theory about children's theories. Children do not start with the knowledge or theories that adults or scientists have, but neither do they start with reflexes, as Piaget claimed. Instead, they are born equipped with some innately released responses and a propensity to make false recognitions or, in the terms of the authors, some specific and false theories, and with an ability to test and reject theories and form new ones. In this fundamental way, children are as rational as scientists, outstripping the everyday activities of normal adults.[1]

Obviously, scientific knowledge cannot grow unless there are individual scientists who are able to employ their own cognitive abilities. Equally unquestionably, the acquisition of language and of knowledge in children involves the use of individual cognitive abilities. A rather noncontroversial or even trivial way to interpret Gopnik and Meltzoff's claim is to say that the mental abilities that enable scientists to engage in scientific activity are the same as the mental abilities we also find in infants. Such an interpretation is supported by claims the authors make that all human beings basically have the same ability to engage in learning about the world because of the facts that (a) they all have the same kind of brain (Gopnik and Meltzoff, 1997, p. 15), (b) they have the same cognitive abilities resulting from the same evolutionary process, and (c) children and scientists are on different ends of the same continuum (p. 213).[2] Such general claims are not new. On the contrary, they are the basis for learning theories as different in other respects as the behavioristic and Piagetian theories. The behaviorists assume that conditioning and association are mechanisms involved in all cognitive growth. Piaget claims that even if children make lots of factual as well as logical mistakes from the standpoint of the adult, children of all ages, as well as adults and scientists, increase their knowledge in the same way through the process of equilibration, utilizing assimilation and accommodation. Thus even if thinking in some respects is qualitatively different in children and adults, the same mental processes are found in all. Gopnik's and Meltzoff's comparison between children and scientists, interpreted this way, turns out to be rather trivial.

The comparison between children and scientists in this general way is only given as a preliminary and supporting argument for their more specific proposal that both scientific activity and cognitive activity in infants involve theory construction and testing. Before discussing this claim, I will discuss the way they misrepresent scientific activity in order to get their comparison with children to work.

In making their analogy between scientific activity and child reasoning, Gopnik and Meltzoff opt for what they call the cognitive view of science: that cognitive changes in the minds of individual scientists are at least partial explanations of scientific growth (Gopnik and Meltzoff, 1997, p. 14). Scientists and their cognitive activity are necessary, but not sufficient, for producing scientific knowledge. The authors seem to assume that the cognitive activity of scientists is both necessary and sufficient. Individual cognitive processes are involved in scientific activity, and these processes or abilities put limits to such activity. To propose rules and methodologies for science that are not compatible with human cognitive functioning is bound to fail. This is a long way from claiming that theoretical change in science is essentially something that is based on the private, subjective conviction of the individual scientist, that is, in cognitive structures in individuals (p. 7), but this is what the authors do. They claim that the most important aspect of scientific activity is the psychological activity of individual scientists who create, test, and reject theories. This is a view that falls back on the philosophical tradition, represented by, for example, Francis Bacon and René Descartes. Their approach to knowledge and knowledge growth assumes scientific growth to be a matter of private experience and certainty. This view does not deny social interaction as part of scientific activity, but it does not take such interaction to be a necessary precondition for it.

As mentioned earlier, the authors acknowledge that science also involves specific social settings, which to a certain extent are different from the ones that children find themselves in. But they do not think that such differences are important enough to reject the comparison they make between children and scientists. On the contrary, they think that there is an important social similarity between children and scientists in that both groups have lots of leisure time (p. 25).

The literature in the philosophy and sociology of science during the last hundred years is very diverse, and there seems to be no agreement about what constitutes science. Yet there is one thing generally agreed upon in this literature: the replacement of the traditional philosophical Robinson Crusoe individualistic view of science with a social conception of science.

There are two related points to be made here. I have already mentioned the first point, that contemporary philosophers of science (for example, Popper and Kuhn) agree on the claim that the objectivity and creativity of science, which set it apart from other activities, are based in special social institutions or traditions. For example, Popper (1963) argues that when science emerged in the Greek pre-Socratic world, dogmatism was replaced with a tradition of critical thinking. This new social tradition of rational interaction, involving free discussion and criticism between pupils and their teachers, was the motor of early as well as contemporary theory change in science. Of course, critical discussion requires the participation of individual persons, but this critical discussion is made possible by a new attitude and a new cultural setting. Furthermore, it is a public discussion of the content of theories and statements, not a matter of individual cognitive certainty. Kuhn (1962), although he focuses on more irrational aspects of scientific growth, makes a similar sociological point when he stresses the importance of paradigms, normal science, and scientific revolutions, which are all social phenomena.

It is not the specific social arrangements at universities or in laboratories that are important for science, but the general fact that science is a public and social activity. Therefore, Gopnik and Meltzoff's claim (1997, p. xx) that since Johannes Kepler and Isaac Newton operated in a very different social setting compared to today's scientists, social arrangements are irrelevant for scientific change and growth misses the mark. Philosophers of science maintain, not that it is certain details of the institutional arrangements in themselves that are important, but that the critical tradition (Popper) or, in the case of Kuhn, the presence of paradigms, normal science, and revolutions (all social activities) sets science apart. Gopnik and Meltzoff thus misrepresent the view they want to reject. The ease by which they do this, I would argue, is based on a confusion of two different meanings of knowledge and knowledge growth.

This brings me to my second point, which can be stated briefly and simply: Scientific change involves changes in the propositional contents of theories. The propositional contents of theories are not psychological entities, but are logical-linguistic entities expressed publicly in language, mathematics, or other symbols. Thus scientific growth is different from individual cognitive development. In ignoring this difference, Gopnik and Meltzoff ignore the distinction between two different senses of knowledge. (See, for example, Popper in *Objective Knowledge*, 1972; see also van Gelder in this volume.)

The first sense of knowledge, distinguished by Popper, refers to thoughts and theories in the subjective or psychological sense, that is, a state of mind, of consciousness, or a disposition to react and behave. The second sense of knowledge refers to knowledge in the objective sense, that is, of propositional content of theories, problems, and arguments. Knowledge in this sense is independent of anyone's claim to know or anyone's having dispositions to behave, although of course such knowledge is used by human beings. Popper asks us to make a distinction between the content of some particular proposition and the mental attitude one can have toward this proposition, like believing, accepting, and so on. Another way to state the same distinction is to say that knowledge in the first, subjective sense refers to individual mental processes, and knowledge in the second sense to the objective content of these thoughts or mental processes. Popper (1972, p. 109) cites Frege's way of making this distinction as follows: "I understand by a *thought* not the subjective act of thinking but its *objective content* . . . ."

There is abundant evidence in the text that Gopnik and Meltzoff do not make this distinction. Both in their descriptions and explanations, they move from one meaning of knowledge to the other without acknowledging the difference. For example, they discuss the process of cognitive development in children and scientists (subjective sense) in one sentence, but in the next sentence they speak about scientific theory change (objective) (Gopnik and Meltzoff, 1997, p. 3). On page 6 we find the same pattern: First they refer to cognitive development, that is, knowledge in the subjective sense, and then to theory change (the objective sense). On page 19 they discuss scientific representations and rules and compare them to children's representations and rules. They refer (p. 18) to close links between science (objective) and childhood cognition (subjective) and (p. 21) to conceptual change in children (subjective) and in science (objective). Furthermore, they describe theory change as cognitive change (p. 39) and even ascribe human-like qualities to theories—for example, they speak about the advances that a theory makes (p. 100).[3]

The discussion of these authors is thus confused. This is serious because it obscures the fact that science and scientific change are not appropriate models for cognitive development. Science and scientific activity are public activities, specifically, changes in the public propositional content of theories, and are not primarily matters concerned with changing psychological processes—although, of course, changes of this last sort always are involved as well. By using science as their model, the authors are appealing to a nonpsychological activity or entity to explain a psychological entity. This means that they are committing what Ryle (1949) called a category mistake. They should have been consistent about comparing the propositional contents of the beliefs of scientists and children, on one side, and their respective cognitive capabilities or skills, on the other. Sometimes they do this (e.g., Ryle, p. 24). But in all these cases their comparisons are very meagre. For example, children and scientists have the same type of facial expressions when they solve difficult problems; both groups have a lot of leisure time; neither group is primarily concerned with making and feeding children; and both groups love truth more than anything else ("Like scientists, babies sometimes prefer truth to love" [p. 152]—said about a child who disobeys its mother). Further similarities, according to the authors, are in that both groups of people belong to the same species and have the same type of brain "designed" by evolution "to get things right." Thus we seem to be back where we started, at the noncontroversial and rather trivial claim that there are similarities in cognitive processing in all humans, be they children or adults, scientists, or people using magic. Furthermore, the comparison between children and science could be rejected without jeopardizing their main claim that children have and use theories. Before turning to this, let me make a few more comments related to their comparison between scientific activity and children's cognitive abilities.

The authors provide a large amount of empirical evidence to support their claims about the cognitive abilities of children, but they provide hardly any empirical evidence concerning the cognitive abilities of scientists. Here instead they fall back on various philosophical views and assumptions, which they ultimately want to replace. My comment about this is that in order to investigate whether scientists are similar to children, one not only needs to study children solving cognitive tasks, but also scientists engaged in scientific activity.

Another consequence of their "theory theory," if it is correct, I think, is that education, especially science education, ought to be changed. This kind of education should aim at encouraging students to become like infants. That is, it should encourage them to regress and rely more on their own subjective convictions than on public and intersubjective interactions. What needs to be taught is not reasoning skills or the importance of intersubjectivity, but only some points about mathematics and statistics, and specific information concerning the problem area. In other words, scientific education is not really needed, since doing science is something even infants master, even if their specific theories are mistaken.

As hinted at earlier, I do not think that the comparison between children and scientists is crucial for the main argument of the book, but is merely a way of gaining attention to the authors' more fundamental claim that children's thought processes are best characterized as theory testing, rejection, and change. This interpretation is supported by the fact that after the first chapters the comparison between children and scientific activity slips into the background, and the claim that children create, test, and change theories comes to the foreground.

Infants and Theories

Gopnik and Meltzoff claim that having a theory means that one makes explanations and predictions, and that one has beliefs, concepts, and ontological commitments concerning an external world independent of one's theorizing about it. This is true both of scientists and of children:

> All these characteristics of theories ought also to apply to children's early cognitive structures if these structures are really theoretical. That is, children's theories should involve appeal to abstract theoretical entities, with coherent causal relationships among them. Their theories should lead to characteristic patterns of predictions, including extensions to new types of evidence and false predictions, not to just more empirically accurate predictions. Their theories should also lead to distinctive interpretations of evidence. . . . Finally, their theories should invoke characteristic explanations phrased in terms of these abstract entities and laws. (Gopnik and Meltzoff, 1997, p. 41)

According to the authors, infants are thus born with crude and mistaken theories and the ability to change and replace them by testing and rejecting them and by creating new ones. All humans are born with theories, which they change and replace by better ones during development. In this respect, individual cognitive development is similar to scientific activity.

To ascribe theories to children is also, according to Gopnik and Meltzoff, to ascribe beliefs to children, including the belief that there is a world independent of thoughts or beliefs about it. But to have beliefs involves having concepts and also having an idea of what is true and false. To test beliefs against experience also involves logical concepts like contradiction. Thus children are born with, and from birth are equipped with all the necessary ingredients of, logical thinking and rationality. The only difference between them and adults, including scientists, is that the contents of children's theories are mistaken and deal only with a limited set of topics.

In this chapter, I do not question whether adults, scientists, or older children have and use theories, or question the account that Gopnik and Meltzoff give of theories, but only ask (1) whether it is justifiable to ascribe theories to preverbal infants, and (2) whether such ascriptions have explanatory value. Remember, they claim that nine-month-old infants create, test, and reject theories. In this context, Gopnik and Meltzoff's references to similarities between scientists and children are relevant because they claim that children literally, and in the same sense as scientists, have, test, and revise theories. They do not mean this in a metaphorical or weak sense, as when we speak about the aims and beliefs of heat-seeking missiles, or sunflowers, or dogs. Infants literally are born with theories and the ability to assess and change them rationally.

Is it justifiable to ascribe beliefs, concepts, and ontological commitments to preverbal infants and young children? The issue under discussion concerning my first point is not whether infants have certain complex behaviors, but whether it is warranted to ascribe concepts and beliefs to them, including the concepts of truth and falsity.

Let me begin by drawing a distinction between having concepts, beliefs, and the like in a strong and in a weak sense. That is, I do not deny that infants have some cognitive capacities, or that they engage in discriminative behavior. Infants, like sunflowers, animals, and other living organisms, behave in ways that are both discriminatory and finely adjusted to the environment. But this in itself does not entitle us to ascribe beliefs, concepts, or ontological commitments to them. Children are creatures that eventually will have all these things. It sometimes makes sense to speak about them as having beliefs, hopes, and ideas, as all parents do. It also sometimes can have predictive value to ascribe such things to infants. But this does not mean that they have beliefs in the strong sense of the word.

Let me try to illustrate what I mean by ascribing beliefs in the strong sense to preverbal children and then explain why we should not fall for this temptation in the course of our attempts to explain children's behavior and cognitive growth. Let us assume that we describe the behavior of a young child by saying that "Sara believes that she is building a snowman." This description of her behavior, if we assume that beliefs are taken in the strong and not metaphorical sense, implies not only that Sara believes that she is building a snowman, but also that she intends to do so, desires to do so, and knows the difference between what a snowman is and what a snowman is not. This in its turn implies that she has an idea of true and false. It also implies that she has an idea of her own subjective judgment, and that this is related to an independent world, which also is accessible to other people, who also have subjective states and the idea of an independent world.

For a belief to be true, it must correspond to the states in the world; but it is not Sara's brain state or something in her mental substance (whatever we take this to be) that corresponds to the world, but the propositional content of the belief. If she believes that p, "the snow in front of her is a snowman and not an igloo," it is implied that she can distinguish the objective content of her belief and relate it to something outside the belief, and also to other people's beliefs. "The basic idea is that one cannot recognize that one's beliefs constitute a subjective point of view on something objective, or independent of one's beliefs, except in so far as one also recognizes other subjective points of view." (Rovane, 1986, p. 423)

Another problem is that if we ascribe a specific belief to a child in the strong sense, we are ascribing not only dispositions to behave, but specific concepts to the child. These must be concepts that the child has learned and is able to apply before he or she participates in various shared linguistic and normative activities. Hence believers must also be communicators or interpreters of others. More specifically, they must be able to interpret the specific objective content of other people's beliefs.

Having theories and testing them involve judging their truth or falsity. If children have theories in the sense that Gopnik and Meltzoff claim, then children at the preverbal stage as well as later would have to have these concepts. But truth and falsity apply to statements and are metalinguistic judgments. Thus they not only require language, but also a way of thinking about language. The psychological literature denies Gopnik and Meltzoff's claim, stating that preschool children lack all metalinguistic awareness. Although children use words like "no" quite early, it is not until they first start school that such words represent a judgment of the truth or falsity of statements. Before that, they simply are used to register disagreement and similar things (Olson, 1997).

Furthermore, Nelson (1996), for example, provides evidence that children under the age of four years do not understand that other people have beliefs, and they also lack the idea that they themselves have beliefs. Children have beliefs without being aware of them, or without being aware that they have beliefs, but to claim that children test their beliefs is to claim that they treat their own beliefs, and the content of those beliefs, as objects of thought. Thus in such cases it is necessary for them to have the conception of beliefs.

In claiming that children are testing theories, Gopnik and Meltzoff are claiming that they are born not only with false theories, but also with a fully developed logical ability—with a language of thought like the ones proposed, for example, by Fodor (1975) and Macnamara (1986). In addition to the problems with such positions that I reviewed earlier, there is another serious problem, namely, that the authors here are presupposing what they claim to explain, rationality.

Rationality Presupposed: The Resemblance Fallacy

One of the most persistent and also one of the most important problems in developmental psychology is constructing a theory capable of accounting for psychological cognitive change. Different suggestions, like association, deduction, and Piaget's explanatory concepts of assimilation and accommodation, all have run into serious problems. Gopnik and Meltzoff's "theory theory" postulates conceptual or theory change as typical of childhood cognitive development, but this idea makes it necessary to ascribe to children all the properties that we associate with reasonable thinking and rationality. Although the specific contents of the theories change, the basic mechanisms for change remain unchanged and are presupposed in the explanational model the authors propose. If children are born with the ability to test, reject, and create theories, there is not really any developmental difference in basic cognitive ability or rationality. In other words, there is no development and no change over time in this fundamental ability, which is shared by all humans. Piaget (1952) calls this position intellectual vitalism, alluding to the vitalist explanation of life in terms of a life force. Gopnik and Meltzoff explain rationality in terms of rationality. At most, according to their proposal, children change the specific contents of their theories over time, but not their own basic ability to reason.

Even more seriously, by confusing knowledge in the objective sense with knowledge in the subjective sense, and by transferring the objective conception both of theory and of theory change to the subjective or psychological sphere, they have not given us a psychological mechanism, but only a redescription of how any reasonable person would argue in similar cases. It is just a reconstruction of a rational argument in the objective sense. By transferring rationality from the public sphere to the private and subjective level, they do not explain the observed level. The unobserved process is as much in need of explanation as the observed.

Instead of providing a psychological theory of rationality, then, they postulate an inner hidden psychological mechanism mirroring the public discourse we use to describe a rational linguistic discourse (see Harré, 1997, and Wittgenstein, 1953). They are committing a fallacy of resemblance — that is, ascribing qualities characteristic of something they are familiar with (as actively working scientists) to what presumably produces this behavior, namely, psychological mechanisms. This fallacy rests on the assumption that what produces apparently rational behavior must itself be rational.

Put another way, they seem to be committing what William James called the "psychologist's fallacy" of ascribing to their objects of study characteristics that belong to themselves (James, 1890, p. 196). As scientists, Gopnik and Meltzoff create, test, and revise theories, and they conclude that children do the same thing. Danziger (1985) describes how Wilhelm Wundt warned against a similar problem, the tendency of psychologists to use logic to characterize behavior and then illegitimately to transfer this same logical language to the level of psychological mechanisms as well.

Conclusion

I strongly endorse theoretical developments in psychology, of which there are far too few in comparison with all the empirical work. With this in mind, Gopnik and Meltzoff are attempting to do the right thing in their book. But in spite of all their theoretical and empirical discussions, the fundamental problems of psychological growth and the nature of rationality remain. The reason for this, I think, is that they are still too much part of the Cartesian-Kantian philosophical tradition, which (1) often confused the objective with the subjective sense of knowledge and belief and (2) as a consequence of this did not distinguish clearly between what one could call cognition, on one side, and the mind, on the other (see van Gelder in this volume).

By cognition I mean all the states and processes that form the causal underpinnings of all our sophisticated behavior, from wine tasting to playing football to doing mental mathematics. The most complex component of cognition is the brain, but our body considered more generally is also important. Cognition is individual and mostly inside the skin or skull, but it also involves skills and behaviors of different kinds. It is a physical process and involves causal mechanisms. There is no mystery about the ontological status of cognition seen in this way. Cognition is simply a physical, biological process.

But the mind includes beliefs and knowledge, which involve something else besides the physical or biological processes or mechanisms of an indvidual. They also involve norms and social institutions. For example, think about what kind of physical structure we would call a church: There is the actual physical building, which is quite complex; but for it to be a church, there has to be agreement among the members of the community to call and use it as church, and for this to be possible, there have to be certain norms and social institutions in place. In a similar way, scientific activity is more than the cognition of scientists. Likewise, being an individual who believes is more than having cognition; it is also participating in a specific social and linguistic setting according to certain norms. In order to understand cognitive development, we need to study both these aspects and see how they interact, not confuse them by trying to reduce the one to the other. Cognition is something that combines brain and culture, but the issue of how this is done is still unresolved by Gopnik and Meltzoff.

Notes

1. Their views of the lack of intellectual activity in adults are mysterious, and I can understand them only as a way of stressing that adults are normally less engaged in intellectual activity than children and scientists. Adults are too busy with more mundane things, like caring for their scientist-children, as Gopnik and Meltzoff point out. I do not think that they seriously maintain that there is any qualitative difference between the intellect of adults as compared to children and scientists, only that they as a group are less interesting, given the authors' problem. This is shown, for example, later in the book when they repeatedly compare children's and adults' reasoning processes.

2. It is worth noting that the authors repeatedly refer to evolution as designing the cognitive processes. Thus they seem to be operating with a non-Darwinian and teleological conception of evolution. Although this is not central to their main argument, it is careless. But it is also not surprising, given the tendency of developmental psychologists to accept such views. See, for example, Morss, 1990.

3. To be fair, Gopnik and Meltzoff sometimes seem to be aware of the distinction between objective and subjective aspects of knowledge. For example, they reject the distinction between context of discovery (subjective) and context of justification (objective) (Gopnik and Meltzoff, 1997, p. 33). But the problem is that they do not maintain and respect this distinction, as I already have indicated. This blurring is especially troublesome when they discuss theories and theory change. That is, they present the logical account of theories as if it were a psychological matter (p. 34).

References

Berkson, W., and Wettersten, J. 1984. *Learning from Error*. La Salle, IL: Open Court.
Cavell, M. 1993. *The Psychoanalytic Mind: From Freud to Philosophy.* Cambridge, MA: Harvard University Press.
Danziger, K. 1985. "The Methodological Imperative in Psychology." *Philosophy of the Social Sciences*, 15, pp. 1–13.

Erneling, C. 1993. *Understanding Language Acquisition: The Framework of Learning.* Albany: State University of New York Press.

Fodor, J. 1975. *The Language of Thought.* New York: Crowell.

Gellner, E. 1985. "The Scientific Status of the Social Sciences." Pp. 101–127 in Gellner, *Relativism and the Social Sciences.* Cambridge, UK: Cambridge University Press.

Gopnik, A., and Meltzoff, A.N. 1997. *Words, Thoughts, and Theories.* Cambridge, MA: MIT Press.

Harré, R. 1997. " 'Berkeleyan' Arguments and the Ontology of Cognitive Science." Pp. 335–52 in D.M. Johnson and C.E. Erneling (Eds.), *The Future of the Cognitive Revolution.* New York: Oxford University Press.

James, W. 1890. *The Principles of Psychology.* New York: Dover Publications Inc.

Johnson, D.M., and Erneling, C.E. (Eds.). 1997. *The Future of the Cognitive Revolution.* New York: Oxford University Press.

Kuhn, T.S. 1962. *The Structure of Scientific Revolutions.* Chicago: University of Chicago Press.

LePore, E. (Ed.). 1986. *Essays on Truth and Interpretation.* Oxford: Blackwell.

Macnamara, J. 1986. *A Border Dispute: The Place of Logic in Psychology.* Cambridge, MA: MIT Press.

Morss, J.R. 1990. *The Biologising of Childhood: Developmental Psychology and the Darwinian Myth.* Hillsdale, NJ: Lawrence Erlbaum.

Nelson, K. 1996. *Language in Cognitive Development: Emergence of the Mediated Mind.* New York: Cambridge University Press.

Olson, D. 1997. "Written Representation of Negation." *Pragmatics and Cognition,* 5(2), pp. 235–52.

Piaget, J. 1952. *The Origins of Intelligence in Children.* New York: International Universities Press.

———. 1970. *Genetic Epistemology.* New York: Norton.

Popper, K. 1963. "Back to the Pre-Socratics." Pp. 136–165 in Popper, *Conjectures and Refutations: The Growth of Scientific Knowledge.* London: Routledge and Kegan Paul.

———. 1972. *Objective Knowledge: An Evolutionary Approach.* Oxford: Clarendon Press.

Rovane, C. 1986. "The Metaphysics of Interpretation," in E. LePore (Ed.), *Essays on Truth and Interpretation.* Oxford: Blackwell.

Ryle, G. 1949. *The Concept of Mind.* London: Hutchinson.

Wittgenstein, L. 1953. *Philosophical Investigations.* Oxford: Basil Blackwell.

28

Mind, Brain, and the Upper Paleolithic

David Martel Johnson

Shortly after Steven Pinker published *How the Mind Works* (1997), I saw him being interviewed on television by science commentator Jay Ingram.[1] As I recall the occasion, the host began with something like the following words: "Here is a person who just has written a book called *How the Brain Works*." I held my breath, waiting for Pinker to correct this obvious mistake about the title of his book, but he did nothing of the sort. Instead, he carried on calmly as if no error had been made, or as if, even though he was aware of the mistake, he considered it such a trivial one that he did not consider it appropriate to say anything about it. Reflecting on this incident later—and after having looked again at the first few pages of Pinker's book—it struck me that his muted reaction to the misstatement probably was not surprising, since it fitted in well with his general way of thinking about the relation between mind and brain. Pinker's basic statement on this subject appears on page 21, where he says, "The mind is what the brain does." Or, as he immediately goes on to explain more fully, "The mind is a system of organs of computation, designed by natural selection to solve the kinds of problems our ancestors faced in their foraging way of life, in particular, understanding and outmaneuvering objects, animals, plants, and other people."

In roughly similar style, linguist George Lakoff and philosopher Mark Johnson claim in a still more recent work (1999) that the most central and characteristic function of the mind is that of generating reasonable thought. Furthermore, according to them, mind (or "reason"—a word they take to be equivalent) always is physically embodied "in such a way that our conceptual systems draw largely upon the commonalities of our bodies and of the environments we live in." This implies in turn that "much of a person's conceptual system is either universal or widespread across languages and cultures" (Lakoff and Johnson, 1999, p. 6). They provide an even more complete summary of their views in the following passage (pp. 3–4):

Reason has been taken for over two millennia as the defining character-istic of human beings. Reason includes not only our capacity for logical inference, but also our ability to conduct inquiry, to solve problems, to evaluate, to criticize, to deliberate about how we should act, and to reach an understanding of ourselves, other people, and the world. . . . Reason is not disembodied, as the tradition has largely held, but arises from the nature of our brains, bodies, and bodily experience. . . . [T]he very struc-ture of reason itself comes from the details of our embodiment. . . . Rea-son is evolutionary, in that abstract reason builds on and makes use of forms of perceptual and motor inference present in "lower" animals. . . . Reason is not "universal" in the transcendent sense; that is, it is not part of the structure of the universe. It is universal, however, in that it is a capacity shared universally by all human beings. What allows it to be shared are the commonalities that exist in the way our minds are em-bodied.

Pinker, Lakoff, and M. Johnson apparently believe that, in principle, one can give an exhaustive and scientifically significant account of every "meaningful" characteristic associated with mind in terms of natural (e.g., physiological) prop-erties of the brain, but not vice versa. (Another way of saying the same thing is to claim that they subscribe to the explanatory program Patricia Churchland calls "neurophilosophy." See Churchland, 1986.) One main motivation for their hold-ing this view might be methodological. Thus, for example, all of them probably would agree with the following principles of a "naturalist methodology," as set forth by Noam Chomsky:

In formulating a constructive research program we depart in various ways from ordinary usage with its teleological and normative conditions, which have no place in a naturalistic inquiry and merely lead to confusion if adopted uncritically. . . . The approach to language . . . mentioned ear-lier—and . . . other work on specific topics within the cognitive sci-ences—adheres more strictly to the naturalistic pattern. We want to dis-cover how actual systems work. Simulation is of value insofar as it contributes to this end, and, that apart, there is no interest in criteria for commonsense notions like intelligence, language, understanding, knowl-edge, aboutness, etc. There is no reason to expect them to find a place, unchanged, in a principled theory of the mind. (Chomsky, 1997, pp. 24, 31; emphasis italics added)

What, more precisely, are the "actual systems" whose workings Chomsky con-siders it the proper object of scientists to discover, describe, and explain whenever they set themselves the task of making sense of the mind? The answer is that he identifies these systems with various parts of the brain, but not with items like, say, an invented cultural or historical tradition, a novel way of thinking, or a new way humans learned to conceive of themselves. Furthermore, his implicit justifi-cation for this answer is that, strictly speaking, only the first and not the second exists. In other words, according to him (and presumably, according to Pinker and the others as well), the job of scientists is to study what is real; and in the naturalistic world picture to which he subscribes, every real entity is (1) physical, (2) individual, and (3) completely determinate.

I agree with at least some of the claims made by Chomsky, Pinker, Lakoff, and the other Johnson. For instance, I see nothing contradictory or otherwise nonsensical in the notion of investigators' eventually connecting all mental acts, powers, and "contents" with roughly corresponding properties of the mind's underlying brain. Nevertheless, this notion strikes me as a trivial rather than a substantive one, since it is a merely utopian ideal with very few practical consequences. More especially, I do not believe that this idea provides an adequate justification for claiming that there is an "explanatory asymmetry" between mind and brain of the sort espoused by the authors mentioned, because I suspect that attempts to employ this ideal as a guide for practical scientific investigations would be, not just unfruitful, but disastrously misleading.

I have three main reasons for saying this. The first is based on what empirical investigations have shown the human brain to be like. The second is a reflection of the general way in which I interpret the history of Western philosophy and science. And the third grows out of some relatively recent scientific discoveries about our species' history.

Thus, research has taught us that the human brain is a pliable organ that is capable of adjusting itself, in both its structure and functioning, to a wide range of external and internal circumstances. (There is a classic expression of this point in Penfield, 1975; a more recent discussion is Donald, 1991, especially p. 13.) But has that same research also established that all the influencing circumstances just mentioned must be narrowly physical ones? For example, is it true to say that although the brain can be influenced by things like temperature, atmospheric pressure, on the amount of alcohol, oxygen, adrenaline, or testosterone in the blood, it cannot be influenced by "meaningful" factors like thoughts, purposes, plans, normative standards, or general patterns of thinking?

A somewhat controversial but nevertheless, in my opinion, clear case to show that the answer is no concerns the example of language. All normal adult human beings alive at the present moment make use of language—that is, a system of expressing and receiving information radically different from all other known natural modes of communication. (Our use of language probably has changed our bodies and nervous systems in various ways. Compare Terrence Deacon's statement [1997, p. 25]: "Such a major shift in behavioral adaptation [as language] could hardly fail to have left its impression on human anatomy.") Nevertheless—pace Chomsky, Pinker, and the others—it cannot be correct to say that language simply and automatically "arose" out of individual human brains as soon as natural selection had brought brains of that sort into existence, for the following reason. We now have extensive experimental evidence to show that children cannot learn the meanings of basic referential terms like "red," "ball," and "hot" unless they participate in situations of shared attention with caregivers to whom the meanings of these terms already are known (see Neisser, 1997, pp. 253–54). In other words, children do not acquire general principles involved in language and meaning simply by "maturation," but instead—at least in part—by a process of genuine learning. And the special sort of learning involved in this achievement needs to occur in a cultural environment where the learner begins by exchanging nonverbal or preverbal information with other individuals.

Thus cognitive scientists need to take account of brain changes that come from things like ideas, meanings, goals, plans, and patterns of thought. Whenever facts lead us to give explanations of this last type, then, I suggest, it is appropriate for us to speak of mind determining the brain, rather than the other way around.[2]

My second reason for opposing the methodologically motivated views of theorists like Pinker, Lakoff, M. Johnson, Chomsky, and Churchland is that even though all these people "tip their hats" in the general direction of Darwinism, I do not think that they have managed to grasp the full significance of the intellectual revolution Darwin introduced. For example, Aristotle maintained that there could not be genuine, "scientific" knowledge of any item that owed its existence to chance events or conditions, and that therefore fell under categories that were artificial, arbitrary, and impermanent (see *Physics*, 2. 4–6). But as opposed to that view, Darwin showed a way of extending one type of rigorously scientific thinking to objects and categories that were neither necessary nor "timeless" (in the Aristotelian sense of eternally present in the world), but were just temporarily effective results of incidental and accidental causes. Because of Darwin's influence, for example, biologists now think of species as historical entities with beginning points in the past and that also will come to an end at certain times in the future. To quote Ian Tattersall (1998, p. 26), "Species . . . turned out to be bounded entities in time as well as in space, with origins, life spans, and extinctions."

Pinker, Lakoff, and M. Johnson go part of the way toward taking account of this Darwinian conception of the world, since they assume that the human body (including the brain) is a chance product of a long series of past evolutionary events. But what they then say about the mind—namely, that it somehow is either embodied in the brain or supervenes on it (see Kim, 1998, p. 10)—reintroduces old-fashioned Aristotelianism by the back door. What I mean is that they thereby commit themselves to the notion that as soon as evolution had created brains of our type, then—automatically, and as a timeless truth—minds also had to be present in, or expressed by, every one of those brains. But this is a defective way of talking because it introduces a scenario where Darwin can only exorcise the ghost of Aristotle in a partial and relative way, rather than completely.

Incidentally, another point the Darwinian revolution apparently implies is that even if there are no such things as meanings, aims, or Aristotelian final causes in inanimate nature, the same is not true of the living world. In Darwin's view, for example, creatures that have relative intellectual complexity are only able to compete in the evolutionary struggle by making something like literal choices, based on something resembling meaningful criteria and values. For example, consider the important role that mating behavior plays in sexual—and thus also in natural—selection. Any animal that cannot distinguish between appropriate and inappropriate mates and behave in significantly different ways toward these two groups also will not succeed in passing on its genes to descendants. Furthermore, what allows animals to engage in behavior of this sort is not just innately given, hardwired programs that prompt them to respond in appropriate ways to correct cues. It is also partly a matter of their employing—that is, giving and receiving—quasi-conventional signals or clues, which have to be acquired by learning. For example, ethologists tell us that if, by switching eggs in a nest, we bring it to pass that a goldeneye duck is raised by a mallard mother and father, then that duck will not be able to reproduce itself later in life, because its early experiences will have caused it to learn sexual signals that other goldeneyes will neither recognize nor respond to.

I now want to explain my third, more historical reason for rejecting the "neurophilosophical" claim that one always can account for mind in terms of brain, but not the other way around. First, although I do not agree with Lakoff and M. Johnson that reason is an innately given brain function shared by all normal, adult humans, it still seems to me that there is an important respect in which these people are right to identify the mind (in a nonontological sense) with reason. To be specific, parts of human history show that reason was an intellectual invention that certain members of a past cultural tradition made at a particular time and place. In fact, in a book and series of articles written over the last decade and a half (1987, 1988, 1997, 2000, and 2003), I defended the quasi-eliminativist thesis that, strictly speaking, there were no human minds anywhere, until the relatively recent date[3] when one or more now unknown individuals living in pre-Socratic Greece thought of, and then began employing in their own practice, the special program of techniques, rules, ideals, and standards of assessing and thinking that we now refer to as "reason."[4]

Nevertheless, I shall not talk here about the considerations just mentioned. Instead, I propose to focus on the additional point that cognitive scientists also need to take account of a second, broader sense of the word "mind" that refers to something much more widely shared among humans (including many who lived before what I call the "Greek revolution"). But it is likewise necessary to think of mind in this wider sense as more than just a set of functions that automatically arises out of brains of a special sort. My main reason for saying this is not a conceptual, but an empirical one.

I consider paleontology and archeology to be important, but often-neglected, cognitive sciences. These disciplines' importance is proved by the fact that their practitioners have discovered significant facts about our species that only could have come to light through consideration of data distinctively associated with those fields. For instance, such data have shown that throughout the long evolutionary process that eventually led to modern humans, there has been a consistent mismatch between physiology on one side and behavior on the other. In particular, there virtually always was a delay between (1) the development of larger and/or more complex brains, and (2) subsequent cultural advances for which, presumably, those larger brains were in part responsible.

Consider a simple example. At the beginning of chapter 5 of *Becoming Human* (1998), paleoanthropologist Ian Tattersall describes the appearance in eastern

Africa, about 1.9 million years ago, of a species "distinctively different from anything previously known." He is referring to the advent of *Homo ergaster* (or "work
man," also sometimes known as the "African *Homo erectus*"), "a creature who
sported a cranium that much more closely resembled that of later humans, boast-
ing a braincase of about 850 ml in volume (above half the modern average),
housed in a relatively high and rounded vault." (p. 136) Despite the physiological
advances of this hominid over its predecessors, however, archeological evidence
shows that as far as *Homo ergaster*'s behavior and culture were concerned—for
example, the animals it hunted and the stone tools it made—the members of this
species remained at essentially the same level as that of their immediate ancestors
for a very long time. Thus Tattersall continues as follows (1998, pp. 137–38):

> Culturally, though, little appears to have changed by the time Turkana
> boy came on the scene [an especially complete, well preserved specimen
> dated about 1.6 million years ago]—although studies of tooth wear in
> *Homo ergaster* suggest a greater amount of meat eating compared to
> *Homo habilis*, which shows the more vegetarian pattern of wear typical
> of *Australopithecus*. The stone tool kit and animal remains found at Tur-
> kana in the time of the earliest *Homo ergaster* do not, for example, differ
> significantly from those associated with *Homo habilis*.

Then he adds the following reflective comment:

> At first, this appears a little counter-intuitive; but a moment's thought
> will contradict intuition. Why should a new species—which inevitably
> emerged out of an old one—necessarily bring with it a new technology?
> Whether physical or cultural, innovations can appear in only one place,
> and that's *within* a species. Any individual who bears a new genetic trait
> or invents a new technology (which is a very different thing) cannot, after
> all, differ too much from his or her parents.

Four hundred thousand years after the first appearance of *Homo ergaster*,
some members of this species—now developed into fully-fledged *Homo erectus*—
made an intellectual advance worthy of their more capacious and complex brains.
Tattersall explains this new development the following way:

> A couple of hundred thousand years after fossils of *Homo ergaster* first
> show up, however, we do see a remarkable cultural innovation in the
> archeological record. Up to that time (about 1.5 myr ago), stone tools
> had been of the simple kind that had been made for the previous million
> years or so, in which the main aim had probably been to achieve a
> particular attribute (a sharp cutting edge) rather than a specific shape.
> Suddenly, however, a new kind of tool was on the scene: the Acheulean
> hand ax and associated tool types, which were obviously made to a stan-
> dardized pattern that existed in the toolmaker's mind before the tool-
> making process began. [In particular, h]and axes are large, flattish,
> teardrop-shaped implements that were carefully fashioned on both sides
> to achieve a symmetrical shape. (1998, p. 138)

To bring our discussion closer to the principal question posed in this chapter, let me now offer a second example of the same phenomenon. This is the re-markable—and remarkably rapid—transition through which our own species passed (in Europe) when its members left behind the behavioral patterns and technologies characteristic of the so-called Middle Paleolithic period and adopted instead the behaviors associated with the Upper Paleolithic era. Archeologists tell us that during more than half the time the species *Homo sapiens* has existed, our ancestors behaved in ways that were almost indistinguishable from the behavior of our closest relatives, members of the "cousin" primate species, *Homo neander-thalensis*. For instance, Alan Thorne and Milford Wolpoff (1992, p. 78) claim that in the Levant (the eastern shore of the Mediterranean Sea), where both species lived in close proximity for a long while, " 'modern' people had a culture that was identical to that of their local Neanderthal contemporaries: they made the same types of stone tools with the same technologies and at the same frequencies; they had the same stylized burial customs, hunted the same game and even used the same butchering procedures" (see also Tattersall, 1998, pp. 150–80; and Tattersall, 1999, chapter 8). That situation changed only at the end of the Middle and beginning of the Later or Upper Old Stone Age or Paleolithic. This revolutionary event took place approximately 40,000 years ago (again, in the case of Europe).[5]

Paul Mellars (1998, pp. 91–92) says that he, along with many other archeol-ogists, considers the beginning of the Upper Paleolithic "the most radical episode of cultural, technological and general behavioral change in the entire history of the European continent." Is this statement an exaggeration? Should Mellars have said instead that the most profound change that ever occurred in the life of Eu-ropean humans happened at the start of the Neolithic or New Stone Age, roughly 10,000 years ago? After all, this last date was the time of the invention of agricul-ture, irrigation, domestication of animals, settled city life, and the institutions of government, military organization, and law. (For example, this is the opinion of University of Frankfort prehistorian Jens Lüning. See Lemonick, 1992, p. 53.)

At least from the perspective of cognitive science, the answer is no. In other words, there is no reason to believe that the Neolithic transition was basic in a cognitive sense of the word, since we know from hindsight that it was a not unexpected—perhaps even inevitable—working out of capacities that humans had acquired much earlier. In fact, it appears that all the intellectual elements that finally produced the Neolithic revolution already were in place 30,000 years before then, at the start of the Upper Paleolithic.

What precisely were the effects on human thought of the event that inau-gurated the Upper Paleolithic? The simplest answer is that what took place at that time enabled humans to begin thinking in explicitly symbolic terms.[6] To get a clear idea of what that means, consider Mellars's following list of seven changes that occurred at the start of the Upper Paleolithic (all of them extensively docu-mented from archeological materials):

(1) The appearance of much more widespread "blade" and "bladelet" as opposed to "flake"-based technologies. . . .

(2) The appearance of a wide range of entirely new *forms* of stone tools, some of which . . . reflect an entirely new component of conceptual or visual form and standardization in the production of stone tools. . . .

(3) The effective explosion of bone, antler and ivory technology, involving . . . a remarkably wide range of new and tightly standardized tool forms. . . .

(4) The appearance of the first reliably documented beads, pendants and other items of personal decoration. . . .

(5) The transportation of sea shells and other materials over remarkable distances . . .

(6) The appearance of the first unmistakable sound-producing instruments. . . .

(7) Most dramatic of all, the sudden appearance of explicitly "artistic" activity, in a remarkable variety of forms. . . . (Mellars, 1998, p. 92)

Did the Middle/Upper Paleolithic transition involve the founding of a new human culture—one that included the invention of an ur-language, from which all other European languages were later to descend?[7] Even if the answer to this question is yes, establishing that culture could not have been the most significant thing that happened then, because of the fact that there were no symbolically based European cultures at all before that date. Presumably, therefore, the most important thing that happened at the beginning of the Upper Paleolithic must have been the introduction of a new way of thinking that had the (indirect) effect of making all such cultures possible. For these reasons, then, I claim that we are entitled to describe the event in question as the inauguration of a new type of shared human mind, after (perhaps as long as 90,000 years after) evolutionary forces already had created our shared human brain.

The point that needs special emphasis here is that the Upper Paleolithic transition was not just a physical (e.g., physiological) occurrence, but was primarily a cultural one. That is, it was not something that simply was produced by changes either in human bodies and brains or in the physical environment in which those bodies then existed. Instead, it occurred at the time it did because certain individuals then managed to solve certain intellectual problems—problems about (or involving) meanings, purposes, and general ways of thinking. One proof of this point is the fact that the revolution happened far too quickly to have been a result of evolved bodily changes. For example, we have no evidence for supposing that it was triggered by the replacement of one population of humans by another (see Tattersall, 1998, pp. 231–32).

Let me now conclude with a few remarks about a single further example. This case (one from my own experience) shows how easy it is for cognitive theorists who have no keen interest in the history of our species to fall into error. For reasons analogous to the three discussed earlier, I speculated in one of the chapters of a recently completed book (2003) that it was appropriate to give a "mental" rather than "physical" hypothetical account of the mysterious historical fact that humans had to wait a very long time after the origin of their species to begin thinking in "modern" terms. In other words, I claimed that even after evolution had brought the modern human body and brain into being, it was necessary for certain cultural developments to take place among early humans before mind in the broad sense could come into existence as well. More concretely, I proposed — in quasi-Freudian terms — that early members of the species *Homo sapiens* (with their improved and more powerful brains) might have been vaguely aware, within themselves, of a new power to conceive of things around them in objective terms, rather than just in relation to their own interests, experience, needs, and the like. Nevertheless, for a long while they did everything in their power to disguise, subvert, and ignore that awareness and that power of thinking, because of the fact that they found these things frightening. In particular, it seemed to them that attempting to exercise that particular intellectual power would threaten them with separation and estrangement from the safety and comfort of the familiar natural world in which they had existed up to that time.

An anonymous editorial reader described this as one of the strangest accounts of the origins of the human mind that he or she ever had read. Furthermore, that person claimed that my account was merely a priori extrapolation into an imaginary past from various known facts about our own, present-day circumstances. In this respect, it was similar to Thomas Hobbes's view that the lives of early humans had been "nasty, brutish, and short." And, the reader finally added, this account had no more scientific warrant or justification than the story that Hobbes had told.

But the empirical facts summarized before should make it clear that this is not a justified objection. Unlike us, Hobbes did not have any means of knowing about the Upper Paleolithic revolution. Therefore, he was not in a position to pose the scientifically substantive question of why it was necessary for humans to wait something like 90,000 years before finally becoming able to exploit potentialities that presumably already were implicitly present in their brains. In conclusion, then, even if there is a grain of truth in claiming — as Pinker does — that human brains were "designed by evolution" for symbolic, representational thought, history also shows that much more had to happen besides the simple fact that evolution produced those brains, before thinking of that sort could begin.

I admit — in fact, the point strikes me as obvious — that further empirical investigation might falsify my suggested story. For example, paleontologists might uncover evidence of a serious, debilitating disease which is consistently present in the bones of all humans who lived before the Upper Paleolithic revolution, but which is not present in the fossil bones of those who lived after this event. If this were to happen, it would give us a convincing reason for concluding that the crucial cause of the transition was not a meaningful or cultural factor after all, but was merely the physical change of humans' coming to be cured of the disease from which they previously had suffered. However, I consider this possibility of refutation a friend and not a foe, since it is that on which I base the claim that my proffered account is not just an a priori, Hobbesean exercise of unfettered imagination, but instead is a fallible interpretation of genuine, concrete facts.

Notes

1. This is an earlier version of material at the beginning of Johnson, 2003, Chapter 1.

2. Although human beings are paradigm cases of "minded creatures," the idea of explanatory asymmetry prompts theorists to ignore the most important characteristic that sets humans apart from intellectually simpler creatures like slime molds, sea squirts, and tapeworms. What I am referring to is the fact that the first, but not the second, live in an environment of socialization, learning, and culture. Thus one can say that the basic mistake involved in the idea of accounting for all differences between humans and other animals just in terms of the physiological and, more especially, neurological properties respectively belonging to each, is that this represents a distinction in kind as if it were nothing more than a difference of degree.

3. Lakoff and Johnson focus attention on what people have thought and said about reason "for over two millennia." But why do they choose that particular number of years, as opposed to some other number? Even if two or three thousand years is a lengthy period from some viewpoints, it represents only a small fraction (a little over 1 percent) of the whole time our species, Homo sapiens, has existed on Earth. My suggestion here is that by picking this number, these authors implicitly are recognizing something about which virtually all present-day historians of the ancient period agree — that the systematic patterns of thinking, inferring, judging, and the like we now call "reason" did not exist before roughly 1000 B.C.E.

4. Of course, the word "reasonable" (in what I think of as the strict, Greek-derived sense) does not mean the same thing as "intelligent," "cultured," or "mature." Therefore, it is not a contradiction for me to claim that at roughly the time of Homer, some humans inaugurated a change from one way of thinking to another, despite the fact that many normal, adult, intelligent, and cultured humans (with normal brains) existed before that time.

5. Steven Mithen says (1996, p. 152):

> Yet if we look a little more closely at the boundary . . . we see that there is not so much a single big bang as a whole series of cultural sparks that occur at slightly different times in different parts of the world between 60,000 and 30,000 years ago. The colonization of Australia, for instance, seems to reflect a cultural spark which happened between 60,000 and 50,000 years ago, yet at this time all remained relatively quiet elsewhere in the world. In the Near East a cultural spark happened between 50,000 and 45,000 years ago when the Levallois technology was replaced by that of blade cores. The cultural spark in Europe seems not to have been until 40,000 years ago with the appearance of the first objects of art. Indeed, it is perhaps only after 30,000 years ago that we can be confident that the hectic pace of cultural change had begun in earnest throughout the globe.

6. The title of Terrence Deacon's book The Symbolic Species (1997) is meant to express something like this same point.

7. In another place, Steven Pinker (1994, p. 254) expresses agreement with the hypothesis that human language "evolved only once," but, consistently with his general principles, he assumes that this original language must have come into existence at exactly the same time — about 200,000 years ago — as the first Homo sapiens. He does not suppose (as, for example, Ian Tattersall does; see 1998, p. 232) that the first human

language began much later—in fact, that it originated 40,000 years ago, as one more part of the Upper Paleolithic revolution.

References

Chomsky, Noam. 1997. "Language and Cognition." Pp. 15–31 in David Martel Johnson and Christina E. Erneling (Eds.). *The Future of the Cognitive Revolution.* New York: Oxford University Press.

Churchland, Patricia Smith. 1986. *Neurophilosophy: Toward a Unified Science of the Mind-Brain.* Cambridge, MA: MIT Press.

Deacon, Terrence W. 1997. *The Symbolic Species.* New York: W.W. Norton.

Donald, Merlin. 1991. *Origins of the Modern Mind: Three Stages in the Evolution of Culture and Cognition.* Cambridge MA: Harvard University Press.

Jablonski, N.G., and Aiello, L.C (Eds.). 1998. *The Origin and Diversification of Language*, Memoirs of the California Academy of Sciences, no. 24. San Francisco: California Academy of Sciences.

Johnson, David Martel. 1987. "The Greek Origins of Belief." *American Philosophical Quarterly*, 24(4), pp. 319–27.

———. 1988. " 'Brutes Believe Not.' " *Philosophical Psychology*, 1(3), pp. 279–94.

———. 1997. "Taking the Past Seriously: How History Shows that Eliminativists' Account of Folk Psychology Is Partly Right and Partly Wrong." Pp. 366–75 in David Martel Johnson and Christina E. Erneling (Eds.), *The Future of the Cognitive Revolution.* New York: Oxford University Press.

———. 2000. "Aristotle's Curse of Non-existence against 'Barbarians.' " Pp. 126–35 in Demetra Sfendoni-Mentzou (Ed.), *Aristotle and Contemporary Science.* Vol. 1. New York: Peter Lang.

———. 2003. *How History Made the Mind: The Cultural Origins of Objective Thinking.* Chicago: Open Court Press.

Johnson, David Martel, and Erneling, Christina E. (Eds.). 1997. *The Future of the Cognitive Revolution.* New York: Oxford University Press.

Kim, Jaegwon. 1998. *Philosophy of Mind.* Boulder, CO: Westview Press.

Lakoff, George, and Johnson, Mark. 1999. *Philosophy in the Flesh: The Embodied Mind and Its Challenge to Western Thought.* New York: Basic Books.

Lemonick, Michael D. 1992. "The World in 3300 B.C." *Time*, October 26, pp. 52–55.

Mellars, Paul. 1998. "Neanderthals, Modern Humans and the Archaeological Evidence for Language." Pp. 89–115 in N.G. Jablonski and L.C. Aiello (Eds.), *The Origin and Diversification of Language.* Memoirs of the California Academy of Sciences, no. 24. San Francisco: California Academy of Sciences.

Mithen, Steven. 1996. *The Prehistory of the Mind: The Cognitive Origins of Art, Religion, and Science.* New York: Thames and Hudson.

Neisser, Ulric. 1997. "The Future of Cognitive Science: An Ecological Analysis." Pp. 247–60 in David Martel Johnson and Christina E. Erneling (Eds.), *The Future of the Cognitive Revolution.* New York: Oxford University Press.

Penfield, Wilder. 1975. *The Mystery of the Mind: A Critical Study of Consciousness and the Human Brain.* Princeton, NJ: Princeton University Press.

Pinker, Steven. 1994. *The Language Instinct: How the Mind Creates Language*. New York: HarperCollins.

———. 1997. *How the Mind Works*. New York: W.W. Norton.

Sfendoni-Mentzou, Demetra (Ed.). 2000. *Aristotle and Contemporary Science*. Vol. 1. New York: Peter Lang.

Tattersall, Ian. 1998. *Becoming Human: Evolution and Human Uniqueness*. New York: Harcourt Brace.

———. 1999. *The Last Neanderthal: The Rise, Success, and Mysterious Extinction of Our Closest Human Relative*. Rev. ed. Boulder, CO: Westview Press.

Thorne, Alan G., and Wolpoff, Milford H. 1992. "The Multiregional Evolution of Humans." *Scientific American* (April), pp. 76–83.

29

Afterword: Between Brain and Culture — The Diversity of Mind

Christina E. Erneling

According to *The Oxford Dictionary of Current English* "between" means

> **1 a** at a point in the area bounded by two or more other points in space, time, etc., **b** along the extent of such an area; **2** separating; **3 a** shared, **b** joint action; **4** to and from; **5** taking one of (*choose between them*).

Throughout the history of psychology and, more recently, in cognitive science (e.g., as represented by the chapters in Johnson and Erneling, 1997, and in this book), the fifth and last of these meanings, exclusive choice, has been at the center of the debate about the scientific study of the mind. Several of the authors in this volume (e.g., Rom Harré, Jerome Bruner) point to the more than hundred-year-old opposition between *Naturwissenschaften* and *Geisteswissenschaften* and to Wundt's division between experimental and folk psychology and then claim that we still ought to be basing our understanding of mind on some such proposed division. They, like Jans Brockmeier and David Bakhurst (part VI), support some sort of cultural psychology. By contrast, others discuss the possible reduction of all supposed aspects of cultural or folk psychology either to neurophysiology or to cognitive psychology (especially parts III and V). Still other authors propose to accept various different kinds of dualism (part II). Yet neither the approaches and theories that take their starting points from the cultural sciences nor the ones that are linked to the brain and cognitive sciences have successfully made the case that they really are capable of providing even tentative answers to all the central questions that concern the mind and its activities.

On the other hand, in several chapters in this volume there also is a tendency to try to overcome this dichotomy without resorting to reductionism (e.g., parts V and VII). Instead, some of the authors in these parts present conceptions of the mind and its activity that are better described by some of the other meanings of the word "between" — that is, at a point in the area bounded by two or more other points in space or time; along the extent of such an area; shared by; joint action;

or to and from. For example, some of these chapters explore the possibility of overcoming the dichotomy by taking an evolutionary or developmental approach (see part V and also the chapters by Gunther Stent and David Olson).

Another possible way of trying to overcome this dichotomy or opposition is critically to examine the very principles we use to classify mental phenomena, both in general, as distinct from other types of phenomena, and in cases of specific mental activities. In his 1997 book *Naming the Mind*, Kurt Danziger shows how the classification of supposedly mental phenomena varies cross-culturally, and how the Western scientific tradition by no means provides the only way of classifying something as mental, or even as something that is an instance of a specific mental phenomenon like memory. For example, Western conventions of distinguishing psychological topics such as motivation, learning, and intelligence make no sense to scholars trained in traditional Indonesian psychological thinking. Although they recognize certain aspects of the mental activities in Western classifications as familiar, they do not group them this way and find the classifications both unnatural and having the result of avoiding interesting issues. It thus is possible to carve up the field of mental phenomena quite differently, depending on one's theoretical system and cultural context. Another strong case against a universal psychological taxonomy is found in Michael Cole's studies of different cognitive systems (see, for example, Cole, 1996).

Further examples of different possible classification schemes are found in Thomas Leahey's chapter in part I and in David Martel Johnson's chapter in part VII. Johnson, for example, by talking about all the important changes that came about as a result of the Upper Paleolithic revolution, tries to show how implausible it is for theorists to insist that all the members of our species who lived before that event (simply because of the fact that they had brains that were essentially like ours) also must have had "minds" as well. Furthermore, he argues that this is true even when one proposes to understand this word not in a way that makes it relative to some particular cultural tradition, but instead in a quite broad and inclusive sense.

Timothy van Gelder and Ian Jarvie (see part VII) in their discussions of beliefs and rationality approach the same issue from a different perspective, by recharacterizing and reclassifying what is usually thought of as individual mental activity, namely, beliefs (van Gelder) and rationality (Jarvie), as something normative and social. For example, van Gelder argues that we mistakenly join together different mental activities as belonging under one umbrella, as it were, when from an ontological point of view they are really very different activities or entities. For instance, beliefs involve norms of correctness, which are grounded in social institutions, but sensations do not. Jarvie makes a similar point in his proposal of how it is possible to overcome the nature-convention distinction. Taking the positions of dogmatism and of skepticism seriously, he argues that these two views are similar in some respects, and that very often they are capable of working quite well. However, they are inferior in his opinion to what he calls the workshop model, which is a social and cultural model of rationality, since such a model provides a better description of scientific rationality and of individual reasoning. These two authors point to the normative aspect of some mental phenomena. In some cases, mental activities can be nonnormative in character (e.g., sensations), but in other cases, they necessarily involve getting something right or wrong (e.g., beliefs — see also Stent's and Olson's chapters) and therefore count as normative activities. Furthermore, van Gelder's and Jarvie's arguments imply that mental activity is not something that is restricted to the individual. For example, there is as much mind manifested in an architect's workshop as there is in some individual contemplating a future course of action.

These chapters also suggest that the mind and mindful activity are much too diverse to be able to be accounted for in terms of one underlying mechanism, either biological or cultural. In much contemporary psychology and philosophy of mind, it is assumed that there is some crucial, common mechanism (neurobiological or computational) that produces all mental phenomena. This is true both of approaches that assume a central process and of modularity theories. The mechanisms of different modules will perhaps vary, but they are fundamentally of the same neurophysiological or computational kind, and they are independent of the context or culture in which these mental activities occur (see part IV). For example, memory is supposed to be governed by this same mechanism, untainted by cultural variations in exhibiting and classifying memory performances. But on the other side, a reduction to cultural mechanisms also seems equally problematic.

This indicates that we need to examine again the tradition of assuming that everything that has to do with the mind and mindful activity must be of the same kind. Can it be that the way we so far have characterized and classified mental phenomena has hindered our efforts to explore the mind's origin and proper explanation?

Problems of Classification

As remarked in the introductions to several parts of this book, and as many of the chapters make evident, most studies of the mind still seem to start from, and to take for granted, the Cartesian-Kantian conception of mind. It should be clear by now that this tradition, with its assumption about mentality that earlier philosophers and psychologists perhaps found sensible and useful, no longer provides many useful hypotheses for the study of mental activity. This point has been made numerous times before, but nevertheless the difficulty and frustration remain. Wittgenstein's claim that in psychology there are experimental methods and conceptual confusion still seems to hold true.

It is in this context that revisions in classification, like the one van Gelder has proposed, might be an important beginning in changing the field of investigation. But revisions of this sort always come hand in hand with theoretical, most typically ontological, changes. The underdetermination of any given theory by any available set of empirical data shows that describing and classifying something requires one's making ontological commitments (Harré, 1997). Clearly the Cartesian ontological commitments that have dominated the scientific study of the mind up to the present have not been helpful.

As scientists and scholars, we are trained to suppose that we see the world objectively—as it is. But in spite of everything written in philosophy of science, for example, it is easy for us to forget that the very conceptions and classifications we use are built on traditions of thought developed for different purposes, and that they are based on beliefs that we no longer employ in other spheres of study. For example, as Jagdish Hattiangadi (part IV) points out, most scholars of mind still adhere to Newtonian physics, long after physicists themselves rejected that theory. This has led to a firm, but perhaps unnecessary, rejection of the mind conceived as emergent (for a discussion of emergence, see also William Seager's Chapter in part II).

Categorization and classification of phenomena—in the case we are discussing in this book, of the mental versus the non-mental and of culture versus brain— ought to relate objects in ways that will help us retrieve information about them and also provide us with a basis for explaining them. Stephen Jay Gould, in a popular article on the classification of fossils (Gould, 1999), tells the story of how the early-sixteenth-century classification of fossils hindered an understanding of them, as well as of geological changes over long periods of time (for a different account of how fossils have been viewed historically, see Mayor, 2000). The convention of placing both inorganic objects and organic remains found in the earth in the same group (fossils) and classifying these objects according to similarity of form hindered the understanding of both the nature and the origin of fossils. It also blocked an understanding of long-term developmental processes in nature. I would like to argue that perhaps the stalemate that is present in the contemporary study of mind is similar to this: We need new categorizations and conceptions of the mental. This is what several chapters in this volume, in a modest way, have started to do.

As just mentioned, one of Gould's examples of how classification can cloud our view is what he calls "conflation of categories"—that is, the normative practice of classifying everything (organic or inorganic in origin) that was dug up from the ground as belonging to the same group of things, namely, fossils. Van Gelder and, following him, Christina Erneling argue that many theories of mind have conflated what van Gelder calls cognition with mind, or more specifically cognition with beliefs, which are ontologically quite different items. When one classifies them together as the same sort of things, it becomes difficult to explain their nature and origin. For a discussion of a concrete example of this, see Erneling's chapter on Gopnik and Meltzoff's theory of cognitive development.

A second case of problems arising from categorization, according to Gould, has to do with the difficulty of distinguishing accidental resemblance (in the case of fossils, the form of the object) from genuine resemblance (organic or inorganic origin). Such confusion makes the discussion of origins as well as of causes difficult. Gould's third example of how classification can lead to confusion is that a person can describe something in a particular way that precludes insight into its origins. Stuart Shanker and Talbot Taylor's chapter is an example of the recate-gorization and redescription of language, which thereby opens up another possible way of understanding the origin of language. Hattiangadi provides still another example (differences between perception and imaging). Jarvie's and van Gelder's chapters also, as mentioned, do something similar for our understanding of rationality.

As Johnson points out, all the chapters in part III on folk psychology defend our commonsense way of describing and classifying the mental and reject the replacement of it with a neurobiological way of classifying the mental, as proposed by the eliminative materialists.

The views expressed in part III thus seem to imply that in order to advance the study of the mind the focus should be our everyday psychological understanding and not their neurobiological enabling conditions. Focusing on the last set of conditions, although important, does not help us understand what is unique about mental phenomena.

The connecting theme of all the chapters included in the part II of the book is to explore different possible versions and interpretations of dualism as a general means of classifying mental versus nonmental phenomena. For example, is it necessary to think about the topic of consciousness in a very different way than we think about all the other aspects of the mind? For another example, should we think of psychology as an applied science or as a type of engineering, as contrasted with physics and chemistry, which are theoretical?

Conclusion: Convention versus Nature

In the introduction to part I, I mentioned the fact that various recent authors have claimed that psychology is dead because it has been replaced by other sciences like neurobiology, or because we do not understand how our minds work, or because the nature of mind is beyond human capacity of understanding. In light of the fresh approaches to the mind that many chapters take in this volume, this pessimistic judgment is premature, partly because the pessimistic judgment pre-supposes a Cartesian view of psychology and of the mind as a scientific object. This conception of the mental is built on an ontology and taxonomy that are atomistic—that is, minds are supposed to be items that are individual and presuppose a sharp distinction between body and mind, or between the outer and the inner. Connected with these ontological views are the taxonomic system of physical versus mental substances, with all mental things and activities being basically of the same kind, and methodological assumptions concerning systematic differences in the study of the mind and the body. Perhaps it is a good thing that psychology, understood as the study of the mind in this sense, is dead or rejected. But this does not rule out a science of the mental that is built on other ontological foundations and on other ways of categorizing mental activity. Several chapters in this volume point in this direction, and an intensive intellectual workshop of the kind Jarvie suggests to iron out these ideas is what we should hope for.

One fruitful way is to return once more to Descartes, who was quite sensitive to the difference between physical and mental phenomena (e.g., sensations as opposed to thoughts), and discuss his views in the light of recent scientific advances. Or, as is suggested directly or indirectly by some of the chapters in this volume, it might be a better idea to affirm again the claim made by Wilhelm Wundt and others that there are two sciences of the mental. Rather than being opposed, as the Cartesian approach assumes, these two sciences complement each other. One is biology, which encompasses the neural processes and structures as well as the genetic source of human behavior. The other science is psychology, but a psychology that is able to deal with the normative aspects of the mental— that is, with meanings, skills, and rules. To ground motor skills, natural expressions of bodily feelings, reason, language, and subjectivity (without which the culturally various and historically contingent psychological traits and activities could neither develop nor be transferred to future generations) in neural processes and structures is not to reduce the one to the other, but to identify the means by which psychological activity is exercised (see Harré, 2000). We need both types of science to understand and explain the ontologically heterogeneous mind.

Let me illustrate how we can begin to think about diversity of mind and of mental activity as incorporating both brain and culture by considering the topics of self-knowledge and language. In his article "Five Kinds of Self-Knowledge" (1988) Ulric Neisser argues that there are five different selves: the ecological or physical self, the interpersonal or social self, the extended or memory-related self, the private or subjective self, and the conceptual self. These selves are seldom experienced as distinct, but "differ in their developmental histories, in the accuracy with which we can know them, in the pathologies to which they are subject, and generally in what they contribute to human experience" (p. 35). Thus to think about the self as unified and as consisting of just subjective awareness of mental processes, in the way the Cartesian conception of mind suggests, is misleading. These five selves are grounded in different mechanisms, according to Neisser. The first two (at least initially) are grounded in direct perception of the physical and social environment, but the other three also involve different aspects of cultural interaction. Consider the private self, which is made up of conscious experiences that are not available to anyone else, which is important to most human beings, and which according to the Western tradition is the center of our psychological being. Young children have conscious experiences, but it is only around the age of three that they notice that certain experiences seem to belong exclusively to them alone. This apparently indicates that the difference between public and private action and discourse is the result of a certain human practice—namely, learning to keep what one thinks, feels, and so on to oneself. The Cartesian distinction and classification of the mental as subjective and body as public is too simple and needs to be rethought. The private self with its subjective experiences involves both brain and culture.

Just as self-knowledge consists of different kinds of skills that are based on different underlying mechanisms, biological as well as cultural, so too does language acquisition (see Erneling, 1993). Although learning language presupposes individual biological structures and skills, coming to be a competent user of language does not and could not occur in any isolated individual. Language mastery is not the result of a neural process or computational process internal to the individual, but is the shaping of such processes, physiological and mental, by the sociolinguistic environment. The framework necessary for language acquisition actually consists of three interacting frameworks: the innate and biological skills of the child, the social context in which the right kinds of conversations occur, and the social and normative institution of language itself.

Becoming a competent user of language is the result of a "domestication" of natural behaviors and reactions that are shaped by sociolinguistic training and interaction. From this perspective it is fruitful to look at language acquisition as assembling and modifying two different sets of skills (natural and conventional), which become interrelated, with one (convention) overruling and shaping the other (nature). Thus learning a language involves a purely linguistic or phonological and syntactic aspect, the perception and production of speech sounds in accordance with syntactic rules; and it also involves a communicative-semantic aspect, the communication of concepts in varying circumstances with different people. A precondition for this interaction is the plasticity and redundancy of the developing brain that only slowly reaches its growth potential. The biological behaviors and skills involved in the phonological and syntactic aspects of language are present from an early age—for example, the ability to discriminate speech sounds already from birth. Others, in particular the capacity to produce distinct speech sounds, come into play when the relevant anatomical structures have matured. But neither of these biological and innate behaviors can be used successfully for the production of anything resembling language until the communicative and semantic skills have developed enough complexity. Thus the natural and biological skills are shaped by the cultural and social skill of communicating with symbols. To understand language as well as self-knowledge, we need to understand both the brain and culture, and how they interact in shaping human psychological activity.

The approach exemplified here condones pluralism and interdisciplinary approaches, conceived as consisting of different approaches to an ontologically heterogeneous object, the mind. On the other hand, it is possible to endorse the relevance of neurobiology for the study of the mind, not as a study of "parts of the mind," but instead as a study of part of the various physical conditions that have to be present in the world in order for there to be a mind, understood as a cultural invention, at all. This is the view that David Johnson asks us to consider. Consistent with what he said in the introduction to this volume—in particular, his rejection of the no-center view and his claim that in the end all theorists will be forced to choose between the view that the mind is identical with the brain or the view that the mind is a product of culture—Johnson does not subscribe to the idea of the mind as some kind of complex. Rather, he believes that even though a person's having a mind presupposes that certain facts are true about the physical world (and more especially, about structures and powers of the brain), the mind amounts to nothing more nor less than an intellectual invention. Therefore, like any other such invention (like, e.g., a nursery rhyme), it is something that is entirely cultural and not at all physical in its ontological nature.

In light of the discussions in this volume and the different ideas of how to conceive of the relationship between brain and culture, I think that what we need at this stage is not grand theory. Instead, what is needed is a reopening of old issues in the open atmosphere of a workshop, as suggested by Jarvie. We need to go back to the drawing board, as it were, and continue to redraw the boundaries between different psychological activities and the intersections between the brain and culture. A modest start is to begin to reevaluate our taxonomy of mental and non-mental and of specific mental phenomena. This is what the contributors to this volume have begun to do. To quote Gould (1999, p. 75), they have started "to expand the realm of conceptual space by the most humble, yet most markedly effective device: the development of a new taxonomic scheme to break a mental logjam."

References

Cole, M. 1996. *Cultural Psychology*. Cambridge, MA: Belknap Press of Harvard University Press.

Danziger, K. 1997. *Naming the Mind: How Psychology Found Its Language*. London: Sage.

Descartes, R. 1641/1968. *Meditations on First Philosophy*. New York: Cambridge University Press.

Erneling, C.E. 1993. *Understanding Language Acquisition: The Framework of Learning*. Albany: State University of New York Press.

Gould, S.J. 1999. "When the Fossils Were Young." *Natural History* (October), pp. 24–26, 70–75.

Harré, R. 1997. " 'Berkeleyan' Arguments and the Ontology of Cognitive Science." Pp. 335–52 in D.M. Johnson and C.E. Erneling (Eds.), *The Future of the Cognitive Revolution*. New York: Oxford University Press.

———. 2000. "The Rediscovery of the Human Mind." http://www.massey.ac.nzl ~alock/virtual/korea.htm.

Johnson, D.M., and Erneling, C.E. (Eds.). 1997. *The Future of the Cognitive Revolution*. New York: Oxford University Press.

Mayor, A. 2000. *The First Fossil Hunters: Paleontology in Greek and Roman Times*. Princeton, NJ: Princeton University Press.

Neisser, U. 1988. "Five Kinds of Self-Knowledge." *Philosophical Psychology*, 1(1), pp. 35–59.

Citation Index

Subject Index

a priori, 153
abductive reasoning, 219–220
abnormal, the, 64
aboutness, 500
absorption spectrum, 21
abstract concepts, 487
abstract entities, 493
abstract objects, 463
accidental causes, 502
accommodation, 21, 489, 495
Acheulean hand ax, 504
acquisition of language, 250, 320, 367,
    489, 516–517
  gradual accretion of practical
    techniques, 372
  not the result of inner neural or
    computational processes, 517
action
  understood in reference to symbolic
    systems, 406
  See also human action
actual systems, 500
adaptation, 61, 402
  human activities work against, 405
  individual, 403
adaptationist thinking, 392
adaptedness, as an emergent property, 182
adaptive resonance theory (ART), 254
addressivity, 438
affect, 27, 371
affection, 294

age of accountability, 162
agency, 435
  primacy of, 425
agents, 417
  bodily, 330
  with inner representations, 330
agriculture, invention of, 505
akrasia, 331
alchemists, 55
Alexandrianism, 41
alien life, 290
altriciality, secondary, 371, 379n2
altruism, genetic, 385
  See also reciprocal altruism
American psychology, 57
American Sign Language, 32
analytic philosophers, 94–95
analyticity, 203, 215
anarchists, 195–196
anger, 249
Anglo-American philosophy, 413, 457
Anglo-American psychology, 59
animal cognition, 319, 323
animal language research, history of, 376
animal psychology, 64
animals, 349
  bifurcated from humans according to
    Western views, 378
  Descartes' theory of, 62–63, 319
  minds of, 63–65
Annales school, 404–405